SOCIOLINGUISTICS

MODERN LINGUISTICS SERIES

Series Editors

Professor Noël Burton-Roberts
University of Newcastle upon Tyne

Dr Andrew Spencer
University of Essex

Each textbook in the **Modern Linguistics** series is designed to provide an introduction to a topic in contemporary linguistics and allied disciplines, presented in a manner that is accessible and attractive to readers with no previous experience of the topic, but leading them to some understanding of current issues.

Noël Burton-Roberts founded the **Modern Linguistics** series and acted as Series Editor for the first three volumes in the series. Andrew Spencer has since joined Noël Burton-Roberts as joint Series Editor.

Titles published in the series

English Syntax and Argumentation Bas Aarts
Phonology Philip Carr
Linguistics and Second Language Acquisition Vivian Cook
Sociolinguistics: A Reader Nikolas Coupland and Adam Jaworski
Morphology Francis Katamba
Contact Languages: Pidgins and Creoles Mark Sebba

Further titles are in preparation

Sociolinguistics

A Reader

Edited by

Nikolas Coupland and Adam Jaworski

St. Martin's Press
New York

SOCIOLINGUISTICS

St. Martin's Press, Scholarly and Reference Division,
175 Fifth Avenue, New York, N.Y. 10010

First published in the United States of America in 1997

This book is printed on paper suitable for recycling and
made from fully managed and sustained forest sources.

Printed in Great Britain

ISBN 0–312–17572–8 (cloth)
ISBN 0–312–17573–6 (paper)

Library of Congress Cataloging-in-Publication Data
Sociolinguistics : a reader / edited by Nikolas Coupland and Adam
Jaworski.
p.   cm. — (Modern linguistics series)
Includes bibliographical references and index.
ISBN 0–312–17572–8 (cloth). — ISBN 0–312–17573–6 (paper)
1. Sociolinguistics.   I. Coupland, Nikolas, 1950–   .
II. Jaworski, Adam, 1957–   .   III. Series.
P40.S5775 1997
306.44—dc21   97–11315
                                                                            CIP

Contents

Acknowledgements

The editors and publishers wish to thank the following for permission to use copyright material:

Arnold for material from M. A. K. Halliday (1973), *Explorations in the Function of Language*, pp. 48–67; Richard H. Bourhis (1982), 'Language policies and language attitudes: le monde de la francophonie' in *Attitudes towards Language Variation: Social and Applied Contexts*, ed. Ellen Bouchard Ryan and Howard Giles, pp. 34–62; Jenny Cheshire (1982), 'Linguistic variation and social function' in *Sociolinguistic Variation in Speech Communities*, ed. Suzanne Romaine, pp. 153–66; and Miles Hewstone and Howard Giles (1986), 'Social groups and social stereotypes in intergroup communication: a review and model of intergroup communication breakdown' in *Intergroup Communication*, ed. W. B. Gudykunst, pp. 10–20; Blackwell Publishers for material from Muriel Saville-Troike (1989), *The Ethnography of Communication: An Introduction*, 2nd edn, pp. 107–38; Lesley Milroy (1987), *Observing and Analysing Natural Language: A Critical Account of Sociolinguistic Method*, pp. 1–11; James Milroy (1992), *Linguistic Variation and Change: On the Historical Sociolinguistics of English*, pp. 177–9; Robert Hodge and Gunther Kress (1988), *Social Semiotics*, Polity Press, pp. 79–83, 91–7; with New York University Press for Peter Trudgill (1983), *On Dialect: Social and Geographical Perspectives*, pp. 141–60; with University of Pennsylvania Press for William Labov (1972), *Sociolinguistic Patterns*, pp. xix–xxiv, 43–54, copyright © 1972 University of Pennsylvania Press; and with The Free Press, an imprint of Simon & Schuster, for William Labov (1972), 'Rules for ritual insults' in *Studies in Social Interaction*, ed. David Sudnow, copyright © 1972 by The Free Press; Cambridge University Press for material from John J. Gumperz (1982), 'Interethnic communication' in *Discourse Strategies*, pp. 172–86; Susan Gal (1978), 'Peasant men can't get wives: language change and sex roles in a bilingual community', *Language in Society*, 7:1, pp. 1–16; Nessa Wolfson (1976), 'Speech events and natural speech: some implications for sociolinguistic methodology', *Language in Society*, 5:2, pp. 189–209; M. Agar (1991), 'The bicultural in bilingual', *Language in Society*, 20:2, pp. 169–70, 172–81; John R. Edwards (1979), 'Social class differences and the identification of sex in children's speech', *Journal of Child Language*, 6, pp. 121–7; Penelope Eckert (1989), 'The whole woman: sex and gender differences in variation', *Language Variation and Change*, 1:1, pp. 245–65; and Peter Trudgill (1974), 'The co-variation of the phonological variables with sociological parameters' in *The Social Differentiation of English in*

Norwich, pp. 90–5; Elsevier Science Ltd for Deborah Cameron, Elizabeth Fraser, Penelope Harvey, Ben Rampton and Kay Richardson (1993), 'Ethics, advocacy and empowerment: issues of method in researching language', *Language and Communication*, 13:2, Pergamon Press, pp. 81–94; Joshua A. Fishman (1972) for material from *The Sociology of Language: An Interdisciplinary Social Science Approach to Language in Society*, Newbury House Publishers, pp. 1–7; Dr. Penelope Gardner-Chloros for reprinting 'Language Selection and Switching in Three Strasbourg Department Stores'; Georgetown University Press for material from John J. Gumperz (1982), 'The linguistic bases of communicative competence' in *Analyzing Discourse: Text and Talk [Georgetown University Round Table on Language and Linguistics 1981]*, ed. Deborah Tannen, pp. 323–34; and Dell Hymes (1974), 'The scope of sociolinguistics', pp. 313–33 and Joshua Fishman (1977), 'Language, ethnicity, and racism', pp. 297–309 from Roger W. Shuy, *Sociolinguistics: Current Trends and Prospects [Monograph Series on Languages and Linguistics, No. 25]*; Harcourt Brace & Co. Ltd for material from Howard Giles and Peter F. Powesland (1975), *Speech Style and Social Evaluation [European Monographs in Social Psychology]*, pp. 154–70; Eva Haugen for material from Einar Haugen (1966), 'Dialect, language, nation', *American Anthropologist*, 68:6, pp. 922–35; Mouton de Gruyter, a division of Walter de Gruyter & Co., for material from Viv Edwards (1989), 'Patois and the politics of protest: Black English in British classrooms' in *English Across Cultures, Cultures across English: A Reader in Cross-cultural Communication*, ed. O. Garcia and R. Otheguy, pp. 359–72; and R. K. Herbert (1991), 'The sociology of compliment work: an ethnocontrastive study of Polish and English compliments', *Multilingua*, 10:4, pp. 381–402; Routledge for material from Deborah Cameron (1990), 'Demythologizing sociolinguistics: why language does not reflect society' in *Ideologies of Language*, ed. John E. Joseph and Talbot J. Taylor, pp. 79–93; and Elinor Ochs (1983) 'Cultural dimensions of language acquisition' in *Acquiring Conversational Competence*, ed. Elinor Ochs and Bambi B. Schieffelin, Routledge & Kegan Paul, pp. 185–91; University of California Press for Suzanne Romaine (1990), 'Pidgin English Advertising' in *The State of the Language*, 1990 edn, ed. Christopher Ricks and Leonard Michaels, pp. 195–203. Copyright © 1989 The Regents of the University of California; and Pamela Fishman (1978), 'Interaction: the work women do', *Social Problems*, 25(4), pp. 397–406. Copyright © 1978 by the Society for the Study of Social Problems; Walter A. Wolfram for Walter A. Wolfram and Ralph W. Fasold (1974), 'Field methods in the study of social dialects' in *The Study of Social Dialects in American English*, Prentice-Hall, pp. 364–45.

Every effort has been made to trace the copyright holders, but if any have been inadvertently overlooked the publishers will be pleased to make the necessary arrangement at the first opportunity.

Also, the editors thank Justine Coupland, Peter Garrett and Gordon Tucker for their generous advice during the compilation of the volume. As it is conventional but necessary to add, the editors alone are responsible for the final form of the book and whatever shortcomings it is felt to have.

Introduction

Nikolas Coupland and Adam Jaworski

Sociolinguistics is the study of language in its social contexts and the study of social life through linguistics.

Broadly defined in this way, sociolinguistics is a vast interdisciplinary field. It subsumes many different traditions of study which have their own titles as well as their own established methods and priorities. The areas which are the main focus for this book are: *urban dialectology* (or *urban variation studies*), *the ethnography of communication* (including work on *language across cultures*), *the sociology of language* (including *multi-lingualism*), and *the social psychology of language* (especially studies of *attitudes towards language varieties*).

Despite this confusing array of titles, there has always been a good deal of overlap and interchange between traditions, and modern sociolinguistics is blurring distinctions between them even further. This means that the structure we have imposed on the book is by no means an absolute or inevitable one. But it should give newcomers a way of appreciating important differences of emphasis within contemporary sociolinguistics, as well as a sense of how the discipline has developed.

We are aware that a few other areas of study can also be included in the term sociolinguistics. In fact, sociolinguistics is the best single label to represent a very wide range of contemporary research at the intersection of linguistics, sociology and social theory, social psychology, and human communication studies. For purely practical reasons, we have largely excluded the areas of study designated by the labels *conversation analysis*, *discourse analysis* and *pragmatics*, which we have dealt with in a companion volume to this one (Jaworski and Coupland, forthcoming).

Defining sociolinguistics has never been without its controversies. Sociolinguistics is probably the most active but also the most diverse area of contemporary language studies. Among its main concerns, all of which are represented in the present volume, have been:

- how are forms of speech and patterns of communication distributed across time and space?
- how do individuals and social groups define themselves in and through language?
- how do communities differ in the 'ways of speaking' they have adopted?
- what are typical patterns in multilingual people's use of languages?

1

– how is language involved in social conflicts and tensions?
– do our attitudes to language reflect and perpetuate social divisions and discrimination, and could a better understanding of language in society alleviate these problems?
– is there a sociolinguistic theory of language use?
– what are the most efficient, and defensible, ways of collecting language data?
– what are the implications of qualitative and quantitative methods of sociolinguistic research?
– what are the relationships between researchers, 'subjects' and data?

So the issues that arise in this book are theoretical and methodological, but also practical. We hope the book reflects the evolution of sociolinguistic answers to these questions, but also its ongoing debates.

With these aims in mind, we see the Reader mainly as a resource book for new undergraduate students of language and communication. Working through an easily accessible and structured selection of important primary sources is probably the best way into the study of language in society. More advanced undergraduate and postgraduate students of sociolinguistics and related disciplines will also benefit from their first, or renewed, acquaintance with the original texts we have included.

The suggestions for further reading that we have included at the end of the introduction to each part of the book do not include the original sources of the chapters themselves. Nor do the further readings repeat references to the many solid, though amongst themselves very different, textbooks in sociolinguistics now available. We have provided a list of textbooks in the Further Reading section at the end of the introduction to Part I. Even new students are well advised to supplement their reading, where possible, by accessing the main international journals in the field. Once again, these are identified at the end of the introduction to Part I.

Our policy has been to reproduce the selected readings as faithfully to their original forms as possible. Despite this, limitations of space have forced us to reduce the length of many original versions. Where we have done this, we have indicated that text has been omitted and, in some instances, we have commented on the content of the sections we have edited out. We have of course made every attempt to maintain the coherence and emphasis of the originals.

Three of the chapters are newly-commissioned texts – the chapters by Bell, Gardner-Chloros and Kristiansen. These scholars were able to offer us newly written summaries of their important original works. We have referenced the original source of each text in a footnote on the title page of each chapter.

A note about style: we have followed a deliberate policy of not regularizing stylistic differences between chapters, such as American and

British English vocabulary and spelling. Sociolinguistics is, after all, the study of linguistic *differences*. The style-norms under which original texts were written, and indeed the decisions made by individual authors about how to represent their work, are of some theoretical interest in this case. There is also the important consideration that many chapters include examples of language data from around the world, where difference is again precisely the focus. We have reproduced these data in their original forms. Therefore, because different writers have followed slightly different conventions in representing and analysing their language data, some inconsistencies remain, for example in how words and sounds are phonetically transcribed.

REFERENCE

Jaworski, A. and Coupland, N. (forthcoming) *Discourse: A Reader and Coursebook.*

Part I
Sociolinguistics: Origins, Definitions and Approaches

In this first part of the book we have assembled extracts from some of the most influential writers in sociolinguistics to illustrate their views on what sociolinguistics is, what it does, and what it might become. From the short chapters by Hymes, Labov, (Joshua) Fishman and Halliday we get a strong sense of the core ideas that have brought sociolinguistics into existence: the limitations of a study of language that ignores the social and contextual basis of language; the need to develop an understanding of what language can *do* socially and communicatively – a functional perspective – as well as understanding what language is like as an abstract system; the need to account for language in use across many formal and informal, casual and ceremonial, ordinary and poetic situations; the commitment to displaying and accounting for variation, at all levels, in social uses of language; the pursuit of equality and social justice in a social world riddled with linguistic prejudice.

This socially-based view of language was a reaction to a more idealized view of language as code, conceptualized by Chomsky as *linguistic competence*: knowledge of the grammatical rules of a language by an idealized speaker-hearer. A degree of idealization will be present in linguistic analysis of any sort (as Halliday points out in Chapter 4 and Milroy in Chapter 8). But from a sociolinguistic point of view, the Chomskyan approach was limited and limiting. Therefore Hymes argued for the broadening of the object of linguistic inquiry into *communicative competence* – knowledge of grammatical but also social and cultural rules of a language, and reflecting the competences of actual speakers, not some idealized norm (see Gumperz's Chapter 5).

At the same time, a sense of history is important in this regard.[1] Although sociolinguistics is still a young discipline, dating mainly from the 1960s, its priorities have shifted over the years. Today, these priorities are being quite vigorously debated and challenged. A close reading of this part's chapters will show up significant differences of emphasis, and these will be repeated in later parts of the book. How we should 'frame' the discipline of sociolinguistics is therefore something of an open question, and it will be valuable to return to this introductory section from time to time to refine your own views. In the meanwhile, we can usefully highlight some of the principal areas of debate.

5

The 'shape' or morphology of the word 'sociolinguistics' sets up an expectation that sociolinguistics is a version of, or a way of doing, linguistics. It seems to be that part of linguistics which attends to 'social' questions. But several writers have pointed to the inaccurate assumptions behind this interpretation. In his short but much-quoted Introduction to the book *Sociolinguistic Patterns* (the extract is reprinted here as Chapter 2), Labov writes that he resisted the term sociolinguistics because it implies, mistakenly, that there *can* be a sort of linguistics that is *not* social. What is language if not a means of establishing contact between people? So isn't language an inherently social process? Doesn't language define the sociality of human beings? Sociolinguists of all persuasions would of course agree that this is the case. To answer the questions that Labov has set for himself, there is no alternative to studying actual uses of language in its natural contexts. Only a 'socially realistic' approach will reveal patterns in the distribution of language forms within communities and over time. Certain truths about language can only emerge from analyses based on real language data.

But other sociolinguists have argued (see, for example, Cameron in Chapter 7) that Labov himself does not go far enough; he doesn't go beyond asking questions about the linguistic system. His work extends the notion of system by accounting for linguistic variation and change, but it does not combine its results with a broader social theory, except in limited respects. Halliday takes Labov's (and others', most notably Bernstein's) work as a starting point in his version of sociolinguistics. He shares Labov's assumptions, but with rather different goals for his analyses. His argument is that we need a social perspective in order to model language, and in particular the meaning-options that are captured in the grammar and vocabulary of any sentence or utterance. Again, then, the general argument is that any adequate account of language – any viable sort of linguistics – needs to be social. Sociolinguistics would be a redundant concept if linguistics properly reflected the social basis of all language use.

Halliday also challenges Hymes's view of communicative competence, conceptualized as knowledge. Halliday argues for studying language as action, or 'doing', in which speakers produce particular forms and meanings by choosing from all those which are potentially available to them. We could say that Halliday's perspective is therefore one which grows out of sociolinguistic assumptions, but moves back into the traditional territory of linguistics – the modelling of grammatical organization at the level of the individual utterance. Most sociolinguists, on the other hand, feel that their analyses should illuminate both language *and* society in some specific respects.

Hymes's chapter, apart from introducing the notion of communicative competence, is helpful in showing us different theoretically possible links between language and society. What Hymes calls *the linguistic and the social* is merely a matter of bringing each of these concepts to bear upon the other – the minimal requirement for sociolinguistics. *Socially realistic linguistics*, Labov's formulation, sets up criteria for basing the study of language on observable instances of language-in-use. But Hymes sets out his case in favour of a *socially constituted linguistics*, an approach in which whatever questions we might ask about language are embedded in a social analysis – language as part of communicative conduct and social action. From this perspective, language and society are not theoretically distinct concepts. Language is itself a form of social action. Speaking and writing are the fulfilment of purposes which are defined socially and culturally. Equally, we might argue that society itself is a concept that depends intimately on exchange of meanings between people, and therefore on language.

Similarly, in (Joshua) Fishman's version of sociolinguistics, or what he prefers to call *the sociology of language*, sociological and linguistic concerns are inextricably linked. Fishman argues that, in multilingual communities, questions of nationalism, group equality, dominance and political change have a strong basis in attitudes to language, language choice and language policies. The sociology of language therefore needs to concern itself with psychological (or, more appropriately, social psychological) questions of attitudes, beliefs, stereotypes, allegiances and antipathies. Its range of research methods (as we shall see in Part II of the Reader) needs to be broad enough to give us access to cognitive processes as well as to the facts of linguistic distribution and patterns of use. This is why sociolinguistics has developed a strong tradition of sociopsychological work, as represented in Part V of the book.

We can therefore ask whether the scope of sociolinguistics in fact needs to be restricted to developing a better understanding of language itself. For Hodge and Kress, the overriding concern is *social semiotics*, or the symbolic and *ideological* meanings that sustain social groups and all social categories. Only some of these meanings will be strictly linguistic, and Hodge and Kress's analyses highlight the social significance of all conventional codes, including visual and behavioural conventions. We might think of Hodge and Kress's social semiotics as a particular version of sociolinguistics which addresses familiar linguistic topics – such as accent, dialect or style – within a distinctively *social* theory of meaning. For them, language styles have symbolic meanings that represent different positions in social conflicts, such as class interests and associated power struggles. Their social theory is influenced by Voloshinov,[2] who insisted that words and other linguistic forms are 'filled with dialogic overtones', echoing the voices of different social experiences and interest groups.

Voloshinov's ideas, developed as early as the 1920s, have attracted renewed interest in recent years as part of a movement towards critical linguistics. Within sociolinguistics, the critical perspective has begun to challenge the orthodoxy of *variationist* sociolinguistic research associated with William Labov. Note how Hodge and Kress, similarly to Cameron, acknowledge the ground-breaking importance of Labov's research in urban settings – his detailed and rigorously conducted observations of language variation in New York City, for example (well overviewed in Cameron's chapter). But these last chapters also criticize Labov for what they see as the narrowness of his social theorizing. Cameron argues that Labov is too ready to accept the belief that language *reflects* society, and that his research is designed on that assumption. Examining how features of pronunciation co-vary with social dimensions like social class, gender or age leaves us unable to explain the symbolic force of such features. Even the most thorough descriptive account of language variation leaves us unable to *explain* the social constitution of linguistic features.

So, for all the obvious successes of sociolinguistics from the 1960s onwards, sociolinguists are reappraising the trust they have placed in objective, observational research, and in quantification as their main research tool. Systematic observation and counting has revealed important facts about how language forms are distributed – between women and men, across age-groups and over time. On the other hand, does commitment to this sort of research limit the questions we can *ask* about language in society? Halliday seemed to suggest so when he wrote that sociolinguistics sometimes appears to be a search for answers which have no questions!

Questions of method are taken up in the chapters in Part II, but there is *more* at stake than methods themselves. If we endorse Hymes's appeal for a 'socially constituted' study of language, do we dare to place language at the centre of our model of social life? If we do, then the agenda for sociolinguistics is, perhaps paradoxically, far broader than that of linguistics. Sociolinguistics can provide a coherent way of investigating social processes generally. This is why it is probably useful to keep the terminological distinction between linguistics and sociolinguistics, despite Labov's wish to do away with the 'socio' element.

There is no reason to expect that a uniform vision of sociolinguistics will prevail, and we have tried to reflect the diversity of sociolinguistic approaches and priorities, past and present, throughout the Reader.

NOTES

1   A sense of history is also important in appreciating the writing conventions of sociolinguists. To contemporary readers, it is very striking that eminent theorists of language and society should have tolerated what are arguably *sexist* modes of reference, such as Labov's 'people...arguing with their wives', the first word of Fishman's chapter, or Halliday's 'language and social man'. It is very largely through the sociolinguistic research which these authors brought into existence that we have become aware of the divisiveness and inequality that such patterns of usage can promote.

2 Hodge and Kress's references to Voloshinov can be taken to refer simultaneously to Bakhtin, who is often thought to be the original source of texts attributed to Voloshinov: Mikhail Bakhtin (1981) *The Dialogic Imagination: Four Essays*, ed. M. Holquist, trans. C. Emerson and M. Holquist (Austin, TX: University of Texas Press).

PART I: FURTHER READING

General

Bolton, K. and Kwok, H. (eds) (1992) *Sociolinguistics Today: Asia and the West* (London: Routledge).

Cameron, D. (ed.) (1990) *A Feminist Critique of Language* (London: Routledge).

Coates, J. (1993) *Women, Men and Language: A Sociolinguistic Account of Gender Differences in Language* (second edition) (London: Longman).

Dittmar, N. (1976) *Sociolinguistics: A Critical Survey of Theory and Application* (London: Arnold).

Figueroa, E. (1994) *Sociolinguistic Metatheory* (Oxford: Pergamon).

Fowler, R., Hodge, R., Kress, G. and Trew, T. (1979) *Language and Control* (London: Routledge & Kegan Paul).

Gee, J. P. (1990) *Social Linguistics and Literacies: Ideology in Discourses* (London: Falmer Press).

Giglioli, P. P. (ed.) (1972) *Language and Social Context* (Harmondsworth: Penguin).

Gumperz, J. J. and Hymes, D. (eds) (1972) *Directions in Sociolinguistics: The Ethnography of Communication* (New York: Holt, Reinhart & Winston; also published by Blackwell).

Halliday, M. A. K. (1978) *Language as Social Semiotic* (London: Arnold).

Hymes, D. (1972) 'On Communicative Competence', in Pride, J. and Holmes, J. (eds) *Sociolinguistics* (Harmondsworth: Penguin) pp. 269–93.

Kress, G. and Hodge, R. (1994) *Language as Ideology* (second edition) (London: Routledge).

McConnell-Ginet, S., Borker, R. and Furman, N. (eds) (1980) *Women and Language in Literature and Society* (New York: Praeger).

McKay, S. and Hornberger, N. H. (eds) (1996) *Sociolinguistics and Language Teaching* (Cambridge: Cambridge University Press).

Pride, J. and Holmes, J. (eds) (1972) *Sociolinguistics: Selected Readings* (Harmondsworth: Penguin).

Robinson, W. P. (1972) *Language and Social Behaviour* (Harmondsworth: Penguin).

Trudgill, P. (ed.) (1984) *Applied Sociolinguistics* (New York: Academic Press).

Williams, G. (1992) *Sociolinguistics: A Sociological Critique* (London: Routledge).

Wolfson, N. (1988) *Perspectives: Sociolinguistics and TESOL* (New York: Newbury House).

Sociolinguistics Textbooks

Bell, R. T. (1976) *Sociolinguistics: Goals, Approaches and Problems* (London: Batsford).

Downes, W. (1984) *Language and Society* (London: Fontana).

Fasold, R. (1984) *The Sociolinguistics of Society* (Oxford: Blackwell).

Fasold, R. (1990) *Sociolinguistics of Language* (Oxford: Blackwell).

Fishman, J. A. (1971) *Sociolinguistics: A Brief Introduction* (Rowley, MA: Newbury House).

Holmes, J. (1992) *An Introduction to Sociolinguistics* (London: Longman).

Hudson, R. A. (1996) *Sociolinguistics* (second edition) (Cambridge: Cambridge University Press).

Montgomery, M. (1986) *An Introduction to Language and Society* (London and New York: Methuen).

Romaine, S. (1994) *Language in Society: An Introduction to Sociolinguistics* (Oxford: Oxford University Press).

Trudgill, P. (1983) *Sociolinguistics: An Introduction* (second edition) (Harmondsworth: Penguin).

Wardhaugh, R. (1992) *An Introduction to Sociolinguistics* (Oxford: Blackwell).

Sociolinguistics Journals

Sociolinguistics is served by several international journals. Of these, *Language and Society* (Cambridge: Cambridge University Press) is the best established. It leans towards ethnographic and anthropological research. The *Journal of Sociolinguistics* (Oxford: Blackwell Publishers) is a new journal, in which both editors of this Reader are also involved editorially, along with Allan Bell; it aims to cover the whole interdisciplinary field and is open to innovative approaches.

Language Variation and Change (Cambridge: Cambridge University Press) gives the best coverage of quantitative variationist approaches. The *International Journal of the Sociology of Language* (Berlin: Mouton de Gruyter), as its title implies, follows the more macro-sociological tradition of Fishman's sociolinguistics; it is an excellent source of information of language communities around the world, sociolinguistic conflicts and language policy debates. *Current Issues in Language and Society* (Clevedon: Multilingual Matters) prints round-table discussions of sociolinguistic topics centring on usually one or two major papers per issue.

Multilingua (Berlin: Mouton de Gruyter) and *Journal of Multilingual and Multicultural Development* (Clevedon: Multilingual Matters) offer broad coverage but with an emphasis on multilingual settings and cultural differences. The *International Journal of Applied Linguistics* (Oslo: Novus), and *Language and Communication* (Oxford and New York: Pergamon/Elsevier) cover sociolinguistic topics amongst others.

The Journal of Language and Social Psychology (London and Thousand Oaks: Sage) is best known for covering quantitative and experimental research, although it is increasingly open to qualitative and less overtly psychological topics and methods. *Applied Linguistics* (Oxford: Oxford University Press) carries sociolinguistic papers but it has in the past interpreted 'applied' linguistics as issues in language learning and teaching.

Many journals represent work on social interaction and discourse which can appropriately be considered to be part of sociolinguistics. (As we noted earlier, this area is covered in a companion reader under our editorship, also published by Macmillan.) Of these journals, *Discourse and Society* (London and Thousand Oaks: Sage) is probably closest in its coverage to the interests of the present book.

1 The Scope of Sociolinguistics

Dell Hymes

COMPETENCE AND PERFORMANCE

Chomsky's (1965) work is a decisive step, not only in extending the scope of linguistic theory, but also in redefining the nature of its object. For 'language' Chomsky substitutes 'competence,' defined as a fluent native speaker's knowledge (largely tacit) of grammaticality – of whether or not putative sentences are part of his language, and according to what structural relationships. The goal of linguistic description is thus changed, from an object independent of men, to a human capacity. Both changes (deep structure, human capacity) are felt to be so great as to lead transformational grammarians to reject 'structural linguistics' as a name for their work, and to use it solely to describe other schools as predecessors. From a social standpoint, transformational grammar might equally well be seen as the culmination of the leading theme of structural linguistics. To center analysis in a deep structure, one grounded in human nature, is to fulfill an impulse of structural linguistics to treat language as a sphere of wholly autonomous form. Such a theory perfects and gives the ultimate justification to a study of language at once of human significance and abstracted from actual human beings.

Chomsky's redefinition of linguistic goals appears, then, a half-way house. The term 'competence' promises more than it in fact contains. It is restricted to knowledge, and, within knowledge, to knowledge of grammar. Thus, it leaves other aspects of speakers' tacit knowledge and ability in confusion, thrown together under a largely unexamined concept of 'performance.' In effect, 'performance' confuses two separate aims. The first is to stress that competence is something underlying behavior ('mere performance,' 'actual performance'). The second is to allow for aspects of linguistic ability which are not grammatical: psychological constraints on memory, choice of alternative rules, stylistic choices and devices in word order, etc. The intended negative connotation of the first sense of 'performance' tends to attach to the second sense; factors of

Source: Hymes, D. (1974) *Foundations in Sociolinguistics: An Ethnographic Approach* (Philadelphia, PA: University of Pennsylvania Press) pp. 92–209.

performance – and the theory must place all social factors here – are generally seen as things that limit the realization of grammatical possibilities, rather than as constitutive or enabling. In fact, of course, choice among the alternatives that can be generated from a single base structure depends as much upon a tacit knowledge as does grammar, and can be studied as much in terms of underlying rules as can grammar. Such things equally underlie actual behavior as facets of knowledge, and would be aspects of competence in the normal sense of the term. On its own terms, linguistic theory must extend the notion of competence to include more than the grammatical. ...

An adequate approach must distinguish and investigate four aspects of competence: (a) *systemic potential* – whether and to what extent something is not yet realized, and, in a sense, not yet known; it is to this Chomsky in effect reduces competence; (b) *appropriateness* – whether and to what extent something is in some context suitable, effective, or the like; (c) *occurrence* – whether and to what extent something is done; (d) *feasibility* – whether and to what extent something is possible, given the means of implementation available.

The last three dimensions would have to be 'performance' in the system of Chomsky's *Aspects* (1965), but knowledge with regard to each is part of the competence of a speaker-hearer in any full sense of the term, and 'performance' should be reserved for a more normal, consistent meaning (see below). There is no notice of occurrence in *Aspects*, or in most current linguistic theory, but it is an essential dimension. Most linguists today scorn quantitative data, for example, but Labov (1973a, 1973b) has shown that systematic study of quantitative variation discloses new kinds of structure and makes possible explanation of change. In general, this theoretical dimension provides for the fact that members of a speech community are aware of the commonness, rarity, previous occurrence or novelty, of many features of speech, and that this knowledge enters into their definitions and evaluations of ways of speaking. ...

GOALS OF SOCIOLINGUISTICS

The term 'sociolinguistics' means many things to many people, and of course no one has a patent on its definition. Indeed not everyone whose work is called 'sociolinguistic' is ready to accept the label, and those who do not use the term include and emphasize different things. Nevertheless, three main orientations can be signaled out, orientations that can be labelled: (1) the social as well as the linguistic; (2) socially realistic linguistics; (3) socially constituted linguistics. Let me characterize each of these orientations in relation to conventional linguistic theory.

1. *The social as well as the linguistic.* Here may be placed ventures into social problems involving language and the use of language, which are not seen as involving a challenge to existing linguistics. American linguistics does have a tradition of practical concerns – one can mention Sapir's semantic research for an international auxiliary language, Bloomfield's work in the teaching of reading, Swadesh's literacy work, the 'Army method' of teaching foreign languages. The salient examples today involve American cities and developing nations, and concern problems of education, minority groups, and language policies. For the most part this work is conceived as an application, lacking theoretical goals, or else as pursuing theoretical goals that are in addition to those of normal linguistics, or perhaps even wholly unrelated to them. When 'sociolinguistics' serves as a legitimizing label for such activity, it is, as said, not conceived as a challenge to normal linguistics; linguists who perceive such a challenge in the label tend to eschew it.

2. *Socially realistic linguistics.* This term is apt[1] for work that extends and challenges existing linguistics with data from the speech community. The challenge, and indeed the accomplishment, might be summed up in the two words, 'variation' and 'validity.' A salient example is the work of William Labov, whose orientation toward linguistics is represented in such papers as 'The Study of Language in its Social Context' (1970) and 'Methodology' (1971) (see now Labov 1973a, 1973b). The expressed theoretical goals are not distinct from those of normal linguistics, e.g. the nature of linguistic rules, the nature of sound change, but the method of work, and the findings, differ sharply. Here might also be put work which recognizes dependence of the analysis of meaning and speech acts on social context (e.g. R. Lakoff 1972, 1973). ...

3. *Socially constituted linguistics.* The phrase 'socially constituted' is intended to express the view that social function gives form to the ways in which linguistic features are encountered in actual life. This being so, an adequate approach must begin by identifying social functions, and discovery the ways in which linguistic features are selected and grouped together to serve them. Such a point of view cannot leave normal linguistic theory unchallenged as does the first orientation, nor limits challenge to reform, because its own goals are not allowed for by normal theory, and cannot be achieved by 'working within the system.' A 'socially constituted' linguistics shares the practical concerns of other orientations; it shares concern for social realism and validity; but even if it could wait for the perfection of a 'linguistic theory' of the normal sort, it could not then use it. Many of the features and relationships with which it must deal would never have been taken up in a 'theory' of the normal sort. (That is why, indeed, 'linguistic theory' of the normal sort is not a 'theory of language,' but only a theory of

grammar.) A 'socially constituted' linguistics is concerned with social as well as referential meaning, and with language as part of communicative conduct and social action. Its task is the thoroughgoing critique of received notions and practices, from the standpoint of social meaning, that is, from a functional perspective. Such a conception reverses the structuralist tendency of most of the twentieth century, toward the isolation of referential structure, and the posing of questions about social functions from that standpoint. The goals of social relevance and social realism can indeed be fully accomplished only from the standpoint of the new conception, for much of what must be taken into account, much of what is there, organized and used, in actual speech, can only be seen, let alone understood, when one starts from function and looks for the structure that serves it. ...

In sum, if our concern is social relevance and social realism, we must recognize that there is more to the relationship between sound and meaning than is dreamt of in normal linguistic theory. In sound there are stylistic as well as referential features and contrasts; in meaning there is social as well as referential import; in between there are relationships not given in ordinary grammar but there for the finding in social life.

From this standpoint, what there is to be described and accounted for is not in the first instance a language (say, English), but *means of speech*, and, inseparably, their meanings *for those who use them*. The set of conventional resources available to a competent member of a community can be so described. As we have seen, this set of resources is more extensive than a single norm, grammar, or language; nor can the nature of its organization be given in those terms. Yet it is *this* set of resources with which one must deal, if 'linguistic theory' is to become synonymous with 'theory of language.'

It is not that phenomena pointing to a more general conception of the relationship between sound and meaning have not long been noted, and often enough studied with insight and care. Expressive language, speech levels, social dialects, registers; functional varieties, code- and style-switching, are familiar and essential concepts; the interlocked subjects of stylistics, poetics, and rhetoric have flourished in recent years. Anything that can be accomplished in theory and method for a socially constituted linguistics must incorporate and build on that work, which has done much to shape what I say here. But the tendency has been to treat such phenomena and such studies as marginal or as supplementary to grammar. (Certainly that has been the tendency of grammarians.) The hegemony of grammar as a genre, and of the referential function as its organizing basis, has been preserved. Whereas the essence of a functional approach is not to take function for ranted, but as problematic; to assume as part of a universal theory of language that a plurality of functions are served by linguistic features in any act and community; to require validation of the relationships between features and functions, and of their organization into varieties, registers, ways of speaking, ethnographically within the community; and to take functional questions, a functional perspective, as having priority, that is, as being fundamental, both in general theory and in specific accounts, to whatever can be validly said as to structure, comptence, universals, etc. (cf. Hymes 1964a).

Such a perspective was present in the structuralism of the period before World War II (cf. Jakobson 1963, Firth 1935, and below), and has never been wholly lost. In Anglo-American circles it has begun to come to the fore in work under the aegis of sociolinguistics in recent years. Salient examples include the work of Labov (1966, 1970, sec. 3) on 'sociolingistic structure,' of Gumperz (1964) on verbal repertoire, of Bernstein (1972) on codes, of Fishman on domains (1966), of Denison (1970) and Le Page (1969) on multilingualism, of Halliday (1970, 1971) on the multifunctional approach to grammar, and of Ervin-Tripp (1972) on sociolinguistic rules. What is important here is the element in each work that contributes to a general methodological perspective. Such work goes beyond the recognition and analysis of particular cases to suggest *a mode of organization of linguistic features other than that of a grammar.* The common implication, which I want to draw, emphasize, and elaborate, is, in its weaker form, that such alternative modes of organization exist; and, in its stronger form, that one or more such alternative modes of organization may be fundamental.

There is a second point, linked to the first, and owing its full recognition to much the same body of work: *a conception of the speech community not in terms of language alone* (especially not just one language, and a fortiori, not just one homogeneous language).

Although they would find the wording odd, many linguists might accept a definition of the object of linguistic description as: the organization of features within a community. From the present standpoint, the wording is not odd, but vital. The two points just stated in negative terms can now be put positively.

1. The organization of linguistic features within a speech community is in terms of ways of speaking within a verbal repertoire.
2. Membership in a speech community consists in sharing one (or more) ways of speaking.

From this standpoint, the usual linguistic description identifies a part (not the whole) of the linguistic features, resources, verbal means, of a community, and says little or nothing about their actual organization. Grammar indeed originated as a pedagogical and literary genre, and has been revitalized as a logical one; neither its traditional nor its mathematical pedigree is much warrant for taking it for granted that it is the form in which speech comes organized in use. Psychologists and psycholinguists have recently discovered and begun to build on recognition of this fact, with regard to the organization of language for production, reception, and acquisition. Those of us interested in the existence of social facts and customary behavior must build on it too. ...

What is the nature of such a reconstruction, of a method of description adequate to the goals of a socially constituted linguistics, as just stated? Briefly and broadly put, 'the task is to identify and analyze the ways of speaking in a community, together with the conditions and meanings of their use. In sociolinguistic description, the first application of the commutation test is to ways of speaking.' In what way is a person speaking? What is the set of such ways? And the contrastive as well as identificational meaning of each? Within ways of speaking, commutation will further discover two mutually implicated modes of meaning, the 'referential' and 'social.' There is the systemic invariance in terms of which two utterances of 'fourth floor' are repetitions, the same utterance, and there is the contrast in virtue of which they may be different (see Labov 1966 on style-shifting in New York City department stores with respect to 'repetitions' of utterances with post-vocalic constriction). Conversely, there is the contrast by which utterances of 'third floor' and 'fourth floor' may differ in what they convey (as to location), and there is the systemic invariance in terms of which they are repetitions, conveying the same meaning (as to social position and speech community identification). It is not obvious, is it, after all, that the energies of linguistics should be devoted entirely to the signals that tell where things can be bought in department stores, and not at all to the signals that tell where the people in department stores have come from, are now, and aspire to be? ...

If we associate 'sociolinguists' with 'socially constituted linguistics,' then there are a number of themes, or indeed slogans, for a sociolinguistics of the scope just sketched.

1. Linguistic theory as theory of language, entailing the organization of speech (not just of grammar).
2. Foundations of theory and methodology as entailing questions of function (not just of structure).
3. Speech communities as organizations of ways of speaking (not just equivalent to the distribution of the grammar of a language).
4. Competence as personal ability (not just grammatical knowledge, systemic potential of a grammar, superorganic property of a society, or, indeed, irrelevant to persons in any other way).
5. Performance as accomplishment and responsibility, investiture and emergence (not just psycholinguistic processing and impediment).
6. Languages as what their users have made of them (not just what human nature has given).
7. *Liberté, Egalité, Fraternité* of speech as something achieved in social life (not just postulated as given as a consequence of language).

THE SCOPE OF SOCIOLINGUISTICS

What, then, is the scope of sociolinguistics? Not all I have just described, but rather, that part of it which linguists and social scientists leave unattended. The final goal of sociolinguistics, I think, must be to preside over its own liquidation. The flourishing of a hybrid term such as sociolinguistics reflects a gap in the disposition of established disciplines with respect to reality. Sometimes new disciplines do grow from such a state of affairs, but the recent history of the study of language has seen the disciplines adjacent to a gap themselves grow to encompass it. Some can recall a generation ago when proper American linguists did not study meaning, and ethnographers had little linguistic method. A study of meaning in another language or culture (say, grammatical categories or kinship terms) could qualify as 'ethnolinguistic' then. Today, of course, semantics is actually pursued in both linguistics and ethnography, and a mediating interdisciplinary label is unnecessary; 'semantics' itself will usually suffice.

Let us hope for a similar history for 'sociolinguistics.' In one sense, the issue again is the study of meaning, only now, social meaning.

What are the chances for such a history to be written, say, from the vantage point of the year AD2000? To see, in retrospect, the flourishing of 'sociolinguistics' as a transitional stage in the transformation of linguistics and adjacent social science disciplines to encompass what I have called 'socially constituted linguistics'? The chances, I think, are quite uncertain.

Clearly recognition of the gap, and advocacy of a perspective to overcome it, are not enough. The future historian will notice that there were 'efforts towards a means–end model of language' between the two world wars (Jakobson 1963). And in the literature of that period, he will find in the writings of another of the five or six great linguists of the century such statements as the following:

> The true locus of culture is in the interaction of specific individuals and, on the subjective side, in the world of meaning which each one of these individuals may unconsciously abstract for himself from his participation in these interactions. [1932, SWES 515].

> For it is only through an analysis of variation that the reality and meaning of a norm can be established at all, and it is only through a minute and sympathetic study of individual behavior in the state in which normal human beings find themselves, namely in a state of society, that it will ultimately be possible to say things about society itself and culture that are more than fairly convenient abstractions. [1938, SWES 576].

> It is not really difficult, then, to see why anyone brought up on the austerities of a well-defined science must, if he is to maintain his symbolic self-respect, become more and more estranged from man himself. [1939, SWES 580].

The very terminology which is used by the many kinds of segmental sciences of man indicates how remote man himself has become as a necessary concept in the methodology of the respective sciences ... In linguistics, abstracted speech sounds, words, and the arrangement of words have come to have so authentic a vitality that one can speak of 'regular sound change' ... without knowing or caring who opened their mouths, at what time, to communicate what to whom. [1939, SWES 578, 579]

As we follow tangible problems of behavior rather than selected problems set by recognized disciplines, we discover the field of social psychology. [1932, SWES 513]

The social psychology into which the conventional cultural and psychological disciplines must eventually be resolved is related to these paradigmatic studies as an investigation into living speech is related to grammar. I think few cultural disciplines are as exact, as rigorously configurated, as self-contained as grammar, but if it is desired to have grammar contribute a significant share to our understanding of human behavior, its definitions, meanings, and classifications must be capable of a significant restatement in terms of a social psychology which ... boldly essays to bring every cultural pattern back to the living context from which it has been abstracted in the first place ... back to its social matrix. [1934, SWES 592–3, 592]

These quotations are from the writings of Sapir's last years, when he began to rethink the nature of language, culture, and society from a standpoint he sometimes called 'psychiatric,' or 'social psychology,' and which today we might more readily label the standpoint of social interaction, or communicative conduct; the standpoint, as I would see it, of sociolinguistics.

Obviously Sapir's intellectual lead did not prevail, after his death in 1939, although its influence can be traced in many quarters. Such a fact must humble expectation. A decade ago (when the introduction to my book of readings was written) I did venture to predict:

It may be that the development of these foci of interest (semantic description, sociolinguistic variation) will lead historians of twentieth-century linguistics to say that whereas the first half of the century was distinguished by a drive for the autonomy of language as an object of study and a focus upon description of structure, the second half was distinguished by a concern for the integration of language in sociocultural context and a focus upon the analysis of function. (Hymes 1964b: 11)

Ten years later, we are, I think, only at a threshold. Whether we pass over and occupy the land will depend crucially upon the commitment of those who have the essential skills, especially linguists. For a criterion of the field I envisage is that it is a linguistics, a functionally oriented, more adequate linguistics, that has at last realized itself as a social science. Perhaps in this respect there will be in the year AD2000 three main branches of linguistic science: psychological, sociological (these two answering to the two directions of explanatory adequacy), and the traditional and indispensable work oriented toward specific languages, language families, and language areas. With regard to the sociological branch of the three, there are many reasons within theoretical linguistics today why it appears a necessary step. But holes in a scientific pattern, like those in a phonological one, may go long unfilled. Perhaps as much or more will depend on practical as on scientific concern. It may not have been accidental that it was the 1930s that saw Sapir's concern with personal meaning and social interaction. Perhaps socially concerned linguistics in the coming decade will discover wisdom in Chairman Mao Tse-tung's remark (1964: 7):

> If you want to know a certain thing or a certain class of things directly, you must personally participate in the practical struggle to change reality, to change that thing or class of things, for only thus can you come into contact with them as phenomena; only through personal participation can you uncover the essence of that thing or class of things and comprehend them.

Certainly it is a sociolinguistic perspective, uniting theory and practice, that is most appropriate to a vision of the future of mankind as one in a world at peace. There are three ways of seeking unity in the phenomena of language. One has been to seek a unity of origin in the past. Comparative-historical linguistics, linguistics oriented toward individual languages and language families, can discover and maintain such unities; indeed, it has had positive effect in that regard (Matthew Arnold pointed to the Indo–European unity of the English and Irish, Sir Henry Maine to that of England and India, as warrant for overcoming prejudice and accepting brotherhood). A second way has been to seek a unity of underlying structure, a timeless or continuing origin, so to speak, in the present. Structural and psychologically-oriented linguistics can point to this. A third way is to seek the origins of a unity in the future – to see the processes of sociolinguistic change that envelop our objects of study as underlain by the emergence of a world society. It is a sociolinguistic perspective that naturally and inevitably considers mankind, not only as what it has been, and is, but also as what it is becoming. Linguistics as sociolinguistics, if it will, can envisage and work toward a unity that is yet to come.

NOTE

1   I owe this term to Maxine Bernstein, in whose dissertation I encountered it.

REFERENCES

Bernstein, B. (1972) *Class, Codes and Social Control, I: Theoretical Papers* (London: Routledge & Kegan Paul).

Chomsky, N. (1965) *Aspects of the Theory of Syntax* (Cambridge, MA: MIT Press).

Denison, N. (1970) 'Sociolinguistic Aspects of Plurilingualism', *Proceedings of the International Days of Sociolinguistics* (Rome: Istituto Luigi Sturzo) pp. 255–78.

Ervin-Tripp, S. (1972) 'On Sociolinguistic Rules: Alternation and Co-occurrence', in *Directions in Sociolinguistics*, Gumperz, J. J. and Hymes, D. (eds) (New York: Holt, Rinehart & Winston) pp. 213–50.

Firth, J. R. (1935) 'The Technique of Semantics', *Transactions of the Philological Society*, London, pp. 36–72.

Fishman, J. (1966) *Language Loyalty in the United States* (The Hague: Mouton).

Gumperz, John J. (1964) 'Linguistic and Social Interaction in Two Communities', in *The Ethnography of Communication*, Gumperz, J. J. and Hymes, D. (eds) Special Issue of *American Anthropologist*, **66**(6), pp. 137–53.

Halliday, M. A. K. (1970) 'Functional Diversity in Language as seen from a Consideration of Modality and Mood in English', *Foundations of Language*, **6**, pp. 322–61.

Halliday, M. A. K. (1971) 'Linguistic Function and Literary Style: An Inquiry into the Language of William Golding's *The Inheritors*', in *Literary Style: A Symposium*, Chatman, S. (ed.) (London: Oxford University Press).

Hymes, D. (1964a) Directions in (Ethno) Linguistic Theory', in *Transcultural Studies of Cognition*, Romney, A. K. and D'Andrade, R. G. (eds) (Special publication, *American Anthropologist*, **66**(3), part 2) (Washington, DC: American Anthropological Association) pp. 6–56.

Hymes, D. (1964b) 'Introduction: Toward Ethnographies of Communication', in *The Ethnography of Communication*, Gumperz, J. J. and Hymes, D. (eds) (Special publication, *American Anthropologist*, **66**(6), part 2) (Washington, DC: American Anthropological Association) pp. 1–34.

Jakobson, R. (1963) 'Efforts Towards a Means-ends Model of Language in Inter-war Continental Linguistics', in *Trends in Modern Linguistics*, Mohrmann, C., Norman, F. and Sommerfelt, A. (eds) (Utrecht: Spectrum Publishers) pp. 104–8. (Reprinted in his *Selected Writings*, **2**, pp. 522–6 (The Hague: Mouton, 1971).)

Labov, W. (1966) *The Social Stratification of English in New York City* (Washington, DC: Center for Applied Linguistics).

Labov, W. (1970) 'The Study of Language in its Social Context', *Studium Generale* **20**, pp. 30–87.

Labov, W. (1971) 'Methodology', in *A Survey of Linguistic Science*, Dingwall, W. O. (ed.) (College Park, MD: University of Maryland, Linguistics Program) pp. 412–91.

Labov, W. (1973a) *Language in the Inner City* (Philadelphia, PA: University of Pennsylvania).

Labov, W. (1973b) *Sociolinguistic Patterns* (Philadelphia, PA: University of Pennsylvania).

Lakoff, R. (1972) 'Language in Context', *Language*, **48**, pp. 907–27.

Lakoff, R. (1973) 'Language and Woman's Place', *Language in Society*, **2**(1), pp. 45–80.

Le Page, R. (1969) 'Problems of Description in Multilingual Communities', *Transactions of the Philological Society* (1968), London, pp. 189–212.

Mao Tse-Tung (1964) *On Practice* (Peking: Foreign Language Press).

Sapir, E. [Papers by Sapir reprinted in Mandelbaum (ed.), *Selected Writings of Edward Sapir* (Berkeley and Los Angeles, CA: University of California Press, 1949) are indicated by 'SWES,' together with their pages in that collection.]

Sapir, E. (1932) 'Cultural Anthropology and Psychiatry', *Journal of Abnormal and Social Psychology*, 27 (SWES 509–21) pp. 229–42.

Sapir, E. (1934) 'The Emergence of the Concept of Personality in a Study of Cultures', *Journal of Social Psychology*, 5 (SWES 590–7) pp. 408–15.

Sapir, E. (1938) 'Why Cultural Anthropology Needs the Psychiatrist', *Psychiatry*, 1 (SWES 569–77) pp. 7–12.

Sapir, E. (1939) 'Psychiatric and Cultural Pitfalls in the Business of Getting a Living', *Mental Health*, Publication No. 9 (American Association for the Advancement of Science) (SWES 578–89) pp. 237–44.

2 Linguistics and Sociolinguistics

William Labov

I have resisted the term *sociolinguistics* for many years, since it implies that there can be a successful linguistic theory or practice which is not social. When I first published the studies of Martha's Vineyard and New York City that form the basis of the first part of this book, it seemed necessary to make that point again and again. In spite of a considerable amount of sociolinguistic activity, a socially realistic linguistics seemed a remote prospect in the 1960s. The great majority of linguists had resolutely turned to the contemplation of their own idiolects. We have not yet emerged from the shadow of our intuitions, but it no longer seems necessary to argue about what is or is not linguistics. There is a growing realization that the basis of intersubjective knowledge in linguistics must be found in speech – language as it is used in everyday life by members of the social order, that vehicle of communication in which they argue with their wives, joke with their friends, and deceive their enemies.

When I first entered linguistics as a student, in 1961, it was my intention to gather data from the secular world. The early projects that I constructed were 'essays in experimental linguistics,' carried out in ordinary social settings. My aim was to avoid the inevitable obscurity of texts, the self-consciousness of formal elicitations, and the self-deception of introspection. A decade of work outside the university as an industrial chemist had convinced me that the everyday world was stubborn but consistently so, baffling at the outset but rewarding in the long run for those who held to its rational character. A simple review of the literature might have convinced me that such empirical principles had no place in linguistics: there were many ideological barriers to the study of language in everyday life. First, Saussure had enunciated the principle that structural systems of the present and historical changes of the past had to be studied in isolation (1962: 124). That principle had been consistently eroded by Martinet (1955) and others who found structure in past changes, but little progress had been made in locating change in present structures. The second ideological barrier

Source: Introduction to Labov, W. (1972) *Sociolinguistic Patterns* (Philadelphia, PA: University of Pennsylvania Press) pp. xix–xxiv. Also published in 1978 (Oxford: Basil Blackwell).

explicitly asserted that sound change could not in principle be directly observed. Bloomfield defended the regularity of sound change against the irregular evidence of the present by declaring (1933: 364) that any fluctuations we might observe would only be cases of dialect borrowing. Next Hockett observed that while sound change was too slow to be observed, structural change was too fast (1958: 457). The empirical study of linguistic change was thus removed from the program of 20th-century linguistics.

A third restriction was perhaps the most important: free variation could not in principle be constrained. The basic postulate of linguistics (Bloomfield 1933: 76) declared that some utterances were the same. Conversely, these were in free variation, and whether or not one or the other occurred at a particular time was taken to be linguistically insignificant. Relations of *more* or *less* were therefore ruled out of linguistic thinking: a form or a rule could only occur always, optionally, or never. The internal structure of variation was therefore removed from linguistic studies and with it, the study of change in progress.

It was also held that feelings about language were inaccessible and outside of the linguist's scope (Bloch and Trager 1942). The social evaluation of linguistic variants was therefore excluded from consideration. This is merely one aspect of the more general claim that the linguist should not use nonlinguistic data to explain linguistic change. Throughout these discussions, we see many references to what the linguist can or cannot do *as a linguist*.

REFERENCES

Bloch, B. and Trager, G. (1942) *Outline of Linguistic Analysis* (Baltimore, MD: Waverley Press).
Bloomfield, L. (1933) *Language* (New York: Henry Holt).
Hockett, C. F. (1958) *A Course in Modern Linguistics* (New York: Macmillan).
Martinet, A. (1955) *Economie des Changements Phonétiques* (Berne: Francke).
Saussure, F. de (1962) *Cours de Linguistique Générale* (Paris: Payot).

3   The Sociology of Language

Joshua A. Fishman

Man is constantly using language – spoken language, written language, printed language – and man is constantly linked to others via shared norms of behavior. The sociology of language examines the interaction between these two aspects of human behavior: the use of language and the social organization of behavior. Briefly put, the sociology of language focuses upon the entire gamut of topics related to the social organization of language behavior, including not only language usage *per se* but also language attitudes and overt behaviors toward language and toward language users.

SOCIOLINGUISTIC HEADLINES

The latter concern of the sociology of language – overt behavior toward language and toward language users – is a concern shared by political and educational leaders in many parts of the world and is an aspect of sociolinguistics that frequently makes headlines in the newspapers. Many French-Canadian university students oppose the continuation of public education in English in the Province of Quebec. Many Flemings in Belgium protest vociferously against anything less than full equality – at the very least – for Dutch in the Brussels area. Some Welsh nationalists daub out English signs along the highways in Wales and many Irish revivalists seek stronger governmental support for the restoration of Irish than that made available during half a century of Irish independence. Jews throughout the world protest the Soviet government's persecution of Yiddish writers and the forced closing of Yiddish schools, theatres, and publications.

Swahili, Filipino, Indonesian, Malay, and the various provincial languages of India are all being consciously expanded in vocabulary and standardized in spelling and grammar so that they can increasingly function as the exclusive language of government and of higher culture and technology. The successful revival and modernization of Hebrew has encouraged other smaller communities – the Catalans, the Provençals, the

Source: 'The Sociology of Language', in Fishman, J. A. (1972) *The Sociology of Language: An Interdisciplinary Social Science Approach to Language in Society* (Rowley, MA: Newbury House Publishers) pp. 1–7.

Frisians, the Bretons – to strive to save *their* ethnic mother tongues (or their traditional cultural tongues) from oblivion. New and revised writing systems are being accepted – and at times, rejected – in many parts of the world by communities that hitherto had little interest in literacy in general or in literacy in their mother tongues in particular.

Such examples of consciously organized behavior toward language and toward users of particular languages can be listed almost endlessly. The list becomes truly endless if we include examples from earlier periods of history, such as the displacement of Latin as the language of religion, culture, and government in Western Christendom and the successive cultivation of once lowly vernaculars – first in Western Europe, and then subsequently in Central, Southern, and Eastern Europe, and finally in Africa and Asia as well. Instead of being viewed (as was formerly the case) as merely fit for folksy talk and for common folk, the vernaculars have come to be viewed, used, and developed as *independent* languages, as languages suitable for *all* higher purposes, and as languages of state-*building* and state-*deserving* nationalities. All of these examples too feed into the modern sociology of language, providing it with historical breadth and depth in addition to its ongoing interest in current language issues throughout the world.

SUBDIVISIONS OF THE SOCIOLOGY OF LANGUAGE

However, the subject matter of the sociology of language reaches far beyond interest in case studies and very far beyond cataloguing and classifying the instances of language conflict and language planning reported in chronicles, old and new. The ultimate quest of the sociology of language is pursued diligently and in many universities throughout the United States and other parts of the world, and is very far from dealing directly with headlines or news reports. One part of this quest is concerned with describing the generally accepted social organization of language usage within a speech community (or, to be more exact, within speech and writing communities). This part of the sociology of language – *descriptive sociology of languages* – seeks to answer the question 'who speaks (or writes) what language (or what language variety) to whom and when and to what end?' *Descriptive sociology of language* tries to disclose the norms of language usage – that is to say, the generally accepted social patterns of language use and of behavior and attitude toward language – for particular social networks and communities, both large and small. Another part of the sociology of language *dynamic sociology of language* seeks to answer the question 'what accounts for different rates of change in the social organization of language use and behavior toward language?' *Dynamic sociology of language* tries to explain why and how the social organization of language use and behavior toward language can be selectively different in the *same* social networks or communities on two different occasions. Dynamic sociology of language also seeks to explain why and how once similar social networks or communities can arrive at quite different social organizations of language use and behavior toward language.

These two subdivisions taken together, i.e. descriptive sociology of language *plus* dynamic sociology of language constitute the sociology of language, a *whole* which is *greater than the mere sum of its parts.*

LANGUAGE IS CONTENT; THE MEDIUM IS (AT LEAST PARTLY) THE MESSAGE

Newspaper headlines, with all of their stridency, may serve to remind us of a truism that is too frequently overlooked by too many Americans, namely, that language is not merely a *means* of interpersonal communication and influence. It is not merely a *carrier* of content, whether latent or manifest. Language itself *is* content, a referent for loyalties and animosities, an indicator of social statuses and personal relationships, a marker of situations and topics as well as of the societal goals and the large-scale value-laden arenas of interaction that typify every speech community.

Any speech community of even moderate complexity reveals several varieties of language, all of which are functionally differentiated from each other. In some cases the varieties may represent different occupational or interest specializations ('shop talk,' 'hippie talk,' etc.), and therefore contain vocabulary, pronunciation, and phraseology which are not generally used or even known throughout the broader speech community. As a result, the speakers of specialized varieties may not always employ them. Not only must they switch to other varieties of language when they interact in less specialized (or differently specialized) networks within the broader speech community of which they are a part, but most of them do not even use their specialized varieties all the time with one another. On some occasions, interlocutors who *can* speak a particular specialized variety to one another nevertheless do not do so, but instead switch to a different variety of language which is either in wider use or which is indicative of quite a different set of interests and relationships than is associated with their specialized variety. This type of switching represents the raw data of descriptive sociology of language, the discipline that seeks to determine (among other things) who speaks what variety of what language to whom, when, and concerning what.

The varieties of language that exist within a speech community need not all represent occupational or interest specializations. Some varieties may represent social class (economic, educational, ethnic) distinctions within coterritorial populations. 'Brooklynese' and 'cockney' English within New York and London, respectively, do not connote foreignness or even a particular section of the city as much as lower-class status in terms of income, education, or ethnicity. Nevertheless, many individuals who have left lower-class status behind can and do switch back and forth between Brooklynese and more regionally standard New York English when speaking to each other, depending on their feelings toward each other, the topic under discussion, where they happen to be when they are conversing, and several other factors, all of which can exhibit variation and, as a result, can be signaled by switching from one variety of English to another.

A speech community that has available to it several varieties of language may be said to possess a *verbal repertoire*. Such repertoires may not only consist of different specialized varieties and different social class varieties, but may also reveal different regional varieties (Boston English, Southern English, Midwestern English, and other widely, and roughly, designated dialects of American English are regional varieties), if the speech community is sufficiently large so that enclaves come to arise within it on a geographic basis alone. Furthermore, multilingual speech communities may employ, for the purpose of *intragroup* communication, all the above types or varieties of language within each of the codes that the community recognizes as 'distinct' languages (e.g. within Yiddish *and* Hebrew, among most pre-World War II Eastern European Jews: within English *and* Hindi, among upper-class individuals in India today, etc.).

Regardless of the nature of the language varieties involved in the verbal repertoire of a speech community (occupational, social class, regional, etc.), and regardless of the interaction between them (for initially regional dialects may come to represent social varieties as well, and vice versa), descriptive sociology of language seeks to disclose their linguistic and functional characteristics and to determine how much of the entire speech community's verbal repertoire is available to various smaller interaction networks within that community, since the entire verbal repertoire of a speech community may be more extensive than the verbal repertoire controlled by subgroups within that community. Dynamic sociology of language, on the other hand, seeks to determine how changes in the fortunes and interactions of networks of speakers alter the ranges (complexity) of their verbal repertoires.

All in all, the sociology of language seeks to discover not only the societal rules or norms that explain and constrain language behavior and *the behavior toward language* in speech communities, but it also seeks to determine the symbolic value of language varieties for their speakers. That language varieties come to have symbolic or symptomatic value, in and of themselves, is an inevitable consequence of their functional differentiation. If certain varieties are indicative of certain interests, of certain backgrounds, or of certain origins, then they come to represent the ties and aspirations, the limitations and the opportunities with which these interests, backgrounds, and origins, in turn, are associated. Language varieties rise and fall in symbolic value as the status of their most characteristic or marked functions rises and falls. Varieties come to represent intimacy and equality if they are most typically learned and employed in interactions that stress such bonds between interlocutors. Other varieties come to represent educated status or national identification as a result of the attainments associated with their use and their users and as a result of their realization in situations and relationships that pertain to formal learning or to particular ideologies. However, these functions are capable of change (and of being consciously changed), just as the linguistic features of the varieties themselves may change (and may be consciously changed), and just as the demographic distribution of users of a variety within a particular speech community may change.

The step-by-step elevation of most modern European vernaculars to their current positions as languages of culture and technology is only one example of how dramatically the operative and symbolic functions of languages can change. Similar changes are ongoing today:

> Since the preservation of adequate control over the labour force loomed so large in the minds of the early planters, various devices have evolved, of which the maintenance of castelike distance was perhaps the one most significantly affecting race relations. One thinks immediately of the frequently cited admonition in the *Rabaul Times* of August 8, 1926, by a veteran Territorian, 'Never talk to the boys in any circumstances. Apart from your house-boy and boss-boy, never allow any native to approach you in the field or on the bungalow veranda.' This free advice to the uninitiated planters was, no doubt, intended to preserve 'White prestige,' but it was also conceived as a protective device to 'keep labour in its place.' So also the Melanesian Pidgin, which had come into being as a medium of interchange in trade, subsequently acquired, on the planta-tions, the character of a language of command by which the ruling caste 'talked down' to its subordinates and 'put them in their place.' A wide range of plantation etiquette symbolizing proper deference by workers toward their masters and expressed in expected form of address and servile conduct gave further protection to the system and any signs of insubordination or 'cheekiness' on the part of the workers might be vigorously punished and rationalised by the planter as a threat to the system. (Lind 1969, p. 36).

Yet today, barely half a century since Melanesian Pidgin began to expand, it has been renamed Neo-Melanesian and is being groomed by many New Guineans to become their country's national language, and as such to be used in government, education, mass media, religion, and high culture more generally (Wurm 1961/62).

The sociology of language is the study of the characteristics of language varieties, the characteristics of their functions, and the characteristics of their speakers as these three constantly interact, change, and change one another, both within and between speech communities.

REFERENCES

Lind, A. W. (1969) 'Race Relations in New Guinea,' *Current Affairs Bulletin* (Sydney: Australia), **XLIV**, iii, pp. 34–48.

Wurm, S. A. and Laycock, D. C. (1961/62) 'The Question of Language and Dialect in New Guinea,' *Oceania*, **XXXII**, pp. 128–43.

4 Language in a Social Perspective

Michael Halliday

A significant fact about the behaviour of human beings in relation to their social environment is that a large part of it is linguistic behaviour. The study of social man presupposes the study of language and social man.

A concern with language and social man has for a long time been one of the perspectives of modern linguistics. In 1935 J. R. Firth, introducing the term 'sociological linguistics', discussed the study of language in a social perspective and outlined a programme of 'describing and classifying typical contexts of situation within the context of culture... [and] types of linguistic function in such contexts of situation'. We tend nowadays to refer to sociolinguistics as if this was something very different from the study of language as practised in linguistics *tout court*; but actually new 'socio-linguistics' is but old 'linguistics' writ large, and the linguist's interests have always extended to language as social behaviour.

It was Malinowski from whom Firth derived his notions of 'context of culture' and 'context of situation' (Malinowski, 1923); and Malinowski's ideas about what we might call cultural and situational semantics provide an interesting starting point for the study of language and social man, since they encourage us to look at language as a form of behaviour potential. In this definition, both the 'behaviour' and the 'potential' need to be emphasized. Language, from this point of view, is a range of possibilities, an open-ended set of options in behaviour that are available to the individual in his existence as social man. The context of culture is the environment for the total set of these options, while the context of situation is the environment of any particular selection that is made from within them.

Malinowski's two types of context thus embody the distinction between the potential and the actual. The context of culture defines the potential, the range of possibilities that are open. The actual choice among these possibilities takes place within a given context of situation.

Firth, with his interest in the actual, in the text and its relation to its surroundings, developed the notion of 'context of situation' into a valuable

Source: 'Language in a Social Perspective', in Halliday, M. A. K. (1973) *Explorations in the Functions of Language* (London: Edward Arnold) pp. 48–71.

tool for linguistic inquiry. Firth's interest, however, was not in the accidental but in the typical: not in this or that piece of discourse that happened to get recorded in the fieldworker's notebook, but in repetitive patterns which could be interpreted as significant and systematizable patterns of social behaviour. Thus, what is actual is not synonymous with what is unique, or the chance product of random observations. But the significance of what is typical – in fact the concept 'typical' itself – depends on factors which lie outside language, in the social structure. It is not the typicalness of the words and structures which concerns us, but the typicalness of the context of situation, and of the function of the words and structures within it. . . .

If we regard language as social behaviour, therefore, this means that we are treating it as a form of behaviour *potential*. It is what the speaker can do.

But 'can do' by itself is not a linguistic notion; it encompasses types of behaviour other than language behaviour. If we are to relate the notion of 'can do' to the sentences and words and phrases that the speaker is able to construct in his language – to what he can say, in other words – then we need an intermediate step, where the behaviour potential is as it were converted into linguistic potential. This is the concept of what the speaker 'can mean'.

The potential of language is a meaning potential. This meaning potential is the linguistic realization of the behaviour potential; 'can mean' is 'can do' when translated into language. The meaning potential is in turn realized in the language system as lexico-grammatical potential, which is what the speaker 'can say'.

Each stage can be expressed in the form of options. The option in the construction of linguistic forms – sentences, and the like – serve to realize options in meaning, which in turn realize options in behaviour that are interpretable in terms of a social theory. . . .

A word or two should be said here about the relation of the concept of meaning potential to the Chomskyan notion of competence. The two are somewhat different. Meaning potential is defined not in terms of the mind but in terms of the culture; not as what the speaker knows, but as what he can do – in the special sense of what he can do linguistically (what he 'can mean', as we have expressed it). The distinction is important because 'can do' is of the same order of abstraction as 'does'; the two are related simply as potential to actualized potential, and can be used to illuminate each other. But 'knows' is distinct and clearly insulated from 'does'; the relation between the two is complex and oblique, and leads to the quest for a 'theory of performance' to explain the 'does'.

This is related to the question of idealization in linguistics. How does one decide what is systematic and what is irrelevant in language – or, to put the question another way, how does one decide what are different sentences, different phrases, and so on, and what are different instances of the same sentence, the same phrase? The issue was raised by Peter Geach in *The State of Language* (1969). His argument is, that in order to understand the logical structure of sentences we have to 'iron out' a lot of the differences that occur in living speech: 'idealization which approximates slightly less well to what is actually said, will, by the standards of logical insight into the structures of sentences, pay off better than some analyses that try to come closer to what is actually said'.

The philosopher's approach to language is always marked by a very high degree of idealization. In its extreme form, this approach idealizes out *all* natural language as irrelevant and unsystematic and treats only constructed logical languages; a less extreme version is one which accepts sentences of natural language but reduces them all to a 'deep structure' in terms of certain fundamental logical relations. Competence, as defined by Chomsky, involves (as Geach objects) a lower degree of idealization than this. But it is still very high from other points of view, particularly that of anyone interested in language as behaviour. Many behaviourally significant variations in language are simply ironed out, and reduced to the same level as stutterings, false starts, clearings of the throat and the like. ...

Sociological theory, if it is concerned with the transmission of knowledge or with any linguistically coded type of social act, provides its own criteria for the degree and kind of idealization involved in statements about language; and Bernstein's work is a case in point (1962, 1967). In one sense, this is what it is all about. There is always some idealization, where linguistic generalizations are made; but in a sociological context this has to be, on the whole, at a much lower level. We have, in fact, to 'come closer to what is actually said'; partly because the solution to problems may depend on studying what is actually said, but also because even when this is not the case the features that are behaviourally relevant may be just those that the idealizing process most readily irons out. An example of the latter would be features of assertion and doubt, such as *of course*, *I think*, and question tags like *don't they?*, which turn out to be highly significant – not the expressions themselves, but the variations in meaning which they represent, in this case variation in the degree of certainty which the speaker may attach to what he is saying (Turner and Pickvance, 1971).

In order to give an account of language that satisfies the needs of a social theory, we have to be able to accommodate the degree and kind of idealization that is appropriate in that context. This is what the notion of meaning potential attempts to make possible. The meaning potential is the range of *significant* variation that is at the disposal of the speaker. The notion is not unlike Dell Hymes's notion 'communicative competence', except that Hymes defines this in terms of 'competence' in the Chomskyan sense of what the speaker knows, whereas we are talking of a potential – what he can do, in the special linguistic sense of what he can mean – and avoiding the additional complication of a distinction between doing and knowing. This potential can then be represented as systematic options in meaning which may be varied in the degree of their specificity – in what has been called 'delicacy'. That is to say, the range of variation that is being treated as *significant* will itself be variable, with either grosser or finer distinctions being drawn according to the type of problem that is being investigated.

Considering language in its social context, then, we can describe it in broad terms as a behaviour potential; and more specifically as a meaning potential, where meaning is a form of behaving (and the verb *to mean* is a verb of the 'doing' class). This leads to the notion of representing language in the form of options: sets of alternative meanings which collectively account for the total meaning potential.

Each option is available in a stated environment, and this is where Firth's category of system comes in. A system is an abstract representation of a paradigm; and this, as we have noted, can be interpreted as a set of options with an entry condition – a number of possibilities out of which a choice has to be made if the stated conditions of entry to the choice are satisfied. It has the form: if *a*, then either *x* or *y* (or . . .). The key to its importance in the present context is Firth's 'polysystemic principle', whereby (again following this interpretation) the conditions of entry are required to be stated for each set of possibilities. That is to say, for every choice it is to be specified where, under what conditions, that choice is made. The 'where', in Firth's use of the concept of a system, was 'at what point in the structure'; but we interpret it here as 'where in the total network of options'. Each choice takes place in the environment of other choices. This is what makes it possible to vary the 'delicacy' of the description: we can stop wherever the choices are no longer significant for what we are interested in.

The options in a natural language are at various levels: phonological, grammatical (including lexical, which is simply the more specific part within the grammatical) and semantic. Here, where we are concerned with the meaning potential, the options are in the first instance semantic options. These are interpreted as the coding of options in behaviour, so that the semantics is in this sense a behavioural semantics.

The semantic options are in turn coded as options in grammar. Now there are no grammatical categories corresponding exactly to such concepts as those of reasoning, pleading or threatening referred to above. But there may be a prediction, deriving from a social theory, that these will be among the significant behavioural categories represented in the meaning potential. In that case it should be possible to identify certain options in the grammar as being systematic realizations of these categories, since presumably they are to be found somewhere in the language system. We will not expect there to be a complete one-to-one correspondence between the grammatical options and the semantic ones; but this is merely allowing for the normal phenomena of neutralization and diversification that are associated with all stages in the realization chain.

There is nothing new in the notion of associating grammatical categories with higher level categories of a 'socio-' semantic kind. This is quite natural in the case of grammatical forms concerned with the expression of social roles, particularly those systems which reflect the inherent social structure of the speech situation, which cannot be explained in any other way. The principal component of these is the system of mood. If we represent the basic options in the mood system of English in the following way:

```
                                    ┌ declarative
                    ┌ indicative  → │
independent    →    │              └ interrogative  →    ┌ yes/no
clause              │                                    │
                    └ imperative                         └ 'WH-'
```

(to be read 'an independent clause is either indicative or imperative; if indicative, then either declarative or interrogative', and so on), we are systematizing the set of choices whereby the speaker is enabled to assume one of a number of possible communication roles – social roles which exist only in and through language, as functions of the speech situation. The choice of interrogative, for example, means, typically, 'I am acting as questioner (seeker of information), and you are to act as listener and then as answerer (supplier of information)'. By means of this system the speaker takes on himself a role in the speech situation and allocates the complementary role – actually, rather, a particular choice of complementary ones – to the hearer, both while he is speaking and after he has finished.

These 'communication roles' belong to what we were referring to as 'socio-semantics'. They are a special case in that they are a property of the speech situation as such, and do not depend on any kind of a social theory. But the relationship between, say, 'question' in semantics and 'interrogative' in grammar is not really different from that between a behavioural-semantic category such as 'threat' and the categories by which it is realized grammatically. In neither instance is the relationship one-to-one; and while the latter may be rather more complex, a more intensive study of language as social behaviour also suggests a somewhat more complex treatment of traditional notions like those of statement and question. Part of the grammar with which we are familiar is thus a sociological grammar already, although this has usually been confined to a small area where the meanings expressed are 'social' in a rather special sense that of the social roles created by language itself. ...

The investigation of language as social behaviour is not only relevant to the understanding of social structure; it is also relevant to the understanding of language. A network of socio-semantic options – the representation of what we have been calling the 'meaning potential' – has implications in both directions; on the one hand as the realization of patterns of behaviour and, on the other hand, as realized by the patterns of grammar. The concept of meaning potential thus provides a perspective on the nature of language. Language is as it is because of its function in the social structure, and the organization of behavioural meanings should give some insight into its social foundations.

This is the significance of functional theories of language. The essential feature of a functional theory is not that it enables us to enumerate and classify the functions of speech acts, but that it provides a basis for explaining the nature of the language system, since the system itself reflects the functions that it has evolved to serve. The organization of options in the grammar of natural languages seems to rest very clearly on a functional basis, as has emerged from the work of those linguists, particularly of the Prague school, who have been aware that the notion 'functions of language' is not to be equated merely with a theory of language use but expresses the principle behind the organization of the linguistic system.

The options in the grammar of a language derive from and are relatable to three very generalized functions of language which we have referred to as the ideational, the interpersonal and the textual. The specific options in meaning that are characteristic of particular social context and settings are expressed through the medium of grammatical and lexical selections that trace back to one or other of these three sources. The status of these terms is that they constitute a hypothesis for explaining what seems to be a fundamental fact about the grammar of languages, namely that it is possible to discern three distinct principles of organization in the structure of grammatical units, as described by Daneš (1964) and others, and that these in turn can be shown to be the structural expression of three rather distinct and independent sets of underlying options.

Those of the first set, the ideational, are concerned with the content of language, its function as a means of the expression of our experience, both of the external world and of the inner world of our own consciousness – together with what is perhaps a separate sub-component expressing certain basic logical relations. The second, the interpersonal, is language as the mediator of role, including all that may be understood by the expression of our own personalities and personal feelings on the one hand, and forms of interaction and social interplay with other participants in the communication situation on the other hand. The third component, the textual, has an enabling function, that of creating text, which is language in operation as distinct from strings of words or isolated sentences and clauses. It is this component that enables the speaker to organize what he is saying in such a way that it makes sense in the context and fulfils its function as a message.

These three functions are the basis of the grammatical system of the adult language. The child begins by acquiring a meaning potential, a small number of distinct meanings that he can express, in two or three functional contexts: he learns to use language for satisfying his material desires ('I want an apple'), for getting others to behave as he wishes ('sing me a song'), and so on. At this stage each utterance tends to have one function only, but as time goes on the typical utterance becomes functionally complex – we learn to combine various uses of language into a single speech act. It is at this point that we need a grammar: a level of organization intermediate between content and expression, which can take the various functionally distinct meaning selections and combine them into integrated structures. The components of the grammatical system are thus themselves functional; but they represent the functions of language in their most generalized form, as these underlie all the more specific contexts of language use.

The meaning potential in any one context is open-ended, in the sense that there is no limit to the distinctions in meaning that we can apprehend. When we talk of what the speaker can do, in this special sense of what he 'can mean', we imply that we can recognize significant differentiations within what he can mean, up to some point or other which will be determined by the requirements of our theory. The importance of a hypothesis about what the speaker can do in a social context is that this makes sense of what he does. If we insist on drawing a boundary between what he does and what he knows, we cannot explain what he does; what he does will appear merely as a random selection from within what he knows. But in the study of language in a social perspective we need both to pay attention to what is said and at the same time to relate it systematically to what might have been said but was not. Hence we do not make a dichotomy between knowing and doing; instead we place 'does' in the environment of 'can do', and treat language as speech potential.

NOTE

The paper on which this chapter is based was first prepared for the Second International Congress of Applied Linguistics, Cambridge, September 1969. A revised version was presented to the Oxford University Linguistic Society, October 1969. It was first printed in *Educational Review*, June 1971.

REFERENCES

Bernstein, B. (1972) 'A Socio-linguistic Approach to Socialization; with Some Reference to Educability', in Gumperz, J. J. and Hymes, D. H. (eds) *Directions in Sociolinguistics* (New York: Holt, Rinehart & Winston).

Danes, F. (1964) 'A Three-level Approach to Syntax', *Travaux Linguistiques de Prague*, 1, pp. 225–240.

Firth, J. R. (1935). 'The Technique of Semantics', *Transactions of the Philological Society*. Reprinted in Firth, J. R., *Papers in Linguistics 1934–1951* (London: Oxford University Press, 1957).

Geach, Peter (1969) 'Should Traditional Grammar Be Ended or Mended? – II', in *The State of Language* (Educational Review, 22.1, pp. 18–25).

Malinowski, B. (1923) 'The Problem of Meaning in Primitive Languages', Supplement I to Ogden, C. K. and Richards, I. A., *The Meaning of Meaning* (London: Routledge & Kegan Paul).

Turner, G. J. and Pickvance, R. E. (1971) 'Social Class Differences in the Expression of Uncertainty in Five-year-old Children', *Language and Speech*, **14**, pp. 303–25.

5 Communicative Competence

John J. Gumperz

The issues I want to discuss in this chapter are questions of linguistic theory that arise from the perspective of interactional sociolinguistics pioneered, among others, by Harold Garfinkel, Erving Goffman and Harvey Sacks (see Shuy 1972). What have we learned over the last decades by applying micro-conversational analyses to conversational data such as have only recently become available for systematic study through innovations in audio and video technology? What does the interactive approach to communication, which sees communicating as the outcome of exchanges involving more than one active participant, imply for the way we look at linguistic data and for our theories of grammar and meaning? What do conversational exchanges tell us about the interplay of linguistic, sociocultural and contextual presuppositions in interpretation?

A key concept we need to reconsider is the notion of communicative competence. The term is a familiar one, coined by Dell Hymes (see Chapter 1 in this volume), to suggest that as linguists concerned with communication in human groups we need to go beyond mere description of language usage patterns, to concentrate on aspects of shared knowledge and cognitive abilities which are every bit as abstract and general as the knowledge that is glossed by Chomsky's more narrowly defined notion of linguistic competence. Among European social scientists the term has become familiar through the writings of Jurgen Habermas, who argues that an understanding of communication is basic to a more general theory of social and political processes. He calls for a theory of communicative competence that would specify what he terms 'the universal conditions of possible understandings.' But it is far from clear exactly what facts of human interaction such a theory must account for and how we can characterize the knowledge speakers must have and the socioeconomic environments that can create these conditions.

Habermas (1970), in his informal discussion, relies on notions of what he calls 'trouble-free communication' and assumptions about sharedness of code which recall Chomsky's ideally uniform communities, as if understanding depended on the existence of a unitary set of grammatical rules.

Source: 'The Linguistic Bases of Communicative Competence', in Deborah Tannen (ed.) *Analyzing Discourse: Text and Talk [Georgetown University Round Table on Languages and Linguistics 1981]* (Washington, DC: Georgetown University Press) pp. 323–34.

Yet sociolinguistic research during the last decade [this chapter was originally published in 1981 – *Eds*] has demonstrated not only that all existing human communities are diverse at all levels of linguistic structure, but also that grammatical diversity, multi-focality of linguistic symbols, and context dependence of interpretive processes are essential components of the signalling resources that members rely on to accomplish their goals in everyday life (Gumperz 1982).

Other empirical findings that by now have become generally accepted are: that generalization about ongoing processes of language change must build on empirical data on everyday speech in a range of natural settings; that basic issues of language acquisition can best be explained by reference to the behavioral facts of mother–child interaction; that the grammaticality judgments which furnish the data for syntactic analysis depend on speakers' ability to imagine a context in which the sentence could occur; and that discourse consists of more than the sum of component utterances. The theoretical linguists' insistence on maintaining a strict separation between linguistic and extralinguistic phenomena has thus become untenable in many key areas of linguistic research.

Yet even though these points are by now gaining acceptance, and context and sociocultural presuppositions are beginning to be brought into our explanatory models, our ideas of what is rule-governed about speaking and about how meaning is conveyed continue to be based on concepts deriving from sentence-based grammatical analysis. We talk about language and culture, language and context, as if these were separate entities, which stand outside the actual message and which, like the ideas in the conduit metaphor (Reddy 1979), can be likened to bounded concrete objects. Moreover, and more importantly perhaps, our methods for analyzing contextual and social aspects of communication rest on procedures of taxonomic categorization and on statistical distribution counts which are quite distinct from the introspective, interpretive methods of linguistic analysis. Many sociolinguistic studies of communicative competence, in fact, aim at little more than statements of regularities that describe the occurrence of utterances or verbal strategies isolated by traditional methods of linguistic analysis in relation to types of speakers, audiences, settings, and situations. This leads to a highly particularistic notion of competence, which some psycholinguists claim has little relevance for basic cognitive processes; they argue that lexical and syntactic measures are the only valid indices of verbal skills.

I believe that we can avoid the difficulties that this raises by integrating the sociolinguistic findings on variability with Habermas's call for a theory of possible human understanding. What is needed is an approach which can relate the specifics of situated interpretation to the panhuman ability to engage others in discourse. I propose therefore that we redefine communicative competence as 'the knowledge of linguistic and related communicative conventions that speakers must have to initiate and sustain conversational involvement.' Conversational involvement is clearly a necessary precondition for understanding. Communication always presupposes some sharing of signalling conventions, but this does not mean that interlocutors must speak a single language or dialect in the sense that linguists use the term.

Code-switching studies over the last ten years have documented a variety of speech situations in societies throughout the world, where speakers build on the contrast between two distinct grammatical systems to convey substantive information that elsewhere, in equivalent situations, can be conveyed by the grammatical devices of a single system. Moreover, participants in a conversation need not agree on the specifics of what is intended. People frequently walk away from an encounter feeling that it has been highly successful only to find later that they disagree on what was actually said. Studies of communicative competence, therefore, must deal with linguistic signs at a level of generality which transcends the bounds of linguists' grammatical system and must concentrate on aspects of meaning or interpretation more general than that of sentence content. It is furthermore evident that the perceptual cues we must process in conversational exchanges are different from those that apply to decoding of isolated sentences.

The following example of a brief recorded exchange between two secretaries in a small university office serves to organize my discussion of relevant interpretive processes.

1. A: Are you going to be here for ten minutes?
2. B: Go ahead and take your break. Take longer if you want.
3. A: I'll just be outside on the porch. Call me if you need me.
4. B: OK. Don't worry.

Brief though it is, this exchange nevertheless contains in itself much of the data we need to determine what participants intended and how it was achieved. Setting aside for the moment our natural tendency to concentrate on the meanings of component utterances, we note that B inerprets A's opening move as a request to stay in the office while she takes a break. By her reply in line 3, A then confirms B's interpretation and B's final 'OK. Don't worry' both reconfirms what was agreed and concludes the exchange.

Given this evidence showing that both speakers have actively participated and have proffered and agreed on (for the moment at least) interpretations, we can proceed to employ the linguist's interpretive, introspective methods of analysis to seek hypotheses as to what knowledge participants rely on and what signalling cues they perceive to accomplish what they do.

Note that B's interpretation is an indirect one which responds to more than the referential meaning or the illocutionary force of A's utterance. The inferential process here seems to have some of the characteristics of Gricean implicature. That is, we assume that B assumes A is cooperating, that her question must therefore be relevant, and that since there is no immediately available referent she searches her memory for some possible context, i.e. some interpretive frame that would make sense. But this begs the question how B arrives at the right inference. What is it about the situation that leads her to think A is talking about taking a break? A common sociolinguistic procedure in such cases is to attempt to formulate discourse rules such as the following: 'If a secretary in an office around break time asks a co-worker a question seeking information about the co-worker's plans for the period usually allotted for breaks, interpret it as a request to take her break.' Such rules are difficult to formulate and in any case are neither sufficiently general to cover a wide enough range of situations nor specific enough to predict responses. An alternative approach is to consider the pragmatics of questioning and to argue that questioning is semantically related to requesting, and that there are a number of contexts in which questions can be interpreted as requests. While such semantic processes clearly channel conversational inference, there is nothing in this type of explanation that refers to taking a break.

Note that all the foregoing arguments rely on sentence-based views of language which assume that the cues that conversationalists process are basically those covered in traditional phonological, syntactic, and semantic analysis. I believe that conversational inference relies on additional types of linguistic signalling and that an understanding of how these signs work to channel interpretation is basic to a theory of communicative competence.

Some of these contextualization cues (Gumperz 1977, Cook-Gumperz and Gumperz 1978, Gumperz and Tannen 1979) have to do with what, following sociological work in conversational analysis, have come to be called sequencing or turn-taking processes. Sacks, Schegloff, and Jefferson (1974) argue that speaker change is a basic conversational process and that turn-taking mechanisms are organized about transition relevance places, which determine when a next speaker can take the floor. But they give no data on how such transition relevance places are signalled. Conversations, unlike sentences, do not come pre-chunked. Conversationalists must process verbal signs to determine when to take turns without interfering with others' rights. For example, B's utterance in line 2 comes in immediately at the end of A's sentence, while A in line 3 waits long enough to allow B to produce not one but two sentences. How is this negotiated?

Moreover, responses in this exchange, as well as in most verbal encounters, are rhythmically organized in such a way that moves follow each other at regular time intervals. This rhythmicity is important in maintaining conversational involvement (Erickson and Shultz 1981). Halliday (1967), in discussing problems of segmentation in longer passages, argues that language is chunked into semantically holistic information units, but his discussion focuses largely on written texts and on the role of syntax in chunking. Chafe (1980) proposes the notion of idea unit to deal with related issues and points to the role of tempo and pausing in segmentation.

These problems are treated in considerable detail in recent work on intonation. Ladd's (1980) comprehensive review of the relevant literature indicates that chunking cannot be described in terms of a single phonetically determined set of signalling cues. Chunking is an act of interpretation involving simultaneous processing of signs at several levels of signalling: prosodic, phonological, syntactic, lexical and rhythmic, which, like the process of phonemic categorization described by structural linguists, depends on learned conventions which differentially highlight or ignore some cues at the expense of others.

Chunking or phrasing of speech, moreover, does more than just signal transition relevance places; it also serves to indicate relationships among items of information and to set off or foreground others. A's utterance in line 1 could have been split by a tone group boundary, while B's line 4 could have been grouped together under a single clause contour.

Another process of key importance for conversational inference is the signalling of utterance prominence to indicate which of several bits of information is to be highlighted or placed in focus. In our English rhetorical tradition this is done partly through syntax and lexical choice and partly through placement of prosodic accent. Given a particular choice of words, we have certain expectations about normal accent placement. These can then be systematically violated to convey additional information not overtly given in the message. If in line 1 'you' had been accented rather than 'be here,' B might have thought the question referred to whether she, as opposed to someone else, was going to stay in the office. She might not have recognized it as a request. As it is, the interpretation B actually does make relies in large part on the fact that 'be here' is emphasized by primary stress, 'ten minutes' carries secondary stress, and the two phrases come under the same contour. We assume that B perceived the question as focusing on her being (i.e. remaining) for a period equivalent to that normally associated with the morning break, and that this led to her inference. Other rhetorical traditions rely on information signalled through a different combination of signalling channels or subsystems. What is important is that perception of focus always relies on expectations of how these channels cooccur, and these expectations are not dealt with in our usual grammatical analyses, which tend to focus on one subsystem at a time.

A final signalling cue of relevance here is the choice of discourse strategy. Note that A could have achieved her end by simply asking 'Can I take my break?,' in which case a simple one-word or one-phrase answer like 'yes' or 'OK' would have been sufficient to complete the exchange. But given her choice of words, our experience with similar situations tells us that more talk is expected. There is something of a formulaic nature about exchanges such as these which affects our interpretations.

This discussion suggests that conversational inference is best seen not as a simple unitary evaluation of intent but as involving a complex series of judgments, including relational or contextual assessments on how items of information are to be integrated into what we know and into the event at hand, as well as assessments of content. ...

One can visualize the process as consisting of a series of stages which are hierarchically ordered so that more general relational assessment serves as part of the input to more specific ones. Perception of contextualization cues, moreover, plays a role at every stage.

It is assumed that the initial assessment in an exchange concerns the nature of the activity being proposed or performed. This sets up expectations about what likely outcomes are, what topics can be covered, what can be put in words and what must be conveyed indirectly; and what counts as suitable styles of speaking and thereby provides the motivation for entering into the interaction in the first place. At the next lower level, decisions are made about the more immediate communicative or discourse tasks such as narrating, describing, requesting, which together make up particular activities. Such discourse tasks have some similarity to the linguists' speech act, but they differ in that they typically consist of more than one utterance and in that they are described in terms of primary semantic relationships that tie together component utterances, rather than in terms of illocutionary force.

Note that whereas activities are often culturally or situationally specific, discourse tasks are universals of human interaction. An understanding of how relational signs function to signal these tasks can provide basic insights into how interpretations are agreed upon and altered in the course of an interaction by differentially foregrounding, subordinating, and associating various information-carrying items. If conversational involvement is to be maintained, higher-level relational signs must be shared, although participants may disagree on the meaning of words and idioms. On the other hand, however, participants may agree on what sentences mean in isolation, yet when relational signals differ, conversational cooperation is likely to break down. Cross-cultural analysis of how discourse tasks are signalled – that is, how focusing, phrasing, coreferentiality and other aspects of cohesion are signaled – can form the basis for empirical investigations of panhuman features of communicative competence.

It must be emphasized that verbal strategies for negotiating conversational interpretations are for the most part indirect. Information is not overtly expressed in surface content, but must be inferred on the basis of tacit presuppositions acquired through previous interactive experience. Indirect signalling mechanisms differ from lexicalized signs in that, like nonverbal signals, they are inherently ambiguous. Any single utterance is always subject to multiple interpretations. One decides on what interpretation to accept by examining what Austin has called 'uptake', that is, the conversational process through which lines of reasoning are developed or altered.

Given the nature of the signalling system, participants, in order to be able to develop their arguments, are constantly required to test and display the tacit knowledge on which they rely to make inferences in the first place. Wherever conversational cooperation is maintained over time, that is, wherever we find evidence that conversationalists actively react to and work with each others' responses to establish cohesive themes, we can assume at least some sharing of tacit contextualization strategies.

Failure to achieve this type of cooperation, on the other hand, may in some cases, although certainly by no means in all, indicate undetected differences in signalling systems. In the midst of an exchange, when conversationalists are faced with the need to respond in time and have little opportunity to reflect, such difficulties tend to go undiagnosed. The fact that they exist must be discovered through *post-hoc* empirical analysis. It is here that the new audiovisual technologies, which for the first time in human history enable us to freeze and preserve for systematic study samples of naturalistic exchanges, can provide truly novel insights into the workings of communicative processes.

Our recent empirical studies in ethnically diverse urban settings indicate that miscommunications attributable to undetected systematic differences in signalling conventions occur considerably more frequently than casual observations would lead one to suspect. A possible linguistic reason for this is that contextualization conventions are distributed along areal networks which do no necessarily coincide with language or dialect boundaries as established through historical reconstruction or typological comparison of grammatical categories. Such conventions are created through prolonged interactive experience in family, friendship, occupational, or similar networks of relationships. Typically, they affect the signalling of contextual and inter-utterance relationships through formulaic expressions, phrasing or chunking, focusing, anaphora, deixis, or other grammatical cohesive mechanisms. Once established through practice, they come to serve as communicative resources which channel inferences along particular lines. Knowledge of how they work becomes a precondition for active participation in verbal encounters. The knowledge is of a kind which cannot easily be acquired through reading or formal classroom instruction. Personal contact in situations which allow for maximum feedback is necessary. ...

To be sure, not all problems of interethnic contact are communicative in nature. Economic factors, differences in goals and aspirations, as well as other historical and cultural factors, may be at issue. But we have reason to suspect that a significant number of breakdowns may be due to inferences based on undetected differences in contextualization strategies, which are after all the symbolic tip of the iceberg reflecting the forces of history. The existence of communicative differences must, of course, be demonstrated. It cannot be presupposed or inferred from grammars or the usual ethnographic descriptions. Here conversational analysis becomes a diagnostic tool to determine whether the linguistic prerequisites of possible communication exist.

How do we go about documenting the functioning of contextualization strategies? One way to accomplish this is to concentrate on naturally occurring events such as court proceedings, job interviews, medical diagnoses, and committee meetings, where discourse strategies play a key role in the evaluation of performance. Let me present some data from transcribed testimony of a Navy hearing held in connection with a perjury trial. The accused was a Navy physician born in the Philippines, who had been indicted for perjury in connection with statements he had made concerning a burn injury he had treated.

A principal goal of the hearing was to document his professional qualifications. He had spent many years in the United States and speaks English well. The questioning deals with his training in burn treatment.

Q.1. Any other sources of burns that you've observed?
A.2. Occasionally from gasoline and kerosene burn because as far as the
  3. situation there, most of the houses don't have any natural gas or
  4. electric stove as here. They use kerosene instead as a means of fuel for
  5. cooking.
  6. The reason why I'm saying this also is because this hospital where I
  7. had my training is a government hospital, so most of the patients that
  8. go there are the poverty-stricken patients unlike you going to a medi-
  9. cal center, it's usually the middle class who go where you don't have
 10. this problem.

In the preceding parts of his testimony dealing with his training in the Philippines, the witness has repeatedly compared conditions there with those in the United States. His argument in lines 2–4 rests on such a contrast, and from the way he begins the second part of his answer, starting in line 6, one would expect a similar comparison of 'there' with 'here.' But the content of his sentences does not seem to bear out these expectations. If one examines what he says, starting with: 'most of the patients who go there are the poverty-stricken patients unlike you going to a medical center,' one is unsure what is being compared: poverty-stricken patients with middle-class patients, or medical centers in the United States with government hospitals in the Philippines?

Participants in an interaction, as well as most casual observers, are unlikely to see such conflicts as reflecting on the witness's credibility, but our experience with similar types of interethnic situations leads us to suspect that in situations like this, where expectations signalled at one level of generality are not borne out by lower-level signalling processes, systematic processing difficulties ultimately attributable to grammatical presuppositions may be at work.

Note that the passage is too long to be processed as a whole. A reader will have to rely on syntactic and prosodic knowledge to sound it out and chunk it into relevant information units. Native speakers of English who do this will have difficulty in assigning the word 'unlike' in line 7 to either the preceding or following clause. The first reading yields the clause 'poverty-stricken patients unlike you'. This not only conflicts with expectations signalled through the preceding context but also renders the remaining passage unintelligible. Speakers of Filipino English who were consulted tended to assign 'unlike' to the following clause and had no difficulty in recognizing the speaker's intent to contrast 'there' with 'here.' Yet native speakers of English are likely to have difficulty in fitting a clause such as 'unlike you going to a medical center' into the surrounding discourse frame.

The problem is a complex one, requiring more detailed analysis than can be presented here. But the most likely explanation lies in the discourse conventions for signalling coreferentiality. To make sense of the 'unlike' clause, an English speaker would have to recognize it as a syntactically incomplete clause in which 'this is' had been deleted or left unexpressed immediately preceding 'unlike.' To recover such unverbalized information, English speakers look for a pronoun or noun phrase that could signal coreferentiality. It is our inability to locate such a phrase in the foregoing passage that leads to processing difficulty. My hypothesis, which will, of course, have to be tested through systematic research, is that Filipino English speakers, even though they speak grammatical English at the sentence level, nevertheless employ discourse principles influenced by Tagalog and similar Austronesian languages, where coreferentiality is signalled by means other than overtly lexicalized pronouns or noun phrases. The same passage can thus be differently interpreted by listeners who process it with different presuppositions.

Investigation of such multilevel signalling processes, and of the role played by contextualization as well as by linguistic and sociocultural presuppositions in the multilevel inferences necessary to sustain verbal exchanges, could lay the foundation of a universal theory of communicative competence capable of providing new insights into the communicative problems that affect our urban societies.

NOTE

Research on the paper on which this chapter is based was supported by grants from the Institute of Advanced Studies in Princeton, NJ, and the National Institute of Health.

REFERENCES

Chafe, W. L. (1980) 'The Deployment of Consciousness in the Production of a Narrative', in Chafe, W. L. (ed.) *The Pear Stories: Cognitive, Cultural, and Linguistics Aspects of Narrative Production* (Norwood, NJ: Ablex).

Cook-Gumperz, J. and Gumperz, J. (1978) 'Context in Children's Speech', in Snow, K. and Waterson, N. (eds) *The Development of Communication* (London: Wiley).

Erickson, F. and Shultz, J. (1981) *Talking to the Man* (New York: Academic Press).

Gumperz, J. (1977) 'Sociocultural Knowledge in Conversational Inference', in Saville-Troike, M. (ed.) *Georgetown University Round Table on Languages and Linguistics 1977* (Washington, DC: Georgetown University Press).

Gumperz, John (1982) *Discourse Strategies* (Cambridge: Cambridge University Press).

Gumperz, J. and Tannen, D. (1979) 'Individual and Social Differences in Language Use', in Fillmore, C. J., Kempler, W. and Wang, W. S.-Y. (eds) *Individual Differences in Language Ability and Language Behavior* (New York: Academic Press).

Habermas, J. (1970) 'Toward a Theory of Communicative Competence', in Dreitzel, H. P. (ed.) *Recent Sociology II* (London: Macmillan).

Halliday, M. A. K. (1967) 'Notes on Transitivity and Theme in English, Part 2', *Journal of Linguistics*, 3(2), pp. 199–244.

Ladd, Robert (1980) *The Structure of Intonational Meaning* (Bloomington, IN: Indiana University Press).

Reddy, M. (1979) 'The Conduit Metaphor: A Case of Frame Conflict in our Language about Language', in Ortony, A. (ed.) *Metaphor and Thought* (Cambridge: Cambridge University Press).

Sacks, H., Schegloff, E. and Jefferson, G. (1974) 'A Simplest Systematics for the Organization of Turn Taking for Conversation', *Language*, **50**, pp. 696–735.

Shuy, R. (ed.) (1972) *Georgetown University Round Table on Languages and Linguistics 1972* (Washington, DC: Georgetown University Press).

6 Social Semiotics, Style and Ideology

Robert Hodge and Gunther Kress

The most convenient starting point for analysis of how metasign systems work is the sound system of spoken languages, including 'accent' in the most limited sense of the word. This is partly because its social function is so easily recognizable and well known. The word 'shibboleth' has come to refer to party labels or slogans, because of an incident recorded in the Bible as occurring over 3000 years ago. In a bloody incident involving two groups of Jews, the Gileadites and the Ephraimites, the victorious Gileadites imposed a linguistic test on their opponents. Those who could not pronounce the 'sh' of 'shibboleth' (meaning a river) but adopted the Ephraimite 's' were to be killed. For this reason, 42,000 men of Ephraim perished (Judges 12: 6). It is a dramatic illustration of the effectivity of a seemingly trivial phenomenon, types of pronunciation. 'Accent' typically plays a similar role to this in communities which have a mutually intelligible common language. In class societies, accents perform the same function as the Jewish shibboleth, usually affecting the social and economic position of millions rather than causing the deaths of thousands. For these purposes speech accents do not usually have to work on their own – there are many other systems of metasigns to supplement them. Nor is the accent powerful in itself. The Ephraimite 's' wouldn't have been fatal if there had not been hostility and conflict of interests between the two tribes. The energies attached to accents are social, not intrinsic to the sounds themselves; but this misperception is what makes conflicts over accents or languages seem so trivial to outsiders.

For social semiotics, the most useful starting point is Voloshinov's concept of the 'multi-accentuality of the sign'. Unlike structuralists, Voloshinov sets this phenomenon at the centre of his semiotic theory. Instead of assuming the coherence of society, Voloshinov posits conflict and contradiction as the norm. He sees language as normally dialogic, as the site of competing voices and competing interests. Where it is monologic, that signals the active suppression of difference, and even the possibility of difference, by an overwhelming social force. Monologic texts, then, rest on strictly policed logonomic rules which do not allow opposition or even

Source: 'Style as Ideology', in Hodge, R. and Kress, G. (1988) *Social Semiotics* (Cambridge: Polity Press in association with Basil Blackwell) pp. 83–91.

participation by the non-powerful. The meaning that they encode is an ideology of absolute power. Dialogic and pluralist codes signify the existence of various kinds of opposition, resistance, negotiation within a group. At the level of the individual sign, this opposition is expressed through the phenomenon of multi-accentuality. If we take individual words as linguistic signs, this principle is realized through the existence of different 'accents' applied to the 'same' word. The example of 'shibboleth' will illustrate the point. This word had the same meaning for both Ephraimites and Gileadites, referring to a river, the same kind of river. Only its phonological substance was slightly different. The difference between 's' and 'sh' did not label reality differently: its main function was in the plane of semiosis, to label the kinds of speaker differently. Social difference can be signified at many other levels of the system of verbal language. We can represent some of the possibilities schematically in a semiotic hierarchy, as in Figure 6.1. Items from any level can be used to mark difference, and there is also 'leakage' between levels within one group's language code. We do not know why, of all the words containing 's', the Gileadites chose 'shibboleth', river, for their test, though a river was the boundary between the two areas, and there were no rivers in the Ephraimites' mountainous region. Shibboleths which draw on accents from several levels function more economically as group labels, though this is not necessary for them to serve their function. The lower down in the table, the less significant the difference seems to be, the less concerned with mimetic (referential) meaning, but this allows them a more exclusive concern with semiosic/ideological reference. This quality is precisely why markers with low mimetic value are so widely used for this social purpose.

Saussure bequeathed to structuralism a precise system for describing the phenomenon of accent in sound, but also acute problems in explaining or accounting for it. For Saussure (1974) the problems focused on sound change. Change in sound systems was evidently ubiquitous, but for Saussure

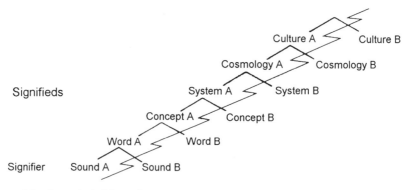

Figure 6.1   A semiotic hierarchy

it was also inexplicable. Saussure could see that the forces producing language change came from outside language, from society itself, but he excluded these dimensions from semiotics and linguistics, and since he regarded the linguistic sign as definitionally non-rational, he had to see language change as both motiveless and meaningless. It has been the sociolinguist William Labov (1978) who has resolved many of the problems left by Saussure. As a sociologist, Labov did not leave out the social dimension of language. On the contrary, the relations between social and linguistic structures were his primary object of study. He integrated historical and sociolinguistic inquiry by a single powerful assumption: that the same forces and processes which create small differences over a short time in a single language community will produce over a longer time the large differences which ultimately constitute separate languages. The motor of linguistic change in the present, and therefore presumably in the past, is the desire to express social difference and its other face, solidarity.

Labov's basic method was to isolate an element subject to significant variation within a linguistic community, that is, an element subject to a social accent, to use Voloshinov's term. One such element he studied was post-vocalic *r* in New York speech (that is, *r* as in *part* or *party*). In order to isolate its effects, he manufactured texts which differed only in terms of this variable. He then established its function as a marker or label of socio-economic position, and for whom it functioned. He found that this variable acted as a prestige-marker, correlating significantly with judgements about the speaker's socio-economic status. He also found that it signified the status of an occasion, ranging from formal to casual. The same marker, therefore, could signify both a prestigious speaker and a formal occasion. That is, it indicated power in the semiosic plane, but ambiguously, referring either to the power of the producer or to power associated with the situation itself.

Labov elicited what he called 'subjective' meanings assigned to these markers, judgements made on speakers purely on the basis of the chosen markers. What he found was a consensus by all classes on some meanings, and divergences on others. In the dimension of power, all classes rated users of prestige forms as possessing high earning power, but in terms of physical power ('good in a fight') those of high socio-economic status tended to rate users of low-prestige forms higher than did those who used those forms. Predictably, in the solidarity dimension, high-status speakers reacted more positively to users of prestige forms, and low-status speakers the opposite. The differences and the agreements form a pattern which fits well with a process in which a common set of metasigns are given different values by different groups.

In broad outline, none of this is surprising. But as well as demonstrating quantitatively what had previously been understood impressionistically as linguistic prejudice, Labov was able to show that these same meanings were present in the atoms of linguistic prejudice (just as the Gileadites had suspected). He also opened up a precise new instrument for studying the mechanisms and processes of group formation, and the complex ideological meanings that sustain them. Since the sounds of language have a material existence, they can be analysed by precise instruments. Labov was able to show both the considerable material difference that is treated as the 'same sound', as non-significant variation, and differences that exist systematically but beneath the level of consciousness, indicating that an incipient change is under way. He was also able to show minute differences between the signals sent, and what was believed to have been sent, or what would be norms for the social group concerned – evidence of ideological shifts and contra-dictions in group allegiance. So, for instance, women often 'hypercorrect' (using 'plummier' vowels than speakers from a higher social group, and/or hearing their own vowels as plummier than they are). Further, Labov was able to explain convincingly why users of non-prestige forms continued to use them when there seemed to be rewards for 'speaking correctly'. Labov pointed out the role of what he called 'covert prestige forms' in low-status groups. In his view, these strengthen solidarity bonds and act as potent carriers of a counter-ideological meaning. All groups have their metasign systems, which are so crucial to group identity and group survival that they won't lightly abandon them.

Labov distinguished between a number of kinds of difference, each with a different social function and meaning. Some differences have expressive value, so that they are meaningful to speakers, but do not mark off speech communities. Other differences have this second function, and Labov called these 'markers'. They are what together constitute an accent. Finally there is a sub-set of markers which have particularly high visibility within and outside the community. These are signs which have a special relationship to the metasign of the accent itself. Labov calls these 'stereotypes'. One important difference with stereotypes is that these are an accent of an accent. They are the selection, inflection and reading of a whole system of accents by a hostile community, a recuperation of the deviancy of the accent by reducing it to something simple, manageable and under the control of people outside the accent-community. So English speakers fancy their 'Irish' accent, Americans do their 'Negro' take-off, and Australians are delighted with their Aboriginal imitations. In each case, the real accent expresses the identity of the community, and excludes all other speakers. The stereotype constitutes the counter-claim that membership of that speech community is easy but worthless.

Labov's work can be complemented by Halliday's (1978) concept of antilanguage, which we have already mentioned. Where Labov worked mostly though not exclusively with sound signifiers, Halliday looked at other levels where meaning was more obviously important, at words and syntax. Halliday was clearer about the social functions of an antilanguage or its antigroup, and how these functions affected the typical forms of the language itself. In an antilanguage, language exists primarily to create group identity and to assert group difference from a dominant group. In Halliday's terms, the interpersonal function predominates over the ideational. In our terms, language is oriented towards the semiosic plane, not to the mimetic plane. One result is deliberate difficulty, often unintelligibility. Antilanguages simultaneously exclude outsiders, and express the ideology of the antigroup. Yet the antilanguage is derived from the dominant language, parasitic on it, typically achieving its incomprehensible forms by a series of simple but *ad hoc* transformations. For example 'look' becomes, by rhyming slang, 'butcher's hook'. Another transformation deletes 'hook', and the phrase 'take a butcher's' (meaning 'take a look') becomes unintelligible to outsiders. In the process of creating the forms of an antilanguage, difference is first created by normal transformational processes. The terms of that difference are then assigned a social label. Finally the transformational processes are suppressed, so that the language becomes exclusive to its users. An antilanguage differs from an accent only in its assertion of stronger difference and more intense opposition; or, conversely, an accent is a partial antilanguage. The meaning at the core of the metasign of antilanguages is hostility and rejection of the dominant order. Where possible, antigroups usually draw on other semiotic systems – such as the use of black clothing, by many outlaw groups – to express the same basic set of meanings.

Antilanguages as studied by Halliday seem to be associated with subordinate oppositional groups – prisoners, thieves, and so on. But a related phenomenon is very general in languages in stratified societies. Many language communities have two distinct languages, one of which is labelled 'high', and is identified with high-status speakers on public occasions, the other 'low', for the converse. Corresponding to 'high' languages, in such communities, there is normally 'high' culture, with the same social meaning and function as the high language, and usually mediated through the relevant 'high' language (cf. Bourdieu 1984). The nature, existence and role of 'high' culture and its opposing category, 'low' or 'popular' culture, have been extensively theorized. From a general semiotic point of view it is necessary to establish the unity of this set of phenomena, so that a 'high' language can be treated as one component of a 'high' culture, which operates ultimately as a single semiotic system that consists of overlapping sets of metasigns. We can also observe that whereas in Halliday's account an 'antilanguage' typically marks an oppositional and marginalized group, a 'high' culture and language normally signify the values of the dominant group. Yet 'high' languages have the typical qualities of an antilanguage. They are oriented towards the semiosic plane rather than the mimetic, they are full of complex transformations that obscure referential meanings while signifying kinds of power and solidarity, and they function to exclude those outside the high-status language community. Similarly, 'high' art, 'high' music, and 'high' culture are themselves characteristically difficult, with mimetic meanings usually made inaccessible. They are full of complex transformations which are valorized to ensure that high culture forms are, for one reason or another, not available to the ordinary person. The metasigns of the élite who control high culture incorporate meanings of hostility towards the majority just as much as do metasigns of punks, bikers and mafiosi...

At this point it will be be useful to draw together a number of observations about the role of metasigns in creating and sustaining difference and identity.

1. The motor of semiotic change is the desire to express difference. This desire proceeds from the need of specific groups to create internal solidarity and to exclude others, as antigroups constructing antilanguages, antimeanings, anti-cultures and antiworlds.

2. Differences can be expressed by marked choices and significant transformations at any level in a semiotic hierarchy, from the micro level ('accent', 'style' or 'grammar') through the meso level (item, phrase, ensemble) to the macro level (topic, theme, cosmology, metaphysics).

3. These differences exist to express group ideology and group identity. They normally form functional sets of metasigns (pervasive markers of group allegiance), whose meaning is social rather than referential, oriented to the semiotic rather than the mimetic plane.

4. Metasigns of group identity are normally constructed out of transparent signifiers. But since antilanguages and anticultures aim to exclude and mystify others, and since metasigns are normally pervasive in the production of texts, an accumulation of transparent metasigns of group identity will normally lead to forms of language and text whose mimetic meanings seem impenetrable, inexplicable and opaque to outsiders. Incomprehensibility, that is, is never an accident.

5. The 'culture' of a group performs the same functions for it as the metasigns in individual codes. A culture, then, is a complex that consists of metasigns from a range of codes (speech, clothing, food, etc.) with a common core of social meanings.

REFERENCES

Bourdieu, P. (1984) *Distinction: A Social Critique of the Judgement of Taste* (trans. Nice, R.) (London: Routledge and Kegan Paul).

Halliday, M. A. K. (1978) *Language as Social Semiotic* (London: Edward Arnold).

Labov, W. (1978) *Sociolinguistic Patterns* (Oxford: Blackwell).

Saussure, F. de (1974) *Course in General Linguistic*, Culler, J. trans. Baskin, W. (ed.) (London: Fontana).

7   Demythologizing Sociolinguistics

Deborah Cameron

INTRODUCTION

> A concept of a language involves, and is most often clearly manifest in,
> acceptance or rejection of what requires explanation about the ways in
> which languages work. This means that a concept of a language cannot
> stand isolated in an intellectual no-man's land. It is inevitably part of
> some more intricate complex of views about how certain verbal
> activities stand in relation to other human activities, and hence,
> ultimately, about no man's place in society and in nature.
>
> (Harris 1980: 54)

Harris's own work represents an attempt to explore the 'intricate complex of
views' that underpin the western tradition of language study. He identifies
what he calls a 'language myth' (Harris 1981): a collection of taken-for-
granted propositions about the nature and workings of language from
which particular questions 'naturally' follow, and lead in turn to particular
kinds of solutions. For example, if one accepts the Lockean idea of
communication through language as 'telementation', the transference of
messages from one mind to another, the obvious question is 'how can this be
accomplished?' and the natural solution is to model language as a 'fixed
code' located in the mind of every speaker.

Harris's project of 'demythologizing' linguistics consists essentially in
making explicit the hidden assumptions which underlie linguists' models,
showing that they are historical constructs (rather than immutable truths
given by the nature of language itself) and subjecting them to critical
scrutiny. By adopting a different concept of a language, Harris points out,
we would inevitably commit ourselves to asking quite different questions
and proposing quite other solutions. In Harris's view this is exactly what
linguistics ought to do; but I should perhaps add that we do not have
to agree with Harris's outright rejection of current linguistic orthodoxy to

Source: 'Demythologizing Sociolinguistics: Why Language Does Not Reflect
Society', in Joseph, J. E. and Taylor, T. J. (eds) (1990) *Ideologies of Language*
(London and New York: Routledge) pp. 79–93.

accept his critical method as a valid and useful tool for reflecting on our practice.

In this chapter, I want to reflect on the practice of sociolinguistics (by which I mean, more or less, the 'variationist' or 'quantitative' paradigm associated with the work of Labov; whether this is an unreasonably narrow definition of the term 'sociolinguistics' is a question to which I shall return). In a demythologizing spirit I shall ask what assumptions about language and society underpin work in the quantitative paradigm, why sociolinguists have invested in these assumptions and whether they are useful, or even tenable. I shall argue that if sociolinguistics is to move forward, or indeed to realize fully its current objectives, it will need to shift its views 'about how certain verbal activities stand in relation to other human activities' – a move whose consequences for sociolinguistic methodology and theory may well prove quite radical.

Let me say immediately that I do not wish to deny the value of work in the quantitative paradigm. Indeed, there is an irony in my attempting to demythologize sociolinguistics, since sociolinguistics itself was conceived as a demythologizing exercise. The name Labov once gave it – 'secular linguistics' – implies a conscious desire to challenge sacred linguistic dogmas.

The doctrine Labov was most concerned to challenge was that of 'the ideal speaker-hearer in a homogeneous speech community' (I use the familiar Chomskyan formulation, but the central point that linguistics must idealize its object in order to describe it goes back through the structuralist paradigm and to Saussure). Labov debunked this as myth by showing that language is not homogeneous, either at the level of the speech community or the individual grammar. Rather, it possesses 'structured variability'. 'Structured' is important here: it means the variation found in language is not a matter of 'free' or random alterations (which mainstream linguists had recognized but excluded from consideration on the grounds that they were superficial, hence uninteresting, and difficult to model elegantly) but is, on the contrary, systematic and socially conditioned. Labov's work demonstrated that variation could be modelled, and that the analysis of variation provided insight into the mechanism of language change. In other words, he argued convincingly that to accept the myth of the ideal speaker-hearer in the homogeneous speech community was not merely to screen out a few surface irregularities, but rather to miss a fundamental general property of language.

By insisting on the importance of heterogeneity, and developing methods of analysing it, sociolinguistics clarified questions of real theoretical importance which were not addressed in any principled way by existing paradigms. Like all myths, the myth of idealized homogeneity had foregrounded some things, making them easier to 'see', while rendering other things (like variation and change) impenetrably obscure. Labov's work may with justice be called 'demythologizing' because it pointed this out, and began the task of bringing what was obscure into the light. But the approach he founded is not without myths and blindspots of its own. Quantitative sociolinguistics has certainly clarified some aspects of language in society. But other aspects remain mysterious, the crucial questions unanswered, or even unasked.

What are these crucial questions? Very briefly, they concern the reasons *why* people behave linguistically as they have been found to do in study after study. Sociolinguistics does not provide us with anything like a satisfactory explanation. The account which is usually given – or, worse, presupposed – in the quantitative paradigm is some version of the proposition that 'language reflects society'. Thus there exist social categories, structures, divisions, attitudes and identities which are marked, encoded or expressed in language use. By correlating patterns of linguistic variation with these social or demographic features, we have given a sufficient account of them. (The account may also be supplemented with crudely functionalist ideas – that speakers 'use' language to express their social identity, for instance – or with a slightly less crude model in terms of group 'norms' at both macro- and micro-levels.)

Two things about this kind of account are particularly problematic. The first problem is its dependence on a naive and simplistic *social* theory. Concepts like 'norm', 'identity', and so on, and sociological models of structures/divisions like class, ethnicity and gender, are used as a 'bottom line' though they stand in need of explication themselves. Secondly, there is the problem of how to *relate* the social to the linguistic (however we conceive the social). The 'language reflects society' account implies that social structures somehow exist before language, which simply 'reflects' or 'expresses' the more fundamental categories of the social. Arguably, however, we need a far more complex model that treats language as *part* of the social, interacting with other modes of behaviour and just as important as any of them.

Before I return to these problems in more detail, it is necessary to ask why sociolinguistics has become caught up in them – why has the quantitative paradigm invested in the whole notion of 'language reflecting society'? This takes us back to the question of what sociolinguistics is, and how the field has been defined.

'SOCIOLINGUISTIC AND SOCIOLINGUISTICS': THE RISE AND RISE OF THE QUANTITATIVE PARADIGM

As I pointed out above, to make sociolinguistics synonymous with the Labovian quantitative is to beg the question. There are other approaches to the study of language in society (such as ethnography of speaking, discourse analysis, sociology of language) which surely have some claim to the title 'sociolinguistics' so that my definition could be construed as unnecessarily narrow and restricted, not to say biased.

To the criticism of narrowness and bias, however, I would respond by asserting that my definition of sociolinguistics reflects a historical (and academic-political) reality: over the last fifteen years the quantitative paradigm has so successfully pressed its claims to the central and dominant position in language and society studies, that for most people in the field (and especially most *linguists* in the field) 'sociolinguistics' does indeed mean primarily if not exclusively 'Labovian quantitative sociolinguistics'. The effect to this shift, for as we shall see it *is* a shift, is to privilege and even to mythologize one kind of approach to linguistic variation. ...

One can point to any number of textbooks by influential authors in which the primacy of linguistic over social issues is vigorously asserted (Hudson 1980; Trudgill 1978 and 1983). In a rather bizarrely titled introductory essay called 'Sociolinguistics and sociolinguistics', Trudgill puts his notion of what he calls 'sociolinguistics proper' in the following terms: 'All work in this category...is aimed ultimately at improving linguistic theory and at developing our understanding of the nature of language...very definitely *not* 'linguistics as a social science', (1978: 3).

Now there is of course nothing wrong with trying to improve linguistic theory and our understanding of the nature of language; it is also quite true that sociolinguistics of the sort Trudgill advocates has enabled progress to be made. But one might ask: why this assiduous policing of the disciplinary borders? What is at stake in the emphatic denial of 'linguistics as a social science'? Is Trudgill's stand well motivated in terms of the overall aims of sociolinguistics, or is it determined by somewhat different considerations?

In my view, what Trudgill says (and he is typical enough) can be interpreted as part of an understandable concern about the academic prestige of sociolinguistics. Many sociolinguists would like to lay claim to the sort of prestige mainstream linguistics has achieved over the last 25 years; conversely, they would like to distance themselves from the more dubious reputation of contemporary sociology. Academic prestige is dependent on various factors, but one of them is *scientific status*: a prestigious discipline will tend to possess qualities associated with science (however erroneously) such as theoretical and methodological rigour, 'objectivity', abstraction, and so on. One achievement of the so-called Chomskyan revolution has been to appropriate this sort of status for linguistics more successfully than previous or alternative paradigms. Little wonder, then, that sociolinguistics should concentrate on the 'linguistics' to the virtual exclusion of the 'socio'. ...

The trouble with concentrating on the purely linguistic and eschewing approaches tainted with the 'social science' tag is that sociolinguistics, however you try to define it, remains the study of language *in society*.

Linguistic variation cannot be described sensibly without reference to its social conditioning; and if sociolinguistics is to progress from description to explanation (as it must unless it wants to be vulnerable to renewed charges of 'butterfly collecting') it is obviously in need of a theory linking the 'linguistic' to the 'socio'. Without a satisfactory social theory, therefore, and beyond that a satisfactory account of the relationship between social and linguistic spheres, sociolinguistics is bound to end up stranded in an explanatory void.

Faced with the problem of explaining variation, and in the absence of a well-thought-out theory of the relation of language and society, socio-linguists tend to fall back on a number of unsatisfactory positions: they may deny that anything other than statistical correlation is necessary to explain variation, they may introduce *ad hoc* social theories of one kind or another, or they may do both. Let us look more closely at the way these positions are taken up in practice and at their adequacy or otherwise as explanatory strategies.

EXPLANATION AND THE LIMITS OF QUANTIFICATION: THE CORRELATIONAL FALLACY

In the quantitative paradigm, statistical correlations are used to relate frequency scores on linguistic variables to nonlinguistic features both demographic (class, ethnicity, gender, age, locality, group structure) and contextual (topic, setting, level of formality). For instance, it is well known that rising frequencies of 'prestige' variants like postvocalic [r] in New York City correlate positively with rising social status and rising levels of formality. This kind of regularity is called a 'sociolinguistic pattern'.

Sociolinguistic patterns are essentially descriptive statements about the distribution of certain variables in the speech community. The question remains how to explain that distribution. As Brown and Levinson (1987) have noted, it is commonplace to take correlation as the terminal point of the account. Thus it could be claimed that my score for the variant [r] is explained by the fact that I belong to a particular social category – say, working-class women of Italian descent aged 50 + and living in New York City – and am speaking in a particular context, say a formal interview with a linguistic researcher. The variable (r) acts as what Scherer and Giles (1979) call a 'social marker'. This whole 'explanation' clearly rests on the perception that 'language reflects society': I shall refer to it as the 'correlational fallacy'.

Why is it a fallacy? Because the purported explanation does not in fact explain anything. Someone who subscribes to the sort of account given above has misunderstood what it means to explain something. One does not explain a descriptive generalization (such as 'older working-class female Italian New Yorkers in formal interviews have average (r) scores of n%') by simply stating it all over again. Rather, one is obliged to ask in virtue of what the correlation might hold. Any account which does not go on to take this further step has fallen into the correlational fallacy.

It is precisely at the point where the further step becomes necessary that *ad hoc* social theories are likely to be invoked. A sociolinguist might assert, for instance, that by using n% of (r), older working-class female Italian New Yorkers are expressing their identity as older working-class female Italian New Yorkers; or they are adhering to the norms of their peer group, or possibly (as in the case of a formal interview) the norms of the larger society which dictate a more standardized speech on certain occasions.

There are various difficulties with these suggestions, not all of which can be gone into here in the detail they deserve, but certain problems can at least be sketched in. Take, for example, the notion of speakers expressing a social identity. It is common currency among sociolinguistics, but a social theorist might pose some awkward questions about it: do people really 'have' such fixed and monolithic social identities which their behaviour consistently expresses? Furthermore, is it correct to see language use as expressing an identity which is separate from and prior to language? To put the point a little less obscurely, is it not the case that the way I use language is partly *constitutive* of my social identity? To paraphrase Harold Garfinkel, social actors are not sociolinguistic 'dopes'. The way in which they construct and negotiate identities needs to be examined in some depth before we can say much about the relation of language to identity.

The suggestion that people's use of language reflects groups norms is a more useful one; it recognizes that human behaviour needs to be explained not in terms of invariant causes and effects but in terms of the existence of social meanings, in the light of which people act to reproduce or subvert the order of things. Unfortunately the account of normativity to be found in sociolinguistics is a curious and extremely deterministic one (a claim which will be illustrated below). There is also the question of where linguistic norms 'come from' and how they 'get into' individual speakers – a problem which becomes all the more acute when, as is often the case, the alleged norms are statistical regularities of such abstraction and complexity that no individual speaker could possibly articulate them either for herself or any other member of the speech community. So once again, the whole issue of norms requires a less *ad hoc* and more sophisticated treatment than it has on the whole received from sociolinguists.

Many of the problems to which I have referred here are also addressed by Suzanne Romaine in an article titled 'The status of sociological models and categories in explaining linguistic variation', which stands as an indictment of the correlational fallacy in sociolinguistics (Romaine 1984). In her article,

Romaine adduces four typical studies in the quantitative paradigm (Labov 1963; Gal 1979; Milroy 1980; Russell 1982) and points out a link between them: they all explain linguistic variation and change in terms of group structure and membership. Tight-knit groups (technically, dense multiplex networks) promote language maintenance whereas looser ties permit linguistic change.

An illustration may make this clearer. Lesley Milroy (1980) devised what she called a 'network strength scale' to measure the integration of her Belfast informants into their peer group. Points were scored for such things as having strong ties of kinship in the neighbourhood; working at the same place as your neighbours; spending leisure time with workmates; and so on. Individuals scored between 0 and 5 for network strength, and high scores were found to correlate positively with the use of certain vernacular variants. People who were less well integrated – for instance because they had been rehoused, were employed outside the neighbour-hood where they lived or had no work at all – used fewer of these vernacular features. This led Milroy to conclude that people in her survey behaved linguistically as they did because of the normative influence of their peer group. Their sources on linguistic variants were determined by how strong or weak the peer group influence was. Tight-knit groups where people spend a lot of time with each other (and less with anyone else) are efficient norm-enforcing mechanisms – hence the finding that they promote the maintenance of traditional vernacular rather than permitting innova-tion to creep in.

All this may seem obvious enough, but as Romaine enquires, what kind of an *explanation* is it? The social network is a theoretical construct which cannot therefore 'make' any individual speaker do anything. Yet if we take away the idea of the network's ability to enforce linguistic norms, all we are left with is statistical correlations. Of these, Romaine comments: 'the observed correlations between language and group membership tell us nothing unless fitted into some more general theory' (1984: 37).

What is this 'general theory' to be? Clearly, it needs to engage with the whole issue of how individuals relate to groups and their norms – in Romaine's words, it must make reference to 'rationality, intentionality and the function of social agents and human actors' (1984: 26). Is it then a theory of individual psychology, which seeks to explain how actors make rational decisions in the domain of linguistic behaviour? This kind of 'rational choice' line is the one often favoured by sociolinguists who do go beyond correlation (cf. Brown and Levinson's explanation (1987) of politeness phenomena in terms of strategies for satisfying universal psychological needs to maintain 'face'). But while an account of individual psychology may be necessary, I think Romaine recognizes it is not sufficient. There is another, neglected area which properly belongs to the study of language in society but which cannot be addressed within the current assumptions of the quantitative paradigm.

Romaine hints at this when she makes the following observation:

> It is legitimate to recognise that an agent's social position and his relations with others may constrain his behavior on a particular occasion in specific ways . . . People are constrained by the expressive resources available in the language(s) to which they have access and by the conventions which apply to their use. (1984: 37).

This can be interpreted as an argument for social or sociological levels of explanation as well as individual or psychological ones. For what Romaine alludes to here is the fact that speakers 'inherit' a certain system and can only choose from the options it makes available. Social agents are not *free* agents, but this does not mean we have to go back to the notion that they are sociolinguistic automata. Rather, we should ask ourselves such questions as 'what determines "the expressive resources available" in particular languages or to particular groups of speakers? Who or what *produces* "the conventions which apply to their use"? How – that is to say, through what actual, concrete practices – is this done?'

To address such issues seriously requires us to acknowledge that languages are regulated social institutions, and as such may have their own dynamic and become objects of social concern in their own right. With its emphasis on microanalysis and its suspicion of social theory, sociolinguistics tends to push this kind of perspective into the background. But if we seek to understand people's linguistic behaviour and attitudes – and, after all, changes in the linguistic system must at some level be brought about by the behaviour and attitudes of actual speakers – an approach to language in society which foregrounds questions like Romaine's is desperately needed. A demythologized sociolinguistics would incorporate such an approach as a necessary complement to quantification and microanalysis. It would deal with such matters as the production and reproduction of linguistic norms by institutions and socializing practices; how these norms are apprehended, accepted, resisted and subverted by individual actors and what their relation is to the construction of identity.

At this point it is helpful to consider in concrete terms how an approach like this would work and what its advantages might be. I shall therefore turn to a case in point: the changes in linguistic behaviour and in certain language systems brought about by the reformist efforts of contemporary feminists. These developments exemplify a kind of linguistic change with which quantitative sociolinguists do not feel at ease, and in relation to which conventional accounts within the 'language reflects society' framework appear particularly lame.

A CASE IN POINT: SEXISM IN LANGUAGE

Over the last fifteen years the question of 'sexism in language' has been a hotly contested topic both inside and outside professional linguistic circles. What is at issue is the ways in which certain linguistic subsystems (conventional titles and forms of address, parts of the lexicon and even of grammar, for instance) represent gender. Feminists have pointed out that the tendency of these representations is to reinforce sexual divisions and inequalities. Salient facts about English include, for example, the morphological marking of many female-referring agent nouns (*actress, usherette*); the availability of more sexually pejorative terms for women than men (Lees 1986); the non-reciprocal use of endearment terms from men to women (Wolfson and Manes 1980); and most notoriously, the generic use of masculine pronouns (Bodine 1975).

It should not surprise us that phenomena like these are widely understood as an instance of 'language reflecting society'. 'Society' holds certain beliefs about men and women and their relative status; language has 'evolved' to reflect those beliefs. Feminists have tried to argue that more is going on than passive reflection: sexist linguistic practice is an instance of sexism in its own right and actively reproduces specific beliefs. But nonfeminist sociolinguists have notably failed to take their point.

This becomes particularly evident in discussions of recent changes in English usage – changes which have occurred under pressure from feminist campaigns against sexism in language. For some time, the view of many linguists was that reforming sexist language was an unnecessary, trivial and timewasting objective, since language merely reflected social conditions. If feminists concentrated on removing more fundamental sex inequalities, the language would change of its own accord, automatically reflecting the new nonsexist reality. (This, incidentally, suggests a view of language which might have been supposed to be obsolete in twentieth-century thought, and which we might label 'the organic fallacy': that language is like an organism, with a life of its own, and evolves to meet the needs of its speakers. Exactly how language does this remains a mystery.)

More recently, however, it has become obvious that linguistic reform as proposed by feminists has enjoyed a measure of success. For instance, it is clear that generic masculine pronouns are no longer uniformly used by educated speakers and writers; even such authoritative sources as Quirk *et al.* (1985) acknowledge the existence of alternatives such as singular *they* and *he or she*. What do sociolinguists make of this change in English pronominal usage? Astonishingly, they tell us it has happened 'naturally', as a reflection of the fact that women's social position has radically altered in the last two decades (cf. Cheshire 1984: 33-4 for a statement to this effect).

It is worth pointing out in detail what is wrong with this sort of claim. One immediate flaw in the argument is that it is patently untrue: without campaigns and debates specifically on the issue of sexism *in language*, linguistic usage would not have altered even though other feminist gains (such as equal pay and anti-discrimination legislation) were made. Historically speaking there is certainly a connection between feminist campaigns for equal opportunities and for nonsexist language, but the one has never entailed the other, nor did either just reflect the other. To repeat the crucial point once more: language-using is a social practice in its own right.

It should also be pointed out that a change in linguistic practice is not just a reflection of some more fundamental social change: it is, itself, a social change. Anti-feminists are fond of observing that eliminating generic masculine pronouns does not secure equal pay. Indeed it does not – whoever said it would? Eliminating generic masculine pronouns precisely eliminates generic masculine pronouns. And in so doing it changes the repertoire of social meanings and choices available to social actors. In the words of Trevor Pateman (1980: 15) it 'constitutes a restructuring of at least one aspect of one social relationship'.

Another problem with the 'language reflects society' argument in relation to changes in English usage is that it makes language change a mysterious, abstract process, apparently effected by the agency of no one at all (or perhaps by the language itself – the organic fallacy rides again). This overlooks the protracted struggle which individuals and groups have waged both for and against nonsexist language (and the struggle continues). It ignores, for instance, the activity of every woman who ever fought to put 'Ms' on her cheque book, every publisher, university committee or trade union working party that produced new institutional guidelines on the wording of documents, not to mention every vituperative writer to the newspapers who resisted, denounced or complained about nonsexist language.

The general point here is that there are instances – this is one – where we can locate the specific and concrete steps leading to an observable change in some people's linguistic behaviour and in the system itself. We can discover who took those steps and who opposed them. We can refer to a printed debate on the subject, examine the arguments put forward on both sides (and it is interesting that those arguments tended to be about language rather than gender: not 'should women be treated equally' but 'what do words mean and is it right to change them?'). The 'language reflects society' model obscures the mechanisms by which sexist language has become less acceptable, evacuating any notion of agency in language change. Crucially, too, the model glosses over the existence of social conflict and its implications for language use. Here as elsewhere in sociolinguistics the underlying assumption is of a consensual social formation where speakers acquiesce in the norms of their peer group or their culture, and agree about the social 'needs' which language exists to serve.

It would of course be wrong to claim that all linguistic change is of this kind – organized and politically motivated efforts to alter existing norms and conventions. But some linguistic changes *are* of this kind, and sociolinguistics should not espouse a concept of language which makes them impossible to account for.

TOWARDS A DEMYTHOLOGIZED SOCIOLINGUISTICS

The campaign against sexism in language is one of instance of a type of metalinguistic practice which we might call 'verbal hygiene' (other examples might include Plain English movements or Artificial Language movements; systems regulating the use of obscenity and insults (cf. Garrioch 1987); and, of course, prescriptivism, standardization and associated activities). Such practices are referred to in sociolinguistic work in passing if at all: doubtless it is thought that they are unlikely to advance linguistic theory, and should therefore be left for sociologists to research.

Yet if the arguments put forward above have any force, it may not be so easy to prise apart the concerns of linguistic theory and those of the sociologist. We have seen that sociolinguists make casual but significant use of notions like 'norm' and 'social identity' in order to explain the variation and the attitudes they observe. And I have argued that one of the problems with this is that we are left with no account of where the norms 'come from' and how they 'get into' individual speakers – it is not good enough simply to situate them in some vague and ill-defined 'society', as though society were homogeneous, monolithic and transparent in its workings, and as if individual language users were pre-programmed automata. A detailed investigation of language users' metalinguistic activities – for instance, forms of 'verbal hygiene' – might well tell us a good deal about the production of norms and their apprehension by individuals.

It is striking, for example, that sociolinguists very often refer to the (overt) 'prestige' of standard English and assume this is impressed on speakers by normative instruction carried out mainly in schools; yet I know of no study of how (or even whether) the norms of standard English are inculcated by teachers. Dannequin (1988) has researched this question in France, and the resulting paper is extremely informative – a model of demythologizing.

Metalinguistic activities and beliefs have received, at least in urban Western societies, less attention than they merit. For it is surely a very significant fact about language in these societies that people hold passionate beliefs about it; that it generates social and political conflicts; that practices and movements grow up around it both for and against the status quo. We may consider the well-attested fact that many people, including those with minimal education, read a dictionary for pleasure; that there is a vast market for grammars, usage guides and general interest publications, radio and TV programmes about the English language; that many large-circulation newspapers and periodicals (such as the *Reader's Digest*) have a regular column on linguistic matters.

Most researchers in the quantitative paradigm are of course well aware of these facts, and more generally of people's keen interest in linguistic minutiae. With some honourable exceptions, though, they tend to treat laypersons' views on usage as manifestations of ignorance to be dispelled, or of crankishness and prejudice to be despised. The axiom that linguistics is 'descriptive not prescriptive', together with the methodological principle that a researcher should influence informants as little as possible, prevent sociolinguists taking folk linguistics seriously. Arguably, though, practices like dictionary reading and writing to the papers on points of usage are striking enough to demand analysis: first, not unnaturally, they demand investigation.

And this is the task I would set for a demythologized sociolinguistics: to examine the linguistic practices in which members of a culture regularly participate or to whose effects they are exposed. As well as being of interest in itself, this undertaking would help us to make sense of the process noted by Romaine: the constraining of linguistic behaviour by the social relations in which speakers are involved and the linguistic resources to which they have access. We might also discover how language change may come about through the efforts of individuals and groups to produce new resources and new social relations. For language is not an organism or a passive reflection, but a social institution, deeply implicated in culture, in society, in political relations at every level. What sociolinguistics needs is a concept of language in which this point is placed at the centre rather than on the margins.

REFERENCES

Bodine, A. (1975) 'Androcentrism in Prescriptive Grammar', *Language in Society*, **4**, pp. 129–46.

Brown, P. and Levinson, S. (1987) *Politeness* (Cambridge: Cambridge University Press).

Cheshire, J. (1984) 'The Relationship Between Language and Sex in English', in Trudgill, P. (ed.) *Applied Sociolinguistics* (London: Academic Press) pp. 33–49.

Dannequin, C. (1988) 'Les Enfants Baillonnés' ['Gagged children'], *Language and Education*, **1**, pp. 15–31.

Gal, S. (1979) *Language Shift* (New York: Academic Press).

Garrioch, D. (1987) 'Verbal Insults in Eighteenth-century Paris', in Burke, P. and Porter, R. (eds) *The Social History of Language* (Cambridge: Cambridge University Press).

Harris, R. (1980) *The Language Makers* (London: Duckworth).

Harris, R. (1981) *The Language Myth* (London: Duckworth).

Hudson, R. (1980) *Sociolinguistics* (Cambridge: Cambridge University Press).

Labov, W. (1963) 'The Social Motivation of a Sound Change', *Word*, **19**, pp. 273–309.

Lees, S. (1986) *Losing Out* (London: Hutchinson).

Milroy, L. (1980) *Language and Social Networks* (Oxford: Blackwell).

Pateman, T. (1980) *Language, Truth and Politics* (Lewes, Sussex: Stroud).

Quirk, R. *et al.* (1985) *A Comprehensive Grammar of the English Language* (London: Longman).

Romaine, S. (1984) 'The Status of Sociological Models and Categories in Explaining Linguistic Variation', *Linguistische Berichte*, **90**, pp. 25–38.

Russell, J. (1982) 'Networks and Sociolinguistic Variation in an African Urban Setting', in Romaine, S. (ed.) *Sociolinguistic Variation in Speech Communities* (London: Arnold) pp. 125–40.

Scherer, K. and Giles, M. (1979) *Social Markers in Speech* (New York: Academic Press) (Cambridge: Cambridge University Press).

Trudgill, P. (1978) 'Introduction: Sociolinguistics and Sociolinguistics' in Trudgill, P. (ed.) *Sociolinguistic Patterns in British English* (London: Edward Arnold) pp. 1–18.

Trudgill, P. (1983) *On Dialect* (Oxford: Blackwell).

Wolfson, N. and Manes, J. (1980) 'Don't "Dear" Me!', in McConnell-Ginet, S., Borker, N. and Furman, R. (eds) *Women and Language in Literature and Society* (New York: Praeger) pp. 79–92.

Part II
Methods for Studying Language in Society

The expression 'language in society' implies a practical as well as a theoretical emphasis. It implies a place where language is to be found, and where it needs to be studied – essentially in social life. Society is of course a very general concept, and we have already considered the argument that all instances of language in use are necessarily situated in some specific social context. But sociolinguistics has been very interested in these specifics – in characterizing what is potentially significant about social contexts for understanding linguistic forms and meanings, in explaining how language bears the imprint of the social contexts in which it has been produced, and in explaining how people actively manipulate the character of social situations through their language.

When it comes to designing investigations of language in society, this emphasis on social context poses tantalizing problems. If we believe that language and context are so inextricably linked, how can we observe language in use without ourselves *influencing* that delicate balance? As observers, aren't we colouring the language behaviours that we have come to observe? Can we study social contexts without being *part of* those contexts? This is the problem of methods that Labov has labelled *the observer's paradox*: how can we observe *un*observed language in society? Many of the chapters in this section comment on this problem, either as a theoretical issue or as a practical problem to be overcome or at least minimized in designing and implementing studies.

But it is also important to appreciate the general assumptions that lie behind the observer's paradox and the view of scientific investigation that it is based on. For example, there is clearly a belief here in the value of *natural* behaviour, and in the importance of naturally occurring linguistic data. The phrase 'field methods' suggests that researchers need to leave the safe places where they plan and interpret their research (usually colleges and universities) and engage with the world of 'real' and 'natural' language use. Observation is considered to be a problem if it interferes with the naturalness of a communicative episode or event.

This in turn implies a belief in *objectivity*, with the researcher's goal being to observe or capture instances of language use which are not 'skewed' or 'tainted' by the observation process. The researcher, it is implied, should be a dispassionate and independent observer, operating at a psychological distance from the events s/he is researching (see Wolfram and Fasold's Chapter 9). Even more strongly implied is a belief in research as an *empirical* process – a set of specific scientific techniques designed to engage with real-world activities such as conversations. Sociolinguists have typically been sceptical about ways of analysing language which don't have an empirical basis. This is one reason why they have been very critical of the 'introspective' (see Lesley Milroy's Chapter 8) or 'intuitive' approach favoured by some grammarians who have felt that their own internalized knowledge of language is an adequate source of knowledge or 'data'. For sociolinguists, 'data' means everyday uses of language observed in their normal social environments.

This set of linked assumptions – naturalism, objectivism, empiricism – is in fact being reappraised by sociolinguists, and by social scientists generally. Are we to accept these as universal principles of scientific research, or do they define only one version of what social research can be? Have we perhaps taken for granted the feasibility of objective sociolinguistic research, and been blinkered to the subjective aspects of how we have posed questions and interpreted results? Does language ever have the purity and uniformity that is implied in the assumption of naturalness? Are quantitative methods actually appropriate for the analysis of language, or do numerical summaries obscure the subtleties of meaning that language is designed to convey?

These are all elements of a grand debate about sociolinguistic methods which is far from resolved. Therefore, the texts in this part of the Reader do more than simply point to 'good' or 'adequate' practical means of collecting information about language in society. They debate the link between methods and theory. They defend rather different positions on what sociolinguistic research can and should achieve, and they therefore reach different conclusions about methods. While every sociolinguist will endorse the importance of some sort of empirical research procedure, different writers can disagree quite fundamentally about naturalism and objectivity.

Wolfram and Fasold introduce the most well-established research tradition in sociolinguistics – the *variationist* tradition, producing statistical information based on relatively large amounts of observed data. This is the technique associated with William Labov's research in New York City, extended and replicated in many urban communities around the world, including Trudgill's study in Norwich in the UK (see Trudgill's Chapter 14). Lesley Milroy's chapter outlines the historical background to modern variationist research. She shows how Labov's approach in fact has a substantial pedigree from research that pre-dates modern sociolinguistics.

Wolfram and Fasold clearly adopt *empiricist* principles. That is, they assume, as much American research has done, that the basic mode of sociolinguistic investigation is controlled and objective surveying. They explain how a random sample of speakers is needed, to make sure that survey findings will be representative of the community being studied. The social characteristics of people in the survey are then described on some objective basis, and statistically correlated with counts of particular linguistic features.

This procedure implies that we accept social dimensions like social class, age or gender as factual and relatively fixed. The method treats linguistic values and social values as equivalent, and examines the degree of co-variation between them. The survey method places the researcher in the role of an orchestrator of research, and, in sociolinguistic survey interviews, as an elicitor of data rather than a *bona fide* conversationalist. If we take these observations together, we might criticize variationist sociolinguistics for being too static in its methods and too rigid in its assumptions. A more radical criticism would have it that language is far too active, creative and influential a phenomenon to be studied within an empiricist tradition. A *social constructivist* model would argue that it is only *through* language that our understanding of society and social categories such as class, gender and age have any meaningful existence. What sociolinguistics needs, by this account, is research methods which can uncover the social meanings that attach to linguistic categories, and how language shapes our social worlds. We should study the processes of linguistic construction rather than their products.

These questions have in fact been addressed within sociolinguistics, which is not limited to observing and analysing the distribution of language forms. Labov himself has made the point that we must also investigate people's subjective beliefs, judgements and reactions if we want to understand why patterns of usage are the way they are. Under the general heading of *language attitudes* research, this sort of sociolinguistics tends to be *experimental*, meaning (as Milroy comments) that studies are even more obviously and rigidly controlled by researchers than in the variationist tradition. As Wolfram and Fasold point out, methods have been developed in the social psychology of language by Lambert, Giles and others for this specific purpose. Ironically enough, we once again find very largely empiricist principles underpinning research which tries to answer questions about social construction! Language attitudes are usually studied quantitatively and in semi-laboratory conditions, by analysing trends in questionnaire-based responses to audio-recorded samples of speech. The so-called *matched-guise technique* uses imitated speech-styles ('guises') specifically to control the differences that always exist between different speakers speaking on different occasions, for example in speech-rate, pitch or voice quality.

The *ethnographic* tradition of sociolinguistic work, associated with Hymes's theoretical contribution (see Chapter 1), is quite different. It is summarized here in Saville-Troike's Chapter 11. Ethnographic research finds strengths in *qualitative* as well as quantitative study, and stresses the importance of the insider's viewpoint, and therefore subjectivity. It will be important to find the areas of overlap and incompatibility between the variationist and the ethnographic programmes, because, despite their differences, both are unquestionably sociolinguistics! Both are empirically grounded approaches to the study of language in society.

As we pointed out earlier, an empirical programme of study bases its analyses on 'data' of some sort. When sociolinguists talk about data, they mean a more or less systematic collection of instances of language in use. Lesley Milroy's Chapter 8 traces the early American linguists' concern with *accountability to the data*, a principle that was given up in Chomsky's influential research on transformational grammar but re-established in sociolinguistics through Labov's work. A cornerstone of modern socio-linguistics was established when Labov and others found that they could only account for their data if they recognized linguistic *variation* within geographical communities, which also fundamentally challenged the idea that 'pure' or 'genuine' linguistic forms exist.

Labov, however, did defend what is in one sense a purist notion – the idea of *natural speech*. For Labov, natural speech was not any particular, describable linguistic variety but a category of situation in which a speaker speaks in his or her least monitored style, what he calls *the vernacular*. Wolfram and Fasold describe techniques that have been developed to try to produce this naturalness, even in semi-structured sociolinguistic interviews. They include the famous 'danger of death' question, which invites speakers to tell an involving personal narrative. But Wolfson's main goal, in Chapter 10, is to challenge this understanding of 'natural speech'. For Wolfson, spontaneous interviews of the sort that sociolinguists have developed to access 'natural speech' are not in fact a recognized type of speech event. For that reason, she argues that the speech that these interviews generate is anything *but* natural.

Wolfson's position is interesting because it introduces what we could call a consideration of 'ecological validity' into the evaluation of sociolinguistic research, in place of 'naturalness': how do informants subjectively orient to research settings, and do research procedures match their expectations? Wolfson asks us to consider the qualitative experience of research episodes, beyond their adequacy as objective data-gathering devices. She does not challenge the main assumptions of variationist sociolinguistics, but moves towards some of the priorities of ethnography.

In the ethnographic tradition of sociolinguistics we find the clearest alternative to empiricism. Saville-Troike argues that it is crucial that ethnographers do *not* approach their research with preconceived categories. The ethnographer's responsibility is to build interpretations of communication in a natural environment, using a wide range of sources of information, open to unplanned as well as planned eventualities. A deeper understanding,

Saville-Troike argues, can be obtained if the researcher can function as a participant in the events being observed. So there is no claim to objectivity or independence, other than through 'keeping a mental distance'. Ethnographers, that is, can be cultural and behavioural *insiders* even though their research goals require them to be analytic outsiders. In ethnographic sociolinguistics, the categories of 'researcher' and 'researched' become less distinct, but this does not weaken the force of ethical considerations.

There is in fact a good deal of overlap between the ethical issues raised by Saville-Troike and those discussed by Wolfram and Fasold, although the intimacy of ethnographic accounts will often mean that findings cannot be generalised as widely as the quantitative results of sociolinguistic surveys. Saville-Troike feels that ethnographic research needs to achieve a balance of usefulness, being of value to the community being investigated as well as to the researcher. It is likely that this sort of consideration will be increasingly important in social science generally, as government-sponsored research agencies (such as the Economic and Social Research Council in the UK) evaluate research proposals more and more in relation to visible achievements for specific 'user groups'.

Here again, particular philosophies and ideologies of research come into play, and we find significantly different interpretations of what an *ethical* approach to sociolinguistics means. In the empiricist tradition, ethics is addressed as the need to observe a set of specific criteria – not betraying informants' confidences, avoiding deception, avoiding intrusiveness, and so on (again, see Wolfram and Fasold). Research is more ethical to the extent that the researcher is more open, respectful and honourable. But the term 'ethics' is given a more specific and technical sense in Cameron, Frazer, Harvey, Rampton and Richardson's account (Chapter 12). For them, an ethical stance in relation to research is a minimalist moral position, narrowly conceived as a policy of reducing imposition while allowing researchers to get on with fulfilling their personal agendas. Cameron *et al.* say that ethical research is the traditional pattern of *research on* subjects. They then challenge these traditional assumptions, suggesting that they are inadequate for sociolinguistics.

A second stance is what they call *advocacy* research, which is research both *on and for* researched populations. Many people embark on sociolinguistic research motivated by concerns about social inequalities, and research has often been designed to expose prejudice or discrimination in the hope of promoting tolerance and improving social circumstances. Labov's involvement in the 'Black English' trial in Ann Arbor, Michigan (discussed in Cameron *et al.*'s chapter) is an excellent example. Even so, Cameron *et al.* find some theoretical problems with the concept of advocacy research. They suggest, for example, that it can easily be paternalistic and that it confuses the principles of objectivity and personal commitment.

The third stance they consider is *empowerment*, and the possibility of doing research *on, for* and *with* social subjects. The concept of empowering communities through researching them is certainly idealistic and even utopian. But Cameron *et al.*'s closely argued rationale for it is perhaps the clearest instance to date of sociolinguists trying to overturn the discipline's dominant empiricist tradition. The stimulus to this debate is a moral rather than a methodological concern. But Cameron *et al.* find that their moral priorities do not allow them to accept the *practices* of empiricist sociolinguistic research. In fact, their chapter challenges us to rethink the definition of research itself, our place in it as an activity, our investment in research, and the politics of the institutions that sustain it.

PART II: FURTHER READING

Baker, G. and Hacker, P. (1984) *Language, Sense and Nonsense* (Oxford: Blackwell).

Berger, P. and Luckman, T. (1966) *The Social Construction of Reality* (Harmondsworth: Penguin).

Botha, R. (1981) *The Conduct of Linguistic Inquiry* (The Hague: Mouton).

Carr, P. (1990) *Linguistic Realities: An Autonomist Metatheory for the Generative Enterprise* (Cambridge: Cambridge University Press).

Chambers, J. K. (1995) *Sociolinguistic Theory: Linguistic Variation and its Social Significance* (Oxford: Blackwell).

Chomsky, N. (1980) *Rules and Representations* (New York: Columbia University Press).

Pateman, T. (1987) *Language in Mind and Language in Society: Studies in Linguistic Reproduction* (Oxford: Clarendon Press).

Romaine, S. (1982) *Socio-historical Linguistics* (Cambridge: Cambridge University Press).

Scherer, K. R. and Howard, G. (eds) (1979) *Social Markers in Speech* (Cambridge: Cambridge University Press).

8 Field Linguistics

Lesley Milroy

DATA AND THEORY

Labov has observed that the general programme of all linguists – not only those who are writing competence grammars – begins with a search for *invariance* (Labov 1975: 7). The context of this remark was an attempt to focus on precisely how one kind of linguistic enterprise differs from another, and Labov argued that good methods and theories could best be developed by considering the important assumptions which linguists shared before examining those which divided them. Commenting on the theory/data relationship in a manner which also tends to emphasize the similarities between different types of linguistic enterprise, Kibrik lists what he considers to be three crucial concepts in any conceivable descriptive linguistic activity:

1. The *subject* of investigation (the language or part of the language).
2. The *object* of the investigation (written texts or tape-recorded data).
3. The *product* of the investigation. This is the *model* of the subject of the investigation which is usually called the *grammar*. Thus, Labov's graphic representations, which model patterns of language variation in New York City, may reasonably be described as grammars.

By using the term 'grammar' in this extension of its usual sense, we can begin to compare and contrast coherently the aims, methods and procedures of, for example, a descriptive linguist and an urban sociolinguist both working on a portion of the verb phrase (see Cheshire 1982 and J. Harris 1984 as examples of sociolinguists with those interests). It is not profitable to see these differences in terms of differences in the amount of idealization of the data base; models are always abstract and indirectly related to data. But using Kibrik's framework, and assuming with Labov (1975) that co-operation is essential if linguists are to benefit from each other's insights, differences between descriptive linguists and sociolinguists may be analysed as differences in the relationship between the investigator, the subject of

Source: 'Field Linguistics: Some Models and Methods', in Milroy, L. (1987) *Observing and Analysing Natural Language: A Critical Account of Sociolinguistic Method* (Oxford: Basil Blackwell) pp. 1–17.

study and the object of study in the process of arriving at the final product
(or model). Differences in the character of these relationships also give rise
to methods which differ in their potential to achieve particular goals.

Following this general line of thinking, we can present in graphic form
(Figure 8.1) three different models of the process by which an investigator
arrives at a product.

Figure 8.1(a) models an investigator/data/grammar relationship whereby
the investigator directly accesses the target language by means of his or her
own linguistic competence. Since the description is based on introspective
self-observation (sometimes checked against the introspections of others), a
body of data (the object of the investigation) is absent. One point which
might be made is that this method cannot be used to study any language
or language variety not known to the investigator, and since academic
linguists are seldom competent speakers of non-standard dialects or
uncodified languages, can in practice be used for describing only fully codified languages. This is not of course to deny that those who have grown up
as native speakers of a dialect (for example, Peter Trudgill in Norwich: see
Chapter 14) may have intuitions about its structure; so also might non-
native speakers who have developed an intimate knowledge of the structure
of a dialect (see J. Milroy 1981 for an example). But descriptions of non-
standard dialects generally use intuition as an aid to focusing the
investigation, rather than as a basic method; for although important facts
about linguistic structure and organization are accessible to introspection,
its applicability is sharply limited.

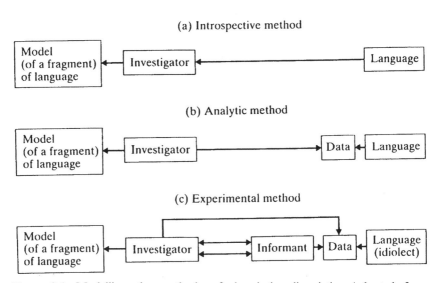

Figure 8.1 Modelling the methods of descriptive linguistics (adapted from
Kibrik 1977: 3)

The method modelled in Figure 8.1(b) also involves knowledge of the target language by the investigator. But rather than accessing intuitions directly, he or she bases generalizations upon a corpus of independently collected data. The clearest example of this method is modern work on discourse analysis and stylistics (see for example Stubbs 1983). The kinds of generalizations made by discourse analysts and stylisticians do not in fact appear to be accessible to intuition.

Much methodological discussion in the writings of the American structuralists implies that the structure of an *unknown* language can be recovered by analysing a corpus, without recourse to any other method; but as Bowman (1959) shows, this does not seem to be feasible. In practice, generalizations based on analyses of corpuses are usually derived using an additional method – either introspection or some kind of experimental procedure. Thus for example the substantial grammar of English written by Quirk and his associates (1972) is based upon both analytic and introspective methods of accessing information about linguistic structure, no clear distinction being drawn between information drawn from a corpus and information drawn from introspection.

In practice then, entirely corpus-based linguistic description of the kind attacked by Chomsky is extremely rare and probably represents a concept whose value is largely polemic. Since most linguists would probably agree that an adequate grammar cannot be derived solely from a corpus, the disagreement does not appear to be about the validity of a corpus-based analysis. Rather, it is about finding a principled way of supplementing or replacing a corpus-based approach. Labov (1975) provides an extended critique of the difficulties associated with introspection as an *alternative* method.

The term 'experimental' , which describes the method modelled in Figure 8.1(c), refers to the investigator's *control* over the data accessed. This method is used in conjunction with data independent of the investigator's own introspective observations, but does not involve inductively deriving linguistic generalizations from that data source. Rather, a native speaker is used to provide specified types of fact about the target language or variety, and most sociolinguists or dialectologists investigating a known language use a combination of this method with (a) and (b). Characteristically, linguists who investigate *unknown* languages use a combination of the experimental and analytic methods; sometimes an interpreter mediates between investigator and native speaker.

The term 'experimental' is used broadly to describe any method which entails the direct manipulation of an informant's responses. Within it is included a heterogeneous collection of procedures ranging from the minimal pair and commutation tests developed by the American structuralists to the formidable battery used by Labov (1966; 1975; 1981) for various purposes. Also included are the matched guise techniques developed by social psychologists (see Giles and Powesland, Chapter 18) and standard methods used in psycholinguistics. ...

EARLIER APPROACHES TO LINGUISTIC DESCRIPTION

The American Descriptivists

The American linguists commonly known as 'structuralists' or 'descriptivists' placed a high premium on the development and practice of a rigorous and accountable set of field methods... For a fuller account the reader is referred to Lepschy (1982), and Hymes and Fought (1980).

The concern with field methods in mainstream American linguistics from about the 1920s until the emergence of Chomsky may be partly attributed to a desire to describe as rapidly and efficiently as possible a large number of dying American Indian languages. Gumperz (1982: 12) contrasts the atmosphere of empiricism at that time in America, where scholars were concerned with working in the field, with that in Europe, where they worked in offices. Many American linguists, following the line of reasoning exemplified by Bloomfield (1926; 1935), associated the development of rigorous methods of description with the accreditation of a *scientific* status to linguistics. They strove to obtain objectivity by developing accountable procedures for inductively deriving linguistic generalizations from observable data, and an important methodological principle springing from this concern was that the phonological, morphological, syntactic and semantic patterns of a language should be analysed separately. They should moreover be analysed in that order, so that the analyst could remain in touch with the 'observable' part of language – the sequence of sound segments which he always began by describing.

This concern with *accountability to the data* (the object of description, in Kibrik's terms) has subsequently been the hallmark of Labov's work; the *principle of accountability* extends the general philosophy of accountability to a specifiable procedure which is the cornerstone of quantitative method. In this respect Labov's views resemble those of earlier American linguists but differ sharply from those of Chomsky and others working within his paradigm. Replacing induction with a hypothetico-deductive mode of reasoning, the generativists argue that no corpus of data, however large, can usefully serve as a basis for linguistic generalizations since any corpus is a partial and accidental collection of utterances (Chomsky 1975: 15). Although Chomsky's general point about the inadequacy of corpuses as the *only* source of information is surely correct (if in practice uncontroversial) one effect of his remarks has been to remove the sense of accountability to an independently collected body of data which was once much more widespread in linguistics than it is now. Field linguists generally – not only those working in the Labovian tradition – have reservations about the consequences of heavy reliance upon introspection: 'whatever may be the difficulties in studying and evaluating human behaviour in relation to language, behaviour is nevertheless more objective and observable than intuition or introspection. We can observe behaviour; we can only affirm intuition' (Longacre 1964: 13). There is no doubt that the revolution in linguistic thinking pioneered by Chomsky has affected the way field linguists go about constructing *models* (see G. Sankoff 1980c: 65 for a discussion). But American descriptivist methods still provide the basis for many contemporary techniques of *data collection* and *data analysis*. The extensive studies of Australian languages by Robert Dixon and his associates are obvious examples. ...

Traditional Dialectology

Many aspects of an approach to the observation and description of language which was developed during the nineteenth and twentieth centuries have been taken over and sometimes adapted by contemporary rural and urban dialectologists. Its main features are described by Petyt (1980) and Chambers and Trudgill (1980). Generally speaking, the aim of dialectological work is to produce a geographical account of linguistic differences, the product often taking the form of a series of maps showing the broad areal limits of the linguistic features (usually lexical or phonological) chosen for study. Boundaries (known as *isoglosses*) are plotted on the map, which show where form A gives way to form B; a *dialect boundary* is said to exist where a number of isoglosses more or less coincide. For example, Wakelin (1972: 102) illustrates the boundary between the Northern and North-Midland dialect areas of England by showing eight isoglosses which mark the approximate southern limit of eight phonological features characteristic of northern English dialect speech.

If we are to understand the field methods of traditional dialectology, it is important to remember that they were devised not in order to survey patterns of contemporary language use as an end in itself, but to offer a means of answering questions about the earlier history of the language. The main objective was to study contemporary reflexes of older linguistic forms in their natural setting, concentrating on speakers and locations which were relatively free from external influence. Associated with this theoretical model was a view of rural life strongly coloured by eighteenth- and nineteenth-century romanticism, as is evident from the following description:

In Europe, the practice has been to confine the survey to the speechways of the folk, and to give prominence to the oldest living generation in rural communities. A predilection for historical problems, the hope of shedding light on processes of linguistic change by observing the linguistic behaviour of the folk, and admiration for the soil-bound 'ethos' or 'world-view' of 'natural' people have been the motives and justification offered for this practice. (Kurath 1972: 13)

With these motives, Gilliéron (1902–10) approached his linguistic survey of France by seeking out older male, uneducated speakers who lived in remote rural communities. Both Orton (1962: 15) and McIntosh (1952: 85) discuss the value to more recent surveys of this type of speaker on whom it does indeed seem sensible to concentrate if the goal is to collect evidence which confirms hypothetical reconstructions of earlier forms. But the problem is that rather different sampling procedures are needed if the survey purports to make a more general statement about patterns of language variation. While nineteenth-century research is overwhelmingly historical in orientation, twentieth-century dialectologists working within the traditional paradigm frequently seem to have shifted their theoretical goal in the direction of an attempt to describe the contemporary language. Thus, the *Linguistic Atlas of the United States and Canada* attempts to adapt the traditional model by selecting informants at three educational levels, each notionally categorized as 'old-fashioned' and 'modern' types. Kurath comments: 'Until recently, large-scale surveys have been deliberately restricted to folk speech, especially to that of the countryside... In *The Linguistic Atlas of the United States* all population centers of any size were regularly included and, in principle, all social levels are represented' (1972: 11).

A similar tendency in more recent British studies to shift the theoretical goal is evident form McIntosh's comment that the Scottish survey will concentrate on older (or, as he calls them, 'resistant') speakers '*only in the first instance*' (1952: 86). Orton on the other hand, while aware of the sensitivity of patterns of language use to factors such as status, age, sex and situational context, is nevertheless quite clear in his view that these facts are irrelevant, since his objective is to locate for the *Survey of English Dialects* speakers who can provide samples of traditional dialect speech (Orton 1962: 15). One of the major points made by Labov in his early comments on the week of the dialectologists is that a realistic account of contemporary language variation necessitates radical alterations to the traditional method; minor adaptations are insufficient.

Moving on from the question of appropriate techniques of speaker selection to consider methods of *data collection* in traditional dialectology, we find that the two major techniques are *on-the-spot phonetic transcription* by a trained fieldworker and *the postal questionnaire*. It is the technique of on-the-spot transcription, adapted in various ways, which has provided the major model for later work. In recent times it has been supplemented or replaced by the tape-recorder, a development which has made possible the study of larger stretches of spontaneous spoken language rather than isolated lexical items. However, twentieth-century dialectology (exemplified by the *Survey of English Dialects*), which works within an only slightly modified framework of the traditional paradigm, has generally not fully exploited in its methods those technological advances which facilitate the study of spontaneous speech. Characteristically, the tape-recorder is used simply as a support for the fieldworker, who proceeds otherwise in much the same way as his or her nineteenth-century equivalent.

The postal questionnaire is an older technique, pioneered in Germany by Georg Wenker, who published his work in 1876. More recently it has been used by McIntosh (1952) and Le Page (1954); see also Le Page and Tabouret-Keller (1985: 83). McIntosh notes the obvious advantage of the method, that it provides an economic means of collecting large volumes of data. Questionnaires are still quite widely used where there is a need to collect a large amount of easily processable data quickly; examples are the ALUS survey of the Linguistic Minorities Project (1985) and Amuda's (1986) study of Yoruba/English code-switching patterns in Nigeria. The main disadvantage of questionnaires is that data may be inaccurately reported by informants who are not trained in phonetic transcription. Thus, McIntosh proposes using a postal questionnaire whenever possible, supplemented by the observations of a trained fieldworker when 'a closer scrutiny of the exact form of the word is necessary' (1952: 78). ...

THE TRADITIONAL MODEL:
SOME ADAPTATIONS AND CRITICISMS

Until the mid-1960s, the general framework offered by the traditional dialectological model was widely used for descriptions of language variation largely because at that time it was the only coherent one available. We look in this section at various attempts to adapt it for purposes other than those for which it was originally intended and the difficulties consequently encountered.

De Camp's Survey of Jamacan Dialects

De Camp began by working within the traditional paradigm, but later abandoned it for a more sophisticated approach to the problems of describing variability in creole languages (De Camp 1971). In his early work, he used traditional dialect-mapping techniques to plot linguistic differences

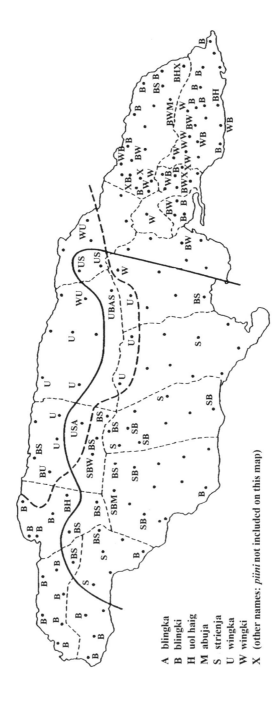

A blingka
B blingki
H uol haig
M abuja
S strienja
U wingka
W wingki
X (other names: *piini* not included on this map)

Figure 8.2 Linguistic dialect differences in Jamaica for 'small firefly' (adapted from De Camp 1961: 78)

between Jamaican dialects (see Figure 8.2), but was clearly unhappy with the implication of *discreteness* underlying the concept of isoglosses. Even though dialectologists have generally acknowledged that dialect boundaries are not in reality sharp divisions, a method of presentation such as Figure 8.2 is difficult to interpret as a satisfying model of contemporary language variation. De Camp comments:

Many people, including some educated Jamaicans, say that there are two distinct kinds of English spoken in Jamaica: 'standard English' and 'the dialect', meaning the folk speech of the uneducated. This is a persistent myth, a dangerous misconception. Indeed there is a great deal of difference between the English one hears at a Parent-teacher Association meeting of a fashionable suburban prep. school and that which one hears at a pocomania street meeting. But one can also find examples of every intermediate variety of English. Nearly all speakers of English in Jamaica could be arranged in a sort of linguistic continuum, ranging from the speech of the most backward peasant or labourer all the way to that of a well educated urban professional. Each speaker represents not a single point but a span of this continuum, for he is usually able to adjust his speech upwards or downwards for some distance on it. The middle-class housewife will understand the informal speech of a market woman, and, if sufficiently provoked, may even retort in kind, though she would probably have difficulty in maintaining an extended conversation on the market woman's level. Similarly the market woman may adapt her speech in the direction of the matron's. Each of them would probably describe the different levels in her own speech as 'standard English' and 'the dialect', yet the market woman's 'standard' might be further down the linguistic continuum than the matron's broadest 'dialect'. Every speaker differs in the span of this continuum which he can command. (De Camp 1961: 81)

It is evident from these remarks that De Camp is interested in finding a way to model patterns of contemporary language use, rather than in applying his data in the manner of the traditional dialectologists to the solution of historical problems. His observations on the nature of the linguistic continuum in Jamaica use the example of creole data to raise objections to underlying assumptions of invariance and discreteness which have proved subsequently to be of considerable theoretical interest. Moreover, dialectological methods were simply not designed to deal with language variation associated with a range of social factors *within* a single geographical area. Nor could existing dialect-mapping techniques deal with the fact that individual speakers vary within a range which might overlap the range controlled by other speakers.

BETWEEN PARADIGMS:
SOME EARLY URBAN STUDIES

One of the most pervasive assumptions underlying traditional dialectological method is that a particular form of a dialect – usually represented by the speech of a conservative, socially marginal speaker – may in some sense be seen as the 'genuine' or 'pure' form. The main difference between early and more recent urban studies is that the latter examine *alternative* linguistic forms, seeing this alternation as a significant property of language rather than admitting the concept of the 'pure' or 'genuine' dialect. As we shall see, this difference in the conception of what constitutes a 'dialect' has important implications for informant selection procedures.

One example of a good traditional study of an urban dialect is Viereck's *Phonematische analyse des Dialekts von Gateshead-upon-Tyne [sic]* (1966), a substantial and clear synchronic phonological account which includes a discussion of the relation between Received Pronunciation and 'local standards' (an idea derived from H. C. Wyld). Viereck considers in some detail how dialect forms might interact with RP forms to produce such urban varieties as that of Gateshead. However, although Gateshead's population is given as 100 000 and consists of persons of both sexes, all ages and various social statuses, the description is based on the speech of twelve men, all retired manual workers, whose average age is seventy-six. This does not seem to be a reasonable basis for a systematic description of an urban dialect.

Gregg's work in Larne, Co. Antrim (1964) resembles Viereck's in that it contains substantial phonological information and shows a similar interest in the emergence of local urban standards. Gregg relates his findings in Larne to data on the local Ulster-Scots dialect, noting that while Larne speakers have a similar phoneme inventory to rural hinterland speakers, they characteristically reorganize it in such a way that the available phonemic contrasts appear in different lexical sets. This kind of systematic difference is what Wells (1982) describes as an *incidential* difference in the distribution of phonemes. Although Gregg's account is sophisticated it is clearly traditional in orientation in so far as it is preoccupied with the 'genuine' speech of Larne as opposed to speech in which influence from nearby Belfast can be detected.

Similar comments might be made about Sivertsen's *Cockney Phonology* (1960). While recognizing that there are various kinds of Cockney which vary according to style and speaker, Sivertsen is explicitly interested in what she describes as 'rough Cockney', and her work is based mainly on the speech of four elderly female informants from Bethnal Green, selected for their relative social isolation, low social status, and lack of education. Although this is a substantial and clear description which includes a number of interesting observations (on, for example, sex-based differences in language), Sivertsen still reveals the traditional preoccupation with the 'pure' form of the dialect, in her view obtainable only from uneducated, old, low-status speakers.

The same preoccupation is revealed in a slightly different form in Weissmann's study of Bristol phonology (1970). Again we have a substantial and clear phonological account supplemented by both a phonemic and a phonetic transcription of spontaneous speech (recall the tendency of traditional dialectology to focus on single lexical items). Weissman's selected informants were all young men, partly because he felt more comfortable with men, but more importantly because he felt (probably correctly) that men would modify their characteristic Bristol speech less than women. Thus we see again a *restriction* in the type of informant selected with a view to producing a static description of some kind of 'extreme' phonological system.

The best of these early urban studies, of which we have discussed only a few examples here, provide valuable sources of data on the phonologies of British urban dialects (see Kurath 1972: 184ff for a discussion of some similar American studies). But they present two main problems which are both exemplified in Sivertsen's study.

First, certain assumptions are inherent in the preoccupation with 'genuine' dialect, the most obvious being that young speakers, by virtue of access to education and modern communications networks, are more likely to be influenced by the standard. This assumption has not in general been borne out by empirical observation. For example, Hurford (1967), discussing the language of three generations of a London family, suggests that Cockney features are advancing among the youngest speakers at the expense of RP features.

Some recent quantitative studies suggest that the kind of age grading in language noted by Hurford in London is in fact rather general, to the extent that researchers now expect to find the most extreme form of an urban vernacular among adolescent speakers and may focus on that age group (see for example Cheshire 1982). It is therefore dangerous to proceed in the manner of the older urban studies on the basis of apparently common-sense assumptions which may, when investigated, turn out to be false.

The second problem with these studies is their lack of *representativeness*. London is one of the largest cities in the world and has probably always been linguistically very heterogeneous. Even if we confine our interest to working-class speech from the East End, we are still talking about hundreds of thousands of people, and so it seems inappropriate, without explicit acknowledgement, to limit the description to a single type of informant. Some scholars have attempted to tackle this problem while still working broadly within the traditional framework, and a brief outline of two such attempts will help to place Labov's subsequent and much more influential work in perspective.

Houck's survey in Leeds was intended to provide a model for the study of urban dialects generally (Houck 1968). Using an extremely sophisticated two-stage sampling procedure, he ended up with a sample of 115, representing a 75 per cent success rate, which is very good for a linguistic survey. Unfortunately, however, Houck gave little indication in his published work of how the speech of his 115 informants was handled; the intention seems to have been to set up a phonological system using minimal pairs elicited by means of sentence frames. Thus, although he succeeded in obtaining a large amount of representative data, he was not in the end able to find a way of handling it.

Heath's survey of the urban dialect of Cannock, Staffordshire, carried out in the late 1960s, is characterized by an equally rigorous approach to sampling (Heath 1980). The 80 informants are divided into five groups, in accordance with the amount of influence upon their speech of the 'extremes' of Received Pronunciation on the one hand and Cannock urban dialect on the other: the influence of traditional studies on Heath's approach, as on that of the other researchers whose urban dialectological work has been considered in this section, is shown by frequent references to the 'pure' Cannock speaker.

Later studies used methods of data collection and analysis which do not oblige us to use the concept of the 'pure' dialect speaker but allow the contemporary language to be modelled in a somewhat more realistic way than was possible by adapting traditional methodology. For although there is much that is valuable and innovatory in Heath's work, which adapted traditional methods quite considerably, he was not able to model the *systematic* character of inter-speaker variation. The major contribution of Labov's methods was that in explicitly recognizing such patterns they provided a means of describing the language of *all* speakers of a dialect, without forcing the investigator to argue (or imply) that the language of one particular group was in some sense more 'genuine' than that of others.

REFERENCES

Amuda, A. (1986) 'Language Mixing by Yoruba Speakers of English'. Unpublished Ph.D. thesis, University of Reading.

Bloomfield, L. (1926) 'A Set of Postulates for the Study of Language', *Language*, 2, pp. 153–64.

Bloomfield L. (1935) *Language* (London: Allen and Unwin).

Bowman, E. (1959) 'An Attempt at an Analysis of Modern Yucatec from a Small Corpus of Recorded Speech', *Anthropological Linguistics*, 1(4), pp. 43–86.

Chambers, J. K. and Trudgill, P. (1980) *Dialectology* (Cambridge: CUP).

Cheshire, J. (1982) *Variation in an English Dialect: A Sociolinguistic Study* (Cambridge: CUP).

Chomsky, N. (1957) *Syntactic Structures* (The Hague: Mouton).

De Camp, D. (1961) 'Social and Geographical Factors in Jamaican Dialects', in Le Page, R. B. (ed.), *Creole Language Studies II* (London: Macmillan) pp. 61–84.

De Camp, D. (1971) 'Implicational Scales and Sociolinguistic Linearity', *Linguistics*, **71**, pp. 30–43.

Gilliéron, J. (1902–10) *Atlas Linguistique de la France*. 13 vols (Paris: Champion).

Gregg R. J. (1964) 'Scotch-Irish Urban Speech in Ulster', in Adams, B. (ed.) *Ulster Dialects: A Symposium* (Hollywood, Co. Down: Ulster Folk Museum) pp. 163–91.

Gumperz, J. J. (1982) *Discourse Strategies* (Cambridge: CUP).

Harris, J. (1984) 'Syntactic Variation and Dialect Divergence', *Journal of Linguistics*, **20**(2), pp. 303–27.

Heath, C. D. (1980) *The Pronunciation of English in Cannock, Staffordshire* (Oxford: Blackwell).

Houck, C. L. (1968) 'Methodology of an Urban Speech Survey', *Leeds Studies in English*. NS II, pp. 115–28.

Hurford, J. R. (1967) 'The Speech of One Family'. Unpublished Ph.D. thesis, University of London.

Kibrik, A. E. (1977) *The Methodology of Field Investigations in Linguistics*. Janua Linguarum. Series Minor (The Hague: Mouton).

Kurath, H. (1972) *Studies in Area Linguistics* (Bloomington, IN: Indiana UP).

Labov, W. (1966) *The Social Stratification of English in New York City* (Washington. DC: Center for Applied Linguistics).

Labov, W (1975) *What is a Linguistic Fact?* (Lisse: Peter de Ridder Press).

Labov, W. (1981) 'Field Methods Used by the Project on Linguistic Change and Variation', *Sociolinguistic Working Paper* 81 (Austin, TX: South Western Educational Development Laboratory).

Le Page, R. B. (1954) 'Linguistic Survey of the British Caribbean: Questionnaire A' (Jamaica: University College of the West Indies).

Le Page, R. B. and Tabouret-Keller, A. (1985) *Acts of Identity* (Cambridge: CUP).

Linguistic Minorities Project (1985) *The Other Languages of England* (London: Routledge).

Longacre, R. E. (1964) *Grammar Discovery Procedures* (The Hague: Mouton).

McIntosh, A. (1952) *An Introduction to a Survey of Scottish Dialects* (Edinburgh: Nelson).

Milroy, J. (1981) *Regional Accents of English: Belfast* (Belfast: Blackstaff).

Orton, H. (1962) *Survey of English Dialects: Introduction* (Leeds: E. J. Arnold).

Petyt, M. (1980) *The Study of Dialect: An Introduction to Dialectology* (London: Deutsch).

Quirk, R., Greenbaum, S., Leech, G. and Svartvik, J. (1972) *A Grammar of Contemporary English* (London: Longman).

Sankoff, G. (1980) 'A Quantitative Paradigm for the Study of Communicative Competence', in Sankoff, G. *The Social Life of Language* (Philadelphia, PA: University of Pennsylvania Press) pp. 47–9.

Sivertsen, E. (1960) *Cockney Phonology* (Oslo: Oslo UP).

Stubbs, M. (1983) *Discourse Analysis* (Oxford: Blackwell).

Viereck, W. (1966) *Phonematische Analyse des Dialekts von Gateshead-upon-Tyne, Co. Durham* (Hamburg: Cram, de Gruyter).

Wakelin, M. (1972) *Patterns in the Folk Speech of the British Isles* (London: Athlone).

Weissmann, E. (1970) 'Phonematische analyse des Stadtdialects von Bristol', *Phonetica*, **21**, pp. 151–81; pp. 211–40.

Wells, J. C. (1982) *Accents of English: An Introduction* (Cambridge: CUP).

9 Field Methods in the Study of Social Dialects

Walt Wolfram and Ralph W. Fasold

In our attempt to collect meaningful data, there are two major areas of concern: (1) the choice of a sample population and (2) the elicitation of adequate speech data.

THE SAMPLE

When a sociolinguist decides to describe the speech behavior of a particular population, he is faced with the problem of defining his universe in such a way as to ensure that his observations adequately represent the population. The first decision he must make, therefore, is to delimit the population from which his sample will be drawn. In some cases, it is quite possible to choose a population that is already defined in terms of some arbitrary boundary, such as a geographical one. For example, we may decide that we are going to study the speech of a given locale, such as Detroit, Michigan, Rochester, New York, or Meadville, Mississippi. For a population of this type, the boundaries of our universe have already been established for us, so that our only task is to select a representative sample from that population. In other cases, we may want to describe the speech behavior of a population defined socially rather than geographically, such as a lower-class inner-city group. If this is our universe, then we need to establish the boundary on the basis of criteria such as social class, age, and so forth. Once we have established who qualifies according to our social criteria, we can decide how to obtain a representative sample of this population.

In some types of sociological studies, *random sampling* is used, in which each person in the total population has an equal chance of being selected from the sample. Random sampling, however, should not be equated with haphazard or casual selection. It is an organized procedure for choosing the informants in such a way as to eliminate selection bias. One of the traditional ways of obtaining an authentic random sample is through the use

Source: 'Field Methods in the Study of Social Dialects', in Wolfram, W. and Fasold, R. W. (1974) *The Study of Social Dialects in American English* (Englewood Cliffs, NJ: Prentice-Hall) pp. 36–72.

of a table of random numbers. This procedure relies on the assignment of a number to each individual in the population. The investigator can then use a table of random numbers, simply following the numbers in consecutive order. (Tables of random numbers can be found in most basic statistics textbooks.) Each individual with an assigned number corresponding to the one selected in the list of random numbers is then chosen for the sample, until the researcher arrives at the number of informants he desires for his study.

Although a list of random numbers is often used in random sampling, this is not the only procedure that can be utilized. The researcher can simply designate every *n*th unit in his population for study; for example, every fifth, tenth, twentieth, hundredth, or other *n*, depending on the ratio of the total population that he chooses for his sample.

Strict random samples, though advantageous for some reasons, have limitations for the investigation of social dialects. They often include numbers of subjects whose speech cannot be considered because they are recent immigrants from another section of the United States or from another country. Labov notes the various types of problems faced by the sociolinguist when dependent on a strict random sample:

A trial random sample of my own involved counting every tenth building in a block, and calling on every seventh apartment. This method seemed to be free from bias, but did not enable me to choose my informants randomly within the family, nor could I predict how large an area I would be able to cover by this method before available resources were expended. Most importantly, any sampling on this basis would be unable to discriminate between native speakers and foreign language speakers, and a great deal of effort would be spent on fruitless calls on the latter type of resident. (1966: 201)

A strict random sample should also result in the representation of population proportionately with respect to the various social groups. For example, if there are large numbers of middle-class whites in a particular area but few working-class whites, this should be represented in the sample. In some cases, this may result in excessive numbers of subjects representing one group while another group is underrepresented for the sake of a sociolinguistic analysis.

As an alternative to strict random sampling, it is often more efficient to obtain a representative sample for predetermined social categories. In this procedure, the social composition of the sample is first determined, then informants are chosen to represent these categories, which are sometimes referred to as *cells* of the sample. Informants can be chosen randomly until an adequate number is obtained to represent each cell. This procedure avoids the problem of over- and underrepresentation for particular social categories, because the investigator stops selecting informants for given cells when a quota is reached. To illustrate, we might set up a hypothetical study in which we decide to investigate the variables of social class, sex, age, and ethnicity. We choose to have a sample representing four social classes, both sexes, three age groups, and both black and white subjects. If we want each of the logically possible social categories represented in our sample, we will have a sample distribution as in Figure 9.1.

In our sample, we want to make sure that all cells (e.g. upper middle-class white 10 to 12-year-old females or lower working-class black 25 to 35-year-old males) are adequately represented, so we choose only a given number of informants for each. The total number of cells in the sample is the number of categories of each social variable multiplied by each other. There are four social classes multiplied by two races, two sexes, and three age groups, and so the total number of cells is 48, $4 \times 2 \times 2 \times 3 = 48$. When speaking of a sample of this type, it is more crucial to speak of the number of informants in each cell than of the total number of informants. For example, if we just had 5 informants in each of the cells in our sample, we would have a sample of 240 subjects. But if we were conducting a study of sex differences in the speech of lower-class whites, we would have only one variable. In this case, a total of 100 subjects would be divided equally into categories of 50 males and 50 females. Thus the total sample in this instance would be considerably smaller, but the representation in each of the two cells much greater. If we have a large number of cells, it may be possible to collapse some of them for some types of analysis, but an analysis of the effect of all the intersecting variables on each other will require adequate representation of all of our cells.

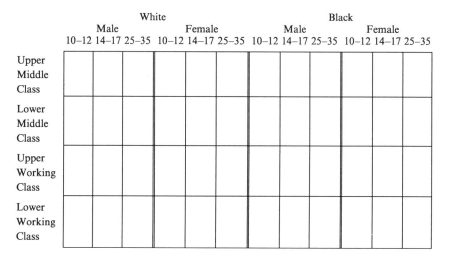

Figure 9.1: Sample distribution of logically possible social categories in a hypothetical field project design.

The question of optimal sample size for the study of social dialects is still undetermined. On the one hand, there is the tradition of linguistics which generally relies on very small samples. In some cases, one or just a few individuals serve as informants, and sometimes the linguist acts as his own informant. On the other hand, the tradition of sociological surveys is to have rather substantial numbers of subjects, often in the hundreds or thousands. The investigation of social dialects must rely on samples that are somewhere in between these two traditions. It is, however, difficult to even approximate what might be a reasonable number of informants in each cell. There are both theoretical and practical considerations. To a certain extent, the size of the sample is dependent upon how homogeneous behavior can be expected to be. The more homogeneous the behavior, the smaller the sample may be. It appears that linguistic behavior is considerably more homogeneous than some other types of behavior, so that we might obtain a reliable sample by using a smaller sample than some types of sociological surveys. Linguists have a tradition of assuming that the speech of a few informants may be sufficient to represent a language system, but exactly how many informants is sufficient in each cell is still difficult to predict for a given study. In part, the size depends on the type of sociolinguistic problem with which we are dealing. If, for example, we are dealing with subjective reactions to speech through a formal questionnaire, there is no reason why we cannot use samples that are rather large in size. A requirement of 10 to 20 subjects in each cell would appear to be a minimum in such a case if we expect to arrive at statistically significant results. On the other hand, if we are doing a quantitative analysis of linguistic variables of the type undertaken by Labov *et al.* (1968), Wolfram (1969, 1973), or Fasold (1972), the sample must be limited in size for quite practical reasons. This type of analysis requires detailed extraction of speech data. The simple procedure of extraction may take several days for each informant, so that a comprehensive analysis of hundreds of tapes is precluded if we are to complete our analysis within a reasonable amount of time. The larger the sample, of course, the more social variables we can examine and the more confidence we can have in our conclusions, but there are sometimes practical limitations of time. It appears, however, that if we have fewer than five informants in each cell for this type of analysis, we run the risk of getting quite skewed results.

So far we have referred only to samples dependent on some type of random selection procedure. But there are studies in social dialects for which we may wish to abandon randomness completely in favor of some structured pattern of informant selection based on other criteria. For example, Labov and his associates' most insightful linguistic data on black adolescent speech in Harlem came not from his random sample, but from his study of selected peer groups. The selection of peer-group informants is described by him as follows:

The next step in approaching the NNE peer group and its use of the basic vernacular was to study a particular recreation center in detail.... In the initial series of discussions and interviews, we located one major peer group at the Stephen Foster Center, and began to study it using the 'S-G-S' [Sociogram Scale] paradigm.... When we speak of 'members' of the group, we man the peer-group structure formed by the daily activities of the boys, and most clearly by the hand-out patterns. (1968: 31)

The sociogram technique mentioned by Labov involves the objective presentation of relationships within groups. It is a diagram showing the informal group structure, including such elements as friendship patterns and the position of each individual among individuals in the group. The actual questions used in sociogram analysis may vary from study to study, but typical types of questions concern friendship and leadership choices within the group. If we are interested in peer-group speech patterns, this type of informant selection is obviously preferred over a random sample.

The crucial consideration in selecting a sample is the goal of the research. If our goal is to describe peer-group adolescent black speech in Harlem, for example, our essential goal is to define the sample in terms of criteria related to the establishment of peer groups. But if we desire to describe the various social parameters of social stratification in the speech of several classes of adult New Yorkers, we want quite a different type of sample. Our sample cannot be selected without prior consideration of what social parameters of speech we want to examine.

Social Status

Any study that attempts to correlate linguistic behavior with social stratification must have not only a clear-cut delimitation of the linguistic data, but valid delimitation of social strata as well. We need to know what the various social levels in a community are, and how we can measure a given individual's status in terms of these levels. In some cases, we may desire to delimit the various social levels before we begin our linguistic analysis, so that we can correlate our linguistic variables with predetermined social levels (see Wolfram 1969). In other cases, it may be advantageous to first delimit the population on the basis of linguistic differences, then examine the social characteristics of the various linguistic groups (see Bickerton 1971). Or we may use a combination, starting with a finely stratified group of informants but combining and manipulating the social groups in such a way as to most clearly reveal patterns of correlation between linguistic phenomena and social stratification (see Labov 1966).

Whatever procedure we choose for the delimitation of social levels, we need a reliable method for assessing social stratification. The essential question is, how do we assess the relative social rank of individuals in the community? There are two main types of procedures for doing this – those dependent on the objective measurement of an outside investigator and those dependent upon the subjective evaluations of the community participants themselves.

Objective Measurements. The objective approach to the study of social stratification is based on the detailed observation of the various strata that exist in a community, regardless of whether or not the strata are recognized by the members. The researcher 'stands outside' the community and attempts to determine the criteria that will divide it into the strata most significantly affecting social behavior. One of the most common types of objective evaluation involves the use of what Warner (1960) has called the Index of Status Characteristics (ISC). (In the UK, the *Registrar-General's Classification of Occupations* serves a similar function.) The ISC is primarily an index of certain socioeconomic factors. Most typically, the criteria used for evaluating subjects are occupation, education, income, house type, and dwelling area. For each of these criteria arbitrary divisions are set up so that a ranking is given in each area. For example, occupations may be divided into seven categories, described roughly as follows:

Class	*Occupation*
1	Major professionals
	Executives of large concerns
2	Lesser professionals
	Executives of medium-sized concerns
3	Semi-professionals
	Administrators of small businesses
4	Technicians
	Owners of petty businesses
5	Skilled workmen
6	Semi-skilled workmen
7	Unskilled workers (Shuy, Wolfram, and Riley 1968: 12)

A fairly typical delimitation of educational rank is given in the following list:

Class	*Level of Education*
1	Any graduate degree (professional)
2	College graduation (four-year)
3	One year or more of college
4	High school graduation
5	Some high school (tenth grade up)
6	Junior high school (seventh through ninth)
7	Less than seven years of school

(Shuy, Wolfram, and Riley 1968: 12)

Two types of income indices are commonly used in ISC evaluations – those which delimit actual salary levels (e.g. above \$30 000, \$20 000–\$30 000, etc. [at 1974 rates!]) and those which delimit the source of the income (e.g. inherited income, profits and fees, etc.). The source of the income is often more reliable than the actual income levels because income levels can become outdated quite rapidly and actual income is not always commensurate with status.

Two types of residency scales are also used, one relating to the individual house type and one to the more general dwelling area. With reference to house type, characteristics such as size, condition, number of inhabitants per room, and plumbing are considered. Dwelling area refers to overall neighborhood conditions (such as nondeteriorating single homes with spacious yards or deteriorating block homes with no yards). Although this type of evaluation may appear to be dependent on the personal impressions of the evaluators, quite objective measures can be set up on the basis of various census tract data.

All ISC evaluation measures do not use the same criteria, so that one study may use the scales of occupation, education, and residency whereas another may use occupation, house type, and dwelling area. It is also possible to assign different values to the various scales used in assessing an overall status ranking. Occupation, for example, may be weighted more heavily than education and residency in computing an overall ISC score. In the Detroit Dialect Study, which used the criteria of occupation, education, and residency to evaluate social status, the following procedure was employed to obtain an ISC rank:

At this point, each informant had three rating numbers: (a) a rating from one to seven on education; (b) a rating from one to seven on occupation; and (c) a rating from one to six on residence . These numbers were then multiplied by factors of 5, 9, and 6, respectively, the sum of these numbers being the informant's position on the scale. For instance, a lawyer who lived in a Class I neighborhood would receive a 1 for education, a 1 for occupation, and a 1 for residence. Multiplied by 5, 9, and 6 respectively, these give a combined score of 20. For a person rated 7 on both education and occupation (a laborer with a third grade education, for example), with a house in a Class VI neighborhood, the score is 134. Obviously, the lower the number the higher the prestige, and vice versa. (Shuy, Wolfram, and Riley 1968: 15)

Once overall scores are computed, it is possible to divide the population into discrete social levels. In the Detroit study cited above, subjects who had status scores between 20 and 48 were classified as upper middle class, those with scores between 49 and 77 lower middle class, those with scores between

78 and 106 upper working class, and those between 107 and 134 lower working class. Subjects whose scores fall at the lower or upper ranges of an individual level are generally considered marginal, so that an individual with a status index score of 76 would be considered as marginally between upper working and lower middle class.

The use of ISC for the measurement of social status is based on two propositions: (1) that certain economic factors are closely correlated with social status, and (2) that these social and economic factors are translated into social-class behavior acceptable to the members of any given level of the community (Warner 1960: 39). ISC presumes a set of values and behavioral patterns. Because it is an indirect method for assessing social class, we must expect that some discrepancies will, of course, occur – some individuals who are given a particular status ranking on an ISC may reflect behavioral characteristics more typical of individuals of a different socioeconomic level.

The fact that ISC is an indirect way of getting at social class is one of the weaknesses of the procedure. It is actual behavioral patterns that are the basis of social class, not an objective ranking on selected socioeconomic indices. The general applicability of objective socioeconomic measures may also vary considerably from community to community. This is particularly true with respect to applicability for various ethnic groups. For example, how important should occupation be considered in the black community, given the history of discrimination which has kept blacks from job opportunities commensurate with their abilities? Even if such scales are applicable to the black community, their weighting may be considerably different from that for the white community. For example, education (not only the amount, but where it was obtained) appears to be more heavily weighted than occupation for some black communities. Various adjustments must be made in ISC weighting from region to region for any group, but quite substantial adjustments may be necessary for its application to various ethnic groups.

Although the ISC method is the most commonly used objective measurement of social stratification, there are other objective approaches not exclusively dependent on socioeconomic ranking. It is quite possible to examine certain types of institutional membership and differential social roles in a community, for example. An investigator may look at such things as church membership, leisure-time activities, or community organizations. In these cases the total configuration of institutional membership is considered, because various affiliations will often imply each other. On the basis of these configurations, different social groupings can be established. On a large scale, this type of objective measurement is not as simple as ISC and is not used nearly as frequently, despite the fact that it is probably more directly related to social class than the simple measurement of economic factors.

Subjective Evaluation. One of the major criticisms of an exclusively objective approach to the measurement of social status is the fact that the differentiation of social strata is determined on the basis of an outsider's criteria. Ultimately, however, the real discriminators of social class are the members of the community themselves. From one perspective, social classes exist because the members of the community believe that they exist. If the community members are the real determiners of social class, then it stands to reason that their judgments about social class might be the primary basis for class delimitation. The method of subjective evaluation referred to by Warner as Evaluated Participation (EP) is based on this proposition. It assumes that the members are implicitly or explicitly aware of the social rank of those around them and can evaluate their social participation into social-class ratings. The investigator asks the community members how they rate each other (and, in some instances, themselves) in terms of social-class categories recognized within the community. This can be done in a number of ways. For example, it is possible to rate informants on the basis of status reputation. Using this technique, community members are asked to evaluate personal acquaintances on the basis of certain imputed character traits. One person may be thought to be 'from the wrong side of the tracks' whereas another may be thought of as 'upper crust'. A community member may be asked to designate his own social categories and then rank other community members. Individuals can also be asked to rate themselves and other community members above or below them in the social hierarchy. This not only gives an indication of how they view other people in terms of social class but also shows how they view themselves. Class is a concept that is generally recognized throughout American society, and a valid picture of social rank would appear to take into account the perceptions of class from the participants within the community class structure.

Although the use of EP techniques seems to avoid some of the pitfalls of the objective approaches, there are both theoretical and practical questions that can be raised concerning their use. We may, for example, receive quite different pictures of social class itself from the various classes – the lower classes may perceive social class quite differently from the upper classes. Which of these reflects an accurate picture, or are there as many structures as there are classes looking at them? We must also recognize that we may not receive a consistent picture of the divisions of social class. One community member may believe there are five social classes and another, three. Are we justified in assuming that the majority opinion of social-class divisions is necessarily the authentic one? These are the kinds of questions that researchers who use an EP procedure must deal with on a theoretical level.

On a practical level, the sociolinguist who wants to use EP as the basis for differentiating social class must recognize that it assumes a certain knowledge of the community beforehand. He must also know the community members who are ranked by a given member. It is difficult to use an EP procedure on a large scale because of the ethnographic knowledge that it presumes.

Ideally, an accurate assessment of social class should combine subjective and objective measurements of many types of behavioral roles and values. For sociolinguistic studies, this is often precluded because of the enormous task this is in itself. Where convenient, it appears reasonable to utilize sociological or anthropological studies that have previously delimited various social strata. This is the procedure, for example, that Labov (1966) adopted in his study of social stratification of English in New York City and that Shuy, Wolfram, and Riley (1968) followed in their study of Detroit speech. Not only does it provide a more practical solution to what may be a very time-consuming problem, but it provides a base for examining the validity of social-class distinctions as reflected in the linguistic data.

ELICITATION OF DATA

Once we decide *who* we want to interview, the next step in research on social dialects is to elicit the data that we want. No study of social dialects can hope to succeed without having adequate data for analysis. As we shall see later, there are a number of different types of data and methods for collecting this data at the disposal of the fieldworker. Before discussing these methods, however, it is appropriate to consider the ethics of fieldwork in sociolinguistics.

Fieldwork Ethics

In recent years, the question of fieldwork ethics has become increasingly important to social scientists and the communities in which they carry out their research. Unfortunately, suspicions have been aroused because some social scientists have misrepresented their intentions to the community or obtained their data through devious means. Understandably, some communities have thus become reticent about cooperating in research projects in which they feel they may be exploited. As a result, an increasing number of professional organizations have come to realize that it is their responsibility to set ethical guidelines concerning data collection.

The first question that arises with respect to an investigator is the role that he assumes in the community. Samarin notes:

There are obviously questions of ethics when one assumes a role and states a purpose in a community. The first one concerns the ethics of role-playing itself. Is it deceitful to assume a role which is in conformity to the local role expectations even when these are far removed from the explicit purpose of the research? The answer to this question will be decided in part by the amount of disparity there is between the role and the purpose. It will be decided also by the expectations of the community. It is not unethical to act in harmony with these expectations. (1967: 61)

To assume a natural role in a community as a means of establishing rapport appears to be quite appropriate, but it is possible for the portrayal of a role for the exclusive purpose of obtaining information to be deceptive and unethical. Much depends on the role one is fulfilling. For example, when one of the authors was investigating the sociolinguistics of glossolalia ('speaking in tongues') among some New England church groups, it would have been possible for him to assume a role as a participant. The productive skill in glossolalia, however, had no religious significance for him. To assume a role as a glossolalist would, no doubt, have helped in the acquisition of data, but this role would have been out of harmony with his own religious beliefs and would have offended the group had they discovered the fraud. It was, therefore, considered inappropriate role-playing.

On the other hand, the same author has participated in 'pick-up' basketball games with informants he wanted to interview during the course of research on social dialects of English. This activity, however, is a natural one for him to engage in, because he still actively plays pick-up basketball games in his leisure time. His participation helped establish rapport with informants and set a casual atmosphere for an interview situation. To adopt this sort of role was not seen as inappropriate, because it was an extension of a natural role, used to alleviate suspicion and create an informal setting.

It should be mentioned that *natural* membership within a group (such as an ethnic group, for example) no more justifies deceit in obtaining data than does pretended membership – in fact, it may be even more pretentious.

Once we have assumed a role in the community, we may ask how we should represent our research to the informants specifically and to the community in general. To what extent is a social scientist responsible for telling his informants exactly what he is doing? One option, of course, is to simply deceive the informants and tell them that we are interviewing for another purpose. This is a practice that social scientists have used in the past, and it is one of the reasons that some communities are suspicious of researchers. Unless we actually intend to investigate the information that we tell the informant we are interested in, this procedure seems unwarranted. On the other hand, there is no need to relate all the precise details of our research. Many of these are irrelevant to the informant. We should be able to reach a compromise without a boring account of all the details. In our recent study of the English of second-generation Puerto Ricans in Harlem, we typically represented our research in the following manner:

> We're interested in what teenagers in different parts of the country are interested in. For example, I'm from Philadelphia and we don't fly pigeons from the top of buildings there so I'm interested in how you do it. We're also interested in how teenagers think about some things, because they look at things differently. For example, teenagers use different words and stuff when they're talking so that we're interested in how teenagers talk and think about some things. We're going to tape record it because we can't remember all the things you might say. (Wolfram *et al.* 1971:14)

In this explanation, we did not attempt to disguise our interest in language or culture, but we were nonspecific in talking about the type of language diversity in which were interested. In most cases, we found that this type of explanation was satisfactory, but any questions were answered by honest but nondetailed comments.

Our representation of interests to informants is often more problematic once the interview has started. We sometimes project interest in the subject matter when what we are really interested in is how the person talks. Are we being dishonest with the informant? In order to elicit speech, we must project personal empathy concerning the informant's interests, and more often than not we do find ourselves quite engrossed in the subject matter, whether it is our central purpose or not. A necessary qualification of a good researcher and interviewer is an honest and sincere interest in his subject and in those who aid him in his study of it.

Another matter that must be considered by fieldworkers is the recording of interviews. Current types of analysis in the study of social dialects make it virtually impossible to operate without tape-recording speech. Are we obligated to tell the informant that he is being tape-recorded? Even though it may present obstacles in obtaining speech samples, we are invading a person's right of privacy unless we do so. Although we may argue that we are not going to use the speech we obtain via a hidden tape recorder or video camera for any exploitative purposes, we still do not have the right to record a person's speech if for some reason he is against it. In some cases, it may be appropriate to 'bug' a room after the informants have been forewarned that this is planned, but all those who are being tape-recorded should be so informed before the fact. Constraints that may arise from the presence of a tape recorder must be neutralized by means other than the deception of informants.

Finally, we must mention the matter of confidence. It is surprising how much privileged information some people will share with an empathetic fieldworker; however, this is given in confidence and should not be used in any way to exploit the informant. Our task is to analyze speech and we should keep in mind that this is why the informant has consented to the interview. What happens if we obtain certain types of information concerning illegal activity (e.g. narcotics, delinquency, etc.) during the course of the interview? In these cases, it seems appropriate to view our role as that of the priest in a confessional, unless there are some very extenuating circumstances to warrant otherwise. Social scientists have an obligation to keep privileged information in the confidence that the informant assumed when he disclosed it.

Obligations to informants also include obtaining proper permission to conduct interviews. If we are conducting research within a school system, we must follow the specified procedures for obtaining this permission. And, in the case of minors, this often involves getting written consent from parents or guardians before conducting our interviews.

At this point, having discussed the very important area of ethics in fieldwork, we return to discussion of the actual strategies used in eliciting meaningful data in investigations of social dialects.

Spontaneous Interviews

The spontaneous or free conversation interview is basic to current sociolinguistic research for a reasonable approximation of how language is actually used. Obtaining data from relatively casual contexts is crucial for current types of sociolinguistic analysis. It serves, for example, as the basis for much of the quantitative tabulation which some types of sociolinguistic analysis call for. Unfortunately, the very fact that a person is being interviewed and tape-recorded is a formidable obstacle to obtaining casual speech. Labov refers to this problem as *the observer's paradox*: 'To obtain the data most important for linguistic theory, we have to observe how people speak when they are not being observed' (1972: 113). By using various techniques, it is possible to neutralize the natural obstacles inherent in any interview situation. The goal of spontaneous interviewing is quite straightforward and simple: the interviewer wants to get as much free conversation as possible. He wants the informant to focus on the topic of his conversation so that he pays minimal attention to the way he is speaking. The less attention paid to his speech, the more informal and natural we can expect his speech to be. In most cases, this means that what informants talk about is less important than the fact that they talk. Therefore, lengthy narratives are tolerated, and in fact encouraged, even though they may be tangential to the specific questions asked.

Individual Interviews. Although fieldworkers must realize the limitations in recording a free conversation with an informant in a one-to-one situation, the effectiveness of this technique should not be underestimated. People like to talk about themselves, and if they are not threatened by the situation many people can become interesting conversationalists even in this type of interview. The fieldworker is a captive audience and if the informant feels him respond to his interests, he will usually give more than adequate amounts of conversation. There are, of course, informants who are reticent about talking because of either the artificial situation or their personal inhibitions, but even the most skilled interviewers will have difficulty obtaining adequate free conversation from these individuals. For the most part, they constitute a small minority of interviews.

A spontaneous conversation calls for considerable flexibility in what the informant talks about, but this should not be interpreted to mean that no general outline is followed for eliciting conversation. Certain types of questions (not always the ones we might predict beforehand) tend to naturally elicit conversation more readily than others. It is possible to informally direct an interview in such a way as to get specific types of sociological information about such things as the informant's peer associations, social status, and general patterning of social interactions, as well as to obtain a natural representation of certain types of linguistic structures. Suppose we wanted to ensure that there was an adequate representation of past-tense constructions in our interview. This could be accomplished by asking the informant to relate an incident from the past. On the other hand, if we wanted to get a representation of present-tense forms, we would have to make sure that we had adequate conversation about present-time activities. In our analysis of the use of invariant *be* in Black English, we observed that its occurrence was often concentrated in stories about the way in which children's games were played (e.g. *We run and hide and the last person that get to base, they be it*). This observation was a cue to the type of conversations from which we might hope to elicit its usage. Our informal direction of spontaneous conversation, then, can elicit both sociological and linguistic data.

There is obviously no certain guarantee for success in the elicitation of free conversation. The observation of certain general common-sense principles, however, may help us to get a maximum amount of conversation. Following are some of the principles that can help obtain free conversation.

1. The use of questions that must be answered by conversation rather than yes-no answers. For obvious reasons, questions that can be answered by yes or no replies are not the most efficient means of getting adequate samples of free conversation. Questions that elicit narratives or descriptive accounts must be used. For example, if we want to discuss children's leisure-time games, we would not ask questions such as 'Did you play hide and seek?' or 'Did you play kick the can?' Rather, we would make requests like 'Describe the types of games you played as a child' or 'Tell me how you played hide and seek, because there are different ways of playing it.'

2. *The use of questions to which informants can relate.* General sets of questions must be adapted according to a number of informant variables, including a person's class, sex, age, ethnicity, and personal interests. Flexibility in this regard is the earmark of the successful interviewer. The use of questions to which informants can easily relate assumes that we have a certain pre-knowledge of the community in which we are interviewing. An interviewer in an inner-city, suburban, or rural area must be aware of the different types of indigenous activities and interests of the respective groups. For example, in inner-city New York, some of our most elegant descriptions of recreational activities involve the hobby of breeding, raising, and training homing pigeons. This activity requires specialized knowledge; it can sometimes elicit long and animated accounts from involved informants. ...

An interviewer who is not aware of some of the indigenous interests and activities of the community is at a serious disadvantage in obtaining relatively natural speech data.

3. *Cues of informants' interests should be pursued.* To a certain extent, a lack of knowledge concerning the community can be compensated for by sensitivity to the interests of the informant as expressed in the interview. Alert fieldworkers should be able to pick up cues concerning subjects for discussion in the interview. For example, Shuy, Wolfram, and Riley cite the following interchange as an example of alertness to the interests of the informant:

Fieldworker: Do you play marbles?
Informant: Yes, I have 197 marbles right now.
Fieldworker: Oh, tell me about them. Ho'd you get them? What are the different ones called?   (1968: 117)

Skill in marble-shooting is something some adolescents can be quite proud of, and naturally would be a matter that a good marble-shooter could describe in some detail. In the above instance, the fieldworker's sensitivity to this fact resulted in a detailed description of the activity. This alertness can be contrasted with the opposite extreme, also illustrated in Shuy, Wolfram, and Riley:

Fieldworker: Did you ever play hide and seek?
Informant: Yes, I played that a lot.
Fieldworker: What other games did you play?   (1968: 118)

In this instance, the fieldworker missed an opportunity to discuss an activity that was quite familiar to the informant. The informant was apparently quite willing to discuss a favorite game, but the fieldworker missed the chance to elicit a detailed account of it.

4. Questions should help alleviate the informant's consciousness of his own speech. Although a tape-recorded interview, by its very nature, is an artificial situation, our goal is to get speech as natural as possible. This can be structured in the interview by asking questions that will focus the informant's attention more on what he is saying than on how he is saying it. Direct questions about speech, though valuable for some purposes, often make a person very aware of how he is talking. Therefore, if we want to ask questions about speech as part of the interview, they should probably be asked after we ask questions that will make him forget about the way he is talking and concentrate on the subject matter. Certain types of topics apparently are more apt to have this effect than others. For example, Labov has noted that when informants are asked if they have ever been in a situation in which they thought they were going to die, many informants will answer in the affirmative. If they are then asked to describe the situation, they will often become so involved in convincing the interviewer that this was an authentic rather than an imagined experience that they will forget about how they are talking in their effort to convince him. We cannot guarantee the types of topics that will have this sort of effect, but the informant's emotional involvement in a conversation is a fairly reliable indicator that he is more engrossed in his subject matter than in his style of speaking.

The style of speech by the interviewer can also help direct the focus away from the speech itself. Interviewers should use a casual style in their own speech repertoire. This does not mean that they should talk exactly like the informant or talk in a manner in which they would not normally talk – this can appear pretentious and insulting to the informant. It would be pretentious for a white middle-class interviewer to try to use Vernacular Black English when interviewing a black informant, but if he can naturally adopt a nonstandard variety of white speech, it may help in setting an informal atmosphere for the interview.

5. Questions should not arouse suspicions about any hidden intentions in interviewing. Even if we represent our purpose for interviewing in a straightforward and honest manner, we must realize that informants can easily become suspicious of our motives. It is sometimes difficult for informants to believe that we are simply interested in speech. We have, on occasion, been suspected of being everything from tape-recorder salesmen to FBI agents. It is, therefore, necessary to be sensitive to these potential suspicions and not pursue topics that will unnecessarily arouse the informants. This observation was forcefully brought home to one of the authors when he was interviewing a working-class adult male in Detroit. In a parenthetical remark, the informant mentioned some of the racial tensions that existed in the city at the time. The interviewer, out of curiosity, pursued the subject. The informant immediately became suspicious of some underlying motive for the interview and became very reticent about discussing anything at length after that point. Thus the elicitation of extended conversation was sacrificed because the interviewer had aroused the informant's suspicions about the true purpose of the interview.

To say that we should not unnecessarily arouse an informant's suspicions does not mean that we can only ask trivial questions. As we mentioned previously, many interviews are used to obtain valuable sociological as well as linguistic data. Our general procedure in eliciting this type of information, however, is to structure it well after we have gotten into the course of the interview. The initial questions are generally quite innocuous, involving such topics as childhood games, leisure-time activity, movies, TV, and the like.

Following is a rough outline of spontaneous interviewing that we conducted in our recent study of the English of second-generation Puerto Rican males in East Harlem. The general outline used here was not completely unique for this research project, but represents a modification of other types of questionnaires that were used for Labov's study of the social stratification of English in New York City (1966), Shuy, Wolfram, and Riley's study of Detroit speech (1968), and Fasold's study of Vernacular Black English in Washington, DC (1972). Specific items are included for the specific population, but a number of questions were simply adopted from previous spontaneous interview outlines.

A. *Games and Leisure*
    What kinds of games do you play around the neighborhood (stickball, games with bottle caps, marbles, handball, flying pigeons, etc.)?
    How do you play these games (rules for the games, deciding who's IT, etc.)?
    Do you follow any of the NY sports teams? What do you think of the Mets this year? How about the Knicks for next year (or Joe Namath and the Jets)?
    What are your favorite TV programs? Describe a recent program.
    What is your favorite movie of all time? What happens? (If you can elicit movies without trouble, ask about *West Side Story* and an opinion of how life in Harlem is portrayed in this movie.)

B. *Peer Group*

How about the guys you hang around with? In this group is there one guy that everybody listens to? How come?

What makes for a leader in the group (tough, hip with girls, good sounder, etc.)?

Do the guys in the group sound on each other? How does this work?

What do you sound on? Can it be true, etc.? (If rapport right, get some sounds.)

What makes a good sounder?

Say a new kid moves into the tenement. Any way he can get into your group?

Who are some of the guys you're tight with? Name some.

Of the guys you named, are there any Negroes? Puerto Ricans in the group? How about Whites?

Any of these guys speak Spanish? How about their parents?

C. *Aspirations*

How about when you're through with school? Any idea of what you might do? What does a _____ do?

If someone came up to you and said, 'Here's all the money in the world,' what would you do with it?

What is a successful man (if informant responds, have him define unsuccessful, good, bad, smart man)?

D. *Fighting and Accidents*

What kinds of things do fights usually start about on the street?

Any rules for a fair fight? (How about if someone was kicking somebody or hitting them with a chain or lead pipe, what would you do?)

Ever see anybody get beat up real bad? What happened?

Do the kids around here still fight in gangs? How do these start?

(If answer negatively, pursue why gang fights have stopped.)

Ever been in a hospital, or automobile accident? Describe.

How about a situation where you thought, 'Man, this is it, I'm gonna die for sure now'? What happened?   (Wolfram *et al.* 1971: 438: 9)

As with all previous questionnaires we have used, the success of particular topics in eliciting conversation varies considerably from informant to informant. And, of course, the actual interview sometimes strays considerably from the structured topics of discussion.

In the final analysis, success in individual interviews is largely dependent on the personalities involved. The qualities of rapport and empathy may be discussed at length, but ultimately they cannot be programmed.

Group Interviews.   Probably the closest we can come to getting completely natural speech in an interview situation is by interviewing groups of peers.

In the group interview, a set of informants is tape-recorded in conversation with each other. The topic for discussion is generally up to the participants rather than the fieldworker. It is expected that natural leaders of the group will direct the conversation, so that the fieldworker, if he is present, will not have to actively participate in the conversation. The greatest advantage of the group interview is that it is the context most conducive to obtaining casual speech. The constraints of the interview either from the tape-recording, the artificial situation, or the presence of an outsider are most readily overcome in this setting. It is also the most natural setting for the elicitation of indigenous themes. Certain types of indigenous verbal activities (e.g. ritualistic insults and singing among black inner-city males), in fact, can only be obtained from a group interview situation.

The group interview has probably been used to its greatest advantage by Labov and his colleagues (1968) in their study of adolescent peer speech in Harlem. First, the fieldworkers conducted some exploratory face-to-face interviews, including some of the peer leaders. Then acquaintance was made with peer groups in various social outings. Finally, group sessions were conducted in which multitrack recordings were made. Much of the interviewing was conducted by a participant observer who used his knowledge of the indigenous community to elicit verbal activity appropriate for peer interactions among members. This procedure resulted in some of the most detailed structural and functional data now available on the speech of this group.

Once the organizer of a group session has arranged for the details of the interview, there is often little that he has to do in terms of participation in the verbal interaction, unless there is some specific topic he wants discussed by the group. In most cases, a natural peer group will follow its own structural procedure for verbal interaction. Leaders should assume their natural roles in directing the session.

In setting up a group interview, researchers should be aware of the technical problems that can arise. Each speaker must be recorded on a different track in a group interview. A single recording for a group interview will often result in data that is unusable for the detailed analysis that is necessary for some types of sociolinguistic analysis. Phonological details, in particular, are almost impossible to transcribe reliably when an entire group is being recorded on one track. Furthermore, it can be extremely difficult to identify speakers on the tape if just one track is used. Even the group members themselves may have difficulty in identifying various speakers. We must also recognize that some speakers will dominate group sessions while others will have very little to say, due to the patterns of social interaction that exist in the group. For some speakers, adequate linguistic data may not be derived from the group session, so that this will have to be compensated for in later individual sessions.

Although a well-defined peer group gives the most authentic type of speech, it is not always necessary to have complete groups. Group interviews can also be conducted with smaller friendship groups or even dyads. In some cases, the selection of just two peer informants may result in quite casual speech. The essential matter in all group interviews is to involve the participating members primarily in conversation with one another rather than having individual responses to interviewer questions.

[We omit valuable, but lengthy, sections on direct questioning, repetition, and structural elicitation as further sources of data. *Eds*]

Reading

In order to get a range in the continuum of informal to formal speech, reading passages are sometimes included in sociolinguistic fieldwork. This represents a context in which one is quite aware of the way he is talking. Data from reading passages do not usually yield essential information in themselves, but when compared with other contextual styles of speech, can provide an important basis for stylistic analysis.

There are several different types of reading that might be included as part of an interview. One might construct a reading passage in which a number of linguistic variables are purposely included for analysis of the realizations of these variables. Following is a sample passage from Labov's work in 1966, in which he investigated the parameters of five phonological variables in several styles of speech in New York City. The particular phonological variables he was analyzing are underlined.

Text for concentrating five
phonological variables
[Underlining added to indicate concentration of the variables.] ...

(oh)
We always had chocolate milk and coffee cake around four o'clock. My dog used to give us an awful lot of trouble: he jumped all over us when he saw the coffee cake. We called him Hungry Sam.

(eh)
We used to play *Kick-the-can*. One man is 'IT': you run past him as fast as you can, and you kick a tin can so he can't tag you. Sammy used to grab the can and dash down the street – we'd chase him with a baseball bat, and yell, 'Bad boy! Bad! Bad!' But he was too fast. Only my aunt could catch him. She had him do tricks, too: she even made him ask for a glass of milk, and jump into a paper bag.

(r)
I remember where he was run over, not far from our corner. He darted out about four feet before a car, and he got hit hard. We didn't have the heart to play ball or cards all morning. We didn't know we cared so much for him until he was hurt.

There's something strange about that – how I can remember
everything he did: this thing, that thing, and the other thing. He
used to carry three newspapers in his mouth at the same time. I
suppose it's the same thing with most of us: your first dog is like
your first girl. She's more trouble than she's worth, but you can't
seem to forget her.   (Labov 1966: 597)

(th)
(dh)

As illustrated in this passage, it is essential to have an adequate representation of the variables to allow for their quantitative measurement. As an added incentive such passages should deal with topics of common interest.

In addition to entire story passages like Labov's, some investigators have used isolated sentences as a basis for focusing on single items. Levine and Crockett describe their use of diagnostic words in sentences.

> First, each word was embedded in a sentence. Each sentence contained from one to four of the words chosen, with no rhymes permitted in any sentence. Further, each sentence contained a blank, to be filled in by the respondents. This device was used to distract respondents from their pronunciation; the blanks were also the vehicles for the collection of data on grammar (e.g., preterite-participle choice, adjective-adverb choice) and on idioms and choices of words (e.g., *sick to-, at-,* or *in my stomach*; *pail* or *bucket,* etc.). The sentences, themselves pretested, were listed in an order which distributed word-types throughout the test instrument. (1967: 80)

Finally, it is possible to give simple word lists that focus on some of the crucial phonological realizations of items when one is most aware of speech. Another type of word list is the minimal pair list, in which two items are read and the informant then decides whether these items sound the same or not. In many cases, the words are distinct in one dialect but potentially homophonous in another dialect (i.e. interdialectal homophony). As illustration, we can consider the following list used in our study of Puerto Rican English in Harlem:

Same/Different Words

rows	rose	side	sod
run	rum	shoe	chew
hut	hot	mass	mask
sold	soul	deaf	death
boat	vote	yellow	jello
sin	sing	time	Tom
rain	reign	pin	pen
west	Wes	watch	wash
bet	bat	boil	ball

(Wolfram et al. 1971: 443)

In the above minimal word-pair list, there are some items that are homophonous in all dialects of English and therefore nondiagnostic. Items like *rows* and *rose* and *rain* and *reign* represent this category. These items are included in order to ensure that the informant understands the task and is responding accordingly. There are also some items we would expect to be homophonous in certain varieties of Spanish-influenced English, including *bet* and *bat* and *shoe* and *chew*. These items give us an indication of the extent of Spanish influence on English in formal style. There are also items we would expect to be homophonous on the basis of the surrounding Black English dialect, such as *deaf* and *death* and *pin* and *pen*. Two main aspects of minimal word lists must be recorded: (1) whether the informant actually pronounces the items the same or differently and (2) whether he says that they sound alike or not. The first qualification gives us objective data while the second gives us an intuitive judgment about the speaker's sound system. Although intuitive reactions may appear to be quite important for an analysis of a phonological system, researchers cannot always take the informant's reactions at face value. In some cases there may be stated differences even though careful analysis (including acoustic analysis) shows the words to be produced similarly, while in other cases the converse may be true.

The Elicitation of Subjective Reactions

Up to this point, we have discussed primarily the elicitation of objective speech data for sociolinguistic analysis. Little mention has been made of the subjective reactions of informants toward either their own or other people's speech. Yet it is the perception of dialect differences and the social evaluation of these differences by participating members of the society which is the real basis for the existence of social dialects. A complete description of social dialects should therefore include examination of the subjective reaction to distinct speech varieties.

There are several different ways in which we can elicit subjective evaluations of speech differences. The most traditional method is through the use of an interview questionnaire. In some cases, it may be useful to ask open-ended questions, in which informants are simply asked to give their opinions on certain speech varieties. For example, in our study of the English spoken by second-generation Puerto Ricans in Harlem, we wanted to ascertain their perception of the way they talked as compared with the speech of the surrounding black community. Informants were simply asked, 'Do you think that Puerto Rican and black teenagers talk alike? In what way do they talk the same or differently?' The informant was to answer this question, being allowed to state whatever reasons he felt were relevant. Similarly, Labov's study of English in New York City included questions designed to elicit how New Yorkers felt about New York speech. These questions allowed the informant to express his reaction toward New York speech and explain why he felt the way he did. Although open-ended questions concerning subjective reactions allow us to gather data we might not anticipate in a nondiscursive questionnaire, it can become difficult to taxonomize and quantify results on this basis. For this reason, many questionnaires are designed to elicit responses in terms of predetermined categories. In some cases, informants may be asked to make a forced choice between a positive and a negative evaluative response. A questionnaire may simply require a subject to respond Yes or No to a statement such as, 'I think nonstandard dialects are as logical as standard dialects of English.' Or we may ask an informant to pick out what he considers the most socially stigmatized and most prestigious dialect, given a list of American English dialects that includes Southern White speech, Black English, New England speech, and Midwestern speech. There are, of course, a number of variations in the types of questions that can be asked in this way. For example, we may ask an informant to place each of the given dialects in rank order in terms of relative prestige rather than make a single choice.

One technique that has become relatively popular in recent subjective reaction questionnaires is that of the semantic differential. This procedure, originally developed by Charles Osgood and his colleagues at Indiana University, attempts to investigate the connotative aspects of a subject's reactions. In the typical semantic-differential task, the subject is asked to judge entities or concepts by means of a series of bipolar, seven-step scales defined in terms of descriptive opposites. The concept is given at the top of the sheet and the subject responds by putting a check mark in the appropriate position on the scale for each of the bipolar opposites. For example, a study of speech identification in Detroit, by Shuy, Baratz, and Wolfram (1969) included the following semantic polar adjectives in the attempt to elicit the connotative aspects that several different speech varieties evoke.

White Southern Speech

worthless	___:___:___:___:___:___:___:___:___	valuable
dull	___:___:___:___:___:___:___:___:___	sharp
difficult	___:___:___:___:___:___:___:___:___	easy
positive	___:___:___:___:___:___:___:___:___	negative
rough	___:___:___:___:___:___:___:___:___	smooth
weak	___:___:___:___:___:___:___:___:___	strong
fast	___:___:___:___:___:___:___:___:___	slow
sloppy	___:___:___:___:___:___:___:___:___	careful
complex	___:___:___:___:___:___:___:___:___	simple
thick	___:___:___:___:___:___:___:___:___	thin
bad	___:___:___:___:___:___:___:___:___	good
smart	___:___:___:___:___:___:___:___:___	dumb

The closer one checks to one of the poles in the scale, the more heavily weighted is his response in terms of the particular extreme. A particular numerical value is assigned on this basis for computation of the results. For example, starting with 0 as the midpoint, each scale may have a value of +1, +2, and +3 (immediately contiguous to the positive side of the adjectival pole), or −1, −2, and −3 (immediately contiguous to the negative side of the pole). Using the technique of factor analysis, researchers have found evidence indicating that the judgments tend to cluster into three main domains of connotative meaning, including the dimension of *evaluation* (e.g., good–bad, positive–negative), *potency* (strong–weak, dull–sharp), and *activity* (fast–slow, difficult–easy). By employing the semantic-differential technique, it is possible to compare reactions to different concepts on a positive–negative continuum rather than by means of binary choice. Used properly, the semantic differential can be a useful tool for getting at subjective reactions to speech and speech concepts.

The typical problem with questionnaires used to elicit subjective reactions involves the disparity between expressed attitudes and overt behavior. In an effort to look at the responses between these two poles, Fishman has designed an instrument labeled the *Commitment Measure*. His study, carried out with respect to bilingualism, sought to determine 'whether commitment items show any greater relationship to pertinent language behavior criteria than do more traditional dispositional or role playing language use and language attitude items' (1969: 5). In addition to the traditional types of attitudinal responses asked on his questionnaire, Fishman included a ten-item commitment scale in which a person's willingness or commitment to respond or perform a particular type of activity with respect to language was measured. The type of questions Fishman asked were calculated to measure a person's willingness to maintain and strengthen the use of Spanish on a personal and community level in New York City, and ranged from willingness to participate in a small-group discussion on the topic of improving the person's command of Spanish to willingness to contribute money to help finance the activities of an association for building up the use of Spanish in New York. When the commitment questions were correlated with the previously given noncommitment attitude scale, a significant difference arose. Commitment measures as a data-gathering technique are more useful than traditional attitude questionnaires because they can more directly get at behavioral tendencies rather than eliciting simple cognitive or evaluative responses.

So far, we have only referred to subjective reactions made on the basis of a fieldworker's questioning or a written questionnaire. But we can also use other types of stimuli in eliciting subjective reactions to speech. The elicitation of responses from tape-recorded samples of speech is one of the current techniques used to considerable extent in the study of social dialects. One such method, originally developed by Lambert and his colleagues at McGill University for evaluating personality traits of bilinguals, has been labeled the *Matched Guise Technique*. In this procedure, a select group of subjects evaluates the personality traits of speakers' voices played to them on the tape recorder. The recording is made by a speaker who has considerable ability in producing different language or dialect varieties. The subjects are not told that the different varieties heard on the tape belong to one speaker, but are simply asked to judge certain traits of the speaker. ... The major advantage of this technique is that it controls a number of variables such as the voice quality and personality of the speaker. One of the disadvantages is that it is sometimes difficult to find speakers who have acquired nativelike control of the various social dialects we might require to produce such a tape.

Rather than use one speaker, some researchers have had speakers from different social groups simply read the same passage. This is the technique that Bryden (1968) used in his study of the identification of social class and race in Charlottesville, Virginia. The use of a tape-recording in this case sets up an artificial situation, however, because most speakers are unable to read in a natural speaking manner. For this reason, other investigators have simply extracted topically comparable passages (e.g. TV programs, games, etc.) from tape-recorded spontaneous interviews rather than using identical passages that have been read. Although variables such as content and voice quality are much more difficult to control, this has the advantage of authenticity. This is the type of stimuli that was used by Shuy, Baratz, and Wolfram in their study of speech identification in Detroit and Washington (1969). In this study 20 to 30-second portions were excerpted for the interviews of four socioeconomic classes of whites and blacks in Detroit. At the conclusion of the main passages, a number of short portions (one sentence of from 3 to 5 seconds) were included in order to determine reactions on the basis of much shorter stimuli. For each of the longer passages, subjects were asked to identify the race of the speaker, as well as the relative socioeconomic class, and to make some attitudinal judgments on a semantic differential. This was presented as follows:

a. What is the race of this speaker? Black ( ) White ( )
b. What is the educational/occupational level of this speaker?
    ( ) 1. College graduate usually with graduate training.
             Dentist, mechanical engineer, personnel manager.
    ( ) 2. High school graduate, probably some college or technical school. Printer, post office clerk, small business owner or manager.
    ( ) 3. Some high school or high school graduate.
             Bus driver, carpenter, telephone lineman.
    ( ) 4. Not beyond 8th grade.
             Dishwasher, night watchman, construction laborer.

c. Rate the speech sample on each of the following scales:

awkward	___:___:___:___:___:___:___:___	graceful
relaxed	___:___:___:___:___:___:___:___	tense
formal	___:___:___:___:___:___:___:___	informal
thin	___:___:___:___:___:___:___:___	thick
correct	___:___:___:___:___:___:___:___	incorrect

In most cases, repeated passages of from 20 to 30 seconds were more than adequate for making judgments of the type we asked above. In fact, fairly accurate identification (over 70 percent) of race and social class was often made just on the basis of the 3 to 5-second sentence. It should be noted that questions concerning a wide range of reactions may be asked on the basis of tape-recorded passages. For example, we have used tape-recorded passages as the basis for obtaining data on language and employability. Labov asked questions about masculine virtues such as toughness on the basis of tape-recorded passages and concluded on this basis that the use of nonstandard dialects has a positive effect for conducting some societal roles that call for expressed toughness. The types of reactions that we may have subjects make on the basis of recorded speech samples are almost limitless.

Recent studies of language attitudes have also utilized videotapes to some advantage (e.g. Williams, Whitehead, and Miller 1971; Williams 1973). In the study of language attitudes and stereotyping reported by Williams (1973), stereotyping was investigated by using videotapes from three different ethnic groups: black, white, and Chicano. In one of the exercises, the respondents were shown side views of children speaking. The respondent could observe the person speaking, but was unable to lip-read what he was saying. Audiotapes of Standard English were then dubbed onto the videotapes of the children from the three different groups to create a type of *ethnic guise*. Stereotyping was measured by looking at the extent to which the visual picture determined a particular reaction despite the constancy of the Standard English. Modern technology affords the creative researcher a great deal of variety in designing ways of 'teasing out' various dimensions of subjective reactions to language differences.

REFERENCES

Bickerton, D. (1971) 'Inherent Variability and Variable Rules', *Foundations of Language*, 7, pp. 457–92.

Bryden, J. D. (1968) *An Acoustic and Social Dialect Analysis of Perceptual Variables in Listener Identification and Rating of Negro Speakers*. USOE Project No. 7-C-003.

Fasold, R. W. (1972) *Tense Marking in Black English: A Linguistic and Social Analysis* (Washington, DC: Center for Applied Linguistics).

Fishman, J. A. (1969) 'Bilingual Attitudes and Behaviors', *Language Sciences*, **5**, pp. 5–11.

Labov, W. (1966) *The Social Stratification of English in New York City* (Washington, DC: Center for Applied Linguistics).

Labov, W., Cohen, P., Robins, C. and Lewis, J. (1968) *A Study of the Non-Standard English of Negro and Puerto Rican Speakers in New York City*. USOE Final Report, Research Project No. 3288.

Levine, L. and Crockett, H. J. (1967) 'Friends' Influence on Speech,' *Sociological Inquiry*, **37**, pp. 109–28.

Samarin, W. J. (1967) *Field Linguistics: A Guide to Linguistic Field Work* (New York: Holt, Rinehart & Winston).

Shuy, R. W., Baratz, J. C. and Wolfram, W. (1969) *Sociolinguistic Factors in Speech Identification*. NIMH Final Report, Project No. MH 15048-01.

Shuy, R. W., Wolfram, W. A. and Riley, W. K. (1968) *Field Techniques in an Urban Language Study* (Washington, DC: Center for Applied Linguistics).

Warner, W. L. (1960) *Social Class in America* (New York: Harper & Row).

Williams, F. (1973) 'Some Research Notes on Dialect Attitudes and Stereotypes', in Shuy, R. W. and Fasold, R. W. (eds), *Language Attitudes: Current Trends and Prospects* (Washington, DC: Georgetown University Press).

Williams, F., Whitehead, J. L. and Miller, L. M. (1971) *Attitudinal Correlates of Children's Speech Characteristics*. USOE Research Report Project No. 0-0336.

Wolfram, W. (1969) *A Sociolinguistic Description of Detroit Negro Speech* (Washington, DC: Center for Applied Linguistics).

Wolfram, W. (1973) 'On What Basis Variable Rules?', in *Studies in New Ways of Analyzing Variation in English* (Washington, DC: Georgetown University Press).

Wolfram, W. in collaboration with Shiels, M. and Fasold, R. W. (1971) *Overlapping Influence in the English of Second-generation Puerto Rican Teenagers in East Harlem*. Final Report, USOE Project No. 3-70-0033(508).

10   Speech Events and Natural Speech

Nessa Wolfson

THE INTERVIEW AS A SPEECH EVENT

The Question/Answer Pattern

For interviews which follow a questionnaire format, the problems involved in collecting anything approaching everyday speech are extremely severe. This is because the interview is, in fact, a speech event, in the technical sense proposed by Hymes (1974: 52):

> The term speech event will be restricted to activities, or aspects of activities that are directly governed by rules or norms for the use of speech. An event may consist of a single speech act, but will often comprise several.

Every society has a variety of types of speech event, in this sense, set off from each other by different rules of speaking. In some cases a single rule of speaking is so strong and so widely recognized by the speech community as to be itself the defining characteristic of the speech event. This is exactly the case for the interview in our society, a fact which may be ascertained very quickly by asking any native speaker to give his definition of an interview. When I asked various people what an interview was, the definitions were all very explicit in mentioning the question/answer pattern:

> ...'An interview is a question and response conversation between two or even more than two people.'
> ...'An interview is a meeting in which one is questioned and one answers.'
> ...'An interview is where someone comes and asks you a lot of questions and you answer them.'
> ...'A meeting for the purpose of finding out information.'

Source: 'Speech Events and Natural Speech: Some Implications for Sociolinguistic Methodology', *Language in Society*, **5**, 2 (1976), pp. 189–209 (Cambridge: Cambridge University Press).

Such definitions show that native speakers of English are quite aware of the rule which gives one of the participants in the interview event the unilateral right to ask questions and the other(s) the obligation to answer them. The distribution of power between the participants is thus clearly delimited and accepted as part of the speech event.

The important point here is that free conversation is not expected. For this reason, an attempt on the part of the interviewer to break out of the question/response format in order to elicit spontaneous conversation will usually arouse surprise and may even lead to suspicion and resentment. This leaves us with a dilemma: the fact that the interview is a speech event in our society makes it legitimate to ask questions of a personal nature of total strangers, but at the same time severely limits the kind of interaction which may take place within it, and therefore the kind of data which one can expect to collect.

Consequences: Interview Narratives vs. Conversational Narratives

Sociolinguists frequently make a great effort to elicit narratives in interviews precisely in order to collect samples of 'natural speech'. The assumption here is that the narratives told in interviews are somehow not part of the question/answer pattern. We will see that this is not the case, however, by looking briefly first at the way narratives are introduced both in interviews and outside them, and secondly, by contrasting the characteristic features of narratives found in interviews with those found in differently structured speech events.

In an interview, a narrative is warranted as a response to a question such as, 'Have you ever been in a bad fight? What happened?' The interview event is so structured, however, that the question which is intended to lead to a story is only one in a series of questions and there is a change in topic immediately following the subject's response. An example from an interview quoted by Shuy, Wolfram and Riley (1968: 86) will serve to show how this works:

FW: 'Okay, good. Did you ever see anybody get beat up real bad?'
IN: 'Yes.'
FW: 'What happened?'
IN: 'Well, this girl was fighting with uh other girl, and she, they was fighting and she gave her a bloody nose and she made her, she broke the girl arm. She made her run into a tree and the girl arm be like that and she couldn't move.'
IN: 'Yes. How about a boy, have you even seen a boy get beat up real bad?'
IN: 'No.'
FW: 'Did you ever get into a fight with a girl bigger than you?'

IN: 'No. Nope. I get into fights with around about the same size but not bigger.'

FW: 'What was that like? Was she tough?'

IN: 'Nope, Everytime I get into a fight with somebody they be smaller than me, the same size, but they be skinny or fat or something like that.'

FW: 'And so you beat them, huh?'

IN: 'Yes.'

FW: 'Uh huh. Do the guys around here usually fight one to one or in gangs?'

IN: 'Nope.'

FW: 'How do they fight?'

IN: 'Fight by theyself.'

FW: 'They never fight in gangs.'

IN: ('No.')

FW: 'Have you ever been in the hospital?'

IN: 'Yep.'

FW: 'Can you tell me about the worst illness you ever had?'

IN: 'A broken arm.'

FW: 'What was it like? How did you do it, what happened and what type of hospital were you in?'

Although this is a series of questions aimed at eliciting narratives, there is only one response, the first, which could be called a narrative at all. The topic of the narrative is introduced not by the teller but by the interviewer. In contrast, it is usually the teller himself who provides the occasion for the narrative in everyday conversation. Some examples from conversations will serve to show how narratives are introduced:

1. 'Goodnow's. That's where we used to take Pat and Mike when I used to go to Washington's Crossing, all that area there, the wildflower show, and uh, we used to have a picnic. Then we would, on our way home, stop in there for dinner. So this one night Pat and Mike ordered a banana split...'

2. 'Let me tell you something. I may not be a sailor and I have to take a dramamine before I go on every time, but I love the water. (To husband): Did you tell them what happened to your Mom?'

3. 'Why don't you come into the store? We got some beautiful things in. In fact something funny happened: I was driving down Broad Street the other day and...'

4. 'Watch how you hold that bag now. People dont' realize how easy it is to spill. There's this one customer, he comes in twice a week. One time he was in here and as he's walking out the door...'

5. 'Talk about serving meat raw! You wouldn't believe what happened to me. A few Sundays ago I was having the kids over for dinner and...'

As the foregoing examples show, the conversational narrative is related to and inspired by the topic under discussion. Changes in topic are usually motivated by something within the conversation. In contrast, the question/answer rule of the interview prevents the speaker from introducing topics of narratives which is, as we have seen, the way they occur in everyday conversation. To be sure, if questions in interviews are of the type which require the subject to talk about his past experiences, he will usually do so. Thus questions about accidents and fights of the 'Have you ever?' variety often do produce narratives as answers. But we cannot assume that the narrative thus elicited has been told as it would have been if the speaker had introduced the topic as part of a conversation between himself and an audience of his own choosing. Clearly, this is an empirical question, requiring analysis and comparison of narratives told in interviews with those told in everyday conversations.

Several crucial consequences follow from this contrast in the structure of interviews and conversations. First, the fact that the subject does not have the right to introduce topics during an interview severely restricts his opportunities for introducing narratives. Secondly, the subject of an interview knows that what he is expected to do is give answers to a series of questions. As a result, his narratives, when he does tell them, are usually in the form of a summary – short and to the point with little detail as to the interaction of the participants. Conversational narratives, on the other hand, are usually full of such detail. This detail appears in a number of features – grammatical, phonologic, stylistic – which are absent from the summary. One such feature, the one which has been the object of my own study, is the historical present tense, the use of the present tense to indicate past action. In collecting data for the study of this form, I found that its use is most fully developed in the performed narrative of everyday conversation, but almost entirely absent in summaries.

Narratives that *are* found in interviews have distinguishing characteristics all their own. Not only are they usually given in summary form, but *there is often elaboration and emphasis on the specific part of the story which answers the question that has been asked.* The point is that people know they are answering a question and for this reason the details which they *do* include in their narratives are frequently directed to the point of the question. ...

SPONTANEOUS INTERVIEWS[1]

The Spontaneous Interview is not a Speech Event

But if people know the rules of speaking for the interview situation and conform to them in the ways which we have just seen, then clearly an interview survey cannot be expected to elicit the kind of data which one would need to study a variable which appears in fully developed narratives. In order to solve the problem of collecting samples of everyday speech which would include lengthy narratives and a good sampling of grammatical structures, many sociolinguists have turned to the so-called spontaneous interview in which the subject is asked a few questions and then encouraged to develop any topic which seems to interest him. The results of such interviews can be very interesting and have often been said to provide excellent material. The question which arises, however, is whether in attempting to overcome the bias of the formal interview one is not simply exchanging one set of biases for another. From an ethnographic point of view, is it fair to say that the spontaneous interview represents a less 'artificial' speech situation than the formal questionnaire interview? A great deal of research has been conducted on this assumption, but my own viewpoint is that the contrary is true. The formal interview is, as we have just seen, a recognized speech event in our society. Members of the speech community know the rules of speaking for interviews. They expect to be asked a series of questions and to answer them. Although being interviewed is hardly an everyday experience for most people, there is nothing 'artificial' or 'unnatural' about it, and there is no reason to believe that the speech produced by the subject in such an interaction is anything but natural – for an interview.

The so-called spontaneous interview, however, *is not a speech event.* It goes by no name which would be recognizable to members of the speech community and it has no rules of speaking to guide the subject or the interviewer. As anyone who has ever done this kind of fieldwork can testify, it can be an exceedingly uncomfortable thing to do. It usually begins as a true interview in that the researcher introduces himself in his official capacity and starts by asking a few questions. He then does everything in his power to encourage the subject to violate the rules of speaking for an interview. His whole aim is to get the subject to speak freely, to introduce topics and to tell stories. He attempts, in fact, to create a completely different speech event, an informal conversation. From the point of view of the subject, this is not only an unexpected turn of events, but a truly unnatural speech situation. The subject is frequently quite mystified about why a total stranger, armed with a tape recorder, should want to engage him in conversation. He feels that something is very wrong and he is correct; the rules have been broken and he has no idea what his role should be.

Reactions to this sort of interviewing vary, but there is ample proof in my data that people feel very uncomfortable when placed in such a situation. Frequently the position of authority which normally belongs to the interviewer is so badly shaken that the subject questions whether the interviewer knows what he is doing. If questions do not follow one upon the other (because the interviewer is trying to elicit conversation) the subject may simply ask for the next question. A typical example is the following: a tape-recorded conversation was in progress between the interviewer and the subject, a middle-aged female schoolteacher. The topic was 'life in Philadelphia' and the conversation had turned to the issue of women's liberation. The interviewer, in an attempt to elicit some narratives, told a little story about a child who had been called a male chauvinist pig by the mother of one of his friends. The subject broke into the conversation and said:

Subj: 'Now what's the story?'
Int: 'What's the story?'
Subj: 'Yeah, what type questions – are you all set up now?'
Int: 'Well, we'll continue with what we've got. Well, I've just got some more, you know.'

Another woman, when interviewed without a questionnaire and asked to tell about growing up in Philadelphia, became very annoyed and told the interviewer to decide exactly what she wanted to know, write down the questions and come back another day when she was better prepared. The subject clearly felt that the interviewer was incompetent and was wasting her time.

Other subjects are very suspicious, and questions like, 'Just what are you trying to find out?' or 'What do you want to know all this for?' are not infrequent.

Relationships between Interviewer and Subject

All this is not to say that spontaneous interviews are valueless, for in spite of the problems mentioned so far, it is still true that these interviews can, under certain circumstances, elicit excellent data. The great difficulty with this technique as a method for collecting sociolinguistic data is that the factors which enable one interviewer to elicit excellent data from one subject may be the very factors which will make it impossible for him to collect anything even resembling casual conversation from another. Basically, the determining factors here are connected with the issue of power and solidarity (Brown & Gilman 1960). Although we have no reason to believe that the conventional distribution of power in a formal interview succeeds in eliminating the influence of the personal attributes of the specific participants on the subject's speech behavior, it is in the spontaneous interview that we can most clearly see this influence at work. This is precisely because the spontaneous interview lacks a structure of its own. Thus, if the interviewer shares with the subject certain personal attributes such as age, sex, general attire, and very importantly, dialect or speech variety, then his chances for involving the subject in conversation and thereby obtaining data approaching the subject's intimate speech are greatly increased, and the reverse is also true.

With respect to the spontaneous interview situation, then, we can say that the degree of solidarity between the participants will affect the verbal behavior of the subject. There are, for instance, rules of speaking in our society which operate very strongly against speaking casually with a stranger of the opposite sex. Teenage girls, when interviewed by a male of approximately their own age and social background, collapse into giggles and are unable to produce anything but self-conscious speech while their male counterparts in the neighborhood (often their own brothers and cousins) are the source of some of the best interview data imaginable (David Depue, personal communication). In addition to this striking contrast along the dimension of sex, we must also recognize that relative age and social status are of extreme importance. In the example cited above, the interviewer's age, sex, and perceived social status worked for him with members of his own sex and against him with those of the opposite sex. If the interviewer is older and/or perceived to be of a higher social status than the subject, there will usually be more of an effort on the part of the subject, but if the reverse is true the results may be very different. In the following interchange, both the restaurant owner and waitress were approximately twenty years older than the interviewer. In addition, the restaurant owner was male, the interviewer female; he is a successful businessman, she a student. After answering a few questions about his birthplace, education and opinions about life in Philadelphia, the subject was led into the beginning of a conversation but suddenly he interrupted by saying:

Owner:	'Let me ask you something. Are you from Philadelphia?'
Int:	'Yes.'
Owner:	'Where were you born?'
Waitress:	(Laughs) 'Now he's gonna question you!'
Int:	'Second and the Boulevard.'
Owner:	'Second and the Boulevard. Uh huh. Do you find Philadelphia different?'
Int:	'Yeah.'
Owner:	'You do? In what respect?'
Int:	'I think people used to be a lot friendlier.'
Owner:	'Well, I think conditions have made it that way.'

Clearly, the restaurant owner has a certain contempt for the line of questioning, and equally clearly, he has no hesitation about expressing it. And this again points up the fact that the distribution of power and/or solidarity among participants in a conversation is always an important determinant of their verbal behavior. ...

A very important consequence follows here: studies which attempt to correlate particular speech forms with the age, sex and social background of stratified samples of speakers cannot make use of interviewing as a technique for data collecting without controlling for the relationship between speaker and interviewer. Whether it is possible to control for this factor in a large-scale statistical survey is a question which has so far not been faced. *There is, in fact, no real justification for using interviews to collect data for use in any kind of systematic comparison of speakers* without controlling for all the other factors in the speech situation. Once this very serious bias is recognized, however, we can continue to make use of data which may be collected in spontaneous interviews for other sorts of studies. As long as we keep in mind that speaker background is far from the only determinant of speech behavior, we may, as Hymes (personal communication) has pointed out, want, for instance, to use spontaneous interviews to learn how people speak *uncomfortably*; to determine, that is, the effect of differences in power and solidarity on speech behavior.

THE AIM: 'NATURAL SPEECH'

Group Sessions

Another method of collecting sociolinguistic data which has been used by a number of researchers, notably Gumperz (1964) and Labov (1972a) is to tape record group session, rather than individuals. That is, people who normally interact socially (Gumperz's closed networks, Labov's adolescent peer groups) are brought together and tape recorded while in the process of interacting with each other. The point of recording group sessions rather than individuals is that the constraints inherent in a one-to-one interview are avoided and the normal patterns of group interaction will, it is hoped, overcome the constraints produced by the subjects' knowledge that they are being observed and recorded. Speakers are said to respond to each other naturally, just as they would if they were not wearing lavalier microphones. As Labov (1972b: 109) explains it:

> In more recent work we have relied more upon group sessions, in which the interaction of members overrides the effect of observation, and gives us a more direct view of the vernacular with less influence of the observer.

It seems reasonable to accept the claim that group interaction will direct attention away from the tape recorder and the observer, but whether the effect of observation is really overridden is a moot question. For the fact is that, try as we may to distract the subject so that he forgets that he is being recorded, we do not have the right to assume that our subjects are unconscious of observation. That the subject is well aware of the presence of the tape recorder, even in the most casual of interviews, is evidenced by the references made to it. An example occurs in one of the interviews conducted by David Depue speaking to a teenager in which the boy tells several long, involved stories which have to do with the brutality of a particular policeman towards one of the boy's friends. The subject remarks that his friend has no proof that he was beaten by the policeman and there follows a discussion about the possibility of using Depue's tape recorder to collect evidence against the policeman. Depue's data contain a great many other tapes in which there are references to the presence of the tape recorder, both in spontaneous interviews with individuals and when he is recording the interaction of natural peer groups. The conversation is often lively, the boys laugh and joke and interrupt each other freely, and the speech style appears to be very casual; nevertheless continual references are made to the recorder. The boys ask if the cord is in the way, they ask if they are speaking loudly enough or 'in too much of a monotone', they suggest that Depue bring more microphones and they occasionally caution each other not to mention someone's name or to speak of certain topics like 'hot merchandise'. In all these cases, the interviewer is an outsider to the group, albeit a well-known one whose frequent visits have made him an acceptable participant in the group and even a confidant. ...

Natural Speech = Appropriate Speech

We have criticized interviews both formal and 'spontaneous' and have said that even group sessions contain a certain bias. All this could be taken to mean that there actually exists such an entity as 'natural speech' which could, if only the researcher were clever enough, be elicited in an experimental situation such as an interview; an entity which, although elusive, has sometimes been glimpsed in interviews. It is, indeed, this sort of reasoning which seems to underlie Labov's isolation of categories of speech styles (casual vs. careful) in interviews. In addition to using devices within the interview itself which are intended to involve the subject in such a way that his attention is focused on what he says rather than on how he says it, Labov also recommends the use of any speech which can be recorded both before and after the interview proper and during any interruptions which may occur during it. ...

The important point to be made here is that there is no single, absolute entity answering to the notion of natural/casual speech. If speech is felt to be appropriate to a situation and the goal, then it is natural in that context. The context itself may be formal or informal, interview or conversation. It is only when norms of speaking are uncertain or violated that one gets 'unnatural' speech. ...

Indeed, unless it is interview speech we wish to study, we cannot expect to obtain valid results from experiments conducted in the form of an interview. Once 'natural speech' is recognized to be nothing more than speech appropriate to the occasion, it can cease to occupy the role of an elusive entity continually being sought by investigators in interviews; natural speech is all around us.

NOTES

I am indebted to Dell Hymes who made many valuable comments on an earlier draft of this chapter, and to John Fought, Daniele Godard, Virginia Hymes, Joan Manes and Susan Thomas for many valuable suggestions. I also want to thank David Depue, William Labov and Roger Shuy for their generosity in giving me access to their data. This chapter is a revised version of the chapter on field methodology from my doctoral dissertation in linguistics at the University of Pennsylvania.

1 'Spontaneous' refers to speech behaviour which the interviewer is attempting to elicit, not the way the interview is conducted. This term is used in the same sense by Wolfram and Fasold (1974: 48).

REFERENCES

Brown, R. and Gilman, A. (1960) 'The Pronouns of Power and Solidarity', in Sebeok, T. A. (ed.) *Style and Language* (Cambridge, MA: The Technology Press) pp. 253–76.

Hymes, D. H. (1974) *Foundations in Sociolinguistics: An Ethnographic Approach* (Philadelphia, PA: University of Pennsylvania Press).

Labov, W. (1972a) 'The Logic of Nonstandard English', in Labov, W. *Language in the Inner City: Studies in the Black English Vernacular* (Philadelphia. PA: University of Pennsylvania Press) pp. 201–40.

Labov, W. (1972b) 'The Isolation of Contextual Styles', in Labov, W. *Sociolinguistic Patterns* (Philadelphia, PA: University of Pennsylvania Press) pp. 70–109.

Shuy, R. W., Wolfram, W. and Riley, W. K. (1968) *Field Techniques in an Urban Language Study* (Washington, DC: Center for Applied Linguistics).

Wolfram, W. and Fasold, R. (1974) *The Study of Social Dialects in American English* (Englewood Cliffs, NJ: Prentice Hall).

11 The Ethnographic Analysis of Communicative Events

Muriel Saville-Troike

In undertaking an ethnography of communication in a particular locale, the first task is to define at least tentatively the speech community to be studied, attempt to gain some understanding of its social organization and other salient aspects of the culture, and formulate possible hypotheses concerning the diverse ways these sociocultural phenomena might relate to patterns of communication. It is crucial that the ethnographic description of other groups be approached not in terms of preconceived categories and processes, but with openness to discovery of the way native speakers perceive and structure their communicative experiences; in the case of ethnographers working in their own speech communities, the development of objectivity and relativity is essential, and at the same time difficult.

Some early steps in description and analysis of patterns of communication include identifying recurrent events, recognizing their salient components, and discovering the relationship among components and between the event and other aspects of society. The ethnographer is also interested in attitudes toward the event, and how both relevant communicative skills and attitudes are acquired. The ultimate criterion for descriptive adequacy is whether someone not acquainted with the speech community might understand how to communicate appropriately in a particular situation; beyond that, we wish to know why those behaviors are more appropriate than alternative possibilities.

Observed behavior is now recognized as a manifestation of a deeper set of codes and rules, and the task of ethnography is seen as the discovery and explication of the rules for contextually appropriate behavior in a community or group; in other words, what the individual needs to know to be a functional member of the community.

Source: 'The Analysis of Communicative Events', in Saville-Troike, M. (2nd edn, 1989) *The Ethnography of Communication: An Introduction* (Oxford: Basil Blackwell) pp. 107–39.

RELATIONSHIP OF ETHNOGRAPHER
AND SPEECH COMMUNITY

... In recent years the awareness has grown that the researcher can develop a deeper understanding of the culture under study by adopting a functional role and becoming a participant. This may in fact be necessary at times if the lack of a defined status and role would cause problems of acceptance by the community. Some kind of rationale may be required for the observer's presence, particularly in studies within his or her own society. When the observer knows the rules of the culture, and the members of the community know that he or she knows the rules of the culture, they expect the observer to behave like a member of the society. Thus, they are likely to find it aberrant for observers to inquire about or record behavior which they are assumed to know, and little tolerance will be shown for violations of rules. There is considerable awkwardness, severe constraints are involved, and problems of ethics emerge. In addition, observers, taking for granted large aspects of the culture because they are already known 'out of awareness,' may find it difficult and less intellectually rewarding to attempt to discover and explicate the seemingly obvious, the 'unmarked' case.

Nevertheless ethnographers, precisely because of this knowledge of a broad range of the world's cultures, are able to bring a comparative perspective to work even within their own society. And by keeping a mental distance from the objects of observation, and by treating subcultures such as that of the school or the factory as 'exotic,' they can maintain some of the detached objectivity for which anthropology is noted.

One of the advantages of studying one's own culture, and attempting to make explicit the systems of understanding which are implicit, is that ethnographers are able to use themselves as sources of information and interpretation. Chomsky's view of the native speaker of a language as knowing the grammar of the language opened the way to introspection by native speakers as an analytical procedure, and recognized that the vastness of this knowledge extended far beyond what had revealed in most linguistic descriptions by non-native speakers. The extension of this perspective to the study of culture acknowledges the member of the society as the repository of cultural knowledge, and recognizes that the ethnographer who already possesses this knowledge can tap it introspectively to validate, enrich, and expedite the task of ethnographic description.

A further advantage to ethnographers working within their own culture is that some of the major questions regarding validity and reliability raised by the quantitatively oriented social sciences can be at least partially resolved. While there may be no one to gainsay claims concerning cultural practices in a remote New Guinea village, any description of activities in the observer's own society becomes essentially self-correcting, both through feedback from the community described and through reactions by readers who are themselves members of the same society.

At the same time, the emphasis in recent ethnographic work on an existential/phenomenological explication of cultural meaning further justifies the value of ethnographers working within their own culture. Combining observation and self-knowledge, the ethnographer can plumb the depths and explore the subtle interconnections of meaning in ways that the outsider could attain only with great difficulty, if at all. In the same way then, with the ethnographer able to function as both observer and informant, some of the problems of verification can be overcome, and a corrective to unbridled speculation provided.

When ethnographers choose to work in other cultures, the need for extensive background study of the community is critical, and a variety of field methods must be employed to minimize imposition of their own cultural categories and perceptions on recording the interpretation of another system. In some cases 'outsiders' may notice behaviors that are not readily apparent to natives of the community, for whom they may be unconscious, but conversely no outsider can really understand the meaning of interaction of various types within the community without eliciting the intuitions of its members. Garfinkel noted:

> The discovery of common culture consists of the discovery *from within* the society by social scientists of the existence of common sense knowledge of social structures. (1967: 76–7; emphasis his)

It is likely that only a researcher who shares, or comes to share, the intuitions of the speech community under study will be able to accurately describe the socially shared base which accounts in large part for the dynamics of communicative interaction. The value of combining perspectives of both insider and outsider as field workers is illustrated by Milroy (1987a).

A second issue is that of community access. Milroy provides good illustrations of how this may be negotiated in her discussion of the methodology used by Blom and Gumperz in Norway and of her own in Belfast:

> I introduced myself initially in each community not in my formal capacity as a researcher, but as a 'friend of a friend' ... so that I acquired some of the rights as well as some of the obligations of an insider. (1987b: 66)

Obtaining access to minority communities which may have a history of exploitation poses ethical as well as practical problems. In the United States, most research on minority communities has traditionally been conducted by members of the majority group or by foreigners (e.g. the work of Madsen, Rubel, and Holtzman and Diaz-Guerrero on Mexican Americans, or

Hannerz and Ogbu on Black Americans). A member of the group under study who is also a researcher will already have personal contacts which should contribute to assuring acceptance, although taking such a role can result in the (sometimes justified) perception that a group member has 'sold out' to the dominant establishment.

The realization of the historical colonialist associations of anthropology has made the science suspect in some communities, and created barriers to access by fieldworkers. One extreme example reportedly occurred in a Pueblo community in New Mexico, where it is said the informant for an anthropologist was killed some years ago after the anthropologist published his study and the community found out how much the informant had divulged.

It is necessary to recognize that sensitivities exist in certain quarters, and that the question of the use to which ethnographic research is to be put has been raised as an ethical issue in the profession. There are many potential applications of data on patterns of communication, ranging from improving education and the delivery of social services (e.g. law and medicine) to contributing to the effectiveness of advertising or propaganda, and it is the ethnographers' responsibility not to exploit the communities in which they work. Often access can be negotiated to the benefit of all by including relevant feedback into the community in a form it may use for its own purposes. Positive examples can be found in the work of a number of anthropological linguists working with Indian groups in the United States. These include Ossie Werner (Northwestern University), whose research on Navajo anatomical terminology and their beliefs about the causes and cures of disease is providing input to improvements in the delivery of health care, and William Leap (American University), whose research on Isletan Tiwa has yielded a written form of the language and bilingual reading materials. These materials were developed in response to community fears that the language is in a state of decline, and to their desire to maintain it.

There are some data that should go unreported if they are likely to be damaging to individuals or the group. Whenever the subjects of research are human beings, there are ethical limits on scientific responsibility for completeness and objectivity which are not only justified but mandated. Furthermore, information which is given confidentially must be kept in confidence. The two linguists whose work with communities was cited above also provide positive examples of this dimension of professional integrity: some of the information about Navajo health beliefs and practices should be disseminated only within the Navajo community, and although the complete data base is being reported by Werner, this portion will remain untranslated into English. Leap made no attempt even to elicit stories which had religious significance for the Tiwa (and thus were secret in nature), while his selection and content for the bilingual readers were submitted to a Parents' Advisory Board for approval prior to publication.

A third issue, partly contained within the second, is that of interviewer race or ethnicity. In the past, when studies were carried out in foreign environments or in minority communities by members of the majority group, the myth of the observer as a detached, neutral figure obscured the social fact that whether a conscious participant or not, the observer was inescapably part of the social setting and affected the behavior of other participants, as well as being influenced and sometimes even manipulated by them. The lack of familiarity of researchers with the culture, the language, and the community often made them vulnerable to such influence, the more so since it was unperceived. ...

At the outset researchers must know the general framework, institutions, and values which guide cultural behavior in the community and be able to behave appropriately, both linguistically and culturally, within any given situation, if their participation is to be genuinely accepted. Similarly, researchers must be able to establish a common basis of shared understandings and rules for behavior if interviews or interactions are to be productive.

Hymes (1978) has distinguished three types of ethnography: *general, topic focused*, and *hypothesis testing*. All are important, and each type is in many respects dependent on the one before. The linguistic and cultural knowledge of the ethnographer can greatly speed the progress of research to the third level, and aid in the generation of hypotheses for testing and further study.

TYPES OF DATA

While not all types of data are necessarily relevant for every study conducted, at least the following should be considered for any ethnographic research on communication:

Background Information

Any attempt to understand communication patterns in a community must begin with data on the historical background of the community, including settlement history, sources of population, history of contact with other groups, and notable events affecting language issue or ethnic relations. A general description is also generally relevant, including topographical features, location of important landmarks, population distribution and density, patterns of movement, sources and places of employment, patterns of religious affiliation, and enrollment in educational institutions. Published sources of information should be utilized as background preparation whenever they are available, and a search should be made of MA and Ph.D. theses to avoid duplication of research effort. Relatively current data may be available from national, state, regional, or local levels of government, or through embassy representatives.

Material Artefacts

Many of the physical objects which are present in a community are also relevant to understanding patterns of communication, including architecture, signs, and such instruments of communication as telephones, radios, books, television sets, and drums. Data collection begins with observation and may include interviewing with such questions as 'What is that used for?' and 'What do you use to...?' The classification and labeling of objects using ethnosemantic procedures is an early stage in discovering how a speech community organizes experience in relation to language.

Social Organization

Relevant data may include a listing of community institutions, identities of leaders and office holders, the composition of the business and professional sectors, sources of power and influence, formal and informal organizations, ethnic and class relations, social stratification, and distribution and association patterns. Information may be available in newspapers and official records of various types, and collected through systematic observation in a sample of settings and interviews conducted with a cross section of people in the community. A network analysis may also be conducted, determining which people interact with which others, in what role-relationships, and for what purposes. The procedure may also be used to identify subgroup boundaries within a heterogeneous community and discover their relative strength.

Legal Information

Laws and court decisions which make reference to language are also relevant: e.g. what constitutes 'slander,' what 'obscenity,' and what is the nature and value of 'freedom of speech,' or how is it restricted. It is of interest, for instance, that a West German court acquitted two former SS members of murder charges in part because 'all the evidence presented was verbal, with not one piece of evidence in writing' (Associated Press 1980). Laws may also prescribe language choice in official contexts, as those enacted in Quebec and Belgium, or as in the Voting Rights Act in the United States, which required ballots to be printed in any language spoken by over 5 per cent of the voting-age citizens in any state or political subdivision. In communities where such information is formally codified, much is available in law books and court records, and in all communities it is accessible through interviews with participants in 'legal' events of various kinds, and observation of their procedures and outcomes.

Artistic Data

Literary sources (written or oral) may be valuable for the descriptions they contain, as well as for the attitudes and values about language they reveal. Additionally, the communicative patterns which occur in literature presumably embody some kind of normative idealization, and portray types of people (e.g. according to social class) in terms of stereotypic use of language. Relevant artistic data also include song lyrics, drama and other genres of verbal performance, and calligraphy.

Common Knowledge

Assumptions which underlie the use and interpretation of language are difficult to identify when they are in the form of unstated presuppositions, but some of them surface after such formulas as 'Everyone knows...,' and 'As they say...,' or in the form of proverbs and aphorisms. These are 'facts' for which evidence is not considered necessary, the 'rules of thumb,' and the maxims which govern various kinds of communicative behavior. Some of the data can be elicited with questions about why something is said the way it is in a particular situation instead of in an alternative way, and even more by studying the formal and informal processes in children's acquisition of communicative competence. Ethnoscience and ethnomethodology are most directly concerned with discovery of this type of data (discussed under Data Collection Procedures below).

Beliefs about Language Use

This type of data has long been of interest to ethnographers, and includes taboos and their consequences. Also included are beliefs about who or what is capable of speech, and who or what may be communicated with (e.g. God, animals, plants, the dead). Closely related are data on attitudes and values with respect to language, including the positive or negative value assigned to volubility versus taciturnity.

Data on the Linguistic Code

Although it is a basic tenet in this field that a perspective which views language only as static units of lexicon, phonology, and grammar is totally inadequate, these do constitute a very important type of data within the broader domain. These, along with paralinguistic and nonverbal features in communication, are included in the model for the analysis of speech events as part of the 'Instrumentality' component (discussed below). Preparation to work within any speech community, particularly if the language used is not native to the ethnographer, should include study of existing dictionaries and grammars. Skills in ethnography of communication are probably best added to skills in linguistic analysis in its narrower sense in order to assure that this component is not neglected or misinterpreted.

SURVEY OF DATA COLLECTION PROCEDURES

There is no single best method of collecting information on the patterns of language use within a speech community. Appropriate procedures depend on the relationship of the ethnographer and the speech community, the type of data being collected, and the particular situation in which fieldwork is being conducted. The essential defining characteristics of ethnographic field procedures are that they are designed to get around the recorders' biased perceptions, and that they are grounded in the investigation of communication in natural contexts. ...

Introspection

Introspection is a means for data collection only about one's own speech community, but it is an important skill to develop for that purpose. This is important not only for data collection *per se*, but for establishing the fact that everyone has a culture, and that questions about various aspects of language and culture require answers from the perspective of researchers' own speech communities as well as those of their subjects. Ethnographers who are themselves bicultural need to differentiate between beliefs, values, and behaviors which were part of their enculturation (first culture learning) and acculturation (second culture learning or adaptation), and this exercise in itself will provide valuable information and insights on the group and on individuals. ...

Participant-Observation

The most common method of collecting ethnographic data in any domain of culture is participant-observation. The researcher who is a member of the speech community was born into that role, and anthropologists have found it possible to perceive and understand patterned cultural behaviors in another society if they are immersed in the community for a year or more. The key to successful participant-observation is freeing oneself as much as humanly possible from the filter of one's own cultural experience. This requires cultural relativism, knowledge about possible cultural differences, and sensitivity and objectivity in perceiving others.

Malinowski was responsible for leading a revolution in fieldwork about 1920, and is credited with the establishment of this approach (see, e.g. Malinowski 1926; 1935). Prior to that date, ethnographers described other cultures on the basis of travelers' reports, or at best lived apart from the group under investigation (often in the more comfortable housing of colonial administrators), merely visiting on a regular basis to observe and take notes.

One of the most important benefits of participation is being able to test hypotheses about rules for communication, sometimes by breaking them and observing or eliciting reactions. Participation in group activities over a period of time is often necessary for much important information to emerge, and for necessary trusting relationships to develop. The role of the outside ethnographer in a community remains problematic, but if at all possible it should be one which contributes to the welfare of the host group in a way they recognize and desire. Whether this is as teacher or construction worker cannot be determined out of context, but the ethnographer should not be 'taking' data without returning something of immediate usefulness to the community. ...

Collecting data in situations in which they themselves are taking part requires ethnographers to include data on their own behaviors in relation to others, and an analysis of their role in the interaction as well as those of others.

Observation

Observation without participation is seldom adequate, but there are times when it is an appropriate data-collection procedure. Some sites are explicitly constructed to allow unobtrusive observation, such as laboratory classrooms with one-way mirrors, or others which allow the researcher to be visible but observe quite passively without being disruptive to the situation. Also, in observing group dynamics in a meeting or other gathering, it is generally better for a marginally accepted observer to refrain from taking active part in the proceedings. Observation from a balcony or porch is usually less disruptive to the patterns of children's interaction when their play is under observation than any attempt at participation.

Observation of communicative behavior which has been videotaped is a potentially useful adjunct to the participant-observation and interview, particularly because of the convenience of replaying for micro-analysis, but it is always limited in focus and scope to the cameraman's perception, and can only be adequately understood in a more holistic context. Furthermore, ethnographers should always remember that the acceptability of taping, photographing, and even note-taking depends on the community and situations being observed. When filming or videotaping is feasible in a relatively fixed context, it is best to use a stationary wide-angle studio camera for 'contextual' footage as well as a mobile camera to focus on particular aspects of the situation. To obtain a visual record of interactional events in which participants are more mobile (such as children playing together out-of-doors, or scenes in a hunting or fishing expedition), a hand-held and battery-operated 8 mm video camcorder is most suitable. In such situations a small radio microphone may be attached to a single focal participant, with a receiver on the camera which records the sound directly on film. Most radio microphones will pick up not only what the focal participant says, but anything said by a speaker within at least three or four feet. When a wider range of audio coverage is needed, a second radio microphone and receiver tuned to a different frequency can provide input to an auxiliary tape recorder. Multiple input from different frequencies directly to the camera audio track requires additional equipment which greatly reduces portability. ...

Since the potential range of settings for observation is enormous, priority must be determined by the focus or primary purpose of investigation. If the focus is on children in an educational situation, for instance, these include most obviously school itself, but also the playground, home, and the social environs most frequented by the child or which appear to have the greatest affective and linguistic effect on the child, such as perhaps the church. The work plan should be sufficiently flexible and open-ended so that important settings which emerge in the course of ethnographic and linguistic research can be added or substituted, as appropriate. It would not be adequate in this education example to limit observation to the classroom setting without taking into account the larger social context of communication.

Persons first developing skill in this method should just report observable behaviors without imposing value judgements or drawing conclusions; more advanced steps involve making inferences about such unobservable aspects of culture as beliefs and values, from the behaviors or things which are observed. The key to successful observation and inference is, again, freeing oneself from one's own cultural filter.

Interviewing

Interviewing may contribute a wide range of cultural information, and may include collection of kinship schedules, information on important religious and community events, and elicitation of folktales, historical narratives, songs, exposition of 'how to' in relation to various aspects of technical knowledge, and descriptions of encounters among members of the community in different contexts. While an interview setting is often formal and contrived, it need not be, and the procedure is an efficient – perhaps necessary – supplement to observation and participation. Types of questions and interviewing styles may be so different that few overall generalizations can be made.

The most common ethnographic interview is composed of questions which do not have predetermined response alternatives. These are appropriate for collecting data on virtually every aspect of communication: what regional varieties are recognized, and what features distinguish them from one another (e.g. Do the people who live on Red Mountain/in Green Valley, etc., talk in a different way from you? Can you understand them? What are some examples?); attitudes toward varieties of language (e.g. Who talks the 'best?' Who talks 'funny?' Why do you think they talk that way?); identification of different kinds of speech events (e.g. What are they doing [with reference to people interacting in various ways]? What kind of talk is that?); social markers in speech (e.g. How do you greet someone who is older than you? Younger? A man? A woman? A servant? Your employer?).

Where possible, it is probably best to impose as little structure as possible on an interview, and to insert questions at natural points in the flow rather than having a rigid schedule of questions to follow.

The essence of the ethnographic interview is that it is open-ended, and carries as few preconceptions with it as possible, or at least constantly attempts to discover possible sources of bias and minimize their effect. The ethnographer must be open to new ideas, information, and patterns which may emerge in the course of interviewing, and to differences between 'ideal' and 'real' culture as reflected in statements of belief or values and in actions, respectively. ...

Among the critical issues in any kind of interviewing are:

(a)   *Selecting reliable informants.* Often the people who make themselves most readily available to an outsider are those who are marginal to the community, and may thus convey inaccurate or incomplete information and interfere with the acceptance of the researcher by other members of the group.

(b)   *Formulating culturally appropriate questions.* This includes knowing what is appropriate or inappropriate to ask about, why, and in what way.

(c)   *Developing sensitivity to signs of acceptance, discomfort, resentment, or sarcasm.* Such sensitivity relates to the first two issues by contributing information on informant reliability and the appropriateness of questions, and on when an interview should be terminated.

(d)   *Procedures for data transcription, arrangement, and analysis.* These will differ to some extent with the kind of information that is being collected and often with the theoretical orientation of the researcher; whenever the interview is conducted in a language not native to the researcher, however, transcription requires skill in using another orthographic system or a phonetic alphabet (even if a tape recorder is in use). ...

Many problems can be avoided by doing a pretest before attempting a large-scale data collection, including an exploration of who can be interviewed, how people within the community exchange information, and what forms of questions are appropriate (Hymes 1970).

The reliability of information can best be judged by asking similar questions of several people in the community and comparing their answers, and by relating information collected through interviews to observations. These should be required steps in all interview procedures.

Ethnosemantics (Ethnoscience)

Ethnosemantics is concerned primarily with discovering how experience is categorized by eliciting terms in the informants' language at various levels of abstraction and analyzing their semantic organization, usually in the form of a taxonomy or componential analysis. Because an adequate ethnography of communication must include the categories and contexts which are culturally significant within the speech community under investigation, including how they group language use into kinds of communicative events, the perspective and methods of ethnosemantics are highly relevant.

A possible initial step in data collection is selecting a domain or genre, and then asking (recursively), 'What kind of -s are there?' One might ask 'What kind of insults are there?,' for instance; if the response were 'Friendly insults and unfriendly insults,' the next question would be 'What kind of friendly insults are there?' in order to elicit subcategories and examples, and then 'What kind of unfriendly insults are there?,' etc. This step is usually followed by questions which elicit the dimensions which the speaker is using for comparison and contrast: e.g. 'In what way are these two things/acts/ events different?' 'How are they the same?' 'Of these three, which two are more alike and in what way?' 'How does the third differ from them?' The first type of questioning strategy yields information primarily about hierarchically structured categories, and the latter primarily about feature sets. Possibilities for applying microcomputer technology to these data collection procedures are discussed in Werner and Schoepfle (1987).

An extension of this method might be called ethnopragmatics, or the discovery of why members of a speech community say they do things as opposed to why ethnographers say they do them: e.g. why people say what they do when someone sneezes.

The ultimate goal of ethnographic description is an *emic* account of the data, in terms of the categories which are meaningful to members of the speech community under study; an *etic* account in terms of a priori categories is a useful preliminary grid for reference and for comparison purposes, but is usually not the ultimate goal of description.

Ethnomethodology and Interaction Analysis

As developed by Harold Garfinkel (1967; 1972), ethnomethodology is concerned primarily with discovering the underlying processes which speakers of a language utilize to produce and interpret communicative experiences, including the unstated assumptions which are shared cultural knowledge and understandings. According to Gumperz (1977; 1984), this is the first tradition to deal with conversations as cooperative endeavors, and to focus on sociological analysis of verbal interaction. To Garfinkel, social knowledge is revealed in the process of interaction itself, and the format required for description of communication is dynamic rather than static.

There are general (perhaps universal) processes through which meaning is conveyed in the process of conversational interaction (Gumperz 1977):

(a)   Meaning and intelligibility of ways of speaking are at least partially determined by the situation, and the prior experience of speakers.
(b)   Meaning is negotiated during the process of interaction, and is dependent on the intent and interpretation of previous utterances.
(c)   A participant in conversation is always committed to some kind of interpretation.
(d)   An interpretation of what happens now is always reversible in the light of what happens later.

A clearly emerging concept is that of the extent to which speakers must share experience to successfully develop conversational exchanges of any depth and duration.

Gumperz builds on this in proposing the outline of a theory of how social knowledge is stored in the mind, retrieved from memory, and integrated with grammatical knowledge in the act of conversing. Conversational inference is 'the "situated"' or context-bound process of interpretation, by means of which participants in a conversation assess others' intentions, and on which they base their responses' (Gumperz 1977: 191).

Because of its cultural base, the 'meaning' that emerges in a conversation is likely to be different for different participants if they are not members of the same speech community. Examples of cross-cultural (mis)communicative events serve to highlight the importance of such factors as the information or presuppositions the communicants bring to the task, the extralinguistic context, and nonverbal cues. For example, I observed the following exchange in a kindergarten classroom on the Navajo Reservation:

A Navajo man opened the door to the classroom and stood silently, looking at the floor. The Anglo-American teacher said 'Good morning' and waited expectantly, but the man did not respond. The teacher then said 'My name is Mrs Jones,' and again waited for a response. There was none.

In the meantime, a child in the room put away his crayons and got his coat from the rack. The teacher, noting this, said to the man, 'Oh, are you taking Billy now?' He said, 'Yes.'

The teacher continued to talk to the man while Billy got ready to leave, saying, 'Billy is such a good boy,' 'I'm so happy to have him in class,' etc.

Billy walked towards the man (his father), stopping to turn around and wave at the teacher on his way out and saying, 'Bye-bye.' The teacher responded, 'Bye-bye.' The man remained silent as he left.

From a Navajo perspective, the man's silence was appropriate and respectful. The teacher, on the other hand, expected not only to have the man return her greeting, but to have him identify himself and state his reason for being there. Although such an expectation is quite reasonable and appropriate from an Anglo-American perspective, it would have required the man to break not only Navajo rules of politeness but also a traditional religious taboo that prohibits individuals from saying their own name. The teacher interpreted the contextual cues correctly in answer to her own question ('Are you taking Billy?') and then engaged in small talk in an attempt to be friendly and to cover her own discomfort in the situation. The man continued to maintain appropriate silence. Billy, who was more acculturated than his father to Anglo-American ways, broke the Navajo rule to follow the Anglo-American one in leave-taking.

This encounter undoubtedly reinforced the teacher's stereotype that Navajos are 'impolite' and 'unresponsive,' and the man's stereotype that Anglo-Americans are 'impolite' and 'talk too much.'

Describing and analyzing the negotiation of meaning requires discovering what aspects of speech signal role and status relations, and serve as a metalanguage for transmitting information about them. The researcher then infers changes in assumptions about the relationships as a conversation progresses.

Potential problems arise in applying these methods to research in other speech communities because speakers' inferences must usually in turn be inferred by the researchers, and this secondary level of inference may be based on quite different assumptions. ...

While the foci and procedures of traditional ethnography and various models of interaction analysis differ, they are in a necessary complementary relationship to one another if an understanding of communication is to be reached. Ethnographic models of observation and interview are most useful for a macro-description of community structure, and for determining the nature and significance of contextual features and the patterns and functions of language in the society; interactional micro-analyses build on this input information, and feed back into an ethnography of communication clearer understandings of the processes by which members of a speech community actually use and interpret language, especially in everyday interaction – a vital aspect of their communicative competence.

Philology

The interpretation and explanation of texts or *hermeneutics* (cf. Soeffner 1985; Tyler 1978), has traditionally been a science or art applied to writing, rather than speech, and especially to Biblical texts. (The Greek term for 'to interpret' derives from *Hermes*, the messenger of the gods.) In addition to the referential meaning of the texts themselves, a variety of written sources may yield information on patterns of use in the language, and on the culture of the people who read and write it.

As discussed under Types of Data above, much of the necessary background information on a community may be found in written sources, including theses and dissertations, governmental publications, old diaries and correspondence, and archival sources. Newspapers and census records may also be used as clues to the social organization of the community, law books and court records to language-related legal information, and literature to idealized patterns of language use, and to attitudes and values about language. ...

Obituary notices in newspapers may provide information on social organization and values by allowing inferences as to who is given special treatment when they die (e.g. is the notice on the front page or near the classified section, and of what length?), what accomplishments are mentioned (e.g. for women, the husband's occupation is mentioned; the reverse is almost never the case), and what is taboo or requires euphemisms. Classified advertising sections are an index to goods and occupations that are available, and their organization indicates salient categories and labels in the community.

For communities with a literate tradition, written sources may be used to document language shifts over time: e.g. historical reconstruction for English speech communities has long included contrasting the forms used in letters versus plays, and secular versus religious writings, and has been used to document changes in such aspects of the language as the use of second-person pronouns, and the relation of such changes to the sociocultural context of time. Changes in the status and functions of languages can be inferred in the shift of language choice for the same genre: e.g. Latin versus English, French versus English.

Old travelers' accounts, texts, dictionaries, and grammars are the only evidence now available from which we may reconstruct cultural information about many groups who have been exterminated or who have fully assimilated to another culture, including many American Indian tribes. A combination of techniques from ethnomethodology and literary analysis has been applied by Hymes (1980; 1981) and others to the oral texts recorded as prose by linguists and anthropologists, uncovering internal poetic structure and coherence, verbal patterns of openings, closings, and transitions, and assumptions about characters and their appropriate behaviors and fates – the 'common knowledge' we seek to understand.

IDENTIFICATION OF COMMUNICATIVE EVENTS

Communication in societies tends to be categorized into different kinds of events rather than an undifferentiated string of discourse, with more or less well-defined boundaries between each, and different behavioral norms (often including different varieties of language) appropriate for each kind. Descriptive tasks include enumerating the kinds of events which are recognized or can be inferred in a community, the nature of boundary markers which signal their beginning and end, and the features which distinguish one type from another.

Since a communicative event is a bounded entity of some kind, recognizing what the boundaries are is essential for their identification. A telephone conversation is a communicative event bounded by a ring of the telephone as a 'summons' and hanging up the receiver as a 'close.' Event boundaries may be signaled by ritual phrases, such as *Did you hear this one?* and then laughter to bound a joke; *Once upon a time* and *They lived happily ever after* to bound a story; or *Let us pray* and *Amen* to bound a prayer. Instead of these, or in addition, there may be changes in facial expression, tone of voice, or bodily position between one communicative event and the next, or a period of silence. Erickson and Schultz (1979) also report changes in gaze direction, change of participants' position in relation to one another, and change of rhythm of speech and body movements. Perhaps the surest sign of a change of events is code alternation, or the change from relatively consistent use of one language or variety to another. Boundaries are also likely to coincide with change of participants, change in topical focus, or change in the general purpose of communication. Major junctures in communication are signalled by a combination of verbal and nonverbal cues.

Consecutive events may be distinguished in a single situation. In a trial, for instance, the opening even begins when the bailiff cries *Hear ye, hear ye* and ends when the judge enters the courtroom and sits down on the bench, and all others are seated. Within the same situation, direct and cross examination of witnesses or the defendant may be identified as separate events because participants are in a different role-relationship, and there is a change in manner of questioning and responding: i.e. different rules for interaction. These events may be bounded by the change in participants, and perhaps by a verbal routine such as *I call – to the stand* to open and *You may stand down* or *Your witness* to close. If a recess is called before a boundary is reached, the interaction can be considered a single discontinuous speech event, even if continued on another day.

Formal ritual events in a speech community have more clearly defined boundaries than informal ones because there is a high degree of predictability in both verbal and nonverbal content of routines on each occasion, and they are frequently set off from events which precede and follow by changes in vocal rhythm, pitch, and intonation. Brief interactions between people almost always consist of routines, such as greetings and leavetakings, and the boundaries of longer and most informal communicative events, such as conversations, can be determined because they are preceded and followed by them (Goffman 1971).

Since the discovery of communicative norms is often most obvious in their breach, examples of boundary violations may highlight what the appropriate boundary behavior is. Some people are annoyed with what they consider to be premature applause by others at the end of an opera, for instance, which indicates differences in what 'the end' of the event is perceived to be: the end of the singing or the end of all music. Still others may whisper through the overture, since for them the event has not yet begun. Christina Paulston (personal communication) reports the occurrence of a serious misunderstanding between Jewish and Christian parents attending an ecumenical service because the Jewish parents continued conversing after entering the place of worship, while the Christians considered this inappropriate behavior once the physical boundary into the sanctuary was crossed.

Micro-analysis of boundary signals is less formal situations commonly requires filming a communicative situation, and then asking participants to view the film themselves and to indicate when 'something new is happening.' The researcher then elicits characterizations of the event, and expectations of what may happen next (and what may *not* happen next), in order to determine the nature of the boundary signals, and how the context has changed from the point of view of the participants.

The communicative events selected initially for description and analysis for one learning to use this approach should be brief self-contained sequences which have readily identifiable beginnings and endings. Further, they should be events which recur in similar form and with some frequency, so that regular patterns will be more easily discernible: e.g. greetings, leavetakings, prayers, condolences, jokes, insults, compliments, ordering meals in restaurants. More complex and less regular events yield themselves to analysis more readily after patterns of use and norms of interpretation have already been discovered in relation to simpler and more regular communicative events.

COMPONENTS OF COMMUNICATION

Analysis of a communicative event begins with a description of the components which are likely to be salient (cf. Hymes 1967; 1972; Friedrich 1972):

1 The *genre*, or type of event (e.g. joke, story, lecture, greeting, conversation).
2 The *topic*, or referential focus.
3 The *purpose* or *function*, both of the event in general and in terms of the interaction goals of individual participants.
4 The *setting*, including location, time of day, season of year, and physical aspects of the situation (e.g. size of room, arrangement of furniture).
5 The *key*, or emotional tone of the event (e.g. serious, sarcastic, jocular).
6 The *participants*, including their age, sex, ethnicity, social status, or other relevant categories, and their relationship to one another.
7 The *message form*, including both vocal and nonvocal channels, and the nature of the code which is used (e.g. which language, and which variety).
8 The *message content*, or surface level denotive references; what is communicated about.
9 The *act sequence*, or ordering of communicative/speech acts, including turn-taking and overlap phenomena.
10 The *rules for interaction*, or what properties should be observed.
11 The *norms of interpretation*, including the common knowledge, the relevant cultural presuppositions, or shared understandings, which allow particular inferences to be drawn about what is to be taken literally, what discounted, etc.

REFERENCES

Erickson, F. and Shultz, J. (1979) 'When is a Context?: Some Issues and Methods in the Analysis of Social Competence'. Manuscript.
Friedrich, P. (1972) 'Social Context and Semantic Feature: The Russian Pronominal Usage', in Gumperz, J. J. and Hymes, D. (eds) *Directions in Sociolinguistics: The Ethnography of Communication* (New York: Holt, Rinehart & Winston) pp. 270–300.
Garfinkel, H. (1967) *Studies in Ethnomethodology* (Englewood Cliffs, NJ: Prentice-Hall).
Garfinkel, H. (1972) 'Remarks on Ethnomethodology', in Gumperz, J. G. and Hymes, D. (eds) *Directions in Sociolinguistics: The Ethnography of Communication* (New York: Holt, Rinehart & Winston) pp. 301–45.
Goffman, E. (1971) *Relations in Public: Microstudies of the Public Order* (New York: Harper & Row).
Gumperz, J. J. (1977) 'Sociocultural Knowledge in Conversational Inference', in Saville-Troike, M. (ed.) *Linguistics and Anthropology* (Washington, DC: Georgetown University Press) pp. 191–212.
Gumperz, J. J. (1984) 'Communicative Competence Revisited', in Schiffrin, D. (ed.) *Meaning, Form, and Use in Context: Linguistic Applications* (Washington, DC: Georgetown University Press) pp. 278–89.

Hymes, D. (1967) 'Models of Interaction of Language and Social Setting', *Journal of Social Issues*, **33**(2), 8–28.

Hymes, D. (1970) Linguistic Aspects of Comparative Political Research', in Holt, R. and Turner, J. (eds) *The Methodology of Comparative Research* (New York: The Free Press) pp. 295–341.

Hymes, D. (1972) 'Models of the Interaction of Language and Social Life', in Gumperz, J. J. and Hymes, D. (eds) *Directions in Sociolinguistics: Ethnography of Communication* (New York: Holt, Rinehart & Winston) pp. 35–71.

Hymes, D. (1978) 'What is Ethnography?', *Texas Working Papers in Sociolinguistics* 45.

Hymes, D. (1980) 'Tonkawa Poetics: John Rush Buffalo's "Coyote and Eagle's Daughter"', in Maquet, J. (ed.) *On Linguistic Anthropology: Essays in Honor of Harry Hoijer* (1979) (Malibu, CA: Undena Publications).

Hymes, D. (1981) *'In Vain I Tried to Tell You': Essays in Native American Ethnopoetics* (Philadelphia, PA: University of Pennsylvania Press).

Malinowski, B. (1926) *Crime and Custom in Savage Society* (London: K. Paul, Trench, Trubner).

Malinowski, B. (1935) *Coral Gardens and their Magic: A Study of Agricultural Rites in the Trobriand Islands*. Vol. II, *The Language of Magic and Gardening* (New York: American).

Milroy, L. (1987a) *Language and Social Networks*. Second Edition (Oxford: Basil Blackwell).

Milroy, L. (1987b) *Observing and Analysing Natural Language: A Critical Account of Sociolinguistic Method* (Oxford: Basil Blackwell).

Soeffner, H-G. (1985) 'Hermeneutic Approaches to Language', *Sociolinguistics* **15**(1), pp. 21–4.

Tyler, S. A. (1978) *The Said and the Unsaid: Mind, Meaning, and Culture* (New York: Academic Press).

Werner, O. and Schoepfle, G. M. (1987) *Systematic Fieldwork. Volume 1: Foundations of Ethnography and Interviewing* (Newbury Park, CA: Sage).

12 Ethics, Advocacy and Empowerment in Researching Language

Deborah Cameron, Elizabeth Frazer,
Penelope Harvey, Ben Rampton
and Kay Richardson

Researching Language, the book-length study on which the following discussion is based, deals with questions about power and method in a range of social science disciplines (anthropology, sociology and sociolinguistics). To put 'power' and 'method' together in such an explicit way, and to foreground them as major concerns, is perhaps an unconventional move. Yet any social researcher who has undertaken fieldwork must at some level be aware that power relations exist in this context as in others; and those power relations are strongly affected by the methods we are constrained to adopt in 'doing research'. That is, they are not entirely determined by pre-existing differences of status imported from other contexts. Something happens within the process of research itself.

Typically, research produces or intensifies an unequal relationship between investigator and informants: authority and control lie with the investigator more often than with the informants, and the whole process benefits the investigator much more than the informants. We want to pose the question, why is this so? What assumptions and practices within social science make it so? Is it inevitable, or can we adopt different assumptions and procedures to produce a different outcome?

Our discussion focuses on linguistic research, though we define that category quite broadly. The disciplines we represent, anthropology and sociology as well as linguistics, are not all concerned with language in the same way or for the same reasons, but they are all, necessarily, concerned with it. For linguistics the point is obvious; but a study of people's religious beliefs or voting intentions must equally be approached by way

Source: 'Ethics, Advocacy and Empowerment: Issues of Method in Researching Language', *Language and Communication*, **13**, 2 (1993) (Oxford: Pergamon Press) pp. 81–94.

of their language, through what they tell you, whether the method used is a questionnaire, a highly-structured 20-minute interview or several years of participant observation. There is nothing controversial in saying this; what is more controversial is the status of language in such investigations. Social scientists have often regarded language as a neutral medium, a window on social reality; so that when someone tells the investigator 'I plan to vote Labour' this is taken as a direct representation of a reality existing outside the language used to describe it. But as many other contemporary social theorists have pointed out, this view is over-simplified. Language is not a neutral medium but itself a social construct; it is partly constitutive of social reality. Therefore, social researchers need to take language *qua* language seriously. In this sense – and whether or not it is made explicit – virtually all social research involves researching language.

The research projects we ourselves have carried out, and to which we will refer later on in this discussion, exemplify 'researching language' in both senses; all of us were interested in some aspect of people's talk, and all of us used talking as the means of finding out about it. At this point, it is helpful briefly to sketch the projects:

(a)   Ben Rampton undertook a sociolinguistic study of adolescent boys in a multiracial peer group, drawing on variationist sociolinguistics and the ethnography of communication. He looked at the use and distribution of syntactic and phonological variables and at their social significance for speakers and educators.

(b)   Penelope Harvey undertook an anthropological study of language use among bilinguals in the Peruvian Andes. She examined the role of language in constructing and maintaining social hierarchies within the peasant culture of a post-colonial state.

(c)   Elizabeth Frazer's was a qualitative sociological project addressing the construction of gender, race and class identities among British teenage girls from different socioeconomic backgrounds. She was especially concerned with the way the girls' talk about themselves related to their experience of themselves.

(d)   Deborah Cameron, a sociolinguist, investigated issues of language and racism with members of a mainly Black youth club in south London, eventually collaborating with them to produce a video on the topic.

These projects will be used in order to illustrate our concerns about power and method in social research. We begin, however, by returning to the more general questions posed above; what assumptions and practices in social science influence relationships between researchers and their subjects when the former go into the 'field' to observe the latter?

POSITIONING RESEARCHER AND RESEARCHED: ETHICS, ADVOCACY AND EMPOWERMENT

In this section we will identify three frameworks for conceptualizing relations between researchers and subjects: the ethical, the advocacy and the empowerment frameworks. Most social research is conducted within the assumptions of the first framework, that of ethics; some is conducted within the assumptions of the second, advocacy. We are most concerned with the possibilities offered by the third, empowerment.

Ethics

All social researchers are expected to take seriously the ethical questions their activities raise. These questions are discussed during postgraduate training, addressed in the guidelines and codes produced by professional bodies, and posed concretely when ethics committees scrutinize particular research proposals. All this institutional activity testifies to a high level of concern about researchers' responsibility to the people they do research on. The nature and limits of that responsibility may be framed, however, in a number of different ways.

Standard frameworks for discussing what is 'ethical' are fairly narrowly conceived. The question they address is how to strike an acceptable balance between potentially conflicting sets of interests. The researcher has an interest in finding out as much as possible; but it may not be in the interests of research subjects to provide information without limits and conditions. Ethical guidelines set out to make clear what the limits and conditions are.

Within such a framework, certain practices are obviously unethical: coercing subjects to participate or neglecting to get informed consent from them; exploiting or abusing them in the course of research; violating their privacy or breaching confidentiality. On the other hand, it is not considered unethical for the researcher to protect their own interests in various ways. They are permitted, or example, to be less than candid about the ultimate purpose of their research. Many research designs require that the investigator conceal their goals; if you tell people you want them to talk so you can measure the frequency with which they pause, say, this may affect their behaviour and so vitiate your results. To avoid this problem, you tell them nothing, or invent some plausible alternative rationale.

In sociolinguistic research, this type of problem has of course been *observer's paradox* agonized over under the heading of 'the observer's paradox' (linguists want to observe how people use language when they are not being observed). Some classical discussions of elicitation technique (e.g. Labov, 1972) have advised the researcher to minimize the problem by using petty deceptions (like leaving the tape recorder running when the informant thinks you have already switched it off). Typically, the question of whether such a proceeding is ethical is treated as a matter of 'balance'; by tacit consent, some deceptions are innocuous, advancing the interests of the researcher without seriously threatening those of the informant. It is worth noting, though, that the judgement of what constitutes an innocuous deception and what would be an unethical one is left to the researcher. The 'ethical' model of relations between researcher and researched is an asymmetrical one in which the researched play a passive role; the legitimate, knowledge-seeking objectives of researchers can be pursued by any means that do not infringe the fundamental rights of informants.

The underlying conception in the 'ethical' model is one of *research on* social subjects. Because these subjects are human beings, they are entitled to special ethical consideration. But the consideration goes only so far, and the researchers rather than the researched decide its limits (e.g. in judging what counts as 'innocuous deception'). Human subjects no more set the social researcher's agenda than a bottle of sulphuric acid sets the chemist's agenda. Nor is it necessarily assumed that social research should produce any positive benefit to the subjects who participate. If it does, this is seen as a bonus; but if it does not, so long as no actual harm is done, it can still be accepted as ethical.

Advocacy

For many social researchers, this ethical model is necessary but not sufficient. Over and above the obligation not to harm informants, researchers often feel a more positive desire to help them. This feeling may be present from the outset, perhaps as a political commitment that has guided the researcher in choosing to work on a particular project. Or it may develop later on, as the researcher forms more complex human relationships with her informants. It is not uncommon for informants themselves to ask researchers for advice, support and help. People are aware that the knowledge, expertise and status of academic social scientists may prove helpful in campaigns for better conditions, and they may ask a researcher to participate in such campaigns, perhaps by acting or speaking publicly on the community's behalf. If the option is taken up, it places the researcher in the position of an *advocate*, engaging in research not only *on* social subjects, as in the ethical framework, but also *for* them.

In the last 15 years [this text published in 1993 – Eds.] there has been a classic case in sociolinguistics of research done within the advocacy framework – that is, research *on* and *for* social subjects: the 'Black English' trial in Ann Arbor, Michigan. Here, a lawsuit brought against the school system by a group of African-American parents came to turn on questions about the community's linguistic variety, American Vernacular Black English (AVBE). The plaintiffs argued that their children were being disadvantaged educationally – for instance, wrongly identified as having 'learning disabilities' – by the schools' failure to make provision for the systemic differences between AVBE and Standard English (SE). Since AVBE is a variety used exclusively by African-Americans, failure to take account of its speakers' needs would constitute racial discrimination. For this argument to succeed, it had to be shown that AVBE was indeed a distinctive variety, highly divergent from SE, specific to African-American communities and reflecting their history of slavery and segregation. In making this case, the advocacy of professional linguists who had studied AVBE was crucial. A number of linguists provided advice, support and eventually expert testimony.

Among those who testified was the sociolinguist William Labov. He subsequently wrote an account of the case whose main title was 'Objectivity and commitment in linguistic science', and this contains a powerful argument about the social responsibilities of sociolinguistic researchers (Labov, 1982). Two principles are laid down for researchers; 'the principle of error correction' (if people believe false and damaging propositions, e.g. 'AVBE is bad English', or 'AVBE is hardly any different from SE', researchers who know better are obliged to try and correct the error); and 'the principle of the debt incurred' (if a community has helped researchers by providing access and information, researchers have a corresponding duty to use their knowledge and expertise for the benefit of the community). This amounts to an argument that advocacy – research *for* as well as *on* social subjects – is not just an optional extra, a bonus researchers may look for or not, as they decide; in the right circumstances it is an obligation.

It should be noted that while Labov speaks powerfully in favour of 'commitment', he is equally concerned with 'objectivity'. This, in fact, is a significant concern which the ethical and advocacy frameworks have in common. Both assume that the first duty of researchers is to pursue the objective truth – a concept which is taken to be unproblematic. Presumably it is this assumption of the overriding claims of truth which legitimates certain 'innocuous deceptions' within the ethical framework; presumably, too, someone like Labov might refuse to act as an advocate if it could not be done without compromising the truth. Most of Labov's paper is devoted to showing that in the Ann Arbor case, objectivity and commitment actually *reinforced one another*. For example, he notes that a number of African-American linguists had studied AVBE at least partly out of political commitment; and he argues that the distinctive knowledge and experience they brought to the field resolved a number of disputes and problems, thus producing a more objective and truthful account. In addition, the stringent requirements of preparing a court case sharpened committed linguists' arguments, obliging them to seek the truth all the more assiduously.

This line of argument takes issue with the more familiar idea that commitment must necessarily threaten a researcher's objectivity. In disciplines which accept a positivist philosophy of science (as quantitative sociolinguistics generally does[1]) there is a distinction made between fact and value, and it is seen as important to keep scientific observations from being tainted by value-judgements. Someone who begins from a partisan standpoint cannot observe objectively; and the problem is compounded if researchers permit their opinions to obtrude in a way that might affect the behaviour being observed. (Hence the kinds of instructions traditionally given to interviewers and discussed by the sociologist Ann Oakley (1981); one handbook advised interviewers to answer informants' questions by saying. 'Well right now your opinions are more important than mine.') Labov does challenge this notion that commitment is totally incompatible with objectivity, but at the same time he appears to accept the positivist fact/value distinction, and the challenge is therefore a limited one. 'Commitment' for Labov seems to lie in the passion with which a researcher pursues the facts, and in what she does with them once she has established them. It does not seem to enter into the processes whereby researchers construct 'facts' – the design of a project, the field methods, the analysis. These are domains where objectivity must prevail.

Problems with Advocacy

This is really where our argument begins. Like many social researchers, including Labov, each of use had sought ways of doing research that would advance our political goals – greater freedom, equality and justice – as well as our intellectual ones. Like Labov we had felt a necessity to go beyond the ethical framework, altering the balance of power between academic researchers and research subjects. Yet the advocacy framework exemplified by Labov's 'Objectivity and commitment' paper also seemed inadequate for two distinct but connected reasons.

The first was that advocacy, as practised by linguists involved in the Ann Arbor case, seemed to beg the following question. If researchers are under an obligation to use their knowledge on behalf of informants, why not go a step further and argue that they should make the knowledge *available to informants* for them to use on their own behalf? For experts to act as advocates is doubtless important (and in present conditions, often vital; we are not suggesting Labov should have refused to testify). But, surely, it would be a positive development if people had the knowledge and skills to act for themselves.

This might seem like an outlandish suggestion, equivalent to saying that everyone should become an academic linguist (and perhaps also, by analogy, a lawyer, a psychologist, a forensic scientist...). Such an extreme proposal is neither necessary, nor necessarily desirable. But consider the implications of a situation where *only* the expert advocate has access to specialist knowledge about a community's language variety. The expert in such a situation retains some very significant powers.

For example, Labov argues that when linguists act as advocates they serve the community and must bow to the political will of the community. Yet he also acknowledges that the 'will of the community' can be hard for an outsider to locate. This is highly relevant to the current politics of AVBE. Although the community involved in bringing the Ann Arbor case seem to have been in agreement about their interests, the wider community of AVBE speakers in the United States certainly is not.[2] Labov did not speak for all African-Americans; he made, in effect, a choice about whose interests he would support. Clearly, it is inevitable that communities will contain a diversity of interests. But if members of those communities do not possess the information needed to engage in internal debate, there is a danger that external advocates will end up making their choices for them.

The matter of intra-community diversity is problematic in another way in Labov's discussion. He emphasizes the contribution of African-American linguists, implying that if researcher and researched are from the same social group, this automatically reduces the potential for conflicts between them. It may well be true that African-American researchers are regarded by African-American communities as less likely to pose a threat than White researchers; but it is questionable whether a shared racial origin reduces the asymmetry of researcher and researched to the point of insignificance. On many criteria, an African-American researcher is likely to be (and be seen as) an outsider to the community (she may differ from most community members in terms of education, occupation, income, residence). But even beyond such crude measures of likeness and difference, attention has to be paid to the complicated, specific ways in which any research process positions those who take part in it. If the goal is to alter the balance of power between researcher and researched, it is not enough to make changes in personnel. There have to be changes in the *process* of research and the social relationships it typically involves, with informants being treated by researchers as 'objects of study', and not as co-participants in a form of social interaction.

One major obstacle to changing the processes and relationships of research is the stringent set of methodological requirements imposed by positivism. And this is the second source of our dissatisfaction with the advocacy framework; it stops well short of a critique of positivist research methods in social science. Arguably, it is positivism more than anything else that prevents many researchers going beyond advocacy. They fear that if they make drastic changes in the relationship they have with subjects, their research will no longer be 'valid'.

We think these anxieties are misplaced, since positivist epistemologies are open to serious criticisms on various grounds. But in the light of the foregoing argument about the politics of social research, their most immediate drawback is that they lead almost inevitably to the objectification of informants by researchers. If, as we would claim, people are not objects and should not be treated like objects, this surely entitles them to more than just respectful (ethical) treatment. It means that researcher and researched should interact; researchers should not try to pretend that their subjects can be studied as if the former were outside the social universe that included the latter.

This is the point at which the political critique of objectification connects to a broader epistemological critique of positivism (a philosophy which favours or even prescribes objectification). Positivists would question whether you can avoid objectification and still do good research. We belive the answer is yes: the claims made for positivist methods are overstated, while non-positivist methods can produce research that is valid and insightful. This argument between positivism and anti-positivism may be pursued with reference to the research tradition of sociolinguistics.

As noted above, variationist sociolinguistics has a longstanding anxiety about the observer's paradox. This rests upon the idea that a researcher's presence (and with a tape recorder, to make things worse) is enough to render the environment hostile for the informant, and to produce a form of linguistic camouflage. Assuming that the researcher and her informants do not share the same linguistic background, it is important for the researcher to minimize her own effect on the speech of the researched.

Behind the various strategies suggested for doing this (e.g. the 'innocuous' deceptions mentioned above, the deflection of informants' questions advised by traditional handbooks, etc.) lies the positivist assumption that there is reality independent of the observer's perception, and that *this* is what all science, natural and social, must aspire to discover. From that perspective, interaction between researcher and researched appears as a source of interference or contamination – hence the need to minimize it or even avoid it altogether.

But critics of positivism find this view naïve. The perspective from which we criticize positivists is one which regards all human behaviour as social and interactive by definition. This is not to deny there is a difference between what people do and what they say, between their behaviour and their accounts of their behaviour. But human meanings – for positivists a realm of the subjective – are for us at least partly constitutive of what a given reality *is*. In other words, a researcher who observes some form of behaviour may properly be interested not only in what the actor appears to be doing, but what the actor herself thinks she is doing. The woman turning a spade in the earth, for instance, may be gardening or preparing to bury a family pet; furthermore, she may be undertaking either task for a variety of reasons which are part of its meaning, and which may only become apparent to an observer if there is interaction between observer and observed.

Returning then to the case of sociolinguistic observation, we can argue along the following lines. If all human behaviour is social behaviour, then interaction between researcher and researched does not produce some anomalous form of communication peculiar to the research situation and misleading as to the nature of 'reality'. Rather such interaction instantiates *normal* communication in one of its forms.

Our own fieldwork convinced us that this is a more insightful way to look at the issue. Talking to us as researchers, informants drew upon their linguistic repertoires as these had been developed in talking to parents, teachers, employers – significant others of various kinds. The roles of 'researcher' and 'informant' are best seen not as pre-given identities which individuals adopt when the situation requires, but as context-dependent identities, negotiated between researcher and researched as part of the process of establishing social relations. The precise content of the 'researcher' role may vary from case to case. On both sides, previous experience informs the way roles are negotiated. So data collected in research situations should not be regarded simply as 'contaminated', a distorted or degenerate version of 'real' interaction; such data provide important insights into the way social relations and identities are constructed through interaction.

Positivists, then, are mistaken in their belief that there is some pristine social reality 'out there' waiting to be discovered by an investigator who is herself neutral and detached from it. And if positivists are thus mistaken, the problem of validity loses its centrality; the scope for introducing a very different kind of research is dramatically widened. If one admits the epistemological and political argument that researchers should interact with the researched instead of trying to remain aloof from them, it becomes possible to do research not just *on* social subjects or *for* social subjects, but also *with* social subjects. The *with* here implies the use of interactive methods, but it also raises two other, connected possibilities. The first is that informants themselves might play a greater role in setting agendas for research than positivist frameworks permit. The second, which goes back to our reservations about Labovian advocacy, is that the knowledge researchers bring to a project or jointly with informants produce in the course of one, might be shared more explicitly with the researched, in an effort to give them a greater measure of control. It is possibilities like these which lead us to label the framework proposed here – research done *on, for* and *with* social subjects – *empowering research*.

Empowerment

It is important to point out that our own focused reflections on 'empowering research' began *after* we had carried out empirical work in situations of evident social inequality. With varying degrees of self-consciousness, we have departed from traditional positivist research methods and introduced into our projects the kinds of concerns we would subsequently relate to the framework of 'empowerment'; the use of interactive methods, the acknowledgement of subjects' own agendas and the sharing of expert knowledge. When we began our discussions, two things quickly emerged. One was that the particular projects we had done would not serve in any simple way as models for empowering research in general. Like most researchers we had designed those projects to address substantive issues, and not to test particular methods. We therefore treated them as case studies rather than recipes, to be discussed and criticized in the light of the theoretical framework we elaborated after finishing them. How 'empowering' were these projects? What problems did they raise?

The second thing that became clear as we reflected on these questions was this: not only were the projects inadequate as models, the whole notion of a model for empowering research was problematic. The argument we have put forward, analysing social research paradigms in terms of ethics, advocacy and empowerment, is in important ways over-simple. Committed though we are to a critique of positivism, we are also aware of a great many crucial questions surrounding the idea of empowerment and complicating any attempt to practise 'empowering research'. Where do we locate 'power'? What are the boundaries of 'research'? Who can define 'subjects' own agendas'? What is the 'knowledge' we propose to share, and how can it be shared?

Every one of the terms we have placed in scare-quotes acquires its meaning within the same set of complex and shifting social relationships we have already referred to in criticizing traditional research methods. If we are not to be as reductive as those we criticize, we cannot produce a *single* account of what would be empowering in every research context. Rather we must point to the kinds of problems a researcher faces whose goal is empowerment, and the questions to which she must pay close attention. In trying to locate various key terms – 'power', 'research' and 'knowledge', for example – we will illustrate the problems and questions at issue with reference to our own case studies.

PROBLEMS OF EMPOWERMENT

Locating Power

An economy of power? Both common-sense discourse and traditional philosophical discussion have a tendency to treat 'power' as the sort of thing individuals and groups can have more or less of. This economic metaphor suggests a fairly simple definition of 'empowerment'; a redistribution which takes power away from some people (the powerful) and gives it others (the powerless). Our own concern about the balance of power between researcher and researched could be addressed in these terms.

But the model of power presupposed here raises a great many problems. The idea of seizing and redistributing power works best if power is taken as a monolith, something with a single point of origin, like ownership of the means of production in classical Marxism, or 'the barrel of a gun' for Maoists. In recent years such monolithic models have been justifiably criticized. There are many simultaneous dimensions of power, interacting with each other in complex ways. It is reductive and inadequate to take one dimension as prior to or more important than all the others – to privilege, say, relations of class over relations of gender and race. Social identity is a fragmented and multiple phenomenon, since social subjects are positioned in many sets of relations, not just one; sometimes the relations are contradictory.

This consideration proved relevant to our case studies. For instance, Elizabeth Frazer studied several groups of girls, among them an upper-class group of public schoolgirls. The privilege these girls enjoyed on one dimension, class, was part of their identity, but not experientially separable from the oppressive gender relations they were also positioned in, and which equally shaped their identity. Privilege and oppression can coexist; a group of people can be both oppressing and oppressed. It is therefore difficult in principle and practice to locate groups of unequivocally 'powerful' and 'powerless' people. And it follows that attempts at 'empowerment' cannot be uncritical; it is not just a matter of giving people 'more power', but of recognizing that every group in a community is itself an arena for conflict and struggle.

Power/knowledge. The work of Michel Foucault (cf. Foucault, 1980) represents a major shift away from economic metaphors of more power and less power. It is therefore of interest to us, but it raises another difficulty, this time about our own position as social researchers. Much of Foucault's work derives from the insight that citizens of modern democracies are controlled less by straightforward violence or economic exploitation than by the pronouncements of expert discourse, organized in 'regimes of truth' – sets of understandings which legitimate certain social attitudes and practices. Programmes of social scientific research on such subjects as 'criminality' or 'sexual deviance' or 'teenage motherhood' organize what we 'know' about certain groups of people – 'criminals', 'deviants', 'teenage mothers' – and contribute to their becoming targets for social control, as well as helping to shape the forms such control will take. (Of course, Foucault also notes that regimes of truth give rise to discourses of resistance which may become powerful in their turn. The process of 'power/knowledge' which brings into existence 'the criminal classes' also brings into existence the threat they represent to bourgeois society; the classification of certain individuals as 'homosexuals' exposes those people to social control, but also gives them a definite identity which they may use to organize for 'gay rights'.)

What are the implications of this analysis for the project of empowering research? Social science is a major contributor to oppressive regimes of truth; perhaps, then, empowering research is a contradiction in terms. There is certainly no denying the non-neutrality of social research, historically and currently; it is strongly implicated in social control. An enormous proportion of social scientific studies focus on relatively powerless people: factory workers, criminals, juvenile delinquents, *not* bosses and directors, judges and jailers. This is not coincidental, and our own case studies (for instance, the fact that three of them involved White researchers working in non-White communities) instantiate a similar pattern. In the specific case of linguistic research, one can point to many studies that have legitimated questionable attitudes and practices. The study of non-European and creole languages contributed in the past to Western notions of 'primitive' culture; the study of working-class speech has fed into victim-blaming educational theories (though to be fair, sociolinguists have also produced a significant challenge to these); allegedly 'descriptive' enterprises like the Summer Institute of Linguistics have disrupted cultural patterns among the researched, and served colonialism by encouraging indigenous people to sign away their lands (Mülhäusler, 1990).

These examples constitute an important critique of social science, and any discussion of empowering research will do well to take them seriously. But returning to the idea of power as a *multiple* phenomenon, we would argue that there is usually more going on in the relationship of researcher and researched than a simple and oppressive 'us/them' opposition. It has been noted already in discussing AVBE that problems of inequality may arise even where researchers are more like 'them', as with Black researchers working in Black communities. But conversely, researchers are not always powerful in an unqualified way. Often, the researched can exert power over researchers by virtue of what they know that researchers do not.

Penelope Harvey found, for instance, that the people of Ocongate in the Peruvian Andes, with whom she lived and worked, very often positioned her not as the omniscient Western expert but as a child needing instruction in the most fundamental ways of behaving. Deborah Cameron, working on a video about language and racism with a group of Black British young people in London, also found her relationship with the researched a shifting one. Sometimes they did treat her as an expert – for example when she was telling them about the history of Caribbean creoles. At other times, however, they consciously enjoyed placing her in different, less powerful positions – when, for example, they cast her as a White racist in sketches performed for the video. In this context, 'White racist' was not a powerful role; it was imposed on Cameron rather than chosen by her, and it placed her, for the moment, outside the locally powerful norms of the group. There are dangers, then, in simply assuming that researchers invariably have absolute power and control while the researched have neither.

Power and representation. This last example – that of the language and racism video – points to a very important form of power, the power to determine how people are represented. And in most research projects, of course, this power does lie with the researcher. At the point when scholars sit down to write their book, thesis, article or report, the complex and shifting interpersonal negotiations that positioned researcher and researched during fieldwork are finally pinned down; fluid and multiple subjectivities become unified and fixed by the writer who must mediate the talk of her subjects for the readers. Furthermore, the interpretations a researcher makes in doing this must inevitably draw on information beyond what was explicitly made available or agreed to by informants.

There is no easy solution for this particular problem of inequality, but it is certainly one argument for the use of interactive methods rather than distanced, 'objective' ones. By talking to the researched and sharing with them, the researcher maximizes their opportunities for defining themselves in advance of being represented. It is also of course possible to use 'feedback' techniques – that is, to present findings to the researched in an effort to get more informed consent to what you will eventually say about them. Ben Rampton used this technique in his work with Asian schoolboys. It is not a novel technique in social science; many researchers have recommended it as a way of checking the validity of results. But while that is one of its functions, it is also a means of continuing dialogue between researcher and researched. The alternative used in Deborah Cameron's project, where the researched represented both themselves and her in a video, is clearly not feasible in every project. Elizabeth Frazer, on the other hand, combined elements of both procedures; she used some feedback techniques, and she also facilitated a further project where two groups of subjects produced their own photo-story magazine, thus representing themselves and the concerns Frazer's research had raised for them.[3]

Locating power. We have argued, then, that 'power' is more difficult to locate than it might seem. We cannot identify some prototypical powerless group to do empowering research with, and we cannot safely assume an unproblematic split between powerful researchers and powerless researched. Power has many dimensions, it is affected by local context and the positions of all involved in fieldwork are shifting and variable rather than static. The more a researcher recognizes the complexities of power that exist both among her informants and in her own relationship with them, the less easy she will find it to formulate a simple agenda for empowerment. That is not, of course, a reason to abandon the *principle* of going research on, for and with social subjects. But it is an argument for awareness of complexity and willingness to engage in a constant negotiation.

Locating 'Research'

'Research' might seem to be a considerably less difficult notion than 'power'. But one of the problems that arises when you try to do research 'on, for and with' subjects, especially if you propose to address their agendas in addition to your own, is precisely whether it can then remain 'research', or whether it collapses into some other activity, like youth work or education or political activism.

The most familiar definition of 'research' is what might be called 'the 'Ph.D. definition'. In order to receive a Ph.D. degree, a researcher must make a substantial and original contribution to the knowledge available in a particular field. What counts as substantial and original is judged by people who have met the same criteria themselves. In other words, to enter the community of qualified researchers one must satisfy someone who belongs already that one has done something they would define as research.

There is a political critique to be made of this definition, just as there is of positivist ideas about validity and objectivity. The Ph.D. definition clearly has a 'gatekeeping' function, and potentially therefore it might work to exclude certain topics and certain ways of pursuing them from the definition of research, on the groups that some subjects and approaches are more valuable than others. But one could ask, more valuable *to whom*? It should surely be open to all who pursue knowledge to participate in shaping new research agendas and new definitions of what constitutes research. If in fact this is discouraged, that has more to do with institutional constraints like the preferences of Ph.D. examiners, journal editors and research funding bodies than with any obvious criteria of value. The value of any project is a matter for debate; and the debate is not settled by appealing to the criterion of whether certain established scholars would accept it as *bona fide* research. That just returns us to the original question: what is research and who decides?

Apart from this point about the internal politics of academe, there is also a more theoretical point to be made in reply to the critic who is worried about blurring the boundaries of 'research'. We have argued already that the researchers, like the researched, are bearers of complex and multiple social identities; the role of 'researcher' is not, in practice, a distinct entity, but draws on other social roles like teacher, youth worker, parent (and indeed child), friend, etc. If this point is accepted, there is no necessary contradiction in taking up more than one role in a research situation; on the contrary, you are always doing that anyway. What Elizabeth Frazer did, for instance, was both research and youth work; one did not vitiate or interfere with the other. We would argue that research methods chosen with the empowerment framework allow you to exploit the potential of the researcher's multiple role, instead of forcing you to deny it. This step – which is only an acknowledgement of the realities of any fieldwork context – has the further virtue of making it easier to take on the agendas of your subjects.

Taking on subjects' agendas does not imply that researchers must subordinate their own agendas. Rather we are arguing that there should be negotiation, aimed at ensuring that the project meets the needs of all involved. This could mean as little as simply making clear that asking questions is not the sole prerogative of the researcher; or as much as organizing additional activities, like Frazer's photo-story. But we would differentiate ourselves from traditions like that of 'action research', in which the main or only criterion of value is utility to the researched. Many of the questions we were interested in when we undertook our projects were entirely without interest or utility to our subjects (Ben Rampton, for example, found his informants relatively unmoved by the incidence of retroflex consonants in their speech). This is no argument for shelving the questions that interest the researcher. Moreover, in other cases informants proved deeply interested in matters we have thought would be regarded as abstruse and irrelevant, like arguments for the autonomy of creoles, or the sociological concept of 'reproduction'.

For us, then, it is important that research as a form of knowledge-producing activity continue to be practised and valued. We question, on the one hand, the narrow institutional criteria which validate certain kinds of knowledge and procedures for producing it, while excluding others; and on the other hand, restrictive political criteria which deem research unproductive if it does not address immediate material needs. The desire to analyse the social world you inhabit is to be encouraged, among both professional academics and other members of society – including, of course, research subjects. This is the goal of social research; to carefully observe and interpret human behaviour with a view to improving our understanding of the social world. And the practice of systematic observation and interpretation that broadly defines the term 'research' is not incompatible with other activities. In real-life research projects it is not even always separable from them. The Ph.D. definition, which would exclude some parts of our own case studies – Frazer's photo-story project, for example, and nearly everything Cameron did – is premised on an oversimplification of what researchers and researched actually do.

We have referred to research as 'knowledge producing', and this introduces another complication. What is 'knowledge'? If pressed, a proponent of the Ph.D. definition of research might well say that research is constituted not only by its procedures and protocols but by the kind of knowledge it produces: expert knowledge, which is systematic, formalized in certain ways and preferably original. This question of expert knowledge is one that has so far been put aside, but it must now be taken up in more detail. It is relevant, not only to the question of whether the empowerment framework produces 'real' research, but also to the question of sharing knowledge with research subjects, which is one of our concerns in proposing the framework.

Locating 'Knowledge'

In one sense, the selection of 'originality' as a mark of expert knowledge is odd. A great deal of the knowledge researchers produce is constructed out of knowledge their research subjects already possess. Labov's account of the ritual insults used by African-Americans in Harlem (Labov, 1972) becomes 'original' only when presented to outside, academic audiences; for the people who provided the data, the content of Labov's article would not be 'original' at all (though the form in which it is rendered might be). This suggests there are different kinds of knowledge; and when we talk about the empowering potential of researchers sharing knowledge it is relevant to reflect on that. A crucial question here is whether expert knowledge is normally privileged over lay knowledge for good and necessary reasons (e.g. Labov's account is more systematic than the lay account he based it on) or for merely contingent ones serving narrow sectarian interests.

Although we would want to demystify the category of expert knowledge, by making explicit its relation to already-existing lay knowledge, our research experiences led us to question the strong thesis that there is no significant difference between the two. Some of us found that sharing expert knowledge can be a valuable mechanism of empowerment.

For example, one characteristic of expert knowledge is the ability to synthesize and relate things, placing them in a broader context. For both Ben Rampton and Deborah Cameron it proved important that the experiences and ideas offered by subjects could be put into a historical context. Rampton related his informants' attitudes concerning aspects of their linguistic repertoires (speaking English, speaking English with a 'Babu' accent, speaking a south Asian language) to the language policies of British imperialists in India, and also to educational theories that were current in Britain during the main immigration period. Cameron, somewhat similarly, approached her informants' ambivalent feelings about patois by giving an account of the history of Caribbean creoles. In both cases, lay knowledge was illuminated by historical contextualization of a kind that had not previously been available to the subjects.

Elizabeth Frazer used a different strategy. On one occasion she asked a group of girls to analyse a transcript of their own previous interaction, with a view to helping them perceive and perhaps resolve certain problems and confusions that had troubled them at the time. The knowledge being shared here was not factual, but processual; Frazer demonstrated the kinds of supervenient reflection, analysis and categorization researchers use in constructing expert knowledge out of informants' talk. These techniques, too, are characteristics of expert discourse, more formalized there than in lay discourse. Frazer's informants reported they found it empowering to have these ways of analysing made accessible and systematic for them. They felt – as did Rampton's and Cameron's informants – that they were learning something about themselves, something they did not know (or know consciously) before.[4]

We believe, then, that expert knowledge does possess certain specific characteristics that make it worth having; and that if it is worth having, it is worth sharing. And once again, we may note that positivist 'ethical' research methods make this kind and degree of sharing difficult or even impossible; to share knowledge is to intervene actively in the understandings of the researched, whereas positivism enjoins on us a responsibility to leave those understandings undisturbed.

CONCLUSION

The question we pose in *Researching Language* is whether the balance of power between researchers and research subjects can be altered, with positive results for both groups; and we answer that question in the affirmative. The prevailing 'ethical' framework – with occasional excursions into 'advocacy' – rests its case for the status quo on the idea that reducing the distance between researcher and researched will destroy the enterprise of research; it will bias the results, muddle the scholarly objectives of academic disciplines and lead researchers into conflicting and irrelevant activities.

We hope we have succeeded in showing that these are unfounded fears, based on a questionable epistemology and politics. To do social research 'on, for and with' subjects is certainly not a simple proceeding; it requires enormous attention to the complexities of any actual research context. But these complexities are present whatever kind of research we do. Traditional frameworks do not make them disappear. The less traditional framework we have argued for acknowledges and works with complexity. In our view, this not only benefits the researched, it benefits the researcher too; for although we have rejected the sociolinguist's traditional Holy Grail – speech unaffected by the presence of the observer – the use of interactive and non-objectifying methods enables us to gain richer insights into subjects' own understandings of their behaviour, and to engage them in dialogue about those understandings. This, we believe, is to our mutual benefit.

Although, like all research paradigms, it must sometimes fall short of the goals it sets itself, empowering research is capable of changing everyone involved in it, providing, not only for researchers but also for their informants, the possibility of constructing new insights and understandings. It is that possibility which should set the standard for all research that concerns itself with language and society.

NOTES

1   An interesting argument could be made that quantitative sociolinguistics is more realist than positivist. Some version of sociolinguistics treat observable variation as the effect of a probabilistic component in speakers' grammars, which in turn are held to be 'real' (a claim which connects with the broader debate in linguistics on the psychological reality of grammar). Nevertheless, variationist linguists' methodological assumptions, and especially their definition of what constitutes good or valid data, may with justification be labelled positivist.

2   There are African-American intellectuals who see any concessions to AVBE as disadvantaging AVBE speakers and reducing their chances of mobility; there are others who feel the Ann Arbor judgement, which made concessions for the specific purpose of teaching SE more effectively, did not sufficiently challenge the dominance of the (White) standard variety. This kind of disagreement should lead social researchers to observe a caveat about the uncritical use of the term 'community', which has come to be used in such extended ways (e.g. 'the business community') that it verges on the vacuous, while at the same time its connotations are manipulated for rhetorical effect.

3   Clearly, the forms of 'self-representation'mentioned here – the video and the photo-story – were not addressed to the conventional audience for academic research and did not use the conventional media for presenting academic research. Furthermore, these non-academic audiences and media are generally accorded lower prestige than, say, a print journal read by academics. But even if 'academic' and 'non-academic' representations are distinct in terms of audience and medium, it would be a mistake for academics to underestimate the potential power and significance of other forms of representation.

4   It is important to acknowledge here that a linguist, or any expert, who tells a group things about itself, is engaging in a form of interaction which requires sensitive handling. Social identities are at stake and face can be seriously threatened.

REFERENCES

Foucault, M. (1980) *Power/Knowledge: Selected Interviews and Other Writings 1972–1977*, Gordon, C. (ed.) (Brighton: Harvester Press).

Labov, W. (1972) 'Rules for Ritual Insults', in *Language in the Inner City* (Philadelphia, PA: University of Pennsylvania Press).

Labov, W. (1982) 'Objectivity and Commitment in Linguistic Science: The Case of the Black English Trial in Ann Arbor', *Language in Society*, **44**, 165–201.

Mühlhäusler, P. (1990) 'Reducing' Pacific Languages to Writing', in Joseph, J. E. and Taylor, T. J. (eds) *Ideologies of Language* (London: Routledge).

Oakley, A. (1981) 'Interviewing Women: A Contradiction in Terms', in Roberts, H. (ed.) *Doing Feminist Research* (London: Routledge).

Part III
Variationist Sociolinguistics

The chapters in this section include extracts from some of the most important empirical studies of language variation, mainly in urban settings. Labov's department-stores study in New York City (Chapter 13), first reported in 1966, was highly influential. It set in motion a wave of quantitative sociolinguistic research. Part of its appeal lies in its boundedness – the fact that Labov was able to draw such theoretically rich findings from such a simple technique and such a limited data base. The procedure he used was rapid and anonymous interviewing, simply repeating the same request for information to 264 different sales assistants spread across three well-known New York City department stores: *excuse me, where are the women's shoes?* The patterns of pronunciation involved in the sales assistants' answers was highly revealing. Labov outlines his methods, findings and interpretations very clearly in the text.

With hindsight, after some thirty years of sociolinguistic research, it is still striking how all the key components of variationism are represented in the department-stores study: a *socially stratified* or ranked community (represented here as the ranked social statuses of the three department stores themselves, and by implication the social statuses of the assistants that were asked the question); a socially sensitive feature of pronunciation, the now-famous postvocalic /r/, potentially realized in words like *fourth* and *floor*; a clear pattern of variation in the frequency of its use, meaning the feature had the potential to mark social differences; and a community where the speech norms are undergoing change.

The study is also a classical piece of empiricist research. Labov stresses the naturalness of the data he was able to gather and the study's objectivity. The findings only emerge as trends in statistical tables and figures, and in degrees of similarity and difference. (Later sociolinguistic studies found it important to use even more rigorous statistical techniques, in particular to help decide which numerical differences were significant in a statistical sense.) The investigation proceeds in the conventional empiricist way, by establishing its hypotheses and its categories in advance (e.g. selecting the three stores in full anticipation of the trends that might emerge) and systematically testing them against the frequency data. There is no commentary on the social context in which the study was made except for the purpose of justifying the categories used in the design, and to justify the claims about objectivity. The study is highly elegant and economical – attributes that are considered positive qualities in controlled experimentation.

It is also important to notice that the study is not designed to tell us anything sociologically novel. The social stratification of the stores was presumed in advance of the investigation, and simply confirmed in the study. What is novel is the precise patterning of the linguistic feature, and perhaps particularly the patterning of (r) as between the first and the second occurrences of the word *floor* in Labov's Figure 13.2 suggesting a stylistic difference between less and more emphatic contexts.

The brief extract (Chapter 14) from Trudgill's Norwich study shows a similar emphasis. It is a replication and elaboration of Labov's survey research method – a far more complex and time-consuming design than the department-stores study, but also applied in New York City. Trudgill's data come from sociolinguistic interviews (of the sort discussed by Wolfson in Chapter 10). He has organized his sample of people being interviewed into five social classes, ranked from high to low. Within each interview, he has then set up four sub-conditions based on different activities in which speakers are involved – from speaking casually to reading lists of words. Detailed analysis and counting of one particular pronunciation feature – (ng) or so-called 'g-dropping', where either a velar [ŋ] or an alveolar [n] nasal sound can be produced – allow Trudgill to produce very consistent numerical patterns, reflecting the social and situational dimensions of context. The pre-established social class groups and the situation-types can be distinguished sociolinguistically.

Trudgill's findings are similar to Labov's and many others' in that they also show regular sex differences, with women tending to produce more standard (or more 'posh') speech variants than men do. At least from one point of view, sex or gender is an obvious and straightforward social variable. It seems entirely reasonable to assume that the world of speakers divides absolutely into males and females. The fact that sociolinguists have often been able to show systematic linguistic variation between males and females perhaps supports this view. However, as we shall see in Eckert's chapter (17) in this section and in the next part of the Reader, there is a danger of underestimating the role of perceptual and other subjective social processes. Individual males and females undoubtedly *differ* in how closely their actions and speech-styles resemble those of prototypical males and females. Being female or male is a more complex social role (gender) than the biological alternative of sex implies. Our reactions to strangers may well be influenced more by our stereotypical views of male and female communication than by people's actual ways of speaking.

When we delve into the theory underlying social class as a social variable, there are even more complications to consider. This is why some chapters in this section have moved on from trying to define 'social class' in simple and apparently objective terms. Cheshire (Chapter 15) divides up her adolescent male[1] speakers into groups depending on how closely they stick to 'the norms of the *vernacular culture*', rather than by social class. The factors she uses are skill at fighting, carrying a weapon, participating in minor crimes, future jobs, dress/hairstyle, and swearing. Cheshire is then able to show that young people's use of some non-standard grammatical features correlates positively with how high they score on an index of vernacular culture. Not surprisingly, the more embedded speakers are in their local, rather anti-social cultural norms, the more non-standard their speech is in certain respects. It may well be true that the people most closely tied to their vernacular culture will be 'working-class' people. But Cheshire's study shows us that *degree* of local affiliation is itself a factor of some consequence for ways of speaking.

The Milroys' chapter takes up closely related questions, through the concept of *social networks* developed in Lesley Milroy's and his work in Belfast, Northern Ireland. Social networks are important for sociolinguistics once again because they help us understand the sorts of pressures that group-membership can exert on speakers. As we have seen, some of the patterns of variation that emerge from sociolinguistic surveys seem self-explanatory. We would have anticipated that high-status speakers would use more standard speech-forms. On the other hand, status itself doesn't give us a way of explaining why lower-class speakers generally cling to their non-standard vernacular speech, when there would appear to be status benefits in using standard forms. Labov's idea of *covert prestige* takes us some of the way to an answer. Non-standard forms *are* in their own way prestigious, via a local and unacknowledged sort of 'prestige'. But the concept of social networks allows us to be rather more precise.

Within a community, people are linked together in different ways. The 'ties' between them can be stronger or weaker. Strong ties result from *dense network* associations, where many people are interlinked by each individual being associated with all or most other individuals. A second criterion is so-called *multiplexity*, when individuals relate to others on more than one basis – for example, working and socializing with the same group. As James and Lesley Milroy argue, these ideas can help us predict how speech-forms may remain stable over long periods, when they are protected by the conservative effects of dense and multiplex social networks. On the other hand, weak ties may provide a crucial means by which change – either linguistic or cultural – infiltrates social networks.

The Belfast data show the differences in network density that can exist within working-class urban groups. In the Ballymacarrett area of Belfast, the study is able to pick out significant positive correlation between network structure and the use of certain local forms of speech. But what is most interesting is that this seems to give us a better explanation for linguistic variation than the apparently clear-cut issue of gender. Ballymacarrett males did use more local vernacular speech forms, but this may have been not so much 'because they were males' but because their patterns of association in the community were more dense and multiplex than those of women. In that area of the city, there was relatively low unemployment and men worked and socialized together far more than the women did. Their networks may well have been an agency for maintaining and focusing local Belfast speech norms.

As we noted above, the term 'sex' implies differences of a purely biological sort. The term 'gender' is more appropriate when we are implying that the relevant differences are more to do with social than biological categorization. Eckert's chapter (17) takes up this issue as a general challenge to variationist sociolinguistics. We have chosen this paper to end the section because Eckert invites variationists (and she herself works in the variationist tradition) to examine the sociological complexities that lie behind apparently simple social categories like age, class, sex and race. In the case of gender, Eckert explores the social structures through which women's roles and statuses have to be established, in adolescence as well as in adulthood, in relation to other women as well as men. Language may generally have a different value for women than for men, if women's reliance on *social symbols* like language to achieve their statuses is greater than men's.

NOTE

1 We have not included the short section from Cheshire's chapter that relates to girls because the female group in her study showed less differentiation of the sort the chapter highlights.

PART III: FURTHER READING

Aitchison, J. (1981) *Language Change: Progress or Decay?* (London: Fontana).

Chambers, J. K. and Trudgill, P. (1980) *Dialectology* (Cambridge: Cambridge University Press).

Dorian, N. (1981) *Language Death* (Philadelphia, PA: University of Pennsylvania Press).

Dorian, N. (1989) *Investigating Obsolence: Studies in Language Contraction and Death* (Cambridge: Cambridge University Press).

Horvath, B. (1985) *Variation in Australian English: The Sociolects of Sydney* (Cambridge: Cambridge University Press).

Labov, W. (1966) *The Social Stratification of English in New York City* (Washington, DC: Center for Applied Linguistics) [also published by Blackwell].

Labov, W. (1972a) *Language in the Inner City* (Philadelphia, PA: Pennsylvania University Press).

Labov, W. (1972b, 1978) *Sociolinguistic Patterns* (Oxford: Basil Blackwell).

Labov, W. (1994) *Principles of Linguistic Change: Internal Factors* (Oxford: Blackwell).

Macaulay, R. K. S. (1977) *Language, Social Class, and Education: A Glasgow Study* (Edinburgh: Edinburgh University Press).

Milroy, J. and Milroy, L. (eds) (1993) *Real English: The Grammar of English Dialects in the British Isles* (London: Longman).

Milroy, L. (1987) *Language and Social Networks* (second edition) (Oxford: Blackwell).

Romaine, S. (ed.) (1982) *Sociolinguistic Variation in Speech Communities* (London: Edward Arnold).

Trudgill, P. (1975) *Accent, Dialect and the School* (London: Edward Arnold).

Trudgill, P. (1983) *On Dialect* (Oxford: Blackwell).

Trudgill, P. (1986) *Dialects in Contact* (Oxford: Blackwell).

Trudgill, P. (1992) *The Dialects of England* (Oxford: Blackwell).

Trudgill, P. (ed.) (1978) *Sociolinguistic Patterns in British English* (London: Edward Arnold).

Wolfram, W. and Schiffrin, D. (eds) (1989) *Language Change and Variation* (Amsterdam/Philadelphia, PA: John Benjamins).

13 The Social Stratification of (r) in New York City Department Stores

William Labov

As this letter is but a jar of the tongue, . . . it is the most imperfect of all the consonants.

(John Walker, *Principles of English Pronunciation*, 1791)

Anyone who begins to study language in its social context immediately encounters the classic methodological problem: the means used to gather the data interfere with the data to be gathered. The primary means of obtaining a large body of reliable data on the speech of one person is the individual tape-recorded interview. Interview speech is formal speech – not by any absolute measure, but by comparison with the vernacular of everyday life. On the whole, the interview is public speech – monitored and controlled in response to the presence of an outside observer. But even within that definition, the investigator may wonder if the responses in a tape-recorded interview are not a special product of the interaction between the interviewer and the subject. One way of controlling for this is to study the subject in his own natural social context – interacting with his family or peer group (Labov, Cohen, Robins, and Lewis 1968). Another way is to observe the public use of language in everyday life apart from any interview situation – to see how people use language in context when there is no explicit observation. This chapter is an account of the systematic use of rapid and anonymous observations in a study of the sociolinguistic structure of the speech community.[1]

This chapter deals primarily with the sociolinguistic study of New York City. The main base for that study (Labov 1966) was a secondary random sample of the Lower East Side. But before the systematic study was carried out, there was an extensive series of preliminary investigations. These

Source: 'The Social Stratification of (r) in New York City Department Stores', in Labov, W. (1972) *Sociolinguistic Patterns* (Philadelphia, PA: University of Pennsylvania Press) pp. 43–54. Also published in 1978 (Oxford: Basil Blackwell).

included 70 individual interviews and a great many anonymous observations in public places. These preliminary studies led to the definition of the major phonological variables which were to be studied, including (r): the presence or absence of consonantal [r] in postvocalic position in *car, card, four, fourth,* etc. This particular variable appeared to be extraordinarily sensitive to any measure of social or stylistic stratification. On the basis of the exploratory interviews, it seemed possible to carry out an empirical test of two general notions: first, that the linguistic variable (r) is a social differentiator in all levels of New York City speech, and second, that rapid and anonymous speech events could be used as the basis for a systematic study of language. The study of (r) in New York City department stores which I will report here was conducted in November 1962 as a test of these ideas.

We can hardly consider the social distribution of language in New York City without encountering the pattern of social stratification which pervades the life of the city. This concept is analyzed in some detail in the major study of the Lower East Side; here we may briefly consider the definition given by Bernard Barber: social stratification is the product of social differentiation and social evaluation (1957: 1–3). The use of this term does not imply any specific type of class or caste, but simply that the normal workings of society have produced systematic differences between certain institutions or people, and that these differentiated forms have been ranked in status or prestige by general agreement.

We begin with the general hypothesis suggested by exploratory interviews: *if any two subgroups of New York City speakers are ranked in a scale of social stratification, then they will be ranked in the same order by their differential use of (r).*

It would be easy to test this hypothesis by comparing occupational groups, which are among the most important indexes of social stratification. We could, for example, take a group of lawyers, a group of file clerks, and a group of janitors. But this would hardly go beyond the indications of the exploratory interviews, and such an extreme example of differentiation would not provide a very exacting test of the hypothesis. It should be possible to show that the hypothesis is so general, and the differential use of (r) pervades New York City so thoroughly, that fine social differences will be reflected in the index as well as gross ones.

It therefore seemed best to construct a very severe test by finding a subtle case of stratification within a single occupational group: in this case, the sales people of large department stores in Manhattan. If we select three large department stores, from the top, middle, and bottom of the price and fashion scale, we can expect that the customers will be socially stratified. Would we expect the sales people to show a comparable stratification? Such a position would depend upon two correlations: between the status ranking of the stores and the ranking of parallel jobs in the three stores; and between the jobs and the behavior of the persons who hold those jobs. These are not unreasonable assumptions. C. Wright Mills points out that salesgirls in large department stores tend to borrow prestige from their customers, or at least make an effort in that direction.[2] It appears that a person's own occupation is more closely correlated with his linguistic behavior – for those working actively – than any other single social characteristic. The evidence presented here indicates that the stores are objectively differentiated in a fixed order, and that jobs in these stores are evaluated by employees in that order. Since the product of social differentiation and evaluation, no matter how minor, is social stratification of the employees in the three stores, the hypothesis will predict the following result: salespeople in the highest-ranked store will have the highest values of (r); those in the middle-ranked store will have intermediate values of (r); and those in the lowest-ranked store will show the lowest values. If this result holds true, the hypothesis will have received confirmation in proportion to the severity of the test.

The three stores which were selected are Saks Fifth Avenue, Macy's, and S. Klein. The differential ranking of these stores may be illustrated in many ways. Their locations are one important point:

Highest-ranking: Saks Fifth Avenue
at 50th St and 5th Ave., near the center of the high fashion shopping district, along with other high-prestige stores such as Bonwit Teller, Henri Bendel, Lord and Taylor

Middle-ranking: Macy's
Herald Square, 34th St and Sixth Ave., near the garment district, along with Gimbels and Saks-34th St, other middle-range stores in price and prestige.

Lowest-ranking: S. Klein
Union Square, 14th St and Broadway, not far from the Lower East Side.

The advertising and price policies of the stores are very clearly stratified. Perhaps no other element of class behavior is so sharply differentiated in New York City as that of the newspaper which people read; many surveys have shown that the *Daily News* is the paper read first and foremost by working-class people, while the *New York Times* draws its readership from the middle-class.[3] These two newspapers were examined for the advertising copy in October 24–27, 1962: Saks and Macy's advertised in the *New York Times*, where Kleins was represented only by a very small item; in the *News*, however, Saks does not appear at all, while both Macy's and Kleins are heavy advertisers.

No. of pages of advertising October 24–27, 1962

	NY Times	*Daily News*
Saks	2	0
Macy's	2	15
S. Klein	1/4	10

We may also consider the prices of the goods advertised during those four days. Since Saks usually does not list prices, we can only compare prices for all three stores on one item: women's coats. Saks: $90, Macy's: $79.95, Kleins: $23. On four items, we can compare Kleins and Macy's:

	Macy's	*S. Klein*
dresses	$14.95	$5.00
girls' coats	$16.99	$12.00
stockings	$0.89	$0.45
men's suits	$49.95–$64.95	$26.00–$66.00

The emphasis on prices is also different. Saks either does not mention prices, or buries the figure in small type at the foot of the page. Macy's features the prices in large type, but often adds the slogan, 'You get more than low prices.' Kleins, on the other hand, is often content to let the prices speak for themselves. The form of the prices is also different: Saks gives prices in round figures, such as $120; Macy's always shows a few cents off the dollar: $49.95; Kleins usually prices its goods in round numbers, and adds the retail price which is always much higher, and shown in Macy's style: '$23.00, marked down from $49.95.'

The physical plant of the stores also serves to differentiate them. Saks is the most spacious, especially on the upper floors, with the least amount of goods displayed. Many of the floors are carpeted, and on some of them, a receptionist is stationed to greet the customers. Kleins, at the other extreme, is a maze of annexes, sloping concrete floors, low ceilings; it has the maximum amount of goods displayed at the least possible expense.

The principal stratifying effect upon the employees is the prestige of the store, and the working conditions. Wages do not stratify the employees in the same order. On the contrary, there is every indication that high-prestige stores such as Saks pay lower wages than Macy's.

Saks is a non-union store, and the general wage structure is not a matter of public record. However, conversations with a number of men and women who have worked in New York department stores, including Saks and

Macy's, show general agreement on the direction of the wage differential.[4] Some of the incidents reflect a willingness of sales people to accept much lower wages from the store with greater prestige. The executives of the prestige stores pay a great deal of attention to employee relations, and take many unusual measures to ensure that the sales people feel that they share in the general prestige of the store.[5] One of the Lower East Side informants who worked at Saks was chiefly impressed with the fact that she could buy Saks clothes at a 25 percent discount. A similar concession from a lower-prestige store would have been of little interest to her.

From the point of view of Macy's employees, a job in Kleins is well below the horizon. Working conditions and wages are generally considered to be worse, and the prestige of Kleins is very low indeed. As we will see, the ethnic composition of the store employees reflects these differences quite accurately.

A socioeconomic index which ranked New Yorkers on occupation would show the employees of the three stores at the same level; an income scale would probably find Macy's employees somewhat higher than the others; education is the only objective scale which might differentiate the groups in the same order as the prestige of the stores, though there is no evidence on this point. However, the working conditions of sales jobs in the three stores stratify them in the order: Saks, Macy's, Kleins; the prestige of the stores leads to a social evaluation of these jobs in the same order. Thus the two aspects of social stratification – differentiation and evaluation – are to be seen in the relations of the three stores and their employees.

The normal approach to a survey of department-store employees requires that one enumerate the sales people of each store, draw random samples in each store, make appointments to speak with each employee at home, interview the respondents, then segregate the native New Yorkers, analyze and resample the nonrespondents, and so on. This is an expensive and time-consuming procedure, but for most purposes there is no short cut which will give accurate and reliable results. In this case, a simpler method which relies upon the extreme generality of the linguistic behavior of the subjects was used to gather a very limited type of data. This method is dependent upon the systematic sampling of casual and anonymous speech events. Applied in a poorly defined environment, such a method is open to many biases and it would be difficult to say what population had been studied. In this case, our population is well-defined as the sales people (or more generally, any employee whose speech might be heard by a customer) in three specific stores at a specific time. The result will be a view of the role that speech would play in the overall social imprint of the employees upon the customer. It is surprising that this simple and economical approach achieves results with a high degree of consistency and regularity, and allows us to test the original hypothesis in a number of subtle ways.

THE METHOD

The application of the study of casual and anonymous speech events to the department-store situation was relatively simple. The interviewer approached the informant in the role of a customer asking for directions to a particular department. The department was one which was located on the fourth floor. When the interviewer asked, 'Excuse me, where are the women's shoes?' the answer would normally be, 'Fourth floor.'

The interviewer then leaned forward and said, 'Excuse me?' He would usually then obtain another utterance, '*Fourth floor*,' spoken in careful style under emphatic stress.[6]

The interviewer would then move along the aisle of the store to a point immediately beyond the informant's view, and make a written note of the data. The following independent variables were included:

the store
floor within the store[7]
sex
age (estimated in units of five years)
occupation (floorwalker, sales, cashier, stockboy)
race
foreign or regional accent, if any

The dependent variable is the use of (r) in four occurrences:

casual: fou_r_th floo_r_
emphatic: *fou_r_th floo_r_*

Thus we have preconsonantal and final position, in both casual and emphatic styles of speech. In addition, all other uses of (r) by the informant were noted, from remarks overheard or contained in the interview. For each plainly constricted value of the variable, (r-1) was entered; for unconstricted schwa, lengthened vowel, or no representation, (r-0) was entered. Doubtful cases or partial constriction were symbolized *d* and were not used in the final tabulation.

Also noted were instances of affricates or stops used in the word *fourth* for the final consonant, and any other examples of nonstandard (th) variants used by the speaker.

This method of interviewing was applied in each aisle on the floor as many times as possible before the spacing of the informants became so close that it was noticed that the same question had been asked before. Each floor of the store was investigated in the same way. On the fourth floor, the form of the question was necessarily different:

'Excuse me, what floor is this?'

Following this method, 68 interviews were obtained in Saks, 125 in Macy's, and 71 in Kleins. Total interviewing time for the 264 subjects was approximately 6.5 hours.

At this point, we might consider the nature of these 264 interviews in more general terms. They were speech events which had entirely different social significance for the two participants. As far as the informant was concerned, the exchange was a normal salesman–customer interaction, almost below the level of conscious attention, in which relations of the speakers were so casual an anonymous that they may hardly have been said to have met. This tenuous relationship was the minimum intrusion upon the behavior of the subject; language and the use of language never appeared at all.

From the point of view of the interviewer, the exchange was a systematic elicitation of the exact forms required, in the desired context, the desired order, and with the desired contrast of style.

OVERALL STRATIFICATION OF (r)

The results of the study showed clear and consistent stratification of (r) in the three stores. In Figure 13.1, the use of (r) by employees of Saks, Macy's and Kleins is compared by means of a bar graph. Since the data for most informants consist of only four items, we will not use a continuous numerical index for (r), but rather divide all informants into three categories.

all (r-1): those whose records show only (r-1) and no (r-0)
some (r-1): those whose records show at least one (r-1) and one (r-0)
no (r-1): those whose records showed only (r-0)

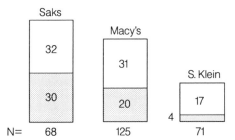

Figure 13.1:   Overall stratification of (r) by store. Shaded area = % all (r − 1); unshanded area = % some (r − 1); % no (r − 1) not shown. N = total number of cases

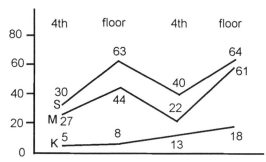

Figure 13.2: Percentage of all (r − 1) by store for four positions
(S = Saks, M = Macy's, K = Kleins)

From Figure 13.1 we see that a total of 62 percent of Saks employees, 51 percent of Macy's, and 20 percent of Kleins used all or some (r-1). The stratification is even sharper for the percentages of all (r-1). As the hypothesis predicted, the groups are ranked by their differential use of (r-1) in the same order as their stratification by extralinguistic factors.

Next, we may wish to examine the distribution of (r) in each of the four standard positions. Figure 13.2 shows this type of display, where once again, the stores are differentiated in the same order, and for each position. There is a considerable difference between Macy's and Kleins at each position, but the difference between Macy's and Saks varies. In emphatic pronunciation of the final (r), Macy's employees come very close to the mark set by Saks. It would seem that r-pronunciation is the norm at which a majority of Macy employees aim, yet not the one they use most often. In Saks, we see a shift between casual and emphatic pronunciation, but it is much less marked. In other words, Saks employees have more *security* in a linguistic sense.

The fact that the figures for (r-1) at Kleins are low should not obscure the fact that Kleins employees also participate in the same pattern of stylistic variation of (r) as the other stores. The percentage of r-pronunciation rises at Kleins from 5 to 18 percent as the context becomes more emphatic: a much greater rise in percentage than in the other stores, and a more regular increase as well. It will be important to bear in mind that this attitude – that (r-1) is the most appropriate pronunciation for emphatic speech – is shared by at least some speakers in all three stores.

Table 13.1 shows the data in detail, with the number of instances obtained for each of the four positions of (r), for each store. It may be noted that the number of occurrences in the second pronunciation of *four* is considerably reduced, primarily as a result of some speakers' tendency to answer a second time, 'Fourth.'

Table 13.1:　Detailed distribution of (r) by store and word position

(r)	Saks				Macy's				S. Klein			
	Casual 4th floor		Emphatic 4th floor		Casual 4th floor		Emphatic 4th floor		Casual 4th floor		Emphatic 4th floor	
(r-1)	17	31	16	21	33	48	13	31	3	5	6	7
(r-0)	39	18	24	12	81	62	48	20	63	59	40	33
d	4	5	4	4	0	3	1	0	1	1	3	3
No data*	8	14	24	31	11	12	63	74	4	6	22	28
Total no.	68	68	68	68	125	125	125	125	71	71	71	71

*The 'no data' category for Macy's shows relatively high values under the emphatic category. This discrepancy is due to the fact that the procedure for requesting repetition was not standardized in the investigation of the ground floor at Macy's, and values for emphatic response were not regularly obtained. The effects of this loss are checked in Table 13.2, where only complete responses are compared.

Since the numbers in the fourth position are somewhat smaller than the second, it might be suspected that those who use [r] in Saks and Macy's tend to give fuller responses, thus giving rise to a spurious impression of increase in (r) values in those positions. We can check this point by comparing only those who gave a complete response. Their responses can be symbolized by a four-digit number, representing the pronunciation in each of the four positions respectively (see Table 13.2).

Thus we see that the pattern of differential ranking in the use of (r) is preserved in this subgroup of complete responses, and omission of the final 'floor' by some respondents was not a factor in this pattern.

Table 13.2:　Distribution of (r) for complete responses

(r)		% of total responses in		
		Saks	Macy's	S. Klein
All (r-1)	1 1 1 1	24	22	6
Some (r-1)	0 1 1 1	46	37	12
	0 0 1 1			
	0 1 0 1 etc.			
No (r-1)	0 0 0 0	30	41	82
		100	100	100
N =		33	48	34

NOTES

1   I am indebted to Frank Anshen and Marvin Maverick Harris for reference to illuminating replications of this study (Allen 1968, Harris 1968).

2   C. Wright Mills, *White Collar* (New York: Oxford University Press, 1956), p. 173. See also p. 243: 'The tendency of white-collar people to borrow status from higher elements is so strong that it has carried over to all social contacts and features of the work-place. Salespeople in department stores... frequently attempt, although often unsuccessfully, to borrow prestige from their contact with customers, and to cash it in among work colleagues as well as friends off the job. In the big city the girl who works on 34th Street cannot successfully claim as much prestige as the one who works on Fifth Avenue or 57th Street.'

3   This statement is fully confirmed by answers to a question on newspaper readership in the Mobilization for Youth Survey of the Lower East Side. The readership of the *Daily News* and *Daily Mirror* (now defunct) on the one hand, and the *New York Times* and *Herald Tribune* (now defunct) on the other hand is almost complementary in distribution by social class.

4   Macy's sales employees are represented by a strong labor union, while Saks is not unionized. One former Macy's employee considered it a matter of common knowledge that Saks wages were lower than Macy's, and that the prestige of the store helped to maintain its nonunion position. Bonuses and other increments are said to enter into the picture. It appears that it is more difficult for a young girl to get a job at Saks than at Macy's. Thus Saks has more leeway in hiring policies, and the tendency of the store officials to select girls who speak in a certain way will play a part in the stratification of language, as well as the adjustment made by the employees to their situation. Both influences converge to produce stratification.

5   A former Macy's employee told me of an incident that occurred shortly before Christmas several years ago. As she was shopping in Lord and Taylor's, she saw the president of the company making the rounds of every aisle and shaking hands with every employee. When she told her fellow employees at Macy's about this scene, the most common remark was, 'How else do you get someone to work for that kind of money?' One can say that not only do the employees of higher-status stores borrow prestige from their employer – it is also deliberately loaned to them.

6   The interviewer in all cases was myself. I was dressed in middle-class style, with jacket, white shirt and tie, and used my normal pronunciation as a college-educated native of New Jersey (r-pronouncing).

7   Notes were also made on the department in which the employee was located, but the numbers for individual departments are not large enough to allow comparison.

REFERENCES

Allen, P. (1968) '/r/ Variable in the Speech of New Yorkers in Department Stores'. Unpublished research paper (SUNY: Stony Brook).

Barber, B. (1957) *Social Stratification* (New York: Harcourt, Brace).

Labov, W. (1966) *The Social Stratification of English in New York City* (Washington, DC: Center for Applied Linguistics).

Labov, W., Cohen, P., Robins, C. and Lewis. J. (1968) 'A Study of the Non-standard English of Negro and Puerto Rican Speakers in New York City', Final Report, Cooperative Research Project 3288, 2 vols (Philadelphia, PA: US Regional Survey, 204 N. 35th St Philadelphia 19104).

Walker, J. (1791) *Principles of English Pronunciation.*

14   The Social Differentiation of English in Norwich

Peter Trudgill

MEASUREMENT OF CO-VARIATION

One of the chief aims of this work is to investigate the co-variation of phonological and sociological variables. In order to measure this type of correlation, a record was first taken of each occurrence of all the variables in the four contextual styles for each informant. Index scores for each informant in each style could then be developed, and, subsequently, the mean index score for each social group calculated. [The following abbreviations are used in this chapter in relation to the social and stylistic stratification of the variable (ng): LWC – lower working-class; MWC – middle working-class; UWC – upper working-class; LMC – lower middle-class; MMC – middle middle-class; WLS – word lists; RPS – reading passages; FS – formal style; CS – casual style – Eds.] By means of these scores we are able: (i) to investigate the nature of the correlation between realisations of phonological variables and social class, social context, and sex; (ii) to discover which variables are subject to social class differentiation and which to stylistic variation; and (iii) to find out which variables are most important in signalling the social context of some linguistic interaction, or the social class of a speaker.

The methods we are using of calculating and portraying individual and group phonological indices were initially developed by Labov (1966). In some respects, however, the present work represents a development of Labov's techniques in that use is made of phonological indices for investigating problems of surface phonemic contrast, and for studying aspects of what is usually termed 'phonological space'. ...

Let us take as an example the phonological variable (ng), the pronunciation of the suffix -*ing*. This is well known as a variable in many different types of English, and seems likely to provide a good example of social class and stylistic differentiation.

Source: 'The Co-variation of Phonological Variables with Social Parameters', in Trudgill, P. (1974) *The Social Differentiation of English in Norwich* (Cambridge: Cambridge University Press) pp. 90–5.

THE VARIABLE (ng)

Table 14.1 shows the average (ng) index scores for the five social classes in each of the four contextual styles: Word List Style (WLS), Reading Passage Style (RPS), Formal Speech (FS), and Casual Speech (CS). Tests of significance have not been carried out on this, or on the data for the other variables. As Labov (1970) has said concerning other sociolinguistic data: 'It is immediately obvious to the sophisticated statistician that tests of significance are irrelevant... even if a particular case were below the level of significance, the convergence of so many independent events carries us to a level of confidence which is unknown in most social or psychological research.' Table 14.1 demonstrates that:

(i)   the Norwich questionnaire has in fact been successful in eliciting four hierarchically ordered and discrete contextual styles, since, for each class, the scores rise consistently from WLS to CS;

(ii)   the social class index has provided a successful basis for the establishment of discrete social classes as these classes are reflected in their linguistic behaviour, since, for each style, the scores rise consistently from MMC to LWC;

(iii) the method of calculating index scores for phonological variables is a successful one and is likely to be useful in the study of Norwich English; and

(iv)   the phonological variable (ng) is involved in a considerable amount of social class and contextual variation, with scores ranging over the whole scale from 000 to 100.

The information given in Table 14.1 is more clearly portrayed in Figure 14.1 Index scores, from 000 representing consistent use of [n], to 100 representing consistent use of [ŋ], are plotted along the ordinate. The four contextual styles, from WLS, the most formal, to CS, the most informal, are shown along the abscissa. The lines on the graph connect scores obtained by each of the five social classes in the four contextual styles.

Table 14.1:   (ng) index scores by class and style

		Style			
Class		WLS	RPS	FS	CS
I	MMC	000	000	003	028
II	LMC	000	010	015	042
III	UWC	005	015	074	087
IV	MWC	023	044	088	095
V	LWC	029	066	098	100

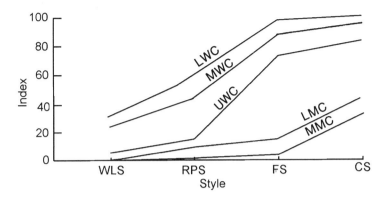

Figure 14.1:   Variable (ng) by class and style

The stylistic variation of this variable is portrayed in the consistent downward slope of the lines from right to left across the graph, representing an increase in [ŋ] endings as we move from everyday speech to more formal styles. The variable (ng), it can be seen, is a very good indicator of social context, with scores ranging, as we have already noted, from 000 (MMC and LMC in WLS; MMC in RPS) to 100 (LWC in CS). Note that stylistic variation is greatest in the case of the UWC, whose range is from 005 to 087, and whose line on the graph consequently has the steepest gradient. The greater awareness of UWC speakers of the social significance of linguistic variables (shown in Figure 14.1) can be explained by the 'borderline' nature of their social position (see Trudgill 1974, chapter 5). The linguistic insecurity revealed here in the large amount of UWC stylistic variation for (ng) is clearly part of the same tendency.

The social class differentiation of (ng) is, of course, shown on the graph by the clear separation of the lines connecting the scores for each class, and by the hierarchical ordering of these lines, LWC–MMC. The amount of differentiation can be gauged from the spatial separation of the lines on the graph. Thus the greatest amount of differentiation occurs in FS, where the two MC groups appear to have the ability to control (ng) forms to a level nearer that of the more formal styles, whereas the three WC groups have scores which more closely approach their CS level. Note that in CS, which we can assume to be reasonably representative of normal, everyday speech in familiar social environments, the three WC groups show only a small amount of differentiation one from the other, 087–100. This is also true of the two MC groups, 028–042. There is, on the other hand, a very significant difference between the (ng) level of the WC as a whole and that of the MC. This underlines once again the importance of this particular social division in the social structure.

We have shown, then, that the proportion of [n] to [ŋ] suffixes that occurs in speech is a function of the social class of the speaker and of the social context in which he is speaking. Moreover, although (ng) quite clearly differentiates between all five social groups, it is most important in distinguishing MC from WC speakers. UWC speakers have the greatest amount of stylistic variation, and MMC speakers the smallest, although it is instructive to note that even this class uses an average of 28 per cent of forms with [n] in CS.

Sex Differentiation of (ng)

Fischer, in his study of this variable in an American locality (1958), found that males used a higher percentage of [n] forms than females. Generally speaking, this is also the case in Norwich, as Table 14.2 shows. In seventeen cases out of twenty, male scores are greater than or equal to corresponding female scores.[1] We can therefore say that a high (ng) index is typical of male speakers as well as of WC speakers. This link between the linguistic characteristics of WC speakers and male speakers is a common one. Almost all the Norwich variables have the same kind of pattern as that shown in Table 14.2, with women having lower index scores than men. This is a fact which is not, on the face of it, particularly surprising, but one that is at the same time in need of some explanation. There would appear to be two interconnected explanatory factors:

1. Women in our society are more status-conscious than men, generally speaking, and are therefore more aware of the social significance of linguistic variables. There are probably two main reasons for this:

Table 14.2:   (ng) indices by class, style and sex

			Style		
Class		*WLS*	*RPS*	*FS*	*CS*
MMC	M	000	000	004	031
	F	000	000	000	000
LMC	M	000	020	027	017
	F	000	000	003	067
UWC	M	000	018	081	095
	F	011	013	068	077
MWC	M	024	043	091	097
	F	020	046	081	088
LWC	M	066	100	100	100
	F	017	054	097	100

Table 14.3: Sample of ten informants: average scores, word-internal and word-final (t) by style

(t)	WLS	RPS	FS	CS
Word-internal, e.g. *better*	029	052	113	134
Word-final, e.g. *bet*	028	089	151	161

(i) The social position of women in our society is less secure than that of men, and, generally speaking, subordinate to that of men. It is therefore more necessary for women to secure and signal their social status linguistically and in other ways, and they are more aware of the importance of this type of signal.

(ii) Men in our society can be rated socially by their occupation, their earning power, and perhaps by their other abilities: in other words, by what they *do*. For the most part, however, this is not possible for women, who have generally to be rated on how they *appear*. Since they cannot be rated socially by their occupation, by what other people know about what they do in life, other signals of status, including speech, are correspondingly more important. This last point is perhaps the most important.

2. The second, related, factor is that WC speech, like many other aspects of WC culture, has, in our society, connotations of masculinity, since it is associated with the roughness and toughness supposedly character-istic of WC life, which are, to a certain extent, considered to be desirable masculine attributes. They are not, on the other hand, considered to be desirable feminine characteristics. On the contrary, refinement and sophistication are much preferred.

This discussion is of course necessarily at a rather simple level, but it is clear that we have reflected in these phonological indices part of the value system of our culture as a whole. From the point of view of linguistic theory, this means that, as far as linguistic change 'from below' is concerned, we can expect men to be in the vanguard. Changes 'from above', on the other hand, are more likely to be led by women.[2] The type of sex differentiation shown in Table 14.2 is, in any case, usual. Only a reversal of this pattern, or a large increase in the normal type of male/female differentiation can be considered to be significantly unusual in any way.

NOTES

1 The low score obtained by male LMC speakers in CS requires some comment. The score is clearly unrepresentative, being lower than both the RPS and

FS scores and the male MMC score, and is due to the fact that only a very small number of instances of this variable happened to be obtained for this group in CS.

2   Labov's terms 'change from below' and 'change from above' refer respectively to changes from below and above the level of conscious awareness. Usually, however, changes from above involve the downward dissemination of prestige features, i.e. they are social changes 'from above' as well. Changes from below, moreover, very often start among lower class groups (see Trudgill, 1972).

REFERENCES

Fischer, J. L. (1958) 'Social Influences on the Choice of a Linguistic Variant', *Word*, **XIV**, 47–56.

Labov, W. (1966) *The Social Stratification of English in New York City* (Washington, DC: Center for Applied Linguistics).

Labov, W. (1970) 'The Study of Language in its Social Context', *Studium Generale*, **XXIII**, 30–87.

Trudgill, P. J. (1972) 'Sex Covert Prestige and Linguistic Change in the Urban British English of Norwich', *Language in Society*, **I**, 179–95.

Trudgill, P. J. (1974) *The Social Differentiation of English in Norwich* (Cambridge: Cambridge University Press).

15 Linguistic Variation and Social Function

Jenny Cheshire

INTRODUCTION

The fact that linguistic variation is correlated with a wide range of sociological characteristics of speakers has been extensively documented over the last 15 years by the many studies that have been inspired by the work of William Labov. It is well established, for example, that the frequency with which speakers use non-standard linguistic features is correlated with their socioeconomic class. More recently, studies involving speakers from a single socioeconomic class have been able to reveal some of the more subtle aspects of sociolinguistic variation. It has been found, for example, that the frequency of use of non-standard phonological features in Belfast English is correlated with the type of social network in which speakers are involved (see Milroy and Margrain 1980). This chapter will show that the frequency with which adolescent speakers use many non-standard morphological and syntactic features of the variety of English spoken in the town of Reading, in Berkshire, is correlated with the extent to which they adhere to the norms of the vernacular culture. It will also show that linguistic variables often fulfil different social and semantic functions for the speakers who use them.

The chapter will consider nine non-standard features of Reading English:

1. the present tense suffix with non-third-person singular subjects
    e.g. we *goes* shopping on Saturdays
2. *has* with non-third-person singular subjects
    e.g. we *has* a little fire, keeps us warm
3. *was* with plural subjects (and singular *you*)
    e.g. you *was* outside
4. multiple negation
    e.g. I'm *not* going *nowhere*

Source: 'Linguistic Variation and Social Function', in Suzanne Romaine (ed.) (1982) *Sociolinguistic Variation in Speech Communities* (London: Edward Arnold) pp. 153–75.

5. negative past tense *never*, used for standard English *didn't*
    e.g. I *never* done it, it was him
6   *what* used for standard English *who, whom, which,* and *that*
    e.g. there's a knob *what* you turn
         are you the boy *what's* just come?
7   auxiliary *do* with third-person singular subjects
    e.g. how much *do* he want for it?
8   past tense *come*
    e.g. I *come* down here yesterday
9   *ain't*, used for negative present tense forms of *be* and *have*, with all
    subjects
    e.g. I *ain't* going
         I *ain't* got any

Many, though not all, of these features function as markers of vernacular loyalty for adolescent speakers in Reading, though some are more sensitive markers than others. *Ain't*, in particular, is able overtly to symbolize some of the important values of the vernacular culture. Furthermore, some features are markers of loyalty to the vernacular culture for adolescent boys but not for adolescent girls, and vice-versa.

THE DATA

The analysis is based on the spontaneous, natural speech of three groups of adolescents, recorded by the method of long-term participant-observation in adventure playgrounds in Reading. The aim was to record speech that was as close as possible to the vernacular, or most informal style, of the speakers. Thirteen boys and twelve girls [the section of Cheshire's original chapter which discussed the speech of girls has been omitted in this version for reasons of space, not because we deem female talk as less important than that of males – *Eds.*] were recorded over a period of about eight months.

Some of the speakers were subsequently recorded at school, by their teacher, with two or three of their friends. The fieldwork procedures are discussed in detail in Cheshire 1978.

THE VERNACULAR CULTURE INDEX

Labov (1966) maintains that the use of non-standard features is controlled by the norms of the vernacular subculture, whilst the use of standard English features is controlled by the overt norms of the mainstream culture in society. Any analysis of variation in the occurrence of non-standard features needs to take this into account, for it means that an adequate sample of non-standard forms is more likely to be found where speakers conform more closely to vernacular norms than to the overt norms of the dominant mainstream culture. The speakers who were chosen for the present study were children who often met at the adventure playgrounds when they should have been at school, and the boys, in particular, were members of a very well-defined subculture. In many respects this culture resembled a delinquent subculture (as defined, for example, by Andry 1960; Cohen 1955; Downes 1966; Willmott 1966 and many other writers). Many of the boys' activities, for example, centred around what Miller (1958) calls the 'cultural foci' of *trouble, excitement, toughness, fate, autonomy* and *smartness* (in the American English sense of 'outsmarting').

Since the vernacular culture was in this case very clearly defined, it was possible to isolate a small number of indicators that could be used to construct a 'vernacular culture index', in the same way that socioeconomic indices are constructed. It seemed reasonable to assume that those aspects of the peer-group culture that were sources of prestige for group members and that were frequent topics of conversation were of central importance within the culture. Six factors that met these requirements were selected. Four of these reflect the norms of trouble and excitement; three directly, and one more indirectly. *Skill at fighting, the carrying of a weapon* and *participation in minor criminal activities*, such as shoplifting, arson, and vandalism, are clearly connected with trouble and excitement. Though interrelated, they were treated as separate indicators because not all boys took part in all the activities to the same extent. The job that the boys hoped to have when they left school was also included as a separate indicator, for the same reason. Again, acceptable jobs reflect the norms of trouble and excitement, though perhaps more indirectly here, and the job that the boys hoped to have when they left school (or, in a few cases, that they already had) was an important contributing factor to the opinion that they formed of themselves and of other group members. Some jobs that were acceptable were slaughterer, lorry driver, motor mechanic, and soldier; jobs that were unacceptable were mostly white-collar jobs. A fifth indicator was 'style': the extent to which dress and hairstyle were important to speakers. Many writers stress the importance of style as a symbolic value within adolescent subcultures (see, for example, Cohen 1972; Clarke 1973), and for many of the boys in the group it was a frequent topic of conversation.

Finally, a measure of 'swearing' was included in the index, since this appeared to be an extremely important symbol of vernacular identity for both boys and girls. Swearing is, of course , a linguistic feature, but this does not affect its use as an indicator here, since it involves only a few lexical items which could not be marked for any of the non-standard features of Reading English.

The behaviour of the boys with regard to each of these factors could be shown on a Guttman scale. The coefficient of reproductability was 0.97, which confirms that the data are scalable (see Pelto 1970, Appendix B).

The boys were then given a score for each of the indicators, and were divided into four groups on the basis of their total score. Group 1 consists of those boys who can be considered to adhere most closely to the norms of the vernacular culture, whilst group 4 consists of boys who do not adhere closely to vernacular norms. Groups 2 and 3 are intermediate in their adherence, with group 2 adhering more closely than group 3.

LINGUISTIC MARKERS OF ADHERENCE TO THE VERNACULAR CULTURE

Table 15.1 shows the frequency of occurrence of the nine non-standard features in the speech of the four groups of boys.

The features are arranged into three classes, which reflect the extent to which they mark adherence to the vernacular culture. Class A contains four features whose frequency is very finely linked to the vernacular culture index of the speakers. The most sensitive indicator is the non-standard present-tense suffix, which occurs very frequently in the speech of those boys who are most firmly immersed in the vernacular culture (group 1), progressively less frequently in the speech of groups 2 and 3, and rather

Table 15.1: Adherence to vernacular culture and frequency of occurrence of non-standard forms

		Group 1	*Group 2*	*Group 3*	*Group 4*
Class A	non-standard -*s*	77.36	54.03	36.57	21.21
	non-standard *has*	66.67	50.00	41.65	(33.33)
	non-standard *was*	90.32	89.74	83.33	75.00
	negative concord	100.00	85.71	83.33	71.43
Class B	non-standard *never*	64.71	41.67	45.45	37.50
	non-standard *what*	92.31	7.69	33.33	0.00
Class C	non-standard aux. *do*	58.33	37.50	83.33	—
	non-standard *come*	100.00	100.00	100.00	(100.00)
	ain't = aux *have*	78.26	64.52	80.00	(100.00)
	ain't = aux *be*	58.82	72.22	80.00	(100.00)
	ain't = copule	100.00	76.19	56.52	75.00

Note: Bracketed figures indicate that the number of occurrences of the variable is low, and that the indices may not, therefore, be reliable. Following Labov (1970) less than five occurrences was considered to be too low for reliability.

infrequently in the speech of boys who are only loosely involved in the culture (group 4). This feature, then, functions as a powerful marker of vernacular loyalty.

The features in Class B (non-standard *never* and non-standard *what*) also function as markers of vernacular loyalty, but they are less sensitive markers than the features in Class A. Significant variation occurs only between speakers in Group 1 and speakers in Group 4, in other words, between the boys who adhere most closely to the vernacular culture, and the boys who adhere least closely. This type of sociolinguistic variation is not unusual: Policansky (1980) reports similar behaviour with subject-verb concord in Belfast English, where significant variation is found only between speakers at the extreme ends of the social network scale (cf. also Jahangiri and Hudson 1982).

The fact that there is some correlation between the vernacular culture index and the frequency of use of Group B features can be clearly seen if the speakers in Groups 2 and 3 are amalgamated into a single group.

Table 15.2 shows that non-standard *never* and non-standard *what* now show regular patterns of variation. These features, then, do function as markers of vernacular loyalty. But they are less sensitive markers than the features in Class A, showing regular patterning only with rather broad groupings of speakers.

Features in class C, on the other hand, do not show any correlation with the speakers' vernacular culture index. For the most part, figures are completely irregular. All these features, however, are involved in other, more complex, kinds of sociolinguistic variation, and this could explain why they do not function as straightforward markers of vernacular loyalty. There is convincing evidence, for example, that non-standard auxiliary *do* is undergoing a linguistic change away from an earlier dialect form towards the standard English form (see Cheshire 1978. See also Aitchison, 1981, for some interesting ideas concerning the mechanism of the change). Some forms of *ain't* appear to function as a direct marker of a vernacular norm, as we will see. We will also see that the use of non-standard *come* bears an interesting relation to the sex of speakers: it functions as a marker of vernacular loyalty for adolescent girls, but for boys it is an invariant feature, occurring 100 per cent of the time in their speech, irrespective of the extent to which they adhere to the vernacular culture.

Table 15.2: Frequency indices of group 1, groups 2 and 3, and group 4

	Group 1	Groups 2 & 3	Group 4
non-standard *never*	64.71	43.00	37.50
non-standard *what*	92.31	18.00	0.00

STYLISTIC VARIATION

We will now consider what happens to the frequency of occurrence of these linguistic features when the boys are at school. The Labovian view of style shifting is that formality–informality can be considered as a linear continuum, reflecting the amount of attention that speakers give to their speech. As formality increases, the frequency of occurrence of some non-standard linguistic features decreases (see Labov 1972, Chapter 3). This approach has been questioned by a number of scholars. L. Milroy (1980) and Romaine (1980), for example, found that reading, where attention is directly focused on speech, does not consistently result in the use of fewer non-standard features. And Wolfson (Chapter 10, this volume) points out that in some situations speakers will monitor their speech carefully to ensure that they use *more* non-standard features, in order to produce an appropriately informal speech style.

The present study also found difficulties in applying the Labovian approach to the analysis of style, for the ability of some linguistic features to signal vernacular loyalty affects the frequency with which they occur in different speech styles.

The recordings made at school were clearly made in a more formal setting than the recordings made in the adventure playgrounds. The speakers were in school, where the overt norms of mainstream society are maintained (see, for example, Moss 1973), the teacher was present, the speaker knew that he was being recorded, and there had been no 'warm-up' session with the tape-recorder before the recording was made. On the other hand, the speaker did have two (at least) of his friends present. This was in an attempt to stop him 'drying up', as he may have done in a straightforward interview situation, and although the intention was to make the situation somewhat more relaxed, it nevertheless clearly represents a more formal setting than the adventure playground.

Unfortunately only eight of the thirteen boys could be recorded at school. Four boys had recently left school, and the fifth was so unpopular with the teacher that she could not be persuaded to spend extra time with him.

Table 15.3 shows the frequency of occurrence of the non-standard linguistic features in the vernacular style and in the school style of these eight speakers. We can see that those features that are sensitive markers of vernacular loyalty (class A) all occur less often in the boys' school style than in their vernacular style, though the difference in frequency is very small in the case of non-standard *was*.

Non-standard *never*, in class B, also occurs less often in the school recordings. Non-standard *what*, however, does not decrease in frequency; instead, it increases slightly in occurrence. The remaining features in the table do not decrease in frequency in the school style, either. Non-standard

Table 15.3: Stylistic variation in the frequency of occurrence of
non-standard forms

		Vernacular style	*School style*
Class A	non-standard -*s*	57.03	31.49
	non-standard *has*	46.43	35.71
	non-standard *was*	91.67	88.57
	negative concord	90.70	66.67
Class B	non-standard *never*	49.21	15.38
	non-standard *what*	50.00	54.55
Class C	non-standard *do*	—	—
	non-standard *come*	100.00	100.00
	ain't = aux. *have*	93.02	100.00
	ain't = copula	74.47	77.78

come remains invariant, and *ain't* increases in frequency by quite a large
amount. (There were no occurrences of third-person singular forms of
auxiliary *do* in the school recordings).

So far, of course, this is quite in accordance with the Labovian view of the
stylistic continuum. Labov classifies linguistic variables into 'indicators' and
'markers', which differ in that indicators show regular variation only with
sociological characteristics of speakers, whereas markers also show regular
correlation with style. We could, therefore, class the linguistic variables in
class A, together with non-standard *never*, as markers in Reading English,
and class the other variables as indicators. But this would be oversimplistic.
As we will see, there are some more complex factors involved in stylistic
variation, which only become apparent if we compare the linguistic
behaviour of individual speakers, rather than of groups of speakers.

Table 15.3 expressed the frequency of occurrence of the non-standard
features in terms of group indices; in other words, the speech of the eight
boys analysed together, as a whole. There are many practical advantages to
the analysis of the speech of groups of speakers, particularly where
morphological and syntactic variables are concerned. One advantage is that
variables may not occur frequently enough in the language of an individual
speaker for a detailed analysis to be made, whereas the language of a group
of speakers will usually provide an adequate number of occurrences of
crucial forms (cf. also the discussion in J. Milroy 1982).

The school recordings consisted of only about half an hour of speech for
each boy. This did not provide enough data for an analysis in terms of
individual speakers, and in most cases it did not even provide enough data for
a group analysis. There was one exception, however. Present-tense verb forms
occur very frequently in speech, so that even within a half-hour recording
there were enough forms for an analysis of their use by individual speakers to

Table 15.4: Frequency of occurrence of non-standard present tense verb forms

	Vernacular style	School style
Noddy	81.00	77.78
Ricky	70.83	34.62
Perry	71.43	54.55
Jed	45.00	0.00
Kitty	45.71	33.33
Gammy	57.14	31.75
Barney	31.58	54.17
Colin	38.46	0.00

be made. This enables us to investigate some of the more subtle aspects of sociolinguistic variation, that would be overlooked in a group analysis.

Table 15.4 shows the frequency of occurrence of non-standard present-tense verb forms in the speech of each of the eight boys, in their vernacular style and in their school style. Noddy, Ricky and Perry are Group 1 speakers, with a high vernacular culture index; Kitty, Jed and Gammy are group 2 speakers, and Barney and Colin are in group 3.

There are considerable differences in the use of the non-standard forms by the different speakers. Noddy's use of the non-standard form, for example, decreases by only 3.22 per cent in his school style, whereas the other group 1 speakers (Ricky and Perry) show a much greater decrease. Jed (a group 2 speaker) does not use the non-standard form at all in his school style, although the other group 2 speakers (Kitty and Gammy) continue to use non-standard forms, albeit with a reduced frequency. Colin, like Jed, does not use the non-standard form in school style; Barney's use of the form, on the other hand, actually increases, by quite a large amount.

Present-tense verb forms are sensitive markers of vernacular loyalty, as we have seen; and a group analysis of their occurrence in different speech styles showed that they were also sensitive to style. We saw that the feature could be classed as a marker, in the Labovian sense. Individual analyses, however, reveal that two speakers do not show the decrease in frequency that we would expect to find in their school style: Noddy, as we have seen, shows only a slight decrease, unlike the other boys in his group, and Barney's frequency actually increases. Their linguistic behaviour does not seem to be related to the vernacular culture index, for Noddy is a group 1 speaker, showing strong allegiance to the peer-group culture, whilst Barney is a group 3 speaker. One factor that could explain Noddy's behaviour is age: Noddy was only 11, whilst the other boys were aged between 13 and 16. Noddy may, therefore, have simply not yet acquired the ability to style shift. Labov (1965) suggested that children do not acquire this ability until the age of about 14, and there is some empirical evidence to support this (see Macaulay, 1977). Other recent studies, however, have found evidence of stylistic sensitivity at a rather younger age (see Reid 1978; Romaine 1975), so that we cannot conclude with any certainty that this is a relevant factor here. In any case, Barney's behaviour cannot be explained this way, for he was 15, and old enough to show some signs of stylistic sensitivity. We need to explore further, then, to discover an explanation for this irregular behaviour.

Barney was recorded with Noddy and Kitty, by their teacher. The teacher was asking them about their activities outside school, and the boys were talking about a disco that they were trying to organize. The teacher was making valiant efforts to understand the conversation, but was obviously unfamiliar with the kind of amplifying equipment and with the situation that the boys were telling him about. It is worth noting that Barney and Noddy hated school and made very derisory remarks about their teachers. Barney had only just returned to school after an absence of a whole term, and Noddy attended school only intermittently. Kitty, on the other hand, attended school more regularly – his father was very strict, and he did not dare to play truant as often as his friends did.

These factors suggest an explanation for the boys' linguistic behaviour. A great deal of insight into linguistic behaviour has been gained from recent research by social psychologists, working within the framework of speech accommodation theory. It has been shown that speakers who are favourably disposed towards each other and who are 'working towards a common goal' adjust their speech so that they each speak more like the other, whereas speakers who are not working towards a common goal may diverge in their linguistic behaviour. One way in which speech convergence is marked is the frequency of occurrence of certain linguistic variables (see Thakerar, Giles and Cheshire 1982).

An explanation along these lines gives some insight into the behaviour of Noddy, Kitty and Barney in the school situation. Kitty knows the teacher, attends school fairly regularly, and we can imagine that he accepts the constraints of the situation. As a result his speech converges towards the teacher's, and he uses fewer non-standard linguistic forms than he does normally. Noddy, on the other hand, hates school and dislikes the teacher; as a result he asserts his allegiance to the peer-group culture rather than to the school, by refusing to acknowledge the situational constraints. The frequency with which he uses the nonstandard form, therefore, does not change (or changes only slightly). Barney, who has only returned to school, asserts his total independence and hostility to the school by using more non-standard forms than he does usually. This is a very clear example of speech divergence. As we saw earlier, Barney is not closely involved in the vernacular culture, and this is reflected in his speech by a relatively low use of non-standard present tense forms. When he wants to assert his independence from the school culture, however, he is able to exploit the resources of the language system, by choosing to use a higher proportion of non-standard forms than he does usually.

Can an explanation in these terms account for the linguistic behaviour of the other boys in this study? For at least three of the boys, it seems that it can.

Ricky, Perry and Gammy were recorded together, by a teacher that they knew and liked. He had taken them on camping and fishing weekend expeditions, with some of their classmates. The conversation was initially about one of these weekends, and then moved on to racing cars and motorbikes, subjects that interested both the teacher and the boys. Speech accommodation theory would predict that in this situation the linguistic behaviour of the boys would converge towards that of their teacher (and, of course, vice-versa). This is precisely what happens – all three boys use a lower proportion of non-standard present tense forms here than they do in their vernacular speech style. The fact that they continue to use *some* non-standard forms, however, means that they are still able to show their allegiance to the vernacular subculture.

Jed and Colin behave rather differently from the other boys, for in their school recordings they do not use any non-standard forms at all. This is surprising, particularly in the case of Jed, who is a Group 2 speaker, like Kitty and Gammy. There are, however, some striking similarities between the linguistic behaviour of these two boys, and the situations in which the school recordings were made. They were recorded at different times, with a different speaker, but both recordings were made in a classroom situation, with about 20 pupils and the teacher. Both Jed and Colin participated a great deal in the discussions, partly because the teacher had purposely chosen topics on which they had strong views (football hooliganism, in Jed's case, and truancy, in Colin's case), and partly because they were encouraged to take part by the teacher. It is possible, though, that the situation was so drastically different from the situation in the adventure playground that the overall formality overrode the option of displaying linguistically their allegiance to the vernacular culture. Or perhaps the fact that no other members of the peer-group were present meant that the boys were more susceptible to the pressures of the norms of the school culture.

It seems, then, that a simple analysis in terms of the formality or informality of the situation cannot fully explain stylistic variation here. A better explanation can, perhaps, be achieved if we think in terms of situational constraints on exploiting the resources of the linguistic system. The non-standard present tense suffix is a powerful indicator of vernacular loyalty, and in some cases this function overrides other situational constraints on linguistic behaviour (as in the speech of Noddy and Barney, for example). In other cases, (as with Jed and Colin), the situational constraints exclude the possibility of using the feature in this way. ...

THE DIRECT REFLECTION OF VERNACULAR NORMS

Non-standard features can sometimes reflect vernacular norms in a more direct way; not just in terms of the *frequency* with which different speakers use the non-standard forms, but also in terms of the specific *form* of a variable that speakers choose to use.

For example, *ain't* has a number of different phonetic realizations in the speech of the adolescent groups. These include [ɪnt], [ænt] and [eɪnt], and can be divided into two main groups – those approximating to *ain't*, and those approximating to *in't*. It is reasonable to expect that [ɪnt] would correspond to standard English *isn't*. This is not the case, however: [ɪnt] forms are used with all subjects, and they are used when the verb is auxiliary *have*, as well as when it is *be*.

The use of *ain't* forms rather than the corresponding standard English forms is subject to a linguistic constraint in Reading English: *ain't* occurs more often in a tag question than it does in any other syntactic environment. The usual function of tag questions is to seek confirmation or corroboration from the hearer for the proposition expressed in the main sentence (see Stockwell, Schachter and Partee 1973). Some tag questions, however, are used by the adolescent groups in a way that does not seek confirmation, but that expresses instead feelings of aggression and assertion. These tags do not require an answer from the hearer, and in most cases the hearer would be unable to provide one.

An example can be found in the interchange below. The boys were going to be taken on a camping weekend by the social worker who was in charge of the adventure playground, and all boys aged 16 and over were supposed to help put up the tents. I was having trouble understanding whether Roger was going on the trip or not, and he was getting impatient:

1 *Jenny*: Aren't you going to help, though?
2 *Roger*: No, I ain't going. I ain't going to help. Bugger that!
3 *Jenny*: Are you staying here?
4 *Roger*: Eh?
5 *Jenny*: Are you staying here?
6 *Colin*: No, he's going camping.
7 *Roger*: No, I'm going, mate, *in I*?
8 *Jenny*: You're going, but you're not going to help?
9 *Roger*: No, I'm not going to help. Bugger that.
10 *Jenny*: Aren't you over 16, though?
11 *Roger*: Yeah, I'm 17.

The effect of Roger's tag question (line 7), which was addressed specifically to me, was (intentionally) to make me feel that I had asked a foolish question, and the general impression was one of aggression. I did not know the answer to his question; in fact, I had been trying to obtain the answer from him.

Another example occurs in the interchange below, between Colin, Puvvy and Roger:

1 *Roger*: He might be taking Britt, he says.
2 *Colin*: Oh, what a thrill. What a name, Britt.
3 *Puvvy*: Who started calling her it?
4 *Roger*: It's her proper name, *in it?*

Again, the effect of Roger's tag question (in line 4) is aggressive: he conveys the impression that Puvvy is foolish not to know that 'Britt' is a real name; and he is *telling* him that it is her proper name, rather than asking for confirmation.

Assertion and aggression, of course, are important elements in the vernacular subculture. Street fights, swearing, shouting and stealing are all aggressive acts. It is significant, therefore, that those tag questions that contain a negative present tense form of *be* or *have* and that are assertive and aggressive in meaning are marked linguistically by the categorical use of the form *in't*. Other phonetic realizations of *ain't* never occur in these tag questions; nor do the corresponding standard English forms. *In't* is used with all subjects, and as both *be* and *have*. In other kinds of tag question, however, *in't* occurs variably with *ain't* and the standard forms.

A full discussion of the use of *ain't* in Reading English can be found in Cheshire 1981. It should be clear, though, that this is an example of a non-standard form that can overtly reflect the norms of the vernacular culture. The use of *in't* in a tag question, then, can fulfil a semantic function for speakers of Reading English.

CONCLUSION

This chapter has focused on the social function of linguistic variation in the speech of adolescent peer-groups. We have seen that non-standard linguistic features function in a number of different ways. Some are very sensitive markers of vernacular loyalty, showing a regular correlation in frequency with the extent to which speakers adhere to the vernacular culture. Others are less sensitive markers of vernacular loyalty. We have also seen that the social function of non-standard features can vary with the sex of the speaker, and that this social function can sometimes override the constraints imposed on speakers by the formality of the situation. Finally, in one case at least, linguistic variation is able to fulfil a semantic function, in that a speaker's choice of a variable form can directly reflect some of the values of the vernacular culture.

REFERENCES

Aitchison, J. (1981) *Language Change: Progress or Decay?* (London: Fontana).

Andry, R. G. (1960) *Delinquency and Parental Pathology* (London: Methuen).

Cheshire, J. (1978) 'Present Tense Verbs in Reading English', in Trudgill, P. (ed.) *Sociolinguistic Patterns in British English* (London: Edward Arnold) pp. 52–69.

Cheshire, J. (1981) 'Variation in the Use of *ain't* in an Urban British English Dialect', *Language in Society*, **10**, pp. 365–81.

Clarke, J. (1973) *The Skinheads and the Study of Youth Culture.* Occasional paper (Birmingham: Centre for Contemporary Cultural Studies).

Cohen, A. K. (1955) *Delinquent Boys* (New York: The Free Press).

Cohen, P. (1972) *Subcultural Conflict and Working-class Community.* Working papers in cultural studies 2 (Birmingham: Centre for Contemporary Cultural Studies).

Downes, D. (1966) *The Delinquent Solution* (London: Routledge & Kegan Paul).

Jahangiri, N. and Hudson, R. (1982) 'Patterns of Variation in Teherani Persian', in Romaine, S. (ed.) *Sociolinguistic Variation in Speech Communities* (London: Arnold) pp. 49–63.

Labov, W. (1965) 'Stages in the Acquisition of Standard English', in Shuy, R. (ed.) *Social Dialects and Language Learning.* Proceedings of the Bloomington, Indiana Conference (1964) (Champaign, IL: National Council of Teachers of English).

Labov, W. (1966) *The Social Stratification of English in New York City* (Washington, DC: Center for Applied Linguistics).

Labov, W. (1970) 'The Study of Language in its Social Context', *Stadium Generale*, **23**, pp. 66–84.

Labov, W. (1972) *Sociolinguistic Patterns* (Philadelphia, PA, Pennsylvania University Press).

Macaulay, R. K. S. (1977) *Language, Social Class and Education: A Glasgow Study* (Edinburgh: Edinburgh University Press).

Miller, W. B. (1958) 'Lower-class Culture as a Generating Milieu of Gang Delinquency', *Journal of Social Issues*, **14**(3), pp. 5–19.

Milroy, J. (1980) 'Lexical Alternation and the History of English', in Traugott, E. *et al.* (eds) *Papers from the Fourth International Congress in Historical Linguistics* (Amsterdam: Benjamins).

Milroy, J. (1982) 'Probing Under the Tip of the Iceberg: Phological Normalisation and the Shape of Speech Communities', in Romaine, S. (ed.) *Sociolinguistic Variation in Speech Communities* (London: Arnold) pp. 35–47.

Milroy, L. and Margrain, S. (1980) 'Vernacular Language Loyalty and Social Network', *Language in Society*, **9**, pp. 43–70.

Moss, M. H. (1973) *Deprivation and Disadvantage?* Open University Course Book E, **262**, 8 (Milton Keynes: Open University Press).

Pelto, P. J. (1970) *Anthropological Research: The Structure of Inquiry* (New York: Harper & Row).

Policansky, L. (1980) *Verb Concord Variation in Belfast Vernacular.* Paper delivered to the Sociolinguistics Symposium, Walsall.

Reid, E. (1978) 'Social and Stylistic Variation in the Speech of Children: Some Evidence from Edinburgh', in Trudgill, P. (ed.) *Sociolinguistic Patterns in British English* (London: Edward Arnold) pp. 158–73.

Romaine, S. (1975) *Linguistic Variability in the Speech of Some Edinburgh Schoolchildren* (University of Edinburgh: M. Litt. thesis).

Romaine, S. (1980) 'Stylistic Variation and Evaluative Reactions to Speech: Problems in the Investigation of Linguistic Attitudes in Scotland', *Language and Speech*, **23**(3), pp. 213–32.

Stockwell, R. P., Schachter, P. and Partee, B. H. (1973) *The Major Syntactic Structures of English* (New York: Holt, Rinehart & Winston).

Thakerar, J. N. Giles, H., and Cheshire, J. (1982) 'Psychological and Linguistic Parameters of Speech Accommodation Theory', in Fraser, C. and Scherer, K. R. (eds) *Advances in the Social Psychology of Language* (Cambridge: Cambridge University Press).

Willmott, P. (1966) *Adolescent Boys of East London* (London: Routledge & Kegan Paul).

16 Network Structure and Linguistic Change

James Milroy and Lesley Milroy

[T]he Belfast research design here depends on the idea of norm maintenance, which we have operationalized in terms of *social network*, and within this model we have distinguished between relatively weak and strong network links. In any real community individuals and groups will vary in the relative intensity of ties, and this is what makes it possible to compare them in these terms. But behind this there lies an idealization which predicts that in a community bound by maximally dense and multiplex network ties linguistic change would not take place at all. No such community can actually exist, but the idealization is important, because it also implies that to the extent that relatively weak ties exist in communities (as in fact they do), the conditions will be present for linguistic change to take place. This perception was partly borne out even in the inner-city research. We noted that very few individuals had markedly low network strength scores, and furthermore that these individuals tended to use language much less close to the core Belfast vernacular, with a much lower use of the 'close-tie' variants (such as [ʌ] in words of the (*pull*) class). The idea that *relative strength of network tie* is a powerful predictor of language use is thus implicit in the interpretative model we have used throughout: it predicts, amongst other things, that to the extent that ties are strong, linguistic change will be prevented or impeded, whereas to the extent that they are weak, they will be more open to external influences, and so linguistic change will be facilitated.

Weak ties are much more difficult to investigate empirically than strong ones, and the instinct of the network-based ethnographer is usually to study relatively self-contained small communities that are internally bound by strong links and relatively insulated from outside influences. The ethnographic work reported in Cohen (1982), for example, focuses on peripheral areas of the British Isles that have a strong sense of local 'community'. Although we may surmise that urban situations (such as Belfast) are likely to exhibit lower density and multiplexity in personal ties than remote rural ones (and are by the same token also likely to be more open to outside influences), many studies, both urban and rural, have shown that a close-knit network

Source: 'Speaker-innovation and Linguistic Change', in Milroy, J. (1992) *Linguistic Variation and Change: On the Historical Sociolinguistics of English* (Oxford: Blackwell) pp. 176–91.

structure functions as a conservative force, resisting pressures for change originating from outside the network; conversely, those speakers whose ties to the localized network are weakest approximate least closely to localized vernacular norms, and are most exposed to external pressures for change (J. Milroy and L. Milroy, 1985). This second observation suggests that since strong network structure seems to be implicated in a rather negative way in linguistic change, a closer examination of *weak* network ties might be profitable.

The difficulty in studying weak ties empirically means that the quantitative variable of network (which can be readily applied to close-knit communities) cannot be easily operationalized in situations where the population is socially and/or geographically mobile. The networks of mobile persons tend to be loose-knit; such persons form (relatively weak) ties with very large numbers of others, and these are often open-ended, seldom forming into close-tie clusters. It is therefore difficult, in studying loose-knit situations, to produce direct empirical (quantitative) evidence of the kind usually used to support sociolinguistic theories, and indeed (as we noted above) the speaker-innovator cannot easily be directly observed and located. However, we have argued (J. Milroy and L. Milroy, 1985) that the speaker-innovator is a necessary theoretical construct if we are to clarify what is involved in solving the actuation problem. Therefore, as we are again dealing with an idealization here, we use a mode of argumentation that differs from the usual inductive mode favoured by quantitative linguists, and to support the argument we adduce evidence from various sources.

This evidence is of several different kinds. As is the case so often in network analysis, we find that anthropological and sociological studies of small-scale communities (as in Cohen, 1982) are illuminating. On the basis of evidence from a number of such studies, Mewett (1982) has observed that *class* differences in small communities begin to emerge over time as the proportion of *multiplex* relationships declines (multiplexity being an important characteristic of a close-knit type of network structure). This observation, in addition to associating social class stratification with the decline of close-knit networks, suggests a framework for linking network studies with large-scale class-based studies in formulating a more coherent multi-level sociolinguistic theory than we have at present. But we have also derived insights from important work by Granovetter (1973, 1982), who has argued that 'weak' and uniplex interpersonal ties, although they may be subjectively perceived as unimportant, are in fact important channels through which innovation and influence flow from one close-knit group to another, linking such groups the wider society. This rather larger-scale aspect of the social function of weak ties has a number of important implications for a socially accountable theory of linguistic change and diffusion, some of which we shall briefly outline.

Granovetter's working definition of 'weak' and 'strong' ties is as follows: 'The strength of a tie is a (probably linear) combination of the amount of time, the emotional intensity, the intimacy (mutual confiding) and the reciprocal services which characterise a tie' (1973: 1361). This is probably sufficient to satisfy most people's feeling of what might be meant by a 'weak' or 'strong' interpersonal tie, and it fits in fairly well with our indicators for measuring network strength in the Belfast inner-city communities. It also fits in with the principles followed in comparing inner-city with outer-city Belfast (see Milroy, J., 1992, Chapter 4): broadly speaking, the former is characterized by stronger and the latter by weaker ties. Thus, although *strength of tie* is a continuous variable, for the purpose of exposition Granovetter treats it as if it were discrete, and we need always to bear in mind that we are speaking in relative terms: a tie is 'weak' if it is less strong than the other ties against which it is measured. Granovetter's basic point is that weak ties between groups regularly provide bridges through which information and influence are diffused. Furthermore, these bridges between groups cannot consist of strong ties: the ties *must* be weak (that is, relatively weak when measured against internal ties). Thus, weak ties may or may not function as bridges, but no strong tie can. This is shown in Figure 16.1.

Strong ties, however, are observed as concentrated within groups. Thus, they give rise to a *local* cohesion of the kind that we explored in inner-city Belfast; yet, at the same time, they lead paradoxically to overall fragmentation. Clearly, this perception is potentially very illuminating in accounting for different language states at different times and places at many levels of generality, ranging from the interpersonal situations, through dialect-divergent, bilingual and code-switching communities to the very broadest of language situations, and it throws light on the question of convergence and divergence. The model of strong and weak ties presented

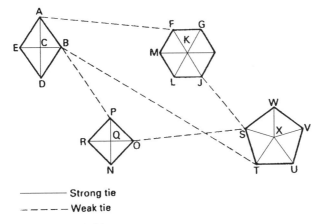

Figure 16.1: Weak ties as bridges

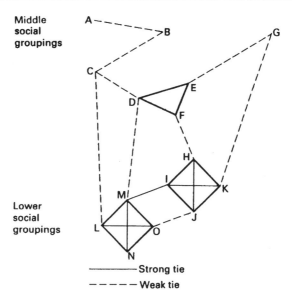

Figure 16.2:   Idealized representation of an urban community in which weaker ties are more numerous in middle social groupings and between the groups

graphically in Figure 16.2 can be thought of as an idealized representation of (for example) an urban community which consists of clumps connected by predominantly strong ties, which in turn are connected to other clumps by predominantly weak ties, but it can of course represent other kinds of language situation that we might conceive of.

The important point (from our perspective) that follows from all this is that weak inter-group ties are likely to be critical in transmitting innovations from one group to another, despite the common-sense assumption that *strong* ties fulfil this role. For example, Downes (1984: 155) suggests that the network concept is important in developing a theory of linguistic diffusion, but assumes that it is strong ties that will be critical. This assumption seems to be shared by many linguists who have considered the matter; indeed, as we have noticed, Labov (1980: 261) presents a model of the innovator as an individual with strong ties both inside *and* outside a local group. Clearly, this conflicts with the arguments presented here, which predict that to the extent that ties are strong, linguistic change will be impeded, not facilitated.

Granovetter's principle seems at first sight to go against 'common sense', and for this reason we need to expound it a little further. First of all, it is likely that weak ties are much more numerous than strong ties, simply because the time and energy invested in the maintenance of strong ties must place an upper limit on how many it is possible to have, whereas weak ties require little effort. Second, many more individuals can be reached through weak ties than through strong ties; consider for example the bridges set up by participants at academic conferences, which link cohesive groups associated with each institution and through which new ideas and information pass. Conversely, information relayed through strong ties tends not to be innovatory, since persons linked by strong ties tend to share contacts (that is, to belong to overlapping networks). So they may, for example, hear the same rumour several times. This general principle entails that mobile individuals who have contracted many weak ties, but who as a consequence of their mobility occupy a position marginal to some cohesive group, are in a particularly strong position to carry information across social boundaries and to diffuse innovations of all kinds.

In view of the norm-enforcing capacities of groups built up mainly of strong ties, it is easy to see why innovators are likely to be persons weakly linked to the group. Susceptibility to outside influence is likely to increase in inverse proportion to strength of tie with the group. Where groups are loose-knit – that is, linked mainly by weak ties – they are likely to be generally more susceptible to innovation. We might note that this contention is consistent with the principle enunciated by Labov and Kroch that innovating groups are located centrally in the social hierarchy, characterized as upper working or lower-middle class (Labov 1980: 254; Kroch 1978). For it is likely that in British (and probably also North American) society the most close-knit networks are located at the highest and lowest strata, with a majority of socially and geographically mobile speakers (whose networks are relatively loose-knit) falling between these two points.

One apparent difficulty with the proposal that innovators are only marginally linked to the group is in explaining how these peripheral people can successfully diffuse innovations to central members of that group, who are of course resistant to innovation. One part of the answer here is that central members often *do not* accept the innovation: hence, for example, the persistence of regional varieties and minority languages in strong-tie situations (compare here Andersen's (1986) idea of *endocentric* dialect communities). But to the extent that they do accept innovations, two related points are relevant. First, since resistance to innovation is likely to be strong in a norm-conforming group, a large number of persons will have to be exposed to it and adopt it in the early stages for it to spread successfully. Now, in a mobile society, weak ties are likely to be very much more numerous than strong ties (especially in urban communities), and some of them are likely to function as bridges through which innovations flow. Thus, an innovation like the London merger between /ð,θ/ (as in *brother, thin*) and /v,f/ reported in Norwich teenage speech (Trudgill 1986: 54ff.) is likely to be transmitted through a great many weak links between Londoners and Norwich speakers, and Trudgill suggests tourists and football supporters as individuals who might contract such links. Quite simply, before it stands any chance of acceptance by central members of a group, the links through which it is originally transmitted *need* to be numerous (compare Granovetter 1973: 1367). Thus, the existence of numerous weak ties is a necessary condition for innovations to spread: it is the quantity as well as the quality of links between people that is crucial here.

The second point we need to make in explaining the success of marginal members of a group as innovators relates more directly to Labov's view of the innovating personality type. As Granovetter suggests, persons central to a close-knit, norm-enforcing group are likely to find innovation a risky activity (indeed it is probably more in their interests to maintain and enforce norms than to innovate); but adopting an innovation that is already widespread on the fringes of the group is very much less risky. There is of course a time dimension involved, and in this dimension a point may be reached at which central members begin to accept that it is in their own interests to adopt the innovation. Informal observation of cultural and political innovation suggests that this is generally true. As an example we may cite the final adoption of a marginal cult (Christianity) in ancient Rome: it took centuries for this innovation to penetrate to the centre. Central members of a group diminish the risk of potentially deviant activity by adopting (after a lapse of time) an innovation from persons who are already non-peripheral members of the group, rather than by direct importation from marginals, who tend to be perceived as deviant. Thus, we can in this way understand how acceptance – under certain conditions –can be a rational strategy on the part of central members of the group.

Within the network model, therefore, the existence of numerous weak ties is a necessary condition for innovation to be adopted. But there must be additional conditions, and at least one of these is psycho-social: this is that speakers from the receptor community want to identify for some reason with speakers from the donor community. Thus, the Norwich speakers cited by Trudgill in some sense view London vernacular speakers as persons with whom, in Andersen's (1986) terms, they wish to express solidarity. Ultimately, for an innovation to be adopted, it seems that the adopters must believe that some benefit to themselves and/or their groups will come about through the adoption of the innovation. The cost of adopting the innovation in terms of effort will thus be perceived by the adopters as less than the benefit received from adopting it. It also seems that an explanation based on the idea of group identity and solidarity is more satisfactory than one that relies on prestige in a social class dimension (see J. Milroy 1992, Chapter 7).

Bearing all these points in mind, it is appropriate now to return to Labov's account of the innovator and compare it with our own. The most general difference is that Labov's account is about a type of person, whereas ours is abstract and structural, focusing on the nature of interpersonal links: it is based on relationships rather than on persons. We might describe

Labov's innovator as a person who is sociable and outgoing, and who has many friends both inside and outside the local group. Intuitively, it seems very likely that information of all kinds (including linguistic innovation) can be diffused by such persons, for the reason that they have many contacts. But according to our account, such individuals could not be near the centre of a close-knit group and at the same time have many strong outside ties. More probably, they would have relatively few multiplex links with others, and many of their links would be open-ended and hence low on density; they would have a predominance of weak links, including many that constitute bridges between groups. In class terms such persons would probably be mobile, and their profile would therefore fit in with Labov's view that socially mobile sectors (upper working to lower-middle class) are the ones in which linguistic innovation and change are carried. It seems, however, that this profile is not that of the innovator at all, but that of an *early adopter*, and we shall consider this point fully in the next section.

What we have presented here is an abstract model, supported by the insights of Granovetter, which in effect implies that a community characterized by maximally strong network ties (and hence maximal norm-enforcement) will not permit change to take place within it. Real communities, however, contain varying degrees of internal cohesions and varying degrees of openness to outside influence through weak ties. The speaker-innovator within this model is not a close-tie person, but one who is marginal to more than one (relatively) close-knit group and who therefore forms a bridge between groups across which innovations pass. . . .

Empirical support for our modelling of the speaker-innovator is provided by Rogers and Shoemaker's (1971) studies of about 1500 cases of innovation in many areas of life, including, for example, innovations in agricultural, educational and technological methods. In the present discussion, the most important principle emerging from this work is the distinction between the *innovator* and the *early adopter*. As the innovator has weak links to more than one group and forms a bridge between groups, he or she is, in relation to the close-tie groups, a marginal individual. Rogers and Shoemaker's studies confirm the marginality of innovators and further suggest that innovators are often perceived as underconforming to the point of deviance. If this is correct, the innovator does not resemble Labov's (1980) characterization (an individual who has 'prestige' both inside and outside the local group), but actually seems to have more in common with the famous 'lames' of the Harlem study (Labov, 1972a). Conversely, Labov's 'innovator' resembles what Rogers and Shoemaker call the 'early adopter'.

Early adopters are relatively central to the group and relatively conforming to the group norms. Once the innovation reaches them, it diffuses to the group as a whole, and at this stage it moves into the middle part of the S-curve structure that is associated with the diffusion of innovations generally. Thus, although linguistic processes are much more complex than many of the other processes that have been studied from this point of view, they share this pattern of diffusion with other kinds of innovation. Later, once the new forms are established in the group, they may diffuse from the centre outwards. At the macro-level, therefore, it is tempting to see these patterns in broad sweeps of cultural and linguistic history (the history of Christianity comes again to mind), but we must leave this speculation aside and return to the matter in hand, because there seems to be no easy way for empirical studies of change in progress to identify in the data the crucial distinction between innovators and early adopters.

However, we should again recall that we are not attempting to describe the characteristics of personality types, but of relations between groups and individuals, and these may vary considerably according to different social and cultural conditions. That is to say that we are not thinking of identifying some individual who lurks around the margins of a group and labelling him or her 'the innovator'. Nor is it a case of 'once an innovator, always an innovator', and it is obviously true that people who are innovative in some ways may not be innovative in others. We are thinking in structural terms, and so we are concerned with the kinds of *relationship between persons* that determine the conditions in which linguistic innovations can be accepted or rejected. Thus, the whole question is relative, just as the definition of the weakness of a tie is relative. What is clear, however, is that if innovations are transmitted across relatively tenuous and marginal links in fleeting encounters that are perceived as unimportant, we are unlikely to observe the actuation of a change. However sophisticated our methods may be, we are much more likely to observe the take-up and diffusion of the innovation by the more socially salient early adopters.

Bearing these difficulties in mind, we now turn to some detailed examples in order to demonstrate how the model developed here affects the interpretation of linguistic variation in speech communities. First, we shall consider two cases of phonological variation from the Belfast inner-city study, and then move on to suggest a tentative analysis of some parts of the Philadelphia data, as reported by Labov and Harris (1986) and Ash and Myhill (1986). Finally, we shall consider a number of more general patterns of change that may be illuminated by the model.

It is usual to suppose that the diffusion of linguistic change is encouraged by relatively open channels of communication and discouraged by boundaries or weaknesses in lines of communication. In Belfast, however, there are many patterns that are difficult to explain in this apparently common-sense way, and we shall consider two of them here. They are: (1) the social configuration of the spread of /a/-backing from the Protestant east of the city into the Clonard, a West Belfast Catholic community; and (2) the city-wide younger generation consensus on the evaluation of the (*pull*)

(a) Index score

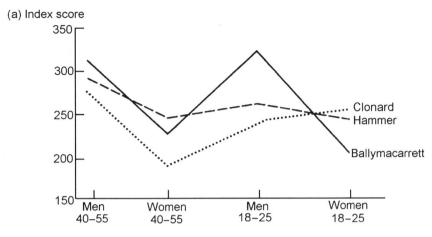

Figure 16.3:   Backing of /a/ in Ballymacarrett, the Clonard and the Hammer

variable, as against conflicting patterns in the older generation. The backing of /a/ is led by East Belfast males. Figure 16.3 shows this, and it also shows that the movement of back /a/ into West Belfast is not led by Protestant males in the Hammer, as might be expected, but by the younger female group in the Catholic Clonard area. This is the group that exhibits the crossover pattern and reverses the generally expected 'stable norm' patterns. In this group the city-wide female movement *away* from /a/-backing is reversed: the incidence of /a/-backing in the group is higher than in the other older and younger female groups, higher than amongst older females in the same area, and – surprisingly – also higher than amongst their young male counterparts in the Clonard. When measured against other groups, these young women are deviant. ...

The social barriers that inhibit contacts between working-class communities have been well described for many locations throughout the world (examples are cited by L. Milroy, 1987), and they were evident in our inner-city fieldwork even *inside* sectarian boundaries. Inter-ethnic conflict in Belfast, however, has had the effect of strengthening the barriers that are present in all such communities (Boal, 1978). In fact, the major sectarian boundary in West Belfast is now marked physically by a brick and barbed-wire structure, which is described by the military authorities, apparently without intentional irony, as the 'Peace Line'. The puzzle is that an East Belfast pattern can be carried across these boundaries, evidently by a group of young women whose movements and face-to-face contacts have been constrained from a very early age. [T]here is a long-term shift in the vowel system towards back /a/, and this diffusion pattern from east to west is a continuation of it. That this shift is continuing across the iron barriers (both physical and psychological) that separate the

Protestant east and Catholic west, is a fact for which we are obliged to seek a principled explanation.

The most accessible, and possibly the only, explanation is one that takes account of weak ties and the distinction between the marginal innovators and the early adopters. It seems that the Clonard young women are central members of the group, and so they resemble early adopters rather than innovators. This is quite clear from their Network Strength score (as reported by L. Milroy, 1987: 204): they all score extremely high on this – much higher than the young Clonard males. Their average score is 4.75 out of a possible maximum of 5.00.

Further personal information about this group points rather clearly to innovation through multiple weak ties. These young women, unlike their male counterparts, were in full employment: they all had regular jobs outside the Clonard community at a rather poor city-centre store. Here they were very likely to be in weak-tie contact with large numbers of people from all over the city, both Catholic and Protestant. Thus, they would be well placed to adopt innovations transmitted by persons peripheral to their core networks, and as a result exposure to innovatory forms would be frequent. Given the large number of service encounters in the store, it becomes possible for the weak-tie encounters with back [a] users to exceed greatly the number of strong-tie encounters with non-back [a] users. Hence the capacity of innovation-bearing weak ties to compete with, and in this case overcome, the innovation-resisting strong ties.

If we have a theoretical perspective such as the one developed here, which explicitly predicts that an innovation will be transmitted through (frequent and numerous) weak ties, we have a solution to the problem of explaining how back [a] can diffuse in this way, and we can present a plausible account of how the innovation can appear to jump across a barrier of brick and barbed wire. If, however, we make the usual assumption that innovations are diffused through strong ties, the pattern is very difficult to explain. Yet, it is only if we make this strong-tie assumption in the first place that [a] diffusion appears to be a puzzle at all.

Whereas back [a] diffusion is mainly a change in a phonetic segment, the change of pattern in the (*pull*) variable is a change of evaluation (or of agreement on norms). This variable is quantified on the basis of a small phono-lexical set consisting of items such as *pull, push, took, shook, foot*, which exhibit vowel alternation between [ʌ] and [u]. Although the [ʌ] variant is recessive, it has very strong affective values and is a very salient marker of casual speech between close acquaintances. But here we wish to point out only one thing – the change in consensus on norms over the generations. Whereas the (*bag*) variable shows consensus across the different groups – old and young, male and female – the (*pull*) variable (shown in Figure 16.4) shows consensus only in the younger generation, where it has become a marker of gender-differentiation. The question is: how can this normative

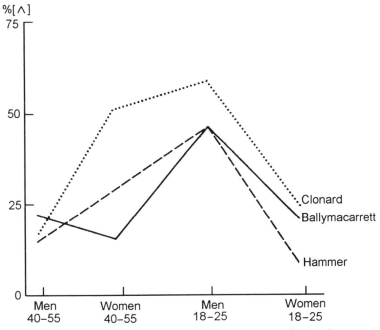

Figure 16.4: Distribution of the (*pull*) variable (percentage of [ʌ] variants are shown) by age, sex and area in inner-city Belfast

consensus come about in this divided city?

The pattern here is one in which the older groups do not agree on the gender marking in use of the 'in-group' variant [ʌ]. In Ballymacarrett, males favour [ʌ], but in the two West Belfast communities, gender preference is reversed: the [ʌ] variant is favoured by the females. The younger groups, however, show the same pattern in all three communities: in all cases [ʌ] preference is stronger among males and weaker among females.

Again the puzzle is to explain how young people living in closed communities, whose outside links are quite tenuous, could reach cross-community consensus on the social value to be attached to the two variants of (*pull*). In their parents' youth there was greater freedom of movement, and people frequently formed friendships across regional and sectarian divisions; however, since the beginning of the civil disorder in 1969, people have been much less able to form strong ties outside their communities. Yet, despite this, the absorption of the (*pull*) variable into the regular socio-linguistic structure of Belfast vernacular has continued unhindered. Again, it is only if we accept that weak ties are the normal channel for the diffusion of innovations that the apparent paradox is resolved.

In these examples, we have selected instances based on extensive quantified information which is very fine-grained and which is fully accountable to the data, but the general pattern here had already become evident from observation of other cases, and the (*pull*) variable can be regarded as testing out a hypothesis that had already been formed. There are many other examples involving different dimensions of variation (including, for example, phonological mergers) that can be observed fairly easily and that appear to show this general pattern of consensus in the inner-city younger generation. Indeed, once you are 'clued in' to the possibilities (especially with regard to gender-differentiation), it is remarkable how readily you can observe the trends in everyday encounters. Perhaps the most dramatic of these trends is the progressive loss of localized lexical items and reduction of phono-lexical variable sets of the (*pull*) type (J. Milroy, 1981). Another example is the three-way merger (or apparent merger) of words of the type *fur/fir/fair*, which are very close to being fully merged amongst younger speakers. The few elderly speakers that we studied (around 70 years old in 1975), however, exhibit a three way differentiation, and middle-aged speakers often have a two-way differentiation. As indications of this greater consensus amongst younger people had already been observed before we started our quantitative analysis, we spoke in terms of 'the rise of an urban vernacular': the first research application in 1975 proposed the hypothesis that we were witnessing in Belfast a fairly early stage in the development of a focused urban vernacular, in which there is a generally observable trend towards greater consensus on norms.

However, we have also emphasized in this chapter the psychosocial barrier of the *sectarian* difference in Belfast, which we might expect to inhibit the trend towards consensus, and from the beginning of our research we naturally wished to discover whether the ethnic difference was consistently and reliably reflected in language. In our pilot research, therefore, we looked at two East Belfast communities, one Catholic and one Protestant (Catholics being a small minority in this part of the city). In our analysis of the tapes, however, we could find no appreciable differences between the two groups: the Catholics spoke with an East Belfast accent (including back varieties of /a/) just as the Protestants did, and their speech was more similar to East Belfast Protestants than it was to West Belfast Catholics. Subsequently, after comparing different communities very fully in our inner-city study, I was able to state, rather cautiously, that 'there is as yet no persuasive evidence to show that the two ethnic groups in Belfast (and Ulster) can be clearly identified by differences in accent' (J. Milroy, 1981: 44). Indeed, it seems that those features of differentiation that in the past could have been seized upon as ethnic markers, have been abandoned in favour of greater inner-city agreement on norms of age, sex and contextual style. In general, the Catholic immigrants arrived in the city later than the Protestants and brought from mid and west Ulster a number of features (such as palatalization of initial [k]) that *could* have been used to reinforce differences, but this does not seem to have happened. Both groups seem to be moving in the same direction in the younger generation even though there may be divergent movements in small details; similarly, both groups appear to evaluate variants in much the same way (and this evaluation is often quite divergent from 'standard' evaluations).

REFERENCES

Andersen, H. (1986) 'Center and Periphery: Adoption, Diffusion and Spread'. Paper delivered to the Conference on Historical Dialectology, Poznán, Poland.

Ash, S. and Myhill, J. (1986) 'Linguistic Correlates of Inter-ethnic Contact', in Sankoff, D. (ed.) *Diversity and Diachrony* (Amsterdam: Benjamins) pp. 33–44.

Boal, F. W. (1978) 'Territoriality on the Shankill-Falls Divide, Belfast: The Perspective from 1976', in Lanegran, D. A. and Palm, R. (eds) *An Invitation to Geography*, 2nd edn (New York: McGraw Hill) pp. 58–77.

Cohen, A. (ed.) (1982) *Belonging* (Manchester: Manchester University Press).

Downes, W. (1984) *Language and Society* (Bungay, Suffolk: Fontana).

Granovetter, M. (1973) 'The Strength of Weak Ties', *American Journal of Sociology*, **78**, pp. 1360–80.

Granovetter, M. (1982) 'The Strength of Weak Ties: A Network Theory Revisited', in Marsden, P. V. and Lin, N. (eds) *Social Structure and Network Analysis* (London: Sage).

Kroch, A. (1978) 'Toward a Theory of Social Dialect Variation', *Language in Society*, **7**, pp. 17–36.

Labov, W. (1972) *Language in the Inner City* (Philadelphia, PA: Pennsylvania University Press).

Labov, W. (ed.) (1980) *Locating Language in Time and Space* (New York: Academic Press).

Labov, W. and Harris, W. (1986) 'De Facto Segregation of Black and White Vernaculars', in Sankoff, D. (ed.) *Diversity and Diachrony* (Amsterdam: Benjamins) pp. 1–24.

Mewett, P. (1982) 'Associational Categories and the Social Location of Relationships in a Lewis Crofting Community', in Cohen, A. (ed.) *Belonging* (Manchester: Manchester University Press) pp. 101–30.

Milroy, J. (1981) *Regional Accents of English: Belfast* (Belfast: Blackstaff).

Milroy, J. (1992) *Linguistic Variation and Change: On the Historical Sociolinguistics of English* (Oxford: Blackwell).

Milroy, J. and Milroy, L. (1985) 'Linguistic Change, Social Network and Speaker Innovation', *Journal of Linguistics*, **21**, pp. 339–84.

Milroy, L. (1987) *Language and Social Networks*, 2nd edn (Oxford: Basil Blackwell).

Rogers, E. M. and Shoemaker, F. F. (1971) *Communication of Innovations*, 2nd edn (New York: Free Press).

Trudgill, P. (1986) 'The Apparent Time Paradigm: Norwich Revisited'. Paper presented at the 6th Sociolinguistics Symposium, University of Newcastle upon Tyne.

17 The Whole Woman: Sex and Gender Differences in Variation

Penelope Eckert

The tradition of large-scale survey methodology in the study of variation has left a gap between the linguistic data and the social practise that yields these data. Since sociolinguistic surveys bring away little information about the communities that produce their linguistic data, correlations of linguistic variants with survey categories have been interpreted on the basis of general knowledge of the social dynamics associated with those categories. The success of this approach has depended on the quality of this general knowledge. The examination of variation and socioeconomic class has been benefited from sociolinguists' attention to a vast literature on class and to critical analyses of the indices by which class membership is commonly determined. The study of gender and variation, on the other hand, has suffered from the fact that the amount of scientific attention given to gender over the years cannot begin to be compared with that given to class. Many current beliefs about the role of gender in variation, therefore, are a result of substituting popular (and unpopular) belief for social theory in the interpretation of patterns of sex correlations with variation.

Sociolinguists are acutely aware of the complex relation between the categories used in the socioeconomic classification of speakers and the social practice that underlies these categories. Thus, we do not focus on the objectivized indices used to measure class (such as salary, occupation, and education) in analyzing correlations between linguistic and class differences, even when class identification is based on these indices. Rather, we focus more and more on the relation of language use to the everyday practice that constitutes speakers' class-based social participation and identity in the community. Thus, explanations take into consideration interacting dynamics such as social group and network membership, symbolic capital and the linguistic marketplace, and local identity. The same can be said to some extent of work on ethnicity and variation, where researchers have

Source: 'The Whole Woman: Sex and Gender Differences in Variation', *Language Variation and Change*, **1**, 1 (1989) (Cambridge: Cambridge University Press) pp. 245–67.

interpreted data on ethnic differences in variation in terms of complex interactions between ethnicity, group history, and social identity. The study of sociolinguistic construction of the biological categories of age and sex, on the other hand, has so far received less sophisticated attention (Eckert, Edwards, & Robins, 1985). The age continuum is commonly divided into equal chunks with no particular attention to the relation between these chunks and the life stages that make age socially significant. Rather, when the full age span is considered in community studies, the age continuum is generally interpreted as representing continuous apparent time. At some point, the individual's progress through normative life stages (e.g. school, work, marriage, childrearing, retirement) might be considered rather than, or in addition to, chronological age. Some work has explored the notion of life stage. The very apparent lead of preadolescents and adolescents in sound change has led some researchers to separate those groups in community studies (Macaulay, 1977; Wolfram, 1969), and some attention has been focused on the significance of these life stages in variation (Eckert, 1988; Labov, 1972b). There has also been some speculation about changes of speakers' relation to the linguistic marketplace in aging (Eckert, 1984; Labov, 1972a; Thibault, 1983). Most interestingly, there have been examinations of the relation of age groups to historical periods of social change in the community (Clermont & Cedergren, 1978; Laferriere, 1979). But taken together, these studies are bare beginnings and do not constitute a reasoned and coherent approach to the sociolinguistic significance of biological age.

Like age, sex is a biological category that serves as a fundamental basis for the differentiation of roles, norms, and expectations in all societies. It is these roles, norms, and expectations that constitute gender, the social construction of sex. Although differences in patterns of variation between men and women are a function of gender and only indirectly a function of sex (and, indeed, such gender-based variation occurs within, as well as between, sex groups), we have been examining the interaction between gender and variation by correlating variables with sex rather than gender differences. This has been done because although an individual's gender-related place in society is a multidimensional complex that can only be characterized through careful analysis, his or her sex is generally a readily observable binary variable, and inasmuch as sex can be said to be a rough statistical indication of gender, it has been reasonable to substitute the biological category for the social sampling. However, because information about the individual's sex is easily accessible, data can be gathered without any enquiry into the construction of gender in that community. As a result, since researchers have not had to struggle to find the categories in question, they tend to fall back on unanalyzed notions about gender to interpret whatever sex correlations emerge in the data and not to consider gender where there are no sex correlations.

Gender differences are exceedingly complex, particularly in a society and era where women have been moving self-consciously into the marketplace and calling traditional gender roles into question. Gender roles and ideologies create different ways for men and women to experience life, culture, and society. Taking this as a basic approach to the data on sex differences in variation, there are a few assumptions one might start with. First, and perhaps most important, there is no apparent reason to believe that there is a simple, constant relation between gender and variation. Despite increasingly complex data on sex differences in variation, there remains a tendency to seek a single social construction of sex that will explain all of its correlations with variation. This is reflected in the use of a single coefficient for sex effects in variable rule or regression analysis of variation. This perspective limits the kind of results that can be obtained, since it is restricted to confirming the implicit hypothesis of a single type of sex effect or, worse, to indicating that there is no effect at all. Second, we must carefully separate our interpretation of sex differences in variation from artifacts of survey categories. I would argue that sociolinguists tend to think of age and class as continua and gender as an opposition, primarily because of the ways in which they are determined in survey research. But just as the class effect on variation may be thought of in terms of the binary bourgeois–working class opposition (Rickford, 1986), and just as there is reason to believe that the age continuum is interrupted by discontinuities in the effects of different life stages on people's relation to society and, hence, on language, variation based on gender may not always be adequately accounted for in terms of a binary opposition. ...

Labov and Trudgill have both emphasized a greater orientation to community prestige norms as the main driving force in women's, as opposed to men's, linguistic behaviour. Trudgill's findings in Norwich led him to see women as overwhelmingly conservative, as they showed men leading in most change. Furthermore, women in his sample tended to overreport their use of prestige forms and men tended to underreport theirs. He therefore argued that women and men respond to opposed sets of norms: women to overt, standard-language prestige norms and men to convert, vernacular prestige norms. Overt prestige attaches to refined qualities, as associated with the cosmopolitan marketplace and its standard language, whereas covert prestige attaches to masculine, 'rough and tough' qualities. Trudgill (1972:182 – and see Chapter 14) speculated that women's overt prestige orientation was a result of their powerless position in society. He argued that inasmuch as society does not allow women to advance their power or status through action in the marketplace, they are thrown upon their symbolic resources, including language, to enhance their social position. This is certainly a reasonable hypothesis, particularly since it was arrived at to explain data in which women's speech was overwhelmingly conservative. However, what it assumes more specifically is that women respond to their powerlessness by developing linguistic strategies for upward mobility, that is, that the socioeconomic hierarchy is the focus of social strategies. There are alternative views of exactly what social strategies are reflected in women's conservatism. An analysis that emphasizes the power relations implicit in the stratificational model was put forth by Deuchar (1988), who argued that women's conservative linguistic behavior is a function of basic power relations in society. Equating standard speech with politeness, she built on Brown's (1980) and Brown and Levinson's (1987) analyses of politeness as a face-saving strategy, arguing that the use of standard language is a mechanism for maintaining face in interactions in which the woman is powerless.

I would argue that elements of these hypotheses are correct but that they are limited by the fact that they are designed to account for one aspect of women's linguistic behavior only: those circumstances under which women's language is more conservative than men's. Based on the multiple patterns of sex, class, and age difference that he found in Philadelphia sound changes in progress, Labov (1984) sought to explain why women are more conservative in their use of stable variables but less conservative in their use of changes in progress and why women lead men in some changes and not in others. Although his data do not show women being particularly conservative, he based his analysis on the assumption that women's linguistic choices are driven by prestige. What he sought to explain, therefore, are cases where women's behavior is not conservative. Based on his Philadelphia data, Labov argued that women lag in the use of variants that are stigmatized within the larger community, that is, stable sociolinguistic variables and changes in progress that are sufficiently old and visible as to be stigmatized within the larger community. Women's behavior in these cases, then, is driven by global prestige norms. At the same time, women lead in changes that are still sufficiently limited to the neighborhood and local community to carry local prestige without having attracted a stigma in the larger Philadelphia community. In this case, Labov argued, women's behavior is driven by local prestige norms. If this explanation account for the Philadelphia data, it does not cover the New York City cases of (aeh) and (oh) (Labov, 1966), where women led in sound changes that had grown old and stigmatized. But more important, I can see no independent reason to seek explanations for women's behavior in prestige. ...

What I will argue is that gender does not have a uniform effect on linguistic behavior for the community as a whole, across variables, or for that matter for any individual. Gender, like ethnicity and class and indeed age, is a social construction and may enter into any of a variety of interactions with other social phenomena. And although sociolinguists have had some success in perceiving the social practice that constitutes class, they have yet to think of gender in terms of social practice.

There is one important way in which gender is not equivalent to categories like class or ethnicity. Gender and gender roles are normatively reciprocal, and although men and women are supposed to be different from each other, this difference is expected to be a source of attraction. Whereas the power relations between men and women are similar to those between dominant and subordinate classes and ethnic groups, the day-to-day context in which these power relations are played out is quite different. It is not a cultural norm for each working-class individual to be paired up for life with a member of the middle class or for every black person to be so paired up with a white person. However, our traditional gender ideology dictates just this kind of relationship between men and women. If one were to think of variables as social markers, then, one might expect gender markers to behave quite differently from markers of class or ethnicity. Whereas the aggressive use of ethnic markers (i.e. frequent use of the most extreme variants) is generally seen as maintaining boundaries – as preventing closeness – between ethnic groups, the aggressive use of gender markers is not. By the same token, the aggressive use of gender markers is not generally seen as a device for creating or maintaining solidarity within the category. To the extent that masculine or feminine behavior marks gender, its use by males and females respectively is more a device for competing with others in the same category and creating solidarity with those in the other category, and aggressive cross-sex behavior is seen as designed to compete with members of the other sex for the attention of members of the same sex.

Two other things follow from the specialization of gender roles, which may apply also to other kinds of differences such as ethnicity.

1. To the extent that male and female roles are not only different but reciprocal, members of either sex category are unlikely to compete with (i.e. evaluate their status in relation to) members of the other. Rather, by and large, men perceive their social status in relation to other men, whereas women largely perceive their social status in relation to other women.[1] Thus, differentiation on the basis of gender might well be sought within, rather than between, sex groups.
2. Men and women compete to establish their social status in different ways, as dictated by the constraints placed on their sex for achieving status. This is particularly clear where gender roles are separate, and in fact when people do compete in the role domain of the other sex, it is specifically their gender identity that gets called into question. ...

Since to have personal influence without power requires moral authority, women's influence depends primarily on the painstaking creation and elaboration of an image of the whole self as worthy authority. Thus, women are thrown into the accumulation of symbolic capital. This is not to say that men are not also dependent on the accumulation of symbolic capital, but that symbolic capital is the *only* kind that women can accumulate with impunity. And, indeed, it becomes part of their men's symbolic capital and hence part of the household's economic capital. Whereas men can justify and define their status on the basis of their accomplishments, possessions, or institutional status, women must justify and define theirs on the basis of their overall character. This is why, in peasant communities as in working-class neighborhoods, the women who are considered local leaders typically project a strong personality and a strong, frequently humorous, image of knowing what is right and having things under control.

When social scientists say that women are more status conscious than men, and when sociolinguists pick this up in explaining sex differences in speech, they are stumbling on the fact that, deprived of power, women must satisfy themselves with status. It would be more appropriate to say that women are more status-*bound* than men. This emphasis on status consciousness suggests that women only construe status as being hier-archical (be it global or local hierarchy) and that they assert status only to gain upward mobility. But status is not only defined hierarchically; an individual's status is his or her place, however defined, in the group or society. It is this broader status that women must assert by symbolic means, and this assertion will be of hierarchical status when a hierarchy happens to be salient. An important part of the explanation for women's innovative and conservative patterns lies, therefore, in their need to assert their membership in all of the communities in which they participate, since it is their authority, rather than their power in that community, that assures their membership. Prestige, then, is far too limited a concept to use for the dynamics at work in this context.

Above all, gender relations are about power and access to property and services, and whatever symbolic means a society develops to elaborate gender differences (such as romance and femininity) serve as obfuscation rather than explanation. Whenever one sees sex differences in language, there is nothing to suggest that it is not power that is at issue rather than gender *per se*. The claim that working-class men's speech diverges from working-class women's speech in an effort to avoid sounding like women reflects this ambiguity, for it raises the issue of the interaction between gender and power. Gender differentiation is greatest in those segments of society where power is the scarcest – at the lower end of the socioeconomic hierarchy, where women's access to power is the greatest threat to men. There is every reason to believe that the lower working-class men's sudden downturn in the use of Australian Question Intonation shown in Guy *et al.* (1986) is an avoidance of the linguistic expression of subordination by men in the socioeconomic group that can least afford to sound subordinate.

For similar reasons of power, it is common to confuse femininity and masculinity with gender, and perhaps nowhere is the link between gender and power clearer. Femininity is a culturally defined form of mitigation or denial of power, whereas masculinity is the affirmation of power. In Western society, this is perhaps most clearly illustrated in the greater emphasis on femininity in the south, where regional economic history has domesticized women and denied them economic power to a greater degree than it has in the industrial north (Fox-Genovese, 1988). The commonest forms of femininity and masculinity are related to actual physical power. Femininity is associated with small size, clothing and adornment that inhibit and/or do not stand up to rough activity, delicacy of movement, quiet and high pitched voice, friendly demeanor, politeness. The relation between politeness and powerlessness has already been emphasized (Brown, 1980) and surfaces in a good deal of the literature on gender differences in language. Although all of these kinds of behavior are eschewed by men at the lower end of the socioeconomic hierarchy, they appear increasingly in male style as one moves up the socioeconomic hierarchy until, in the upper class, what is called effeminacy may be seen as the conscientious rejection of physical power by those who exercise real global power (Veblen, 1931) by appropriating the physical power of others.

The methodological consequence of these considerations is that we should expect to see larger differences in indications of social category membership among women than among men. If women are more constrained to display their personal and social qualities and memberships, we would expect these expressions to show up in their use of phonological variables. This necessitates either a careful analysis of statistical interaction, or separate analysis of the data from each gender group, before any comparison.

GENDER AND ADOLESCENT SOCIAL CATEGORIES

In this section, I discuss some evidence from adolescent phonological variation to illustrate the complexity of gender in the social scheme of things. Adolescents are quite aware of the gender differences I have discussed, particularly since they are at a life stage in which the issue of gender roles becomes crucial. By the time they arrive in high school, adolescent girls (particularly those who have been tomboys) are getting over the early shock of realizing that they do not have equal access to power. One girl told me of the satisfaction it still gives her to think back to the time in elementary school when she and her best friend beat up the biggest male bully in their class and of the different adjustment it had been to finding less direct means of controlling boys. In fact, she was very attractive and was aware but not particularly pleased that her power in adolescence to snub troublesome males was as great as her past power to beat them up.

Whether or not they wielded any direct power in their childhoods, adolescent girls know full well that their only hope is through personal authority. In secondary school, this authority is closely tied up with popularity (Eckert, 1989a, 1990), and as a result, girls worry about and seek popularity more than boys. And although boys are far from unconcerned about popularity, they need it less to exert influence. For a boy can indeed gain power and status through direct action, particularly through physical prowess. Thus, when they reach high school, most girls and boys have already accepted to some extent that they will have different routes to social status. In many important ways, boys can acquire power and status through the simple performance of tasks or display of skills. A star varsity athlete, for instance, regardless of his character or appearance, can enjoy considerable status. There is virtually nothing, however, that a girl lacking in social or physical gifts can do that will accord her social status. In other words, whereas it is enough for a boy to have accomplishments of the right sort, a girl must be a certain sort of person. And just as the boy must show off his accomplishments, the girl must display her persona. One result of this is that girls in high school are more socially constrained than boys. Not only do they monitor their own behavior and that of others closely, but they maintain more rigid social boundaries, since the threat of being associated with the wrong kind of person is far greater to the individual whose status depend on who she appears to be rather than what she does. This difference plays itself out linguistically in the context of class-based social categories.

Two hegemonous social categories dominate adolescent social life in American public high schools (Eckert, 1989a). These categories represent opposed class cultures and arise through a conflict of norms and aspirations within the institution of the school. Those who participate in school activities and embrace the school as the locus of their social activities and identities constitute, in the high school, a middle-class culture. In the Detroit area, where the research I report on was done, members of this category are called 'Jocks' whether or not they are athletes, and they identify themselves largely in opposition to the 'Burnouts.' Burnouts, a working-class culture oriented to the blue-collar marketplace, do not accept the school as the locus of their operations; rather, they rebel to some extent against school activities and the authority they represent and orient themselves to the local, and the neighboring urban, area. The Burnouts' hangouts are local parks, neighborhoods, bowling alleys, and strips. They value adult experience and prerogatives and pursue a direct relation with the adult community that surrounds them. The school mediates this relation for the Jocks, on the other hand, who center their social networks and activities in the school. The Jocks and the Burnouts have very different means of acquiring and defining the autonomy that is so central to adolescents. Whereas the Jocks seek autonomy in adult-like roles in the corporate context provided by the school institution, the Burnouts seek it in direct relations with the adult resources of the local area.

Within each category, girls and boys follow very different routes to achieve power and status. The notion of resorting to the manipulation of status when power is unavailable is in fact consciously expressed in the adolescent community. Girls complain that boys can do real things, whereas boys complain that girls talk and scheme rather than doing real things. By 'real' things, they mean those things that reflect skills other than the purely social and that reflect personal, and specifically physical, prowess. Boys are freer in general. For example, Burnout boys can go to Detroit alone, whereas girls must go under their protection; this seriously curtails a Burnout girl's ability to demonstrate urban autonomy. The Jock boys can also assert their personal autonomy through physical prowess. Although it is not 'cool' for a Jock boy to fight frequently, the public recognition that he could is an essential part of the Jock image. In addition, Jock boys can gain public recognition through varsity sports on a level that girls cannot. Thus, the girls in each social category must devote a good deal of their activity to developing and projecting a 'whole person' image designed to gain them influence within their social category. The female Jocks must aggressively develop a Jock image, which is essentially friendly, outgoing, active, clean-cut, all-American. The female Burnouts must aggressively develop a Burnout image, which is essentially tough, urban, 'experienced.' As a result, the symbolic differences between Jocks and Burnouts are clearly more important for girls than for boys, In fact, there is less contact between the two categories among girls, and there is far greater attention to maintaining symbolic differences on all levels – in clothing and other adornment, in demeanor, in publicly acknowledged substance use and sexual activity. There is, therefore, every reason to predict that girls also show greater differences than boys in their use of any linguistic variable that is associated with social category membership or its attributes.

I have shown elsewhere that the most extreme users of phonological variables in my adolescent data are those who have to do the greatest amount of symbolic work to affirm their membership in groups or communities (Eckert, 1989b). Those whose status is clearly based on 'objective' criteria can afford to eschew symbolization. It does not require much of a leap of reasoning to see that women's and men's ways of establishing their status would lead to differences in the use of symbols. The constant competition over externals, as discussed in Maltz and Broker (1982), would free males from the use of symbols. Women, on the other hand, are constrained to exhibit constantly who they are rather than what they can do, and who they are is defined with respect primarily to other women.

PHONOLOGICAL VARIATION

The following data on phonological variation among Detroit suburban adolescents provide some support for the discussion of the complexity of gender constraints in variation. The data were gathered in individual sociolinguistic interviews during two years of participant observation in one high school in a suburb of Detroit. During this time, I followed one graduating class through its last two years of high school, tracing social networks and examining the nature of social identity in this adolescent community. The school serves a community that is almost entirely white, and although the population includes a variety of eastern and western European groups, ethnicity is downplayed in the community and in the school and does not determine social groups. The community covers a socioeconomic span from lower working class through upper middle class, with the greatest representation in the lower middle class.

The speakers in the Detroit area are involved in the Northern Cities Chain Shift (Labov, Yaeger, & Steiner, 1972), a pattern of vowel shifting involving the fronting of low vowels and the backing and lowering of mid vowels (Figure 17.1). The older changes in this shift are the fronting of (æ) and (a), and the lowering and fronting of (oh). The newer ones are the backing of (e) and (uh).

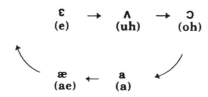

Figure 17.1: The Northern Cities Chain Shift

The following analysis is based on impressionistic phonetic transcription of the vocalic variables from taped free-flowing interviews.[2] A number of variants were distinguished for each vowel in the shift. Both (e) and (uh) have raised, backed, and lowered variants. Backing is the main direction of movement of both (e) and (uh). In each case, two degrees of backing were distinguished:

$$[\varepsilon] > [\varepsilon^>] > [\Lambda]$$

$$[\Lambda] > [\Lambda^>] > [\mathfrak{d}]$$

Both variables also show lowering: [æ] for (e) and [ɑ] for (uh). There are also some raised variants [ε^] and [ɪ] for (e) (the latter occurs particularly in *get*) and [ə] and [U] for (uh). The lowest value for (ae) is [æ^]. The movement of the nucleus of (ae) has clearly been toward peripherality (Labov, Yaeger, & Steiner, 1972), as the higher variants show fronting:

$$[æ^] > [\check{æ}] > [\varepsilon] > [\varepsilon^<] > [e]$$

Two degrees of fronting were distinguished for (a):

[ɑ] > [a] > [æ⁾]

(a) also showed some raising to [aˆ] and [ʌ]. Finally, three degrees of fronting were distinguished for (oh):

[ɔ] > [ɔ<ˇ] > [ɑ] > [a]

(oh) also fronted occasionally to [ʌ]. Extreme variants in the main direction of change were chosen for each of the variables to represent rule application. These extreme variants are:

  (ae) nucleus = [e] or [ɛ<], with or without offglide

  (a)   [æ] or [a<]

  (oh) [a<] or [a]

  (uh) [ɑ] or [ɔ]

  (e)   [ʌ] or [U]

Table 17.1: Percentage of advanced tokens of the five vowels for each combination of social category and sex (numbers of tokens in parentheses)

	Boys		Girls	
	Jocks	*Burnouts*	*Jocks*	*Burnouts*
(ae)	39.7 $\left(\frac{211}{531}\right)$	35.3 $\left(\frac{101}{286}\right)$	62.2 $\left(\frac{244}{392}\right)$	62 $\left(\frac{178}{287}\right)$
(a)	21.4 $\left(\frac{117}{548}\right)$	22 $\left(\frac{77}{350}\right)$	33.8 $\left(\frac{152}{450}\right)$	38.2 $\left(\frac{134}{350}\right)$
(oh)	7.4 $\left(\frac{44}{598}\right)$	10.2 $\left(\frac{34}{333}\right)$	29.8 $\left(\frac{134}{450}\right)$	38.7 $\left(\frac{131}{338}\right)$
(e)	26.2 $\left(\frac{146}{557}\right)$	33.2 $\left(\frac{113}{340}\right)$	23.8 $\left(\frac{103}{433}\right)$	30.9 $\left(\frac{103}{333}\right)$
(uh)	24.6 $\left(\frac{122}{496}\right)$	35.3 $\left(\frac{65}{184}\right)$	25.8 $\left(\frac{94}{364}\right)$	43 $\left(\frac{107}{249}\right)$

The two common social correlations for phonological variables in these data are social category membership and sex. Sex and category affiliation are not simply additive but manifest themselves in a variety of ways among these changes. They interact in ways that are particularly revealing when seen in the context of the overall pattern of linguistic change. Table 17.1 contains a cross-tabulation by social category and sex of the percentage of advanced tokens for each vowel. Differences in the percentages shown in Table 17.1 between boys and girls and between Jocks and Burnouts for each of the changes are displayed in Figure 17.2: one line shows the lead of the girls over boys, whereas the other shows the lead of the Burnouts over the Jocks, for each of the changes in the Northern Cities Shift. As Figure 17.2 shows, the girls have the clearest lead in the oldest changes in the Northern Cities Chain Shift whereas social category differences take over in the later changes. Note that each line dips into negative figures once – at each end of the shift. The boys have a slight lead in the backing of (e) and the Jocks have a slight lead in the raising of (ae). The statistical significance of each of the differences is given in Table 17.2. A treatment of variation that views variables as markers would call the fronting of (ae) and (a) 'sex markers,' the backing of (uh) and (c) 'social category markers,' and the fronting of (oh) both.

In the earlier article, I expressed some puzzlement about the lack of sex differences in the backing of (uh), having expected a simple relation between sex and any sound change (Eckert, 1988). More careful examination of the backing of (uh), however, shows that a simplistic view of the relation between gender and sound change prevented me from exploring other ways in which gender might be manifested in variation. In fact, gender plays a role

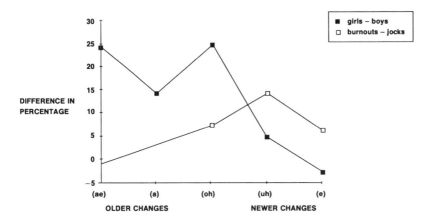

Figure 17.2: Contrast between girls and boys and between Burnouts and Jocks as differences in percentages when calculated for the combined data in Table 17.1

Table 17.2: Significance (yes or no) of social constraints on the vowel changes that constitute the Northern Cities Chain Shift (pl-values of log-likelihood test calculated for each constraint separately using variable rule program on data of Table 17.1)

	Sex	Social category
(ae)	yes ($p < .001$)	no ($p < .77$)
(a)	yes ($p < .001$)	no ($p < .16$)
(oh)[a]	yes ($p < .0001$)	yes ($p < .001$)
(uh)	no[b] ($p < .04$)	yes ($p < .001$)
(e)	no ($p < .38$)	yes ($p < .004$)

Notes
[a] Both constraints remain significant for (oh) when the effects of the other are taken into account.
[b] The sex effect loses significance ($p < .19$) for (uh) when social category is taken into account.

in four out of the five changes in the Northern Cities Chain Shift, although it correlates only with three out of five of the changes, and the role it plays is not the same for all changes.

As can be seen in Table 17.2 and Figure 17.2, the oldest change in the Northern Cities Chain Shift, the raising of (ae), shows no significant association with category membership in the sample as a whole. The same is true within each sex group taken separately (girls: $p < .96$; boys: $p > .22$). However, the girls lead by far in this change. The second change in the Northern Cities Shift, the fronting of (a), also shows only a sex difference, once again with the girls leading. The lack of category effect holds true within each sex group considered separately (girls: $p < .19$; boys: $p > .76$).

The lowering and fronting of (oh) shows a significant difference by both sex and social category, and these effects appear to operate additively in a variable rule analysis:

Overall tendency: 0.182
boys: 0.300   girls: 0.700
Jocks: 0.452   Burnouts: 0.548

When the sexes are separated, however, it turns out that the category difference is only significant among girls ($p < .099$) and not the boys ($p < .14$).

In the backing of (uh), category membership correlates significantly with backing for the population as a whole, with Burnouts leading, but sex does not. When each sex is considered separately, however, it is clear that the

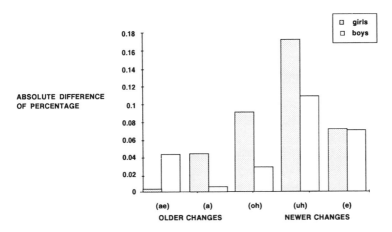

Figure 17.3:   Absolute differences of percentages for Burnouts and Jocks, calculated separately for girls and boys (note that for (ae), Burnouts actually trail Jocks)

category difference is much greater among the girls. The backing of (e) shows a significant category difference, with the Burnouts leading, but no significant sex difference. In this case, when the two sexes are considered separately, the category difference is the same among the girls and among the boys.

Figure 17.3 compares the differences in the percentages in Table 17.1 between the Jocks and Burnouts, within the girls' and boys' samples separately. None of these differences is significant for (a) and for (ae). For (e) they are significant and identical for the two sexes. For (oh) and (uh), however, there is a clear tendency for there to be greater social differentiation among the girls than among the boys.

These results throw into question general statements that women lead in sound change or that sex differences are indicative of sound change. In fact, in my data, the greatest sex differences occur with the older – and probably less vital – changes, involving (ae), (a), and (oh). I would venture the following hypotheses about the relation of gender to the older and the newer changes in these data. It appears that in both sets of changes, the girls are using variation more than the boys. In the case of the newer ones, the girls' patterns of variation show a greater difference between Jocks and Burnouts than do the boys'. In the case of the older ones, all girls are making far greater use than the boys of variables that are not associated with social category affiliation. I have speculated elsewhere that the newer changes, which are more advanced closer to the urban center, are ripe for association with counteradult norms (Eckert, 1987). The older changes, on the other hand, which have been around for some time and are quite advanced in the adult community, are probably not very effective as carriers of counteradult adolescent meaning, but they have a more generalized function associated with expressiveness and perhaps general membership. In both cases – the girls' greater differentiation of the newer changes and their greater use of older changes – the girls' phonological behavior is consonant with their greater need to use social symbols for self-presentation.

CONCLUSIONS

I would not, at this point, claim that the relation shown in these data between new and old changes is necessary, particularly in view of the fact that Labov (1984) found that women in Philadelphia led in new sound changes, whereas sex differences tended to disappear in older changes. It is apparent, then, that generalizations about the relation between sound change and gender are best deferred until more communities have been examined.

The first clear conclusion from these data is that sex and social category are not necessarily independent variables but that they can interact in a very significant way. It is the nature of that interaction, which occurs here with (oh) and (uh), that is of interest in this chapter. It is not the case with these phonological variables that there are large sex differences in one category and not in the other. In other words, sex is rarely more 'salient' in one category than the other. One certainly cannot say that the boys and/or girls are asserting their gender identities through language more in one category than in the other. Rather, there are greater category differences in one sex group than the other. In other words, category membership is more salient to members of one sex than the other; girls are asserting their category identities through language more than boys. This is consonant with the fact that girls are more concerned with category membership than boys, as well as with the fact that girls must rely more on symbolic manifestations of social membership than boys. And this is, in turn, the adolescent manifestation of the broader generalization that women, deprived of access to real power, must claim status through the use of symbols of social membership.

These data make it clear that the search for explanations of sex differences in phonological variation should be redirected. All of the demographic categories that we correlate with phonological variation are more complex than their labels would indicate. Indeed, they are more complex than many sociolinguistic analyses give them credit for. Some analyses of sex differences have suffered from lack of information about women. But it is more important to consider that where most analyses have fallen short has been in the confusion of social meaning with the analyst's demographic abstractions.

NOTES

This work was supported by the Spencer Foundation and the National Science Foundation (BNS 8023291). I owe a great debt of thanks to David Sankoff for his very generous and important help with this chapter. The value of his suggestions for strengthening both the conception and the presentation of these arguments is immeasurable.

1   This is an oversimplification. Gender inequality imposes a canonical comparison, whereby higher and lower status accrue automatically to men and women, respectively. It is this inequality itself that leads to the tendency for intrasex comparisons and for the different terms on which men and women engage in these comparisons. Men tend to compare themselves with other men because women don't count, whereas women tend to compare themselves with other women with an eye to how that affects their relation to male-defined status. (My thanks to Jean Lave for helping me work out this tangle.)
2   The transcription of these data was done by Alison Edwards, Rebecca Knack, and Larry Diemet.

REFERENCES

Brown, P. (1980) 'How and Why Women are More Polite: Some Evidence from a Mayan Community', in McConnell-Ginet, S., Borker, R. A. and Furman, N. (eds) *Women and Language in Literature and Society* (New York: Praeger) pp. 111–36.

Brown, P. and Levinson, S. (1987) *Politeness* (Cambridge: Cambridge University Press).

Clermont, J. and Cedergren, H. (1978) 'Les 'R' de ma Mère Sont Perdus dans L'air', in Thibault, P. (ed.) *Le Français Parlé: Études Sociolinguistiques* (Edmonton, Alberta: Linguistic Research) pp. 13–28.

Deuchar, M. (1988) 'A Pragmatic Account of Women's Use of Standard Speech', in Coates, J. and Cameron, D. (eds) *Women in Their Speech Communities* (London: Longman) pp. 27–32.

Eckert, P. (1984) 'Age and Linguistic Change', in Keith, J. and Kertzer, D. I. (eds) *Age and Anthropological Theory* (Ithaca, NY: Cornell University Press) pp. 219–33.

Eckert, P. (1987) 'The Relative Values of Variables', in Denning, K., Inkelas, S., McNair-Knox, F. and Rickford, J. (eds) *Variation in Language: NWAV-XV* (Stanford: Department of Linguistics) pp. 101–10.

Eckert, P. (1988) 'Adolescent Social Structure and the Spread of Linguistic Change', *Language in Society*, **17**, pp. 183–207.

Eckert, P. (1989a) *Jocks and Burnouts* (New York: Teachers' College Press).

Eckert, P. (1989b) 'Social Membership and Linguistic Variation,' paper presented at NWAVE, Duke University.

Eckert, P. (1990) 'Cooperative Competition in Adolescent "Girl Talk"', *Discourse Processes*, **13**, pp. 91–122.

Eckert, P., Edwards, A. and Robins, L. (1985) *Social and Biological Categories in the Study of Linguistic Variation.* Paper presented at NWAVE IV, Washington, DC.

Fox-Genovese, E. (1988) *Within the Plantation Household* (Chapel Hill, NC: University of North Carolina Press).

Guy, G., Horvath, B., Vonwiller, J., Daisley, E. and Rogers, I. (1986) 'An Intonational Change in Progress in Australian English', *Language in Society*, **15**, pp. 23–52.

Labov, W. (1966) *The Social Stratification of English in New York City* (Washington, DC: Center for Applied Linguistics).

Labov, W. (1972a) 'Hypercorrection by the Lower Middle Class as a Factor in Linguistic Change', in Labov, W. (ed.) *Sociolinguistic Patterns* (Philadelphia, PA: University of Pennsylvania Press) pp. 122–42.

Labov, W. (1972b) 'The Linguistic Consequences of Being a Lame', in Labov, W. (ed.) *Sociolinguistic Patterns* (Philadelphia, PA: University of Pennsylvania Press) pp. 255–92.

Labov, W. (1984) *The Intersection of Sex and Social Factors in the Course of Language Change.* Paper presented at NWAVE, Philadelphia.

Labov, W., Yaeger, M. and Steiner, R. (1972) *A Quantitative Study of Sound Change in Progress.* Report on NSF project No. 65-3287.

Laferriere, M. (1979) 'Ethnicity in Phonological Variation and Change', *Language*, **55**, pp. 603–17.

Macaulay, R. K. S. (1977) *Language Social Class and Education* (Edinburgh: University Press).

Maltz, D. and Borker, R. (1982) 'A Cultural Approach to Male–Female Miscommunication', in Gumperz, J. J. (ed.) *Language and Social Identity* (Cambridge: Cambridge University Press) pp. 195–216.

Rickford, J. (1986) 'The Need for New Approaches to Class Analysis in Sociolinguistics', *Language and Communication*, **6**, pp. 215–21.

Thibault, P. (1983) *Equivalence et Grammaticalisation.* Ph.D. dissertation, Université de Montréal.

Trudgill, P. (1972) *The Social Differentiation of English in Norwich* (Cambridge: Cambridge University Press).

Veblen, T. (1931) *The Theory of the Leisure Class* (New York: Viking).

Wolfram, W. A. (1969) *A Sociolinguistic Description of Detroit Negro Speech* (Washington, DC: Center for Applied Linguistics).

Part IV
Stylistic Variation

The chapters in Part III showed sociolinguistic variation, mainly in the sense of quantitative differences in the language use of different groups or sub-groups of people. This is the dimension of linguistic variation that Labov simply called the 'social' dimension, where language reflects the social stratification of groups within a speech community. But sociolinguistic surveys also produced data on *stylistic* variation, which Labov represented as a second dimension cutting across social variation. As we saw, for example in Trudgill's Norwich data (in Chapter 14), there is a plane of variation through which individual speakers will vary their speaking styles, from situation to situation and even from moment to moment.

This basic, two-dimensional model of linguistic variation has surfaced in other theorists' work too. Halliday, for example, described linguistic variation as being of two broad sorts: variation 'according to the user', which he labelled *dialect* variation (in a rather specialist sense of the term dialect), and variation 'according to use', which he labelled *register* variation. Sociolinguistic surveys can demonstrate that there is a 'situational' dimension of linguistic variation, but there have been relatively few attempts to understand 'register' or *stylistic variation* in more precise terms.

One concerted attempt to do this is found in *accommodation theory*, developed since the 1970s by Giles and his associates. Chapter 18 is an extract taken from one of the earliest statements of accommodation theory, by Giles and Powesland. The central insight is that sociolinguistics needs a sharper focus on social context than on the individual speaker speaking as a group member. Giles argues that the *relational* context of talk is crucial, and that we need to study linguistic variation that is occasioned by who a particular speaker is addressing. That is, speakers can be expected to adjust or *accommodate* aspects of their speech styles towards, or away from, those of their addressees. The model is explicitly a social psychological model, partly because accommodation is a cognitive (as well as a linguistic) adjustment, but also because the model tries to specify the attitudinal conditions under which speakers will and will not make linguistic adjustments. For example, as Giles and Powesland's chapter claims, a speaker draws inferences about the characteristics of a speaking partner and will then 'move closer' or *converge* in speech style to that person, *if* the speaker wants to gain the other's approval.

There are different possible accommodation *strategies*, with convergence (moving closer) and divergence (moving further apart) being the most obvious. Later versions of the model identified more and more specific categories of conditions under which accommodation would or would not happen, and identified exceptions to the central predictions. But even in this early statement of the theory, we can see the dynamic basis of the accommodation model, and how it brings an interactional focus into the analysis of linguistic variation. Also, the general notion of accommodation is applicable to several different 'levels' of sociolinguistic analysis. It was originally applied to accent (phonological) variation, where it could explain the familiar experience of speakers shifting their accents, e.g. from 'broader' to 'milder' in the presence of someone speaking a more vernacular or more 'posh' variety. But, as Giles and Powesland's chapter itself shows, the model has been valuable in accounting for speakers' functionally and symbolically motivated choice of languages, such as choosing to converse in French versus English in particular speaking contexts in Quebec. (There are clear points of contact, then, with all the chapters in Part V and especially with Bourhis's discussion of Quebec in Chapter 24.)

There is a particularly close resemblance between accommodation theory and Bell's research on *audience design* (Chapter 19). For Bell too, the main motivating principle behind style is the addressee or the audience. What separates Giles's and Bell's approaches is mainly the disciplines in which each is being developed. Giles and his colleagues are building a complex psychological theory which identifies speakers' motives and orientations to other speaking participants, but also the importance of social norms and the constraints of appropriate behaviour. Language is actually only one of several key theoretical issues in this model. Bell, on the other hand, is working largely within the Labovian tradition, and accounting for statistical data on linguistic variation. For example, the fact that the quantitative scope of social variation in speech is typically greater than the scope of stylistic variation suggests to him that style variation derives from social variation.

The first two chapters in this section deal with the topic of style in a rather abstract way. The third chapter gives an illustration of speech style-selection that will be familiar to fans of 1960s and 1970s British popular music. (The periodic relaunches of collections of music by the Beatles and the Rolling Stones should allow most readers to listen in to the relevant data – as music historians if not as fans!) In Chapter 20, Trudgill describes the norms of *sung pronunciation* in rock and pop songs, and how these norms shifted during the careers of some influential bands. Pop-song pronunciation is a good instance of a sociolinguistic register because it is so strictly tied to a particular communicative situation and to a set of associated social norms.

At the same time, the pop-song instance is intriguing precisely because it shows the limitations of any single explanation for style-selection. Trudgill opts for an interpretation based on Le Page's 'acts of identity' model. Americanized pronunciation in British pop and rock music is not in any direct sense an 'accommodated' or 'audience-designed' style, even though it does clearly show an orientation to American speech norms. It is designed on semiotic principles (see Hodge and Kress, in Chapter 6). It is designed to convey the symbolic meanings appropriate to a particular (sub)cultural identity and value system. As Trudgill shows, an ideological shift – like the assertion of British, working-class, anti-establishment values in the era of punk music – demands a different set of symbols. It would be informative to extend and update Trudgill's analysis by applying his ideas to current popular music trends in different communities.

PART IV: FURTHER READING

Biber, D. (1988) *Variation Across Speech and Writing* (Cambridge: Cambridge University Press).

Coupland, N. (1988a) *Dialect in Use* (Cardiff: University of Wales Press).

Coupland, N. (ed.) (1988b) *Styles of Discourse* (London: Croom Helm).

Coupland, N. and Giles, H. (eds) (1988) *Communicative Accommodation: Recent Developments*. Double special issue of the journal *Language and Communication*, **8**, 3/4.

Finegan, E. and Biber, D. (1994) *Perspectives on Register: Situating Register Variation within Sociolinguistics* (New York: Oxford University Press).

Giles, H. (ed.) (1984) *The Dynamics of Speech Accommodation*. Special issue of the *International Journal of Sociology of Language*, **46**.

Joos, M. (1962) *The Five Clocks* (Bloomington, IN: Indiana University Research Center in Anthropology, Folklore, and Linguistics).

Rampton, B. (1995) *Crossing: Language and Ethnicity among Adolescents* (London: Longman).

Rickford, J. and Eckert, P. (eds) (1997) *Style* (Cambridge: Cambridge University Press).

18 Accommodation Theory

Howard Giles and Peter Powesland

Fischer (1958) found in a linguistic survey in New England, when he interviewed 24 children, that the 'choice between the participle ending /ing/ and the /in/ variant, appear to be related to sex, class, personality and mood of the speaker, to the formality of the conversation and to the specific verb spoken...(and doubtless of the person spoken to, although this was not investigated)'. But more importantly, Fischer advocated a series of studies involving the interaction of different dialect speakers which he proposed to term 'comparative idiolectology' where

> one might concentrate on a single informant...and note changes in his speech in different settings and situations and with different conversants. Moreover, since language is phenomenologically as much listening as speaking one would be led to analyse what was said comprehensibly to him by others, as well as what he said himself.

The present chapter is in fact an attempt to provide a starting point for the construction of a theoretical framework for such a comparative idiolectology.

Since 1958 much research has accrued [this text published in 1975 – *Eds*] which demonstrates that an individual's speech patterns are in part dependent on the person to whom he is talking, the topic of the discourse and the setting in which it takes place. The bilingual's and bidialectal's choice of language and dialect respectively have been shown to be a function of these three factors as has the monolingual's choice of speech style. Indeed it is, according to Hymes (1972), this notion of code variation and speech diversity that has been singled out as a hallmark of sociolinguistics. The models of speech dynamics that have emerged (e.g. those of Ervin-Tripp, 1964: Hymes, 1967; Sankoff, 1971) have relied, as has already been stated, on a descriptive approach in terms of presenting a taxonomy of factors influencing code variations, such as

Source: 'A Social Psychological Model of Speech Diversity', in Giles, H. and Powesland, P. F. (1975) *Speech Style and Social Evaluation* [European Monographs in Social Psychology] (New York: Harcourt Brace) pp. 154–70.

topic, setting and so forth. This initial work has been extremely important since 'the work of taxonomy is a necessary part of progress towards models (structural and generative) of sociolinguistic description, formulation of universal sets of features and relations, and explanatory theories' (Hymes, 1972). However, owing to the fact that our taxonomies have changed little over the past few years, Giles, Taylor and Bourhis (1973) felt the need to develop a tentative, explanatory sociolinguistic theory to account for at least specific types of speech diversities. The strategy at this initial stage was to formulate a theory which focused on one taxonomic level, in this case, the interpersonal aspects of speech diversity. And it is an elaboration of this theory that this chapter is about, together with a discussion of its usefulness in describing shifts at one particular linguistic level – accent usage. It is hoped that through the elaboration of this theory the two areas of speaker evaluation and speech diversity can be conceptually linked. ...

The essence of the theory of accommodation lies in the social psychological research on similarity-attraction. This work suggests that an individual can induce another to evaluate him more favourably by reducing dissimilarities between them. The process of speech accommodation operates on this principle and as such may be a reflection of an individual's desire for social approval. It seems likely that the accommodative act may involve certain costs for the speaker, in terms of identity-change and expended effort, and so such behaviour may be initiated only if potential rewards are available. If one can accept the notion that people find social approval from others rewarding, it would not seem unreasonable to suppose that there may be a general set to accommodate to others in most social situations. ... This accommodative set is, however, not unresponsive to possible contrary demands of the specific situation, as can be inferred from the reference to speech divergence earlier. It has been suggested that the accommodative act provides the sender with rewards referred to in general terms as the receiver's approval. What specifically these rewards may be in more concrete terms (e.g. increased perceived status) would depend upon the situation itself and the particular linguistic level upon which accommodation occurred. We shall discuss the nature of these rewards shortly when we concentrate upon one particular linguistic level. It is important to note that the receiver's approval does not necessarily imply liking for the sender – just as an employer's approval of a man as suitable for employment does not necessarily imply liking for him.

Accommodation through speech can be regarded as an attempt on the part of a speaker to modify or disguise his persona in order to make it more acceptable to the person addressed. The speaker's rationale, of which he is not necessarily consciously aware, is represented in the following schema:

There is a dyad consisting of speakers A and B
Assume that A wishes to gain B's approval
A then
1. Samples B's speech and
    (i)   draws inferences as to the personality characteristics of B (or at least the characteristics which B wishes to project as being his)
    (ii) assumes that B values and approves of such characteristics
    (iii) assumes that B will approve of him (A) to the extent that he (A) displays similar characteristics
2. Chooses from his speech-repertoire patterns of speech which project characteristics of which B is assumed to approve.

The effect of this decision process is that A produces speech similar – or at least more similar than his normal speech would be – to the speech of B. There is therefore speech convergence. If B at the same times goes through a similar process there is mutual convergence. One effect of the convergence of speech patterns is that it allows the sender to be perceived as more similar to the receiver than would have been the case had he not accommodated his style of speaking in this manner. But in addition, speech accommodation may be a device by the speaker to make himself better understood. The more the sender reflects the receiver's own mode of communication, the more easily will his message be understood. However, Triandis (1960) claims that increased communicative effectiveness between members of a dyad increases interpersonal attraction anyway. It could be suggested that in certain interaction situations the emphasis with regard to accommodation is on increasing comprehensibility whilst in others it may be on causing the sender to be perceived more favourably. But since both processes produce interpersonal attraction, it may not be worthwhile at this point to attempt to disentangle them.

What is the empirical evidence for such a model? Since the desire for social approval is assumed to be at the heart of accommodation, it could be hypothesized that people high on a scale of need for social approval would accommodate more than those having a low need in this regard. Although this has not been tested directly, some encouragement can be derived from the study by Mehrabian (1971) in which he found the subjects highest on a measure of affiliative needs showed the greatest tendency to reciprocate positive verbal and nonverbal signals provided by their dyad partners. With regard to the idea that a person who accommodates would be perceived more favourably than one who does not, the evidence is more substantial. Dabbs (1969) found that a person who exhibited response-matching in respect of the gestures and postures of the person with whom he was interacting was liked more than someone who did not behave in this manner. Moreover, the person who matched responses was considered to have better ideas and be more persuasive than the person who did not.

Although this example is outside the field of speech it does appear to be an instance of accommodation.

With regard to bilingual accommodation in Quebec, Giles *et al.* (1973) had a taped French Canadian (FC) stimulus speaker provide a message to bilingual English Canadians (EC) in either French (no accommodation), a mixture of French and English (partial accommodation) or English (full accommodation). It was found that the FC was perceived more favourably in terms and considerateness and of his effort to bridge the cultural gap the more he accommodated to the EC listeners. Moreover, when the subjects were given the opportunity to return a communication to their FC partner, subjects who were spoken to in English accommodated the most (i.e. spoke French). Subjects in the mixed language condition showed less accommodation and those who were spoken to in French showed least. The results clearly support the theoretical model thus far formulated. A follow-up study by Simard, Taylor and Giles (1976) has shown that such patterns are in evidence when the roles of the two ethnolinguistic groups are reversed. These findings complement those of Feldman (1968) who found that certain cultural groups are more favourably disposed toward assisting foreigners who accommodate to their language than those who do not. ...

Cross-cultural interaction in a realistic context suggests the need for further elaborations of the accommodation model. In the experiment by Giles *et al.* the EC listeners were fully aware that the stimulus speaker was bilingual and had voluntarily chosen to speak the language he adopted. However, in everyday life, we are very often unaware of the background information surrounding an accommodative or nonaccommodative act. For instance, we sometimes do not know whether or not a speaker who failed to accommodate to us had the necessary language skills to do so. Even when a person does accommodate we can often not be sure whether he was under pressure to do so, or whether he voluntarily made the effort to reduce the dissimilarities. The accommodation model thus far described does not take into account such attributed motives underlying accommodative behaviour and implicitly assumes that the perception of all linguistic adjustments *per se*, regardless of the motives attributed to them, will be equally effective. Similarly, different attributed motives underlying nonaccommodative behaviour have not been taken into account and the model has simply regarded the maintenance of regular speech habits as being unfavourably perceived by the listener.

Simard, Taylor and Giles suggested that developments in causal attribution theory could provide useful guidelines for an extension of the accommodation model. Heider (1958), for example, suggests that we understand a person's behaviour, and hence evaluate the person himself, in terms of the motives and intentions that we attribute as the cause of his actions. He proposes that a perceiver considers three factors when attributing motives to an act, namely, the other's *ability*, his *effort* and the *external pressures* impelling him to perform in the manner in which he did. In order to illustrate these factors in operation, Heider gives the example of someone rowing a boat across a stream where the perceiver's evaluation of the actor will depend upon the perception of the actor's *ability* to row, the amount of *effort* exerted and *external* factors such as wind and current prevailing at the time. Analyzing the study by Giles *et al.* (1973) in causal attribution terms provides a clear understanding of the subjects' behaviour. The EC subjects knew that the FC speaker was capable of speaking in English (ability) and that there were no external pressures on him to select one language rather than the other. Thus, subjects were likely to have assessed the FC's accommodative or nonaccommodative behaviour solely in terms of the perceived effort he was prepared to make them. The greater the amount of effort perceived in accommodation when there were no external pressures, the more effective this behaviour was shown to be.

The implication of attribution theory for the present context therefore is that a listener can make a variety of attributions regarding accommodation and nonaccommodation. For example, since a person who accommodates clearly has the linguistic ability to do so, the listener can attribute this behaviour either to the speaker's being forced to converge by some external pressures or to his voluntarily making an effort to reduce dissimilarities between them.

Simard, Taylor and Giles (1976) designed a study primarily to determine whether accommodation was differentially perceived and could be classified according to the motives attributed to it by the listener, Specifically, the study examined whether the attribution factors of ability, effort and external pressure influenced listeners' reactions to accommodative and nonaccommodative speech acts. For example, how would the occurrence of nonaccommodation be attributed when listeners had little knowledge about the speaker's motives – to a lack of ability, to a lack of effort or to the existence of external pressures? Would voluntary accommodation be more effective than forced accommodation in terms of evaluation of the speaker and reciprocated accommodation?

The experiment had three major conditions, the first of which was designed to replicate the findings of Giles *et al.* (1973) using FC listeners with an EC speaker – the reverse of the original study. In this condition, the listener knew that the EC speaker was capable of speaking both English and French and was not under any external pressure to use one language or the other. For the second condition, the 'no information' condition, the listener was not aware of the speaker's linguistic abilities or of any external pressure. For the final condition, the listener knew that the speaker did not choose the language of communication but that external pressure was placed on him to use one language rather than the other. In each of these three conditions, different FC subjects heard the EC stimulus speaker either accommodate to them in French or not accommodate to them by using his native tongue, English.

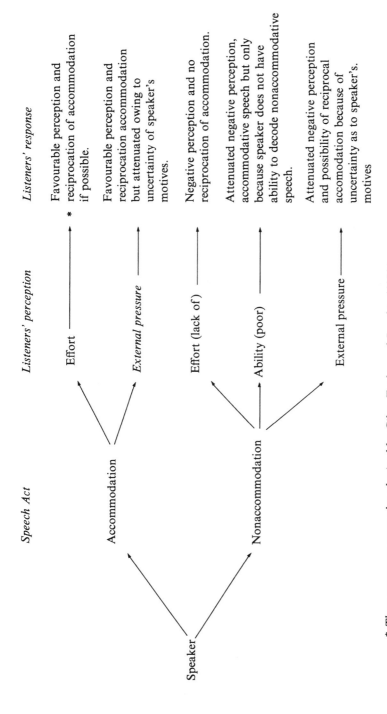

Speaker → Accommodation → Effort → * Favourable perception and reciprocation of accommodation if possible.

External pressure → Favourable perception and reciprocation accommodation but attenuated owing to uncertainty of speaker's motives.

Speaker → Nonaccommodation → Effort (lack of) → Negative perception and no reciprocation of accommodation.

Ability (poor) → Attenuated negative perception, accommodative speech but only because speaker does not have ability to decode nonaccommodative speech.

External pressure → Attenuated negative perception and possibility of reciprocal accomodation because of uncertainty as to speaker's motives

Speech Act — *Listeners' perception* — *Listeners' response*

* *These responses were also obtained by Giles, Taylor and Bourhis (1973).*

Figure 18.1: A revised version of the accommodation model (after Simard, Taylor and Giles, in press)

The tape-recorded message from the EC speaker was a three-minute description of a route to be followed on a city map. The FC listeners were required to trace the route on a blank map in front of them as the description was being given by the speaker. However, each of these descriptions was preceded by one of three different taped instructions apparently being given to the stimulus speaker; these instructions corresponded to the major manipulations in the study. The listeners were told that they would hear their speaker being given his instructions to ensure that they understood completely the nature of the task. In each introduction, it was made clear to the speaker that his listening partner would be a FC. After the description was completed and the subject had traced the route, he or she was presented with a map similar to the one used earlier. This map had a new route traced on it and subjects were asked to describe this route on tape to the EC who had just given them their description and to describe it in the language of their choice. The dependent measures used in the study included: perceptions of the stimulus speaker's language abilities and of his efforts to bridge the cultural gap; the number of errors made in interpreting the message; and the choice of language for the returned communication.

On the basis of their findings, Simard, Taylor and Giles (1976) proposed a revision of the accommodation model, a schematic representation of which appears in Figure 18.1. It suggests that the perception of accommodation is effective in terms of speaker evaluation and reciprocal accommodation. However, a qualification needs to be considered in that if accommodation is attributed to external pressures rather than voluntary effort, then it is likely to be less effective.

REFERENCES

Dabbs, J. M. Jr. (1969) 'Similarity of Gestures and Interpersonal Influence', Proceedings of the 77th Annual Convention of the American Psychological Association.

Ervin-Tripp, S. M. (1964) 'An Analysis of the Interaction of Language, Topic and Listener', in supplement to *American Anthropologist*, **66**, pp. 86–102.

Feldman, R. E. (1968) 'Response to Compatriots and Foreigners Who Seek Assistance', *Journal of Personality and Social Psychology*, **10**, pp. 202–14.

Fischer, J. L. (1958) 'Social Influences in the Choice of a Linguistic Variant', *Word*, **14**, pp. 47–56.

Giles, H., Taylor, D. M. and Bourhis, R. Y. (1973) 'Towards a Theory of Interpersonal Accommodation Through Language: Some Canadian Data', *Language in Society*, **2**, pp. 177–92.

Heider, F. (1958) *The Psychology of Interpersonal Relations* (New York: Wiley).

Hymes, D. (1967) Models of the Interaction of Language and Social Setting', *Journal of Social Issues*, **23**, pp. 8–28.

Hymes, D. (1972) 'Models of the Interaction of Language and Social Life', in Gumperz, J. J. and Hymes, D. (eds) *Directions in Sociolinguistics: The Ethnography of Communication* (New York: Holt, Rinehart and Winston) pp. 35–71.

Mehrabian, A. (1971) 'Verbal and Nonverbal Interaction of Strangers in a Waiting Situation', *Journal of Experimental Research in Personality*, 5, pp. 127–38.

Sankoff, G. (1971) 'Language Use in Multilingual Societies: Some Alternative Approaches', in Pride, J. B. and Holmes, J. (eds) *Sociolinguistics* (London: Penguin).

Simard, L., Taylor, D. M. and Giles, H. (1976) 'Attribution Processes and Interpersonal Accommodation in a Bilingual Setting', *Language and Speech*, 19, pp. 374–87.

Triandis, H. C. (1960) 'Cognitive Similarity and Communication in a Dyad', *Human Relations*, 13, pp. 175–83.

19 Language Style as Audience Design

Allan Bell

WHAT IS STYLE?

Language style is one of the most challenging aspects of sociolinguistic variation. The basic principle of language style is that an individual speaker does not always talk in the same way on all occasions. Style means that speakers have alternatives or choices – a '*that* way' which could have been chosen instead of a '*this* way'. Speakers talk in different ways in different situations, and these different ways of speaking can carry different social meanings.

Style constitutes one whole dimension of linguistic variation – the range of variation within the speech of an individual speaker. It intersects with what William Labov has called the 'social' dimension of variation – differences between the speech of different speakers (see Chapter 2 in this volume). In sum, style involves the ways in which the same speakers talk differently on different occasions rather than the ways in which different speakers talk differently from each other.

STYLE IN SOCIOLINGUISTICS

We can distinguish two main approaches to the study of style in sociolinguistics. The first, associated with Dell Hymes (see Chapter 1), encompasses the many ways in which individual speakers can express themselves differently in different situations. This recognizes that style can operate on the full range of linguistic levels – in the phonology or sound system of a language, in its syntax or grammar, in its semantics or the lexicon, and in the wider patterns of speaking across whole discourses and conversations. So style may be expressed in different forms of address, in the use of tag questions such as *isn't it*, in different ways of asking a question, in choosing one word over another, as well as in the ways that different vowels and consonants are pronounced. On the social side, Hymes has proposed a

---

Source: Written specially for this collection.

240

wide range of factors that may affect the way an individual talks, including audience, purpose, topic, mode, channel and genre (see Chapter 1).

The second approach to style in sociolinguistics is much more strictly defined on both the social and linguistic dimensions. Labov pioneered in his 1966 New York City study a means of eliciting different styles of speech from people within a single interview. In his recorded interviews, as well as conversing with his informants, he had them carry out a series of language tasks, each of which was designed to focus more and more of the speaker's attention on to their speech. When the speaker talked to someone else rather than the interviewer, or discussed topics which got them particularly involved, they were likely to be paying the least attention to their speech, and Labov called this 'casual' speech. When the speaker was answering questions in typical interview fashion, they would be paying rather more attention to their speech and so produced 'careful' style. When they read aloud a brief passage of a story, they would give still more attention to their pronunciation. Reading out a list of isolated words focused more attention again, and reading a set of minimal pairs – words which differ only by a single sound such as *reader* and *raider* – would make the speaker pay the maximum amount of attention to their speech.

On the social side, therefore, this represents what we might call a minimalist approach, compared with what we might call the 'maximalist' view of the more ethnographic work. Labov has also usually worked with micro aspects of linguistic structure – specific sounds which can alternate as two or more variants of one linguistic 'variable', such as the choice between a 'standard' -*ing* pronunciation and a 'non-standard' -*in'* pronunciation in words such as *leaving* and *building*. These are classed as different ways of saying the same thing, and analyses of such sociolinguistic variables have produced findings which, when graphed, have become classics of the sociolinguistic literature.

Peter Trudgill studied the (ng) variable, and Figure 14.1 on p. 181 of this volume from his work on Norwich English is typical of a social class by style graph. Five social groups are distinguished, ranging from the Lower Working Class to the Upper Middle Class, using four different styles. The pattern of the lines of this graph shows two things. First, as we move from the middle-class groups to the working-class groups the use of the -*in'* variant increases and, conversely, the use of the prestigious -*ing* variant decreases. Secondly, the rise of the lines from word lists to casual speech shows that each group style-shifts towards less -*in'* and more -*ing* with each attention-increasing task in the interview. So all four classes use most -*in'* in casual speech, less in careful speech, still less in the reading passage, and least of all in the word lists.

Labov's techniques for eliciting styles have been used in countless studies in many languages and countries since 1966, and in many cases a similar kind of gradient of style-shifting has been found. However, some of the subsequent research has had different findings, and some researchers have questioned whether these styles really apply outside the confines of the sociolinguistic interview. Many have also questioned whether attention to speech is the factor which is operating here. Some have found that attention could be directed to producing all levels of linguistic alternatives, not just the more prestigious forms such as -*ing* rather than -*in*'. Isn't it also possible for speakers to attend to their speech and rather consciously sound *more* non-standard?

AUDIENCE DESIGN

One critique and development of earlier sociolinguistic approaches to style was the Audience Design framework outlined in Bell (1984). I proposed that style shift occurs primarily in response to the speaker's audience rather than to amount of attention or other factors. This approach grew out of one particular study on style. While researching the language of radio news in New Zealand, I came across an unanticipated situation which proved to be tailored to locating and explaining style shift (Bell 1991). The organization of the New Zealand public broadcasting system at the time meant that two of the radio stations being studied both originated centrally in the same suite of studios. The same individual newsreaders could be heard reading news bulletins on both of these networks. Station YA was 'National Radio', the prestige service of New Zealand's public corporation radio. It had an audience with higher social status than the audience for station ZB, which was one of a network of local community stations.

Figure 19.1 shows the percentage of intervocalic /t/ voicing for four newsreaders recorded on both these stations. When it occurs between two vowels, usually voiceless /t/ can be pronounced like a voiced /d/, making

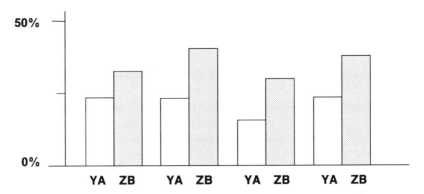

Figure 19.1: Percentage of intervocalic /t/ voicing by four newscasters on two New Zealand radio stations, YA and ZB (from Bell 1982: 162)

words such as *writer* and *latter* sound like *rider* and *ladder*. The six newsreaders shifted on average 20 per cent between YA and ZB. Single newsreaders heard on two different stations showed a remarkable and consistent ability to make considerable style shifts to suit the audience. These switches between stations were at times very rapid: at off-peak hours a single newsreader might alternate between YA and ZB news with as little as ten minutes between bulletins on the different stations.

What could be the cause of these shifts? There is after all just one individual speaker producing two divergent styles. The institution is the same in both cases. The topic mix of the news is similar (in some cases, even the actual scripted news stories are the same). The studio setting is the same. And there is no reason to suppose that the amount of attention paid to speech is being systematically varied. Of all the factors we might suggest as possible influences on news style, only the audience correlated with these shifts.

Looking beyond this particular study, it seemed clear that the same regularities which were amplified in the media context are also operating in face-to-face communication. In mass communication, a broadcaster's individual style is routinely subordinated to a shared station style whose character can only be explained in terms of its target audience. When we look at ordinary conversation, we can also see the important effect that an audience has on a speaker's style, although the impact is less obvious than for broadcasters. In particular, we know that mass communicators are under considerable pressure to win the approval of their audience in order to maintain their audience size or market share. In ordinary conversation the urge to gain the approval of one's audience is similar in kind although less in degree.

The audience design framework was developed to account for these patterns in face-to-face as well as mass communication. The main points can be summarized like this:

1. *Style is what an individual speaker does with a language in relation to other people.* The basic tenet of audience design is that style is oriented to people rather than to mechanisms such as attention. Style is essentially a social thing. It marks interpersonal and intergroup relations. It is interactive – and active. Although audience design and its hypotheses are based on evidence behind this proposition, this is really a premise rather than a hypothesis. Our view of style is ultimately derived from our view of the nature of human persons. Behind audience design there lies a strong and quite general claim that the character of (intra-speaker) style shift derives at a deep level from the nature of (inter-speaker) language differences between people.

2. *Style derives its meaning from the association of linguistic features with particular social groups.* The social evaluation of a group is transferred to the linguistic features that are associated with that group. The link between

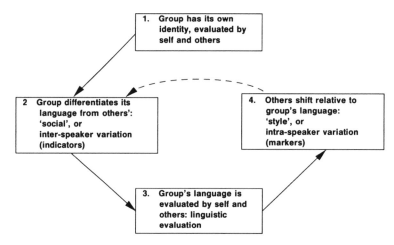

Figure 19.2: The derivation of style from inter-speaker variation

differences in the language of different groups ('social' variation in Labov's terms) and within the language of individual speakers (stylistic variation) is made by society's evaluation of the group's language (Figure 19.2). Sociolinguists have noted this at least since Ferguson and Gumperz (1960). Evaluation of a linguistic variable and style shift of that variable are reciprocal, as Labov (1972) demonstrated in identifying these 'marker' variables. Evaluation is always associated with style shift, and style shift with evaluation. Those few variables which do not show style shift (indicators) are also not evaluated in the speech community. Stylistic meaning therefore has what we can call a normative basis. A particular style is *normally* associated with a particular group or situation, and therefore carries with it the flavour of those associations.

3.   *Speakers design their style primarily for and in response to their audience.*   This is the heart of audience design. Style shift occurs primarily in response to a change in the speaker's audience. Audience design is generally manifested in a speaker shifting their style to be more like that of the person they are is talking to – this is 'convergence' in the terms of the Speech/Communication Accommodation Theory developed by Giles and associates (see Chapter 18). Response is the primary mode of style shift. Style is a responsive phenomenon, but it is actively so, not passive.

This can be seen in a study of the speech of a travel agent carried out by Coupland (1984). Coupland recorded an assistant in a travel agency in conversation with a wide social range of clients. He quantified the assistant's level for the intervocalic (t) voicing variable when speaking to different groups of clients, and compared that with the levels the clients use in their own speech. Figure 19.3 shows how the travel assistant accommodates

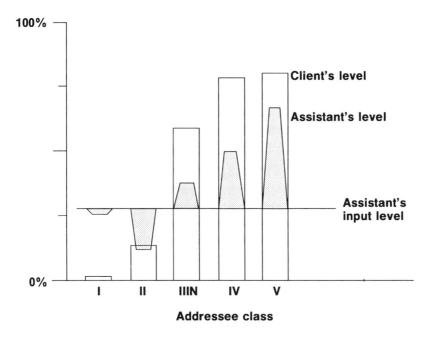

Figure 19.3:   Travel assistant's convergence on intervocalic (t) voicing variable to five occupational classes of clients. Input level taken as assistant's speech to own class. IIIN (derived from Coupland 1984: Figure 4).

towards the clients' own levels of (t) voicing, shifting to more (t) voicing for lower-class clients who use more voicing themselves, and to less (t) voicing with higher-class clients. In this style shift she goes on average at least half-way to meet her clients.

4.   *Audience design applies to all codes and levels of a language repertoire, monolingual and multilingual.* Audience design does not refer only to quantitative style shift of individual sociolinguistic variables such as (ng). Within a single language, it involves features such as choice of personal pronouns or address terms (Ervin-Tripp 1972) and politeness strategies (Brown and Levinson 1987), as well as quantitative style-shifting. Audience design also applies to all codes and repertoires within a speech community, including the switch from one complete language to another in bilingual situations (see Chapter 28). It has long been recognized that the processes which make a monolingual shift styles are the same as those which make a bilingual switch languages. Where a monolingual speaker of English will make quantitative shifts on a number of linguistic variables when talking to a stranger rather than to a family member, a bilingual speaker in parts of Scotland, for example, will shift from talking Gaelic to a family member into English to address a stranger.

5. *Variation on the style dimension within the speech of a single speaker derives from and echoes the variation which exists between speakers on the 'social' dimension.* This style axiom (Bell 1984: 151) claims that the inter-relation between intra-speaker style shift and inter-speaker dialect differences is a derivation. The axiom refers both to the historical origins of styles, and to the present basis on which styles carry social meaning. That is, distinct styles originated in past differences in the language of different groups. And styles carry a particular social meaning now in the present because of their association with the language of particular groups.

The style axiom encapsulates the often-noted fact that the same linguistic variables operate simultaneously on both social and stylistic dimensions, so that for one isolated variable it may be difficult to distinguish a 'casual salesman from a careful pipefitter' (Labov 1972: 240). It also reflects the quantitative relationship of the social and stylistic dimensions: the maximum style shift on graphs such as Figure 14.1 in Chapter 14 (i.e. Trudgill's (ng)) is usually less than the maximum difference between social groups. On Trudgill's graph, the greatest style shift is by the Upper Working Class and is about 80 per cent, while the maximum difference between the different classes is some 95 per cent in style B.

6. *Speakers show a fine-grained ability to design their style for a range of different addressees, and to a lesser degree for other audience members.* These are the classic findings of Giles's accommodation model (e.g. Giles and Powesland 1975; see Chapter 18). In its essence, speech accommodation theory proposed that speakers accommodate their speech style to their hearers in order to win approval. Although the theory was extensively expanded and revised during the 1980s, its principal insight has been that speakers respond primarily to their audience in designing their talk. As well as changing the way they talk when addressing different people, there is good evidence that speakers can make even finer shifts to cater to a range of different people within their audience.

Not all audience members are equally important. We can distinguish and rank their roles according to whether or not they are known, ratified or addressed by the speaker. We can picture them as occupying concentric circles, each one more distant from the speaker (Figure 19.4). The main character in the audience is the second person, the *addressee*, who is known, ratified and addressed. Among the other, third persons who may be present, the *auditors* are known and ratified interlocutors within the group. Third parties whom the speaker knows to be there, but who are not ratified as part of the group, are *overhearers*. And other parties whose presence the speaker does not even know about are *eavesdroppers*.

Speakers are able to subtly adjust their style when a stranger joins a group and becomes an 'auditor' – present in the group but not directly addressed. They even respond to the presence of an overhearer who is within earshot

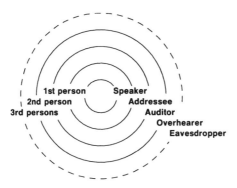

Figure 19.4:   Persons and roles in the speech situation

but is not part of the speaker's conversational circle. In a bilingual community in Hungary, for instance, the arrival of a monolingual German speaker at an Hungarian-speaking inn can be enough to make the conversation switch into German (Gal 1979). The switch between different languages is a much more obvious manifestation of overhearer design than the quantitative style shifts within the same language by a monolingual speaker, but the process is basically the same.

7.   *Style shifts according to topic or setting derive their meaning and direction of shift from the underlying association of topics or settings with typical audience members.*   This tentative hypothesis suggests that when speakers shift their style because of a change of topic, this is an echo of the kind of shift that occurs when a speaker style-shifts in response to the kind of addressee a particular topic is associated with. It implies that we talk about education in a style that echoes how we talk to a teacher, or about work in a style that echoes how we talk to the boss. Thus Coupland's study mentioned above also found that the travel agent shifted her style significantly between work-related topics and other topics.

8.   *As well as the 'responsive' dimension of style, there is the 'initiative' dimension.*   Here the style shift itself *initiates* a change in the situation rather than *resulting* from such a change.

Sociolinguists have drawn attention to this distinction at least since Blom and Gumperz (1972). In responsive style shift, there is a regular association between language and social situation. The entry of outsiders to a local group, for example, triggers a switch from local dialect to standard speech. These situational shifts reflect the speech community's norms of what is appropriate speech for certain audiences. Initiative style trades on such regular associations, infusing the flavour of one setting into a different context. Here language becomes an independent variable which itself shapes the situation. So we find bilingual speakers who switch out of their usual home language into the prestige language of the wider community in order to clinch an argument with a family member. In initiative style shift, the individual speaker makes creative use of language resources often from beyond the immediate speech community, such as distant dialects, or stretches those resources in novel directions. Literary examples of this kind of 'stylization' (Bakhtin 1981) are well known in the use that J. R. R. Tolkien and James Joyce, for example, have made of other dialects or languages to create their own unique voices.

9. *Initiative style shifts are in essence 'referee design', by which the linguistic features associated with a group can be used to express identification with that group.* Initiative style shifts derive their force and their direction of shift from their underlying association with kinds of persons or groups. They focus on an absent reference group rather than the present addressee, for example by adopting a non-native accent. Referees are third persons who are not physically present at an interaction but who are so salient for a speaker that they influence style even in their absence. Initiative style shift is essentially a redefinition by the speaker of their own identity in relation to their audience. So in many New Zealand television commercials, non-New Zealand accents are used in order to call up desirable associations with aristocracy through use of British Received Pronunciation, or with the streetwise wheeler-dealer through imitation of Cockney (Bell 1992). Trudgill's study of the accents of pop singers (see Chapter 20) shows how British singers have adopted features of American English in order to associate with the prestige of American popular music. They have also been known to adopt British working-class features in singing music (such as punk) which is associated with the values of that class.

CONCLUSION

The study of style has had a chequered career in sociolinguistics. In 1972 Labov wrote that 'the most immediate problem to be solved in the attack on sociolinguistic structure is the quantification of the dimension of style'. However, in the intervening years there has been much less study of stylistic variation than of variation between different groups of speakers. Style is attracting more interest again, and as the American scholars Rickford and McNair-Knox have written (1994: 52): 'With respect to theory development, stylistic variation seems to offer more potential for the integration of past findings and the establishment of productive research agendas than virtually any other area in sociolinguistics.' .

Style research seems to be taking two directions. One of these is manifested in the work of Finegan and Biber (1994), whose 'multi-dimensional' approach developed as an alternative to the one I have taken above. The other direction responds to criticisms of both attention and audience factors as inadequate to account for the pervasiveness of initiative style and for the fact that language is not just a reflection of social structure. Recent critical social theorizing stresses that language is not independent of society. The linguistic and the social are not two cleanly separate dimensions, and language constitutes social reality as well as reflecting it. Identity may be revealed and expressed by language on its own, as for instance when we can tell what kind of person a speaker is just from hearing them on the radio, with no other clues to their character. This approach promises new insights into the nature of sociolinguistic style (Coupland 1997).

REFERENCES

Bakhtin, M. M. (1981) *The Dialogic Imagination* (Austin, TX: University of Texas Press).

Bell, A. (1984) 'Language Style as Audience Design', *Language in Society*, **13**(2), pp. 145–204.

Bell, A. (1991) 'Audience Accommodation in the Mass Media', in Giles, H., Coupland, N. and Coupland, J. (eds) *Contexts of Accommodation – Developments in Applied Sociolinguistics* (Cambridge: Cambridge University Press) pp. 69–102.

Bell, A. (1992) 'Hit and Miss: Referee Design in the Dialects of New Zealand Television Advertisements', *Language & Communication*, **12**(3–4), pp. 327–40.

Blom, J-P. and Gumperz, J. J. (1972) 'Social Meaning in Linguistic Structure: Code-switching in Norway', in Gumperz, J. J. and Hymes, D. (eds) *Directions in Sociolinguistics* (New York: Holt, Rinehart & Winston) pp. 407–34.

Brown, P. and Levinson, S. C. (1987 [1978]) *Politeness: Some Universals in Language Usage* (2nd edition) (Cambridge: Cambridge University Press).

Coupland, N. (1984) 'Accommodation at Work: Some Phonological Data and Their Implications', *International Journal of the Sociology of Language*, **46**, pp. 49–70.

Coupland, N. (1997) 'Language, Context and the Relational Self: Re-theorising Dialect Style in Sociolinguistics', in Eckert, P. and Rickford, J. (eds) *Style* (Cambridge: Cambridge University Press).

Dorian, N. C. (1981) *Language Death: The Life Cycle of a Scottish Gaelic Dialect* (Philadelphia, PA: University of Pennsylvania Press).

Ervin-Tripp, S. M. (1972) 'On Sociolinguistic Rules: Alternation and Co-occurrence', in Gumperz, J. J. and Hymes, D. (eds) *Directions in Sociolinguistics*, (New York: Holt, Rinehart & Winston) pp. 213–50.

Ferguson, C. A. and Gumperz, J. J. (eds) (1960) 'Linguistic Diversity in South Asia', *International Journal of American Linguistics*, **26**(3), part 3 (Bloomington, IN: Indiana University Press).

Finegan, E. and Biber, D. (1994) 'Register and Social Dialect Variation: An Integrated Approach', in Biber, D. and Finegan, E. (eds) *Sociolinguistic Perspectives on Register* (Oxford: Oxford University Press) pp. 315–47.

Gal, S. 1979. *Language Shift: Social Determinants of Linguistic Change in Bilingual Austria* (New York: Academic Press).

Giles, H. and Powesland, P. F. (1975) *Speech Style and Social Evaluation* (London: Academic Press).
Labov, W. (1972) *Sociolinguistic Patterns* (Philadelphia, PA: University of Pennsylvania Press).
Rickford, J. R. and McNair-Knox, F. (1994) 'Addressee- and Topic-influenced Style Shift: A Quantitative Sociolinguistic Study', in Biber, D. and Finegan, E. (eds) *Sociolinguistic Perspectives on Register* (Oxford: Oxford University Press) pp. 235–76.

20 Acts of Conflicting Identity: The Sociolinguistics of British Pop-song Pronunciation

Peter Trudgill

Anyone with an interest in British rock and pop songs will have observed that there are 'rules' concerning the way in which the words of these songs are pronounced.[1] The label 'tendencies' might be more appropriate than 'rules' in some instances, but in any case it is clear that singers of this form of music employ different accents when singing from when they are speaking, and that deviations from their spoken accents are of a particular and relatively constrained type. This phenomenon of employing a modified pronunciation seems to have been current in popular music for some decades, probably since the 1920s, and has involved a number of different genres, including jazz , 'crooning', and so on. It became, however, especially widespread and noticeable in the late 1950s with the advent of rock-and-roll and the pop-music revolution.

Analysis of the pronunciation used by British pop singers at around that time, and subsequently, reveals the following rules and tendencies. (We ignore features such as the pronunciation of *-ing* as [ɪn] which are typical of most informal styles.)

1. The pronunciation of intervocalic /t/ in words like *better* as [t] or [ʔ], which are the pronunciations used by most British speakers, is generally not permitted. In pop-singing, a pronunciation of the type [d̠] (a voiced alveolar flap of some kind) has to be employed.

2. It is not permitted to pronounce words such as *dance, last* with the /aː/ that is normal in speech in south-eastern England. Instead they are pronounced with the /æ/ of *cat* (as in the north of England, although the realization is usually [æ] rather than the northern [a]). In addition,

Source: 'Acts of Conflicting Identity: The Sociolinguistics of British Pop-song Pronunciation', in Trudgill, P. (1983) *On Dialect: Social and Geographical Perspectives* (Oxford and New York: Basil Blackwell and New York University Press) pp. 141–60.

words such as *half* and *can't*, which are pronounced with /aː/ by most of those English speakers, of north and south, who have the /æ/ – /aː/ distinction, must also be pronounced with /æ/. Thus:

	cat	dance	half
South-eastern England	/æ/ = [æ]	[aː/	/aː/
Northern England	/æ/ = [a]	/æ/	/aː/
Pop-song style	/æ/ = [æ]	/æ/	/æ/

3. Words such as *girl*, *more* tend to be pronounced with an /r/ even by those English English speakers (the majority) who do not have non-prevocalic /r/ in their speech.
4. Words such as *life*, *my* tend to be sung with a vowel of the type [a·] although they are normally pronounced by a majority of British speakers with a diphthong of the type [aɪ ∼ ɑɪ ∼ ʌɪ].
5. Words such as *love*, *done* tend to be pronounced with a vowel of the type [ə·] rather than with the [ä ∼ ɐ] typical of the south of England or the [ʊ ∼ ɤ] typical of the north.
6. Words such as *body*, *top* may be pronounced with unrounded [ɑ] instead of the more usual British [ɒ].

There are, of course, British varieties which do have these features: most English northern and midland varieties have /æ/ in *path* and a few have /æ/ in *can't*, while some south-western English and most Scottish varieties have no /æ/ – /aː/ distinction and may have an [æ]-like vowel in all those words; many south-western English varieties have [d] in *better*; many western, north-western and Scottish (and other) varieties do have non-prevocalic /r/; some north-western accents do have /aɪ/ as [a·]; many midland and south-western varieties have [ə], although not usually [ə·], in *love*; and some East Anglian and south-western varieties have [ɑ] in *body*. The point is, however, that no single British variety has all these features, and the vast majority of singers who use these forms when singing do not do so when speaking. There can be no doubt that singers are modifying their linguistic behaviour for the purposes of singing.

EXPLANATIONS FOR LINGUISTIC MODIFICATION

An interesting question, therefore, is: why do singers modify their pronunciation in this way? One theory that attempts to deal with language modification of this kind is the socio-psychological *accommodation theory* of Giles (see Giles and Smith, 1979). This, briefly, attempts to explain temporary or long-term adjustments in pronunciation and other aspects of linguistic behaviour in terms of a drive to approximate one's language to that of one's interlocutors, if they are regarded as socially desirable and/or if the speaker wishes to identify with them and/or demonstrate good will towards them. This may often take the form of reducing the frequency of socially stigmatized linguistic forms in the presence of speakers of higher prestige varieties. The theory also allows for the opposite effect: the distancing of one's language from that of speakers one wishes to disassociate oneself from, or in order to assert one's own identity.

Accommodation theory does go some way towards accounting for the phenomenon of pop-song pronunciation. It is clearly not sufficient, however, since it applies only to conversational situations. And we cannot assume that pop musicians adjust their pronunciation in order to make it resemble more closely that of their intended audience, since what actually happens is in many respects the reverse.

Another, less elaborate way to look at this problem is simply to discuss it in terms of the sociolinguistic notion of 'appropriateness'. As is well known, different situations, different topics, different genres require different linguistic styles and registers. The singing of pop music in this way, it could be argued, is no different from vicars preaching in the register appropriate to Church of England sermons, or BBC newsreaders employing the variety appropriate for the reading of the news. Certainly 'appropriateness' is obviously a relevant factor here. But, equally obviously, it is not on its own to provide an explanation for why it is this type of singing which is regulated in this way, nor why it is characterized by this particular set of pronunciation rules and tendencies rather than some other.

A more helpful approach, it emerges, is the theory of linguistic behaviour developed by Le Page. Indeed, the pronunciation of pop-song lyrics provides a useful site for a microstudy which exemplifies many aspects of Le Page's thinking. This theory, expounded by Le Page in a number of writings (see Le Page 1968, 1975, 1978; Le Page *et al.*, 1974) seeks to demonstrate a general motive for speakers' linguistic behaviour in terms of attempts to 'resemble as closely as possible those of the group or groups with which from time to time we [speakers] wish to identify'. ...

In Le Page's terms, British pop singers are attempting to modify their pronunciation in the direction of that of a particular group with which they wish to identify – from time to time (i.e. when they are singing). This group, moreover, can clearly, if somewhat loosely, be characterized by the general label 'Americans': the six pronunciation rules and tendencies outlined above are all found in American accents, and are stereotypically associated by the British with American pronunciation. (If there were any doubt about the identity of the model group, this could be confirmed by reference to the words of pop songs themselves which, even if written by British composers for British consumption, tend to include forms such as *guy* (= *chap, bloke*), *call* (*phone*), etc., which are still Americanisms for many British speakers today, and were certainly Americanisms in the 1950s and 1960s. [They are even less clearly Americanisms in Britain today – Eds.]

The next question therefore is: why should singers attempt to imitate what they consider to be an American accent? The reason for this is reasonably apparent, even if somewhat intuitively arrived at, and without empirical verification. Most genres of twentieth-century popular music, in the western world and in some cases beyond, are (Afro-)American in origin. Americans have dominated the field, and cultural domination leads to imitation: it is appropriate to sound like an American when performing in what is predominantly an American activity; and one attempts to model one's singing style on that of those who do it best and who one admires most.

There are parallels here with other musical genres: British folk-singers often adopt quasi-rural accents; and singers of songs in the reggae style often attempt Jamaican accents. We also have to note that, in many European countries at least, it is not a particular variety of English but simply English itself that has become associated with pop music: at one time, for example, many West German pop groups had English-language names and sang songs, written by Germans, in English – a phenomenon which cannot be entirely explained by a desire to conquer international markets. (It is difficult to think of precise parallels of cultural domination in fields other than music, but one candidate might be the quasi-English accents adopted by American Shakespearean actors even when acting in plays set in, for example, Verona.)

CONSTRAINTS ON LINGUISTIC MODIFICATION

British pop singers, then, are aiming at an American pronunciation. The end-product of this language modification is, however, by no means entirely successful. One obvious measure of their lack of success is that many American listeners are utterly unaware that this is what British singers are trying to do. The results of this modification, too, are complex and subject to change.

This also can be accounted for in Le Page's theory. The theory provides for the fact that, in modifying our linguistic behaviour, our performance as speakers 'is constrained by considerations which fall under one or another of four riders to the general hypothesis'. We will discuss these riders in turn. The first of Le Page's (1978) riders is that our modification of our linguistic behaviour is constrained by:

(i)   the extent to which we are able to identify our model group.

We have already seen that British pop singers have, presumably without giving it too much conscious thought, successfully identified their model group as 'Americans', and that they attempt, again presumably for the most part below the level of conscious awareness, to model their language behaviour on that of American singers. More detailed study, however, suggests that they have not been especially successful in identifying *exactly which* Americans it is they are trying to model their behaviour on. Comparison with the linguistic behaviour of American pop singers is instructive at this point, for there is a strong tendency for them, too, to modify their pronunciation when singing. Modifications made by American singers include (a) the use of the monophthong [a·] in *life*, etc. by singers who have diphthongs in their speech (i.e. the same modification made by British singers); and (b) the *omission* of non-prevocalic /r/ in *car*, etc. by singers who are normally r-ful in their speech. A good example is provided by Bob Dylan, who is from Minnesota, in the American Mid-West, and who has /ai/ = [ai] and non-prevocalic /r/ in his speech. His singing style incorporates frequent use of [a·] and r-loss:

You may be an ambassador [æm'bæsədə]
To England or [ə] France
You may like [la·k] to gamble
You might [ma·t] like [la·k] to dance
               ('Gotta serve somebody', *Slow Train Coming*, 1979)

These two features suggest that the model group whose pronunciation is being aimed at by American singers consists of Southern and/or Black singers, since the combination of [a·] = /ai/ and r-lessness is most typical of the varieties spoken by these groups. The reason for this is again clear: it is in the American South and/or amongst Blacks that many types of popular music have their origins. (This is most obviously true of jazz, rhythm-and-blues, and rock-and-roll.) Cultural domination therefore causes singers with White non-Southern accents to modify their pronunciation when singing.[2]

This leads us to suppose that it is these same groups whose accents British singers too are aiming at, since they also, as we have already seen, have the [a·] = /ai/ feature in their singing styles. This supposition is strengthened, first, by the fact that other features of Southern and Black pronunciation, in addition to [a·], can be heard to occur from time to time in British pop songs:

1.   pronunciations such as *boring* [bourɪn], and the occasional rhyming of words such as *more* with words such as *go*;

2.   the occasional inhibition of the pronunciation of linking /r/, as in *four o'clock*, without the insertion of a pause or glottal stop;

3.   the pronunciation of /ɪ/ as [ɛ ~ æ] before /n/, /ŋ/, as in *thing* [θæŋ], in imitation of the Southern and Black merger of /ɪ/ and /ɛ/ before nasals.

Secondly, it is also confirmed by the occurrence, even in songs written by British pop musicians, of grammatical features associated with Southern and Black dialects:

1. *copula deletion*
   'He livin' there still'   (Beatles *White Album*)
   'My woman she gone'   (Dire Straits *Dire Straits*)

2. *3rd-person -s absence*
   'She make me cry'   (Stranglers *Rattus Norvegicus*)

   'Here come old flat top'   (Beatles *Abbey Road*)

3. *negativized auxiliary pre-position*
   'Ain't nothin' new in my life today'   (Supertramp *Breakfast in America*)

If this is so, then in one respect the British singers are in error. Blacks and Southerners are typically *r*-less. This fact is, as we have seen, recognized by many American singers, who (variably) delete non-prevocalic /r/ when singing even though their speech is *r*-ful. British singers, on the other hand, do the reverse: they insert non-prevocalic /r/ in singing even though their speech is *r*-less. (This contrast between British and American singers was particularly marked in the late 1950s when singers such as Cliff Richard, who were to a considerable extent imitators of Elvis Presley, attempted the pronunciation of non-prevocalic /r/ in their songs, even though Elvis himself was for the most part *r*-less.) We do not deny, of course, that some Southern varieties are *r*-ful. Nevertheless, it is possible to argue that, in their performance of pop songs, British singers exhibit a certain lack of success in identifying who their model group is. The two perceptions – that the model group consists of (a) Americans in general, and (b) Southerners and/or Blacks in particular – conflict when it comes to non-prevocalic /r/, since the case of the particular model group being aimed at, the stereotype that 'Americans are *r*-ful' is inaccurate.

Le Page's second rider also turns out to be relevant for our study of the linguistic behaviour of British pop singers. This rider states that our linguistic behaviour is constrained by:

(ii)   the extent to which we have sufficient access to [the model groups] and sufficient analytical ability to work out the rules of their behaviour.

There is evidence that British singers' analytical abilities are in fact sometimes not sufficient. This is provided, again, by the case of non-prevocalic /r/. Like, for example, many British actors attempting to imitate *r*-ful rural accents, British pop singers often insert non-prevocalic /r/s where they do not belong. This is a form of hypercorrection. Singers know that, in order to 'sound like an American', one has to insert an /r/ after the vowels /aː/ as in *cart*; /ɔː/ as in *fort*; /ɜː/ as in *bird*; /ɪə/ as in *beard*; /ɛə/ as in *bared*; and /ə/ as in *letters*. The problem is that some singers have not mastered the principle behind where this should and should not be done; they are liable to insert an /r/ after the above vowels even where an /r/ is not required, as in *calm, taught, ideas, Americas* (*bird* and *bared*-type words are not a problem, since these vowels occur only before a potential /r/). The correct strategy to follow (except in the case of the word *colonel* – which does not occur too often in pop songs) is to use the orthography, which always has *r* where an /r/ is required... Examples of complete lack of success in analysing the model accent correctly include:

1. Cliff Richard, 'Bachelor Boy' (1961):
    'You'll be *a bachelor boy*...' /ər bæčələr bɔi/ – repeated many times.

2. Kinks, 'Sunny Afternoon' (1966):
    '...*Ma and Pa*' /maːr ən paːr/

3. Paul McCartney, 'Till there was you' on *With the Beatles* (1963):
    'I never *saw them* at all' /sɔːr ðɛm/...

Le Page's fourth rider (we shall return to the third shortly) is:

(iv) our ability to modify our behaviour (probably lessening as we get older).

We have already touched on this point in our discussion of hypercorrection: it is possible that imperfection in imitation is due to lack of ability. We can further demonstrate the validity of this rider by pointing to the fact that most of the modifications British singers make in their pronunciation are variable, irregular, and inconsistent. We can assume, for instance, that many singers would pronounce all non-prevocalic /r/s if they could. It is simply that, in the flow of the song, they are not consistently able to do so. It is also of interest to observe that some phonological environments cause more difficulty than others. Most difficult, apparently, is the insertion of non-prevocalic /r/ in an unstressed syllable before a following consonant, as in *better man*. Here, fewest /r/s are pronounced by British singers. Correspondingly, it is in exactly the same environment that *fewest* /r/s are *deleted* by American singers.

The observation that non-prevocalic /r/ is only spasmodically inserted in singing can be confirmed quite simply by counting. For instance, in spite of a strong impression, to British listeners, that they are in this respect successfully imitating Americans, the Beatles, on their first British LP, *Please Please Me* (1963), manage to pronounce only 47 per cent of potential non-prevocalic /r/s.

CHANGING PATTERNS OF LINGUISTIC MODIFICATION

To count /r/s in this way is to acknowledge that, in British pop music, (r) is a linguistic variable in the Labovian sense. Employing the concept of the linguistic variable in this way, to examine this and the other features typical of British pop-song pronunciation, opens up the possibility of examining Le Page's theory in more detail, especially in so far as it allows for the possibility of accounting for conflict and change.

It permits, for example, the quantitative comparison of the pronunciation of pop songs from the late 1950s and early 1960s with that of later periods. This turns out to be very instructive. For example, an analysis of four LPs from the period 1963–65 (the first two British albums produced by the Beatles and Rolling Stones respectively) gives an overall (r)-count, based on 372 tokens, of 36 per cent (i.e. 36 per cent of potential non-prevocalic /r/s were pronounced). On the other hand, analysis of four British albums, selected at random, from 1978 and 1979 (Dire Straits *Dire Straits*; Supertramp *Breakfast in America*; Clash *The Clash*; Sham '69 *Hersham Boys*) gives an (r)-count, based on 546 tokens, of 4 per cent. Obviously it would not be legitimate to draw any conclusions from such a haphazard and small-scale comparison. At the same time, it does suggest that something has happened to pop-song pronunciation, and it does tally well with casual observations to the effect that things have changed.

This is further reinforced by Figure 20.1. This figure portrays the (r) scores per album for ten of the eleven LPS released by the Beatles in Britain between 1963 and 1971, and paints rather a surprisingly dramatic picture. During the Beatles' recording life there was a very considerable falling-off in non-prevocalic /r/ usage. From a high of 47 per cent in 1963 this falls to a low of 3 per cent in 1970.

The same pattern is repeated in Figure 20.2. This graph deals with the same ten Beatles records, together with scores for four records by the Rolling Stones. In addition to (r) scores, it also shows the percentage of intervocalic /t/s realized as [d] = (t), and a less dramatic but equally clear picture emerges. (In calculating (t) scores, both environments such as *better* and *get a* have been included. The phrase *at all* has been omitted from calculations since British speakers, unlike Americans, have for the most part resyllabified this as *a # t all*. In the case of (t), the phonological environment which causes British singers most difficulty is as in *adversity, nobility*, where there is some variability even in American English.)

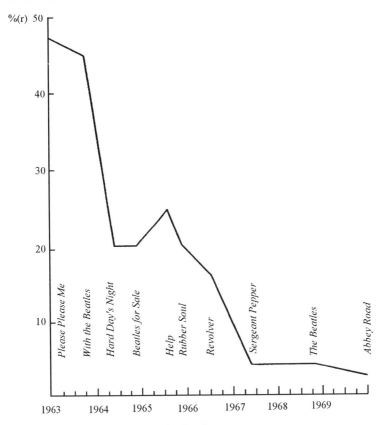

Figure 20.1: Non-prevocalic /r/: the Beatles

Other quasi-American features, too, can be shown to have declined in frequency. We can draw no conclusions from the Beatles' pronunciation of *dance*, *past*, etc., as their native northern (Liverpool) English accents have /æ/ in these words in any case. It is, however, possible to detect a change in their treatment of items such as *can't* and *half* which have /æ/ in the USA but /aː/ in the north as well as the south of England. The progression is:

	Album	*can't, half*
1963	Please Please Me	/æ/
1963	With The Beatles	/æ/
1964	Hard Day's Night	/æ/
1964	Beatles for Sale	/æ/
1965	Help	/æ/
1967	Sergeant Pepper	/æ/ ~ /aː/
1968	The Beatles (White Album)	/æ/ ~ /aː/
1969	Abbey Road	/aː/

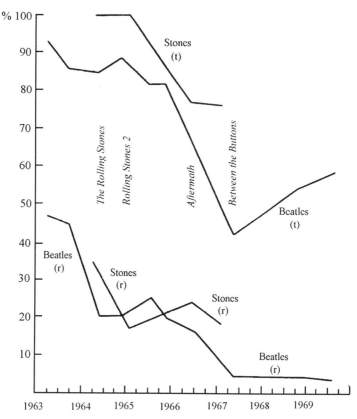

Figure 20.2:   (r) and (t): the Beatles and the Rolling Stones

(The Rolling Stones, on the other hand, have always been /æ/-users, their lead singer Mick Jagger consistently scoring 100 per cent on all albums.)

So what has happened? One factor that may be important in examining the performance of a group such as the Beatles is that it could be argued that their change in pronunciation reflects a change in genre. Their early songs are often clearly in the rock-and-roll mould, while later songs tend to be more complex, contemplative, poetic, and so on. The subject-matter of the songs changes, too, and the later songs, now written entirely by themselves, show an increase in more obviously British themes and locales. (It may also be of some relevance that songs written by British composers tend, naturally enough, to have *r*-less rhymes of the type *bought-short* (Beatles *Revolver*), *Rita-metre* (Beatles *Sergeant Pepper*) (cf. Zwicky, 1976).) The particular 'image' that particular groups try to project will also be a factor.

But it is also clear that, from around 1964 on, British singers generally began trying less hard to sound like Americans. Why should this have been? Within the framework provided by Le Page, we can say that the strength of the motivation towards the American model has become weaker. If this is the case, then this change can in turn be ascribed to developments within the world of pop music itself. The enormous popularity of the Beatles, which extended to the USA by 1964, and, in their wake, of other Liverpool-based (and other British) groups, led to a change in the pattern of cultural domination. For a while, it was Britain that dominated America in this field, and, while this is no longer the case [this text published in 1983 – Eds], the *strength* of American domination was permanently weakened. British pop music acquired a validity of its own, and this has been reflected in linguistic behaviour.

CONFLICTING MOTIVATIONS

Le Page's third rider is:

(iii)   the strength of various (possibly conflicting) motivations towards one or another model and towards retaining our own sense of our unique identity.

As we have just seen, the strength of the motivation towards the American model diminished from 1964 on. Imitation of this model, however, was not in conflict with any other, and the American model remained the sole motivation there was for pop singers to modify their pronunciation. British singers were indeed trying *less hard* to sound like Americans; but it cannot be said that they were actually trying to sound *more British*. Nor does it actually appear to be true, although it was often claimed to be the case at the time, that from 1963 on singers from elsewhere tried to imitate a Liverpool accent. (The Beatles themselves sounded both more American, as we have seen, *and* more Liverpudlian on their early records than on their later records. Obviously Liverpool features included: the heavy aspiration/ affrication of voiceless stops (*passim*); the rhyming of *gone* and *one* (*With The Beatles*); the rhyming of *aware* and *her* (*Rubber Soul*); the pronunciation of *book*, etc. with long /uː/ (as late as *Sergeant Pepper*); the pronunciation of *hang a* . . . and *long ago* with [ng] (*Revolver*).)

In more recent years, however, especially since 1976, this situation has changed. A new and conflicting motivation *has* arisen. This new motivation is most apparent in the performance of music by pop groups categorized under the heading of 'punk-rock' and/or 'new wave'. The music of 'punk' groups is typically loud, fast and aggressive, and the songs concerned, often, with themes such as violence, underprivilege, alienation, and rejection. The songs are also frequently – in non-punk mainstream societal terms – in bad taste. The intended primary audience is British urban working-class youth.

'Punk-rock' singers, like their antecedents, modify their pronunciation when singing. Analysis of their pronunciation, however, shows that there has been a reduction in the use of the 'American ' features discussed above, although they are still used, and an introduction of features associated with low-prestige south of England accents. These features, crucially, are employed in singing even by those who do not use them in speech. They include:

1. the use of wide diphthongs, as /ei/ = [æɪ] *face*, and /ou/ = [æʉ] *go*;
2. the pronunciation of /ai/ as [ɑɪ] *sky*, and of /au/ as [æu ~ɛu] *out*;
3. the vocalization of /l/, as in *milk* [mɪʊk]:
4. the (occasional) deletion of /h/;
5. the use of [ʔ] realizations of /t/ not only finally, as in *get*, but also intervocalically, where it is most socially stigmatized and conspicuous, as in *better*.

The use of these low-status pronunciations is coupled with a usage of non-standard grammatical forms, such as multiple negation and third-person singular *don't*, that is even higher than in other sub-genres of pop music, and the intended effect is assertive and aggressive. There is also clearly an intention to aid identification with and/or by British working-class youth, and to appeal to others who wish to identify with them, their situation and their values. The 'covert prestige' [see Chapters 14 and 22] of non-standard, low-prestige linguistic forms is clearly in evidence, and the overall motivation, conflicting with that towards the American model, is clearly towards a working-class British model, and towards retaining, although at a group rather than individual level, a sense of a unique (and non-American) identity. (Note that accommodation theory (see above) might be applicable here.)

The continued use in punk-rock of 'American' forms, however, shows that the assertion of a unique British working-class identity is not the whole story. The old motivation of sounding American has not been replaced by the new motivation, but remains in competition with it. Not only, for instance, are American pronunciations retained, but American locutions, such as *real good*, continue to be employed. Moreover, many obvious British features are not employed – intrusive /r/, for example, is extremely rare, even on recent recordings. And at points where the two pronunciation models are in direct conflict, such as the realization of /ai/, forms like [a·] and [ɑɪ] alternate, even in the same song.

We therefore have, in Le Page's terms, conflicting motivations towards different models – the American and the British working class. This conflict, however, is not equally apparent in all types of British pop music. This is clearly revealed in Table 20.1. This table is based on data from seven albums only, and can again therefore be no more than suggestive. These albums are nevertheless possibly quite representative of those produced by many other singers and groups. The albums are: Rolling Stones *Some Girls* (1978);

Table 20.1: Usage of 'American' and 'British' features (percentages)

	'American'			'British'
	(r)	*(t)*	*/æ/*	*[ʔ]*
Rolling Stones	19	46	100	0
Supertramp	7	81	—	0
Dire Straits	1	92	—	0
Stranglers	0	88	80	0
Clash	6	71	24	10
Sham '69	1	57	50	9
Ian Dury	0	5	0	22

Supertramp *Breakfast in America* (1979); Dire Straits *Dire Straits* (1978); Stranglers *Rattus Norvegicus* (1977); Clash *The Clash* (1978); Sham '69 *Hersham Boys* (1979); and Ian Dury *Do It Yourself* (1979). The Rolling Stones, Supertramp and Dire Straits represent the 'mainstream' pop-music tradition, while the other performers represent the newer, punk-rock-oriented school. Information is given in the table on the percentage of non-prevocalic /r/s pronounced = (r); the percentage of intervocalic /t/s realized as [d] = (t); the percentage of /æ/ rather than /aː/ in the lexical set of *path, dance* (except for Supertramp and Dire Straits, whose singers are from the north of England); and the percentage of intervocalic /t/s pronounced as a glottal stop.

It can be seen from Table 20.1 that the Rolling Stones, so far as their pronunciation is concerned, are still at the no-conflict, semi-American stage typical of the mid-1960s (and indeed it has always been apparent that Mick Jagger has more self-consciously than most in many respects modelled his singing style on that of Black American rhythm-and-blues singers.) The Stones' (r) and (t) scores are, however, still much lower than they would have been in the early 1960s.

The two newer mainstream groups, Supertramp and Dire Straits, represent the phase after the weakening of American influence. This is apparent from a comparison of their (r) scores with that of the Rolling Stones: the very low (r)-count is typical of nearly all recent British singers. These two groups, however, still heavily favour the 'American' realization of (t) – unlike the Rolling Stones (their low score on *Some Girls* may be influenced by one particular song where the word *pretty* is repeated many times with [tʰ]). It seems, in fact that British singers now have considerable freedom in the extent to which they feel obliged to conform to the earlier 'American' norm for (t). (It is perhaps relevant that the Supertramp record was recorded in the USA, is entitled 'Breakfast in America', and expresses sentiments such as 'Like to see America/See the girls in California...'.)

The supposedly 'punk' group the Stranglers also come out has having an orientation only towards the American model, in that they closely resemble the 'mainstream' groups in their linguistic behaviour. (This is probably of more interest to rock musicologists than to linguists, but it is interesting to note that The Stranglers have been one of the groups accused of having 'sold out' and of not being 'really punk'. Perhaps giving your records Latin titles does not help here either.)

The Clash and Sham '69, on the other hand, can clearly be placed, on phonological grounds alone, in the punk-rock category. In their scores the conflict between the 'American' and 'British' motivations is clearly portrayed. Scores for (r) and /æ/ are low, and [ʔ] is quite heavily used (scores for word-final [ʔ] would be considerably higher than these intervocalic (t) scores). And, interestingly enough, the orientation towards the 'British' model receives overt recognition in one of the songs on the Clash album, which is entitled 'I'm so bored with the USA.' On the other hand, 'American' forms are still used extensively. Punk-rock singing style is probably the only accent of English where the combination of *can't* /kaːnt/, *high* [haˑ] and *face* [fæɪs] is possible.

The scores given for Ian Dury are interesting in a different respect. These show no real signs of any conflict at all: his single model is clearly that of the speech of working-class London. Not too much, however, should be concluded from this as far as pop-song pronunciation in general is concerned. Dury is in some respects on the fringes of the pop-music tradition, and his bawdy and amusing lyrics owe perhaps as much to the comic tradition of the music hall as to pop. His extensive usage of [ʔ], for instance, can certainly be attributed in part to the aggressive style of punk-rockers, but it can also be attributed to the music-hall tradition which has often used Cockney pronunciation for comic effect. (A similar interpretation has to be placed on pronunciations used in the Kinks' 'Little bit of real emotion' (1979) where [lɪʔɫ bɪʔ əv] alternates, in the chorus, with [tʰ] and [d] allophones of /t/. The effect of this is certainly not aggressive, and is perhaps more whimsical than anything else.)

NOTES

1   I would like to thank the following for comments on an earlier draft of this paper; for the loan of their records; for messages run; and/or for information provided: Jim Birnie, Neil Brummage, Alice Davison, Georgia M. Green, Jean Hannah, Chuck Kisseberth, Margi Laff, Jerry L. Morgan, Mark Seidenberg, and Bruce Sherwood.

2   There are other (e.g. choral) American singing styles which are deliberately r-less. These, however, have /aɪ/ as [aɪ], and are probably modelled on Eastern and/or English English accents.

REFERENCES

Giles, H. and Smith, P. (1979) 'Accommodation Theory: Optimal Levels of Convergence', in Giles, H. and St Clair, R. (eds) *Language and Social Psychology* (Oxford: Blackwell).

Le Page, R. B. (1968) 'Problems of Description in Multilingual Communities', *TPS* 1968, pp. 189–212.

Le Page, R. B. (1975) 'Polarizing Factors: Political, Social, Economic, Operating on the Individual's Choice of Identity Through Language Use in British Honduras', in Savard, J. G. and Vigneault, R. (eds) *Les États Multilingues* (Quebec: Laval University Press).

Le Page, R. B. (1978) 'Projection, Focussing, Diffusion', *Society for Caribbean Linguistics Occasional Paper* 9.

Le Page, R. B., Christie, P., Jurdant, B., Weekes, A. and Tabouret-Keller, A. (1974) 'Further Report on the Sociolinguistic Survey of Multilingual Communities', *Language in Society*, **3**, pp. 1–32.

Zwicky, A. (1976) 'Well, This Rock and Roll Has Got to Stop. Junior's Head is Hard as a Rock', in Mufwene, S. *et al.* (eds) *Proceedings of the 12th Annual Meeting of the Chicago Linguistic Society* (Chicago: University of Chicago Press).

Part V
Language, Attitudes and Social Stereotypes

The phrase 'sociolinguistic variation' can refer to how groups of people, their speech or their ways of speaking are *perceived*, as well as referring to differences in their speech itself. This psychological dimension of language in society has been quite extensively studied within a sub-branch of socio-linguistics usually referred to as *the social psychology of language*. The main tradition of research in this area is *language attitudes* study.

In this sort of research, facts about language use have no intrinsic relevance. For many social purposes, facts are less important than *beliefs*, especially where beliefs can be shown to be regularly and systematically held. To take one example, we might be more inclined to learn and use a minority language like Welsh if we believe that Welsh is undergoing a significant revival; or if we believe that Welsh is a beautiful and historic language, or that Welsh speakers have certain sorts of status and career opportunities in contemporary Wales, or that they are more pleasant and likeable people. In this case, our beliefs may be the factor motivating our behaviours, whatever the objective truths. (In fact, Welsh *is* undergoing a revival, at least in terms of its overall numbers of speakers, and it *does* confer certain job opportunities in certain parts of the country. We cannot vouch for the truth value of the other suggestions!)

So we are concerned here with social stereotypes. Hewstone and Giles's chapter (21) gives very useful insights into the general nature of *social stereotypes* and how they are liable to affect communication between social groups. The categories they introduce impose a much-needed discipline on how sociolinguists should understand the process of stereotyping. For example, stereotypes are ubiquitous, but we should only talk of *social* stereotypes when we have evidence that group-relevant beliefs are widely shared. Stereotypes can be positive as well as negative, accurate as well as wrong-headed, positively functional as well as socially dysfunctional. They can be held about one's own group as well as about an outgroup. Hewstone and Giles's comments about the durability of social stereotypes gives us another way of understanding linguistic change and resistance to change. For example, whatever social (including social network) forces may exist to deter groups from changing the way they speak, those same groups may be

267

actively encouraged to adopt the speaking norms of groups for whom they hold strongly positive social stereotypes.

The power and influence of stereotyped judgements about language are clearly shown in John Edwards's study (Chapter 22). This study addresses the claim originally made by Labov (and discussed in Chapter 14 by Trudgill in Part III) that working-class speech generally sounds more 'masculine' than middle-class speech, and vice versa. Studying *children's* speech presents an opportunity to test for these stereotypes, because pre-pubescent males do not have the lower pitch usually associated with male speech. Asking adults, in a controlled experimental design, to guess the sex of children, based only on hearing their voices, might show up the stereotyped association between sex and social class. As Edwards shows, although the adults were generally quite accurate in judging sex from voice, working-class voices (including girls' voices) did indeed tend to be heard as boys' voices, and middle-class boys' voices as girls' voices.

The core method for studying language attitudes has been the matched-guise technique (MGT), and it was discussed in outline by Wolfram and Fasold (Chapter 9, Part II). However, some research has shown that there can be direct, behavioural consequences of holding stereotyped views about language. In Chapter 23, Kristiansen describes a simple but revealing study, replicating and extending an earlier study by Bourhis and Giles. Kristiansen investigated film audiences' reactions to the same message, conveyed to them in four different ways over a loudspeaker system. The speech varieties used were: a standard Danish accent, an urban Copenhagen accent and two versions (mild and broad) of the tradional Zealand accent. On different occasions, a public announcement was relayed to audiences, asking them to co-operate in a survey that the cinema was conducting. The number of questionnaires returned by each audience-group gave a simple index of their level of co-operation. The study provides insight into the social images that Danish people have of the main language varieties available in their community. For example, the local dialect is generally downgraded relative to the standard variety, and younger audience members are better disposed to the Copenhagen voice than older people.

In his chapter on language attitudes in the French-speaking world, Bourhis points out that it was very largely in Quebecois studies that the MGT was developed and refined. But in addition to summarizing the most significant findings from the early *Quebec* attitudes studies, Bourhis's review explains how attitudes to French were partly formed and indeed historically *imposed* by political actions in France itself. This is an important reminder that sociolinguistics needs to consider processes of conscious linguistic control and manipulation, over and above 'natural' processes of language maintenance and change. This is a theme taken up again in Part VI, where we consider multilingualism, including processes of so-called 'language planning'.

So the study of language attitudes, and of subjective processes generally, needs to be linked to the study of language variation. This part of the Reader emphasizes the importance of the subjective perspective, both theoretically and practically. If we look again at the theoretical work done under the heading of *accommodation theory* (see Giles and Powesland's discussion in Chapter 18), we can see how it is possible to link social psychological insights with the study of linguistic variation quite directly in one theoretical statement.

PART V: FURTHER READING

Baker, C. (1992) *Attitudes and Language* (Clevedon: Multilingual Matters).

Giles, H. and Robinson, W. P. (eds) (1990) *Handbook of Language and Social Psychology* (Chichester: John Wiley & Sons).

Giles, H. and Coupland, N. (1991) *Language: Contexts and Consequences* (Buckingham: Open University Press).

Milroy, J. and Milroy, L. (1991) *Authority in Language: Investigating Language Prescription and Standardisation*. Second edition (London: Routledge).

Preston, D. (1989) *Perceptual Dialectology* (Dordrecht: Foris).

Smith, P. M. (1985) *Language, the Sexes and Society* (Oxford: Basil Blackwell).

21 Social Groups and Social Stereotypes

Miles Hewstone and Howard Giles

A series of studies by Taylor and Simard (1975) demonstrated that cross-cultural communication can be, in objective terms, as effective as within-group communication. We should ask then, why this is not always the case, and subjectively too. A major part of the answer, we believe, lies in the role played by stereotypes. We therefore consider the nature of stereotypes, their cognitive foundations and consequences, social functions, resistance to change, and relationship to behaviour.

THE NATURE OF SOCIAL STEREOTYPES

Fishman (1956, 27) stated that stereotype is 'one of the oldest and most frequently employed constructs in the domain of social psychology'. To some, stereotypes are 'traditional nonsense' (Hayakawa 1950); to others, they contain a 'kernel of truth' and a 'well-deserved reputation' (Zawadski 1948); still other researchers accept stereotyping as a necessary, timesaving evil (Bogardus 1950).

Lippman's (1922, 1) distinction between 'the world outside and the pictures in our heads' not only led him to the first discussion of stereotypes, but also neatly encapsulates the essence of cognitive social psychology. This emphasis on cognitions has focused on the study of perception, evaluation, interpretation, attribution, and so on. As Pettigrew (1981) has pointed out, the core idea is that what people perceive as 'real' is in fact real in its social consequences.

Definitions of stereotypes vary widely and cannot be considered in detail here. Instead, we adopt Allport's (1954, 191) classic definition, which still seems to us to be both basically correct and to provide a focus for theory and research:

> ...a stereotype is an exaggerated belief associated with a category. Its
> function is to justify (rationalize) our conduct in relation to that category.

Source: 'Social Groups and Social Stereotypes in Intergroup Communication: A Review and Model of Intergroup Communication Breakdown', in Gudykunst, W. B. (ed.) (1986) *Intergroup Communication* (London: Edward Arnold) pp. 10–20.

Social categorization is a core cognitive process by which is meant the segmentation and organization of the social world into social categories or groups (see Tajfel and Forgas 1981; Mervis and Rosch 1981). It serves several important functions: reducing the complexity of incoming information; facilitating rapid identification of stimuli; and predicting and guiding behaviour. Perhaps because of these functions, Allport (1954) recognized that categorical judgement and erroneous generalization were *natural and common* capacities of the human mind.

Stereotypes can be seen as providing the content of social categories. Three essential aspects of stereotyping can be identified.

1. Other individuals are categorized, usually on the basis of easily identifiable characteristics such as sex, ethnicity, speech style.
2. A set of traits, roles, emotions, abilities, interests, etc., is attributed to all (or most) members of that category. Individuals belonging to the stereotyped group are assumed to be similar to each other, and different from other groups, on this set of attributes.
3. The set of attributes is attributed to any individual member of that category.

Issues raised in relation to stereotypes have differed as widely as the definitions themselves. In the following pages, we are only able to consider selected topics, but some of the key questions to pose are still those noted by Fishman (1956, 30):

Why are we so often misinformed about groups, and about which sorts of groups, or concerning which aspects of groups, are we misinformed? Why is it so difficult to combat the misinformation with information? How does misinformation arise and what conditions hamper or strengthen the growth of misinformation? ...

POSITIVE AND NEGATIVE STEREOTYPES

Many authors agree that stereotypes are inherently 'bad' or 'wrong' because they are illogical in origin, resistant to contradiction, morally wrong, and so on. A reading of Lippman (1922) shows that he certainly considered stereotypes to be essentially incorrect, inaccurate, contrary to fact, and therefore undesirable. But was he correct?

Allport (1954) did acknowledge that stereotypes were not always negative, but this fact has often been overlooked. Taylor and Simard (1975) make the valid point that outgroup stereotypes may lead to the positive outcome of mutual social differentiation. Each group is seen as it wishes to be seen and desired differences are highlighted. In the absence of further information, this chapter will focus on the perhaps more widespread, and certainly more socially divisive, issue of negative outgroup stereotypes. This has been the topic of most social psychological work.

INGROUP AND OUTGROUP STEREOTYPES

In dealing primarily with negative stereotypes, most research has perforce concentrated on stereotypes of the outgroup, although the existence of both in- and outgroup stereotypes has long been recognized. This focus is understandable given that outgroups are referred to as though they were 'homogeneous and monolithic', while ingroups are seen as 'variegated and complex' (Rothbart *et al.* 1984). Similarly, it is reported that people perceive more variability within ingroups than outgroups (Park and Rothbart 1982; Quattrone and Jones 1980). However, this does not mean that stereotypes of the ingroup do not exist. Research also shows that outgroup images are impoverished relative to their ingroup counterparts (Linville and Jones 1980), and ingroup stereotypes appear to precede outgroup stereotypes developmentally (Lambert and Klineberg 1967).

   Triandis and Vassiliou (1967) used the terms auto- and heterostereotypes, respectively, for in- and outgroup images; they argued that agreement between the two may be an indication of stereotype validity. Here we must be careful given that some minority groups come to develop a negative autostereotype in line with the heterostereotype of a dominant outgroup. ... This apparent agreement should surely not be taken as evidence of stereotype validity and is, like other notions of stereotype veridicality, a very difficult hypothesis to verify. Nonetheless, we should expect and demand assessment of auto- and heterostereotypes ... if we are to understand fully the role of social stereotypes in intergroup communication. In terms of Tajfel's (1978) theory, we need to know how a group stereotypes itself in order to predict when its sense of psychological distinctiveness will be threatened by the claims of a rival group.

SOCIAL AND INDIVIDUAL STEREOTYPES

Researchers have long recognized the distinctions between shared stereotypes, defined by consensus, and those ideas about groups held by one individual. Newcomb and Charters (1950) contrasted 'group-shared' and 'private' stereotypes. The attributes that most subjects ascribe to a large percentage of the target group constitute the social stereotype of that group; the attributes ascribed by an individual to a large percentage of the target group constitute the individual stereotype. Which kind of measure should be the object of research is a moot point. We suggest that researchers should consider their own goals before choosing their approach. If studying the extent to which an outgroup image is shared, then a social stereotype is relevant. If trying to predict an individual's behaviour in a given situation (e.g. whether she/he will converge linguistically towards an outgroup member), then an individual stereotype measure will surely provide a better predictor.

The individual versus social distinction has obvious implications for the definition and measurement of stereotypes. In some studies, items are selected only if a majority of respondents agree that they apply to one, but not the other, group (e.g. Broverman *et al.* 1972). Other researchers (see Ashmore and Del Bocca 1979; McCauley and Stitt, 1978) deliberately exclude consensus from their definition, calling a socially shared stereotype a 'cultural stereotype'. McCauley *et al.* (1980) do provide one compelling argument against consensus. They provide an example of half a sample of respondents agreeing on three traits as typical of a group while the other half agree on three different traits. The usual social stereotypes for this sample would then include six traits, but this constellation of traits would not have been indicated by a single respondent. Notwithstanding the danger identified by McCauley *et al.*, we agree with Tajfel (1981) that stereotypes only become social when shared, and we believe social stereotypes have far greater importance for the study of intergroup communication than do individual measures. We also agree with Fishman (1956) that a wholly private stereotype is unlikely to be a stable phenomenon (or an important one in intergroup encounters), because of the need for, and influence of, consensual validation from others (especially ingroup members).

DIMENSIONS OF STEREOTYPES

Pettigrew (1981) emphasizes that stereotypes are patterns of traits rather than individual characteristics, and that they can be fused when a target is classified under two relevant group labels (e.g. female and Black). At one level, it is important to focus on the different content of stereotypes ascribed to different groups, but theoretical knowledge is also advanced by integrating the findings of various studies in terms of underlying dimensions. This may be illustrated by work on the indirect assessment of speech style and social evaluations (Ryan and Giles 1982). Although judgements are based on one speaker (or a few exemplars), the stimulus person is taken as an exemplar of the group in question.

Research in various parts of the world (Ryan *et al.* 1984) has shown that speakers of 'high' or 'powerful' speech styles are stereotyped in terms of competence and traits related to socioeconomic status, while speakers of 'low' or 'powerless' speech styles are stereotyped less favourably along these dimensions. In other social contexts, however, the language varieties of many of the latter groups may be imbued with pride by their own speakers (and sometimes this is conceded by the dominant group) and subordinate group members are stereotyped in terms of the more 'human' traits of solidarity, integrity, social attractiveness, and so on.

Two key dimensions appear to underlie these ratings: status and solidarity. Brown (1965) sees status differences in terms of influence, power and control. Thus, ratings along this dimension (e.g. intelligence, expertise, ambition) tend to reflect the dominant socioeconomic status of the so-called superior group. Solidarity is seen in terms of similarity between speaker and listener, frequent interaction, self-disclosure and intimacy. This dimension operates orthogonally to status and reflects the social pressures to support one's own group and maintain its linguistic variety.

Although we have concentrated here on the content of stereotypes, other dimensions are also important. Tiandis *et al.* (1982) suggest reporting the uniformity (or agreement across subjects), and the intensity (use of extreme categories) of stereotypes as well. Intuitively, a more uniform and intense stereotype (e.g. 80 per cent of Welsh speakers think that 90 per cent of all English speakers are arrogant) appears more likely to have social significance and to predict other important responses. We suggest therefore that in the search for content, researchers should not forget some of the basic judgmental dimensions of stereotypes which may help us to predict their impact on intergroup communication.

FOUNDATIONS AND CONSEQUENCES OF STEREOTYPING

Contrasting recent North American and European work on stereotyping, we might say that the former has concentrated on the cognitive processes underlying and issuing from stereotyping, while the latter has dealt with some of its social functions. We deal in this section with the American work, considering functions in the following section.

Following Hamilton (1979), we can distinguish usefully three important issues in the study of stereotypes:

1. Cognitive biases that result *in* stereotypical perceptions of social groups;
2. Cognitive biases that result *from* stereotypical perceptions of social groups;
3. Behavioural consequences of stereotyping.

Perhaps the clearest example of a cognitive bias that results *in* stereotypical perception is Hamilton's own work on 'illusory correlation'. This deals with how people develop correlational concepts, relating group membership to a psychological attribute (e.g. 'French speakers are intolerant'). Hamilton argues that normal cognitive functioning alone can lead to differential perception of groups. In this research (Hamilton and Gifford 1976), subjects read a number of statements describing behaviour performed by members of two groups, A and B. In two studies, there were twice as many statements concerning group A. Thus, group B became a distinctive stimulus. In the two studies, statements more frequently described desirable and undesirable behaviour respectively. The ratio of desirable–undesirable behaviours was the same for both groups in each experiment, thus no true relationships existed between group membership and the attribute. However, subjects overestimated the frequency with which group B had been described by the undesirable/desirable (infrequently occurring) type of behaviour. In a later study, Hamilton and Rose (1980) reported overestimation of the frequency with which stereotypically expected descriptions had occurred (e.g. 'Blacks are lazy'). They also showed that when a correlation does exist in the stimulus information, that relationship will be perceived as stronger if it confirms a stereotype (Hamilton *et al.* 1985).

Hamilton describes cognitive biases that result *from* stereotypic conceptions by considering a stereotype as a 'structural framework' having the properties of a schema. Thus, stereotypes influence information processing about persons in a variety of ways. For example, they may lead to selective attention and also biased interpretations of selective retrieval of information. Often, stereotypes lead the perceiver 'to go beyond the information given' (Bruner 1957) whereby people 'see' what is not there at all (and fail to see what actually occurs).

The influence of stereotypes on memory is revealed in a strong tendency to remember more favourable ingroup and more unfavourable outgroup behaviours (Howard and Rothbart 1980). Individuals also appear to remember and interpret past events in ways that support current stereotypical beliefs. Snyder (1981) provides evidence of biases in reconstructing the past. Asked to recollect details of a person (someone only later labelled as a lesbian/heterosexual), perceivers reconstructed in ways that supported their *post hoc* sexual stereotype. Whatever people recalled, they interpreted it as evidence of a suggested categorization. Relatedly, evidence that confirms stereotypes is apparently more easily noticed, more easily stored in memory, and more easily activated than is disconfirming evidence (Snyder 1981). Looking forwards, as well as backwards, perceivers reveal the same influence of stereotypes. Snyder and Swann (1978a; 1978b) examined how people tested a hypothesis they were given about another person. Results showed a strong tendency towards hypothesis-confirmation. For example, asked to test whether someone was an extrovert, people would ask questions to support, not disconfirm, the hypothesis.

In short, stereotypes generate expectancies, and perceivers seem to want to see expectancies confirmed. This affects the behaviour of the perceiver and the interpretation of the target's action. People tend to see behaviour that confirms their expectancies, even when it is absent. When stereotypes set up expectations of behaviour, disconfirming evidence tends to be ignored, but confirming evidence remembered.

Perhaps the central effect of stereotypes is on causal attributions. Pyszczynski and Greenberg (1981) suggest that when perceivers see their expectancies confirmed, they may simply rely on dispositions implied by the stereotype, not even bothering to consider additional causal factors. Behaviour inconsistent with expectancies, on the other hand, tends to be attributed to external factors. At the level of attributions for in- and outgroup members, these processes help to explain why stereotypes are so pervasive and difficult to change. Because stereotypes refer to people's assumptions about the *dispositional* attributes of in-and outgroup members, any behaviour violating the stereotype could be avoided on the basis that it reflected situational influences and thus did not derive from the personal characteristics of the actor (Hamilton 1979). Summarizing the evidence for cognitive biases resulting from stereotypes, it is clear that a set of processes conspire to ensure that outgroup members are 'damned if they do and damned if they don't'.

It also appears that stereotypes are used to constrain the behavioural alternatives of others, and to engender stereotype-confirming behaviour from a target. In short, stereotypes become self-fulfilling prophecies. Snyder *et al.* (1977) demonstrated this effect by observing very different behaviour from males who believed that they were interacting with a physically attractive versus unattractive female. A female partner in a telephone conversation (who did not know when was perceived as physically attractive) came to behave in a more friendly, likeable and sociable manner (according to independent judges) than a female stereotypes as unattractive.

An equally convincing demonstration for intergroup communication is the study by Word *et al.* (1974). White interviewers were found to be less verbally immediate, to make more speech errors and to give shorter interviews to Black compared to White interviewees. A second study manipulated this previously-observed communication pattern as an independent variable, but using White interviewees. Recipients of what might be called the 'Black interviewee' communication style were themselves judged less adequate and more nervous than were those accorded 'normal' interviews. While this study has implications for the behavioural confirmation of Whites' stereotypes about Blacks, such stereotypes may often be bolstered simply because members of different groups are not aware of the meaning of different communication behaviours (see Gumperz, Chapter 5 in this volume). Shuter (1982) has shown that Blacks and Whites use different strategies in initial conversation; Black males talked longer to females and asked them more direct questions. One can easily imagine that if White females begin with a feeling of apprehension anyway, this form of communication might easily be negatively perceived as 'stereotypical Black hostility' (rather than a display of 'friendly interest'). In fact, Shuter proposes that Blacks and Whites simply employ quite different approaches to information-seeking.

Such studies illustrate how perceivers put their stereotypes into action; the findings support Snyder's view that various social cognitive processes 'conspire to turn social stereotypes into self-perpetuating stereotypes' (1981, 201). More generally, some researchers have attempted to examine the relationship between stereotypes and behaviour. A problem here is that while stereotypes are usually measured as judgements about a group, one can usually assess behaviour only towards an individual. Behaviour targets may then be perceived as individuated and atypical. It is therefore not surprising that results relating stereotypes to behaviour are unclear. Brigham (1971b) reported that an overall stereotyping measure showed no direct relationship at all to behavioural intentions although it was related to the evaluation of individual 'Negroes', yet evaluation was significantly related to behavioural intentions toward individuals. Brigham's (1971a, 29) conclusion is therefore appropriately cautious in that 'there is not a simple relationship between the expression of ethnic stereotypes and their use in behaviour towards specific ethnic group members'.

The whole purpose of relating stereotypes to behaviour is to see what stereotypes do, not just what they are. Given this aim, a much broader range of behaviours should be considered and we focus here on the diversity of communicative behaviour. Lukens (1979) proposes that ethnocentrism may be expressed on different linguistic levels, such as variations in phonology, syntactic structures, semantics, discourse structures and choice of idiomatic expressions which might usefully be related to stereotypes in future work. Considering Black–White encounters, one could relate stereotypes to White people's discourse and negotiation styles, their choice of lexical items to refer to Black people and phrases adopted, or verbal humour. A powerful argument for the use of linguistic dependent variables is provided by Weitz (1972). She found a negative correlation between friendliness of verbal attitude and both voice tone and behaviour, suggesting a repressed affect model. Those people with the *most* extremely favourable attitudes towards Blacks had the *least* friendly voice tone and behaviour towards Blacks. Weitz therefore suggests that linguistic measures may provide a more trustworthy index of ethnic attitudes than do verbal statements (which can be monitored more easily).

Two further studies reveal alternative methodological possibilities for relating stereotypes to communication. Bourhis and Giles (1977) showed that when ingroup members (in this case learners of the Welsh language) were ethnically threatened by an outgroup (English) speaker, they conveyed their attitudes by, for example, broadening their Welsh accent. Bourhis *et al.* (1979) found that Flemish-speaking students in Belgium reacted similarly to a Francophone speaking English whom they perceived as ethnically threatening. The exact nature of divergence (e.g. switching between Flemish and English, switching entirely to Flemish) depended on the strength of the perceived threat. Thus, stereotypes could be related to strategies derived from speech accommodation and ethnolinguistic identity theories (see Giles and Powesland, Chapter 18 in this volume).

While we would welcome further research on the stereotype–behaviour relationship, the cognitive and functional aspects of stereotyping appear to be worthy of study in their own right. It is arguably just as important that stereotypes engender behavioural confirmation, help to sustain a positive social identity and so on, as that they should relate simply and directly to behaviour. Notwithstanding this view, a fair statement on current knowledge is that of Cauthen *et al.* (1971, 118) that 'stereotypes do not initiate behaviour, but rather serve as guides for behaviour'. Modest as this view is, it still supports the claim that stereotypes constitute a crucial aspect of intergroup communication.

SOCIAL FUNCTIONS OF STEREOTYPES

We agree that while the cognitive approach is necessary, it is not sufficient. Its shortcomings include a failure to look at the functions of stereotypes – other than the broad notion of simplifying information processing – and to examine the link between social or group functions of stereotypes and their common espousal by large numbers of people (Tajfel 1981). A purely cognitive approach also provides no explanations or why one particular minority is singled out for discrimination (or why some, but not other, aggregates of individuals are stereotyped); why various minorities may be liked and disliked with varying intensity; and why some minorities are respected, even liked, rather than despised (see Westie 1964).

Despite the contemporary dominance of the cognitive approach, early writers did not ignore the functions of stereotyping. Fishman (1956) enumerated the functions of rationalization, self-justification, and defence of loved-ones; he concluded that 'stereotypes, not unlike folk proverbs, represent a unique combination of insight, projection, rationalization, and out-and-out gratification'. A more systematic view of functions has been developed by Katz (1960) who identifies four functions of attitudes: instrumental, value-expressive, knowledge, and ego-defensive. Respectively, these functions propose that individuals will develop attitudes which help them achieve desired goals, are consistent with their broader value system, impose structure on their social environment and protect them from recognition of their own inadequacies. These functions certainly cover quite a broad perspective, and they are arguably as applicable to stereotypes as to attitudes. These functions are, however, rather individualistic.

Tajfel's (1981b) analysis is more embracing because he has attempted to specify the individual and collective functions served by stereotypes in intergroup relations. Two individual cognitive functions were proposed with reference to principles of categorization and physical judgements. The first of these is to make a complex social world orderly and predictable by, for example, accentuating intracategory similarities and intercategory differences. The second function is to preserve and defend the individual's value system a function that arises from judgements of categories associated with socially valued rather than neutral differentials. Stereotypes serve two major collective functions for group members as a whole in intergroup contexts. The first may be termed a 'social explanatory' function and refers to the creation and maintenance of group ideologies that justify and explain intergroup relations, particularly reactions to and treatment of outgroup members. ... The second collective function concerns the role of stereotyping in preserving, creating or enhancing positively valued differentiations between the ingroup and relevant outgroups. Traits will be selected as stereotypic, and judgements accentuated, if they are relevant to a particular intergroup situation. Tajfel argues that the contents of stereotypes, which vary from one intergroup relationship to another, will depend on which group function(s) they serve in the context under consideration.

As Tajfel (1984) warns, we must not over-simplify or over-extend his model of social stereotypes. An analysis of, for example, racist stereotypes will immediately provide further functions which may be both more social and more important – such as defending the division of labour or preventing subordinate groups from challenging the status quo. Nonetheless, Tajfel's approach to the social functions of stereotypes does provide a heuristic, in initial taxonomy that is a necessary counterweight to the cognitive perspective.

THE STABILITY OF STEREOTYPES

Having looked at both cognitive and functional underpinnings of stereotypes, we can already begin to understand why stereotypes are so difficult to change. First, one should not ignore the extensive social support that usually accompanies stereotypes (Pettigrew 1981). If society substantiates people's views that certain minorities are second class, then negative stereotypes will become entrenched. Thus (following Hartman and Husband 1974), as long as Blacks, Gastarbeiter, or Mexican Americans are badly housed, employed in menial work, poorly educated and stereotyped in the media, it will be almost impossible to alter traditional racist stereotypes.

Much hope has been invested in the idea that stereotype-disconfirming contact with individual outgroup members will reduce or erase stereotypes (see Brewer and Kramer 1985; Hewstone and Brown, 1976). However, most prejudiced people faced with one atypical outgroup member simply exclude the 'special case' from the category, and hold the category intact. Allport (1954) called this response 're-fencing', by which the exception maintains, rather than questions, the rule. In our opinion, this reaction of prejudiced persons questions the value of trying to 'dilute' stereotypes by providing individuating information. Naturally, the cognitive processes discussed above can also be mustered to support a stereotype, and attribution processes may be used to 'explain away' any positive behaviour by members of negatively stereotyped outgroups (Pettigrew 1979). Some evidence even suggests that disconfirmation of stereotypes is cognitively uncomfortable for the perceiver. Gardner and Taylor (1968) found that a speaker who contradicted his group stereotype was evaluated more neutrally on stereotypical items (than a speaker who confirmed the stereotype), but less positively on dimensions such as likeability and friendliness.

Despite the cognitive and functional supports for stereotypes, we know that group images can and do change with real (albeit often drastic) changes in political, economic and social conditions (e.g. Seago 1947; Sinha and Upadhyay 1960). Nonetheless, we believe that our review has implications for attempts to bring about change. It is simply time that social scientists acknowledged the importance of groups, and group images, for the healthy functioning of many individuals. If as Westie (1964, 208) has argued, 'one is one's groups, and vice-versa', then further attempts to reduce stereotyping by cleaving the individual from the group will surely be futile. Given the pervasiveness of stereotypes, and the insatiable need for categorization and simplification, it would seem a more realistic aim to replace negative with positive stereotypes, rather than eradicate group images altogether. Pettigrew (1981) suggests an additionally useful strategy, that of increasing the number of positive subgroup stereotypes, thereby countering the view of outgroups as homogeneous masses.

REFERENCES

Allport, G. (1954) *The Nature of Prejudice* (Reading, MA: Addison-Wesley).

Ashmore, R. D. and Del Bocca, F. K. (1979) 'Sex Stereotypes and Implicit Personality Theory: Toward a Cognitive–Social Psychological Conceptualization', *Sex Roles*, **5**, pp. 219–48.

Bogardus, E. S. (1950) 'Stereotypes Versus Sociotypes', *Sociological and Social Research*, **34**, pp. 286–91.

Bourhis, R. Y. and Giles, H. (1977) 'The Language of Intergroup Distinctiveness', in Giles, H. (ed.) *Language, Ethnicity and Intergroup Relations* (London: Academic Press).

Bourhis, R. Y., Giles, H., Leyens, J. and Tajfel, H. (1979) 'Psycholinguisic Distinctiveness: Language Divergence in Belgium', in Giles, H. and St Clair, R. (eds) *Language and Social Psychology* (Oxford: Basil Blackwell).

Brewer, M. B. and Kramer, R. M. (1985) 'The Psychology of Intergroup Attitudes and Behaviour', *Annual Review of Psychology*, 36, pp. 219–43.

Brigham, J. (1971a) 'Ethnic Stereotypes', *Psychological Bulletin*, 76, pp. 15–38.

Brigham, J. (1971b) 'Racial Stereotypes, Attitudes and Evaluations of and Intentions Toward Negroes and Whites', *Sociometry*, 34, pp. 360–80.

Broverman, I. K., Vogel, S. R., Broverman, D. M., Clarkson, F. E. and Rosenkrant, P. S. (1972) 'Sex-role Stereotypes: A Current Appraisal', *Journal of Social Issues*, 28, pp. 59–78.

Brown, R. (1965) *Social Psychology* (New York: Free Press).

Bruner, J. (1957) 'On Perceptual Readiness', *Psychological Review*, 64, pp. 123–52.

Cauthen, N. R., Robinson, I. A. and Krauss, H. H. (1971) 'Stereotypes: A Review of the Literature, 1926–1968', *Journal of Social Psychology*, 84, pp. 103–25.

Fishman, J. A. (1956) 'An Examination of the Process and Function of Social Stereotyping', *Journal of Social Psychology*, 43, pp. 27–64.

Gardner, R. C. and Taylor, D. M. (1968) 'Ethnic Stereotypes: Their Effects on Person Perception', *Canadian Journal of Psychology*, 22, pp. 267–74.

Hamilton, D. L. (1979) 'A Cognitive-attributional Analysis of Stereotyping', in Berkowitz, L. (ed.) *Advances in Experimental Social Psychology*, vol. 12 (New York: Academic Press).

Hamilton, D. L., Dugan, P. M. and Trolier, T. K. (1985) 'The Formation of Stereotypic Beliefs: Further Evidence for Distinctiveness-based Illusory Correlations', *Journal of Personality and Social Psychology*, 48, pp. 5–17.

Hamilton, D. L. and Gifford, R. K. (1976) 'Illusory Correlation in Interpersonal Perception: A Cognitive Basis of Stereotypic Judgements', *Journal of Experimental Social Psychology*, 12, pp. 392–407.

Hamilton, D. L. and Rose, T. L. (1980) 'Illusory Correlation and the Maintenance of Stereotypic Beliefs', *Journal of Personality and Social Psychology*, 39, pp. 832–45.

Hartman, P. and Husband, C. (1974) *Racism and the Mass Media* (London: Davis-Poynter).

Hayakawa, S. L. (1950) 'Recognizing Stereotypes as Substitutes for Thought', *Review of General Semantics*, 7, pp. 208–10.

Hewstone, M. and Brown, R. J. (eds) (1976) *Contact and Conflict in Intergroup Encounters* (Oxford: Basil Blackwell).

Howard, J. W. and Rothbart, M. (1980) 'Social Categorization and Memory for Ingroup and Outgroup Behavior', *Journal of Personality and Social Psychology*, 38, pp. 301–10.

Katz, D. (1960) 'The Functional Approach to the Study of Attitudes', *Public Opinion Quarterly*, 24, pp. 164–204.

Lambert, W. E. and Klineberg, O. (1967) *Children's Views of Foreign People: A Cross-national Study* (New York: Appleton-Century-Crofts).

Linville, P. W. and Jones, E. E. (1980) 'Polarized Appraisals of Outgroup Members', *Journal of Personality and Social Psychology*, 38, pp. 689–703.

Lippmann, W. (1922) *Public Opinion* (New York: Macmillan).

Lukens, J. (1979) 'Interethnic Conflict and Communicative Distance', in Giles, H. and Saint-Jacques, R. *Language and Ethnic Group Relations* (Oxford: Pergamon Press).

McCauley, C. and Stitt, C. L. (1978) 'An Individual and Quantitative Measure of Stereotypes', *Journal of Personality and Social Psychology*, **36**, pp. 929–40.

McCauley, C., Stitt, C. L. and Segal, M. (1980) 'Stereotyping: From Prejudice to Prediction', *Psychological Bulletin*, **87**, pp. 195–208.

Mervis, C. B. and Rosch, E. (1981) 'Categorization of Natural Objects', in Rosenzweig, M. R. and Porter, L. M. (eds) *Annual Review of Psychology* 32.

Newcomb, T. M. and Charters, W. W. (1950) *Social Psychology* (New York: Dryden Press).

Park, B. M. and Rothbart, M. (1982) 'Perception of Outgroup Homogeneity and Levels of Social Categorization: Memory for the Subordinate Attributions of Ingroup and Outgroup Members', *Journal of Personality and Social Psychology*, **42**, pp. 1051–68.

Pettigrew, T. F. (1979) 'The Ultimate Attribution Error: Extending Allport's Cognitive Analysis of Prejudice', *Personality and Social Psychology Bulletin*, **5**, pp. 461–76.

Pettigrew, T. F. (1981) 'Extending the Stereotype Concept', in Hamilton, D. L. (ed.) *Cognitive Processes in Stereotyping and Intergroup Behaviour* (Hillsdale, NJ: Lawrence Erlbaum).

Pyszczynski, T. A. and Greenberg, J. (1981) 'Role of Disconfirmed Expectancies in the Instigation of Attributional Processing', *Journal of Personality and Social Psychology*, **40**, pp. 31–8.

Quattrone, G. A. and Jones, E. E. (1980) 'The Perception of Variability Within Ingroups and Outgroups: Implications for the Law of Small Numbers', *Journal of Personality and Social Psychology*, **38**, pp. 141–52.

Rothbart, M., Dawes, R. and Park, B. (1984) 'Stereotyping and Sampling Biases in Intergroup Perception', in Eiser, J. R. (ed.) *Attitudinal Judgment* (New York: Springer Verlag).

Ryan, E. B. and Giles, H. (eds) (1982) *Attitudes Toward Language Variation* (London: Edward Arnold).

Ryan, E. B., Hewstone, M. and Giles, H. (1984) 'Language and Intergroup Attitudes', in Eiser, J. (ed.) *Attitudinal Judgment* (New York: Springer Verlag).

Seago, D. W. (1947) 'Stereotypes: Before Pearl Harbor and After', *Journal of Psychology*, **23**, pp. 55–63.

Shuter, R. (1982) 'Initial Interaction of American Blacks and Whites in Interracial and Intraracial Dyads', *Journal of Social Psychology*, **117**, pp. 45–52.

Sinha, A. K. P. and Upadhyay, O. P. (1960) 'Change and Persistence in the Stereotypes of University Students Toward Different Ethnic Groups During Sino-Indian Border Dispute', *Journal of Social Psychology*, **52**, pp. 31–9.

Snyder, M. (1981) 'On the Social Self-perpetuating Nature of Social Stereotypes', in Hamilton, D. L. (ed.) *Cognitive Processes in Stereotyping and Intergroup Behaviour* (Hillsdale, NJ: Lawrence Erlbaum).

Snyder, M. and Swann, W. B. (1978a) 'Hypothesis-testing Processes in Social Interaction', *Journal of Personality and Social Psychology*, **36**, pp. 1202–12.

Snyder, M. and Swann, W. B. (1978b) 'Behavioral Confirmation in Social Interaction: From Social Perception to Social Reality', *Journal of Experimental Social Psychology*, **14**, pp. 148–62.

Snyder, M., Tanke, E. D. and Berscheid, E. (1977) 'Social Perception and Interpersonal Behavior: On the Self-fulfilling Nature of Social Stereotypes', *Journal of Personality and Social Psychology*, **35**, pp. 656–66.

Tajfel, H. (ed.) (1978) *Differentiation Between Social Groups* (London: Academic Press.

Tajfel, H. (1981) 'Social Stereotypes and Social Groups', in Turner, J. C. and Giles, H. (eds) *Intergroup Behaviour* (Chicago: University of Chicago Press).

Tajfel, H. (1984) 'Intergroup Relations, Social Myths and Social Justice in Social Psychology', in Tajfel, H. (ed.) *The Social Dimension: European Developments in Social Psychology* (Cambridge: Cambridge University Press).

Tajfel, H. and Forgas, J. P. (1981) 'Social Categorization: Cognition, Values and Groups', in Forgas, J. (ed.) *Social Cognition: Perspectives on Everyday Understanding* (London: Academic Press).

Taylor, D. M. and Simard, L. M. (1975) 'Social Interaction in a Bilingual Setting', *Canadian Psychological Reviews*, **16**, pp. 240–54.

Triandis, H. C., Lisansky, J., Setiadi, B., Chang, B., Marin, G. and Betancourt, H. (1982) 'Stereotyping Among Hispanics and Anglos: The Uniformity, Intensity, Direction, and Quality of Auto- and Heterostereotypes', *Journal of Cross-cultural Psychology*, **13**, pp. 409–26.

Triandis, H. C. and Vassiliou, V. (1967) 'Frequency of Contact and Stereotyping', *Journal of Personality and Social Psychology*, **7**, pp. 316–28.

Weitz, S. (1972) 'Attitude, Voice and Behavior: A Repressed Affect Model of Interracial Interaction', *Journal of Personality and Social Psychology*, **24**, pp. 14–21.

Westie, F. R. (1964) 'Race and Ethnic Relations', in Faris, E. L. (ed.) *Handbook of Modern Sociology* (Chicago: Rand McNally).

Word, C. O., Zanna, M. P. and Cooper, J. (1974) 'The Nonverbal Mediation of Self-fulfilling Prophecies in Interracial Interaction', *Journal of Experimental Social Psychology*, **10**, pp. 109–20.

Zawadski, B. (1948) 'Limitations of the Scapegoat Theory of Prejudice', *Journal of Abnormal and Social Psychology*, **43**, pp. 127–41.

22 Social Class Differences and the Identification of Sex in Children's Speech

John R. Edwards

INTRODUCTION

It is a truism that, in learning and using language, people are susceptible to social influences in their environment. At a gross level this is shown by the fact that, for example, Chinese children learn Chinese and American children learn English. Within such broad linguistic categories, however, there may exist many regional and social accent and dialect varieties. In addition, varying degrees of prestige and value attach to different language varieties (see, for example, Giles & Powesland 1975 and see Chapter 18 in this volume). Thus within a given society the social conventions relating to language may be many and varied.

One important dimension along which linguistic perceptions may vary is that of social class. In both America and Britain, for example, an association between working-class speech and masculinity and 'toughness' has been noted. Labov (1966) pointed to the positive masculine values associated with working-class speech patterns in New York City. Perception of these values is apparently not restricted to members of the working class, but is shared to some degree by middle-class speakers as well. Whether speakers are aware of these values or whether, because of middle-class pressures, they do not readily admit to them, such values do appear to have general appeal. Thus Labov noted that 'masculinity is unconsciously attributed to the unmodified native speech pattern of the city' (1966: 501). The attribution of masculinity to working-class speech has been termed 'covert prestige', which seems apt, both in view of what has just been mentioned and, as well, in the light of information deriving from a study of English in Norwich (Trudgill 1972). Here, among both working-class and middle-class males, covert prestige was demonstrated by the fact that as many as 54% *claimed* to use non-standard speech forms (e.g. for the word *tune*, use of [tʉːn] rather than [tjʉːn]), even when they did not actually do so.

Source: 'Social Class Differences and the Identification of Sex in Children's Speech', *Journal of Child Language*, **6** (1979), pp. 121–7 (Cambridge: Cambridge University Press).

The covert prestige of working-class speech obviously attracts men rather than women. Indeed, Labov (1966) noted that the positive masculine associations of working-class speech for men do not appear to be balanced by any similar positive values ascribed by women to non-standard speech. Female speech, in general, has been found to be more disposed towards standard, middle-class styles (Fischer 1958, Thorne & Henley 1975, Trudgill 1972, 1974). Allowing for social class and age, women tend to produce 'politer' and more 'correct' speech than their male counterparts. Thus it appears that, as Trudgill (1974) has suggested, covert prestige is more powerful for men and standard prestige is more powerful for women.

Further to this, Mattingly (cited in Sachs 1975) has suggested that linguistic conventions relating to men's and women's speech may cause, in adults, exaggeration of voice differences beyond those accounted for physiologically. Similar conventions may operate for children's speech as well (Meditch 1975). In general, children's early learning of social conventions can hardly be doubted. In the learning of sex-trait stereotypes, for example, Williams, Giles & Edwards (1977) have shown that children as young as five years of age may be quite aware of socially determined stereotypes concerning characteristics of men and women.

Among prepubertal children, certain physiological sex differences relating to speech production are not very marked; the lower fundamental frequency (pitch) typical of male speech, for instance, is produced with the onset of puberty. Similarly, formant (overtone) frequencies are, physiologically, unlikely to be very different among prepubertal boys and girls (Sachs, Lieberman & Erickson 1973). Nevertheless, the sex of prepubertal children can be identified with a high degree of accuracy by judges listening to tape-recorded speech samples. Thus, Weinburg & Bennett (1971) reported 74% accuracy with five- and six-year-olds; Meditch (1975) found 79% correct guesses made of the sex of three- to five-year-old children; Sachs *et al.* (1973) recorded 81% accuracy in judges' identifications of the sex of children whose ages ranged from four to fourteen years. It seems likely that, as Sachs (1975) has suggested, the cues in the speech of prepubertal children which allow accurate identification of sex are at least partly related to children's early conformity to appropriate social norms.

If young children reflect social norms in their speech, and if these norms themselves vary along sex and social class dimensions, then one might expect judgements of prepubertal children's sex to illuminate these phenomena. The purpose of the present study, therefore, was to consider whether differences in the accuracy of sex identification may be related to the social class of the speaker. In addition, the nature of the investigation suggested that the sex of those making the identifications might also prove relevant. Meditch (1975), for example, found that female judges were more accurate in sex-identification than were males. Therefore, both male and female judges participated in this study. In order to be better able to interpret any findings showing differences related to social class, attention was also given to the perceptions of middle-class and working class speech along the masculinity–feminity dimension.

Overall, this study sought to give some practical insights concerning the identification/misidentification of children's sex which may be useful to workers in the general area of child language. Condry & Condry (1976) have provided a general example of the influence of sex stereotypes; ratings of the emotions suggested by the videotaped behaviour of a nine-month-old were quite different, according to whether judges thought they were observing a boy or a girl. More specifically, a recent review by Thorne & Henley (1975) has shown that sex stereotypes operate in connection with speech. In general, the sex (actual or guessed) of a child whose language is under study may be a potent factor in any interpretations of speech behaviour, and one worthy of investigation.

METHOD

The subjects comprised 20 lower-working-class children and 20 middle-class children, whose average age was 10 years (SD approximately 6 months).[1] Within each group were 10 boys and 10 girls. Each child read a prose passage – a 99-word description of school life – which was selected with the assistance of teachers. All the children were given a practice trial following which their second reading was tape-recorded. The reading took place at school, where the investigator was a familiar figure, and the children appeared at ease; the reticence sometimes shown by working-class children in such situations was not evident here (see also Edwards 1976). The judges in this study were 14 teachers-in-training at a Dublin college. There were seven females and seven males. All judges heard all the children's taped voices, in a randomized order, and were asked to identify the sex of each child. Five other adults (2 males and 3 females) were asked to listen to all the voices and to rate each one, using 7-point scales, on four traits: rugged-delicate, low–high, masculine–feminine, rough–smooth. These scales were taken from Sachs (1975) and were included here to see whether, over both boys and girls, working-class speech was in fact perceived as more masculine in character than middle-class speech. The scales were scored by averaging the ratings (from 1 to 7) given by the judges for each child.

RESULTS

Overall, the judges showed 83.6% accuracy in identifying the children's sex, which is of the same order as that obtained in previous studies (see above). The major interest here, however, arises from the distribution of the

Table 22.1: Errors made in the identification of children's sex

		Male judges	Female judges
Working class	Boys	3	1
	Girls	21	9
Middle class	Boys	26	17
	Girls	10	5

incorrect identifications; there were 92 errors made in all, 16.4% of the total number of guesses ($14 \times 40 = 560$). An analysis of variance was performed on the errors (3-way: social class × child sex × judges' sex) in which the last factor was a replicated one. The cell totals for this analysis are shown in Table 22.1. The main effect due to the judges' sex was found to be significant ($F = 15.83$, d.f. $= 1,36$, $P < 0.01$) – the female judges being more accurate overall than were their male colleagues. There was also a significant interaction found between social class and child sex ($F = 10.80$, d.f. $= 1, 36$, $P < 0.01$). This interaction is depicted in Figure 22.1. It is apparent that relatively few errors were made in identifying the sex of working-class boys; more were made with girls. For the middle-class children, the pattern is reversed with more errors being made with boys than with girls.

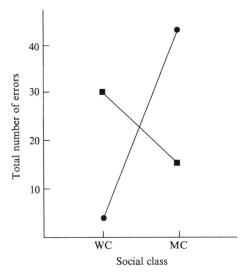

Figure 22.1: Interaction between social class (WC = working class; MC = middle class) and child sex in terms of errors of sex identification. ●—●, boys; ■—■, girls

On each of the four rating scales, the means for the middle-class and working-class groups were compared using one-tailed t-tests. On the scale rugged–delicate, although there was a tendency for working-class children's voices to be perceived as more rugged, no significant different was detected ($t = 1.57$, d.f. $= 38$, $P > 0.05$). However, looking at the other three dimensions, the working-class children were seen as having lower voices ($t = 1.72$, $P < 0.05$), rougher voices ($t = 4.35$, $P < 0.01$) and more masculine voices ($t = 1.86$, $P < 0.05$) than their middle-class counterparts.

DISCUSSION

The finding that female judges were more accurate than the males in identifying the children's sex is in accord with similar results reported by Meditch (1975). Although there is little in the literature on this specific point, Mazance & McCall (1976) found that females were more sensitive than males in interpersonal relationships, especially with regard to verbal styles. If this is the case, then the present results are at least partly explicable (see also Kramer 1977).

Of greater interest here, however, is the interaction, shown in Figure 22.1, between social class and child sex. Among the working-class children, few boys were mistaken as girls; this is consistent with a view of working-class speech as rougher and more masculine than that of the middle class. This view received additional support in the present study from the results of the subjective ratings of the speech samples: the working-class voices were perceived as being lower, rougher and more masculine than the middle-class voices. The fact that more working-class girls were mistaken as boys is interesting, since there is evidence from several sources (see above) that female speech is politer and more correct (i.e. more approaches a middle-class standard) than that of males. In this connection, Labov (1966) has noted that, in showing a tendency towards more standard speech, females exhibit much greater linguistic insecurity than males. It is possible, of course, that status-consciousness of this sort is not highly developed among young girls, although early learning of social norms seems fairly general. In addition, Fischer's (1958) results would seem to belie such a view. He found, among children aged between three and ten years, that girls were much more likely than boys to use the more standard *-ing* rather than *-in* for the ending of the present participle. It may, in fact, be the case that working-class girls are misidentified as boys because the general masculinity of working-class speech is strong enough to cover any stratus strivings on the girls' part. And, in his work on covert prestige, Trudgill (1972) has noted that, although covert prestige itself is primarily a male phenomenon, it is also evident among younger females. It remains to be seen, according to Trudgill, whether the attraction of covert prestige for females is repeated by the youth of each generation or whether it is a new, and perhaps stable, change.

Among the middle-class children, more errors were made with the boys than with the girls. Even though, physiologically, prepubertal boys and girls are more or less equivalent in terms of speech production, the observation that 'boys sound like girls' is more common, perhaps, than 'girls sound like boys'. This is presumably because it is the boys' speech which is going to change markedly at puberty, developing into stereotypical male adult speech, while the differences between girls' and women's speech are less marked. In general terms, of course there is also the fact that, if working-class speech is seen as relatively more masculine than middle-class speech, then the other side of the coin is that middle-class speech is relatively more feminine. Trudgill (1974) pointed out that some males may associate standard speech with feminity, and has also suggested (1972) that middle-class speech may carry feminine connotations because schools, which generally support middle-class speech, are staffed largely by women. In general, the findings reported here support the view that working-class speech is characterized as more masculine than middle-class speech, and this is reflected in the way errors in sex identification are made.[2]

The results of the present study have some implications for those who work with children's speech. Condry & Condry (1976), in their discussion of the influence of sex stereotypes upon the observation of a child's behaviour (see Introduction), suggested caution in interpreting studies of children in which the sex is known, and in which the behaviour has some relation to commonly held sex stereotypes. Such stereotypes are clearly important in the area of speech (Sachs 1975, Thorne & Henley 1975). Where the sex of the child is known, one may at least attempt to interpret results in the light of sex stereotypes which can themselves be investiged. Where the sex is unknown, however, interpretation may be more difficult since, although stereotypes still operate, one cannot be sure if judges have accurately identified the child's sex. The present study indicates that, although there may be a high overall degree of accuracy in guessing the sex of prepubertal children from speech samples, errors made may not be randomly distributed. Consequently, unless they have specific reasons for not doing so, researchers may wish to ensure that the sex of children is known to those who are to assess or interpret some aspects of the children's language.

NOTES

1 The author is aware that terms like 'working class' and 'middle class' are very general. Considerable background data, available upon request, show that for the children in the present study the terms are reasonably applied and reflect such indices as the overall socioeconomic status of the home, characteristics of the home area, parental occupation, etc.

2 An interesting extension of this work would be to employ working-class judges.

REFERENCES

Condry, J. and Condry, S. (1976) 'Sex Differences: A Study of the Eye of the Beholder', *Child Development*, **47**, pp. 812–19.

Edwards, A. D. (1976) 'Social Class and Linguistic Choice', *Sociology*, **10**, pp. 101–10.

Fischer, J. L. (1958) 'Social Influences on the Choice of a Linguistic Variant', *Word*, **14**, pp. 47–56.

Giles, H. and Powesland, P. F. (1975) *Speech Style and Social Evaluation* (London: Academic Press).

Kramer, C. (1977) 'Perceptions of Female and Male Speech', *Language and Speech*, **20**, pp. 151–61.

Labov, W. (1966) *The Social Stratification of English in New York City* (Washington, DC: Center for Applied Linguistics).

Mazanec, N. and McCall, G. J. (1976) 'Sex Forms and Allocation of Attention in Observing Persons', *Journal of Psychology*, **93**, pp. 175–80.

Meditch, A. (1975) 'The Development of Sex-specific Speech Patterns in Young Children', *Anthropological Linguistics*, **17**, pp. 421–33.

Sachs, J. (1975) 'Cues to the Identification of Sex in Children's Speech', in Thorne, B. and Henley, N. (eds) *Language and Sex: Difference and Dominance* (Rowley, MA: Newbury).

Sachs, J., Lieberman, P. and Erickson, D. (1973) 'Anatomical and Cultural Determinants of Male and Female Speech', in Shuy, R. W. and Fasold, R. W. (eds) *Language Attitudes: Current Trends and Prospects* (Washington, DC: Georgetown University Press).

Thorne, B., and Henley, N. (eds) (1975) *Language and Sex: Difference and Dominance* (Rowley, MA: Newbury).

Trudgill, P. (1972) 'Sex, Covert Prestige and Linguistic Change in the Urban British English of Norwich', *Language and Society*, **1**, pp. 179–95.

Trudgill, P. (1974) *Sociolinguistics: An Introduction* (Harmondsworth: Penguin).

Weinburg, B. and Bennett, S. (1971) 'Speaker Sex Recognition of 5- and 6-year-old Children's Voices', *Journal of the Acoustical Society of America*, **50**, pp. 1210–13.

Williams, J. E., Giles, H. and Edwards, J. R. (1977) 'Comparative Analyses of Sex-trait Stereotypes in the United States, England and Ireland', in Poortinga, Y. H. (ed.) *Basic Problems in Cross-cultural Psychology* (Amsterdam: Swets and Zeitlinger).

23 Language Attitudes in a Danish Cinema

Tore Kristiansen

The phenomena of language variation and change raise an important problem which is often neglected in sociolinguistics. In Labovian socio-linguistics the problem is known as *the evaluation problem* (Labov 1972: 162). Social evaluations of language variants and varieties are also referred to as *language attitudes*. Especially when it comes to explanations, the need to study the social evaluations or attitudes which accompany variation and change becomes pressing.

THE VALIDITY PROBLEM IN LANGUAGE ATTITUDES RESEARCH

Language attitudes are complex psychological entities which involve knowledge and feeling as well as behaviour, and are sensitive to situational factors (e.g. the formality of the situation, or the salience of language in the situation). As a consequence, the problem of validity is conspicuous in this field of research: Can we be sure that what we are measuring are really people's attitudes? One might suspect, for instance, that a standard procedure in which a researcher asks for some kind of evaluative reaction (in an interview, in a questionnaire, or in a matched-guise experiment) will prompt subjects to reproduce generally-held opinions rather than display their particular 'real' attitudes.

Thus, one can argue that 'the problem of relating empirical findings to natural behaviour – while hardly unique to language attitude theorists – should be of some particular concern' (Edwards 1982: 32). In fact, it has long been realized that 'if this research area is not to be characterized by 'experiments in a vacuum' (Tajfel 1972) then this method [the matched-guise technique] must be elaborated in such a way as to elicit behavioural, as well as attitudinal, reactions in more real life settings (Giles and Bourhis 1976: 296). A more recent state-of-the-art article makes it a priority of the field to 'free ourselves from the safe haven of studying students or

---

Source: Written specially for this collection.

pen-prone, form-familiar literate, middle class informants' (Ryan, Giles and Hewstone 1988: 1076).

There seems to be fairly general agreement, then, that the best way of detecting 'real' attitudes is to register behavioural reactions to language in real-life situations – in situations in which 'subjects' are unaware that they are taking part in an 'experiment'. However, naturalistic studies of this kind are not easy to design or implement; the literature has not provided us with much more than agenda-setting statements.

THE LANGUAGE OF CO-OPERATION IN WALES

An important exception is a study from Cardiff (reported in Bourhis and Giles 1976) in which the subjects were cinema- and theatre-goers, who made up two types of audiences: (1) an audience attending two films in English was assumed to reflect the language situation in Cardiff, and to consist mainly of monolingual English speakers; (2) an audience attending a play staged in Welsh was assumed to consist of Welsh–English bilinguals. Both the films and the play were shown with an interval, and at the beginning of this interval the audiences were asked over the loudspeaker system to help plan future programmes. To this end, they were required to obtain and complete questionnaire forms in the foyer and return them to the box-office.

A male bilingual speaker had been tape-recorded reading versions of the announcement in: (1) standard Received Pronunciation (RP), (2) a broad South Welsh-accented English, (3) a mild South Welsh-accented English, and (4) standard non-localized Welsh. These versions, which all represent linguistic norms that are relevant to the speech community of Cardiff and South Wales, were presented to audiences on several nights, one version per night. (The Welsh version was of course presented only to the bilingual theatre-goers.)

The behavioural reactions of the two kinds of audience were measured as the ratio between completed questionnaires and tickets sold. In the mainly monolingual audience, one out of every four responded positively to RP and to the mildly Welsh-accented variety of English (22.5% and 25.0%), whereas significantly fewer people (8.2%) completed a questionnaire in response to the broader-accented English. In the bilingual audience attending a play in the Welsh language, it was the request in standard Welsh that gained compliance from one out of every four (26%), whereas both the mildly and broadly Welsh-accented English produced significantly fewer responses (9.2% and 8.1%), and RP even fewer (2.5%).

In addition to being measures of co-operation with differently voiced requests, the percentages of completed questionnaires can be interpreted as measures of language attitudes. It seems reasonable to assume that these data reflect 'real' attitudes fairly well. I leave it here to the reader to reflect on what the data tell us about language and its social meanings in Cardiff, and go on to present a study in which the 'theatre audience method' was used and elaborated in a very different sociolinguistic setting (originally reported in Kristiansen 1991, Kristiansen and Giles 1992).

THE NÆSTVED SETTING

Copenhagen is by far Denmark's largest city; out of a national total of some 5 million inhabitants, 1.5 million live in the conurbation of the capital city. Næstved is a middle-sized Danish town with 38 000 inhabitants, 80 kilometres to the south of Copenhagen. Although a regional centre of considerable importance, Næstved is in every respect heavily influenced by Copenhagen, and some 2600 people travel to work there every day. Both Copenhagen and Næstved are situated on the island of Zealand.

The kind of language variation to be found in the speech of native Næstveders indicates that growing up in this town means relating to three norms of Danish language use. (1) The *Standard* norm represents a language use traditionally associated with high social status and commonly thought of as the 'correct' language; it is the norm of language use in the national mass media and is propagated by schools all over Denmark. (2) The *Copenhagen* norm represents a language use traditionally associated with the working class of that city. During the last decades characteristic features of Copenhagen speech have spread throughout the whole of Denmark in the speech of young people, irrespective of social status, and are increasingly being heard on national radio and television. (3) The *Zealand* norm represents the local language use, which nowadays is associated with older people in the countryside, if not with peasantry and boorishness. Only very few Zealand features are nowadays heard in the speech of young people.

An intriguing question with regard to a sociolinguistic situation like that in Næstved is whether a 'mild' local language has a future. If the few remaining local features are not just reminiscences of a dying norm, we should be able to register positive attitudes towards 'mild' local language use, in the sense of such language use being accepted and preferred in public – like in a movie-theatre – and not just *in private* with family and friends.

Given the relative statuses of the dialects as described, the most likely pattern of response to emerge in a cinema experiment would be: most responses to a request in the Standard accent, least to a request in a broad Zealand accent, somewhere in between in response to the Copenhagen and mild Zealand accents.

STIMULUS TAPES AND LINGUISTIC VARIABLES

Since it was not possible to find a speaker who was able to perform all four accents in a satisfactory, authentic manner (as in the case of the classical matched-guise technique), the four versions of the request were read by four different people. The broad Zealand version was read by a 75-year-old woman from the countryside surrounding Næstved, and the mild version was read by a Næstved woman aged about 40. The Standard and Copenhagen versions were read by two women from Copenhagen, both about 40 years old. All four versions were competently read and differred minimally with regard to features such as speech rate and fluency.

The main linguistic differences between the voices will be described briefly here, partly in order to stress the desirability that this be done in language attitudes studies, partly in order to give an idea of the nature of the linguistic variation in the Næstved area – which is generally limited to the phonological level of language:

– [ε ~ æ] Before dentals and in word-final position (e.g. in words like *kasse*, 'box' and *ka* 'can'), the *Standard* and *Zealand* norms have a less fronted variant [æ] than the *Copenhagen* norm [ε]. On the tape, the Standard and broad Zealand voices have only the [æ] variant; the Copenhagen and the mild Zealand voices have both variants, with the [ε] variant predominating in the Copenhagen voice.

– [ʌ ~ ɒ] In most linguistic contexts (e.g. in words like *oppe*, 'up' and *om*, 'about', the *Standard* norm has a more fronted and less rounded variant [ʌ] than the *Copenhagen* and *Zealand* norms [ɒ]. On the tape the Standard voice has only the [ʌ] variant; the other three voices have both, with the [ɒ] variant predominating in the Copenhagen voice.

– [æ ~ a] After r-, the *Copenhagen* norm has [a] in words which according to the *Standard* and *Zealand* norms have [æ] (e.g. in words like *ret*, 'rather' and *interesser*, 'interests'). On the tape the Standard and broad Zealand voices have [æ], the Copenhagen and mild Zealand voices have [a]. In some of the relevant words the *Zealand* norm has [e]. On the tape one example of this is present in both the mild and broad Zealand voices (the word *forresten*, 'by the way').

– *stød* This is a prosodic feature, linked to the syllable, most frequently manifested as a glottal constriction. The feature is present in all three norms, but it is assigned to more words in the *Zealand* norm than in the other two; in addition it is characteristic of Zealand speech that the *stød* is pronounced more vigorously (often as a glottal stop). On the tape both Zealand voices show assignment and realization of *stød* that differ from the Standard and Copenhagen voices, but there are far more instances in the broad version than in the mild one. (The broad version shows other 'old' features of the *Zealand* norm as well.)

PROCEDURE

There is only one cinema in Næstved, but it has five theatres which show different films. Two of the films that were shown in the theatre at the time of the study (April 1988) are double-length films, and the other three are of normal length and were played twice nightly. This means that the experiment could be conducted at 8 performances each night, thereby accessing 32 audiences over a four-day period.

Each audience was addressed for one minute over the loudspeaker system in both the theatre and the foyer just before the film started. They were asked to fill out a questionnaire containing four questions about their habits as cinema-goers, and were offered the opportunity to comment on the cinema's film programme. (The answers to these questions have been analysed and the results submitted to the cinema owners, so their participation in a survey was real enough). They were also asked to provide information about their sex, age, and occupation, as well as about where they grew up, where they lived now, and where they worked or attended school.

The questionnaires had been placed on the stage at the front of the theatre. For the normal-length films, people were invited to collect the questionnaires after the film had finished, answer them and put them into a box by the stage. A short reminder of some 20 seconds was transmitted when the film had finished. For double-length features, people were invited to fill out the questionnaire during the interval, at which time a reminder was transmitted. This procedure was repeated on four nights of the same week (Monday–Thursday to avoid the potentially different weekend audiences). The addresses to the audiences (both initial and reminder) were presented in a different guise every evening, in the following order: Standard, mild Zealand, Copenhagen, and broad Zealand. This order was based on the hypothesis that the Standard would be the expected variety in a cinema context, whereas the other varieties might represent increasing degrees of unexpected language use.

As in the Bourhis and Giles study, the measure of behavioural co-operation was the ratio between the number of completed questionnaires and the number of tickets sold each night, the last number, of course, being the number of questionnaires that potentially could have been filled out.

THE AUDIENCES

Five theatres showing different films provide an opportunity to explore the reactions of potentially different categories of audiences. The audiences were characterized on the basis of two kinds of data. (1) By drawing on information about the films – content, purpose, addressees, time on screen – these and their audiences were ranked on a five-point 'entertaining/ light–intellectual/serious' scale. (2) On the presupposition that the respondents are representative of their audiences, these were characterized with regard to the background variables used in the questionnaires: age, sex, education/occupation and geographical affiliation. The audiences were equally distributed as to sex, but differently – in a statistically significant way – as to the other variables. These characteristics will be presented and drawn upon in the next section, which presents and discusses the participation patterns in the different audiences as a picture of language attitudes.

RESULTS AND DISCUSSION: LANGUAGE ATTITUDES AS REVEALED IN BEHAVIOURAL CO-OPERATION

When we look at the behavioural reaction of the audience as a whole (i.e. the five audiences taken together), we find that, just as in the Cardiff study, one out of four responded positively to the standard voice, i.e. the kind of language use that people expect to hear over the loudspeaker of a cinema. This was, as hypothesized, significantly more responses than for the other voices. Contrary to expectation, there was no difference in response to the non-standard voices (see Figure 23.1).

Out of the five audiences, two were classified as *adult* (mean ages of 31.0 and 30.4), three as *young* (mean ages of 17.1, 17.9 and 19.5). The responsiveness of the total young audience (i.e. the three young audiences taken together) exhibits the expected pattern, but the differences between the non-standard voices are not significant (see Figure 23.2).

When we examine the five audiences separately, we find important within-community differences, which the general pattern disguises (see Figures 23.3–7).

Cry Freedom (directed by Richard Attenborough)

Let us start by looking at the *Cry Freedom* audience, which is the only one that produces no significant variation in its co-operative response pattern. In addition, we note that a very high percentage of the audience were responsive on all four days (see Figure 23.3).

This audience was ranked as the most 'intellectual/serious' of the cinemagoers. The film they saw – about the founder of the Black Consciousness Movement in South Africa (Steve Biko) – was the most obvious 'message-film' of the five. It attracted enough people to remain on the bill for only two weeks in Næstved, and obviously had little appeal beyond a narrowish 'special-interest' circle. The audience was dominated by adults, the majority of whom were employed in the education/healthcare sector.

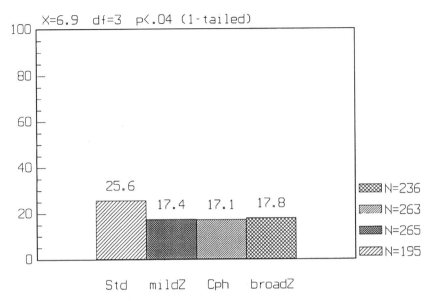

Figure 23.1:   Total audience

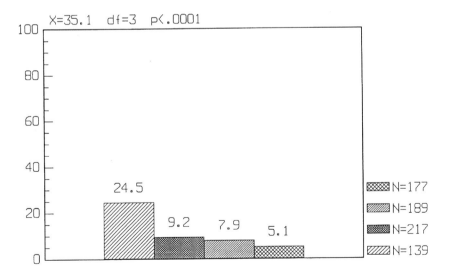

Figure 23.2:   Young audience

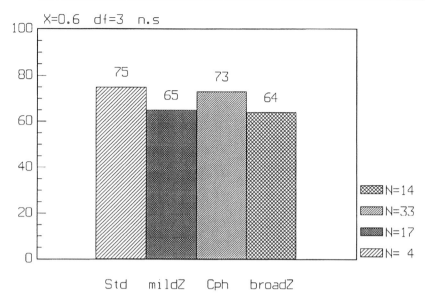

Figure 23.3:   *Cry Freedom*

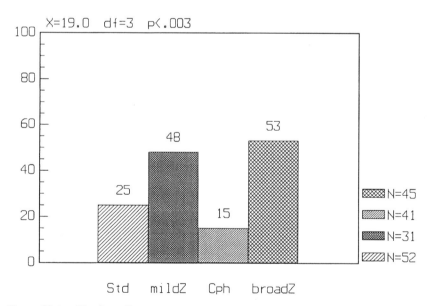

Figure 23.4:   *The Last Emperor*

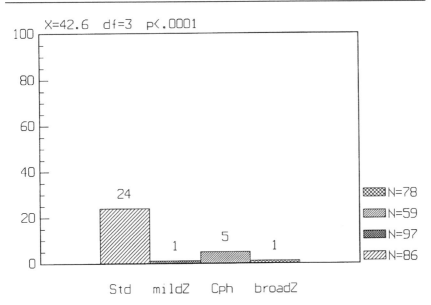

Figure 23.5: Three Men and a Baby

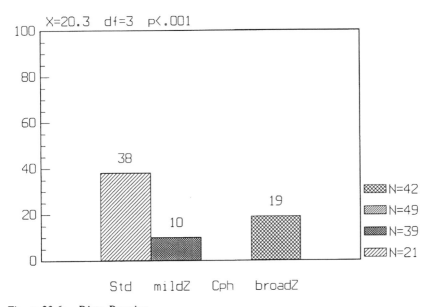

Figure 23.6: Dirty Dancing

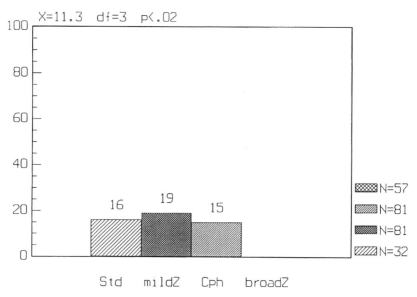

Figure 23.7:   Wish You Were Here

Regarding the size of the participation ratio, it would not be irrelevant to point out that, in general, people in this audience were no doubt more accustomed to handling questionnaires than people in the other audiences. As to the consistency of the participation ratio, a possible explanation might be a particularly high interest in this audience in the actual *content* of the request, i.e. in the possibility of commenting upon the film programme of the only Næstved cinema. However, even though this audience had the highest percentage of respondents who took the opportunity to add comments and views, this was not significantly different from the other audiences.

Interpreted as a pattern reflecting language attitudes, the audience's responsiveness must be said to reflect tolerance and acceptance of sociolinguistic variation and diversity.

Turning now to consider the participation patterns in the other four audiences that do vary as a function of language use, we should first of all note that the degree of co-operation with the Standard voice is approximately the same across these audiences (differences are not significant), whereas the reactions to the other voices vary quite considerably (differences are significant). The uniform reaction to the Standard voice is notable because it corresponds to the assumption that this is the unmarked language used in the cinema setting. Therefore, for further analyses we can take reactions to the Standard as the baseline in each of the audiences, and then characterize the reactions to the other voices as either positive or negative if the difference in participation is significantly above or below this baseline.

The Last Emperor (directed by Bernardo Bertolucci)

This audience shows positive reactions towards both the mild and broad Zealand voices; the reaction towards the Copenhagen voice is neutral, i.e. not significantly different from the reaction towards the Standard voice (see Figure 23.4).

The film, which tells the life-story of the last Chinese Emperor, was ranked as the second most 'serious' one. It had a broader appeal than *Cry Freedom*, and was screened for six weeks. This was the other adult audience; most respondents listed an occupation, and those were (unlike the respondents in the *Cry Freedom* audience) equally distributed among the three sectors of industry/craft, office/trade, and education/healthcare. Neither was there anything special in terms of 'geographical affiliation' that might offer an explanation for the positive reaction to Zealand-accented speech in this audience. All in all, this was probably a very 'ordinary' adult audience.

Its response pattern could be seen as a case of upgrading (or maybe only defending) the local values against the intruding values of the larger society.

Three Men and a Baby (directed by Leonard Nimoy)

Coming to the young audiences, we start with the main audience responsible for the total pattern (in Figures 23.1 and 23.2): this audience reacts very negatively and unresponsively to all three non-standard varieties (see Figure 23.5).

The film was ranked as the most 'light/entertaining' of the five. It attracted a lot of people, and was shown for 11 weeks in the Næstved cinema; during the week of the experiment it was by far the best-attended, and accounted for one-third of the total sample. The majority were students or occupational trainees. Characteristic of the audience is its anonymity: it showed the lowest level of participation, and gave very few comments about the film programme. The audience might be said to present itself as the 'silent majority'.

Nevertheless, it still produces a participation ratio of about 25 per cent as its reaction to the Standard voice. Interpreted as a language attitudes finding, this co-operative pattern suggests that the young 'silent majority' is consequently negative towards non-Standard language use in a public place. When in a cinema, the prototypical 'light' audience of young people in education or training dissociate themselves from anything but the 'correct' (the expected) accent.

Dirty Dancing (directed by Emile Ardolino)

This young audience shows the same negative rection as the previous one towards the mild Zealand and Copenhagen voices. But, unlike in the *Three Men and a Baby* audience, the response to the broad Zealand voice is neutral, i.e. not significantly different from the response to the Standard voice (see Figure 23.6).

The film was ranked next to *Three Men and a Baby* as a 'light' film. It was seen by a lot of people and stayed on the screen for 12 weeks. The audience shares all characteristics with the *Three Men and a Baby* audience – with the one exception that it attracted far more viewers from Næstved's surrounding area. This particular feature can be explained by the fact that *Dirty Dancing* had been on the bill in Næstved for much longer than any of the other films at the time of the experiment (it played in its tenth week). There is a clear pattern in the data indicating that a film first draws its potential audience from the centre, and then attracts more and more of its potential audience from the geographical periphery.

Thus, one might say that the neutral reaction to the broad Zealand voice, which does seem surprising in this young audience, finds a plausible explanation in the audience's high degree of affiliation with the countryside. The countryside character of the audience may also be part of the explanation for its negative reaction towards the Copenhagen and mild Zealand accents, in as far as these are perceived as 'town accents'.

Wish You Were Here (directed by David Leland)

This audience's response pattern is clearly different from the pattern in the two other young audiences. The reaction was neutral in response to the mild Zealand and Copenhagen voices, and negative only in response to the broad Zealand voice, which gained no participation at all (see Figure 23.7).

Which audience characteristics might explain this response pattern? Firstly, we should note that the film did not attract as broad an audience – it was taken off after six weeks; being good entertainment but certainly not just completely frivolous, it was ranked in the middle on the 'light-serious' scale. Secondly, we may also note that the respondents of this audience showed a higher mean age than the respondents of the other two young audiences (19.5 versus 17.1 and 17.9); this was not statistically significant, however. On the other hand, the audience differed significantly from the other two young audiences in comprising more employed people. In other words, this audience's greater resemblance with the adult audiences may to some extent account for its response pattern.

However, the very negative reaction towards the broad Zealand voice does not resemble the reaction in any of the adult audiences, so it seems reasonable to point to another factor as the more decisive one in the *Wish You Were Here* audience: the audience differed significantly from the others in being predominantly from the town itself; very few were from the surrounding area. It can be argued that this was due to the fact that the film ran in its first week at the Næstved cinema (cf. the centre/ periphery conditioned pattern mentioned above in the discussion of *Dirty Dancing*).

The response pattern supports the assumption that the Copenhagen and mild Zealand accents are conceived of as 'town accents'. To this particularly town-affiliated audience these accents are no less acceptable in the cinema situation than the Standard, whereas the countryside accent (broad Zealand) is strongly rejected.

IMPLICATIONS

This study of language attitudes in a naturalistic setting is part of a larger sociolinguistic study of the ongoing language change processes in the Næstved area. The main theoretical interest of the project as a whole is the role of social evaluations in language change, with a particular focus on how people's attitudes are dependent on whether they are aware or not that they are making some kind of evaluation – the assumption being that the 'real' attitudes are those that seem to have an impact on language use and, hence, on language change.

In other studies, in which subjects were aware of displaying attitudes towards accents, the local accent is evaluated positively by native adolescents of the Næstved area, on a par with the Standard, whereas the Copenhagen accent is evaluated significantly more negatively. Such an evaluative pattern is in contradiction with the changes in language use. As mentioned earlier, traditional dialect variants are to a great great extent being replaced by Standard variants, or more frequently by Copenhagen variants among young people.

However, the attitudes which young people displayed in the cinema, i.e. when not being aware of displaying attitudes, are more in accordance with what is happening on the level of language use. The evaluative pattern of the total young cinema audience (see Figure 23.2) shows clearly that the local dialect is dowgraded in comparison with the Standard. And the Copenhagen accent is upgraded, in the sense that it is no longer evaluated more negatively than the local dialect but on a par with it.

In a matched-guise experiment conducted within the Næstved project – an experiment in which subjects were also not aware of assessing speakers of Standard, Copenhagen and mild Zealand accents – adolescents evaluated the Copenhagen accent significantly more positively than the other two accents (with regard to status as well as to solidarity). The lack of an equivalent upgrading in the young cinema audience may have been due to the fact that the Copenhagen voice over the cinema loudspeaker belonged to a 40-year-old woman (whereas the speakers in the matched-guise experiment were young men).

There is, however, a clear indication in the cinema data to the effect that younger people are more positive than older people towards the Copenhagen accent. If we take the total number of adult respondents (those more than 20 years old, $N = 93$) and look at their mean ages across the four nights, i.e. their mean ages as a function of the accent used in the request, we find the following pattern: Standard 34.3 years, mild Zealand 37.5 years, Copenhagen 28.9 years, broad Zealand 37.1 years ($F = 3.02$, $p < .04$). Under the assumption that the mean age of the audience is approximately the same every night, the variation in the mean age of the respondents indicates that co-operation with the local voices was obtained mostly from the older section of the adults, whereas co-operation with the Copenhagen voice was obtained mostly from the younger adults.

All in all, we can be fairly certain that the language attitudes which were displayed in the cinema are 'real' attitudes in the speech community of the Næstved area: they seem to be governing the ongoing language change.

Finally, let us briefly consider whether the cinema data shed any light on the future of the local dialect. A regional centre like Næstved might be the hotbed of renewed feelings of local identity and positive attitudes towards the few remaining local features in the speech community. It might stand up, so to speak, against the general influence from Copenhagen in its region. The role of the town in this respect emerges as rather ambiguous.

On the one hand the town clearly functions as a spearhead of the Copenhagen dialect advance. We saw how the young audience characterized by a high degree of Næstved- affiliation showed a neutral reaction towards the Copenhagen voice (see Figure 23.7), which was a more positive reaction than with the two other young audiences (see Figures 23.5 and 23.6). And if we do the same analysis as with age above, and look at how the geographical affiliation of the respondents varies across the four nights, we find that they were significantly more Næstved-affiliated on the Copenhagen night than on the other nights.

On the other hand, the young audience characterized by Næstved-affiliation did also react more positively towards the mild Zealand voice (see Figure 23.7) than did the young audience affiliated to the surrounding area (see Figure 23.6). The same, significant, difference was obtained in the matched-guise experiment (in the status dimension). In other words, there is also some evidence that Næstved as a regional centre may secure a future for a mild local accent.

REFERENCES

Bourhis, R. Y. & Giles, H. (1976) 'The Language of Cooperation in Wales: A Field Study', *Language Sciences*, **42**, pp. 13–16.

Edwards, J. R. (1982) 'Language Attitudes and Their Implications Among English Speakers', in Ryan, E. B. & Giles, H. (eds) *Attitudes towards Language. Social and Applied Contexts* (London: Edward Arnold) pp. 20–33.

Giles, H. & R. Y. Bourhis (1976) 'Methodological Issues in Dialect Perception: A Social Psychological Perspective', in *Anthropological Linguistics*, **19**, pp. 294–304.

Kristiansen, T. (1991) *Sproglige Normidealer på Næstvedegnen. Kvantitative Sprogholdningsundersøgelser*. Dissertation, University of Copenhagen.

Kristiansen, T. & Giles, H. (1992) 'Compliance-gaining as a Function of Accent: Public Requests in Varieties of Danish', *International Journal of Applied Linguistics*, **2**(1), pp. 17–35.

Labov, W. (1972) (1985) *Sociolinguistic Patterns* (Oxford: Basil Blackwell).

Ryan, E. B., Giles, H. & Hewstone, M. (1988) 'The Measurement of Language Attitudes', in Ammon, U., Dittmar, N. & Mattheier, K. J. (eds) *Sociolinguistics. An International Handbook of the Science of Language and Society* (Berlin – New York: Walter de Gruyter) pp. 1068–81.

Tajfel, H. (1972) 'Experiments in a Vacuum', in Israel, J. & Tajfel, H. (eds) *The Context of Social Psychology: A Critical Assessment* (London: Academic Press).

24 Language Policies and Language Attitudes: Le Monde de la Francophonie

Richard Y. Bourhis

Attitudes towards the French language in 'le monde de la francophonie' have been deeply influenced by language policies developed in France since the seventeenth century. Through vigorous and sometimes brutal language planning programmes, multilingual France emerged in this century as a unilingual French state. In addition to legislating against non-French languages, policy makers in France insured that only the 'Ile de France' dialect emerged as the prestige standard form of the language. By virtue of its population and cultural vitality, France today can still be considered the heart of the francophone world. Consequently, it seems appropriate to devote the first part of this chapter to the development of language attitudes in France.

Social psychological research has already shown that a prestige standard form of a language has no *inherent* aesthetic or linguistic advantage over nonstandard varieties of this or other languages. Rather, the prestige ascribed to the standard form of a language is usually the product of culture-bound stereotypes passed on from one generation of speakers to the other. In France, the history of language planning efforts in favour of the Ile de France dialect demonstrates that the prestige attained by a standard form of a language may not be just the product of a cultural accident favouring its use, but the result of centuries of systematic efforts to impose *one* variety as the prestige norm to the exclusion of all other varieties.

[Only the sections on France, English Canada and Quebec are included here, because of restrictions on space. The original chapter also discusses language attitudes in Algeria, Tunisia, Morocco, Lebanon, South East Asia, Haiti, Martinique, Guadeloupe, Belgium, Switzerland, and the French language situation in the USA—*Eds.*]

Source: 'Language Policies and Language Attitudes: Le Monde de la Francophonie' in Ryan, E. B. and Giles, H. (eds) (1982) *Attitudes towards Language Variation: Social and Applied Contexts* (London: Edward Arnold) pp. 34–62.

Three major points emerge from this overview. First, as in France, very little *empirical* data exist on attitudes towards the French language in 'le monde de la francophonie'. The notable exception to this state of affairs is the situation in Quebec, which remains the most active centre for the investigation of language attitudes in the francophone world (Douaud 1979). Indeed, much of the techniques and knowledge developed for the social psychological investigation of language attitudes was generated in the Quebec setting (Lambert 1967; Giles and Powesland 1975; Giles and Bourhis 1976). One aim of this chapter is to provide a sociohistorical context for broadening empirical work on language attitudes to all parts of the francophone world.

The second point that emerges from the overview is that from existing anecdotal evidence and secondary sources, it seems that relative to indigenous speech varieties, standard French remains the prestige norm for many francophones across the world. Indeed, diglossia (Ferguson 1959; Fishman 1967) seems to be an important legacy of the French colonial presence in the francophone world. Contributing to this state of affairs is the fact that France imposed standard French as the only language of civilization throughout its empire. Also, the ruling elites of many francophone states have been trained in France where standard French has long been the prestige norm in educational circles. To this day, economic, cultural and educational activities in France promote the use of standard French as the prestige norm across the world. Finally, standard French remains the target norm taught to those learning French as a second language in most parts of the world. These four sociostructural factors help account for the maintenance of standard French as the prestige norm across the francophone world.

The third point to emerge is that though 75 million people still speak French in the world today, French language usage seems to have decreased in former French colonies. Many Third-World countries whose own language was displaced by French during colonial days today reassert their identity by replacing French with a modernized version of their own language. For such countries the reintroduction of a strong ancestral language as a symbol of identity is seen to have the advantage of promoting the group solidarity necessary for successful nation building (Deutsch 1953; Fishman 1977). ...

LANGUAGE ATTITUDES IN FRANCE

Current attitudes towards the French language in 'le monde de la francophonie' have been shaped by the notion of 'le bon usage' developed in Paris in the seventeenth century. This notion was introduced by Claude Favre de Vaugelas in his work entitled *Les remarques sur la Langue*

Française published in 1647. Vaugelas maintained that there was only one correct way of speaking the French language. 'Le bon usage' could only consist of the French spoken by esteemed members of the King's Court. Vaugelas expected the best authors of the day to enshrine the best forms of courtly French in their writing. According to Vaugelas, reading the best authors was not sufficient to guarantee appropriate usage, as correct French pronunciation could only be acquired through regular attendance at the Court. Since the King's Court was established in Le Palais du Louvre, the Ile de France dialect spoken by the King and his entourage became the prestige form of the language to the exclusion of other French dialects spoken in other parts of France.

Vaugelas was also an influential member of l'Académie Française (its 40 members called 'les Immortels'). Established in 1637 by Cardinal Richelieu, l'Académie Française had the task of purifying and perpetuating correct French usage as rendered by the Court and esteemed authors. Vaugelas fully expected that the elite constituting Les Immortels would guarantee the harmonious development of correct French through the ages. It was during the reign of Louis XIV, whose cultural policy encouraged the great French literary masters, that the French language was standardized. The literary works of Corneille, Molière and Racine became the models of good style and correct spoken French.

In the eighteenth century the myth of French as a classical language blessed with unique virtues such as clarity, purity, rationality and discipline was widely accepted and propagated by the French ruling elites throughout Europe. To this elite, changing aspects of French vocabulary and grammar, or adopting foreign borrowings could only lead to the corruption of the French language. More importantly, it was felt that only the Ile de France dialect could be considered as the vehicle of French civilization. All other forms of French spoken in France were dismissed as 'degenerate patois' best left to the abuse of the 'common people'. By the end of the eighteenth century the test of whether a person could be classed as belonging to 'les honnêtes gens' came to depend on the quality of his or her spoken French.

Nation building in France was facilitated by language legislation promoting French *language* unilingualism. As early as 1539, François I decreed French as the only official language of France. This decree banned the use of the Latin, Breton, Basque and Occitan languages from the courts and enshrined French in texts of laws. Until the French Revolution no systematic attempt was made by the monarchy or ruling elites to impose 'le bon usage' on the common people. But, with the French Revolution in 1793 France disposed of the monarchy as a unifying symbol. It is during this period that standard French emerged as a potentially unifying symbol to inspire the nationalism of the new Republic. The victorious bourgeoisie needed to suppress existing regional commercial and language barriers to establish its economic control across France. The Ile de France dialect adopted by the Parisian bourgeoisie was seen as a tool to suppress competing regional, economic and language interests in the name of the new Republic. Simultaneously, Parisian proletarian elements associated strong regional language groups in the provinces with feudalism and the counterrevolution. Therefore, bourgeois and proletarian interests converged to favour a strong, centralized nation–state cemented by the imposition of French unilingualism in all the regions of France. In 1793 Abbé Grégoire was commissioned by the National Convention to undertake a language survey aimed at determining the number of French speakers in France. Grégoire was forced to report that out of a population of 26 million in France, only 3 million inhabitants could speak the Ile de France dialect fluently. In his report, Grégoire identified patriotism with the speaking of French while non-French speakers were viewed as potential traitors to the Revolution and a threat to the political unity of the emerging French Republic. As advocacy for French unilingualism the title of Grégoire's Report is revealing: 'Report on the needs and means to destroy the 'patois' and to universalize the use of the French language'.

Between 1793 and 1794 the National Convention passed a series of laws which made the teaching of French compulsory in primary school and proclaimed French unilingualism in all parts of France including Brittany, the Basque country, Alsace, Corsica and the whole of southern France known as l'Occitanie. This first attempt at language planning resulted in a complete failure for linguistic unity in France. By late 1794, faced with the strength of regional languages and a desperate lack of French teachers, the National Convention was compelled to pass a law allowing bilingual education in primary schools.

After the revolution of 1830 a law was passed requiring clerks and administrators seeking public office in any region of France to demonstrate mastery of written French. For the aspiring middle classes of the regions this law meant that access to civil service positions could only be achieved through mastery of French. By 1850 numerous French dictionaries served the needs of the upwardly mobile, eager to learn the standard Ile de France dialect as enshrined by the prescriptions of l'Académie Française.

Between 1881 and 1884 the laws of Jules Ferry successfully entrenched French unilingualism in France. As primary education became compulsory, so was the teaching of all disciplines to be made exclusively in the medium of French. This time an adequate number of teachers had been made available through 'les Ecoles normales'. These institutions trained elementary school teachers to become proficient language teachers in standard literary French. For the ruling elites and the growing middle class, French was the language of civilization destined to replace not only the Occitan and Breton languages in France but also to replace Arab and African languages in the expanding French colonies. The contempt for non-French languages in France was epitomized in Brittany, Occitanie, Alsace and Corsica, where students caught speaking their non-French mother tongue on school premises were punished by being forced to wear the infamous 'signum' or Token. Pupils wearing the Token at the end of the school day were severely punished by the teacher. A pupil could only dispose of the Token by catching another student using the patois and reporting him to the teacher before the end of the school day. Such practices fostered distrust between non-French speakers and made schoolchildren ashamed of using their parents' language both at school and at home. Compulsory military service in the French army also contributed to the decline of non-French languages in France. During the 1914–18 war, recruits from linguistically diverse regions of France were systematically assigned to regiments where only French could serve as a lingua franca. At the end of the First World War, non-French languages were in decline while the linguistic unification of France was well underway. Indeed, by the late 1960s apart from the German/French bilinguals in Alsace and migrant workers throughout France, 95 per cent of the 53 million inhabitants in France were of French mother tongue.

Language standardization in favour of the Ile de France *dialect* was always viewed as a way of promoting linguistic unity in France. From the Revolution onwards attempts were made in the school system to ensure that no other dialect of French be taught than the standard Ile de France variety. In the French educational system, official attitudes towards nonstandard dialects were generally hostile. For instance, official directives issues by the Ministry of Education from the 1920s to the 1970s emphasized the teachers' duty of fostering correct oral and written French to offset the 'debasing influence of ordinary usage' (Marks 1976, 212). More recent directives for preschool education assumed that the mother tongue of the preschool years only meant the Ile de France standard. Only 20–30 per cent of preschool pupils in France came from homes where the standard form of French was the mother tongue. For 70–80 per cent of preschoolers using German, Arabic or French nonstandard dialects, the teacher's standard dialect constituted an almost foreign language. For many of these nonstandard speakers, the disadvantage was further increased by teachers who judged the correctness of the child's language by reference to the norms of standard French.

In 1972 a series of recommendations for French language teaching in elementary school was proposed in Le Plan Rouchette. This government-sponsored document pointed out that over 50 per cent of elementary school pupils (mostly working class) spoke nonstandard dialects, which made learning to read and write standard French as difficult as learning a second language. With evidence that over 50 per cent of French children left elementary school only bordering on literacy, Le Plan Rouchette recommended that French be taught in elementary school using *second* language techniques. The Plan Rouchette was vehemently attacked by numerous academics, politicians and members of l'Académie Française who felt that the new methods of teaching French would fail and thus threaten the very existence of the French language. To cool the debate, a new Ministry of Education document was quickly published recommending a compromise between the traditional and new approaches to mother-tongue instruction in the primary school system. It is clear that to this day French educational policies are aimed at promoting language standardization in favour of the Ile de France dialect. Government guidelines remain designed to discourage nonstandard pronunciation in the school setting (Marks 1976).

Indications are that the repressive policies and attitudes towards nonstandard usage take their toll in the French educational system as is evident from the high proportion of failures in the school system. It is probable that nonstandard speakers experience a considerable degree of linguistic insecurity by the time they have completed their education. Goosse (1970) remarks that many secondary school leavers 'feel paralysed by the fear of making a mistake in their written or oral French'. Anecdotal evidence reported by Laks (1977) also supports this observation. Using techniques developed by Labov (1972), Laks compared the ability of middle-class *vs* working-class French pupils to switch from colloquial French to the prestige Ile de France pronunciation. Laks (1977) reported a considerable amount of linguistic insecurity, especially amongst working-class respondents who were aware of their inability to switch to the prestige pronunciation. Laks quotes a working-class pupil named Jean Pierre as saying: 'Il faut savoir quand même ton français, si c'est du français arabe t'es dedans. A l'école je suis nul, alors je suis dedans' ('But you need to know about your French, whether it's Arabic French that you're into. At school I'm out of it, when I use it.')

Jean Pierre refers to his nonstandard French as being as bad as 'français Arabe', an allusion to the low status ascribed to Arab-accented migrant workers in France. Feeling useless in school, speaking as bad as 'français Arabe', Jean Pierre considers himself 'out of it' with little hope of 'ever making it'.

The imposition of standard French and the chastising of nonstandard speech styles was not limited to the educational system. Since the introduction of radio and television in France the prestige and diffusion of the Ile de France dialect has increased to the detriment of nonstandard dialects and non-official languages. As Bourdieu (1977) points out, even in university texts such as those of Guiraud (1956, 1965, 1968), colloquial French, regional and urban accents and dialects are often described using derogatory and value-laden terms. For instance, Guiraud (1956) unleashes his most vehement attacks on nonstandard speakers when he describes the special vocabulary of the Parisian proletariat (known as '*l'Argot*') in the following terms:[1]

the vocabulary of the vulgar Parisian is almost exclusively concrete...it is based on a narrow reality devoid of culture and literature...the degradation of its sentimental values is only matched by the degradation of its aesthetic values. The masses have few words to express beauty...In any event, the materialism and obscenity of the vulgar Parisian glares in the vocabulary of these masses. (pp. 42–6)

Guiraud (1968) distinguished between accent deviations from the norm which could be tolerated and those which he felt must be stamped out. On this issue Goosse (1970) is less rigid and concedes that it is illusory to attempt the elimination of all nonstandard accents in France or elsewhere. Instead he proposes 'to correct the most visible and shocking departures' while noting that amongst those who have been 'better educated', many have succeeded in 'correcting their faulty pronunciation'. The eminent French linguist, Martinet (1969) expressed most tolerance by pointing out that a French speaker should never be denigrated on the basis of accent or dialect as long as he/she 'uses impeccable syntax and vocabulary'. In fairness to the above scholars, it must be pointed out that in more recent times French linguists have adopted a more sociolinguistic approach to the study of dialectal diversity in France.

From this overview it seems that to this day a majority of academics, educators, policy makers and mass media specialists favour one standard norm of French which happens to be the Ile de France dialect. Nonstandard dialects and accents are not much tolerated as these are viewed as a threat to both the linguistic unity of France and to the purity and universality of the French language. No study of the type reviewed in Giles and Powesland (1975) has investigated empirically the impact of the above policies and views on attitudes towards standard and nonstandard speech styles in France. Indeed J. R. Ross (1979) pointed out that:

little systematic work, apart from dialect studies, has been done on nonnormative descriptions of French...and, indeed, in nonlinguistic circles there is still a tendency towards a folklore denying the existence of socially conditioned or status-indicative variants of French...but the tradition of one France, one French seems unreasonable and can be refuted on endless anecdotal grounds.

Thus, one might expect that on a prestige (high–low status) and evaluative (good–bad) continuum of speech styles in France, the Ile de France standard would be rated very favourably by both standard and nonstandard speakers. Conversely, one could expect regional accents and dialects to be rated below the Ile de France style, while urban nonstandard and ethnic speech styles would be rated even lower on this prestige and evaluative continuum. Finally the Parisian Argot and the foreign ethnic-accented

French of migrant workers from North Africa and Eastern Europe would most probably receive the lowest ratings on this continuum. On the other hand, one might also expect each of the above nonstandard varieties of French to be rated favourably in their respective milieus for usage in informal settings. The above speculations are necessarily subject to empirical verification using survey and experimental procedures of the type developed by Lambert (1967), Giles and Bourhis (1976) and Bourhis (1981).

Not all nonstandard speakers in France could be expected to denigrate their own speech style in favour of the standard norm. Loyalty to nonstandard speech styles could be expected amongst cultural nationalists and urban activists in numerous parts of France. Intellectuals such as Lafont (1973), Person (1973) and Calvet (1974) have argued that the history of language and cultural policies in France amounts to a linguistic and cultural genocide against most dialect and language groups other than the Ile de France elite. Since the Second World War, reactions against the government's centralist linguistic, cultural and economic policies culminated in numerous ethnic revival movements. Regionalist demands were so great after the war that a law called 'Loi Deixonne' was passed in 1951 allowing for the teaching of regional languages such as Breton, Occitan, Catalan and Basque as second languages in schools of these respective regions. By 1970, Corsican was allowed to be taught as a second language in Corsica, while Flemish and German were allowed in their respective regions as 'foreign languages' (Marcellisi 1979). However, the 'Loi Deixonne' is seen by many as too limited since these second language classes are only optional, often scheduled at inconvenient times and are assigned to teachers who lack proper second language training skills (Marcellisi 1975). Today, ethnic revival movements can be found in Occitanie with its *langues d'oc* made up of numerous dialects including Gascon, Provençal, Limousin and Auvergnat. Other movements emerged in Brittany around the Breton language: in the Basque Country with the Basque language, in Catalogna with the Catalan language, in Corsica with the Italian dialect, in Alsace with German, and in French Flanders with Flemish. As in Wales and other parts of the world, these cultural nationalists and regional activists reject standard French in favour of their own distinctive accent, dialect or language which they use as symbols of group identity. Though no empirical study has yet addressed this issue in France, evidence suggests that loyalty to nonstandard languages and dialects persists in the above regions of France.

Though loyalty to nonstandard speech styles exists in certain regions of France, it is likely that such loyalties are seriously undermined as institutional support in favour of the Ile de France standard grows more overwhelming for each new generation of Frenchmen. To many a Frenchman, attachment to standard French has grown deep as a symbol of the unity, prestige and vitality of French culture in the world. In this respect, it seems that language policies aimed at the linguistic unification of France have been so successful that the future of nonstandard accents, dialects and languages is bleak in France (Tabouret-Keller 1981).

THE FRENCH LANGUAGE BEYOND FRANCE

In the eighteenth century the prestige of standard French as a universal language and culture was well established amongst the elites in both France and across Europe (Gordon 1978; Viatte 1969). In the nineteenth century, the French colonial empire guaranteed the spread of standard French as the language of civilization beyond Europe. In each of its new colonies, standard French was established as the language of administration and the linguistic tool needed by local elites to share in the 'universality' of French civilization. As in France, non-French languages encountered in the colonies were usually dismissed as mere patois or vulgar vernaculars best left to the 'unassimilable masses'. By the beginning of the First World War, France's colonial empire was second only to that of Britain. On the eve of the Second World War the French colonial empire stretched across five continents, with Paris still considered the cultural capital of the world.

It is not surprising then, to find that long after decolonization standard French still commands much prestige in the world. To this day, the Ile de France dialect remains the prestige norm against which francophone speakers across the world are most likely judged. Indeed Goosse (1970), a Belgian linguist, reiterated the necessity of maintaining the Ile de France dialect as the universal standard for French by concluding that 'the history of the French language, the numerical importance of the French in France and the cultural role of France virtually dictates no other choice but that of standard French as the universal norm for French'.

To this day, much emphasis has been placed on teaching standard French rather than local varieties of French to pupils in schools across the world. ...

Language Attitudes in English Canada

Since Lord Durham's Report of 1839 which advocated the full assimilation of francophones to the English culture, French Canadians have usually been a minority everywhere in Canada except Quebec. Both before and after the British North American Act (BNA) of 1867, French Canadians from Quebec settled in English Canada seeking better jobs as labourers, farmers and small entrepreneurs. The French linguistic presence in English Canada has been most important in Ontario and New Brunswick. According to

Canadian Census figures of 1971, 9.6 per cent of the Ontario population was of francophone origin while in New Brunswick 37 per cent of the population was of French background. In the other English provinces, French Canadians have not been so numerous and assimilation to the English majority has been predicted to be close to complete in the near future (FFHQ 1978; Joy 1972, 1978).

Across English Canada, French-Canadian assimilation has usually gone through a phase of individual French/English bilingualism followed by English unilingualism. Indeed, Stanley Lieberson (1970) in his now classic *Language and Ethnic Relations in Canada* concluded that 'Patterns of bilingualism in recent decades in Canada have very much favoured the English language...there is little doubt that a French Canadian who becomes bilingual is increasingly likely to raise his children in English'. The Anglicization of French Canadians residing in English Canada has been facilitated by the omnipresence of English as the language of work, business, administration, mass media and leisure. Historically, assimilation has also been accelerated by English Canadian discrimination against French Canadians (*Royal Commission on Bilingualism and Biculturalism*, 1969) and by Public Education Acts banning French-medium schools in Ontario (Law 17, 1917) or laws banning the teaching of French as a second language in public schools such as those of Manitoba (1916) and Saskatchewan (1929). Indeed, a survey of language and education policies enacted in English Canada since the BNA Act of 1867 shows that many of these laws contributed to the assimilation of francophones in English Canada (FFHQ 1978).

Today, more tolerant language laws allow French-medium schools in Ontario (1968) and Manitoba (1980), while the Canadian Official Languages Act (1969) declared English and French the official languages of the Federal Parliament and Government services. Nevertheless, the Canadian Census showed that the rate of Anglicization of francophones (or language transfer in favour of English) in the nine English provinces was an impressive 27 per cent in 1971. Indeed, of the 1.4 million respondents who acknowledged their French Canadian origin (6.6 per cent) in English Canada, 65 per cent claimed French as their mother tongue while only 48 per cent claimed French was still the most often spoken language at home (FFHQ 1978). The census data also showed that language transfer in favour of English occurred mostly for francophones between the ages of 20 and 44, this age group having an anglicization rate of 35 per cent (Castonguay and Marion 1975). This latter trend suggests that francophone anglicization in English Canada may be even higher by the 1981 Canadian Census (FFHQ 1978).

Patterns of language use and francophone assimilation in English Canada suggest that French-Canadian attitudes towards their own language may be less positive than those they have towards the English language. In addition, standard French rather than local-accented Canadian French has long been taught as the prestige form of French in both English and French-medium schools across English Canada. Consequently, one may expect both French and English Canadians to perceive standard French more favourably than local-accented Canadian French on prestige dimensions.

In Ontario, Mougeon and Canale (1979) identified Franco-Ontarian French as a linguistically distinctive dialect of French which, they note, is perceived negatively by most Anglo-Ontarians and numerous Franco-Ontarians. Indeed, survey results obtained by Léon (1976) showed that working-class speakers of Franco-Ontarian French felt linguistically insecure relative to both standard French and the English language. Nevertheless, as the largest group of francophones outside Quebec (pop. 737,360), Franco-Ontarians have recently emerged as culturally and politically more active in their defence of broader language rights in Ontario. This recent militancy on the part of Franco-Ontarians may herald more positive views towards Franco-Ontarian French as a possible badge of Franco-Ontarian identity distinct from English Canadian and Québécois identity.

By virtue of their numbers (pop. 235,000) and their demographic concentration in the northern and eastern parts of New Brunswick known as Acadia, French-speaking Acadians have not only resisted assimilation (only 7.7 per cent in 1971), but have recently emerged as an assertive ethnic group in eastern Canada. Since the last decade, Acadians and English Canadians have clashed over language and cultural issues in Moncton and other parts of Acadia. The Acadian ethnic revival movement recently culminated in the creation of 'Le Parti Acadien' which seeks the establishment of Acadia as a new francophone province within the Canadian Confederation.

Acadians have long been made ashamed of their distinctive Acadian dialect both by teachers of standard French and by New Brunswich English Canadians. The struggle of the Acadians for fairer treatment fostered a resurgence of the distinctive Acadian cultural and linguistic identity. Pride in Acadian identity peaked in 1979 when Antonine Maillet received France's most prestigious literary aware (le Prix Goncourt) for her recent novel written in the distinctive Acadian dialect. It now appears that amongst students and cultural nationalists at least, the Acadian accent and dialect (Chiac) has come to serve as a symbol of pride in Acadian identity and group solidarity. A study by Larimer (1970) in the late 1960s showed that amongst Acadian respondents, the Acadian accent was evaluated as favourably as Canadian-accented English and more favourably than Québécois-accented French. Studies contrasting attitudes towards standard *vs* Acadian *vs* Québécois-accented French should reveal whether or not Acadian French has emerged as a symbol of positive identity for substantial portions of the Acadian population.

Language Attitudes in Quebec

Beyond France, Quebec today represents the largest native French-speaking population in the world (5 million). Under the influence of the Catholic Church, the French-Canadian population in Quebec during the 90 years following the British conquest rose from 70 000 in 1763 to a staggering 670 000 by 1850. A prodigious birth rate and loyalty to both Catholicism and the French language are important factors which prevented the Anglicization of French Canadians in Quebec. Unlike the situation in English Canada where the Anglicization of dispersed French Canadians increased with each generation, French Canadians held their own as a majority concentrated in the province of Quebec.

Though a majority in Quebec (80 per cent of the population), French Canadians have been the economic underdogs in a province controlled by a powerful English-Canadian minority. Studies such as the *Royal Commission on Bilingualism and Biculturalism* (1969) showed that French Canadians in Quebec have long been discriminated against by members of the English-Canadian bourgeoisie. But the modernization of Quebec society in the 1960s gave rise to an ethnic revival movement which asserted the distinctiveness of the Québécois linguistic and cultural presence in North America. In the 1970s the Québécois nationalist movement fostered both democratic and paramilitary political movements which sought Quebec's independence from the rest of Canada. By 1976 the pro-independence Parti Québécois led by René Levesque was elected and promptly passed Bill 101 in 1977, making French the official language of Quebec. Essentially, Bill 101 was drafted with the aim of making Quebec a completely French-speaking society within North America. From the evidence so far it seems that this linguistic legislation has been successful in reaching its immediate goals.

As elsewhere in the francophone world, has standard French emerged as the prestige form relative to the local Québécois-style French? Following the defeat of the French army on the Plains of Abraham in 1760 the French population of Quebec was cut off from the influence of Metropolitan France. Consequently, French in Quebec developed for more than 200 years without the normalizing influence of the standard Ile de France dialect. This led Spilka (1970) to note that 'The French spoken in Quebec today by all but a small academic and professional elite differs at all levels of linguistic analysis from the accepted prestige form spoken in France'. Before the substantial impact of modernization, education and improved Franco-Quebec relations, it is likely that French Canadians had positive views towards their own style of Québécois French. But early efforts of Quebec language planners in the 1960s may have inadvertently denigrated Québécois-style French by introducing language planning favouring standard French. This effect was also compounded by the negative views towards Québécois French held by some French-Canadian elites and by

English Canadians (Lambert 1967). For instance a study of Bourhis, Giles and Lambert (1975), using a dialogue refinement of the matched-guise technique, showed that French-Canadian listeners rated a French-Canadian speaker to be more intelligent and educated when she switched to standard French than when she maintained or accentuated her Québécois-style French. Most studies up to 1975 contrasting attitudes towards standard French *vs* Québécois middle-class and working-class French showed that French Canadians downgraded their own mode of speaking relative to standard French.

Political, cultural and linguistic events favouring the Québécois cause were expected to have an impact on the value attached to Québécois speech styles relative to standard French. Daoust (1982) reports the results of a yet unpublished study which indicates a:

> perceptible change in the attitudes of the French-speaking student population in favour of Quebec French. The preliminary analysis of part of the secondary school students' sample seems to reveal that Quebec French is perceived more favourably and that the group studied feels less need to fall into line with standard European French... although we cannot draw any final conclusions, it is tempting to suppose that this apparent change in attitude is an indication of a trend toward an improved self-image.

Future language-attitude studies should help determine which styles of French French Canadians consider most appropriate for formal and informal usage in Quebec. From recently released language planning documents, there are indications that l'Office de la Langue Française in Quebec supports the re-evaluation of middle-class Québécois French relative to standard French. Indeed, it would seem that of all the francophone communities beyond France, Quebec has the demographic and institutional means needed to imbue its own middle-class Québécois-style French with as much prestige as standard French. In this sense, the emerging strong position of Québécois French relative to standard French is becoming more similar to the strong position of American English relative to the British standard and to Mexican Spanish relative to the Castilian standard in Spain. In these three cases demographic and institutional support built up in favour of the New World renderings of these languages have grown to the point of matching the prestige ascribed to the Old World standards of these languages.

As elsewhere in the francophone world it is noteworthy that local Québécois French must not only coexist with standard French but must also compete with the predominance of the English language in the North American continent. Traditionally in Quebec, the English language has dominated over the French language in prestige value and as the language of business and economic advancement. Language policies in Quebec favoured institutional French/English bilingualism until the passage of Bill 22 in 1974. As early as 1864 both English and French were declared the two official languages of Parliament and of the Legisla-ture. In addition to providing bilingual civil services, Quebec, to this day, maintains two parallel government-financed systems of primary, secondary and higher education servicing both the French majority and the English minority. Freedom of choice for the language of education became an important political issue when the French-Canadian birth rate dropped dramatically in the 1960s and when statistics showed that immigrants to Quebec chose English rather than French as the language of adoption for themselves and their children. Both Bill 22 and Bill 101 addressed this issue by maintaining freedom of choice for the language of education of English Canadians but restricting the choice to French for recently-landed migrants to Quebec.

The historically dominant position of English Canadians and the subordinate position of French Canadians in Quebec was reflected in Lambert's classic series of studies using the matched-guise technique (Lambert *et al.* 1960; Lambert 1967, 1979). The results of Lambert's studies and of others reviewed by Giles and Powesland (1975) showed that English Canadians in Quebec tended to evaluate English-speaking representative speakers of their own group more favourably than French Canadian speakers, while French Canadians showed the *same* tendency in a *more exaggerated* form, that is, they too rated English-Canadian speakers more favourably than French-Canadian speakers. In addition to showing that the English language had more prestige than French, these results were also interpreted as indicating that French Canadians had accepted for themselves the negative stereotypes English Canadians had of them in the context of French/English relations.

The Québécois nationalist movement of the 1970s was expected to have a positive effect on French-Canadian identity in Quebec. Preliminary results to this effect were obtained in the study by Bourhis and Genesee (1980). One of the patterns of results obtained in this recent study showed that instead of denigrating representative speakers of their own group, French-Canadian students rated a speaker of their own group more favourably than an outgroup English-Canadian speaker. Such results remain to be corroborated in further studies, but the general atmosphere in favour of French in Quebec seems to have raised the status of Québécois French relative to both the English language and standard French.

NOTES

I would like to express my gratitude to E. B. Ryan, H. Giles, B. Weinstein, B. Saint-Jacques, I. Sachdev, R. Clément, M. Daly and R. Day for their useful comments on earlier drafts of this chapter. I also wish to thank Beverly Pitt for her cheerful patience in typing various versions of this chapter.

1 Most translations into English are mine and have been phrased so as to capture the flavour of the originals.

REFERENCES

Boudieu, P. (1977) 'L'Économie des Échanges Linguistiques', *Langue Française*, **34**, pp. 17–34.

Bourhis, R. Y. (1981) 'Cross-cultural Communication in Montreal: Some Survey and Field Data After Bill 101', Paper Presented at the 42nd Annual Convention of the Canadian Psychological Association, Toronto.

Bourhis, R. Y. and Genesee, F. (1980) 'Evaluative Reactions to Code-switching Strategies in Montreal', in Giles, H., Robinson, W. P. and Smith, P. (eds) *Language: Social Psychological Perspectives* (Oxford: Pergamon Press) pp. 335–43.

Bourhis, R. Y., Giles, H. and Lambert, W. E. (1975) 'Social Consequences of Accommodating One's Style of Speech: A Cross-national Investigation', *International Journal of the Sociology of Language*, **6**, pp. 55–72.

Calvet, L. J. (1974) *Linguistique et Colonialisme* (Paris: Petite Bibliothèque Payot).

Castonguay, C. and Marion, J. (1975) 'L'Anglicisation du Canada', *La Monda Lingvo-Problemo*, **5**, pp. 145–56 (now: *Language Problems and Language Planning*).

Daoust, D. (1982) 'Corpus and Status Language Planning in Quebec', in Cobrarrubias, J. (ed.) *Progress in Language Planning: International Perspective* (The Hague: Mouton).

Deutsch, K. W. (1953) *Nationalism and Social Communication* (Cambridge, MA: MIT Press).

Douaud, P. (1979) 'Canada and France: Main Trends in the Sociolinguistics of French', *Anthropological Linguistics*, **21**, pp. 163–81.

Ferguson, C. (1959) 'Diglossia', *Word*, **15**, pp. 325–40.

FFHQ (1978) *The Heirs of Lord Durham: Manifesto of a Vanishing People* (Ottawa: Fédération des Francophones Hors Québec).

Fishman, J. A. (1967) 'Bilingualism and Diglossia', *Journal of Social Issues*, **23**, pp. 29–37.

Fishman, J. A. (1977) 'Language and Ethnicity', in Giles, H. (ed.) *Language, Ethnicity and Intergroup Relations* (London: Academic Press) pp. 15–57.

Giles, H. and Bourhis, R. Y. (1976) 'Methodological Issues in Dialect Perception: Some Social Psychological Perspectives', *Anthropological Linguistics*, **18**, pp. 294–304.

Giles, H. and Powesland, P. F. (1975) *Speech Style and Social Evaluation* (London: Academic Press).

Goosse, A. (1970) 'La Norme et les Écarts Régionaux', *Annales de la Faculté des Lettres et Sciences Humaines de Nice*, **12**, pp. 91–105.

Gordon, D. C. (1978) *The French Language and National Identity* (The Hague: Mouton).

Guiraud, P. (1956) (7th edition, 1976) *L'Argot*. Collection Que Sais-Je? (Paris: Presses Universitaires de France).

Guiraud, P. (1965) (4th edition, 1978) *Le Française Populaire*. Collection Que Sais-Je? (Paris: Presses Universitaires de France).

Guiraud, P. (1968) (2nd edition, 1971) *Patois et Dialectes Français*. Collection Que Sais-Je? (Paris: Presses Universitaires de France).

Joy, R. J. (1972) *Languages in Conflict* (Toronto: McClelland & Stewart).

Joy, R. J. (1978) *Les Minorités des Langues Officielles au Canada* (Montreal: C.D. Howe Institute).

Labov, W. (1972) *Sociolinguistic Patterns* (Philadelphia, PA: University of Pennsylvania Press).

Lafont, R. (1973) 'Sur le Problème National en France: Aperçu Historique', *Les Temps Modernes*, **324–6**, pp. 21–53.

Laks, B. (1977) 'Contribution Empirique a l'Analyse Socio-differentielle de la Chute de /r/ dans les Groupes Consonantiques Finals', *Langue Française*, **34**, pp. 109–25.

Lambert, W. E. (1967) 'A Social Psychology of Bilingualism', *Journal of Social Issues*, **23**, pp. 91–109.

Lambert, W. E. (1979) 'Language as a Factor in Intergroup Relations', in Giles, H. and St Clair, R. N. (eds) *Language and Social Psychology* (Oxford: Basil Blackwell and Baltimore: University Park Press) pp. 186–92.

Lambert, W. E., Hodgson, R., Gardner, R. C. and Fillenbaum, S. (1960) 'Evaluational Reactions to Spoken Languages', *Journal of Abnormal and Social Psychology*, **60**, pp. 44–51.

Larimer, G. S. (1970) 'Indirect Assessment of Intercultural Prejudices', *International Journal of Psychology*, **5**, pp. 189–95.

Léon, P. (1976) 'Attitudes et Comportements Linguistiques: Problèmes d'Acculturation et d'Identité', *Cahier de Linguistique*, **6**, pp. 199–221.

Lieberson, S. (1970) *Language and Ethnic Relations in Canada* (New York: Wiley).

Marcellisi, J. B. (1975) 'L'Enseignement des Langues Régionales', *Langue Française*, **25**, pp. 1–12.

Marcellisi, J. B. (1979) 'Quelques Problèmes de l'Hégémonie Culturelle en France: Langue Nationale et Langues Régionales', *International Journal of the Sociology of Language*, **21**, pp. 63–80.

Marks, C. T. (1976) 'Policy and Attitudes Towards the Teaching of Standard Dialect: Great Britain, France, West Germany', *Comparative Education*, **12**, pp. 199–218.

Martinet, A. (1969) *Le Français sans Fard* (Paris: Presses Universitaires de France).

Mougeon, R. and Canale, M. (1979) 'Maintenance of French in Ontario: Is Education in French Enough?' *Interchange*, **9**, pp. 30–9.

Person, Y. (1973) 'Impérialisme Linguistique et Colonialisme', *Les Temps Modernes*, **324–6**, pp. 90–118.

Ross, J. R. (1979) 'Where's English?' in Fillmore, C. J., Kempler, D. and Wang, W. S. Y. (eds) *Individual Differences in Language Ability and Language Behaviour* (New York: Academic Press) pp. 127–63.

Royal Commission on Bilingualism and Biculturalism, Book 1–4, (1969) (Ottawa: Queen's Printer).

Spilka, I. V. (1970) *Force Study of Diglossia in French Canada* (Montreal: Mimeo Université de Montréal).

Tabouret-Keller, A. (1981) 'Introduction: Regional Languages in France: Current Research in Rural Situations', *International Journal of the Sociology of Language*, **29**, pp. 5–14.

Viatte, A. (1969) *La Francophonie* (Paris: Larousse).

Part VI
Multilingualism

If one way of defining sociolinguistics is the study of speakers' socially motivated linguistic choices, then one of the fundamental questions within the discipline is: which languages or language varieties are spoken by members of different speech communities in different situations and why? This part of the Reader represents several sociolinguistic studies which have helped to provide answers.

Language is one of the most important forms of human symbolic behaviour and is a key component of many groups' social *identities*. Because people belong to different groups and have many potential identities (see, for example, Chapters 3, 20 and 24), different codes will serve as markers or even tools for forging these identities. A separate, national language, for example, is often perceived as a necessary condition for a nation to exist. But definitions of languages can be very subjective. Seemingly identical linguistic codes can be identified as separate languages if distinct identities need to be established for two, otherwise similar, ethnic groups.

Serbian and Croatian are good examples of languages which, until the war which broke out in the former Yugoslavia in 1991, were treated as one language, Serbo-Croat. The main difference between the two varieties was that they were written in two alphabets, Cyrillic and Roman respectively. But after the war started, linguists and non-linguists in the former Yugoslavia went to considerable lengths to establish the varieties as separate languages by asserting how much the two codes differed structurally.[1] If, say, British English and American English were to undergo similar political 'theorizing', one could imagine claims being made that they were radically different languages. In fact, we currently think of them as dialects of a common code, distinguished by minor matters of vocabulary, pronunciation and orthography (or normative spelling). What was at stake in the former Yugoslavia was not a linguistic reality but a set of political and social realities.

But there are notable exceptions to the generalization that national or ethnic identity is tied to a national or ethnic language. For example, the Irish have largely lost Irish Gaelic but not a sense of nationhood. Some American Aboriginal peoples have lost their indigenous languages but have not necessarily lost their ethnic identity or cultural vitality. Even in cases like these, language can be a source of national or ethnic identity, although in a rather negative way – through a sense of loss. For example, when asked about their linguistic and cultural heritage, many Welsh monoglot English speakers invoke their Welshness in terms of a national language which has been denied to them. For other Welsh people, and particularly those whose learning of Welsh halted the decline in the overall numbers of Welsh speakers at the 1991 census, a Welsh identity is likely to be linked to the language in a less abstract way.

This part's opening chapter, by Joshua Fishman, debates some of the political and moral questions surrounding *language and ethnic identity*. Fishman's celebratory view of ethnic and linguistic diversity has been very influential in sociolinguistics. He has also established the importance of sociolinguistic ideas in key areas of social and political life, for example in relation to language planning. In this reflexive and largely philosophical essay, Fishman points out the damaging and dangerous (Eurocentric?) myth of 'one nation, one state, one language' which became well established in the nineteenth century and persisted in the political and popular conception of nationhood until late-modern times. Today, such an ideology can too easily be a tool of reactionary propaganda, in the rhetoric of such groups as 'English Now' in the USA. This movement calls for the linguistic cleansing of America by imposing English as the official language in the country. Such legislation could lead to a ban on bilingual education and might also spark off some version of ethnic cleansing, on the grounds of the supposed superiority of English over other languages spoken in America; that is, *racism* in Fishman's terms.

In contrast to the view of a nation as an ethnic and linguistic monolith, Fishman proposes ethnic and linguistic diversity not only as a universal and normal condition, but as a necessary and desirable one, if we are to celebrate the human race in all its manifestations. For Fishman, ethnicity is a non-discriminatory, value-free notion, which he opposes theoretically to racism – the prejudicial, essentially hierarchical, value-laden notion that one group and its language is inferior to another. All countries in the world have ethnic and linguistic minorities within their boundaries. To construe them as a problem for national identity is to assert a divisive monocultural and purist ideal. Against this, the primary goal of sociolinguistics has been to assert principles of *linguistic and cultural pluralism*.

There is no denying that languages and language varieties are socially and politically stratified. Haugen's chapter outlines the mechanisms by which some varieties emerge as fully-fledged languages and symbols of national or group identity and power. Others, in contrast, can remain stigmatized, functionally underdeveloped and aesthetically undervalued languages, associated with groups and minorities adjudged to be inferior. Haugen makes us aware that most of the processes that establish or change a language's status in a community – such as *standardization, codification*, the development of a *writing system*, and so on – are not only linguistic but political acts. Similarly, it is not only the institutions (such as language academies, parliaments, or newspapers) or authority figures (writers, politicians, journalists) who promote these decisions, but *all* language users. A good example is what Ferguson called a *diglossic* situation, when 'high' and 'low' language codes or dialects exist alongside each other in a community (for example, Classical Arabic versus a regional form of Arabic). In a diglossic community, political, religious and educational views and values are established and perpetuated.

The sociolinguistics of language choice needs to consider many practical questions too. The early characterization of multilingualism proposed by Fishman operated across different *domains* of language use, such as the family, school, playground, church, and so on. These domains were thought to trigger the bilingual speaker's choice of one language or the other. More recent studies of code-switching (see, for example, Chapters 28 and 29 by Gardner-Chloros and Gal) have dealt with a much broader range of linguistic, pragmatic and social aspects of multilingualism. Through investigating particular forms and functions of code-choice, they have also addressed problems of language change, shift and death, pointing out the crucial link between ethnic and linguistic group vitality.

Romaine (Chapter 27) describes the use of Tok Pisin, the English based creole of Papua New Guinea, as an advertising medium. Tok Pisin is one of the three official languages of Papua New Guinea, and it has undergone considerable development from being an 'inferior' variety to a 'full' standard. It has been selected as a national language (alongside English and another pidgin language, Hiri Motu), and it has gained partial acceptance – 44 per cent of the population of New Guinea claim to speak it. It is now a written language and it is used extensively in the House of Assembly, although, as Romaine points out, English is the official medium of education. The vocabulary of Tok Pisin is undergoing rapid development to increase its range of uses and to fill in lexical gaps, partly by borrowing words from other languages. Romaine deals with the expansion of Tok Pisin into the domain of newspaper advertising (functional elaboration) and the expanding and fixing of Tok Pisin's resources to serve this new function (codification).

Western companies trying to advertise their products in Tok Pisin have to realize that Tok Pisin has come to use some words for various household goods that derive from specific brand-names with generic meanings. For example, soap powder translates into Tok Pisin as *omo*, which poses serious linguistic problems in advertising Omo-brand soap powder in Tok Pisin. Similarly, different styles or registers in Tok Pisin make use of phrases which cannot be used in advertising without invoking unintended connotations. As Romaine points out, biscuit advertisers need to know that the Tok Pisin word *switbisket* (from English 'sweet biscuit') and *draibisket* have metaphorical meanings. 'Switbisket' can refer to a sexually attractive woman, and 'draibisket' to an older and less attractive woman. Also, certain culturally-based assumptions about what sells products well through the

Western media will not always work effectively in Papua New Guinea. For example, sexual innuendo is likely to be found offensive, not persuasive.

None of these practical problems facing the codification and expansion of Tok Pisin are stopping the language from being used in advertising. The social gains of this ongoing language shift (from English to Tok Pisin) very easily outweigh a certain amount of effort on the part of advertising copy-writers. For their part too, in adopting Tok Pisin as their communication medium, advertisers can create a sense of solidarity with the educated élite of the country and potentially appeal to a new consumer group. Their products can be promoted to a wider group than the expatriates, the group they traditionally appealed to through English.

In her study of code-switching between French and Alsatian in Strasbourg, Gardner-Chloros (Chapter 28) borrowed and extended Labov's method-ology from his original department-stores study (see Chapter 13). In Strasbourg, French is the 'high' and dominant language and Alsatian the 'low' and 'dying' one. Gardner-Chloros hypothesized that the choice of high and low forms would correlate with degrees of prestige across three economically and socially stratified department stores. What is interesting about this chapter from the methodological point of view is that, still using Labov's survey technique, it extends the notion of the linguistic variable from the pronunciation of a single sound to the choice of language code. But as Gardner-Chloros admits, showing correlations between social context and language choice does not in itself explain the psychological motivation for switching in individual speakers.

To capture the psychological reality of language choice, Gal explains how a shift from speaking one language to another can symbolize changes in the status and sex roles of speakers, and shifting values associated with both languages. The study deals with a language shift from Hungarian–German bilingualism to German monolingualism among young females in a small community of *Oberwart* in eastern Austria. The hardship of farm-work and the far-from-glamorous image of peasant life were part of the traditional values of this community, which were in turn symbolized for these women in the use of the Hungarian language. A shift to German monolingualism became symbolic of their wish to free themselves from peasant status and to move into a preferred worker status. This could only be achieved through marriage to young working men who were (or declared themselves to be) German monolingual speakers. In this way the language choices of young women in Oberwart, and the general pattern of language shift that followed, can be described as socially motivated. They were a response to the psychological realities of people's lives; a change of linguistic identity was a passport to a new identity and an easier life.

The theme of language and gender is therefore given another interpre-tation in Gal's work. With reference to Trudgill's work in Norwich (see Chapter 14), and similarly to Eckert (in Chapter 17), Gal argues against a deterministic view of women's (and men's) sex as the only or the main agent for linguistic conservatism or innovation. She advocates a more dynamic view of men and women as occupying variable positions in society and strategically working towards altering them.

NOTE

1 Another, probably more evident difference between the two groups is their 'national' religion, the Serbs being Orthodox Christians and the Croats Catholics.

PART VI: FURTHER READING

Ager, D. E. (1990) *Sociolinguistics and Contemporary French* (Cambridge: Cambridge University Press).

Baetens Beardsmore, H. (1982) *Bilingualism: Basic Principles* (Clevedon: Multilingual Matters).

Bickerton, D. (1981) *Roots of Language* (Ann Arbor, MI: Karoma).

Cheshire, J. (ed.) (1991) *English Around the World* (Cambridge: Cambridge University Press).

Clyne, M. (1995) *The German Language in a Changing Europe* (Cambridge: Cambridge University Press).

de Klerk, V. (ed.) (1996) *Focus on South Africa*. Varieties of English Around the World, **15** (Amsterdam, PA: John Benjamins).

Edwards, J. (1985) *Language, Society and Identity* (Oxford: Blackwell in association with André Deutsch).

Ferguson, C. A. and Heath, S. B. (eds) (1981) *Language in the USA* (Cambridge: Cambridge University Press).

Heath, S. B. (1983) *Ways with Words: Language, Life, and Work in Communities and Classrooms* (Cambridge: Cambridge University Press).

Heller, M. (ed.) (1988) *Codeswitching* (Berlin: Mouton de Gruyter).

Hewitt, R. (1986) *White Talk Black Talk* (Cambridge: Cambridge University Press).

Le Page, R. B. and Tabouret-Keller, A. (1985) *Acts of Identity: Creole Based Approaches to Language and Ethnicity* (Cambridge: Cambridge University Press).

Mühlhäusler, P. (1986) *Pidgin and Creole Linguistics* (Oxford: Blackwell).

Myers-Scotton, C. (1993a) *Duelling Languages* (Oxford: Clarendon).

Myers-Scotton, C. (1993b) *Social Motivation for Code-Switching: Evidence from Africa* (Oxford: Clarendon).

Romaine, S. (1988) *Pidgin and Creole Languages* (London: Longman).

Romaine, S. (1995) *Bilingualism*. 2nd Edition (Oxford: Blackwell).

Sebba, M. (1993) *London Jamaican* (London: Longman).

Shopen, T. (ed.) (1979a) *Languages and their Speakers* (Philadelphia, PA: University of Pennsylvania Press).

Shopen, T. (ed.) (1979b) *Languages and their Status* (Philadelphia, PA: University of Pennsylvania Press).

Skutnab-Kangas, T. (1984) *Bilingualism or Not: The Education of Minorities* (Clevedon: Multilingual Matters).

Todd, L. (1984) *Modern Englishes: Pidgins and Creoles* (Oxford: Basil Blackwell).

Trudgill, Pe. (ed.) (1984) *Language in the British Isles* (Cambridge: Cambridge University Press).

Williams, C. H. (1994) *Called unto Liberty!: On Language and Nationalism* (Clevedon: Multilingual Matters).

25 Language, Ethnicity and Racism

Joshua A. Fishman

LANGUAGE AND ETHNICITY: OVERLOOKED VARIABLES IN SOCIAL THEORY AND SOCIAL HISTORY

Many discussions of ethnicity begin with the struggle to define 'it'. While I am certainly interested in defining (or delimiting) ethnicity, I am even more interested in what the definitional struggle in this day and age reveals, namely, that the social sciences as a whole still lack an intellectual tradition in connection with this topic. Social scientists and social theorists have neither reconstructed nor developed with respect to ethnicity (nor, indeed, with respect to language and ethnicity) either a sociology of the phenomenon *per se* or a sociology of knowledge concerning it, much less a synchronic view of the link between the two, in any major part of the world of social life and social thought. Thus, here we are, in the late twentieth century, with God only knows how few or how many seconds remaining to the entire human tragi-comedy on this planet, still fumbling along in the domain of ethnicity, as if it had just recently appeared and as if three millenia of pan-Mediterranean and European thought and experience in connection with it (to take only that corner of mankind with which most of us are most familiar) could be overlooked. Obviously that is not our attitude toward other societal forms and processes such as the family, urbanization, religion, technology, etc. For all of these we manifestly delight in the intellectual traditions surrounding them. I must conclude that our intellectual discomfort and superficiality with respect to ethnicity and our selective ignorance in this connection are themselves ethnicity-related phenomena, at least in part, phenomena which merit consideration if we are ultimately to understand several of the dimensions of this topic that we are still waiting to be revealed.

This is not the place to undertake so grand an expedition, nor have I the ability to take you everywhere that this topic (the sociology of language and

Source: 'Language, Ethnicity and Racism', in Fishman, J. A. (1989) *Language and Ethnicity in Minority Sociolinguistic Perspective* (Clevedon: Multilingual Matters) pp. 9–22.

ethnicity and the sociology of knowledge with respect to it) must lead us. Suffice it to say that we must try to carry both the reconstruction and the analysis of social history and social theory from classical Hebrew and Greek times through to the twentieth century, up to and including the 'rebirth of ethnicity' in many Western locales during the past decade. In the process we must attend to the Roman Empire, both in the West and in the East; to the early Church and the Church Fathers; to Islam as a Euro-Mediterranean presence, to medieval and renaissance life and thought throughout Europe; to the reformation and counter-reformation; to the commercial and industrial revolutions viewed both as social change/continuity and as stimulants to social thought and social theory; and finally, to the rise of modern intellectual schools and social movements. In this last we must particularly examine the capitalist–Marxist clash, and the Marxist–Herderian–Weberian differences in sociological and anthropological thought and in political and economic action, both in the ominous nineteenth and in the cataclysmic twentieth centuries. At this time I can only try to select a few themes here and there that may provide some clues to language and ethnicity viewed in such a perspective.

WHAT IS ETHNICITY?

Since one of my objectives (in what might very well be a life-time task in and of itself) is to disclose what social theorists have said about ethnicity, including how they have defined it, my initial definitional passions can be satisfied at a general orientional level which gives me as much latitude as possible to attend to all forms and definitions of ethnicity (see Isajiw, 1974, for detailed attention to the definitional issue). What I am interested in is both the sense and the expression of 'collective, intergenerational cultural continuity', i.e. the sensing and expressing of links to 'one's own kind (one's own people)', to collectivities that not only purportedly have historical depth but, more crucially, share putative ancestral origins and, therefore, the gifts and responsibilities, rights and obligations deriving therefrom. Thus, what I am interested in may or may not be identical with all of society and culture, depending on the extent to which ethnicity does pervade and dictate all social sensings, doings and knowings, or alternatively (and as is increasingly the case as society modernizes) only some of these,[1] particularly those that relate to the questions: Who are we? From where do we come? What is special about us? I assume (together with Le Page & Tabouret-Keller, 1982) that these questions can be answered differently at different times by the same respondents (and, all the more so, by different respondents). It is in this context that I also want to monitor whatever link there may be to language as an aspect of presumed ethnic authenticity.

THE THEME OF FUNDAMENTAL 'ESSENCE'

Both ancient Israel and ancient Greece conceived of the world as made up of a finite number of ethnicities with characteristic and fundamental biological 'essences' and, therefore, histories or missions of their own. This theme, with its undercurrent of bodily continuity and triumph over death, has its counterpart in modern Herderian and nationalist thought and has been continually present in the pan-Mediterranean and European world, as well as in much of the African, Asian, and Native American worlds. This essence is transcendental and ultimately of superhuman origin, and language is naturally a co-occurring part of the essential blood, bones, or tears. Thus, the view that the deity (or deities) necessarily speak(s) to each ethnicity in its own language and could not conceivably do otherwise, is also a recurring view (albeit one that is not always accepted and, therefore, one that is also contradicted). It is a view related to a cosmology in which language-and-ethnicity collectivities are seen as the basic building blocks of all human society. In more modern thought, the superhuman origin of this co-occurrence and its dependence on biological essences are questioned. However, many theoreticians and philosophers still hold that ethnicity and ethnogenesis (i.e. the coming into being of ethnicities and of language-and-ethnicity linkages) is a natural and necessary fact of human social life (for a Soviet view along these very lines, see Bromley, 1974). Eastern European and Eastern Mediterranean thought is particularly noteworthy along these latter lines (Jakobson, 1945) and it is here in the Euro-Mediterranean complex that we find today most generally and insistently the view that language authenticity is a natural and necessary part of a mystically inescapable physical/cultural collective continuity.

THE THEME OF METAMORPHOSIS

Seemingly at odds with the above view, but at times syncretistically subscribed to in addition to it, is the view that ethnicities can be transcended and that new or 'higher' levels of ethnic integration can be arrived at, including the level of terminal de-ethnicization, i.e. of no ethnicity at all. The argument between those who view ethnicity as fixed and god-given and those who view it as endlessly mutable begins with Plato and Aristotle, the former proposing that a group of de-ethnicized Guardians of the City be created so that uncorrupted and uncorruptable, altruistic and evenhanded management of the polity could be attained. There would be no husband–wife relationships among them since all women would belong to all men and vice versa. Similarly their offspring would have no fathers and no mothers since all male adults would be fathers to all children, all female adults would be their mothers, all children would belong equally to all adults and vice versa. Only a group such as this – a group whose members had no differentiating intergenerational biological continuities – could devote itself to the public weal, since, having neither property nor family, it could view the general need without bias, without favoritism, without greed, without conflict of interest, all of which Plato considered necessary accompaniments of ethnicity. Aristotle hotly contested this view and stressed that, whatever the dangers of ethnicity might be, those who do not initially love and feel uniquely bound to specific 'others' could not then love mankind nor have the benefit of generalized 'others' firmly in mind. A child who belongs equally to one and all belongs to no one. The challenge of ethnicity, as Aristotle saw it, was one of augmenting familial love, expanding the natural links to one's own 'kind', so that these links also include others who are more distantly related, rather than doing away with the initial links and bonds as such.

This theme too is developed consistently – the expansion and transmutation of language and ethnicity to a higher, more inclusive level of both being repeatedly expressed by early Christian thought, e.g. St. Augustine, Roman thought, medieval thought (including much of moral philosophy) and by capitalist statism. Going even further, de-ethnicization and linguistic fusion are expressed as ultimate, millenial goals by some modern Christian social theorists, by classical Marxists as well as classical capitalists, and as inevitable if regrettable outcomes of modern industrial society by Weber and the entire 'grand tradition' of modern social theory from Saint-Simon to Parsons.

ETHNICITY AS DISRUPTIVE, IRRATIONAL, AND PERIPHERAL

The darker side of ethnicity is commented on by almost all ancient and medieval thinkers, but usually as only one side of the coin, i.e. as only half of the entire phenomenon which has both positive and negative features. However, the more completely negative view begins with Plato, as already mentioned, in relation to matters of state. In this connection it receives its quintessential formulation by Lord Acton, John Stuart Mill, and other establishment-oriented defenders of Western capitalist democracy. For them, state-forming ethnicity was nothing but the democracy. For them, state-forming ethnicity was nothing but the disrupter of civility, a base passion, a nightmare, a wild evil that still lurked in the backward parts of Europe but that had, thank God, already been tamed and superseded in Great Britain, France, Spain, Holland, and in the other early and enlightened beneficiaries of political consolidation and econo-technical growth.

This view coincided with a developmental theory defining 'legitimate' language-and-ethnicity, namely, that the link between them and the currency that they both enjoyed *in the West* were by-products of political and economic stability. That is, they were the legitimate creations of centuries of continuous governmental, commercial, military, and religious stability. This view, that the benign, wise and stable state creates its corresponding and legitimate nationality, was long the dominant view in the West. The thought that the nationality might undertake to create a state for itself was anathema, viewed as unnatural, unjust, unwise, and simply a wild and wanton disruption of peace and civility. The thought of a Breton or Romanian ethnicity was as roundly abhorred by 'proper' society *then* as the thought of a Quebecois ethnicity is in some circles *today*. Indeed, the evil, instinctual penchant of 'illegitimate' language-and-ethnicity movements to undertake disruptive state-formation was thought to be the basic negative dynamic of minority ethnicity, and so it is for some to this very day. Thus, the confusion of ethnicity with politically troublesome collectivities, with rambunctious minorities, with 'difficult' peripheral and vestigial populations, began long ago.

However, classical Marxism was not very different from capatilist establishment statism in this respect. Mill had held that the language and ethnicity movements, particularly in their nationality-into-state phase, were despicable 'irrationalities' that had to be contained at all costs, evils to be compromised with only grudgingly if the established political order was to be maintained (note, for example, the compromise escape clause of 'once defeated but historical nations' as an interstitial category between Mill's and Acton's two major categories: 'goodies': 'peoples with histories', and 'baddies': 'peoples without histories'). Initially, Marx and Engels were equally vituperative with respect to nation-into-state language and ethnicity movements (and, ultimately, made equally grudging and opportunistic exceptions in connection with them), due to their obviously disruptive impact on the class struggle and on proletarian unity. However, if language-and-ethnicity movements for Mill were merely vile passions, they were for Marx and many of his followers also vile figments, lies, and chimeras, objectively no more than mere by-products of more basic economic causes, phantoms manipulated by leading capitalist circles in order to fragment and weaken the international proletariat.

Needless to say, both Mill and Marx have their followers today, who ascribe to language and ethnicity linkages all manner of evil and evil alone, including genocide. Furthermore, this purportedly objectivist view is still very much alive among these social scientists who deny any subjective validity or functional need for ethnicity, and who see it only as an essentially manipulated (and therefore, basically inauthentic), manufactured by-product of élitist efforts to gain mass support for political and economic goals (Gellner, 1964). They basically sympathize with Engels's lament of more than a century ago (1866):

There is no country in Europe where there are not different nationalities under the same government. The Highland Gaels and the Welsh are undoubtedly of different nationalities to what the English are, although nobody will give to these remnants of people long gone by the title of nations, any more than to the Celtic inhabitants of Brittany in France...The European importance, the vitality of a people, is as nothing in the eyes of the principle of nationalities; before it the Roumans [*sic*] of Wallachia, who never had a history, nor the energy required to have one, are of equal importance to the Italians who have a history of 2,000 years, and an unimpaired national vitality: the Welsh and Manxmen, if they desired it, would have an equal right to independent political existence, absurd thought it be, with the English! The whole thing is absurdity. The principle of nationalities, indeed, could be invented in Eastern Europe alone, where the tide of Asiatic invasion, for a thousand years, recurred again and again, and left on the shore those heaps of intermingled ruins of nations which even now the ethnologist can scarcely disentangle, and where the Turk, the Finnic Magyar, the Rouman, the Jew and about a dozen slavonic tribes live intermixed in interminable confusion.

To this very day ethnicity strikes many Westerners as being peculiarly related to 'all those crazy little people and languages out there', to the unwashed (and unwanted) of the world, to phenomena that are really not fully civilized and that are more trouble than they are worth.

ETHNICITY AS CREATIVE AND HEALING

Autochthonous ethnicity theories commonly refer to the responsibilities incumbent upon the carriers of the intergenerational essence, i.e. to the duties that those of 'one's own kind' have, duties to be and to do in particular authentic ways; and of course, these theories also refer to the individual and collective rewards of such faithfulness. However, various more generalized ethnicity theories have taken this kind of thinking a step higher. Classical Hebrew thought contains a recurring emphasis on the perfectability of ethnicity, i.e. an emphasis on its highest realization via sanctification. It was not only Jewish ethnicity which could be so elevated and attuned with the Creator's designs and expectations (Fishman, Mayerfeld & Fishman, 1985), although Hebrew thought is, understandably, repeatedly more concerned with the theoretical perfectability of Hebrew ethnicity (just as it is with the actual shortcomings of Hebrew ethnicity). Hebrew thought is an early source for the recurring message that sanctified ethnicity is ennobling, strengthening, healing, satisfying. Its thought proclaims the message of the joy, the wholeness, the holiness of embodying and expressing language-and-ethnicity in accord with the commandments of the Master of the Universe: 'for they are our life and the length of our days'. Whosoever lives in the midst of his own kind, speaking his own language and enacting his own most divinely regulated traditions in accord with these imperatives, has all that one could hope for out of life (also see Fishman, 1978).

The joys of one's own language and ethnicity are subsequently expressed over and over again, from every corner of Europe and in every period. In modern times this feeling has been raised to a general principle, a general esthetic, a celebration of ethnic and linguistic diversity *per se*, as part of the very multisplendored glory of God, a value, beauty, and source of creative inspiration and inspiring creativity – indeed, as the basic human good. It is claimed that it is ethnic and linguistic diversity that makes life worth living. It is creativity and beauty based upon ethnic and linguistic diversity that make man human. Absence of this diversity would lead to the dehumanization, mechanization, and utter impoverishment of man. The weakening of this diversity is a cause for alarm, a tendency to be resisted and combatted. In Herder and in Mazzini, in the Slavophiles and in Kallen – indeed, in much of modern anthropology and anthropological linguistics – the theme of ethnic diversity and the sheer beauty of cultural pluralism provide an unending rhapsody. This view both tantalizingly merges with and also separates from general democratic principles, with the rights of man, and the inalienable privilege to be one's self, *not only to be free but to be free to be bound together with 'one's own kind'* (Talmon, 1965). On the one hand, democracy also subsumes an alternative right, namely, to be free from ethnicity, i.e. the right and opportunity to be a citizen of the world rather than a member of one or another traditioned ethnic collectively. On the other hand, democracy guarantees the right to retain one's own ethnicity, to safeguard collective ethnic continuity, to enable one's children to join the ranks of 'one's own kind', to develop creativity, and to reach their full potential without becoming ethnically inauthentic, colorless, lifeless, worse than lifeless: nothingness.

DIMENSIONS OF LANGUAGE-AND-ETHNICITY

The foregoing themes provide us with many insights into language and ethnicity, and into how language and ethnicity have been viewed in a particularly influential part of the world as well. The themes themselves are not independent of each other. Many of them relate to a putative ethnic essence that is intergenerationally continuous among 'one's own kind' and is absorbed via the mother's milk. Thus, there is commonly a 'being' component to ethnicity, a bodily mystery, a triumph over death in the past as well as a promise of immortality in the future, as the putative essence is handed on generation after generation. There are a few escape hatches in, and a few escape hatches out, and a terrifying state of liminality in between, but the physical continuity of a *corpus mysticum* continues. And language is part of that corpus. It issues authentically from the body, it is produced by the body, it has body itself (and, therefore, does not permit much basic modification).

Just as commonly, language is part of the authentic 'doing' constellation and the authentic 'knowing' constellation that are recurringly assumed to be dimensions of ethnicity. Ethic doing and knowing are more mutable and, therefore, in danger of inauthenticity. Ethnic doing is a responsibility that can be shirked. Ethnic knowing is a gift that can be withheld. The basic desideratum, ethnic being, is necessary but not sufficient. There is everything to be gained and everything to be lost, and language is recurringly part and parcel of this web (Fishman, 1977). In premobilization ethnicity it is naturally, unconsciously so (Fishman, 1965), whereas in mobilized ethnicity it is a rallying call, both metaphorically and explicitly (Fishman, 1972).

Autochthonous theories gravitate toward the metaphorical and meta-physical views of the language and ethnicity link. External objectivists reduce the mystery to the needs of the military and the economy, with the school system merely exploiting language and ethnicity in preparing recruits for both. Autochthonists see language and ethnicity as initial essences, or causes. External objectivists see them as manipulable by-products. However, both agree that they are generally there together. Hovering over them both is the problem of how to interpret the 'we–they' differences that are, unconsciously or consciously, part of the experience of ethnicity, which brings me to racism.

ETHNICITY AND RACISM

Racism is one of many words that have been so broadened in modern, popular usage as to have lost their utility. Democracy and socialism are two other such terms, but whereas the latter have become all-purpose terms of approbation (viz., people's democracy, guided democracy, National Social-ism, etc.), the former has become an all-purpose put-down. I would like to rescue *racism* from that dubious distinction, to limit its semantic range, in order more clearly to distinguish between ethnicity and racism as social phenomena and as social theories, and thereby, to focus pejorative usage more tellingly.

Relative to ethnicity, racism is not only more focused on the 'being' component (therefore having even fewer escape hatches from it than does ethnicity), but it also involves an evaluative ranking with respect to the discontinuity between ethnic collectivities. Ethnicity is an enactment (often unconscious) and a celebration of authenticity. Racism inevitably involves more heightened consciousness than does ethnicity, not only because it is an 'ism', but because its focus is not merely on authenticity and the celebration of difference or collective individuality, but on the evaluation of difference in terms of inherent better or worse, higher or lower, entirely acceptable and utterly objectionable. Ethnicity is less grandiose than racism. It has no built-in power dimension while racism, being essentially hierarchical, must have the concept of dominance in its cosmology and requires the constructs of superior races, dominant stocks, master peoples. By their words and deeds, ethnicity and racism are importantly different.

Herder, though anti-French to the hilt (like many German intellectuals struggling against French cultural hegemony within the disunited German princedoms at the beginning of the nineteenth century), is rarely, if ever, racist. He proclaims:

No individual, no country, no people, no history of a people, no state is like any other. Therefore, the true, the beautiful and the good are not the same for them. Everything is suffocated if one's own way is not sought and if another nation is blindly taken as a model (Herder, *Sammtliche Werke*, v. 4, p. 472).

Is not this still a dominant ethic and motivating dynamic in cultural anthropology to this very day? Herderian views must be understood as a plea and a rhapsody for an ethnically pluralistic world in which each ethnicity can tend its own vineyard as a right, a trust, and a point of departure for new beauty and creativity yet undreamed of. Such pluralism is, however, strange to racism, since the dynamics of racism represents a call and rationale for domination rather than for coexistence. While ethnicity can proclaim live and let live, racism can proclaim only bondage or death to the inferior.

Of course, every ethnicity runs the risk of developing an ethnocentrism, i.e. the view that one's own way of life is superior to all others. It may even be true that some degree of ethnocentrism is to be found in all societies and cultures, including the culture of secular science itself, to the degree that they are all-encompassing in defining experience and perspective. The antidote to ethnocentrism (including acquired anti-ethnic ethnocentrism, which may be just as supercilious and uncritically biased as is ethnic conditioning) is thus comparative cross-ethnic knowledge and experience, transcending the limits of one's own usual exposure to life and values (a theme which has long appeared in the literature on ethnicity). Characteristic of postmodern ethnicity is the stance of simultaneously transcending ethnicity as a complete, self-contained system, but of retaining it as a selectively preferred, evolving, participatory system. This leads to a kind of self-correction from within and from without, which extreme nationalism and racism do not permit.

The modern heroes of racism are Gobineau in France (see, for example, Biddess, 1966, 1970a,b), Houston Stewart Chamberlain (1899) in

England, and a chorus of German philosophers, scientists, and politicians (see, for example, Barzun, 1937; Gasman, 1971; Mosse, 1966; Weinreich, 1946). From their works it becomes clear that the language link to racism is an invidious as racism *per se*. Hermann Gauch, a Nazi 'scientist', was able to claim:

> The Nordic race alone can emit sounds of untroubled clearness, whereas among non-Nordics the pronunciation is...like noises made by animals, such as barking, sniffing, snoring, squeaking...That birds can learn to talk better than other animals is explained by the fact that their mouths are Nordic in structure (quoted in Mosse 1966: 225).

Here we have the ultimate route of racist thought: the demotion of the 'others' to a subhuman level. They are animals, vermin, and are to be subjected to whatever final solution is most effect and efficient.

CONCLUDING SENTIMENTS

These remarks must not be taken simply as a defense of ethnicity. Ethnicity has been recognized since ancient times as capable of excess, corruption, and irrationality, this capacity being one of the basic themes accompanying its preregrination across the centuries. The very term *ethnicity*, derived from the Greek *ethnos* (used consistently in the Septuagint to render the Hebrew *goy*, the more negative term for nationality, as distinct from *'am*, the more positive term), has a decided negative connotation in earliest English usage (see OED: *ethnic* 1470, *ethnist* 1550 and 1563, *ethnicize* 1663, *ethnicity* 1772, *ethnize* 1847). These connotations – heathenness, superstition, bizarreness – have not fully vanished even from modern popular usage, e.g. ethnic dress, ethnic hair-dos, ethnic soul. Thus, we need not fear that the excesses of ethnicity will be overlooked.

Racism itself is one of the excesses into which ethnicity can develop, although racism has often developed on pan-ethnic and perhaps even on nonethnic foundations as well.[2] However, the distinction between ethnicity and racism is well worth maintaining, particularly for those in the language-related disciplines and professions. It clarifies our goals, our problems, and our challenges as we engage in bilingual education, in language planning, in language maintenance efforts, and in a host of sociolinguistic and anthropological enterprises. The distinctions between religion and bigotry, sexuality and sexism, socialism and communism, democracy and anarchy, are all worth maintaining. No less worthwhile is the distinction between ethnicity and racism. Unfortunately, we know more about racism that about ethnicity, and more about the conflictual aspects of ethnicity than about its integrative functions. This is a pity, particularly for American intellectuals, since we too (regardless of our pretense to the contrary) live in a world in which the ethnic factor in art, music, literature, fashions, diets, childrearing, education and politics is still strong, and needs to be understood and even appreciated. Not to know more about ethnicity, about the ethnic repertoires of modern life, the endless mutability of ethnicity since the days of ancient Israel, the variety of prior thought concerning ethnicity (e.g. the various and changing views as to its power or centrality as a factor in societal functioning and social behavior) is also to limit our understanding of society and of the role of language in society. Language and ethnicity have been viewed as naturally linked in almost every age of premodern pan-Mediterranean and European thought. When ethnicity disappeared from modern social theory in the nineteenth century, language, too, disappeared therefrom. We may now be at the point of reappearance of both in modern social theory and we must prepare ourselves, accordingly, to benefit from and to contribute to the sensitivities and perspectives that a knowledge of language and ethnicity can provide, without overdoing them. Only in this way can the 'ethnic revival' in the United States be fully understood.

NOTES

1 For an account of racism's more complete domination of modern culture, see Banton's paper in Zubaida (1970). For a preliminary differentiation between ethnicity and racism, see the penultimate section of this chapter.
2 The terminology of ethnicity often included the word *race* (e.g. *raza*) in the sense of ethnicity as employed in this chapter. This is but one of the semantic alternatives that a sociology and a sociology of knowledge pertaining to ethnicity must be aware of and must hurry to illuminate.

REFERENCES

Barzun, J. (1937) *Race: A Study in Superstition* (New York: Harper).
Biddess, M. D. (1966) 'Gobineau and the Origin of European Racism', *Race: Journal of the Institute of Race Relations*, 7, pp. 225–70.
Biddess, M. D. (ed.) (1970a) *Gobineau: Selected Political Writings* (London: Cape).
Biddess, M. D. (1970b) *Father of Racist Ideology: The Social and Political Thought of Count Gobineau* (London: Weidenfeld and Nicolson).
Bromley, Yu V. (1974) 'Soviet Ethnology and Anthropology', *Studies in Anthropology I* (The Hague: Mouton).
Chamberlain, H. S. (1899) *The Foundations of the Nineteenth Century* (New York: Fertig).
Engels, F. (1866) 'What Have the Working Class to do with Poland?' *Commonwealth*, **24**, 31 March and 5 May.

Fishman, D. E., Mayerfield, R. and Fishman, J. A. (1985) '*Am* and *Goy* as Designations for Ethnicity in Selected Books of the Old Testament', in Fishman, J. A. *et al. The Rise and Fall of the Ethnic Revival* (Berlin: Mouton de Gruyter) pp. 15–38.

Fishman, J. A. (1965) 'Varieties of Ethnicity and Varieties of Language Consciousness', *Georgetown University Roundtable on Languages and Linguistics, 1965*, Kreidler, C. W. (ed.) pp. 69–79.

Fishman, J. A. (1972) *Language and Nationalism* (Rowley: Newbury House).

Fishman, J. A. (1977) 'Language and Ethnicity', in Giles, H. (ed.) *Language and Ethnicity in Intergroup Relations* (New York: Academic Press) pp. 15–57.

Fishman, J. A. (1978) 'Positive Bilingualism: Some Overlooked Rationales and Forefathers', *Georgetown University Roundtable on Languages and Linguistics, 1978*, Atlantis, J. E. (ed.) pp. 42–52.

Gasman, D. (1971) 'The Scientific Origins of National Socialism', *Social Darwinism in Ernest Haeckel and the German Monist League* (London: Macdonald).

Gellner, E. (1964) *Thought and Change* (Chicago: University of Chicago Press).

Herder, J. G. *Sammtliche Werke.* 33 vols. Suphan, B., Redlich, E. *et al.* (eds) Berlin, pp. 1877–1913.

Isajiw, W. W. (1974) 'Definitions of Ethnicity', *Ethnicity*, **1**, pp. 111–24.

Jakobson, R. (1945) 'The Beginnings of National Self-determination in Europe', *Review of Politics* (1968), **2**, pp. 29–42. Reprinted in Fishman, J. A. (ed.) *Readings in the Sociology of Language* (The Hague: Mouton).

Le Page, R. B. & Tabouret-Keller, A. (1982) 'Models and Stereotypes of Ethnicity and Language', *Journal of Multilingual and Multicultural Development*, **3**, pp. 161–92.

Mosse, G. L. (1966) *Nazi Culture: Intellectual, Cultural and Social Life in the Third Reich* (London: W. H. Allen).

Talmon, J. L. (1965) *The Unique and the Universal* (London: Secker and Warburg).

Weinreich, M. (1946) *Hitler's Professors: The Part of Scholarship in Germany's Crimes Against the Jewish People* (New York: Yiddish Scientific Institute-YIVO).

Zubaida, S. (ed.) 1970), *Race and Racism* (London: Tavistock).

26 Language Standardization

Einar Haugen

The taxonomy of linguistic description – that is, the identification and enumeration of languages – is greatly hampered by the ambiguities and obscurities attaching to the terms 'language' and 'dialect.' Laymen naturally assume that these terms, which are both popular and scientific in their use, refer to actual entities that are clearly distinguishable and therefore enumerable. A typical question asked of the linguist is: 'How many languages are there in the world?' Or: 'How many dialects are there in this country?'

The simple truth is that there is no answer to these questions, or at least none that will stand up to closer scrutiny. Aside from the fact that a great many, perhaps most, languages and dialects have not yet been adequately studied and described, it is inherent in the very terms themselves that no answer can be given. They represent a simple dichotomy in a situation that is almost infinitely complex. Hence they have come to be used to distinguish phenomena in several different dimensions, with resultant confusion and overlapping. The use of these terms has imposed a division in what is often a continuum, giving what appears to be a neat opposition when in fact the edges are extremely ragged and uncertain. Do Americans and Englishmen speak dialects of English, or do only Americans speak dialect, or is American perhaps a separate language? Linguists do not hesitate to refer to the French language as a dialect of Romance. This kind of overlapping is uncomfortable, but most linguists have accepted it as a practical device, while recognizing, with Bloomfield, 'the purely relative nature of the distinction' (1933: 54). ...

[Here Haugen discusses the French and Classical Greek usages which gave rise to the current usage of the English terms 'language' and 'dialect' – *Eds.*]

Due to various historical processes, the two terms are cyclically applicable, with 'language' always the superordinate and 'dialect' the subordinate term. This is also clear from the kind of formal structures into which they can be placed: 'X is a dialect of language Y,' or 'Y has the dialects X and Z' (never, for example, 'Y is a language of dialect X'). 'Language' as the superordinate term can be used without reference to

Source: 'Dialect, Language, Nation', *American Anthropologist*, **68**, 6 (1966), pp. 922–35, reprinted in Dil, A. S. (sel. and intro.) (1972) *The Ecology of Language: Essays by Einar Haugen* (Stanford, CA: Stanford University Press) pp. 237–54.

dialects, but 'dialect' is meaningless unless it is implied that there are other dialects and a language to which they can be said to 'belong.' Hence every dialect is a language, but not every language is a dialect. ...

General usage has limited the word ['dialect'] largely to the regional or locally-based varieties, such as 'Lancashire dialect' or 'Irish dialect' in reference to varieties of English. It is less customary to speak of 'London dialect' or 'Boston dialect,' except in reference to the lower-class speech of those cities. Nor is it common to speak of 'British dialect' in reference to cultivated English speech, and Americans are generally resentful of being told they speak 'American dialect' when reference is had to the speech of educated people. Martinet is therefore beside the mark when he writes that in America 'the term denotes every local form of English but without any suggestion that a more acceptable form of the language exists distinct from the dialects' (1964: 146). It is quite different with the word 'accent:' an American may inoffensively be described as having a 'New England accent' or a 'Southern accent,' and, of course, all Americans speak of the English as having an 'English accent.' 'Dialect' is here as elsewhere a term that suggests informal or lower-class or rural speech. In general usage it therefore remains quite undefined whether such dialects are part of the 'language' or not. In fact, the dialect is often thought of as standing outside the language: 'That isn't English.' This results from the *de facto* development of a standard language, with all the segregation of an élite and the pyramidal power structure that it has usually implied.

As a social norm, then, a dialect is a language that is excluded from polite society. It is, as Auguste Brun (1946) has pointed out, a language that 'did not succeed.' In Italy, Piedmontese is from every linguistic point of view a language, distinct from Italian on the one hand and French on the other, with a long tradition of writing and grammatical study. But because it is not Tuscan, and Tuscan became the standard language of all Italy, Piedmontese is only a 'dialect,' yielding ground to Italian with every generation and kept alive only by local pride and linguistic inertia (Clivio 1964). Only if a 'dialect' is watered down to an 'accent' – that is, an intonation and a set of articulations, with an occasional lexical item thrown in for color – does it (say in Germany or Italy or England) become 'salonfähig.' As a complete structure it is out in the cold limbo of modern society. In America the stigma is placed not so much on local dialects, since these are few and rarely heard, as on 'bad' English, which is quite simply lower-class dialect. The language of the upper classes is automatically established as the correct form of expression. They cannot only say, 'L'état, c'est moi,' but also 'Le langage, c'est le mien.'

In trying to clarify these relationships, linguistic science has been only moderately successful. Even in the Renaissance it was perfectly clear to serious students of the subject of that the term 'language' was associated with the rise of the nation to conscious unity and identity. George

Puttenham wrote in his book *The Arte of English Poesie* (1589): 'After a speech is fully fashioned to the common understanding, and accepted by consent of a whole country and nation, it is called a language.' This kind of historical development, by which convergence was achieved at the expense of deviating varieties, was familiar to the men of that age. But the arbitrary tower-of-Babel approach to linguistic divergence was dispelled by the discovery, in the early 19th century, of historical regularity. The realization that languages have resulted from dialect-splitting gave a new content to the terms and made it possible to begin calling languages like English and German 'dialects' of a Germanic 'language.'

But in the mid-19th century, when scientific study of the rural and socially disadvantaged dialects began, a generation of research was sufficient to revolutionize the whole idea of how a dialect arises. The very notion of an area divided into a given number of dialects, one neatly distinct from the next, had to be abandoned. The idea that languages split like branches on a tree gave way to an entirely different and even incompatible idea, namely, that individual linguistic traits diffused through social space and formed isoglosses that rarely coincided. Instead of a dialect, one had a 'Kernlandschaft' with ragged edges, where bundles of isoglosses testified that some slight barrier had been interposed to free communication. ...

There are two clearly distinct dimensions involved in the various usages of 'language' and 'dialect.' One of these is *structural*, that is, descriptive of the language itself; the other is *functional*, that is, descriptive of its social uses in communication. Since the study of linguistic structure is regarded by linguists as their central task, it remains for sociologists, or more specifically, sociolinguists, to devote themselves to the study of the functional problem.

In the *structural* use of 'language' and 'dialect,' the overriding consideration is genetic relationship. If a linguist says that Ntongo has five dialects, he means that there are five identifiably different speech-forms that have enough demonstrable cognates to make it certain that they have all developed from one earlier speech-form. He may also be referring to the fact that these are mutually understandable, or at least that each dialect is understandable to its immediate neighbors. If not, he may call them different languages, and say that there is a language Ntongo with three dialects and another, Mbongo, with two. Ntongo and Mbongo may then be dialects of Ngkongo, a common ancestor. This introduces the synchronic dimensions of comprehension, which is at best an extremely uncertain criterion. The linguist may attempt to predict, on the basis of his study of their grammars, that they should or should not be comprehensible. But only by testing the reactions of the speakers themselves and their interactions can he confirm his prediction (Voegelin and Harris 1951; Hickerson *et al.*, 1952). Between total incomprehension and total comprehension there is a large twilight zone of partial comprehension in which something occurs that we may call 'semicommunication.'

In the *functional* use of 'language' and 'dialect,' the overriding consideration is the uses the speakers make of the codes they master. If a sociolinguist says that there is no Ntongo language, only dialects, he may mean that there is no present-day form of these dialects that has validity beyond its local speech community, either as a trade language or as a common denominator in interaction among the various dialect speakers. A 'language' is thus functionally defined as a superposed norm used by speakers whose first and ordinary language may be different. A 'language' is the medium of communication between speakers of different dialects. This holds only within the limits established by their linguistic cognacy: one could not speak of Ntongo as a dialect of English just because its speakers use English as a medium of intercommunication. The sociolinguist may also be referring to the fact that the 'language' is more prestigious than the 'dialect.' Because of its wider functions it is likely to be embraced with a reverence, a language loyalty, that the dialects do not enjoy. Hence the possibility of saying that 'Mbongo is only a dialect, while Ngkongo is a language.' This means that Ngkongo is being spoken by people whose social prestige is notoriously higher than that of people who speak Mbongo. When used in this sense, a dialect may be defined as an undeveloped (or underdeveloped language. It is a language that no one has taken the trouble to develop into what is often referred to as a 'standard language.' This dimension of functional superiority and inferiority is usually disregarded by linguists, but it is an essential part of the sociolinguist's concern. It becomes his special and complex task to define the social functions of each language or dialect and the prestige that attaches to each of these.

What is meant by an 'undeveloped' language? Only that it has not been employed in all the functions that a language can perform in a society larger than that of the local tribe or peasant village. The history of languages demonstrates convincingly that there is no such thing as an inherently handicapped language. All the great languages of today were once undeveloped. Rather than speak of undeveloped languages as 'dialects,' after the popular fashion, it would be better to call them 'vernaculars,' or some such term, and limit 'dialect' to the linguist's meaning of a 'cognate variety.' We are then ready to ask how a vernacular, an 'undeveloped language,' develops into a standard, a 'developed language.' To understand this we will have to consider the relation of language to the nation.

The ancient Greeks and Romans spread their languages as far as their domains extended, and modern imperialists have sought to do the same. But within the modern world, technological and political revolutions have brought Everyman the opportunity to participate in political decisions to his own advantage. The invention of printing, the rise of industry, and the spread of popular education have brought into being the modern nation-state, which extends some of the loyalties of the family and the neighborhood or the clan to the whole state. Nation and language have become inextricably intertwined. Every self-respecting nation has to have a language. Not just a medium of communication, a 'vernacular' or a 'dialect,' but a fully developed language. Anything less marks it as underdeveloped.

The definition of a nation is a problem for historians and other social scientists; we may accept the idea that it is the effective unit of international political action, as reflected in the organization of the United Nations General Assembly. As a political unit it will presumably be more effective if it is also a social unit. Like any unit, it minimizes internal differences and maximizes external ones. On the individual's personal and local identity it superimposes a national one by identifying his ego with that of all others within the nation and separating it from that of all others outside the nation. In a society that is essentially familial or tribal or regional it stimulates a loyalty beyond the primary groups, but discourages any conflicting loyalty to other nations. The ideal is: internal cohesion – external distinction.

Since the encouragement of such loyalty requires free and rather intense communication within the nation, the national ideal demands that there be a single linguistic code by means of which this communication can take place. It is characteristic that the French revolutionaries passed a resolution condemning the dialects as a remnant of feudal society. The dialects, at least if they threaten to become languages, are potentially disruptive forces in a unified nation: They appeal to local loyalty. This is presumably the reason that France even now refuses to count the number of Breton speakers in her census, let alone face the much greater problem of counting the speakers of Provençal. On the other hand, a nation feels handicapped if it is required to make use of more than one language for official purposes, as is the case in Switzerland, Belgium, Yugoslavia, Canada, and many other countries. Internal conflict is inevitable unless the country is loosely federated and the language borders are stable, as is the case in Switzerland.

Nationalism has also tended to encourage external distinction, as noted above. In language this has meant the urge not only to have one language, but to have one's own language. This automatically secludes the population from other populations, who might otherwise undermine its loyalty. Here the urge for separatism has come into sharp conflict with the urge for international contact and for the advantages accruing both to individual and nation from such contact. Switzerland is extreme in having three languages, no one of which is its own; Belgium has two, both of which belong to its neighbors. The Irish movement has faltered largely under the impact of the overwhelming strength of English as a language of international contact. The weakness of the New Norwegian language movement is due to the thorough embedding of Danish in the national life during four centuries of union; what strength the movement has had is derived from the fact that Danish was not one of the great international languages.

Whenever any important segment of the population, an élite, is familiar with the language of another nation, it is tempting to make use of this as the medium of government, simply as a matter of convenience. If this is also the language of most of the people, as was the case when the United States broke away from England, the problem is easily solved; at most it involves the question of whether provincialisms are to be recognized as acceptable. But where it is not, there is the necessity of linguistically re-educating a population, with all the effort and disruption of cultural unity that this entails. This is the problem faced by many of the emerging African and Asian nations today (Le Page 1964). French and English have overwhelming advantages, but they symbolize past oppression and convey an alien culture. The cost of re-education is not just the expense in terms of dollars and cents, but the malaise of training one's children in a medium that is not their own, and of alienation from one's own past.

The alternative is to develop one's own language, as Finland did in the 19th century, or Israel did in the 20th. Different languages start at different points: Finland's was an unwritten vernacular, Israel's an unspoken standard. Today both are standards capable of conveying every concept of modern learning and every subtlety of modern literature. Whatever they may lack is being supplied by deliberate planning, which in modern states is often an important part of the development process.

It is a significant and probably crucial requirement for a standard language that it be written. This is not to say that languages need to be written in order to spread widely or be the medium of great empires. Indo-European is an example of the first, Quechua of the Inca Empire an example of the second (Buck 1916). But they could not, like written languages, establish models across time and space, and they were subject to regular and inexorable linguistic change. It is often held that written language impedes the 'natural' development of spoken language, but this is still a matter of discussion (Zengel 1962; Bright and Ramanujan 1964). In any case the two varieties must not be confused.

Speech is basic in learning language. The spoken language is acquired by nearly all its ushers before they can possibly read or write. Its form is to a great extent transmitted from one generation of children to the next. While basic habits can be modified, they are not easily overturned after childhood and are virtually immovable after puberty. The spoken language is conveyed by mouth and ear and mobilizes the entire personality in immediate interaction with one's environment. Writing is conveyed by hand and eye, mobilizes the personality less completely, and provides for only a delayed response. Oral confrontation is of basic importance in all societies, but in a complex, literate society it is overlaid and supplemented by the role of writing.

The permanence and power of writing is such that in some societies the written standard has been influential in shaping new standards of speech.

This is not to say that writing has always brought them into being, but rather to say that new norms have arisen that are an amalgamation of speech and writing. This can of course take place only when the writing is read aloud, so that it acquires an oral component (Wessen 1937). There is some analogy between the rise of such spoken standards and that of pidgin or creole languages (Meillet 1925: 76; Sommerfelt 1938: 44). The latter comprise elements of the structure and vocabulary of two or more languages, all oral. They have usually a low social value, compared to the oral standards, but the process of origin is comparable. The reawakening of Hebrew from its century-long dormant state is comprehensible only in terms of the existence of rabbinical traditions of reading scripture aloud (Morag 1959). Modern Hebrew has shown a rapid adaptation to the underlying norms of its new native speakers, so that it has become something different from traditional Hebrew. Similarly with the standard forms of European languages: one is often hard put to say whether a given form has been handed down from its ancestor by word of mouth or via the printed page. 'Spelling pronunciations' are a well-known part of most oral standards, even though purists tend to decry them.

While we have so far spoken of standard languages as if they were a clear and unambiguous category, there are differences of degree even among the well-established languages. French is probably the most highly standardized of European languages, more so than, for example, English or German. French, as the most immediate heir of Latin, took over many of its concepts of correctness and its intellectual elaboration. French in turn became a model for other standard languages, and its users were for centuries nothing loth to have it so considered. When English writers of the 18th century debated whether an English academy should be established to regulate the language, the idea of such an institution came from France. The proposal was rejected largely because the English did not wish to duplicate what they regarded as French 'tyranny.'

While making a survey of the world's standard languages, Ferguson proposed (1962) to classify them along two dimensions: their degree of standardization (St. 0, 1, 2) and their utilization in writing (W 0, 1, 2, 3). Zero meant in each case no appreciable standardization or writing. St. 1 meant that a language was standardized in more than one mode, as is the case, for example, with Armenian, Greek, Serbo-Croat, and Hindi-Urdu. He also included Norwegian, but it is at least arguable that we are here dealing with two languages. St. 2 he defined as a language having a 'single, widely accepted norm which is felt to be appropriate with only minor modifications or variations for all purposes for which the language is used.' W 1 he applied to a language used for 'normal written purposes,' W 2 to one used for 'original research in physical sciences,' and W 3 to one used for 'translations and résumés of scientific work in other languages.'

These categories suggest the path that 'underdeveloped' languages must take to become adequate instruments for a modern nation. The 'standardization' to which Ferguson refers applies primarily to developing the form of a language, i.e. its linguistic structure, including phonology, grammar, and lexicon. We shall call this the problem of *codification*. Ferguson's scale of 'utilization in writing' applies rather to the *functions* of a language. We shall call this the problem of *elaboration*, a term suggested by a similar usage of Bernstein's (1962). As the ideal goals of a standard language, codification may be defined as *minimal variation in form*, elaboration as *maximal variation in function*.

The ideal case of minimal variation in form would be a hypothetical, 'pure' variety of a language having only one spelling and one pronunciation for every word, one word for every meaning, and one grammatical framework for all utterances. For purposes of efficient communication this is obviously the ideal code. If speakers and listeners have identical codes, no problems of misunderstanding can arise due to differences in language. There can be none of what communication engineers call 'code noise' in the channel (Hockett 1958: 331–2). This condition is best attained if the language has a high degree of stability, a quality emphasized by many writers on the subject. Stability means the slowing down or complete stoppage of linguistic change. It means the fixation forever (or for as long as possible) of a uniform norm. In practice such fixation has proved to be chimerical, since even the most stable of norms inevitably changes as generations come and go. At all times the standard is threatened by the existence of rival norms, the so-called 'dialects,' among its users. It is liable to interference from them and eventually to complete fragmentation by them.

Apparently opposed to the strict codification of form stands the maximal variation or elaboration of function one expects from a fully developed language. Since it is by definition the common language of a social group more complex and inclusive than those using vernaculars, its functional domains must also be complex. It must answer to the needs of a variety of communities, classes, occupations, and interest groups. It must meet the basic test of *adequacy*. Any vernacular is presumably adequate at a given moment for the needs of the group that uses it. But for the needs of the much larger society of the nation it is not adequate, and it becomes necessary to supplement its resources to make it into a language. Every vernacular can at the very least add words borrowed from other languages, but usually possesses devices for making new words from its own resources as well. Writing, which provides for the virtually unlimited storage and distribution of vocabulary, is the technological device enabling a modern standard language to meet the needs of every specialty devised by its users. There are no limits to the elaboration of language except those set by the ingenuity of man.

While form and function may generally be distinguished as we have just done, there is one area in which they overlap. Elaboration of function may lead to complexity of form, and, contrariwise, unity of form may lead to rigidity of function. This area of interaction between form and function is the domain of *style*. A codification may be so rigid as to prevent the use of a language for other than formal purposes. Sanskrit had to yield to Prakrit, and Latin to the Romance languages, when the gap between written and spoken language became so large that only a very few people were willing to make the effort of learning them. Instead of being appropriate for 'all purposes for which the language is used,' the standard tends to become only one of several styles within a speech community. This can lead to what Ferguson (1959) has described as 'diglossia,' a sharp cleavage between 'high' and 'low' style. Or it may be a continuum, with only a mild degree of what I have called 'schizoglossia,' as in the case of English (Haugen 1962). In English there is a marked difference between the written and spoken standards of most people. In addition, there are styles within each, according to the situation. These styles, which could be called 'functional dialects,' provide wealth and diversity within a language and ensure that the stability or rigidity of the norm will have an element of elasticity as well. A complete language has its formal and informal styles, its regional accents, and its class or occupational jargons, which do not destroy its unity so long as they are clearly diversified in function and show a reasonable degree of solidarity with one another.

Neither codification nor elaboration is likely to proceed very far unless the community can agree on the *selection* of some kind of a model from which the norm can be derived. Where a new norm is to be established, the problem will be as complex as the sociolinguistic structure of the people involved. There will be little difficulty where everyone speaks virtually alike, a situation rarely found. Elsewhere it may be necessary to make some embarrassing decisions. To choose any one vernacular as a norm means to favor the group of people speaking that variety. It gives them prestige as norm-bearers and a headstart in the race for power and position. If a recognized élite already exists with a characteristic vernacular, its norm will almost inevitably prevail. But where there are socially coordinate groups of people within the community, usually distributed regionally or tribally, the choice of any one will meet with resistance from the rest. The resistance is likely to be the stronger the greater the language distance within the group. It may often be a question of solidarity versus alienation: a group that feels intense solidarity is willing to overcome great linguistic differences, while one that does not is alienated by relatively small differences. Where transitions are gradual, it may be possible to find a central dialect that mediates between extremes, one that will be the easiest to learn and most conducive to group coherence.

Where this is impossible, it may be necessary to resort to the construction of a new standard. To some extent this has happened naturally in the rise of the traditional norms; it has been the aim of many language reformers to duplicate the effect in new ones. For related dialects one can apply principles of linguistic reconstruction to make a hypothetical mother tongue for them all. Or one can be guided by some actual or supposed mother tongue, which exists in older, traditional writings. Or one can combine those forms that have the widest usage, in the hope that they will most easily win general acceptance. These three procedures – the comparative, the archaizing, and the statistical – may easily clash, to make decisions difficult. In countries where there are actually different languages, amounting in some African nations to more than a hundred, it will be necessary either to recognize multiple norms or to introduce an alien norm, which will usually be an international language like English or French.

Finally, a standard language, if it is not to be dismissed as dead, must have a body of users. *Acceptance* of the norm, even by a small but influential group, is part of the life of the language. Any learning requires the expenditure of time and effort, and it must somehow contribute to the well-being of the learners if they are not to shirk their lessons. A standard language that is the instrument of an authority, such as a government, can offer its users material rewards in the form of power and position. One that is the instrument of a religious fellowship, such as a church, can also offer its users rewards in the hereafter. National languages have offered membership in the nation, an identity that gives one entrée into a new kind of group, which is not just kinship, or government, or religion, but a novel and peculiarly modern brew of all three. The kind of significance attributed to language in this context has little to do with its value as an instrument of thought or persuasion. It is primarily symbolic, a matter of the prestige (or lack of it) that attaches to specific forms or varieties of language by virtue of identifying the social status of their users (Labov 1964). Mastery of the standard language will naturally have a higher value if it admits one to the councils of the mighty. If it does not, the inducement to learn it, except perhaps passively, may be very low; if social status is fixed by other criteria, it is conceivable that centuries could pass without a population's adopting it (Gumperz 1962, 1964). Both in our industrialized and democratic age there are obvious reasons for the rapid spread of standard languages and for the importance in the school systems of every nation.

The four aspects of language development that we have now isolated as crucial features in taking the step from 'dialect' to 'language,' from vernacular to standard, are as follows: (1) selection of norm, (2) codification of form, (3) elaboration of function, and (4) acceptance by the community. The first two refer primarily to the form, the last two to the function of language. The first and the last are concerned with society, the second and the third with language. They form a matrix within which it should be possible to discuss all the major problems of language and dialect in the life of a nation:

	Form	Function
Society	Selection	Acceptance
Language	Codification	Elaboration

REFERENCES

Bernstein, B. (1962) 'Linguistic Codes, Hesitation Phenomena and Intelligence', *Language and Speech*, **5**, pp. 31–46.

Bloomfield, L. (1933) *Language* (New York: Holt).

Bright, W. and Ramunujan, A. K. (1964) 'Sociolinguistic Variation and Language Change', *Proceedings, IX International Congress of Linguists* (The Hague, Mouton) pp. 1107–14.

Brun, Auguste (1946) *Parlers Régionaux: France Dialectale et Unité Française* (Paris and Toulouse: Didier).

Buck, C. D. (1916) 'Language and the Sentiment of Nationality', *American Political Science Review*, **10**, pp. 44–69.

Clivio, G. (1964) *Piedmontese: A Short Basic Course*. Mimeographed ed. Center for Applied Linguistics, Washington, DC.

Ferguson, C. A. (1959) 'Diglossia', *Word*, **15**, pp. 325–40.

Ferguson, C. A. (1962) 'The Language Factor in National Development', *Anthropological Linguistics*, **4**, 1, pp. 23–7.

Gumperz, J. (1962) 'Types of Linguistic Communities', *Anthropological Linguistics*, **4**, 1, pp. 28–40.

Gumperz, J. (1964) 'Hindi-Punjabi Code Switching in Delhi', *Proceedings, IX International Congress of Linguists* (The Hague: Mouton) pp. 1115–24.

Haugen, E. (1962) 'Schizoglossia and the Linguistic Norm', *Monograph Series on Languages and Linguistics* (Washington, DC: Georgetown University) No. 15, pp. 63–9.

Hickerson, H., Turner, G. D. and Hickerson, N. P. (1952) 'Testing Procedures for Estimating Transfer of Information Among Iroquois Dialects and Languages', *IJAL*, **18**, pp. 1–8.

Hockett, C. F. (1958) *A Course in Modern Linguistics* (New York: Macmillan).

Labov, W. (1964) 'Phonological Correlates of Social Stratification', in Gumperz, J. J. and Hymes, D. (eds) *The Ethnography of Communication*, American Anthropologist **66**, No. 6, pt 2, pp. 164–76.

Le Page, R. B. (1964) *The National Language Question: Linguistic Problems of Newly Independent States* (London: Oxford University Press).

Martinet, A. (1964) *Elements of General Linguistics* (Chicago: University of Chicago Press).

Meillet, A. (1925) *La Méthode Comparative en Linguistique Historique* (Oslo, Institutet for Sammenlignende Kulturforskning).

Morag, S. (1959) 'Planned and Unplanned Development in Modern Hebrew', *Lingua*, **8**, pp. 247–63.

Sommerfelt, A. (1938) 'Conditions de la Formation d'une Language Commune', *Actes du IV Congrès International de Linguistes*, Copenhagen, pp. 42–8.

Voegelin, C. F., and Harris, Z. S. (1951) 'Methods for Determining Intelligibility Among Dialects of Natural Languages', *Proceedings of the American Philosophical Society*, **95**, pp. 322–9.

Wessen, E. (1937) 'Vaårt Riksspraåk: Naågra Huvudpunkter av Dess Historiska Utveckling', *Modersmålslärarnas Förenings Arsskrift*, pp. 289–305.

Zengel, M. S. (1962) 'Literacy as a Factor in Language Change', *American Anthropologist*, **64**, pp. 132–9.

27 Pidgin English Advertising

Suzanne Romaine

There have recently been attempts to use pidgin English as a medium of advertising in Papua New Guinea, and these have given rise to a number of linguistic and cross-cultural dilemmas. Tok Pisin ('talk pidgin') is an English-based pidgin spoken in Papua New Guinea. Like all pidgin languages, it arose as a lingua franca among speakers of many different languages. It shares with other pidgin languages the characteristic that its lexicon is drawn mainly from one language, in this case English (hence it is referred to as an English-based rather than, say, a French-based pidgin). Its grammar is drawn from another source, in this case, the numerous indigenous languages of Melanesia. This means that even when items derived from English are used to express grammatical categories in pidgin, the syntactic patterning and meanings of them often follow structures found in the indigenous languages. One such instance can be found in the distinction between inclusive and exclusive first person plural pronouns, which is made in Tok Pisin and most, if not all, of the indigenous languages of Melanesia but not in English. Thus, where English has only *we*, Tok Pisin has *yumi* (from English *you + me*), which is inclusive in its reference, and *mipela* (from English *me + fellow*), which is exclusive. One must always distinguish in pidgin between 'we' which includes the speaker and addressee(s) and 'we' which includes the speaker and others, but not the addressee(s). Although the lexical material used to make this distinction is clearly drawn from English, the meanings encoded by it can be understood only by reference to grammatical categories present in Melanesian languages. The use of the suffix *-pela* (from English *fellow*) is another case in point. While *fellow* does not have any grammatical function in English, it has been taken over into pidgin as an affix or classifier marking the word class of attributive adjectives. Thus, we have *gutpela man* ('good man'), *naispela haus* ('a nice house'), *wanpela meri* ('a/one woman'), and so on. In the pronoun system it appears as a formative in the first and second person plural, *mipela* ('we' exclusive) and *yupela* ('you' plural).[1]

Tok Pisin is the descendant of a number of varieties of a Pacific Jargon English which was spoken over much of the Pacific during the nineteenth

Source: 'Pidgin English Advertising', in Ricks, C. and Michaels, L. (eds) (1990 edn) *The State of the Language* (Berkeley, CA and London: University of California Press and Faber & Faber) pp. 195–203.

century and used as a lingua franca between English-speaking Europeans and Pacific Islanders. This jargon was learned by Papua New Guineans on plantations in Queensland, Samoa, Fiji, and in Papua New Guinea itself. The typical pattern of acquisition was for Melanesian workers to pick up the pidgin or jargon on the plantation and then bring it back to villages, where it was passed on to younger boys. Tok Pisin crystallized in a distinctive form in the New Guinea islands and spread from there to the mainland.

Although Tok Pisin was born in and kept going by colonialization, it quickly became more than just a means of communication between the indigenous population and their European colonizers. Since its origin in about 1880, Tok Pisin has become the most important lingua franca for Papua New Guineans, who, according to one estimate, have around 750 indigenous languages. Although it was originally learned as a second language, it is now being acquired by children as their first language. When this happens in the life-cycle of a pidgin language, we can speak of creolization. In sociolinguistic terms, then, Tok Pisin can be described as an expanded pidgin which is currently undergoing creolization. It now has a sizable number of native speakers (about 20 000), and roughly 44 per cent of the population claim to speak it. Indeed, the question of whether Tok Pisin should become the national language of Papua New Guinea has recently been the subject of much discussion. At the moment it has official status, along with two other languages: English, and another pidgin, Hiri Motu, which is based on Motu, one of the indigenous languages of what was, until independence in 1975, the Territory of Papua. Hiri Motu is, however, regionally restricted, and only about 9 per cent of the population speak it. The name Tok Pisin was officially adopted for English-based pidgin in 1981. It had been previously referred to as Neomelanesian, Melanesian pidgin, *Tok boi* (from English *talk + boy*), or just pidgin.[2] It is now, since independence, the preferred language in the House of Assembly, though English is the official medium of education.

One of the things which happens when a pidgin expands and stabilizes, and possibly then creolizes, is that new linguistic resources have to be created or borrowed to fulfil the new functions to which the language is put. For instance, there is an increase in vocabulary so that new concepts can be expressed: *nesional baset* ('national budget'), *minista bilong edukesan/ edukesan minista* ('education minister'). More complicated syntactic structures such as relative clauses emerge, which allow the creation of more sophisticated discourse and stylistic alternatives. Tok Pisin is used now in political debates in the House of Assembly, in media broadcasts, and in journalism.

Tok Pisin has drawn heavily on English in all its new functions. So much English has been borrowed into the language, particularly by urban educated speakers, that many linguists have recognized two separate varieties of the language, urban and rural (or bush) pidgin. Consider this example in which a student being interviewed on a radio broadcast in 1972 said:

Mi salim eplikeson bilong mi na skul bod [me send application belong me and school board i konsiderim na bihain ekseptim mi na mi go [consider and behind accept me and me go] long skul long fama [to school of farmer].[3]

'I sent my application to the school board and then they considered and accepted me and I'm going to agricultural school.'

Here *eplikeson, skul bod, konsiderim,* and *ekseptim* are all recent loans from English. In some cases there are established pidgin equivalents which could have been used. For example, instead of *ekseptim,* one could say *ol givim orait long dispela* or *long mi* ('they gave the okay for this/to me'). Nowadays students would probably not use the term *skul long fama* but say *agricultural college.* In many cases we can see that borrowing a word in English fills a lexical gap or expresses a concept which is foreign and which could be expressed in pidgin only by means of a lengthy circumlocution. For example, *baset* ('budget') could be paraphrased as *ol man i lukautim mani bilong gavman i raitim daun ol samting bilong mani bilong gavman* ('the people who look after the government's money write down things having to do with the government's money'). The circumlocution is self-explanatory, whereas the borrowing is not. People often do not understand the meanings of very frequently used English borrowings. When the country became independent in 1975, the term *independens* was used, but many people then did not understand what it meant, and still do not. I worked with bush informants in 1986 and 1987 who said they were happy their country was independent because it meant that Australia would help them, when in fact it means just the opposite. In practical terms, increased borrowing from English in urban areas has the effect of making town pidgin unintelligible to rural dwellers. But in other cases, though there are equivalent pidgin words, English is borrowed simply because English has more prestige. For example, pidgin uses the term *askim* (from English *ask*) as both a verb and a noun, but increasingly in urban pidgin a more recently borrowed term, *kwesten* (from English *question*), appears too. Thus, one could say either *mi gat askim* or *mi gat kwesten* ('I have a question') or *mi laik askim kwesten* ('I want to ask a question'). Another example is *informesen* (from English *information*) and *toksave* (from Tok Pisin *tok + save,* that is, talk know), which means 'information, knowledge, advice.' Tok Pisin *toksave* can be used as either a noun or verb, whereas the English *infomesen* can be used only as a noun.[4] There has also been an increase in the use of English plurals ending in *-s – ol gels* (from English *girls*), for example, as opposed to *ol meri* ('the girls/women').

Until the last few decades Tok Pisin was only a spoken language. Now it is written too and more and more literature is published in it. One main vehicle for Tok Pisin as a written language is the weekly newspaper *Wantok*, founded in 1970. (The word *wantok* means 'one language' and is used to refer to a person who is part of the same social or kin group, or village.) Written almost entirely in pidgin, Wantok has a circulation of over 10 000 and more than 50 000 readers in Papua New Guinea, and its staff now consists entirely of nationals. Most of the material that appears in it is a translation of news releases from the Department of Information and Extension Services in Port Moresby. It is in Wantok that we find the most extensive use of pidgin in advertising.

Advertising creates special problems for newspapers aimed at a Papua New Guinea public. Most of the products are Australian and geared to western lifestyles, which were originally accessible only to expatriates. Now, increasingly a new market is found in the indigenous urban élite. While products like cars, trucks, and refrigerators are still luxuries for the average Papua New Guinean and therefore advertised largely in English, even in *Wantok*, it is no longer uncommon for Highlanders at the end of the coffee season to come into town and pay cash for a vehicle. Consequently, ads for cars and trucks – for instance, Toyota – are starting to appear occasionally in pidgin. While the names of such products mean something to Australians, they carry no meaning, and correspondingly have no use, for most Papua New Guineans. Products like Vegemite, Omo, and Pine-O-Cleen are just foreign words. For advertising to be successful, the product has to be not only advertised, but also explained in such a way as to create a need for it. One very simply ad which is effective, at least from the advertiser's point of view, is that used by the Wopa biscuit company. The Wopa ad shows a muscular man holding the product and saying, 'Mi kaikai' (I eat). The implication is that the product is good for you because it makes you strong and big. Bread and flour-based products are not part of traditional diets, so they have to be explained and made appealing, whether they are nutritious or not. These products increasingly find their way into every village trade store.

The ad for Sunflower tinned fish, in which the product is clearly illustrated, is effective primarily because of its use of idiomatic Tok Pisin. The slogan says: *Em i bun bilong mi stret* ('it bone belong me straight'), a colloquial expression which means that it is just the thing to serve as the foundation of a good diet. In the literal sense *bun* means 'bone' or 'skeleton'; one who is *bun nating* (from English *bone + nothing*) would be very skinny.

The ad for Paradise Pineapple Crunch biscuits, however, is probably much less effective bcause it relies too heavily on English borrowing. The ad boasts of *tropikal fleva insait long bisket* ('tropical flavor inside a biscuit'). The words *tropikal* and *fleva* are new English borrowings and won't be understood by those who do not know English. The Anchor milk company uses a heavily anglicized description of the product, next to which is a photograph of a jug of milk, a cup of coffee, and a can bearing a label in English, 'full cream vitamin enriched instant milk powder.' To a reader who knows no English, it could as well be an ad for coffee. Most Papua New Guineans have no experience of real milk, let alone powdered milk.

The kinds of clever and catchy advertising slogans typical in Western societies like *drinka pinta milka day*, *go to work on an egg*, and *if your clothes aren't becoming to you, you should be coming to us* are impossible to translate literally into another language because they rely on linguistic devices like vowel reduction ('*drink a pint of milk a day*'), alliteration, rhyme ('*Beanz meanz Heinz*'), and so on. Although presumably these strategies are available to some degree in most languages, the extent to which they are used and the purposes for which they are used will vary.

There are also other kinds of difficulties in literal translations of slogans, even where special devices like rhyme or punning are not brought into play in the original. For example, the Omo soap company wanted to advertise their product in *Wantok* and say simply that this is the best powdered soap you can buy. But in pidgin two product names for soap powder have become generic now in the same way as the brandname Hoover is used in Britain to refer to any vacuum cleaner or the name Jello is used in the United States for any fruit-flavored gelatin. (One can even use the name Hoover as a verb, at least in Britain, where it is more usual to 'hoover' a carpet than to 'vacuum' it.) Pidgin speakers use both *rinso*, another brandname, and *omo* to refer to all soap powders, which would lead to an advertisement that said something like: Omo is the best rinso you can buy, or Rinso is the best omo you can buy.[5] It would be like saying in English: I've just bought an Electrolux hoover.

The difference here is that English already has generic terms like soap powder, detergent, vacuum cleaner, carpet sweeper, and so on, whereas pidgin did not until it pressed a particular brandname into service. In the case of pidgin omo and rinso, the particular brand provides the first name for such a substance and thus is synonymous with it. The status and desirability of brandnames used as generics are debatable. The American Heritage Dictionary includes an entry for example for Kleenex ('a trademark for a soft cleansing tissue') and one for Jello ('a trademark for a gelatin dessert'). But of course the whole point of brandnames is to establish uniqueness. On can assume from the advertising campaign mounted by the Coca Cola Company – 'Coke is the real thing' or simply 'Coke is it' – that it is not unequivocally pleased with the use of Coke as a generic term for a cola drink. Nevertheless, it can also be advantageous for a company's product to become a 'household' word. If Kleenex is synonymous with tissues, then the consumer may be predisposed to seek this brandname when buying tissues.

A related problem arises from the lack of specialized terms in pigin to refer to foodstuffs which have already undergone a certain degree of processing and are therefore 'table-ready' or 'oven-ready.' (Traditionally, of course, Papua New Guineans do not sit down at tables to eat.) The distinction between English 'pork' and 'pig' and 'beef' and 'cow' is of course well known. Interestingly, English has borrowed from French the terms which refer to the edible version of the animal on the table, while it has used its own native terms to refer to the animal on the hoof, so to speak. There is a current ad for chicken which mixes English and pidgin and refers to its product in a confusing way as *Niugini table birds kakaruk* ('New Guinea table birds chicken'). This is also the company's name. The term *table bird* is a collocation specific to English referring to the product in a-ready-to-cook-and-serve state (and possibly even grown for that special purpose). Neither the term nor its concept is known to pidgin speakers. Presumably the idea is to establish an equation between ready-to-cook (as opposed to live) chickens and this particular company through invoking the pidgin term *kakaruk*, 'chicken.'

At the moment there is very little exploitation of linguistic devices like rhyme, alliteration, and punning to achive catchy slogans in Tok Pisin. I found only one example in an advertisement for eggs, and it plays on the English word *eggs* rather than the Tok Pisin term *kiau* (from Tolai, one of the indigenous languages of Papua New Guinea). It describes eggs as 'eggcellent', 'eggciting', and 'ineggspensive', and then says in pidgin that they are good value for money. A pidgin speaker who does not know English will not of course know what these blends mean. There is plenty of scope for creative advertising slogans drawing on native pidgin terms and devices. For instance, one Australian rice producer has named its product *Trukai* (Tok Pisin *tru + kaikai* – 'true food').

Tok Pisin also has a number of named special registers which could provide a productive source for advertisers. *Tok piksa* ('talk picture') is a term for a way of speaking which relies on analogy and similes. *Tok pilai* ('talk play') refers to the jocular use of extended metaphors. *Tok bilas* ('talk decoration') is used to say things which are potentially offensive but can later be denied. *Tok bokis* ('talk box') is a deliberate attempt to disguise meaning by the substitutionh of familiar words with hidden meanings. There are many others. Advertisers would, however, have to be careful here because some brand names already figure in certain registers. For instance, a common *tok piksa* term for beer is *spesel Milo* ('special Milo'), and Milo is already a brand name for a chocolate drink. Biscuit advertisers would benefit from knowing that Tok Pisin *switbisket* (from English *sweet biscuit*) and *draibisket* from English *dry biscuit*) have metaphorical meanings. The former can refer to a sexually attractive woman, and the later to a woman past her prime.

Some of the advertising techniques used by Western advertisers would simply not work in Papua New Guinea because they would be offensive and/or culturally inappropriate – for example, the innuendo and overt display of sexuality in the sale of perfumes, cars, and other luxury items. The *Wantok* newspaper refused an ad from the Gillette company because it showed a European couple in the bathroom nude from the waist up, the woman admiring the face of the smoothly shaven man. Shaving does not interest women in Papua New Guinea, and sexuality would not sell razor blades. On the contrary, it would discourage them.[6]

Conversely, however, many bodily functions do not have the same taboo surrounding them in Papua New Guinea as they do in Western culture, and euphemisms for these things are only just beginning to emerge in Tok Pisin under the influence of western practices. Euphemism is widely used in advertising, even for non-taboo subjects. Take, for instance, the use of 'fun-size' for small candy bars. I was amazed when a young schoolgirl I was interviewing used a new euphemistic term, *troimwe excretia* ('to throw away excretia'), for the normal pidgin *pekpek* ('to defecate'), which is used in all contexts. Similarly, *pispis* is the normal term for 'urinate,' though there is a new Tok Pisin euphemism now: *kapsaitim wara* (from English *capsize* + *water*). The kind of subtlety and allusion used by Western advertisers to sell toilet tissue (for example, fluffy puppies playing with toilet rolls in gleaming bright bathrooms) and sanitary products (not even advertised until recently in Western media) will be lost on most Papua New Guineans from rural areas who have no experience of modern sanitation facilities. Ads for sanitary napkins, which have just recently begun to appear in *Wantok*, do not explicitly describe or depict the product. Although the language itself is not heavily Anglicized and would be intelligible, the advertisers do not explain what the product is or does. Thanks to western taboo, the reader is simply told that Johnson and Johnson have *ol gutpela samting* ('good things'), and shown a picture of a girl daydreaming. The dividing line between euphemism and mystification is very fine in this case. It may well be, however, that this phrase does carry unintended sexual overtone and would therefore offend, because the Tok Pisin term *samting* ('somthing') is used in *tok bokis* to refer to genitals.

Other familiar Wester-style household products are increasingly aimed at Papua New Guineans: for example, Pine-O-Cleen, Mortein, and similar detergents and cleaning agents, and insect sprays. Here it is essential that the product be displayed as well as explained. In these ads an appeal is typically made to the notion of protecting your family against disease. We see here the introduction of Western metaphors into local culture.[7] When such products are advertised in Western media, women are usually portrayed as the protectors of the household, warding off dirt, germs, and other hazards with the right product. Ads for insurance also use the protection metaphor. Then there are also many ads which are used to explain institutions that are culturally alien: banks, taxes, telephones. The effectiveness of the ads depends on how successfully they can render into pidgin the concepts involved. For example, in an ad for PTC (Post and Telecommunication Corporation) the Western metaphor 'time is money' (*yu save olsem taim em i mani* – 'you know that time is money') is invoked to get people to use the telephone to conduct transactions which would ordinarily be done face-to-face in casual encounters and not by appointment. The concepts 'social call' and 'business call' are thus introduced.

These are a few of the difficulties presented by advertising in pidgin English. Some of these derive from the problems of the linguistic medium itself, which is in the process of expanding, while others have more to do specifically with the pragmatics of cross-cultural communication. In order to resolve some of the difficulties I have noted here, co-operation between linguists, manufacturing industries, and advertising agencies is essential.

NOTES

1　See S. Romaine, *Pidgin and Creole Languages* (London, 1988).
2　This word order pattern in *tok boi* also illustrates the use of English items in compound constructions based on those found in indigenous languages. Compare *kot ren* (from English *coat + rain* – 'raincoat'), *haus man* (from English *house + man* – 'men's house'), and so on. The word *boi* was used by Europeans to refer to an indigenous man of any age, particularly in indentured service. It has recently been 'reborrowed' in its English sense to refer to young men in order to replace Tok Pisin *mangki* (from English *monkey*).
3　This example is taken from L. R. Healey, 'When is a Word not a Pidgin Word?', *Tok Pisin i go we?* (Where is Tok Pisin going?), ed. K. McElhanon. Special Issue of *Kivung* (Linguistic Society of Papua New Guinea, 1975), pp. 36–42.
4　The word *save* is from Spanish/Portuguese (*sabir/saber* – 'to know') and is widespread in pidgin and creole languages throughout the world and not just in those of Spanish/Portuguese base. This is one of the few cases where English has borrowed a term from pidgin: that is, *savvy*. Though it can be used only as a noun or adjective in English, in Tok Pisin it can be used as a noun or verb.
5　See the comments of the first editor and founder of *Wantok* in F. Mihalic, 'Interpretation Problems from the Point of View of a Newspaper Editor', in *New Guinea Area Languages and Language Study*, ed. S. A. Wurm, vol. 3 of *Language, Culture, Society and the Modern World* (Canberra, 1977), pp. 1117–26.
6　See Mihalic, 'Interpretation Problems', for his discussion of the newspaper's policy.
7　See G. Lakoff and M. Johnson, *Metaphors We Live By* (Chicago, 1980), for their discussion of some of these metaphors.

28 Code-switching: Language Selection in Three Strasbourg Department Stores

Penelope Gardner-Chloros

INTRODUCTION

Code-switching (CS) can be defined as the use of two or more languages in the same conversation or utterance. This is a common occurrence in many parts of the world in situations of native bi- or multilingualism (e.g. Africa, India), immigration (Europe, the United States), and regional minorities. As millions of people use more than one language in their daily lives, it is no surprise to find that CS is a far from homogeneous phenomenon and that the actual behaviour involved varies depending on the sociolinguistic circumstances as well as the language combination concerned.

Within sociolinguistics, many attempts have been made to identify the main sub-categories of CS. One of the earliest was Gumperz's (1982: 60–61) distinction between *situational* and *conversational* CS. *Situational* CS could be regarded as changes in language choice rather than CS proper; it refers to language switches which coincide with a change of interlocutor, setting or topic. *Conversational* CS, which many authors would now regard as CS proper, does not necessarily coincide with any such changes but is motivated by factors within the conversation itself. A subdivision of conversational CS which Gumperz described and which is sometimes confused with conversational CS itself is *metaphorical* CS, where a switch carries a particular evocative purpose, for example, speaking about a place in the variety which is used there.

A considerable practical problem in distinguishing different *types* of CS is that they tend to occur in the same context and often involve the same speakers. For example, in Alsace a conversation involving two middle-aged, one adolescent and one older participant might well involve interlocutor-related switching, the adolescent being addressed in French and speaking

---

Source: Written specially for this collection.

mainly French, the older person giving and receiving almost exclusive Alsatian, and the two middle-generation speakers code-switching at a conversational/metaphorical level, and being fully understood by the younger and the older participants.

At a linguistic level, a frequently proposed distinction is between CS, in which the two varieties involved are held to preserve their monolingual character, and instances of contact where various forms of convergence occur. The latter are called by other terms such as 'code-mixing' or 'interference' (Hamers and Blanc 1989; Kachru 1978). Such a distinction may be found in the work of Poplack (1980), Sankoff and Poplack (1981) and Poplack and Sankoff (1984). In their study of Spanish–English CS in the Puerto-Rican community in New York, they described a type of CS where English and Spanish preserved their monolingual characteristics; instances which did not conform to this pattern were held to be loans.

The idea that CS was a type of rule-governed juxtaposition of two distinct systems gave rise to a copious literature on the 'grammar' of CS (for a summary see Muysken 1995). For the greater part, these studies apply existing models to CS. Myers-Scotton (1992), however, describes a set of rules which are held specifically to govern CS. Her proposals rely on the assumption that there is always a *matrix language* which determines the fundamental form of a code-switched utterance, while the other language, known as the *embedded language*, contributes specific elements.

Others have found the existence of a matrix language impossible to establish on any objective criterion (e.g. Moyer 1994). In Strasbourg, for example, where this study was carried out, the majority of the population is bilingual and there is a fluid relationship between French and the Alsatian dialect. Many common words including greetings, culinary terms, kinship terms and numbers are identifiably French in origin but synchronically are part of a repertoire which consists of elements from both languages. Certain fields of activity give rise to a high rate of vocabulary transfer from French to Alsatian (for example, business and office terminology). At a phonological level, the Alsatian accent carries over to the local form of French and blurs the distinction between the two languages, and Bickel-Kaufmann (1983) has shown that among the younger generation, French also has a phonological influence on the pronunciation of the dialect. A variety of mixing patterns can be found, which depend on the participants' respective competence in the different varieties and on sociolinguistic factors. Therefore in this context it seems less appropriate to search for generalizable 'rules' governing how two languages are juxtaposed than to compare the patterns of mixing found among different age groups and social groups (see Bentahila and Davies 1991, for a similar approach in a Moroccan context).

BACKGROUND

Strasbourg is the capital of Alsace and the Bas-Rhin region in Eastern France, and a city of some quarter of a million inhabitants. Alsace has belonged alternately to France and Germany since 1648 and since the end of the Occupation in the Second World War has been resolutely French. French is therefore the language of the State, of education and the media and, increasingly, the mother-tongue of the younger generations. Surveys reveal, however, that the Germanic dialect which has always distinguished the area from other parts of France, and which is on a dialectal continuum with dialects spoken in the adjoining areas of Germany, is still widely spoken by various sectors of the population (see Gardner-Chloros 1991 for an overview and further references). Its use is not exclusively tied to rural areas, or to the age and gender of the speaker, but it is true that it is spoken most by the sociolinguistic group that one would expect to speak a traditional dialect: older, rural males. In Strasbourg it also functions as a marker of Alsatian identity, in contrast to French people from other parts of France ('les Français de l'Intérieur', or 'French from the Interior', as they are known in Alsace), and also to the sizeable international population associated with the Council of Europe and the European Parliament, who may speak French but certainly not Alsatian. The dialect is therefore taken up in adolescent groups as well as by local comedians, playwrights and poets, used for humorous, emotional and vernacular purposes of all kinds. In Strasbourg it is more often than not mixed with French, the type of mixing which occurs being a function of the interlocutors, the setting, the topic and purpose of the conversation, etc.

THE PRESENT STUDY

The following study represents an early attempt to sort out the basic parameters influencing language choice in Strasbourg. CS was not subdivided in any way, merely representing instances where speakers do not make exclusive use of one or the other language. The results highlighted the interdependence of language choice and CS. Although CS has sometimes been viewed as a variety in its own right (see Scotton's 1983 concept of *unmarked* CS), it still needs to be understood as part of the overall pattern of language use in the community.

Before finding out what types of CS exist, it seemed an important first step to find out where in Strasbourg it was most likely to occur, and among which speakers. Various anonymous surveys, of which this is the largest, were therefore carried out. The not altogether expected, but welcome consequence of this was to shed some light on some likely motivations for CS.

LANGUAGE SELECTION AND SWITCHING AMONG STRASBOURG SHOPPERS

> Future studies of language in its social context should rely more heavily on rapid and anonymous studies as part of a general programme of utilising unobtrusive measures to control the effect of the observer.... They represent a form of nonreactive experimentation in which we avoid the bias of the experimental context and the irregular interference of prestige norms but still control the behaviour of subjects (Labov 1972: 69).

The aim of this survey, which is broadly based on Labov's (1972) well-known survey in three New York department stores (see also Chapter 13, this volume), was to collect quantitative data on the use of French and Alsatian in Strasbourg, and on switching between the two. Age, context, and topic are all-important in determining language selection; in addition to expectations deriving from the presence of these factors, an understanding of the appropriate *situational norms* is relevant. These norms are, on the one hand, common to many different social groups, such as the rule that 'the customer is always right', which makes the customer's variety dominate in customer–salesperson interactions (Genesee and Bourhis 1982), and, on the other hand, they are enmeshed with the particular diglossic configuration in question: thus in Strasbourg an Alsatian-speaking customer might well refrain from imposing her language because there is a conflicting norm tending to prefer French as the language of public conversations with interlocutors one does not know personally.

HYPOTHESES AND VARIABLES

The hypotheses tested in the study were therefore derived both from existing information on language use in Alsace and from the norms which were expected to govern the situation being observed. The first parameter was social class: it was expected that in stores of higher social standing, more French and less Alsatian would be spoken than in those of lower prestige, the independent variable being the *store*.

Older customers were expected to use more Alsatian and less French than younger customers, the independent variable being *age*; the age of the salesperson with whom they were communicating was also expected to affect language choice, though less so than the age of the customer.

Both *topic* and *setting* affect language choice. Topic in the strict sense could not be used as a variable here, owing to the limited nature of the exchanges observed. Setting was represented by the different *departments*: departments selling *necessities* such as food or other practical items were expected to call forth more Alsatian than those selling *luxuries* such as perfume or hi-fi, which are tied up with social aspirations and the aesthetic side of life.

Since conversations in department stores are public rather than intimate, it was expected that both customers and salespersons would gravitate towards the prestige norm, i.e. speak more French and less Alsatian than in private. It was therefore predicted that whatever the figures obtained, less Alsatian and more French would be spoken between customers and salespersons than within groups of customers or within groups of salespersons: the independent variable was therefore the *ingroup/outgroup* distinction.

It is known from studies in different parts of the world that switching between languages or varieties need not always have the same motivation or significance (Singh 1983). The intermittent use of a variety in which one is not fully competent may, for instance, be used to indicate ethnic allegiance to that variety. Alternatively, switching may be used by speakers who wish to converge towards a prestige norm but are unable to sustain discourse all the time in that variety. This second possibility provides a likely explanation for much of the switching from French to Alsatian in Strasbourg, since French enjoys more social prestige than Alsatian but not all speakers are perfectly at ease in it. It was hoped that the amount of switching observed when different combinations of factors were at play would, first, indicate whether this hypothesis was worth pursuing and, second, suggest further lines of enquiry regarding language switching in Strasbourg.

METHOD

While providing less commercial scope than New York, Strasbourg conveniently possesses three departmental stores of distinct social character: *Printemps*, a branch of the well-known Paris store, just off Place Kléber, the main square in Strasbourg's commercial centre; *Magmod*, equally central and having if anything a larger surface area, but more old-fashioned both inside and out, noticeably dowdier, and less luxuriously appointed; and *Jung*, in the suburb of Schiltigheim which, though attached to Strasbourg geographically, has its own identity, its own politics, and its own shopping centre.

Preliminary discussions with a number of Strasbourgeois revealed a clear consensus as to the stores' social stratification, *Printemps* being considered the most modern, chic, and pricey and therefore likely to be the most French-speaking. *Magmod* was felt to have an 'older', dustier image, while keeping up with *Printemps* in some respects – for example, both *Printemps* and *Magmod* devote their whole ground floor to luxuries such as cosmetics, leather goods, gifts, and jewellery. *Jung* was considered to offer goods of a lower quality, to be cheaper and more provincial. Its ground floor is the main hub of sales activity: women's clothes, men's clothes, food, stationery, records, jewellery, cameras, and so forth are displayed alongside each other on small counters. Only furniture, hardware, and a few other departments are on other floors. The top floor of *Jung* is devoted to furniture, but I was never able to observe language use in that department, as it was usually empty. Only once, an elderly female customer and a saleswoman of similar age were observed, having a thoroughly enjoyable gossip, in very loud voices, as they had the floor to themselves. The language used was, predictably, Alsatian.

Jung and *Magmod*, on the other hand, are more similar to each other as regards food sales, each incorporating large supermarket-style food departments with checkout counters at the end. *Printemps* has instead a small exclusive food hall on the top sales floor, where some of the choicest Strasbourg suppliers have individual counters.

Customers' and salespersons' language use was observed and recorded on small pre-divided cards in each of the three stores. Only women were considered since men were in a tiny minority in both groups (the fieldwork was carried out on weekdays when women formed the majority of shoppers). The main focus of the survey was the language used by customers in speaking to salespersons, of which *254* instances were observed, sometimes by making repeated use of the same salesperson, as in the case of queues at the checkout counters. *Ingroup* conversations between customers and between salespersons were also observed, amounting to a further *292* instances. The collection of these data took some 35 hours. This contrasts with the six and a half hours taken by Labov to gather *264* instances of possible use of postvocalic (r). The longer time required here is explained by the fact that whereas Labov was able to elicit the data by asking for an item which he knew to be on the 'fourth floor', the data in this case were simply observed without any intervention by the researcher.

Greetings and thanks in French were ignored, since *bonjour, merci*, etc., are used in Alsace regardless of the language in which the rest of the conversation is held. Where the salesperson spoke first, the language she used was not recorded either. As one would predict for such a relatively public and formal situation in Alsace, this language was always French – with one interesting exception. The exception was observed in the china department of *Magmod*, where a young customer was asking a young saleswoman – in French, as one would expect – where to go to make arrangements to deposit her wedding list. The young saleswoman hesitated, whereupon another middle-aged saleswoman who had been involved in a conversation in Alsatian with a colleague, but who had overheard the question, interrupted herself, came over to the customer, and directed her to the appropriate department in Alsatian. The incident was so exceptional that one can safely attribute it to an oversight, a failure to switch when circumstances required it, resulting from the saleswoman being immersed at the time in an Alsatian conversation. A mental note was therefore kept of the first language which the customer was heard to use. Where this was French, further eavesdropping revealed whether the customer subsequently switched to Alsatian. If she did, this was recorded as a *switch*. Where the customer *started* in Alsatian, this was simply recorded as a conversation in Alsatian. It was not expected that a customer starting in Alsatian (and so, in a sense, *conceding* her inability to carry out the discussion in French) would switch into French. No separate category was therefore provided for this.

However, I remained alert to the possibility of this happening and the consequent necessity to provide such a category. In the event, the original expectation was fully confirmed and it was not necessary to provide a category for switches from Alsatian into French on behalf of customers. There were, however, some instances of customers who started in French, switched to Alsatian, then back to French, back to Alsatian, and so on. These cases were simply counted as *switches* – meaning from French to Alsatian, since in this study it was not the details of the CS, but whether CS took place at all which was being ascertained. The third possible category provided on the cards was for conversations entirely in French.

Both customers' and salespersons' approximate ages were noted, permitting an analysis not only by age of customer but also of the interaction between different age groups. Three age categories were used: under 30, 30 to 45, and over 45.

The language used in conversations between customers or between salespersons – classed as *ingroup* conversations – was more summarily recorded without note being taken of the speakers' ages or the departments in which they were. The same three categories of language use were employed, thus permitting a comparison between these *ingroup* conversations and the customer–salesperson *outgroup* exchanges. The switching category, while still representing a middle category between pure French and pure Alsatian, was somewhat more broadly defined than in outgroup conversations: discussions between customers and between salespersons have a less specific purpose and are less brief than those between customers and salespersons. Consequently, the switching category here included any kind of switching to and fro, regardless of whether the beginning of the conversation had been overheard.

One problem was that many department-store transactions are frustratingly silent: the customer browses, chooses, hands the item to the salesperson operating the cash register together with the required sum and walks away with her purchase and her change, not having exchanged a word. In other cases, it was not possible to overhear the very beginning of the conversation, and some conversations recorded as 'Alsatian' may in fact have been conversations which started in French and switched to Alsatian ('switches'); thus the amount of switching is, if anything, underestimated.

Finally, there appeared to be no case in which a salesperson, however young, failed to reply in Alsatian to a customer who addressed her in Alsatian (though there must presumably have been some non-Alsatian salespersons). There may also have been non-Alsatian customers in the sample who spoke only French and who remain unidentified, since it was possible to avoid only the two or three customers who were evidently not Alsatian from their physical characteristics.

All in all, the method used and the situations observed would tend to underestimate the amount of Alsatian and of switching among Strasbourgeois in general. This is illustrated in the disparity between the number of customers starting conversations in Alsatian or switching to Alsatian in this survey, which averaged out at a mere 28 per cent overall, and 55 per cent of families in the Bas-Rhin who claim to speak Alsatian 'often' or 'always' when doing the shopping (Schuffenecker 1981; although the survey reported here included local shopping rather than being limited to the big stores in Strasbourg).

RESULTS AND DISCUSSION

Stores

As can be seen from Table 28.1, almost 30 per cent of customers in *Jung* started speaking to salespersons in Alsatian, compared with just under 20 per cent in *Magmod* and 8 per cent in *Printemps*. This follows the expected pattern, and a chi-square performed on the data was significant at one per cent level ($\chi^2 = 17.491$, dfs = 4, p < 0.01 > 0.001). Switching, however, does not follow the same pattern: just under 15 per cent of customers switched in *Jung*, but the next highest was *Printemps* where over 10 per cent switched. Under 5 per cent of customers switched in *Magmod*.

More Alsatian and less French were spoken in *necessity* than in *luxury* departments, though the results were not statistically significant. This may be because food and clothes cannot really be considered necessities when sold in expensive stores.

Table 28.1: Use of Alsatian, French, and switching by store (%)

	Jung	Magmod	Printemps
Alsatian	28.1	19.1	8.0
French	57.3	76.1	81.8
Switching	14.6	4.8	10.2
N	82.0	84.0	88.0

More interestingly, in *Jung*, the most Alsatian speaking store, there was more than twice as much switching (21.2 per cent of conversations) in departments selling luxuries as in those selling necessities (10.2 per cent), indicating some linguistic insecurity on behalf of Alsatian-dominant speakers.

Customer Age

The customer's age was the single most significant factor determining language use, and the biggest difference is to be found between the over-45 age group and the two younger groups (see Table 28.2). Chi-square was significant at the 0.1 per cent level ($\chi^2 = 57.193$, dfs = 4, $p < 0.001$) – it should of course be recalled that it was only possible to guess customers' ages. Note also that switching does not only occur in the group where *most* pure Alsatian is spoken, but also in the group where *least* pure Alsatian is spoken, that is the youngest group.

The breakdown by customer age and store shows that the oldest age group speaks most Alsatian in *Jung*, less in *Magmod*, and less still in *Printemps*, where, however, they go in for a lot of switching (see Table 28.3). The group which switches most *overall*, interestingly, is the youngest group of shoppers in *Jung*. For that reason *Jung* shows a marked difference between age groups 1 and 2, unlike *Magmod* or *Printemps*.

Table 28.2: Use of Alsatian, French, and switching by age of customers (%)

	→30	30–45	45+
Alsatian	2.9	5.6	40.2
French	86.8	87.7	47.4
Switching	10.3	6.7	12.4
N	68	89	97

Table 28.3: Use of Alsatian, French, and switching by customer, age and store (%)

	Jung			Magmod			Printemps		
	→30	30–45	45+	→30	30–45	45+	→30	30–45	45+
Alsatian	4.2	16.7	60.7	0.0	0.0	39.0	4.0	0.0	21.4
French	70.8	73.3	28.6	100.0	95.8	53.7	92.0	94.3	57.2
Switching	25.0	10.0	10.7	0.0	4.2	7.3	4.0	5.7	21.5
N	24.0	30.0	28.0	19.0	24.0	41.0	25.0	35.0	28.0

Table 28.4: Use of Alsatian, French, and switching by age of customers and age of salespersons (%)

Customer age	→30			30–45			45+		
Salesperson age	→30	30–45	45+	→30	30–45	45+	→30	30–45	45+
Alsatian	0.0	3.1	15.4	0.0	7.1	13.3	20.0	28.1	68.6
French	95.5	84.4	76.9	93.9	78.6	86.7	70.0	56.3	22.8
Switching	4.5	12.5	7.7	6.1	14.3	0.0	10.0	15.6	8.6
N	22.0	32.0	13.0	33.0	42.0	15.0	30.0	32.0	35.0

The same trend was reflected in each of the three stores taken separately (see Table 28.4).

As Table 28.5 reveals, in *Jung* salespersons also spoke more Alsatian among themselves than did customers, but adapted as in the other stores to speaking more French when in outgroup conversation with the latter. In *Magmod*, customers and salespersons behaved in a similar fashion when engaged in their respective ingroup conversations, and, notably, spoke as much Alsatian as did customers in *Jung*, but the amount of Alsatian spoken in customer–salesperson interaction was dramatically lower. In *Printemps*, there is less Alsatian overall; unlike the situation in *Jung*, salespersons speak less Alsatian among themselves than do customers but are among the highest switching groups (18.2 per cent). As in the other cases, when interacting with customers the amount of Alsatian drops. Switching is highest within salesperson groups in *Printemps* and *Magmod*, but within customer groups and between customers and salespersons in *Jung*.

Table 28.5: Use of Alsatian, French, and switching by groups of interlocutors and store

	Alsatian %	French %	Switching %	N
Jung ingroup customer–customer	34.0	51.1	14.9	47
Jung ingroup salesperson–salesperson	60.0	30.0	10.0	30
Jung outgroup customer–salesperson*	28.1	57.3	14.6	82
Magmod ingroup customer–customer	37.2	58.1	4.7	43
Magmod ingroup salesperson–salesperson	37.7	49.1	13.2	53
Magmod outgroup customer–salesperson*	19.1	76.1	4.8	84
Printemps ingroup customer–customer	20.0	77.3	2.7	75
Printemps ingroup salesperson–salesperson	13.6	68.2	18.2	44
Printemps outgroup customer–salesperson*	8.0	81.8	10.2	88

*Figures are from Table 28.1.

Patterns of Switching and their Social Motivation

It is clear from an overall view of the data that, whereas the selection of French and Alsatian provides support for the original hypotheses, the pattern of switching is not a function of the same rules. For example, whereas French is spoken most in the order *Printemps, Magmod, Jung*, and Alsatian in the opposite order, switching takes place most in *Jung*, then in *Printemps*, and least of all in *Magmod* (see Table 28.1), that is, it is most prevalent in the two extreme linguistic environments. The same comment applies to customer age: whereas customers speak French in the order young, middle, old, and Alsatian in the reverse order, switching takes place in the order old, young, middle (see Table 28.2). The same amount of switching can occur where there is a very high use of Alsatian (e.g. customers over 45 in *Jung*) and where there is a very low use of Alsatian (e.g. customers between 30 and 45 in *Jung* or customers under 30 in general; see Table 28.3).

Careful study of the results reveals several patterns which cast light on the social motivations of switching. The first likely motivation to emerge for switching can be termed *accommodation* to the linguistic environment. Such a motivation fits in well with approaches which consider switching to be a 'compromise' way of speaking, a means of reconciling opposites (Scotton 1976), since the relevant situations are marked by contrasts or opposition in the data. More recent studies have confirmed the existence of the 'accommodative' motivation for code-switching, in particular when code-switching is taken to mean, as here, sequences of linguistic choices (see Lawson-Sako and Sachdev 1996). The highest rate of switching (25 per cent) is found among the youngest group of shoppers, who are also the most French-speaking, when they are in *Jung*, i.e. the most Alsatian-speaking store. The second highest rate is found among the oldest shoppers, who are the most Alsatian-speaking, in *Printemps*, the most French-speaking store. Relatively high rates of switching (not indicated in any of the tables due to space limitations) were also found in the luxury – and so French-speaking – departments of *Jung*, the store where people are most likely to be Alsatian speakers, as well as in the opposite situation of the shoppers buying necessities in *Printemps*, the most French-speaking store.

This interpretation of the facts is reinforced by the lack of switching in the most neutral linguistic environment, that of *Magmod*, which occupies the middle rank as regards the use of Alsatian overall but the lowest rank as regards switching (see Table 28.1). The youngest and the middle age group in *Magmod* use very little Alsatian and switch very little also (see Table 28.3). The older group of customers uses quite a lot of pure Alsatian (39 per cent) but also switches relatively little (7.3 per cent). Both customer and salesperson ingroups use quite a lot of Alsatian (37.2 per cent and 37.7 per cent, respectively; see Table 28.5). Customers, in fact, use slightly *more*

Alsatian among themselves in *Magmod* than in *Jung*, but the rate of switching between customers is much lower than amongst salespersons indicating less linguistic insecurity.

All the data on *Magmod* suggest that it imposes relatively little pressure on speakers to use one or the other language, so their language selection is more a function of characteristics independent of the immediate environment (such as age) than of the context in which it occurs, and they have little tendency to switch.

The second type of motivation or reason for switching appears to tie in with external pressures to use one language rather than the other, which can be due to the situational norm or to other social expectations. With regard to the first kind of pressure, we note that older customers switch to Alsatian slightly more often with young salespersons than do young customers when speaking to older salespersons (10 per cent and 7.7 per cent, respectively; see Table 28.4). This would appear to confirm that although there is accommodation in both kinds of circumstances, the customer's variety is more often imposed on the salesperson than vice versa.

As far as other expectations are concerned, we turn here to the figures for switching in ingroup conversations between salespersons. This occurs in the order *Printemps* (18.2 per cent), *Magmod* (13.2 per cent), and *Jung* (10 per cent; see Table 28.5), which is the exact reverse of the order in which these same groups use Alsatian. It seems more than likely that there is an expectation that sales staff will use French, be it a specific expectation formulated by employers or a general expectation on the part of customers or society at large. In *Printemps*, salespersons are awarded a bonus for linguistic competence in languages other than French, but Alsatian does not count as a language in the bonus system. But many salespersons prefer to use Alsatian among themselves, so they switch to and fro by way of compromise, most of all in the store in which they are under the heaviest pressure to speak French, and in decreasing order of that pressure.

The last possible factor affecting the rate of switching which will be discussed here is the influence of *the interlocutor*. It is fairly clear that mutual accommodation takes place from the data on language selection. Whereas customers over 45 address sales staff in the same age group in Alsatian in 68.6 per cent of cases, they only address sales staff under 30 in Alsatian in 20 per cent of cases. Equally, young customers appear never to address young salespersons in Alsatian, but do speak Alsatian to salespersons over 45 in 15.4 per cent of cases (see Table 28.4). Switching, however, is most prevalent among all three customer age groups when the salesperson is in the *middle* age group. This may betray uncertainty about the linguistic preferences of the salesperson. The customers' own preferences are also reflected in the fact that older shoppers switch most with this ambiguous group, shoppers in the middle group slightly less, and the youngest shoppers least (15.6 per cent, 14.3 per cent, and 12.5 per cent, respectively). The influence of the interlocutor is perhaps the most intangible of the three types of motivation which have been discussed, due to the complexity of speakers' reactions to one another and the difficulty of apprehending which aspect of their identity they are bringing to the fore.

An interesting case in point is the language selection and switching pattern for customers between 30 and 45 in conversation with salespersons over 45. Whereas this group switches quite a lot with salespersons in the same group (14.3 per cent), no switching was encountered when this group spoke to older salespersons. Instead, more pure French was spoken than with the middle group (86.7 per cent instead of 78.6 per cent), which is the reverse of what interpersonal accommodation would indicate.

The 30–45 age group is probably made up of more balanced bilinguals than either of the other groups, that is of people who have a real choice as to which language to use, yet their lack of switching and low use of Alsatian with older salespersons stands out from the normal pattern of differences between the age groups. Their usage is therefore likely to be the result of a deliberate policy, which in turn probably rests on a heightened awareness of linguistic issues and differences. Its motivation requires further investigation. They might be paying their older interlocutors a deliberate compliment in treating them as French speakers, or they might be indicating their own allegiance to a younger, more French-speaking generation, or even both at once. The interlocutor has, here, still exercised an influence on language selection but not one which at first sight goes in the direction of interpersonal accommodation.

CONCLUDING REMARKS

The study provided useful quantitative data which supported the original hypotheses of language selection in a relatively formal and constrained situation in Strasbourg. Further attempts to quantify selection and switching patterns were based on different constraints: for example, language use as regulated by the different conventions of conversations in small local shops or other workplaces (Gardner-Chloros 1991).

Furthermore, although it is true that such studies 'avoid the bias of the experimental context' and also 'control the effect of the observer', correlations between language use and apparently objective variables such as the store, the department, etc., reflect social reality better than psychological reality: the shoppers in *Printemps* who used a lot of French were not doing so merely because they were in *Printemps*, but also because they were different people from those in *Jung*. Psychological reality is less amenable to objective verification, but quantitative data relating to it can at least clear the ground for a more qualitative analysis.

Thus this study has not exhausted the question of motivations underlying language switching in Strasbourg but has at least made it easier to ask relevant questions about those motivations. It is now clear, for example, that the original assumption that switching reveals a desire to converge to the prestige norm is inadequate. The group which switches more than any other appears to do so in order to fit in with its surroundings, since it is made up of people who are more at ease in the prestige norm, French, than in Alsatian. Accommodation would therefore appear to be as relevant a motive as prestige. This, in turn, underlines that code-switching can have several different *motives/raisons d'être* within a single sociolinguistic context.

It is at least clear that, although some instances of code-switching are so distinctive and sophisticated as to constitute a separate mode of speaking, CS cannot be studied entirely independently of factors governing the selection of the two varieties which make it up. The results of this study show that, at least in this context, an understanding of language selection is a necessary, though not a sufficient, condition for understanding switching.

REFERENCES

Bentahila, A. and Davies, E. E. (1991) 'Constraints on Code-switching: A Look Beyond Grammar', *Papers from the Symposium on Code-switching in Bilingual Studies: Theory, Significance and Perspectives. Barcelona, 21–23 March 1991* (Strasbourg: European Science Foundation) pp. 369–403.

Bickel-Kaufmann, M.-M. (1983) 'Les Consonnes du Parler D'Andolsheim: Étude Expérimentale en Milieu Bilingue', Thèse IIIe Cycle, Univ. des Sciences Humaines de Strasbourg.

Gardner-Chloros, P. (1991) *Language Selection and Switching in Strasbourg* (Oxford: Clarendon Press).

Genesee, F. and Bourhis, R. Y. (1982) 'The Social Psychological Significance of Code-switching in Cross-cultural Communication', *Journal of Language and Social Psychology*, 1(1), pp. 1–27.

Gumperz, J. J. (1982) *Discourse Strategies* (Cambridge: Cambridge University Press).

Hamers, J. F. and Blanc, M. (1989) *Biliguality and Bilingualism* (Cambridge: Cambridge University Press).

Kachru, B. B. (1978) 'Code Mixing as a Communicative Strategy', in Alatis, J. (ed.) *International Dimensions of Bilingual Education* (Washington, DC: Georgetown University Press) pp. 107–21.

Labov, W. (1972) 'The Social Stratification of (r) in New York City Department Stores', in *Sociolinguistic Patterns* (Philadelphia, PA: University of Pennsylvania Press) pp. 43–70.

Lawson-Sako, S. and Sachdev, I. (1996) 'Ethnolinguistic Communication in Tunisian Streets', in Suleiman, Y. (ed.) *Language and Ethnic Identity in the Middle East and North Africa* (Richmond, Surrey: Curzon Press).

Moyer, M. (1994) 'On Defining Matrix Language in Sentential Code-switching: A Syntactic Approach', *Summer School Code-switching and Language Contact. Ljouwert/Leeuwarden 14–17 September 1994*, Fryske Akademy, pp. 192–205.

Muysken, P. (1995) 'Code Switching and Grammatical Theory', in Milroy, L. and Muysken, P. (eds) *One Speaker, Two Languages: Cross-disciplinary Perspectives on Code-switching* (Cambridge: Cambridge University Press) pp. 177–98.

Myers-Scotton, C. (1992) 'Comparing Codeswitching and Borrowing', *Journal of Multilingual and Multicultural Development*, 13(1–2), pp. 19–39.

Poplack, S. (1980) 'Sometimes I'll Start a Sentence in English y Terminó en Español: Toward a Typology of Code-switching', *Linguistics* 18, pp. 581–618.

Poplack, S. and Sankoff, D. (1984) 'Borrowing: The Synchrony of Integration', *Linguistics*, 22, 99–135.

Sankoff, D. and Poplack, S. (1981) 'A Formal Grammar for Code-switching', *Papers in Linguistics*, 14(1), pp. 3–46.

Schuffenecker, G. (1981) 'Mode de Vie en Alsace, Institut National de la Statistique et des Études Économiques', *Dernières Nouvelles d'Alsace* (February 1981), pp. 6–15.

Scotton, C. M. (1976) 'Strategies of Neutrality: Language Choice in Uncertain situations', *Language*, 52(4), pp. 919–41.

Scotton, C. M. (1983) 'The Negotiation of Identities in Conversation: A Theory of Markedness and Code Choice', *International Journal of Sociology of Language*, 44, pp. 115–36.

Singh, R. (1983) 'We, They, and Us: A Note on Code-switching and Stratification in North India', *Language in Society*, 12(1), pp. 71–3.

29   Language Change and Sex Roles in a Bilingual Community

Susan Gal

INTRODUCTION

Linguistic differences between men and women can appear at various levels of grammar: in phonology, in syntax and pragmatics, in choice of lexical items, in choice of language by bilinguals, as well as in patterns of conversational interaction.

However, the effects of such sex differences on linguistic *change* have so far been noted only with respect to phonology, where it has been demonstrated that, along with other social correlates of synchronic linguistic diversity such as class and ethnicity, 'the sexual differentiation of speech often plays a major role in the mechanism of linguistic evolution' (Labov 1972: 303). The substantive aim of this chapter is to describe the way in which the women of a Hungarian–German bilingual town in Austria have contributed to a change in patterns of language choice. The entire community is gradually and systematically changing from stable bilingualism to the use of only one language in all interactions. Sex-linked differences in language choice have influenced the overall community-wide process of change.

In the language usage patterns to be described here, young women are more advanced or further along in the direction of the linguistic change than older people and young men. This is one of the patterns which has been noted in correlational studies of phonological change in urban areas. Most such studies report that women use the newer, advanced forms more frequently than men. Newly introduced forms used mostly by women are sometimes prestigious (Trudgill 1972) and sometimes not (Fasold 1968). In many cases women, as compared to men of the same social class, use more of the new non-prestigious forms in casual speech, while moving further

Source: 'Peasant Men Can't Get Wives: Language Change and Roles in a Bilingual Community', *Language in Society*, **7**, 1 (1978), pp. 1–16 (Cambridge: Cambridge University Press).

towards prestige models in formal speech. In other cases women do not lead in the course of linguistic change (reported in Labov 1972).

Although such findings are well documented, adequate explanations of them have not been offered. General statements about the linguistic innovativeness or conservatism of women will not account for the data. Neither Trudgill's (1972) suggestion that women are 'linguistically insecure', nor Labov's (1972) allusion to norms of linguistic appropriateness which allow women a wider expressive range than men, can convincingly explain why women are linguistically innovative in some communities and not in others (Nichols 1976). Women's role in language change has rarely been linked to the social position of women in the communities studied and to the related questions of what women want to express about themselves in speech. In the present study, men's and women's ways of speaking are viewed as the results of strategic and socially meaningful linguistic choices which systematically link language change to social change: linguistic innovation is a function of speakers' differential involvement in, and evaluation of, social change.

Specifically, in the linguistic repertoire of the bilingual community to be described here, one of the languages has come to symbolize a newly available social status. Young women's language choices can be understood as part of their expression of preference for this newer social identity. The young women of the community are more willing to participate in social change and in the linguistic change which symbolizes it because they are less committed than the men to the traditionally male-dominated system of subsistence agriculture, and because they have more to gain than men in embracing the newly available statuses of worker and worker's wife. In order to make this argument in detail several words of background are necessary, first about the community and second about its linguistic repertoire.

THE COMMUNITY

Oberwart (Felsöör) is a town located in the province of Burgenland in eastern Austria. It has belonged to Austria only since 1921 when as part of the post-World War I peace agreements the province was detached from Hungary. The town itself has been a speech island since the 1500s when most of the original Hungarian-speaking population of the region was decimated by the Turkish wars and was replaced by German-speaking (and in some areas Croatian-speaking) settlers. In Oberwart, which was the largest of the five remaining Hungarian-speaking communities, bilingualism in German and Hungarian became common.

During the last thirty years Oberwart has grown from a village of 600 to a town of over 5000 people because, as the county seat and new commercial centre, it has attracted migrants. These new settlers have all been monolingual German speakers, mainly people from neighboring villages, who have been trained in commerce or administration. The bilingual community today constitutes about a fourth of the town's population.

The indigenous bilinguals who will be the focus of this discussion have until recently engaged in subsistence peasant agriculture. Since World War II, however, most of the agriculturalists have become industrial workers or worker-peasants. By 1972 only about one-third of the bilingual population was employed exclusively in peasant agriculture.

In short, Oberwart is an example of the familiar post-war process of urbanization and industrialization of the countryside often reported in the literature on the transformation of peasant Europe (e.g. Franklin 1969).

THE LINGUISTIC REPERTOIRE

Bilingual communities provide a particularly salient case of the linguistic heterogeneity which characterizes all communities. In Oberwart the linguistic alternatives available to speakers include not only two easily distinguishable languages but also dialectal differences within each language. These 'dialects' are not homogeneous, invariant structures, but rather are best characterized as sets of covarying linguistic variables which have their own appropriate social uses and connotations (cf. Gumperz 1964; Ervin-Tripp 1972). It is possible for bilingual Oberwarters to move along a continuum from more standard to more local speech in either of their languages (cf. Gal 1976).

Of the many functions that code choice has been shown to serve in interaction (Hymes 1967) this paper focuses on just one and on how it is involved in change. As Blom & Gumperz (1972) have argued, alternate codes within a linguistic repertoire are usually each associated with subgroups in the community and with certain activities. It has been pointed out that a speaker's choice of code in a particular situation is part of that speaker's linguistic presentation of self. The speaker makes the choice as part of a verbal strategy to identify herself or himself with the social categories and activities the code symbolise. The choice, then, allows the speaker to express solidarity with that category or group of people. ...

THE MEANING OF CODES

Although bilingual Oberwarters use both standard and local varieties of German as well as of Hungarian, and although the choice between local and standard features in either language carries meaning in conversation, here we will be concerned only with the symbolically more important alternation between German of any sort (G) and Hungarian of any sort (H).

Today in Oberwart H symbolizes peasant status and is deprecated because peasant status itself is no longer respected. 'Peasant' is used here for a native cultural category that includes all local agriculturalists and carries a negative connotation, at least for young people. Young bilingual workers often say, in Hungarian, that only the old peasants speak Hungarian. There is no contradiction here. The young workers know that they themselves sometimes speak Hungarian and they can report on their language choices accurately. The saying refers not to actual practice but to the association of the Hungarian language with peasant status. All old peasants do speak Hungarian and speak it in more situations than anyone else.

The preferred status for young people is worker, not peasant. The world of work is a totally German-speaking world, and the language itself has come to represent the worker. The peasant parents of young workers often say about their children 'Ü má egisz nímët' (He/she is totally German already).[1] This is not a reference to citizenship, nor to linguistic abilities. Oberwarters consider themselves Austrians, not Germans, and even young people are considered bilingual, often using Hungarian in interactions with elders. The phase indicates the strong symbolic relationship between the young people's status as workers and the language which they use at work.

German also represents the money and prestige available to those who are employed, but not available to peasants. German therefore carries more prestige than Hungarian. The children of a monolingual German speaker and a bilingual speaker never learn Hungarian, regardless of which parent is bilingual. In addition, while in previous generations the ability simply to speak both German and Hungarian was the goal of Oberwarters, today there is a premium not just on speaking German, but on speaking it without any interference from Hungarian. Parents often boast that in their children's German speech 'Něm vág bele e madzsar' (The Hungarian doesn't cut into it). That is, passing as a monolingual German speaker is now the aim of young bilingual Oberwarters.

Such general statements about symbolic associations between languages, social statuses and the evaluations of those statuses do not in themselves predict language choice in particular situations. For instance, although H is negatively evaluated by young people it is nevertheless used by them in a number of interactions where, for various reasons, they choose to present themselves as peasants. Besides the values associated with languages, the three factors which must be known in order to predict choices and to describe the changes in these choices are the speaker's age and sex and the nature of the social network in which that speaker habitually interacts.

HOW DO LANGUAGE CHOICE PATTERNS CHANGE?

In any interaction between bilingual Oberwarters a choice must be made between G and H. While in most situations one or the other language is chosen, there are some interactions it is impossible to predict which language will be used by which speaker and both are often used within one short exchange. Gumperz (1976) has called this conversational code-switching. When both languages may appropriately be used Oberwarters say they are speaking 'ehodzsan dzsün' (as it comes). A description of language choice in such situations must include such variation and in this sense is comparable to the rule conflicts described for syntactic change by Bickerton (1973).

In predicting an individual's choice between the three possibilities – G, H or both – the habitual role-relationship between participants in the interaction proved to be the most important factor. Other aspects of the situation such as locale, purpose or occasion were largely irrelevant. Therefore, specification of the identity of the interlocutor was sufficient to define the social situation for the purposes of the present analysis.

We can think of informants as being ranked along a vertical axis and social situations being arranged along a horizontal axis, as in Tables 29.1 and 29.2. Note that all speakers listed in these tables are bilingual. The information is drawn from a language usage questionnaire which was constructed on the basis of native categories of interlocutors and linguistic resources. Similar scales based on systematic observation of language choice were also constructed. There was a high degree of agreement between observed usage and the questionnaire results (average agreement for men 86%, for women 90%). That is, the questionnaire results were corroborated by direct observation of language choice.

The language choices of a particular informant in all situations are indicated in the rows of Tables 29.1 and 29.2 and the choices of all informants in a particular situation are indicated in the columns. The choices of Oberwarters, arranged in this way, form a nearly perfect implicational scale. Note that for all speakers there is at least one situation in which they use only H. For almost all speakers there are some situations in which they use both G and H and some in which they use only G. Further, for any speaker there are no bilingual interlocutors with whom she or he speaks both G and H unless there are some, listed to the left of that interlocutor, with whom the speaker uses H. With few exceptions, if G is used with an interlocutor then only G is used to interlocutors listed to the right of that, and GH or H are used with those listed to the left. The occurrence of any of the three linguistic categories in a cell implies the occurrence of particular others in the cells to the left and right.

Table 29.1:   Language choice pattern of women

| | | Social situations (identity of participant) | | | | | | | | | | |
Informant	Age	1	2	3	4	5	6	7	8	9	10	11
A	14	H	GH		G	G	G			G		G
B	15	H	GH		G	G	G			G		G
C	25	H	GH	GH	GH	G	G	G	G	G		G
D	27	H	H		GH	G	G			G		G
E	17	H	H		H	GH	G			G		G
F	39	H	H		H	GH	GH			G		G
G	23	H	H		H	GH	H		GH	G		G
H	40	H	H		H	GH		GH	G	G		G
I	52	H	H	H	GH	H		GH	G	G	G	G
J	40	H	H	H	H	H	H	GH	GH	GH		G
K	35	H	H	H	H	H	H	H	GH	H		G
L	61	H	H		H	H	H	H	GH	H		G
M	50	H	H	H	H	H	H	H	H	H		G
N	60	H	H	H	H	H	H	H	H	H	GH	G
O	54	H	H		H	H	H	H	H	H	GH	H
P	63	H	H	H	H	H	H	H	H	H	GH	H
Q	64	H	H	H	H	H	H	H	H	H	H	H
R	59	H	H	H	H	H	H	H	H	H	H	H

No. of informants = 18   Scalability = 95.4%
1 = to god   7 = spouse
2 = grandparents and their generation   8 = children and their generation
3 = bilingual clients in black market   9 = bilingual government officials
4 = parents and their generation   10 = grandchildren and their generation
5 = friends and age-mate neighbors   11 = doctors
6 = brothers and sisters

G – German, H – Hungarian, GG – both German and Hungarian.

In addition, looking at the columns instead of the rows in Tables 29.1 and 29.2, and considering not one speaker at a time but the group of speakers as a whole, we see that if a speaker high on the list uses both G and H in a particular situation, then speakers lower down can be expected to use H or both in that situation. But if the speaker at the top of the list uses H, then all others use H in that situation as well. The presence of any one of the three linguistic categories in a cell restricts which of the three may occur in the cells above and below that one. When one speaker's choice of language in a particular situation is known it also gives information about the possibilities open to those lower on the list and those higher on the list. The closer an informant is to the top of the list the more situations there are in which he or she uses G. The closer to the bottom, the more H he or she uses. Tables 29.1

Table 29.2: Language choice pattern of men

		Social situations (identity of participant)										
Informant	Age	1	2	3	4	5	6	7	8	9	10	11
A	17	H	GH			G	G	G		G		G
B	25	H	H		GH	G	G			G		G
C	42		H		GH	G	G	G	G	G		G
D	20	H	H	H	H	GH	G	G	G	G		G
E	22	H	H		H	GH	GH			G		G
F	62	H	H	H	H	H	H	GH	GH	GH	G	G
G	63	H	H		H	H	H	H		GH		G
H	64	H	H	H	H	H	H	H	GH	GH		G
I	43	H	H		H	H	H	H	G	H		G
J	41	H	H	H	H	H	H	H	GH	H		H
K	54	H	H		H	H	H	H	H	H		G
L	61	H	H		H	H	H	H	H	G	GH	G
M	74	H	H		H	H	H	H	H	H	GH	H
N	58	G	H		H	H	H	H	H	H	H	H

No. of informants = 14   Scalability = 95.2%
1 = to god   7 = spouse
2 = grandparents and their generation   8 = children and their generation
3 = bilingual clients in black market   9 = bilingual government officials
4 = parents and their generation   10 = grandchildren and their generation
5 = friends and age-mate neighbors   11 = doctors
6 = brothers and sisters

G – German, H – Hungarian, GG – both German and Hungarian.

and 29.2 have scalabilities of 95.4% and 95.2% respectively, showing that there are only a few exceptions to these generalizations.[2]

Given this, it is worth considering the factors that determine the place of a speaker on the scale. Two factors determine the degree to which a person uses H as opposed to G: the person's age and her or his social network. Because historical evidence (cf. Imre 1973; Kovács 1942: 73–6) shows that present-day age differences are not due to age-grading of language choice, we can take age (apparent time) as a surrogate for repeated sampling over real time (cf. Labov 1972 for details of this strategy).

Social network is defined here as all the people (contacts) an individual spoke to in the course of a unit of time. The average amount of time for all informants was seven days. Each of these network contacts was assigned to one of two categories: (a) those who lived in households which owned either pig or cows, (b) those who lived in households which owned neither pigs nor cows. Oberwarters themselves define those who own cows and pigs as peasants. The peasantness of a person's network, expressed as the percentage of contacts who fit into category (a) is, in effect, a measure of that person's social involvement with the category of persons with which the use of H is associated.

The more peasants the individual has in her or his social network the greater the number of social situations in which that individual uses H. In fact, in most cases a *person's own status*, whether peasant, worker or some gradation in between, *was not as accurate a predictor of his or her choices as the status of the person's social contacts*. These results lend support to the notion that social networks are instrumental in constraining speakers' linguistic presentation of self.

The three-way relationship between language choices, age, and peasantness of social network can be demonstrated by ranking informants on each of the measures and then correlating the rankings with each other. Table 29.3 shows the correlations for this sample of informants. All are significant at the 0.01 level. Note that this group of informants was not formally selected as a representative sample of the bilingual community, but rather was chosen to represent the entire range of the two variables – age and social network – so that conclusions could be drawn about the effect of each variable on changing language choices. In order to distinguish the effects on language choice of time on the one hand and the effects of changing social networks on the other, both old people who had never been totally involved in peasant agriculture and young people who were very much involved were included in the sample.

On the basis of the rank correlations the following brief outline of the synchronic pattern of language choice can be drawn. For the sample as a whole, the more peasants in one's social network the more likely it is that one will use H in a large number of situations. The older one is the more likely it is that one will use H in a large number of situations. Young people who interact only with workers use the least H, older people who interact mostly with peasants use the most H. Older people who associate mostly with workers are closest in their language choices to people much younger than themselves, while very young people who associated mostly with peasants use more H than others their own age.

Table 29.3: Correlations between language choice and age, language choice and peasantness of network*

	All informants	*Women*	*Men*
Language choice and age	0.82	0.93	0.69
Language choice and peasantness of network	0.78	0.74	0.78
	N = 32	N = 18	N = 14

*Spearman rank correlation coefficients all significant at the 0.01 level.

Because historical evidence rules out the possibility of age-grading and because the sample allows one to disentangle the effects of time and that of networks, it is possible to hypothesize the following process of change. Changes in language choices occur situation by situation. The rule for one situation is always first categorical for the old form (H), then variable (GH), before it is categorical for the new form (G). As speaker's networks become less and less peasant they use H in fewer and fewer situations. And, in a parallel but separate process, as time passes new generations use H in fewer and fewer situations regardless of the content of their social networks.

DIFFERENCES BETWEEN MEN AND WOMEN

The implicational scales describing choices seem to indicate no differences between men and women. Both men and women show the same kinds of implicational relationships in the same ordered list of situations. However, the rank correlations of language choice, age and peasantness of network, summarized in Table 29.3, present a more complicated picture. Here the issue is whether age and social networks are equally well correlated with language choice for men and women. In fact they are not: for men the correlation between social network and language choice is about the same as the correlation between age and language choice (0.78 and 0.69 respectively). For women age alone is more closely correlated with language choice (0.93) than is the social network measure (0.74). This difference between men and women is significant at the 0.05 level.

In short, there is a difference between men and women in the way each is going through the process of change in language choice. If we distinguish three twenty-year generations, separate the men from the women and those with very peasant networks from those with non-peasant networks, it is possible to illustrate the process at work. Informants' networks ranged from 13 per cent peasant contacts to 94% peasant contacts. This continuum was divided into two parts. All those scoring at or above the median were put in the peasant network category in Figure 29.1, all those scoring below the median were in the nonpeasant network category.

Figure 29.1 illustrates the fact that for men there is a very regular pattern in the correlations. From the oldest to the youngest generation use of G increases, but for each generation this increase is greatest for those whose social networks include a majority of non-peasants. Among the men the youngest group as a whole uses less H than any of the others. But those young men with heavily peasant networks do use more H. Regardless of the negative evaluations, for these young men expression of peasant identity is still preferred for many situations.

For women the process is different. First we find that in the oldest generation this sample includes not one person with a non-peasant network.

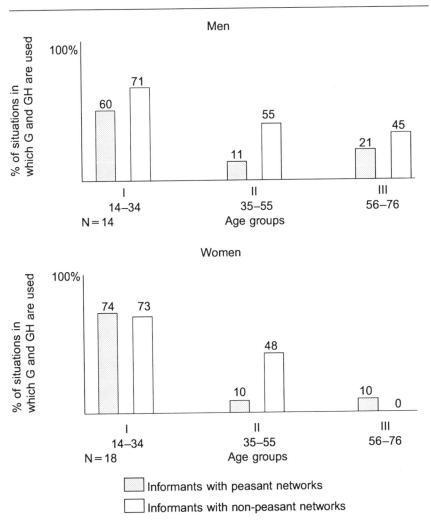

Figure 29.1: Percentage of G and GH language choices of informants with peasant and non-peasant social networks in three age groups

This is not a sampling error but reflects the limited range of activities, and therefore of social contacts, open to women before World War II. In the middle generation the women's pattern matches that of men exactly. Many women of the generation reaching maturity during and after World War II left the peasant home, if only temporarily, to work in inns, factories and shops. Often they remained in contact with those they befriended. As with the men, those who have heavily peasant networks use more H than those who do not.

The youngest generation of women differs both from the older women and from the men. First, these youngest women use more G and less H than anyone else in the community, including the youngest men. In addition, for these women, *peasantness of social network makes no difference in language choice*. Young women with peasant networks use Hungarian as rarely as young women with non-peasant networks. Recall that for all the men, including the youngest, peasantness of network did make a difference since it was associated with more use of H.

To understand these differences it is necessary to go back to the activities from which the languages derive their meanings and evaluations. For the most recent generation of women, peasant life is a much less attractive choice than it is for men. Now that other opportunities are open to these young women, they reject peasant life as a viable alternative. It will be argued here that their language choices are part of this rejection.

There are some young men who, despite a general preference for industrial and commercial employment, want to take over family farms. Some of these young men have the newly developing attitude that farming can be an occupation, a 'Beruf', like any other. These are men whose families own enough land to make agriculture if not as lucrative as wage work at least a satisfactory livelihood. In contrast, young women, since World War II, have not been willing to take over the family farm when this opportunity is offered to them. More importantly, they specifically state that they do not want to marry peasant men. The life of a peasant wife is seen by Oberwart young women as particularly demeaning and difficult when compared to the other choices which have recently become available to them.

Let us compare the choices open to Oberwart young men and women as they see them. For men the life possibilities are (a) to be an industrial or construction worker (usually a commuter coming home only on weekends), (b) to be a peasant-worker, holding two full-time jobs, and (c) to be a full-time agriculturalist. This last is felt by Oberwart men to have the advantage of independence – no orders from strangers – and the disadvantage of lack of cash and prestige. But it is generally agreed that while agricultural work was once more grueling and difficult than factory and construction work, this is no longer the case. Although peasant men still work longer hours than those in industry, machines such as the tractor and the combine make men's farm work highly mechanized and considerably less difficult than it once was.

For women the life possibilities depend mainly on whom they marry. The peasant wife typically spends the day doing farm work: milking, feeding pigs, hoeing, planting and harvesting potatoes and a few other rootcrops. Her evenings are spent doing housework. Industriousness is traditionally considered a young peasant wife's most valuable quality.

There are machines now available which lighten the work of the peasant wife considerably, including the washing machine, the electric stove and the silo (which eliminates the need for rootcrops as cattle feed). But in peasant households the male labor-saving machines are always acquired before any of the ones which lighten women's work. For instance the silo, which is perhaps the most substantial work-saver for the peasant wife, is never built before a combine is purchased, and the combine itself is among the last and most expensive of the machines acquired. In this Oberwart exemplifies the pattern all over Europe, where, for instance, the German small peasant's wife in 1964 averaged over the year 17 more work hours per week than her husband (Franklin 1969: 37–44). In addition, although peasant life in Oberwart is less male-dominated than, for instance, in the Balkans (compare Denich 1974 with Fél & Hofer 1969: 113–44), nevertheless for the peasant wife the independence which is said to compensate the peasant man for his work is not freely available. In fact, being a young peasant wife often means living under the authority of a mother-in-law who supervises the kitchen and women's farm work generally.

In marked contrast, marriage to a worker involves only household tasks and upkeep of a kitchen garden. Wives of workers are sometimes employed as maids or salespersons, but mostly they hold part-time jobs or are not employed at all. Because of the increased access to money, because agricultural equipment is not needed and because some of the women themselves contribute part of the money, electric stoves and washing machines are among the first appliances bought by working married couples, thereby further lightening the wife's work load. Peasant wives work far more than peasant men. Peasant men work more hours than worker men. Worker's wives, especially if not employed, often work fewer hours than their husbands.

This contrast is not lost on young Oberwart women. When discussing life choices they especially dwell on the dirtiness and heaviness of peasant work. Rejection of the use of local Hungarian, the symbol of peasant status, can be seen as part of the rejection, by young women, of peasant status and life generally. They do not want to be peasants; they do not present themselves as peasants in speech.

Mothers of marriageable daughters specifically advise them against marriage to peasants. Oberwarters agree that 'Paraszt legin nëm kap nüöt' (Peasant lads can't get women). For instance, in reference to a particular young couple an old man remarked: 'Az e Trüumfba jár, az fog neki tehen szart lapáni? Abbu má paraszt nëm lesz, az má zicher!' (She works at the [local bra factory], *she's* going to shovel cow manure for him? She'll never be a peasant, that's for sure.) Although the young men themselves are usually also reluctant to become peasants, for those who nevertheless choose family agriculture as their livelihood, the anti-peasant attitudes of the community's young women present a problem.

If in recent years Oberwart young women have not wanted to marry peasant men, and if they have acted on this preference, then Oberwart peasant men must have found wives elsewhere. The town's marriage records

Table 29.4:   Endogamous marriages of all bilingual
Oberwarters and bilingual male peasant Oberwarters

	% Endogamous marriages of all marriages	% Endogamous marriages of male peasants
1911–40	71%	87%
1941–60	65	54
1961–72	32	0

Source: Marriage Register, City of Oberwart.

should provide evidence for the difference in attitudes between young men
and young women.

The general trend in Oberwart in the post-war years has been away
from the traditional village endogamy and towards exogamy. For instance,
Table 29.4 shows that between 1911 and 1940 72% and 1940 72% of the
marriages of bilinguals in Oberwart were endogamous. Between 1961 and
1972 only 32% were. But for the bilingual peasant men of Oberwart the
figures are different. As Table 29.4 indicates, between 1911 and 1940 a
larger percentage of peasant men married endogamously than all bilingual
Oberwarters (87%). Between 1941 and 1960, however, this was reversed.
Finally, by 1961–72, when 32% of all bilingual Oberwarters married
endogamously, not one peasant man married endogamously. Those
peasant men who did marry during those years found wives in the
neighbouring small German monolingual villages where being a peasant
wife has not been negatively valued. In short, the marriage records provide
evidence that young Oberwart women's stated attitudes towards peasant
men have been translated into action. The effect of this is discussed below.

CONCLUSION

There are two ways, one direct and one indirect, in which the attitudes and
choices of young bilingual women are changing the language usage pattern
in this community. Directly, the young women, even those with heavily
peasant networks refuse, in most situations, to present themselves as
peasants by using H. This contrasts with the language choices of older
women and has the general effect that more German is used in more
interactions in the community. It also contrasts with the choices of young
men, who use Hungarian in more interactions than the young women and
who are constrained by the peasantness of their social networks so that
those with heavily peasant networks choose local Hungarian in more
interactions than those with nonpeasant networks.

Indirectly, young women's marriage preferences are also having a linguistic effect. They refuse to marry local peasant men, preferring workers instead. As a result, exactly that small group of young men most likely to be using Hungarian in many situations, that is the ones engaged in peasant agriculture, are the ones who have married German monolingual women with the greatest frequency in the last decade or so. Because the children of marriages between monolingual German speakers and bilingual Hungarian–German speakers in Oberwart rarely if every learn Hungarian, in an indirect way the present generation of young women is limiting the language possibilities of the next generation.

In exploring the reasons for the difference between young men's and young women's language choices, evidence was presented showing that in their stated attitudes and their marriage choices the women evaluate peasant life more negatively than the men and reject the social identity of peasant wife. The women of Oberwart feel they have more to gain then men by embracing the new opportunities of industrial employment. Also, considering the male-dominated nature of East European peasant communities generally and the lives of Oberwart women in particular, women have less to lose in rejecting the traditional peasant roles and values.

This paper has argued that women's language choices and their linguistic innovativeness in this community are the linguistic expressions of women's greater participation in social change. The linguistic pattern is best understood by considering the social meanings of the available languages and the strategic choices and evaluations which men and women make concerning the ways of life symbolized by those languages.

NOTES

The data reported here were gathered during 1974 as part of dissertation fieldwork supported by a NIMH Anthropology Traineeship at the University of California, Berkeley. My thanks to Paul Kay, John Gumperz and E. A. Hammel for their many suggestions. An earlier version of this paper was presented at the symposium on 'Language and Sex Roles' at the 74th Annual Meeting of the AAA, December 1975.

1 The orthography is a modified version of Imre (1971) and of the Hungarian dialect atlas.
2 'Scalability' is the proportion of cells that fit the scale model. Inapplicable cells (those left empty in Tables 29.1 and 29.2) were omitted from the denominator.

REFERENCES

Bickerton, D. (1973) 'The Nature of a Creole Continuum', *Language*, **44**, pp. 640–69.
Blom, J. P. & Gumperz, J. J. (1972) 'Social Meaning in Linguistic Structures: Code Switching in Norway', in Gumperz, J. J. & Hymes, D. (eds) *Directions in Sociolinguistics* (New York: Holt, Rinehart & Winston).

Denich, B. (1974) 'Sex and Power in the Balkans', in Rosaldo, M. S. & Lamphere, L. (eds) *Woman, Culture and Society* (Stanford, CA: Stanford University Press).

Ervin-Tripp, S. (1972) 'On Sociolinguistic Rules: Alternation and Co-occurrence', in Gumperz, J. J. & Hymes, D. (eds) *Directions in Sociolingusitics* (New York: Holt, Rinehart & Winston).

Fasold, R. (1968) 'A Sociolinguistic Study of the Pronunciation of Three Vowels in Detroit Speech' (Washington, DC: Center for Applied Linguistics) Mimeo.

Fél, E. and Hofer, T. (1969) *Proper Peasants* (Chicago: Aldine).

Franklin, S. H. (1969) *The European Peasantry* (London: Methuen).

Gal, S. (1976) *Language Change and its Social Determinants in a Bilingual Community* (Ann Arbor, MI: University Microfilms).

Gumperz, J. J. (1964) 'Linguistic and Social Interaction in Two Communities', *American Anthropologist*, **66**(6), Part II, pp. 137–54.

Gumperz, J. J. (1976) 'The Sociolinguistic Significance of Conversational Code-switching', Ms.

Hymes, D. (1967) 'Models of the Interaction of Language and Social Setting', *Journal of Social Issues*, **23**(2), pp. 8–28.

Imre, S. (1971) 'A Felsoori Nyelvjárás (The Oberwart Dialect)', *Nyelvtudományi Értekezések* 72 (Budapest).

Imre, S. (1973) 'Az Ausztriai (Burgenlandi) Magyar Azorványok (The Hungarian Minority Group in Austria)', in *Népi Kultura – Népi Társadalom* (Folk Culture – Folk Society) (Budapest: Akadémiai Kiadó).

Kovács, M. (1942) 'A Felsoori Magyar Népsziget (The Hungarian Folk-Island of Oberwart)' (Budapest: Sylvester-Nyomda).

Labov, W. (1972) *Sociolinguistic Patterns* (Philadelphia, PA: University of Pennsylvania Press).

Nichols, P. (1976) 'Black Women in the Rural South: Conservative and Innovative', Paper presented to the Conference on the Sociology of the Languages of American Women (New Mexico: Las Cruces).

Trudgill, P. (1972) 'Sex, Covert Prestige and Linguistic Change in the Urban British English of Norwich', *Language in Society*, **1**, pp. 179–95.

Part VII
Interactional Sociolinguistics

Calling one approach to sociolinguistics 'interactional', and so seeming to suggest that most of sociolinguistics in not interested in communicative interaction, is potentially misleading. Many of the chapters in previous parts of the Reader have examined language in interactional settings. But there is some substance to the claim that many traditions in sociolinguistics have not *explicitly* treated language use in interactional terms. They have examined the distributions of speech-forms or languages within and between social groups, or attitudes to particular varieties, or considered broader socio-logical or social policy questions relating to such distributions. Interactional sociolinguistics, if we give it a special place in the discipline, is different in that it sets out to understand language in society *in and through* the dynamic processes of talk itself.

The questions asked by interactional sociolinguistics may not be fundamentally different from those asked in other sociolinguistic approaches. How do language and social identity relate to one another, what forms does linguistic prejudice take, or what happens when language groups come into contact with one another? But an interactionally designed study will be based on a commitment to the particular moment (rather than analytical deduction), to 'on-line' analysis (rather than abstraction), and to the insiders' perspective (rather than the interpretations of an objective researcher). So there are direct connections to be made with the ethnographic priorities of Hymes and Gumperz (Chapters 1 and 5) and the arguments that have surfaced in several places against a strictly empiricist model of sociolinguistics (e.g. Chapters 6, 7, 11 and 12).

Interactional sociolinguistics aligns with *social constructivist* approaches in social science. More accurately, social constructivism was partly *founded* on the theoretical and interpretive work of ethnographic sociolinguists. As we acknowledged in the Introduction to the book, we have had to draw a rather arbitrary dividing line between work which is uncontroversially socio-linguistics and the many other sorts of research that have focused on discourse, conversation and social interaction. This problem is particularly acute in this section of the Reader. One way of exploring this overlap is through this book's companion volume: *Discourse: A Reader and Coursebook*.

Interactional sociolinguistics is most closely associated with the work of John Gumperz, and his chapter (30) in this section establishes the theoretical basis and the practical usefulness of this approach. Gumperz's first example is of how a small detail of speech style, a falling rather than a rising intonation pattern on a single word, can trigger complex patterns of interpretation and misinterpretation between members of different cultural groups. Gumperz's label for this general process is *conversational inferencing*, and he refers to the linguistic or communicative features that trigger it as *contextualization cues*. In ways that are very reminiscent of the social psychological research in Part IV, Gumperz emphasizes that what is sociolinguistically significant in interethnic interaction may not in fact be the styles or codes themselves that are being used. Instead, it is participants' culture-bound processes of perception, evaluation and interpretation. The sources of people's inferences may be details of speech rhythm or the placement of words and phrases. This is why detailed transcripts of particular episodes have to be the focus of analysis, rather than, say, summary statistics.

Viv Edwards continues the theme of inter-ethnic communication introduced in Gumperz's chapter. She deals with the use of Patois (or Creole speech styles) by Afro-Caribbean schoolchildren in Britain, with the interactional contexts and consequences of using Patois, as well as with speakers' perceptions of its use. One of the main social psychological concepts underlying the folk notions of Patois is the negative stereotype (see Hewstone and Giles in Chapter 21) of Patois speakers being predominantly young, disaffected, academically underachieving males. As Edwards points out, this is a misplaced stereotype. Many Patois speakers are females. Many do well at school and show little hostility towards the white community.

Edwards's interactional model of Patois use departs from the speaker-centred, stereotyping approach. She argues that Black pupils' shifting between Patois and the local dialect of English depends on the context of interaction and other local concerns. For example, in pupil–pupil interaction, Patois, which has a strong bonding value for some Black adolescents, is the normal, expected, or 'unmarked' code. If a speaker uses English instead of Patois with peers, she or he is likely to be perceived as betraying his or her roots. In Black–White interactions, Patois can be used symbolically to exclude White pupils from the Black community. Similarly, the marked use of Patois in the classroom when addressing a teacher or in classroom asides is most likely to mark the pupil's defiance of the teacher's power and authority.

Edwards's data are not always interactional in the same sense as Gumperz. She relies on her subjects' self-reports and accounts of interactional situations where Patois and English are used, as well as on transcripts of interaction itself. Even so, the data show how both codes are perceived to be manipulated in interaction, to construct solidarity and shared identity between Black interactants, and isolation, distance and defiance of authority in Black–White interaction.

Questions of *power, control and dominance* are again of crucial importance in Pamela Fishman's chapter. On more than one occasion Gumperz mentions that there is no inherent difference between intercultural and intracultural communication when it comes to interpretive problems or 'miscommunication'. Disparities in power expressed through interaction and resulting social inequalities are very much a feature of communication within monolingual or monocultural groups. Fishman's chapter in this section is an analysis of the conversational roles adopted by White, middle-class Americans in *male–female interactions*. Fishman's data are on a small scale. Only three couples are involved, but they were audio-recorded over several months. Her findings were that women did more conversational *work* than men. They asked questions and used many attention-getting devices, particularly in attempts to keep conversation going in the face of men's relative silence. Women were supportive in their uses of particles like *yeah*, *umm* and *huh*; when men used them, it was in the expression of lack of interest!

There is a methodological tension in Fishman's study. She needs to examine the particularities of interaction in order to make the rather subtle interpretations of communicative function on which her study depends – for example the functioning of a *yeah* particle. On the other hand, her conclusions are very clearly couched in terms of frequencies (e.g. women asking more questions), when her methods do not fully allow her to support distributional claims. Fishman's study was, quite rightly, very influential in opening up an interactional basis for sociolinguistic studies of gender. But the problem of needing to bring together qualitative and quantitative insights in sociolinguistic research is far from being resolved.

With Ochs's chapter, we return once again to the ethnographic approach advocated by Hymes and Saville-Troike (Chapters 1 and 11). Ochs examines the principles and organization of the acquisition of conversational competence by children in Samoa and compares them with those in (broadly defined) middle-class Western society. Research needs to avoid making culturally limited interpretations and generalizations. The cultural tradition in sociolinguistics (see Part VIII) has continually questioned whether research-based claims do in fact carry over from the research context (which is often European or North American) into other cultural settings. Ochs undermines some Western assumptions about the 'universal' principles and organization of child language acquisition – what she calls *language socialization*. She examines patterns of interaction between Samoan children and their caregivers.

Ochs finds that in Samoan society language acquisition tends *not* to take place through one-to-one, direct, verbal interaction common in much of Western, middle-class society. Instead, children are cared for and talked to by a larger number of caregivers, including other children (e.g. older siblings). Samoan children hear plenty of language, but little of it is directed at them. According to Ochs, this culture-specific patterning of interaction during socialization gives children from different backgrounds varied experiences of their own place in a community and of societal hierarchies. This position can be linked with the Whorfian idea that the 'fashions of speaking' of a community shape its cognitive and cultural world view (see Chapter 34).

PART VII: FURTHER READING

Brown, P. and Levinson, S. (1987) *Politeness: Some Universals in Language Usage* (Cambridge: Cambridge University Press).

Goffman, E. (1959) *The Presentation of Self in Everyday Life* (Harmondsworth: Penguin).

Gumperz, J. J. (ed.) (1982) *Language and Social Identity* (Cambridge: Cambridge University Press).

Kendon, A. (1990) *Conducting Interaction* (Cambridge: Cambridge University Press).

Kramarae, C. (1981) *Women and Men Speaking: Frameworks for Analysis* (Rowley, MA: Newbury House).

Peräkylä, A. (1995) *AIDS Counselling: Institutional Interaction and Clinical Practice* (Cambridge: Cambridge University Press).

Preisler, B. (1986) *Linguistic Sex Roles in Conversation: Social Variation in the Expression of Tentativeness in English* (Berlin: Mouton de Gruyter).

Sudnow, D. (ed.) (1972) *Studies in Social Interaction* (New York: Free Press).

Tannen, D. (1984) *Conversational Style: Analyzing Talk among Friends* (Norwood, NJ: Ablex).

Tannen, D. (ed.) (1993) *Gender and Conversational Interaction* (New York and Oxford: Oxford University Press).

Taylor, T. J. and Cameron, D. (1987) *Analysing Conversation* (Oxford: Pergamon).

30 Interethnic Communication

John J. Gumperz

On the practical level, the study of conversational inference may lead to an explanation for the endemic and increasingly serious communication problems that affect private and public affairs in our society. We can begin to see why individuals who speak English well and have no difficulty in producing grammatical English sentences may nevertheless differ significantly in what they perceive as meaningful discourse cues. Accordingly, their assumptions about what information is to be conveyed, how it is to be ordered and put into words and their ability to fill in the unverbalized information they need to make sense of what transpires may also vary. This may lead to misunderstandings that go unnoticed in the course of an interaction, but can be revealed and studied empirically through conversational analysis. ...

To begin with, let me give one brief example to illustrate the scope of the analysis and the subconscious nature of the interpretive process involved.

In a staff cafeteria at a major British airport, newly hired Indian and Pakistani women were perceived as surly and uncooperative by their supervisor as well as by the cargo handlers whom they served. Observation revealed that while relatively few words were exchanged, the intonation and manner in which these words were pronounced were interpreted negatively. For example, when a cargo handler who had chosen meat was asked whether he wanted gravy, a British assistant would say 'Gravy?' using rising intonation. The Indian assistants, on the other hand, would say the word using falling intonation: 'Gravy.' We taped relevant sequences, including interchanges like these, and asked the employees to paraphrase what was meant in each case. At first the Indian workers saw no difference. However, the English teacher and the cafeteria supervisor could point out that 'Gravy,' said with a falling intonation, is likely to be interpreted as 'This is gravy,' i.e. not interpreted as an offer but rather as a statement, which in the context seems redundant and consequently rude. When the Indian women heard this, they began to understand the reactions they had been getting all

Source: 'Interethnic Communication' in Gumperz, J. J. (ed.) *Discourse Strategies* (1982) (Cambridge: Cambridge University Press) pp. 172–86.

along which had until then seemed incomprehensible. They then spontaneously recalled intonation patterns which had seemed strange to them when spoken by native English speakers. At the same time, supervisors learned that the Indian women's falling intonation was their normal way of asking questions in that situation, and that no rudeness or indifference was intended.

After several discussion/teaching sessions of this sort, both the teacher and the cafeteria supervisor reported a distinct improvement in the attitude of the Indian workers both to their work and to their customers. It seemed that the Indian workers had long sensed they had been misunderstood but, having no way of talking about this in objective terms, they had felt they were being discriminated against. We had not taught the cafeteria workers to speak appropriate English; rather, by discussing the results of our analysis in mixed sessions and focusing on context-bound interpretive preferences rather than on attitudes and stereotypes, we have suggested a strategy for self-diagnosis of communication difficulties. In short, they regained confidence in their own innate ability to learn.

The first of the longer case studies examines excerpts from an interview–counselling session recorded in an industrial suburb in London. The participants are both educated speakers of English; one is a Pakistani teacher of mathematics, who although born in South Asia went to secondary school and university in England. The other is a staff member of a center funded by the Department of Employment to deal with interethnic communication problems in British industry. The teacher has been unable to secure permanent employment and having been told that he lacks communication skills for high school teaching, he has been referred to the center. While both participants agree on the general definition of the event as an interview–counselling session, their expectations of what is to be accomplished, and especially about what needs to be said, differ radically. Such differences in expectation are of course not unusual even where conversationalists have similar cultural backgrounds. Conversations often begin with an introductory phase where common themes are negotiated and differences in expectation adjusted. What is unusual about this situation is that participants, in spite of repeated attempts at adjustment over a period of more than an hour, utterly fail to achieve such negotiation. Our analysis concentrates on the reasons for this failure and shows how it is based on differences in linguistic and socio-cultural knowledge.

Methods used for the discovery of contextualization cues rely partly on comparative analysis of a wide variety of ethnically homogeneous in-group and ethnically mixed encounters. Indirect elicitation procedures are used, along with experiments in which participants in a conversation or others of similar background listen to tape-recorded passages and are questioned to discover the perceptual cues they use in arriving at their interpretation.

Case study 1

A: Indian male speaker
B: British female speaker
The recording begins almost immediately after the initial greetings.
B has just asked A for permission to record the interview, and A's first
utterance is in reply to her request.

1. A: exactly the same way as you, as you would like
2.   ⌈ to put on
3. B: ⌊ Oh no, no
4. A: there will be some of ⌈ the things you would like to
5. B: ⌊ yes
6. A: write it down
7. B: that's right, that's right (laughs)
8. A: but, uh ... anyway it's up to you
        (pause, about 1 second)
9. B: um, (high pitch) ... well ... ⌈ I I Miss C.
10. A: ⌊ first of all
11. B: hasn't said anything to me you see
        (pause, about 2 seconds)
12. A: I am very sorry if ⌈ she hasn't spoken anything
13. B: (softly)   ⌊ doesn't matter
14. A: on the telephone at least,
15. B: doesn't matter
16. A: but ah ... it was very important uh thing for me
17. B: ye:s. Tell, tell me what it ⌈ is you want
18. A: ⌊ umm
19.   Um, may I first of all request for the introduction please
20. B: Oh yes sorry⌈
21. A: ⌊ I am sorry
        (pause, about 1 second)
22. B: I am E.
23. A: Oh yes ⌈ (breathy) I see ... oh yes ... very nice
24. B: ⌊ and I am a teacher here in the Center
25. A: very nice │
26. B: ⌊ and we run ⌈
27. A: ⌊ pleased to meet you (laughs) ⌈
28. B: ⌊ different
29.   courses (A laughs) yes, and you are Mr A?
30. A: N.A.
31. B: N.A. yes, yes, I see (laughs). OK, that's the
32.   introduction (laughs)
33. A: would it be enough introduction?

Note that apart from a few seemingly odd phrases the passage shows no readily apparent differences in linguistic code, yet the oddness of A's question, (33) 'Would it be enough introduction?' coming as it does after B's (31) 'Okay, that's the introduction,' clearly suggests that something is going wrong. Normally one might explain this sort of utterance and the awkward exchanges that precede it in psychological terms as odd behavior, reflecting participants' personal motives. But a closer examination of the interactive synchrony of the entire passage, as revealed in the coordination of speakers' messages with backchannel cues such as 'um,' 'yes' or 'no no,' suggests that the problem is more complex than that.

Studies of interactive synchrony (Erickson & Schultz 1982), focusing primarily on nonverbal signs, have shown that in conversation of all kinds, speakers' moves and listeners' responses are synchronized in such a way as to conform to a regular and measurable rhythmic beat. Most longer encounters alternate between synchronous or smooth phases exhibiting a high degree of coordination and phases of asychrony which Erickson calls 'uncomfortable moments.' Experiments carried on at Berkeley (Bennett, Erickson & Gumperz 1976, Bennett 1981) with ethnically mixed student groups reveal that the relationship of back-channel signals to speakers' utterances is closely related to interactional synchrony at the nonverbal level. In synchronous phases back-channel signals stand in regular relationship to points of maximum information content in the speaker's message, as marked by stress and intonation contour. Asynchronous phases lack such coordination. It has furthermore been noted that when participants are asked to monitor video- or audiotapes of their own encounters, they have little difficulty in agreeing on the boundaries between synchronous and asynchronous phases. But when they are asked to interpret what was going on in these phases, their interpretations tend to differ. Conversational synchrony thus yields empirical measures of conversational cooperation which reflect automatic behavior, independent of prior semantic assumptions about the content or function of what was said. Analysis of conversational synchrony can form a useful starting point for comparative analysis of interpretive processes.

In interactions among individuals who share socio-cultural background, which are not marked by other overt signs of disagreement, asynchronous movements tend to reflect the initial negotiation transititions in verbal activity or routines, or unexpected moves by one or another participant, and are relatively brief. In our passage here, however, lack of coordination is evident throughout.

Note, for example, the placement of B's 'oh no' (3). In a coordinated exchange this should appear shortly after A's verb phrase 'write it down' (6). Here it occurs after the auxiliary 'like.' Similarly B's 'yes' (5) overlaps with A's 'the' (4). The same is true of B's 'doesn't matter' (13) and A's 'umm' (18). Similar asynchronous overlaps are found throughout the tape. In line 9

B shifts to a high-pitched 'um, well,' and as she is about to go into her message, A simultaneously begins with 'first of all.' In addition there are premature starts, i.e. starts which lack the usual rhythmic interval, in lines 21, 23 and 25; in lines 8, 11 and 21, we find arhythmic pauses of one, two, and one seconds respectively.

Lack of coordination seems to increase rather than decrease with the progress of the interaction, culminating in several bursts of nervous laughter (27, 29, 31, 32) which suggest that both participants are becoming increasingly ill at ease. Given what we know about conversational rhythm and synchrony there is strong evidence for systematic differences in contextualization and interpretive strategies in this interaction.

To find out what these differences are, we must turn to content. The passage divides into roughly three sequentially ordered subepisodes. These are distinct in manifest topic. But beyond that, they also have semantic import in terms of the role relations and expected outcomes they imply, and can thus be seen as reflecting distinct activity types.

The first subepisode begins with A's response to B's request for permission to tape record. This gives A the option either to agree or to refuse, and further to explain or justify his decision. His words here indirectly suggest that he is agreeing and is taking advantage of his option, in order to comment on the importance of his problem. B, however, does not seem to understand what he's trying to do. Her 'no, no' (3) suggests she is defensive about her request to record, and her 'that's right' (7) seems intended to cut short the preliminaries. In line 9, B attempts to lead into the interview proper. Her rise in pitch is of the type English speakers use elsewhere in our comparative tapes to mark shifts in focus to introduce important new information. A's interruption here suggests that he either does not recognize or disagrees with her change in focus.

Subepisode 2, lines 9–17, consists of B's indirect attempts to get A to state his problem. These are temporarily sidetracked by his responses. In subepisode 3 B once more tries to get started with the interview proper, whereupon A responds with an asynchronous 'umm' and counters by asking for an introduction. The remainder of the passage then focuses on that introduction.

Looking in more detail at the process of speaker–listener coordination, we note than in line 11, B simply ignores A's interruption. Her message is followed by a long pause of two seconds. A's statement following that pause is marked by what, when compared to his preceding and following statements, is unusually slow rhythm and highly contoured intonation. 'Very sorry' (12) and 'very important' (16) are stressed. Many Indian English speakers readily identify the prosody here as signalling that the speaker is seriously concerned and wants the listener to understand the gravity of his situation before he goes on to give more detail. Similarly contouring occurs in a number of other interethnic encounters as well as elsewhere in the present interview. Listeners of English background tend not to be attuned to the signalling value of such cues; those who notice this shift in prosody tend to dismiss it as a rather minor and somewhat misplaced indication of affect. What we seem to be faced with is an ethnically specific signalling system where contoured prosody and slowed rhythm contrast with flattened contours and normal rhythm to suggest personal concern.

In this episode, B is either unaware of this signalling convention or has decided to ignore it, since she fails to respond. In Western English conventions her statement 'Miss C. hasn't said anything to me' counts as an indirect request for more detail as to what the problem is. She seems to want to go on with the interview and when A does not respond as expected she twice interrupts with 'doesn't matter' (13, 1ʃ). Both her interruptions are asynchronous with A's talk. She seems to be interpreting A's statement as a somewhat irrelevant formulaic excuse, rather than as a preamble, or an attempt to prepare the ground for what is to come. As A continues, 'it was very important,' she responds with a 'yes' spoken with normal intonation, and without raising her pitch at all she attempts once more to begin the interview proper. When A then asks for the introduction, she counters with 'oh yes sorry,' whereupon A immediately, i.e. without the normal rhythmic interval, says: 'I am sorry.' Now B seems thrown off balance. She takes a full second to formulate her reply, and it is easy to see why. Her own 'sorry' indicates that she interprets A's preceding remark as implying she has been remiss, but when he himself then replies with 'I am am sorry' he seems to be suggesting it is his own fault.

When B then gives her name in line 22, A replies with a very breathy and contoured 'very nice.' Indian English speakers who listen to the tape will readily identify this last as a formulaic utterance. It is the Indian English equivalent of Urdu *bǝhut ǝccha* which is used as a back-channel sign of interest similar to our 'OK, go on.' The breathy enunciation and contoured intonation are signs of polite emphasis. For Western English speakers, however, the meaning is quite different. 'Very nice' is used to respond to children who behave properly. In this situation moreover, it might be interpreted as having sexual overtones. In any case, B ignores the remark and in line 26 attempts to shift the focus away from herself to talk about the center where she works. A does not follow her shift in focus, however. His 'pleased to meet you' focuses once more on her as a person. This is either intentional or it could be the result of his slowness in following her shift in focus. In any case his laughing now suggests lack of ease or nervousness.

B continues as if he hadn't spoken and then when A laughs again asks 'and you are Mr A?' When A then gives his name she repeats it. Her subsequent laugh and her concluding statement, 'OK, that's the introduction,' indicate that she has interpreted A's original suggestion that they introduce each other as simply a request to exchange names, which given her frame of reference she regards as somewhat superfluous in this situation.

A's subsequent 'would it be enough introduction?' in line 33, however, shows that he has quite different expectations of what the introduction was to accomplish. We can begin to see what these expectations are by examining the following exchange which takes place much later in the interview.

Case study 2

1. A: then I had decided because I felt all the
2.   way that whatever happened that was totally
3.   wrong that was not, there was no trace of
4.   truth in it. I needed teaching. I wanted
5.   teaching, ⌈ I want teaching
6. B: ⌊ hu
7. A: I want to um um to waive ⌈ that
8. B: ⌊ hu
9. A: ⌈ condition so that by doing
10. B: ⌊ hu
11. A: some sort of training ⌈ language training
12. B: ⌊ hu
13. A: I can fulfill the condition and then I can
14.   come back
15. B: hu
16. A: and reinstate in ⌈ teaching condition
17. B: ⌊ hu
18. A: this is what I had the view to write to
19.   the Department of Education and Science and
20. B: yes I see
21. A: with the same view I approached
22. B: Twickenham
23. A: Twickenham as well as Uxbridge ⌈ University
24. B: ⌊ yes
25. A: as well as Ealing Technical College
26. B: college
27. A: and at the end they had directed me to
28.   ⌈ give the ⌈ best possible advice
29. B: ⌊ yes   ⌊ yes
30. A: by doing some sort of language course in
31.   which I could best help, so I can be reinstated
32.   and I can do something productive rather
33.   than wasting my time ⌈ and the provincial and
34. B: ⌊ yes I see, yes I understand
35. A: the money and time
36. B: OK now the thing is Mr A there is no course here
37.   which is suitable for you at the moment

38. A: this I had seen the ⌈pro...prospectus ⌈this
39. B: ⌊yes   ⌊yes
40. A: teachers' training ⌈(   )
41. B: ⌊yes that's teachers' training
42.   is for teachers who are employed doing language
43.   training in factories
44. A: per...perhaps perhaps there will be
45.   some way out for you for to for to to
46.   ⌈to help me
47. B: ⌊to help there might be but I can't tell you now
48.   because I shall have to, you see at the moment there
49.   is no course sui...suitable for you ⌈the
50. A: ⌊um
51. B: Teachers' training course is run one day here, one
52.   day there, two days here, two days there and these are
53.   connected with a specific project
54. A: I don't mind doing any sort of ⌈pro...project but
55. B: ⌊no but th...
56.   th...that's not suitable, I can tell you honestly
57.   you won't find it suitable for you, ⌈it won't
58. A: ⌊but
59. B: is is ⌈nothing to do what you want
60. A: ⌊but no it is not what actually I want I want
61.   only to waive the condition, waive the condition
62.   which I have been ⌈restricted from the admission
63. B: ⌊but you see it it
64.   would only be may five days a year, it's only
65.   conferences, we don't have a teachers' training
66.   course here
67. A: nothing (looks at program)
68. B: Yes, oh that's the RSA course
69. A: Yes
70. B: that's at Ealing Technical College, that isn't here
71. A: But it's it's given here
72. B: Yes that's ⌈right it's at Ealing Technical College
73. A: ⌊it's it's

A has here completed his story of the experiences that led to his present predicament, and begins to explain what he wants. The phrase 'I want to waive that condition ' (7, 9) and his repeated use of the word 'condition' (13, 16) are his references to the fact that he has been told that he needs additional communication skills. He then proceeds to ask to be admitted to a training course. When, in line 36, B tells him that there is no course which is suitable for him, he disputes this by mentioning the center's prospectus.

Then in response to B's remarks in lines 51–3, he says 'I don't mind doing any sort of project.' When B then insists that this would not be suitable, and is not what he wants, he says once more, repeating the same phrase twice, that all he wants to do is to 'waive the condition.' In other words he wants another certificate, not more training.

From this, from our analysis of similar situations, and from our interviews with Asians in British industry, we can see that A, along with many others of similar background, views these counselling situations in terms which are similar to the way many Indians view contacts between government functionaries and members of the lay public in general. Following a type of cultural logic which is perhaps best illustrated in Dumont (1970), these situations are seen as basically hierarchical situations in which the counselee acts as a petitioner requesting the counselor to facilitate or grant access to a position. It is the petitioner's role in such situations to plead or present arguments based on personal need or hardship (as in A's expressions of concern in case study 1, lines 12ff.), which the functionary then either grants or refuses.

In the present case, having been told he lacks communication skills, A interprets this to mean that he needs to get another certificate to qualify for a new teaching post. What he wants to ask of B is that she help him get such a certificate. Before he can make his request, however, he needs to find out what her position in the organization is so that he can judge the extent to which she is able to help him. This is what he wants to accomplish with his request for introductions. His awkward-sounding comments are simply attempts at using indirect verbal strategies to get the information he needs.

Seen from this perspective B's response is clearly insufficient. We know, for example, that although B is a trained teacher and does occasionally teach, her main function is that of assistant director of the center in charge of curriculum planning. In identifying herself as a teacher she follows the common English practice of slightly understating her actual rank. Most of us would do likewise in similar situations. If someone were to ask me to introduce myself, I might say that I teach anthropology at Berkeley, but I would certainly not identify myself directly as a full professor, and list my administrative responsibilities. Anyone who needs this type of information would have to elicit it from me. To do so requires command of indirect strategies which could induce me to volunteer the required information, strategies which are dependent on socio-culturally specific background knowledge. A's probes in case study 1, lines 23, 25, 27 and 33 fail because he has neither the socio-cultural knowledge to know what to expect, nor the contextualization strategies needed to elicit information not freely offered.

What B's expectations are emerges from the following passage which in the actual interview follows immediately after case study 1.

Case study 3

1. B: well tell me what you have been studying...
2. A: um...
3. B: up till now
4. A: um, I have done my M.Sc. from N. University
5. B: huh
6. A: I have done my graduate certificate in Education from L. Uni-
7.   versity. I had been teaching after getting that teachers' training in
8.   H., in H.
9. B: Oh, so you have *done* some teaching
10. A: Some ⌈I have done I have done some ⌈ teaching
11. B: ⌊in H.   ⌊ I see
12. A: Um...I completed two terms...uh, unfortunately I had to
13.   leave from that place because ⌈uh I was appointed only
14. B: ⌊oh
15. A: for two terms
16. B: Oh so you didn't get to finish your probation, I suppose
17. A: (sighs) so that is uh ⌈ my start was all right but later
18. B: ⌊ oh
19. A: on what happened it is a mi – a great chaos, I don't know
20.   where I stand or what I can do...um, ⌈after
21. B: ⌊and now you find
22.   you can't get a job
23. A: no this is not actually the situation, ⌈I have not
24. B: ⌊oh
25. A: completely explained ⌈my position
26. B: ⌊yes yes
27. A: After um completing two um um terms of my probation ⌈teaching
28. B: ⌊huh huh
29. A: I had to apply somewhere else. I, there was a job in the borough,
30.   London borough of H., I applied and there that was first applica-
31.   tion which I made and I got the job, but since the beginning the
32.   teach–teaching situation was not suitable for a probationary
33.   teacher.

The initial question here calls for information about the subjects A has studied. Yet A responds first with an asynchronous 'um' and then, following the amplification, 'up till now,' he gives a list of his degrees starting with his first degree. B's 'so you have done some teaching' (10) focuses on 'done' and is thus an indirect probe for more details on A's actual work experience. A's response to this probe is rhythmically premature and simply copies the last phrase of her remark. It almost sounds as if he were mimicking her, rather than responding to the question.

When interpreted in the light of what transpired later, A's next remarks (12–15) are intended to lead into a longer narrative. He starts by mentioning the first of several teaching posts he has held, a temporary appointment which lasted for two terms. However his contextualization practices create problems. Following the initial stressed sentence 'I completed two terms,' his voice drops and the tempo speeds up. Thus the key bit of information about the limited nature of this first appointment is appended to what to English ears must sound like a qualifying remark, which moreover starts with the word 'unfortunately.'...

In the present case B clearly does not respond to what is intended. Being familiar with personnel policies in British education, she knows that new graduates usually begin probationary appointments which last for three terms. Her asynchronous 'oh' (14) and the subsequent response in (16) show that she assumes that A is talking about such a post and that something may have happened to cause his premature dismissal. Given A's prosody and his use of 'unfortunately,' her conclusion seems justified. When A continues with, 'so that is uh my start was all right' (17), she interjects another surprised 'oh.' Viewed purely in terms of its propositional content, A's remark could count as a repair or a correction. What he is saying is that the teaching experience he has just referred to was satisfactory. But his choice of words and prosody again go counter to English speakers' expectations. Repairs and corrections imply that new or non-shared information is being introduced. Ordinarily this is conventionally marked by accent or rise in pitch and by lexicalized transitions such as 'no' or 'I mean.' In the Western English system his initial 'so that is...' implies that he thinks that what he is saying follows from his previous remarks. He seems to be inconsistent and moreover he is not responding to B's reply. This explains her second interjection.

In line 19 A continues once more with unmarked prosody, but after the initial phrase ending with 'chaos' there is a short pause. This is followed by 'I don't know where I stand or what I can do' spoken with countoured intonation similar to that found in Case study 1 (lines 12–16). As was pointed out before, Indian English speakers interpret this type of contouring as a signal that what is to come is of great concern to the speaker. In other words A would seem to be saying: 'now listen to what I have to say next, it's important.' But when he is about to go on to his next point and starts with 'after,' B interrupts to continue her own line of reasoning with 'and now you find you can't get a job.'

Notice that the 'can't' here can refer either to the addressee's qualifications or to outside circumstances which prevent the desired condition from coming about. A, having been interrupted and recognizing that he is not begin listened to, seems to adopt the first interpretation. His reply 'no this is not the actual situation' has the prosodic characteristics of his earlier phrase 'Would it be enough introduction?' (Case study 1, line 33) and suggests annoyance. He then goes on to insist on explaining his case in minute detail.

Line 29 marks the beginning of his narrative which lasts for more than half an hour. Throughout this period B makes regular attempts to get him to concentrate on what she thinks is the point of the interview: talk about the skills he has acquired, about his classroom experiences and about the kind of training he might still need to improve his skills. But the interaction is punctuated by long asides, misunderstandings of fact and misreadings of intent. A, on the other hand, finds he is not being listened to and not given a chance to explain his problem. Neither participant can control the interview. More importantly the fundamental differences in conceptions of what the interview is about that emerge from our discussion of Case study 2 are never confronted. ...

Even when participants have the same background, it is by no means uncommon for counselling interviews to end in mutual frustration. What is important about this case is not the misunderstanding as such but the fact that, in spite of repeated attempts, both speakers utterly fail in their efforts to negotiate a common frame in terms of which to decide on what is being focused on and where the argument is going at any one time. As one Indian English speaker put it in connection with a similar case study, 'they're on parallel tracks which don't meet' (Gumperz & Roberts 1980).

The fact that two speakers whose sentences are quite grammatical can differ radically in their interpretation of each other's verbal strategies indicates that conversational management does rest on linguistic knowledge. But to find out what that knowledge is we must abandon the existing views of communication which draw a basic distinction between cultural or social knowledge on the one hand and linguistic signalling processes on the other. We cannot regard meaning as the output of nonlinear processing in which sounds are mapped into morphemes, clauses and sentences by application of the grammatical and semantic rules of sentence-level linguistic analysis, and look at social norms as extralinguistic forces which merely determine how and under what conditions such meaning units are used. Socio-cultural conventions affect all levels of speech production and interpretation from the abstract cultural logic that underlies all interpretation to the division of speech into episodes; from their categorization in terms of semantically relevant activities and interpretive frames, to the mapping of prosodic contours into syntactic strings and to selection among lexical and grammatical options. The failure to recognize this is another consequence of the fact that linguistic analysis has been sentence-based and influenced by the culture of literacy.

This view of social knowledge is implicit in modern theories of discourse. But work in this tradition has been limited by an unnecessarily diffuse view of extralinguistic knowledge as 'knowledge of the world,' and by its failure to account for the interactive nature of interpretive processes and the role of linguistic contextualization processes in retrieving information and in processing of verbal messages. We can avoid some of the ambiguities inherent in linguists' notions of meaning and intent by concentrating on what participants have to know in order to enter into a conversation and on the inferences they must make to maintain thematic progression. This is essentially what sociolinguists concerned with conversational analysis have begun to do. But in dealing with these problems we cannot assume that interpretive processes are shared. Only by looking at the whole range of linguistic phenomena that enter into conversational management can we understand what goes on in an interaction.

REFERENCES

Bennett, A. (1981) 'Everybody's Got Rhythm', in *Aspects of Non-Verbal Communication*, von Raffler-Engel, W. and Hoffer, B. (ed.) (San Antonio, TX: Trinity University Press).

Bennett, A. F., Erickson, F. and Gumperz, J. J. (1976) 'Coordination of Verbal and Non-verbal Cues in Conversation', Ms. (Report on Workshop at the University of California, Berkeley, January 1976).

Dumont, L. (1970) *Homo Hirarchicus* (London: Weidenfeld and Nicolson).

Erickson, F. and Schultz, J. J. (eds) (1982) *The Counselor as Gatekeeper: Social and Cultural Organization of Communication in Counselling Interviews* (New York: Academic Press).

Gumperz, J. J. and Roberts, C. (1980) 'Developing Awareness Skills for Inter-ethnic Communication', in *Occasional Papers*, no. 12 (Singapore: Seameo Regional Language Center).

31 Patois and the Politics of Protest: Black English in British Classrooms

Viv Edwards

INTRODUCTION

The presence of a large and highly visible minority of non-White children in British schools over the last thirty years has raised many questions about the most appropriate and effective routes to education for a multiracial – and a multilingual – society. Many of these children spoke a language other than English on arrival and most of them have made strenuous attempts to maintain their mother tongue (Linguistic Minorities Project 1985). Many other children arrived speaking an Afro-Caribbean English Creole.

The linguistic situation of the Creole speakers has proved to be simultaneously more straightforward and more complex than that of other recent immigrants. It is more straightforward in that the vast bulk of their vocabulary was English in origin and that communication between speakers of British dialects and speakers of Afro-Caribbean English Creoles, although occasionally difficult, was feasible. It is more complex because the educational establishment was confused about the status of their language. Whereas non-English speakers were provided with English language teaching, support for West Indian children was often non-existent. As a result, children undoubtedly experienced communication difficulties. They were also disadvantaged by negative teacher attitudes towards their language, and lowered expectations of their educational potential.

The position of Black children has changed in many important ways over the last thirty years, but language still remains an important issue. The main focus of this chapter will be on the kind of linguistic interactions which regularly take place in multiracial classrooms – between pupils, and between pupils and teachers – and on the implications of different responses to the use of distinctively Black speech. ...

Source: 'Patois and the Politics of Protest: Black English in British Classrooms', in Garcia, O. and Otheguy, R. (eds) (1989) *English Across Cultures, Cultures Across English: A Reader in Cross-cultural Communication* (Berlin: Mouton de Gruyter) pp. 359–72.

THE LANGUAGE OF BLACK CHILDREN

Until immigration from the Caribbean stopped at the end of the 1960s, the main linguistic issue was the inability of most West Indian children to speak either standard English or the local variety of British English. Attitudes were consistently negative and can be usefully summed up by reference to teacher literature of this period. The National Association of School Masters (1969) refers to West Indian language as 'plantation English which is socially unacceptable and inadequate for communication'. A report on West Indian children produced in 1970 by the Birmingham branch of the Association of Teachers to Pupils from Overseas described their language variously as 'babyish', 'careless and slovenly', 'lacking proper grammar' and even 'very relaxed like the way they walk.'

It seems highly probable that linguistic differences, or more accurately, teacher attitudes towards these differences, played an important part in the educational underperformance of Black children (Edwards 1983). Recognition of this possibility, however, came too late for it to serve any useful purpose, since the predominantly Caribbean speech patterns of the 1960s gradually merged into the predominantly local British speech patterns of the 1970s with the transition from the West Indian-born to the British-born generation.

The first important survey of language use in British Schools became available with the publication of *Languages and Dialects of London School Children* (Rosen & Burgess 1980). The authors concluded on the basis of teacher reports that as few as 10–20 per cent of British Black children have Creole as their dominant speech or use it regularly in certain contexts. There is evidence, however, that this finding is a gross oversimplification of the facts. In particular, a study of British-born Black adolescents in a West Midlands community (Edwards 1986) points to very different patterns of language behaviour.

The West Midlands study abandons the linguist's preferred term, *Creole*, in favour of *Patois*, the most common community term for distinctively Black speech. The Patois spoken by British Black youths in the West Midlands is characterized by the same range of linguistic features associated with Jamaican Creole, but there are important differences between the linguistic situations in Jamaica and the West Midlands. The most important of these differences would appear to lie in the extensive code-switching behaviour of British Black speakers who have at their disposal both English and Patois. Although there is considerable overlap, distinctive phonologies and voice sets usually make it possible to assign speech unambiguously to one variety or the other. British Black speech characteristically switches between English and Patois from sentence to sentence and even clause to clause, and is thus reminiscent of the speech of stable bilingual communities in many parts of the world (cf. Hernández-Chávez *et al.* 1975).

Three different measures were applied to the speech of the young people in the study: frequency of Patois features; competence in Patois; and patterns of Patois usage. Three explanatory variables were found to exert a statistically significant influence on the first of these measures, frequency of Patois features: social network (the more integrated into the Black community a young person is, the more frequent the use of Patois features); attitudes towards mainstream white society (the more critical, the higher the frequency); and education (the lower the level of education, the higher the number of Patois features, but only in the case of the young men).

Patois competence and patterns of Patois usage, however, were found to be significantly affected only by the social networks of the speaker. The more proficient a young person is at speaking Patois, the more likely he or she is to have predominantly Black social relationships. Similarly, the speakers who use Patois in the widest range of situations are those who are most integrated into the Black community. These findings challenge conventional wisdom in a number of important respects. The popular stereotype of the Patois speaker is the disaffected, underachieving male. Some of the most competent speakers in the sample, however, showed little hostility to mainstream White society; some were female; and many had done well at school.

LINGUISTIC SYMBOLISM AND CLASSROOM INTERACTION

One of the most obvious implications of this finding that different patterns of language use exist within the British Black community is that many children who are assumed to be monoglot speakers of an indigenous British dialect, do in fact have access to a much broader linguistic repertoire. Another implication is that for any given situation there will be marked and unmarked language choices (cf. Scotton 1980), and that any departure from the expected code will carry important symbolic messages for participants in the conversation.

PATOIS IN PUPIL–PUPIL INTERACTIONS

Some, though not very many, young people choose to use distinctively Black speech in all situations, including school. In behaving in this way, they are making a very clear statement: the use of Patois is a positive assertion of their Black identity and a rejection of the negative connotations placed on Black language and culture by the dominant White society. The young people who took part in the West Midlands study demonstrated in their own language behaviour, and also in their discussions of that behaviour, a very keen awareness of the kind of conscious decisions which Black people have to make. All the speakers were sensitive to situation. Most of them showed this sensitivity by monitoring out all Patois features in certain situations. However, some achieved the same end by reducing the frequency and range of Patois features. The young people who followed this latter course, attracted a good deal of comment from those who chose the former:

Polly: When Jackie talks to anybody she just talks in the same way so therefore they say she can't speak English. She *can* speak English...

Marie: She can but she don't want to.

Significantly, the use of Patois in the classroom begins in most cases only with the onset of adolescence, and prior to this point Black children tend to adhere very closely to local White speech norms. It is very important to recognize that this kind of behaviour is a deliberately social and psychological protest and not a language teaching problem.

At the other end of the continuum, we find children who are extremely reluctant to use Patois, even in the most private of peer-group conversations. The young people in the study were generally a good deal more critical of this kind of behaviour than they were of the use of Patois in all situations. Nora, for instance, was clearly exasperated by what when perceived to be her sister's snobbiness and misplaced sense of her own importance:

My sister, she's a right little snobby...if she came here now she'd speak plain English, but she can speak Patois better than me. She speaks it to me, to some of her coloured friends who she knows speak Patois, but to her coloured snobby friends she speaks English. She talks Queen English, brebber. She's the snotty one of her family.

It would appear that most young British Blacks occupy the mid-points of the continuum between these two extremes. The use of Patois in the classroom is rare: it is confined to a small number of speakers and a small proportion of exchanges. None the less, it is important to understand that virtually all of the Black children in the class will understand Patois and use certain Patois features in at least some situations; and that the symbolic functions of Patois are part of the shared knowledge of the group. One important function is clearly to express solidarity and to establish yourself as a member of the group. If this kind if linguistic choice is made within the context of a racially mixed situation such as school, it can also have he function of excluding outsider.

Sometimes the outsiders will be teachers; on other occasions they will be White pupils. It is not always the case, however, that White children are excluded. Also pertinent to mention at this point is the question of Patois usage by certain White pupils. There are reports of young Whites who gravitate towards Black or mainly Black friendship groups and who seek to assert their membership of these groups by using Patois speech (Hewitt 1982). The degree of competence exhibited by White children is highly variable and can range from a few set phrases to far more proficient performances. It would appear that some young Black people are amused and even very accepting of his behaviour.

Leighton:	What about if you have a white friend who talk Patois?
Ray:	Yea, like Sean Cooper, well me speak Patois den, ennit?
Andy:	I like it
Ray:	Yea, from me know im say im speak Patois, me speak Patois to im same way
Andy:	All me try to do is, well try and talk Patois to kill im off one time.

However, most appear to dislike White people using something which they perceive to be distinctively Black.

Royston:	I find it hard to speak to them
Elliot:	I don't like it, I don't like it ... it doesn't blend
Royston:	Most of it doesn't sound right ..
Elliot:	It's the White girls that make me sick

In a large proportion of pupil exchanges, Patois will signal inclusion and acceptance by the group. By far the largest number of such interactions will be exclusively Black, though, on occasions, White children will also be included. Patois can also be used to considerable effect to exclude an outsider from the group.

PATOIS IN PUPIL–TEACHER INTERACTIONS

This exclusion function can be seen very clearly in certain teacher–pupil interactions. In a school situation the clear expectation is that English is the language of interaction. Children who make the marked choice and use Patois features when talking to a teacher are minimizing the social distance between them and rejecting the inferior status associated with Patois within their role relationship. In this way, they are failing to observe widely agreed-upon social norms for this kind of interaction and are making statements not only about the immediate situation but their attitudes towards the dominant White society as a whole. These attitudes are understood by Black and White participants alike.

In the West Midlands study, various young people referred to the use of Patois in a school setting as a means of expressing defiance of teachers. The teacher's reaction to the use of Patois in these situations is critical. Many people feel threatened and fear losing control of the situation when a young person uses Patois either as an aside or in a more directly confrontational way. Teachers who, through their own insecurities, respond punitively to this kind of linguistic behaviour are more likely to provoke an escalation of hostilities than to reach a satisfactory resolution.

Take, for instance, Ray and James's account of the kind of incident which apparently occurred with alarming regularity during their time at school.

Ray: Mi used to use Patois a lot, you know and just cuss dem.

James: You go, 'You blood clart' and the teacher goes 'What did you say?'

Ray: 'I know what that was, I know what that was!' and all dat, dat time dem no know what you say. Dem say, 'You say bastard' and all dis.

James: Yes, dem say you swear, they say, 'Well, you did swear, didn't you? Go to the headmaster' or some daftness like that.

Ray: And di headmaster say, 'What did you say?' You no go say to di headmaster seh you say 'blood clart', you say, 'I said "baby"' or something like that.

James: You mumble, behind your words, you mumble.

Even allowing for distortion and bias in the young men's description of events, it would seem that both the class teacher and head teacher failed to understand precisely why Ray was behaving as he did. Any White teacher who simply dismisses the reasons for the kind of language choice which he was making is seriously underestimating the complexities of life in a predominantly White society for Black people and is likely to exacerbate the situation still further.

Not all of teacher–pupil exchanges are quite so confrontational. The young people in the sample also provided examples of quite different patterns of response to the use of Patois. Julie, for instance, recalls an incident at school in the following terms:

I remember a boy at school right and . . . when [the teacher] used to really go at him, he used to go back at her in Patois. So one morning when we got in school right, she had this book in her bag and on the side of the book you could see 'Talk Patois' and all that. I says to Carlton, 'Look at that book. It's about Patois. She soon get to understand it when you read fi cuss her!' . . .

CONCLUSIONS

The language behaviour of Black British children in the 1980s is very different from that of their parents who first arrived in the 1950s and 1960s. In the early days of migration, teachers were faced with children whose speech patterns were markedly different from their own, but there was little understanding of the practical difficulties which this posed for the children or how these might be remedied. By the time that communication problems were finally addressed, however, the situation had radically changed. By 1970 immigration from the Caribbean had come to a virtual halt and teachers were now dealing with a generation of British-born children whose speech closely resembled that of their White peers.

The educational underperformance of Black children had often been linked with their inability to speak British English. It is noteworthy, however, that patterns of underperformance do not seem to have changed significantly even though children have learned to use the local British speech variety. Many other aspects of life in Britain have also remained largely unchanged for Black people, including poor employment prospects and housing conditions. Young Black people are expressing increasing anger at continuing racial inequality and on a number of occasions this anger has taken to the streets.

Teachers have tended to interpret the changed linguistic behaviour of British Blacks in a very narrow way: Patois has ceased to be a 'problem', since the majority of Black children speak a variety of British English. However, this view seriously underestimates the range and richness of language which form the repertoires of most British Blacks. It also shows a lack of understanding of the symbolic value of Patois for both those young people who openly use Patois in a classroom situation and for those who confine their Patois to more private peer-group situations. Patois serves to mark a young person's group membership and is a positive assertion of Black identity. But, in addition to its solidarity functions, it can be used most effectively or expressing rejection of the mainstream White value system, and for excluding outsiders.

The issue of Patois usage in the classroom needs to be examined from two quite different perspectives. First, there is the question of pupils excluding or challenging teachers by using Patois in asides to other pupils, or in more confrontational comments to the teacher. Punitive approaches to this kind of behaviour tend to be born from teacher's own insecurities and limited grasp of why the child is behaving in this way, and will inevitably lead to an escalation of hostilities.

NOTE

This chapter is based on the research project 'Patterns of Language Use in a British Black Community' which was funded by the Economic and Social Research Council.

REFERENCES

Association of Teachers to Pupils from Overseas (AETEPO) (Birmingham branch) (1970) *Work Group on West Indian Pupils Report.*

Edwards, V. (1983) *Language in Multicultural Classrooms* (London: Batsford).

Edwards, V. (1986) *Language in a Black Community* (Clevedon, Avon: Multilingual Matters).

Hernández-Chávez, E., Cohen, A. and Beltramo, A. (1975) *El Lenguaje de Los Chicanos* (Arlington, VA: Center for Applied Linguistics).

Hewitt, R. (1982) 'White Adolescent Creole Users and the Politics of Friendship', *Journal of Multilingual and Multicultural Development*, 3, pp. 217–32.

Linguistic Minorities Project (1985) *The Other Languages of England* (London: Routledge and Kegan Paul).

National Association of School Masters (NAS) (1969) *Education and the Immigrants* (Hemel Hempstead, Herts: Educare).

Rosen, H., and Burgess, T. (1980) *Language and Dialects of London School Children* (London: Ward Lock Educational).

Scotton, C. (1980) 'Explaining Linguistic Choices as Identity Negotiations', in Giles, H., Robinson, P. and Smith, P. (eds) *Language: Social Psychological Perspectives* (Oxford: Pergamon) pp. 359–66.

32 Interaction: The Work Women Do

Pamela M. Fishman

The oppression of women in society is an issue of growing concern, both in academic fields and everyday life. Despite research on the historical and economic basis of women's position, we know little about how hierarchy is routinely established and maintained. This chapter attempts to direct attention to the reality of power in daily experience. It is an analysis of conversations between men and women in their homes. The chapter focuses on how verbal interaction helps to construct and maintain the hierarchical relations between women and men.

Weber (1969: 152) provided the classic conception of power as the chances of one actor in a social relationship to impose his or her will on another. Recently, Berger and Luckmann (1967: 109) have discussed power from a perspective which broadens the sense of 'imposing one's will' on others. They define power as a question of potentially conflicting definitions of reality; that of the most powerful will be 'made to stick.' That particular people have the power to construct and enforce their definition of reality is due to socially prevalent economic and political definitions of reality.

Imposing one's will can be much more than forcing someone else to do something. Power is the ability to impose one's definition of what is possible, what is right, what is rational, what is real. Power is a product of human activities, just as the activities are themselves products of the power relations in the socio-economic world.

Power usually is analyzed macrosociologically: it cannot be solely a result of what people do within the immediate situation in which it occurs. What people do in specific interactions expresses and reflects historical and social structural forces beyond the boundaries of their encounters. Power relations between men and women are the outcome of the social organization of their activities in the home and in the economy. Power can, however, be analyzed microsociologically, which is the purpose of this chapter. Power and hierarchical relations are not abstract forces operating on people. Power must be a human accomplishment, situated in everyday interaction. Both

Source: 'Interaction: The Work Women Do', *Social Problems*, **25**, 4 (1978) (Society for the Study of Social Problems) pp. 397–406.

structural forces and interactional activities are vital to the maintenance and construction of social reality.

Work on gender and the English language shows that the male–female hierarchy is inherent in the words we use to perceive and name our world: the use of the male generic 'man' to refer to the human species (Miller and Swift, 1976); the addition of suffixes ('authoress,' 'actress,' 'stewardess') when referring to female practitioners (Miller and Swift, 1976); the asymmetrical use of first and last names (women are more often called by their first, men by their last, even when they are of equal rank) (Thorne and Henley, 1975); women's greater vocabulary for sewing and cooking, men's for mechanics and sports (Conklin, 1974).[1] These studies of grammatical forms and vocabulary document the male-dominated reality expressed through our language.

Much less attention has been directed toward how male–female power relations are expressed in conversation.[2] By turning to conversation, we move to an analysis of the interactional production of a particular reality through people's talk.

This activity is significant for intimates. Berger and Kellner (1970: 64) have argued that at present, with the increasing separation of public and private spheres of life, intimate relationships are among the most important reality-maintaining settings. They apply this arrangement specifically to marriage. The process of daily interaction in the marital relationship is, ideally:

> ...one in which reality is crystallized, narrowed, and stabilized. Ambivalences are converted into certainties. Typifications of self and other become settled. Most generally, possibilities become facilities.

In these relationships, in these trivial, mundane interactions, much of the essential work of sustaining the reality of the world goes on. Intimates often reconstruct their separate experiences, past and present, with one another. Specifically, the couple sustain and produce the reality of their own relationship, and, more generally, of the world.

Although Berger and Kellner have analyzed marriage as a reality-producing setting, they have not analyzed the interaction of marriage partners. I shall focus upon the interactional activities which constitute the everyday work done by intimates. It is through this work that people produce their relationship to one another, their relationship to the world, and those patterns normally referred to as social structure.

WORK IN INTERACTION[3]

Sometimes we think of interaction as work. At a party or meeting where silence lies heavy, we recognize the burden of interaction and respond to it as work. The many books written on 'the art of conversation' call attention to the tasks involved in interaction. It is not simply an analogy to think of interaction as work. Rather, it is an intuitive recognition of what must be accomplished for interaction to occur.

Interaction requires at least two people. Conversation is produced not simply by their presence, but also by their display of their continuing agreement to pay attention to one another. That is, all interactions are potentially problematic and occur only through continual, turn-by-turn, efforts of the participants.

The work of Sacks and his followers (Sacks *et al.*, 1974; Schegloff and Sacks, 1974; Schegloff, 1972) attempts to specify how conversationalists work to accomplish such things as beginnings and endings. They have ignored, however, the interaction between intimates. Schegloff and Sacks (1974: 262) characterize intimates in home situations as 'in continuing states of incipient talk.' Thus, they contend that their analysis of the activities involved in opening and closing conversations, as well as those involved in keeping conversation going, do not apply to intimate conversations. But this perspective disregards the many conversations which do not begin with greetings nor end with good-byes. If one sees a movie with friends, conversation afterwards does not begin again with greetings. In social gatherings lulls occur and conversation must begin anew. In any setting in which conversation is possible, attempts at beginning, sustaining, and stopping talk still must be made. And these attempts must be recognized and oriented to by both parties for them to move between states of 'incipient' and 'actual' conversation.

In a sense, every remark or turn at speaking should be seen as an *attempt* to interact. It may be an attempt to open or close a conversation. It may be a bid to continue interaction: to respond to what went before and elicit a further remark from one's interlocutor. Some attempts succeed; others fail. For an attempt to succeed, the other party must be willing to do further interactional work. That other person has the power to turn an attempt into a conversation or to stop it dead.

METHOD

The data for this study consists of fifty-two hours of tape-recorded conversation between intimates in their homes. Three couples agreed to have a Uher 400 tape recorder in their apartments. They had the right to censor the taped material before I heard it. The apartments were small, so that the recorders picked up all conversation from the kitchen and living room as well as the louder portions of talk from the bedroom and bath. The tapes could run for a four-hour period without interruption. Though I had timers to switch the tapes on and off automatically, all three couples insisted on doing the switching manually. The segments of uninterrupted recording vary from one to four hours.

The three couples had been together for varying amounts of time – three months, six months, and two years. The two couples who had been together the longest were recently married. All were White and professionally-oriented, between the ages of twenty-five and thirty-five. One woman was a social worker and the other five people were in a graduate school. Two of the women were avowed feminists and all three men as well as the other woman described themselves as sympathetic to the women's movement.

The tape recorders were present in the apartments from four to fourteen days. I am satisfied that the material represents natural conversation and that there was no undue awareness of the recorder. The tapes sounded natural to me, like conversation between my husband and myself. Others who have read the transcripts have agreed. All six people also reported that they soon began to ignore the tape recorder. Further, they were apologetic about the material, calling it trivial and uninteresting, just the ordinary affairs of everyday life. Finally, one couple said they forgot the recorder sufficiently to begin making love in the living room while the recorder was on. That segment and two others were the only ones the participants deleted before handing the tapes over to me.

I listened to all of the tapes at least once, many two or three times. During this period, I observed general features and trends of the interactions as a whole. Three transcripts were chosen from five hours of transcribed conversations for closer, turn-by-turn analysis of the progress of concrete, interactional activities. I chose these three because they were good examples of conversation that appeared to be problematic for the man, for the woman, and for neither.

PRELIMINARY EVIDENCE

Some evidence of the power relations between couples appeared while I was still in the process of collecting the tapes. During casual conversations with the participants after the taping, I learned that in all three couples the men usually set up the tape recorders and turned them on and off. More significantly, some of the times that the men turned the recorders on, they did so without the women's knowledge. The reverse never occurred.

To control conversation it is not merely to choose the topic. It is a matter of having control over the definition of the situation in general, which includes not only what will be talked about, but whether there will be a conversation at all and under what terms it will occur. In various scenes, control over aspects of the situation can be important. The addition of a tape recorder in the home is an example of a new aspect to the routine situation. The men clearly had and actively maintained unilateral control over this new feature in the situation.

In this research, there is also the issue of a typically private interaction becoming available to a third party, the researcher. Usually the men played the tapes to censor them, and made the only two attempts to exert control over the presentation of the data to me. One case involved the 'clicks' that are normally recorded when the recorder is turned off. Since more than one time segment was often on the same side of a tape, I relied on the clicks, as well as my sense of the conversations, to know when a newtime segment began. One man carefully erased nearly all the clicks on the tapes, making it difficult to separate out recordings at different time periods.

The second instance was a more explicit illustration of male censorship. Early on, I made the error of asking a couple to help transcribe a segment of their tape. The error was doubly instructive. First, I saw that the participants could rarely hear or understand the problem areas any better than I even though they had been 'on the spot,' and were hearing their own voices. Second, the man kept wanting to know why I was interested in the segment, repeatedly guessing what I was looking for. At the time, I only knew that it was an example of decision-making and did not know specifically what I wanted. He never accepted this explanation. He became irritated at my continued attempt at literal transcription and kept insisting that he could give me the sense of what occurred and that the exact words were unimportant. He continued the attempt to determine the meaning of the interaction retrospectively, with constant references to his motives for saying this and that. It took hours to withdraw from the situation, as he insisted on giving me the help that I had requested.

The preliminary data suggest that the men are more likely than the women to control conversation. The men ensured that they knew when the tape recorder was on and, when their interaction was available to a third party. They were unconcerned, however, if the women also knew. Further, in at least two cases they attempted to control my interpretation of the tapes.

FINDINGS: INTERACTIONAL STRATEGIES

Textual analysis revealed how interactants do the work of conversation. There are a variety of strategies to insure, encourage, and subvert conversation.

Asking Questions

There is an overwhelming difference between male and female use of questions as a resource in interaction. At times I felt that all women did was ask questions. In seven hours of tapes the three men asked fifty-nine questions, the women one hundred and fifty, nearly three times as many.

Other research (Lakoff, 1975) notes that women ask more questions then men. Lakoff has interpreted this question-asking as an indication of women's insecurity, a linguistic signal of an internal psychological state resulting from the oppression of women. But a psychological explanation is unnecessary to reveal why women ask more questions than men. Since questions are produced in conversations, we should look first to how questions function there.

Questions are interactionally powerful utterances. They are among a class of utterances, like greetings, treated as standing in a paired relation; that is, they evoke further utterance. Questions are paired with answers (Sacks, 1972). People respond to questions as 'deserving' answers. The absence of an answer is noticeable and may be complained about. A question does work in a conversation by opening a two-part sequence. It is a way to insure a minimal interaction – at least one utterance by each of two participants. It guarantees a response.

Once I noted the phenomenon of questions on the tapes, I attended to my own speech and discovered the same pattern. I tried, and still do try, to break myself of the 'habit,' and found it very difficult. Remarks kept coming out as questions before I could rephrase them. When I did succeed in making a remark as a statement, I usually did not get a response. It became clear that I asked questions not merely out of habit nor from insecurity but because it was likely that my attempt at interaction would fail if I did not.

Asking 'D'ya Know'

In line with the assumption that children have restricted rights to speak in the presence of adults, Harvey Sacks (1972) describes a type of question used extensively by children as a conversational opening: 'D'ya know what?' As with other questions, it provides for a next utterance. The next utterance it engenders is itself a question, which provides for yet another utterance. The archetype is, 'D'ya know what?' 'what?' 'Blahblah (answer).' Sometimes, of course, the adult answers with an expectant look or a statement like, 'Tell me what.' Whatever the exact form of that response, the idea is that the first question sets off a three-part sequence, Q-Q-A, rather than a simple Q-A sequence.

Sacks points out that the children's use of this device is a clever solution to their problem of insuring rights to speak (at the same time, their use of this strategy acknowledges those restricted rights). In response to the 'What?' the children may say what they wanted to say in the first place. Finding such three-part 'D'ya know' sequences in interaction informs us both about the work of guaranteeing interaction and the differential rights of the participants. In the five hours of transcribed material, the women used this device twice as often as the men.

Attention Beginnings

The phrase, 'This is interesting,' or a variation thereof, occurs throughout the tapes. When conversation is not problematic, the work of establishing that a remark is interesting ideally is done by both interactants, not one. The first person makes a remark; the second person orients to and responds to the remark, thus establishing its status as something worthy of joint interest or importance. All this occurs without the question of its interest ever becoming explicit.[4] The use of 'This is really interesting' as an introduction shows that the user cannot assume that the remark itself will be seen as worthy of attention. At the same time, the user tries single-handedly to establish the interest of their remarks. The user is saying, 'Pay attention to what I have to say, I can't assume that you will.' In the five hours of transcribed material, the women used this device ten times, the men seven.[5]

There are also many instances of 'y'know' interspersed throughout the transcripts. While this phrase does not compel the attention one's partner as forcefully as 'this is interesting' does, it is an attempt to command the other person's attention. The phrase was used thirty-four times by the women and three times by the men in the transcribed conversations.

Minimal Response

Another interaction strategy is the use of the minimal response, when the speaker takes a turn by saying 'yeah,' 'umm,' 'huh,' and only that. Men and women both do this, but they tend to use the minimal response in quite different ways. The male usages of the minimal response displayed lack of interest. The mono-syllabic response merely filled a turn at a point when it needed to be filled. For example, a woman would make a lengthy remark, after which the man responded with a 'yeah,' doing nothing to encourage her, nor to elaborate. Such minimal responses are attempts to discourage interaction.

The woman also made this type of minimal response at times, but their most frequent use of the minimal response was as 'support work.' Throughout the tapes, when the men are talking, the woman are particularly skilled at inserting 'mm's,' 'yeah's,' 'oh's,' and other such comments throughout streams of talk rather than at the end. These are signs from the inserter that she is constantly attending to what is said, that she is demonstrating her participation, her interest in the interaction and the speaker. How well the women do this is also striking – seldom do they mistime their insertions and cause even slight overlaps. These minimal responses occur between the breaths of a speaker, and there is nothing in tone or structure to suggest they are attempting to take over the talk.

Making Statements

Finally, I would like to consider statements, which do nothing to insure their own success, or the success of the interaction. Of course, a statement does some interactional work: it fills a space and may also provide for a response. However, such statements display an assumption on the part of the speaker that the attempt will be successful as is: it will be understood, the statement is of interest, there will be a response. It is as if speakers can assume that everything is working well; success is naturally theirs.

In the transcribed material, the men produced over twice as many statements as the women, and they almost always got a response, which was not true for the women. For example: many times one or both people were reading, then read a passage aloud or commented on it. The man's comments often engendered a lengthy exchange, the woman's comments seldom did. In a discussion of their respective vitas [CVs – Eds], the man literally ignored both long and short comments from the woman on her vita, returning the conversation after each remark of hers back to his own. Each time, she respectfully turned her attention back to his vita, 'as directed.' Listening to these conversations, one cannot conclude from the substance of the remarks that the men talk about more interesting things than the women. They take on that character by virtue of generating interaction.

INTERACTIONAL PROGRESS

The simple narration of the use of strategies obscures one important quality of interaction, its progression. The finding and frequency of strategies are of interest, but seeing the use of strategies in the developing character of interaction reveals more about the differential work done by the sexes.

In the transcript, a short segment of conversation is reproduced.[6] It is from the transcript originally chosen for analysis because the conversation appeared problematic for the woman. We can see why from the transcript: she documents her problems by the use of strategies that insure some type of response.

This segment is the beginning of an interaction during which the woman is reading a book in her academic specialty and the man is making a salad. The woman's opening remarks set up two 'd'ya know' sequences, demonstrating her lack of certainty, before anything has been said, that the man will pay attention. A safe assumption, since the conversation never gets off the ground. The 'd'ya know' only solves the minimal problem of getting a response. She cannot get a continuing conversation going.

Her second attempt at a conversation, in set 5, is a two-fold one, using both the 'd'ya know' strategy and an attention beginning of 'That's very

TRANSCRIPT

1
F: I didn't know that. (=)　　　　　　　Um you know that ((garbage disposal on)) that organizational
M:　　　　　　　　Hmmm? (=)

2
F: stuff about Frederick Taylor and Bishopsgate and all that stuff? (=)　　　　⌐In the early
M:　　　　　　　　　　　　　　　　　　　　UmHm ((yes))⌐

3
F: 1900's people were trying to fight favoritism to the schools (4)
M:　　　　　　　　　　　　　　　　　That's what we needed. (18) I

4
F:
M: never did get my smoked oysters, I'm going to look for ((inaudible)) (14) Should we try the

5
F:　　　　　　　　OK. That's a change. (72) Hmm. That's very interesting. Did
M: Riviera French Dressing? (=)

6
F: you know that teachers used to be men until about the 1840's when it became a female occupa-
M:

7
F: tion? (2)　　　　　　　　Because they needed more teachers because of the increased enroll-
M:　　　Nhhmm ((no)) (=)

8
F: ment. (5)　　　　　　　　　　　　Yeah relatively and the status (7)
M:　　　And then the salaries started going down probably. (=)

9
F:　　　　　　　　　　　⌐There's two bottles I think⌐
M: Um, it's weird. We're out of oil again. ⌊Now we have to buy that.⌋ ((whistling)) (8) Dressing

10
F:　　　　　　　　　It does yeah. (76) That's really interesting. They didn't start
M: looks good. See? (2) See babe? (1)

11
F: using the test to measure and find the you know categorize and track people in American
M:

12
F: schools until like the early 1900's after the army y'know introduced their array alpha things
M:

13
F: to the draftees (?) And then it caught on with schools and there was a lot of opposition right
M:

14
F: at the beginning to that, which was as sophisticated as today's arguments. The same argu-
M:

15
F: ments y'know (=)　　　But it didn't work and they came (4)　　　　　　⌐heh
M:　　　Yeah (=)　　　　　　　　Leslie White is probably right. ⌐

interesting.' This double attempt to gain his participation manages to evoke one statement of continuation out of him in set 8, but her follow-up calls forth only silence.

Her third attempt, in set 10, uses the attention beginning which had some small success the last time. She adds a few 'y'know's' throughout her utterance, asking for attention. She finally achieves a minimal response, when she repeats something. Though she makes further attempts in the remainder of the interaction (not reproduced here), a conversation on the topic never does develop. After three or four more minutes, she finally gives up.

One might argue that because the man was making a salad he could not pay attention to the conversation. However, while still at work on the salad, the man introduces his own topic for conversation, remarking that then-President Nixon was a former lawyer for Pepsi-Cola. This topic introduction engenders a conversation when the responds to his remark. They go through a series of exchanges which end when he decides not to continue. This conversational exchange demonstrates that the man was willing to engage in discussion, but only on his own terms.

The transcript demonstrates how some strategies are used in actual conversation. It also documents the woman working at interaction and the man exercising his power by refusing to become a fully-fledged participant. As the interaction develops and she becomes more sure of her difficulties, she brings more pressure to bear by an increased use of strategies. Even so, she is only able to insure immediate, localized responses, not a full conversational exchange.

CONCLUSIONS

There is an unequal distribution of work in conversation. We can see from the differential use of strategies that the women are more actively engaged in insuring interaction than the men. They ask more questions and use attention beginnings. Women do support work while the men are talking and generally do active maintenance and continuation work in conversations. The men, on the other hand, do much less active work when they begin or participate in interactions. They rely on statements, which they assume will get responses, when they want interaction. Men much more often discourage interactions initiated by women than vice-versa.

Several general patterns of male–female interactional work suggest themselves. The women seemed to try more often, and succeeded less often than the men. The men tried less often and seldom failed in their attempts. Both men and women regarded topics introduced by women as tentative; many of these were quickly dropped. In contrast, topics introduced by the men were treated as topics to be pursued; they were seldom rejected. The women worked harder than the men in interaction because they had less certainty of success. They did much of the necessary work of interaction, starting conversations and then working to maintain them.

The failure of the women's attempts at interaction is not due to anything inherent in their talk, but to the failure of the men to respond, to do interactional work. The success of the men's remarks is due to the women doing interactional work in response to attempts by the men. Thus, the definition of what is appropriate or inappropriate conversation becomes the man's choice. What part of the world the interactants orient to, construct and maintain the reality of, is his choice, not hers. Yet the women labor hardest in making interactions go.

It seems that, as with work in its usual sense, there is a division of labor in conversation. The people who do the routine maintenance work, the women, are not the same people who either control or benefit from the process. Women are the 'shitworkers' of routine interaction, and the 'goods' being made are not only interactions, but, through them, realities.

Through this analysis of the detailed activity in everyday conversation, other dimensions of power and work in interaction are suggested. Two interrelated aspects concern women's availability and the maintenance of gender. Besides the problems women have generating interactions, they are almost always available to do the conversational work required by men and necessary for interactions. Appearances may differ by case: sometimes women are required to sit and 'be a good listener' because they are not otherwise needed. At other times, women are required to fill silences and keep conversation moving, to talk a lot. Sometimes they are expected to develop others' topics and at other times they are required to present and develop topics of their own.

Women are required to do their work in a very strong sense. Sometimes they are required in ways that can be seen in interaction, as when men use interactional strategies such as attention beginnings and questions, to which the women fully respond. There are also times when there is no direct, situational evidence of 'requirement' from the man, and the woman does so 'naturally.' 'Naturally' means that it is a morally required and highly sanctionable matter not to do so. If one does not act 'naturally,' then one can be seen as crazy and deprived of adult status. We can speculate on the quality of doing it 'naturally' by considering what happens to women who are unwilling to be available for the various jobs that the situation requires. Women who successfully control interactions are derided and doubt is cast on their status of female. They are often considered 'abnormal' – terms like 'castrating bitch,' 'domineering,' 'aggressive,' and 'witch' may be used to identify them. When they attempt to control situations temporarily, women often 'start' arguments. Etiquette books are filled with instructions to women on how to be available. Women who do not behave are punished by deprivation of full female status. One's identity as either male or female is the most crucial identity one has. It is the most 'natural' differentiating characteristic there is.

Whereas sociologists generally treat sex as an 'ascribed' rather than as an 'achieved' characteristic, Garfinkel's (1967, ch. 5) study of a transsexual describes one's gender as a continual, routine accomplishment. He discusses what the transsexual Agnes has shown him, that one must continually give off the appearance of being male or female in order for your gender to be unproblematic in a given interaction. Agnes had to learn these appearances and her awareness of them was explicit. For 'normally-sexed' people, it is routine.

The active maintenance of a female gender requires women to be available to do what needs to be done in interaction, to do the shitwork and not to complain. Since interactional work is related to what constitutes being a women, with what a woman *is*, the idea that it *is* work is obscured. The work is not seen as what women do, but as part of what they are. Because this work is obscured, because it is too often seen as an aspect of gender identity rather than of gender activity, the maintenance and expression of male–female power relations in our everyday conversations are hidden as well. When we orient instead to the activities involved in maintaining gender, we are able to discern the reality of hierarchy in our daily lives.

The purpose of this study has been to begin an exploration of the details of concrete conversational activity of couples in their homes from the perspective of the socially structured power relationship between males and females. From such detailed analysis we see that women do the work necessary for interaction to occur smoothly. But men control what will be produced as reality by the interaction. They already have, and they continually establish and enforce, their rights to define what the interaction, and reality, will be about.

NOTES

An earlier version of this chapter was presented at the 1975 ASA Meetings, San Francisco, I am indebted to Harvey Molotch, under whose encouragement I began the research. I am grateful to Myrtha Chabrán, Mark Fishman, Drew Humphries, Linda Marks, Florence Tager, and Susan Wolf for their support, discussions, and criticisms throughout work on this and earlier drafts, and to Malcolm Spector for his comments on the final version.

1   An excellent summary and analysis of this literature can be found in Thorne and Henley's introduction to their book, *Language and Sex: Difference and Dominance* (Thorne and Henley, 1975). Miller and Swift's (1976) encyclopedic work, *Words and Women*, catalogues the innumerable ways our language upholds the inferior position of women.

2 A notable exception is the work on interruptions in conversation by West (1977), West and Zimmerman (1977), and Zimmerman and West (1975). Hirschman (1974, 1973) has also examined the interactive production of language in male–female settings.

3 Throughout this chapter, I use the terms interaction and conversation interchangeably, although it is not meant to suggest that conversation covers all the essential components of interaction.

4 The notion that joint expression of interest is a necessary feature of conversation is discussed by Garfinkel (1967: 39–42).

5 Unlike the use of questions and 'D'ya know,' which are randomly scattered throughout the transcripts, six of the seven male usages occurred during one lengthy interaction. The conversation had been chosen because it was one of the very few cases when the man was having trouble maintaining interaction. In contrast, four of the female usages were from one transcript and the other six were scattered. My impression from listening to all the tapes was that a complete count would show a much larger proportion of female to male usage than the ten to seven figure indicates.

6 The numbers in parentheses indicate number of seconds of a pause '(=)' means the pause was less than one second. My own comments on the tape are in double parentheses. M and F stand for male and female speaker, respectively. The conversation is presented in paired exchanges, sections 1–15. The sections ideally would be joined up in ticker tape fashion and would read like a musical score. Brackets between lines indicate overlapping talk.

REFERENCES

Berger, P. and Kellner, H. (1970) 'Marriage and the Construction of Reality,' in Dreitzel, H. P. (ed.) *Recent Sociology No. 2* (London: Macmillan) pp. 50–72.

Berger, P. and Luckman, T. (1967) *The Social Construction of Reality* (New York: Anchor Books).

Conklin, N. F. (1974) 'Toward a Feminist Analysis of Linguistic Behavior,' *The University of Michigan Papers in Women's Studies*, 1(1), pp. 51–73.

Garfinkel, H. (1967) *Studies in Ethnomethodology* (Englewood Cliffs, NJ: Prentice-Hall).

Hirschman, L. (1973) 'Female–Male Differences in Conversational Interaction.' Paper presented at Linguistic Society of America.

Hirschman, L. (1974) 'Analysis of Supportive and Assertive Behavior in Conversations.' Paper presented at Linguistic Society in America.

Lakoff, R. (1975) *Language and Woman's Place* (New York: Harper Colophon Books).

Miller, C. and Swift, K. (1976) *Words and Women* (New York: Anchor Press).

Sacks, H. (1972) 'On the Analyzability of Stories by Children,' in Gumperz, J. J. and Hymes, D. (eds) *Directions in Sociolinguistics: The Ethnography of Communication* (New York: Holt, Rinehart and Winston) pp. 325–45.

Sacks, H., Schegloff, E. and Jefferson, G. (1974) 'A Simplest Systematics for the Organization of Turn-taking for Conversation,' *Language*, **50**, pp. 696–735.

Schegloff, E. (1972) 'Sequencing in Conversational Openings,' in Gumperz, J. J. and Hymes, D. (eds) *Directions in Sociolinguistics: The Ethnography of Communication* (New York: Holt, Rinehart and Winston) pp. 346–80.

Schegloff, E. and Sacks, H. (1974) 'Opening up Closings.' in Turner, R. (ed.) *Ethnomethodology* (Middlesex, England: Penguin Education) pp. 197–215.

Thorne, B. and Henley, N. (1975) *Language and Sex: Difference and Dominance* (Rowley, MA: Newbury House).

Weber, M. (1969) *The Theory of Social and Economic Organization* (New York: Free Press).

West, C. (1977) 'Against Our Will: Negotiating Interruption in Male–Female Conversation.' Paper presented at New York Academy of Science Meeting of Anthropology, Psychology and Linguistics Sections, 22 October, New York.

West, C. and Zimmerman, D. (1977) 'Women's Place in Everyday Talk: Reflections on Parent–Child Interaction,' *Social Problems*, **24**, pp. 521–9.

Zimmerman, D. and West, C. (1975) 'Sex Roles, Interruptions and Silences in Conversation,' in Thorne, B. and Henley, N. (eds) *Language and Sex: Difference and Dominance* (Rowley, MA: Newbury House) pp. 105–29.

33 Cultural Dimensions of Language Acquisition

Elinor Ochs

Work on how children acquire language tells us that caregivers, particularly mothers, are highly instrumental in this process. This is accomplished in several ways: mothers simplify their syntax, reduce their utterance length, reduce their vocabulary, repeat and paraphrase their utterances, when speaking to young children (Ferguson, 1977; Snow, 1972, 1977, 1979; Newport, 1976; Cross, 1975, 1977).

Further, while mothers don't overtly correct the form of a child's utterance, they will often repeat what the child says, using correct adult syntax. These are referred to as *expansions* in the literature (Brown *et al.*, 1969; Cazden, 1965, 1972; Cross, 1977) and are illustrated in sequences such as the following:

Child: *down/*
Mother: *You want to get down.*

Child: *Daddy go car/*
Mother: *Right. Daddy is going in the car.*

Child: *baby diaper/*
Mother: *Baby is wearing a diaper.*

Another reported practice of mothers is asking the child to clarify unintelligible utterances. In this way, mothers encourage children to express their thoughts more clearly and in a more acceptable form (Scollon, 1976; Atkinson, 1979).

What I want to discuss here is the cultural nature of these observations of the way in which mothers speak to children. I want to persuade you that what has been observed is *not universal*, is *not a fact* about normal mother–child interaction. These observations are largely based on middle-class, Anglo-American mothers or on middle-class European mothers.

Source: 'Cultural Dimensions of Language Acquisition', in Ochs, E. and Schieffelin, B. B. (1983) *Acquiring Conversational Competence* (London: Routledge and Kegan Paul) pp. 185–91.

If you are an educator or a clinician involved with communicative disorders, it is crucial to separate biological patterns from cultural patterns, to distinguish between a child or a caregiver who does not conform to a cultural norm from a child or caregiver who deviates from a *biological* norm. This is particularly the case when dealing with young children and families of non-Anglo, non-middle-class backgrounds. For these children, it is crucial to know what are the normal and appropriate ways in which young children communicate. Children from different ethnic and class backgrounds may use language in ways that differ from middle-class American children. The diagnosing of their language as disordered or deviant in some way must be based on deviance with respect to their own cultural norms for child language and not with respect to norms of the therapist's or educator's culture, where it differs from that of the child. In other words, it is important to distinguish *difference* from *deviance*.

To this end, I would like to report on an important difference between Anglo-American mother–child interaction and mother–child interaction in a non-Western, traditional society. The society is Samoan, a Polynesian society, and the study is based on 13 months' intensive observation of children's language and socialization in a Western Samoan village. Our study audio- and videotaped twenty-three children under the age of six interacting with caregivers and peers.

Samoan traditional caregiving patterns differ significantly from what most Americans are exposed to. Infants and small children are cared for by a wider range of caregivers. A child's mother is the primary caregiver in the first year of life, but typically she is assisted by another, older child within the household. As young children learn to walk and talk, mothers assume fewer caregiving responsibilities and more responsibility is handed over to the older sibling of the child. This type of caregiving is characteristic of over one third of the world's societies, but it has rarely been described in depth and its consequences to the child's cognitive and linguistic competence has been minimally addressed (Weisner and Gallimore, 1977).

As the Samoan child grows somewhat older, around the age of three, she or he spends most of the day with other children of roughly the same age. These children form age-graded peer groups (*aukegi*) with members drawn primarily from the local extended household.

We should notice right here a major difference between Western Samoan and middle-class American social environments. Americans tend to live in nuclear households (a mother, a father and their direct descendants). Typically there is only one caregiver and typically, in middle-class families, there are fewer than three children.

It is important to point out here that the observations of Anglo-American mother–child interaction from which we have drawn so many conclusions examine one mother interacting with one child. In structured observations by psychologists (e.g. in university observation rooms), the mother has only one personal focus, the child; and the child has only one personal focus, the mother. In naturalistic observations, it is typical for psychologists and linguists to document interactions between a mother and the *first* child. No siblings are present.

This setting contrasts dramatically with that typical of Western Samoan households, where several mothers may be together in a single compound along with nine or ten children in caregiving or cared-for roles. There caregivers must attend to a number of persons and a young child is most often not a central focus of attention.

A second major difference in caregiving concerns the kind of care that mothers are expected to give and the kind of care siblings are expected to provide. In traditional Samoan communities, age is a determinant of status. Older persons have more status than young persons, adults more than children. In the household, *mothers* are high-status caregivers and siblings are low-status caregivers.

One behaviour that distinguishes high and low status is action, motion, movement, involvement. High status persons ideally remain stationary. Lower-status individuals are active and provide most of the physical work within the community. With respect to giving care to children, this means that high-status caregivers, e.g. mothers and grandmothers, tend to move very little. It is the *sibling caregiver who provides the more activecare*. They are primarily the ones to change wet diapers, dress and undress and clean a young child. They are also the ones to prepare and bring food to a young child.

What are the consequences of this social organization of caregiving to mother–child interactions? The result produces a very different type of verbal interaction pattern than that found in middle-class Anglo-American homes. In middle-class homes, we typically find mother and child engaged in a *dialogue*. If a child is distressed, she voices this distress to her mother, expecting a direct response. Under normal circumstances, the mother does respond directly to the child's communication. This produces a direct, two-party conversational sequence in which child talks to mother, mother talks to child, child talks to mother again, mother talks to child again, and so on (ABABAB...).

In the traditional Samoan household, these same expectations and norms do not exist. A child exhibiting some distress – wet diapers, hunger, thirst, etc. – may express this information to her mother. However, typically the mother does not then respond directly to the child. Rather, the mother will turn to an older sibling of the child who is responsible for active care and direct that sibling to respond to the child's distress. At that point the sibling responds verbally or nonverbally directly to the child. Instead of the American mother–child dialogue, we find typically the *child participating in three-party conversations*. Child speaks to mother, mother speaks to sibling, sibling speaks/responds to child (ABCA...).

Samoan children, then, have quite different expectations from American children concerning how mothers will respond to their needs. In the American case the mother's response is direct. In the Samoan case the mother's response is mediated through a sibling. In parallel fashion, Samoan children have quite different expectations concerning how and when mothers will talk to them. Samoan children usually do not expect a direct verbal response to a notification for their needs. Indeed under certain circumstances, such as when the mother is talking with another adult, the child learns to expect no response at all from the mother. Under these circumstances the older guest takes precedence over the child in occupying the mother's attention.

Thus far, the discussion has focused on differences in social organization of caregiving and has outlined its effect on child–adult communication. I turn now to another cultural dimension that affects the way in which young children and their caregivers converse with one another. This cultural dimension involves cultural beliefs about the nature of children. It is important to realize that when an American mother responds to her infant in a particular way, she is doing so not because of *innate biological* patterning but because she is acting on cultural assumptions about qualities and capacities of young children.

For example, middle-class American mothers see even young infants as distinct individuals. These mothers often will look for personality traits in a young infant and interpret behaviours of the infant as expressive of the infant's basic character – easy-going, fussy, serious, pensive, extroverted, excitable, and so on. In this perspective, the child is seen as acting the way he does because of his particular personal nature.

But not only are these infants seen as having individual personalities, they are also seen as capable of acting in a purposeful and goal-directed manner. Middle-class Anglo-American mothers very often interpret infants' verbal and nonverbal behaviours as conscious, motivated, intentional, directed to some end. A hand gesture is interpreted as a reach, an offer, a display. A vocalization is interpreted as a summons to attend, a greeting, a noticing, a request for some object or a rejection and so on.

The child development literature is filled with detailed descriptions of such maternal interpretation of and response to pre-language child behaviours (Stern, 1974, 1977; Bates *et al.*, 1979; Shotter, 1978; Trevarthen, 1979). Trevarthen, who has filmed dozens of British mothers interacting with infants, reports:

As a rule, prespeech with gesture is watched and replied to by exclamations of pleasure or surprise like 'Oh, my my!', 'Good heavens!', 'Oh, what a big smile!', 'Ha! That's a big one!' (meaning a story), questioning replies like, 'Are you telling me a story?', 'Oh really?', or even agreement by nodding 'Yes' or saying 'I'm *sure* you're right' (1979).

Trevarthen and his colleague Sylvester-Bradley see these maternal responses as expressive of their perception of infants. They conclude: 'A mother evidently perceives her baby to be a person like herself. Mothers interpret baby behaviour as not only intended to be communicative, but as verbal and meaningful' (1979).

These perceptions of young humans are not, however, shared by mothers in all cultures. The maternal worldview described by Trevarthen and his colleague is not, for example, shared by most Western Samoan mothers living in traditional villages. Concepts of infancy differ radically in Samoan and Anglo-American communities. I have mentioned that American mothers often assign a particular personality to their infant. There is not even a word in the Samoan language for 'personality'. The idea that a given individual has a basic, consistent character is not part of the Samoan worldview (Shore, 1977). People are seen as constantly changing their demeanour, behaviour and mood in response to particular situations. People are said to have many sides (*itū*) and different sides emerge in different events (Shore, 1977). There is no core personality, however, that holds these sides together into a coherent individual.

Further, Samoans generally do not believe that an individual has a strong capacity to control and direct emotions and actions. Emotions and thoughts are often described as 'springing up suddenly' (Shore, 1977), outside the control of the individual. This type of springing up or impulse leads people to act in socially destructive ways – to fight or show disrespect, for example.

This belief contrasts sharply with that of Anglo-American culture. Anglo-American culture places a strong emphasis on *intentionality*, the ability to act in a self-conscious, goal-directed manner. As a member of this culture, I believe that individuals have the capacity to act *intentionally* as well as *unintentionally*. This distinction and this belief is very important and underlies the way in which members of the culture interpret acts and events. For example, I assess an act in terms of whether an individual acted intentionally or unintentionally. If damage was caused, I excuse it if it were unintentional but not if it were intentional. Our legal code responds to this distinction as well; sanctions are based in part on the extent to which the individual consciously performed the act.

This concern with intentionality is not present to the same extent in traditional Western Samoan communities. In assessing an act of a person, it is not relevant whether or not the person did so intentionally or unintentionally. What counts is the social consequences and the act and its impact on the family and community. An act will be negatively sanctioned if it has damaged the social order, regardless of whether or not the actor did so knowingly, consciously.

This worldview has an effect on the way in which Samoan caregivers interact with their infants and young children. Whereas the Anglo-American mother looks for individual personality traits of her infants, traits that distinguish that child from others, the Samoan mother does not. Whereas the Anglo-American mother responds to her infant as if that young infant were capable of conscious, intentional communication, the traditional Western Samoan mother does not.

The traditional Samoan mother operates in the belief that young children, particularly infants, have no control over their behaviour. They are born with certain natural impulses and it is these impulses that control the child's action. In the first year of life there is very little attempt to constrain the behaviours of the child and very little social instruction is directed to the child. The child, as Margaret Mead discovered, is not considered socially responsive or responsible during this period. Caregivers, then, have little inclination to search for the intentions behind infant behaviours or to engage in the type of pre-language communication reported over and over in the literature on maternal input. In the second year of life, caregivers begin to instruct children in publicly acceptable conduct – how to sit, how to eat, how to interact with siblings and elders and how to speak. This process of socialization produces a communicative relationship in which caregivers introduce and control topics. The very young, language-learning child is neither expected nor encouraged to initiate topics of talk.

What is the import of these behaviours to therapists, clinicians and educators? American society is filled with children of diverse ethnic backgrounds. Many ethnic groups share the cultural patterns just described for Samoan households. These cultural patterns are maintained inside individual households within the United States. The child is socialized inside the household, according to traditional norms and child-rearing practices. But once the child reaches the age of five or six, his days are spent outside the household, in formal classroom settings, where typically someone from outside his culture is the socializing agent. These children find themselves face-to-face with educators who do not share the same expectations as to how children and adults communicate with one another. These children may experience considerable distress in classroom settings or other settings in which they are expected to engage in a direct dialogue with an adult authority figure.

The educator without any background concerning the child's cultural values and norms may see the child's problem as a problem concerning knowledge of *English*. The child's problem is diagnosed as a *language proficiency* problem. The child might then be assigned to a professional who will work on facilitating the child's linguistic competence. Many minority children do have language learning problems. However, in the case at hand, the educator does not grasp the full nature of the minority child's problem. His problem is one of *cultural* interference rather than linguistic interference, a conflict in cultural norms for using language (Hymes, 1974) rather than a conflict in grammatical structure between first and second language.

The transition from monolingualism to bilingualism has been facilitated over the past several years by the availability of numerous language materials that outline points of contrast between a child's first language and English. The number and variety of materials that exist on cultural differences in conversational procedures and conventions is dramatically low. Basic observations have hardly been carried out and those that have been are by and large not communicated to educators and others who interact with ethnically diverse children on a day-to-day basis. Thus the ability of these children to make the transition from monoculturalism to biculturalism is severely hampered.

NOTE

This research is supported by the National Science Foundation, Grant no. 53-482-2480. principal investigator: Elinor Ochs.

REFERENCES

Atkinson, M. (1979) 'Prerequisites for Reference', in Ochs, E. and Schieffelin, B. B. (eds) *Developmental Pragmatics* (New York: Academic Press).

Bates, E., Camaioni, L. and Volterra, V. (1979) 'The Acquisition of Performatives Prior to Speech', in Ochs, E. and Schieffelin, B. B. (eds) *Developmental Pragmatics* (New York: Academic Press).

Brown, R., Cadzen, C. and Bellugi, U. (1969) 'The Child's Grammar from I to III', in Hill. J. P. (ed.) *Minnesota Symposia on Child Psychology*, vol. 2 (Minneapolis: University of Minnesota Press) (Reprinted as 'The Child's Grammar from I to III', in Ferguson, C. and Slobin, D. (eds) (1973) *Studies of Language Development* (New York: Holt, Rinehart & Winston)).

Cazden, C. (1965) *Environmental Assistance to the Child's Acquisition of Grammar*, Ph.D. thesis, Harvard University.

Cazden, C. (1972) *Child Language and Education* (New York: Holt, Rinehart & Winston).

Cross, T. (1975) 'Some Relationships Between Motherese and Linguistic Level in Accelerated Children', *Papers and Reports on Child Language Development*, no. 10 (Stanford, CA: Stanford University Press).

Cross, T. (1977) 'Mothers' Speech Adjustments: the Contribution of Selected Child Listener Variables', in Snow, C. and Ferguson, C. (eds) *Talking to Children*, (Cambridge: Cambridge University Press).

Ferguson, C. (1977) 'Baby Talk as a Simplified Register', in Snow, C. and Ferguson, C. (eds) *Talking to Children* (Cambridge: Cambridge University Press).

Hymes, D. (1974) *Foundations in Sociolinguistics: An Ethnographic Approach* (Philadelphia, PA: University of Pennsylvania Press).

Newport, E. (1976) 'Motherese: The Speech of Mothers to Young Children', in Castellan, N., Pisoni, D. and Potts, G. (eds) *Cognitive Theory*, Vol. II (Hillsdale, NJ: Lawrence Erlbaum).

Scollon, R. (1976) *Conversations with a One Year Old* (Honolulu: University of Hawaii Press).

Shore, B. (1977) *A Samoan Theory of Action: Social Control and Social Order in a Polynesian Paradox*, Ph.D. thesis (Chicago: University of Chicago).

Shotter, J. (1978) 'The Cultural Context of Communication Studies: Theoretical and Methodological Issues', in Lock, A. (ed.) *Action, Gesture and Symbol: The Emergence of Language* (London: Academic Press).

Snow, C. (1972) 'Mothers' Speech to Children Learning Language', *Child Development*, **43**, pp. 549–65.

Snow, C. (1977) 'The Development of Conversation Between Mothers and Babies', *Journal of Child Language*, **4**, pp. 1–22.

Snow, C. (1979) 'Conversations with Children', in Fletcher, P. and Garman, M. (eds) *Language Acquisition* (Cambridge: Cambridge University Press).

Stern, D. (1974) 'Mother and Infant at Play: The Dyadic Interaction Involving Facial, Vocal and Gaze Behaviors', in Lewis, M. and Rosenblum, L. (eds) *The Effect of the Infant on its Caregiver* (New York: John Wiley).

Stern, D. (1977) *The First Relationship: Infant and Mother* (London: Fontana/Open Books).

Trevarthen, C. (1979) 'Communication and Co-operation in Early Infancy: A Description of Primary Intersubjectivity', in Bullowa, M. (ed.) *Before Speech*, (Cambridge: Cambridge University Press) pp. 321–49.

Weisner, T. S. and Gallimore, R. (1977) 'My Brother's Keeper: Child and Sibling Caregiving', *Current Anthropology*, **18**(2), pp. 169–90.

Part VIII
Language and Culture

There is a risk that the sequential nature of any anthology, including this Reader, might suggest that what comes at the end of the book is somehow less important than what precedes it. That is not the case here. *Culture* is a key term in sociolinguistics generally, and sociolinguistics inherited a rich seam of scholarship about culture and cultural diversity from its beginnings. It will be useful, after reading the chapters in this section, to review many of the previously presented studies and reinterpret them from a cultural perspective.

The work of American anthropologists and linguists like Boas, Sapir and Whorf in the USA since the early twentieth century has spawned a large body of literature in the area known as *anthropological linguistics*. The early work was very largely concerned with Native American (what were once called 'American Indian' or 'Amerindian') languages, but soon spread over other geographical and linguistic territories. With its shifting focus, it acquired new labels: the ethnography of speaking, the ethnography of communication, and, more broadly, language and culture.

Anthropological linguists were primarily concerned with the structural properties of languages at all levels of linguistic analysis – phonology, morphology, lexis and syntax – and with the relations between those linguistic structures and the social, perceptual and cognitive structures of their speakers. Not unlike the German philosophers John Herder and Willhelm von Humboldt in the late eighteenth and early nineteenth centuries, they emphasized the great structural diversity across major language families and a strong link between linguistic structure and thought. This led Sapir, and later, more explicitly, Whorf, to formulate what is known today as the principle of *linguistic relativity* or *linguistic determinism*. It holds that languages, because of their differences in structure or 'fashions of speaking', influence the world-views of their speakers in different ways. This view is also known as the *Sapir–Whorf hypothesis*.

The first chapter of this section is one of Whorf's most important papers, expounding the ideas behind his linguistic relativity principle. Much controversy has arisen around Whorf's work, and this makes it particularly important to have some first-hand acquaintance with his writing. Reading Whorf's chapter, it is clear, for example, that his argument is not based on the simple mechanical correlation of certain types of languages (such as those with particular patterns of word-building – so-called 'isolating', 'synthetic' and 'agglutinating' languages) with agricultural, religious, or hunting patterns found in different communities. Whorf did not see language and culture to be as separable as this. Instead, he argued that there is an intimate link between the concepts of language and culture, and that the one cannot be studied without the other. The influence of language on culture, he felt, could only be studied with reference to the effect that habitual linguistic behaviour has on habitual thought.

Potentially, Whorf believed, all people are capable of perceiving the same states and relationships in the world. This is why a degree of success in translation from one language to another is always possible. But it is 'what is actually done', in Hymes's formulation of communicative competence (see Chapters 1, 5 and 11), which makes us limit our verbal repertoires, with consequences for how we see the world.

One of Whorf's best-known examples, described in detail in Chapter 34, is how *time* is conceptually represented by English and Hopi speakers. According to Whorf, through the grammatical patterning of 'number' (singular and plural) in English, speakers of English 'objectify' time. That is, they impose upon one the imaginary entity of 'time' an interpretation of time as a perceptible object which can be dissected into smaller units or chunks, and treated like any other mass noun (such as 'cheese'). From this follows the perception of time units, including past, present and future, as discrete entities, and time in general as a spatial–linear concept.

On the other hand, Hopi speakers have a more abstract view of time. To conceive of time 'becoming later' in Hopi does not mean observing a succession of hours, days or years (i.e. containers filled with time, as English models them) passing in front of our eyes. Time-flow for Hopi speakers, who do not have the grammatical requirement of objectifying time, is described more in terms of greater or lesser intensities of duration. Because, for Hopi people, time is consolidated, the units of time do not 'go away' but form a unitary concept in which *cyclicity* is experienced as a reappearance of the same day, season or year, and not a collection of different days, seasons or years. It is in this sense that historicity is not experienced by Hopi speakers in the same way as by the English speakers. For Hopis, the past cannot be 'cast off' from the rest of their temporal experience, and it 'resides' in the present.

Agar follows the Whorfian tradition, although he is not concerned with the structural differences between English and German. He is intrigued by the *connotational meaning* associated with culture-specific ways of speaking or speech events. He demonstrates, largely on the example of his own experiences as an adult learner of Austrian German, how successful communication in a (second) language implies participation in the culture of the native community. To put this differently, an ability to take a meaningful part in all the physical and cognitive activities of a community presupposes the knowledge of *interpretive frames* for the use of language in that community.

The notion of interpretive frames was borrowed by Agar from Artificial Intelligence studies and, generally speaking, much of anthropological linguistic research. Frames are patterns of expectations about what goes on in communication. They provide information about how to interpret and analyse utterances in interaction, which Agar finds useful from the point of view of an analyst and second language learner. This frame-analysis approach to cultural diversity and relativity gives Agar a necessary meta-language with which to compare communication in different systems. In this way Agar agrees with Whorf, who, despite his relativist position, searched for linguistic and non-linguistic means of what he called *calibration*: a method of linguistically unbiased description of the same situation or experience (see Lucy 1992: 32–3).

Labov's chapter in this part of the book reports a study which combines ethnographic and discourse analytic methods. His data were tape-recorded and then analysed to find the regularities of sequencing and interaction that govern the making of *ritual insults* among adolescent Blacks in Harlem. Linguistic and cultural knowledge prove to be inseparable for young people who want to be successful participants in certain speech events – here, the speech event of *sounding* or *playing the dirty dozens*. A speaker's verbal performance is favourably evaluated by peers only if she or he uses structurally and aesthetically effective ways of speaking. Rhythm, rhyme and alliteration, and smart, timely and appropriate responses, are needed to maintain one's reputation or to 'cut it'. There is also a tacit rule that the speaker shouldn't cross a fine line between ritual and personal insulting, so the speech event is morally regulated despite its obvious obscenity.

Finally, Chapter 37 again shows how ethnographic sociolinguistic research can contribute to cultural understanding of a community under study, and how the analysis of a specific type of speech act can illuminate rather general social and cultural patterns. Studies of requests, apologies, compliments, and other types of speech acts have used different data elicitation procedures, for example, written questionnaires and role-play. The most successful ones have relied on bodies of examples collected in naturally occurring situations. Herbert's study of Polish *compliments*, which he contrasts with compliments from different varieties of English, is of this sort. Differences between the contents, contexts of use and forms of Polish and English compliments lead Herbert to make observations about the Polish community's cultural values and informal patterns of social organization.

Herbert argues that the particularly high incidence of compliments about new possessions in Polish, as opposed to their English counterparts, can be related to the general unavailability of consumer goods in Poland (in the 1980s, i.e. before free-market economy reforms which followed the fall of Communism in Poland). A speaker offering a compliment acknowledges the addressee's good luck or admires the special effort s/he has invested in getting hold of something, through persistence or perhaps through setting up an elaborate social network. So what seems to be (*eti*cally – that is, at the level of observed phenomena) a compliment in Polish is in fact an *emic* (culturally meaningful) act of congratulations (see Saville-Troike, Chapter 11).

REFERENCE

Lucy, J. A. (1992) *Language, Diversity and Thought: A Reformulation of the Linguistic Relativity Hypothesis* (Cambridge: Cambridge University Press).

PART VIII: FURTHER READING

Bauman, R. (1983) *Let Your Words Be Few: Symbolism of Speaking and Silence among Seventeenth-century Quakers* (Cambridge: Cambridge University Press).
Bauman, R. and Sherzer, J. (eds) (1974) *Explorations in the Ethnography of Speaking* (Cambridge: Cambridge University Press).
Carbaugh, D. (ed.) (1990) *Cultural Communication and Intercultural Contact* (Hillsdale, NJ: Lawrence Erlbaum).
Garcia, O. and Otheguy, R. (eds) (1989) *English across Cultures, Cultures across English: A Reader in Cross-cultural Communication* (Berlin: Mouton de Gruyter).
Hymes, D. (ed.) (1964) *Language, Culture and Society: A Reader in Linguistics and Anthropology* (New York: Harper and Row).
Hymes, D. (1996) *Ethnography, Linguistics, Narrative Inequality: Toward an Understanding of Voice* (London: Taylor and Francis).
Leach, E. R. (1976) *Culture and Communication: The Logic by which Symbols are Connected. An Introduction to the Use of Structuralist Analysis in Social Anthropology* (Cambridge: Cambridge University Press).
Philips, S. U., Steele, S. and Tanz, C. (eds) (1987) *Language, Gender, and Sex in Comparative Perspective* (Cambridge: Cambridge University Press).
Saltzman, Z. (1993) *Language, Culture & Society* (Boulder, CO: Westview Press).
Sarangi, S. (1995) 'Culture', in Verschueren, J., Östman, J-O. and Blommaert, J. (eds) *Handbook of Pragmatics.* (Amsterdam: John Benjamins).
Scollon, R. and Scollon, S. W. (1981) *Narrative, Literacy and Face in Interethnic Communication* (Norwood, NJ: Ablex).
Sperber, D. (1996) *Explaining Culture: A Naturalistic Approach* (Oxford: Blackwell).
Ting-Tooney, S. and Korzenny, F. (eds) (1989) *Language, Communication and Culture: Current Directions* (Newbury Park, CA: Sage).
Valdes, J. M. (ed.) (1988) *Culture Bound: Bridging the Cultural Gap in Language Teaching* (Cambridge: Cambridge University Press).

34 The Relation of Habitual Thought and Behavior to Language

Benjamin Lee Whorf

Human beings do not live in the objective world alone, nor alone in the world of social activity as ordinarily understood, but are very much at the mercy of the particular language which has become the medium of expression for their society. It is quite an illusion to imagine that one adjusts to reality essentially without the use of language and that language is merely an incidental means of solving specific problems of communication or reflection. The fact of the matter is that the 'real world' is to a large extent unconsciously built up on the language habits of the group ... We see and hear and otherwise experience very largely as we do because the language habits of our community predispose certain choices of interpretation.

Edward Sapir

There will probably be general assent to the proposition that an accepted pattern of using words is often prior to certain lines of thinking and forms of behavior, but he who assents often sees in such a statement nothing more than a platitudinous recognition of the hypnotic power of philosophical and learned terminology on the one hand or of catchwords, slogans, and rallying cries on the other. To see only thus far is to miss the point of one of the important interconnections which Sapir saw between language, culture, and psychology, and succinctly expressed in the introductory quotation. It is not so much in these special uses of language as in its constant ways of arranging data and its most ordinary everyday analysis of phenomena that we need to recognize the influence it has on other activities, cultural and personal.

Source: 'The Relation of Habitual Thought and Behavior to Language', in Carroll, J. B. (ed. and intro.) (1956) *Language, Thought, and Reality: Selected Writings of Benjamin Lee Whorf* (Cambridge, MA: MIT Press), pp. 134–59 (this chapter was written in 1939).

THE NAME OF THE SITUATION AS AFFECTING BEHAVIOR

I came in touch with an aspect of this problem before I had studied under Dr Sapir, and in a field usually considered remote from linguistics. It was in the course of my professional work for a fire insurance company, in which I undertook the task of analyzing many hundreds of reports of circumstances surrounding the start of fires, and in some cases, of explosions. My analysis was directed toward purely physical conditions, such as defective wiring, presence or lack of air spaces between metal flues and woodwork, etc., and the results were presented in these terms. Indeed it was undertaken with no thought that any other significances would or could be revealed. But in due course it became evident that not only a physical situation *qua* physics, but the meaning of that situation to people, was sometimes a factor, through the behavior of the people, in the start of the fire. And this factor of meaning was clearest when it was a *linguistic meaning*, residing in the name or the linguistic description commonly applied to the situation. Thus, around a storage of what are called 'gasoline drums,' behavior will tend to a certain type, that is, great care will be exercised; while around a storage of what are called 'empty gasoline drums,' it will tend to be different – careless, with little repression of smoking or of tossing cigarette stubs about. Yet the 'empty' drums are perhaps the more dangerous, since they contain explosive vapor. Physically the situation is hazardous, but the linguistic analysis according to regular analogy must employ the word 'empty', which inevitably suggests lack of hazard. The word 'empty' is used in two linguistic patterns: (1) as a virtual synonym for 'null and void, negative, inert,' (2) applied in analysis of physical situations without regard to, e.g., vapor, liquid vestiges, or stray rubbish, in the container. The situation is named in one pattern (2) and the name is then 'acted out' or 'lived up to' in another (1), this being a general formula for the linguistic conditioning of behavior into hazardous forms.

In a wood distillation plant the metal stills were insulated with a composition prepared from limestone and called at the plant 'spun limestone.' No attempt was made to protect this covering from excessive heat or the contact of flame. After a period use, the fire below one of the stills spread to the 'limestone,' which to everyone's great surprise burned vigorously. Exposure to acetic acid fumes from the stills had converted part of the limestone (calcium carbonate) to calcium acetate. This when heated in a fire decomposes, forming inflammable acetone. Behavior that tolerated fire close to the covering was induced by use of the name 'limestone,' which because it ends in 'stone' implies non-combustibility. ...

Such examples, which could be greatly multiplied, will suffice to show how the cue to a certain line of behavior is often given by the analogies of the linguistic formula in which the situation is spoken of, and by which to some degree it is analyzed, classified, and allotted its place in that world which is 'to a large extent unconsciously built up on the language habits of the group.' And we always assume that the linguistic analysis made by our group reflects reality better than it does.

GRAMMATICAL PATTERNS AS INTERPRETATIONS OF EXPERIENCE

The linguistic material in the above examples is limited to single words, phrases, and patterns of limited range. One cannot study the behavioral compulsiveness of such material without suspecting a much more far-reaching compulsion from large-scale patterning of grammatical categories, such as plurality, gender and similar classifications (animate, inanimate, etc.), tenses, voices, and other verb forms, classifications of the type of 'parts of speech,' and the matter of whether a given experience is denoted by a unit morpheme, an inflected word, or a syntactical combination. A category such as number (singular vs. plural) is an attempted interpretation of a whole large order of experience, virtually of the world or of nature; it attempts to say how experience is to be segmented, what experience is to be called 'one' and what 'several.' But the difficulty of appraising such a far-reaching influence is great because of its background character, because of the difficulty of standing aside from our own language, which is a habit and a cultural *non est disputandum*, and scrutinizing it objectively. And if we take a very dissimilar language, this language becomes a part of nature, and we even do to it what we have already done to nature. We tend to think in our own language in order to examine the exotic language. Or we find the task of unraveling the purely morphological intricacies so gigantic that it seems to absorb all else. Yet the problem, though difficult, is feasible; and the best approach is through an exotic language, for in its study we are at long last pushed willy-nilly out of our ruts. Then we find that the exotic language is a mirror held up to our own.

In my study of the Hopi language, what I now see as an opportunity to work on this problem was first thrust upon me before I was clearly aware of the problem. The seemingly endless task of describing the morphology did finally end. Yet it was evident, especially in the light of Sapir's lectures on Navaho, that the description of the *language* was far from complete. I knew for example the morphological formation of plurals, but not how to use plurals. It was evident that the category of plural in Hopi was not the same thing as in English, French, or German. Certain things that were plural in these languages were singular in Hopi. The phase of investigation which now began consumed nearly two more years.

The work began to assume the character of a comparison between Hopi and western European languages. It also became evident that even the grammar of Hopi bore a relation to Hopi culture, and the grammar of European tongues to our own 'Western' or 'European' culture. And it appeared that the interrelation brought in those large subsummations of experience by language, such as our own terms 'time', 'space,' 'substance,' and 'matter.' Since, with respect to the traits compared, there is little difference between English, French, German, or other European languages with the *possible* (but doubtful) exception of Balto-Slavic and non-Indo-European, I have lumped these languages into one group called SAE, or 'Standard Average European.'

That portion of the whole investigation here to be reported may be summed up in two questions: (1) Are our own concepts of 'time,' 'space,' and 'matter' given in substantially the same form by experience to all men, or are they in part conditioned by the structure of particular languages? (2) Are there traceable affinities between (a) cultural and behavioral norms and (b) large-scale linguistic patterns? ...

PLURALITY AND NUMERATION IN SAE AND HOPI

In our language, that is SAE, plurality and cardinal numbers are applied in two ways: to real plurals and imaginary plurals. Or more exactly if less tersely: perceptible spatial aggregates and metaphorical aggregates. We say 'ten men' and also 'ten days.' Ten men either are or could be objectively perceived as ten, ten in one group perception[1] – ten men on a street corner, for instance. But 'ten days' cannot be objectively experienced. We experience only one day, today; the other nine (or even all ten) are something conjured up from memory or imagination. If 'ten days' be regarded as a group it must be as an 'imaginary,' mentally constructed group. Whence comes this mental pattern? Just as in the case of the fire-causing errors, from the fact that our language confuses the two different situations, has but one pattern for both. When we speak of 'ten steps forward, ten strokes on a bell,' or any similarly described cyclic sequence, 'times' of any sort, we are doing the same thing as with 'days.' *Cyclicity* brings the response of imaginary plurals. But a likeness of cyclicity to aggregates is not unmistakably given by experience prior to language, or it would be found in all languages, and it is not.

Our *awareness* of time and cyclicity does contain something immediate and subjective – the basic sense of 'becoming later and later.' But, in the habitual thought of us SAE people, this is converted under something quite different, which though mental should not be called subjective. I call it *objectified*, or imaginary, because it is patterned on the *outer* world. It is this that reflects our linguistic usage. Our tongue makes no distinction between numbers counted on discrete entities and numbers that are simply 'counting itself.' Habitual thought then assumes that in the latter the numbers are just as much counted on 'something' as in the former. This is objectification. Concepts of time lose contact with the subjective experience of 'becoming later' and are objectified as counted *quantities*, especially as lengths, made up of units as a length can be visibly marked off into inches. A 'length of time' is envisioned as a row of similar units, like a row of bottles.

In Hopi there is a different linguistic situation. Plurals and cardinals are used only for entities that form or can form an objective group. There are no imaginary plurals, but instead ordinals used with singulars. Such an expression as 'ten days' is not used. The equivalent statement is an operational one that reaches one day by a suitable count. 'They stayed ten days' becomes 'they stayed until the eleventh day' or 'they left after the tenth day.' 'Ten days is greater than nine days' becomes 'the tenth day is later than the ninth.' Our 'length of time' is not regarded as a length but as a relation between two events in lateness. Instead of our linguistically promoted objectification of that datum of consciousness we call 'time', the Hopi language has not laid down any pattern that would cloak the subjective 'becoming later' that is the essence of time.

NOUNS OF PHYSICAL QUANTITY IN SAE AND HOPI

We have two kinds of nouns denoting physical things: individual nouns, and mass nouns, e.g., 'water, milk, wood, granite, sand, flour, meat.' Individual nouns denote bodies with definite outlines: 'a tree, a stick, a man, a hill.' Mass nouns denote homogeneous continua without implied boundaries. The distinction is marked by linguistic form; e.g., mass nouns lack plurals,[2] in English drop articles, and in French take the partitive article *du, de la, des.* The distinction is more widespread in language than in the observable appearance of things. Rather few natural occurrences present themselves as unbounded extents; 'air' of course, and often 'water, rain, snow, sand, rock, dirt, grass.' We do not encounter 'butter, meat, cloth, iron, glass,' or most 'materials' in such kind of manifestation, but in bodies small or large with definite outlines. The distinction is somewhat forced upon our description of events by an unavoidable pattern in language. It is so inconvenient in a great many cases that we need some way of individualizing the mass bound by further linguistic devices. This is partly done by names of body-types: 'stick of wood, piece of cloth, pane of glass, cake of soap'; also, and even more, by introducing names of containers though their contents be the real issue: 'glass of water, cup of coffee, dish of food, bag of flour, bottle of beer.' These very common container formulas, in which 'of' has an obvious, visually perceptible meaning ('contents'), influence our feeling about the less obvious type-body formulas: 'stick of wood, lump of dough,' etc. The formulas are very similar: individual noun plus a similar relator

(English 'of'). In the obvious case this relator denotes contents. In the inobvious one it 'suggests' contents. Hence the 'lumps, chunks, blocks, pieces,' etc., seem to contain something, a 'stuff,' 'substance,' or 'matter' that answers to the 'water,' 'coffee,' or 'flour' in the container formulas. So with SAE people the philosophic 'substance' and 'matter' are also the naive idea; they are instantly acceptable, 'common sense.' It is so through linguistic habit. Our language patterns often require us to name a physical thing by a binomial that splits the reference into a formless item plus a form.

Hopi is again different. It has a formally distinguished class of nouns. But this class contains no formal subclass of mass nouns. All nouns have an individual sense and both singular and plural forms. Nouns translating most nearly our mass nouns still refer to vague bodies or vaguely bounded extents. They imply indefiniteness, but not lack, of outline and size. In specific statements, 'water' means one certain mass or quantity of water, not what we call 'the substance water.' Generality of statement is conveyed through the verb or predictor, not the noun. Since nouns are individual already, they are not individualized by either type-bodies or names of containers, if there is no special need to emphasize shape or container. The noun itself implies a suitable type-body or container. One says, not 'a glass of water' but *kə·yi* 'a water,' not 'a pool of water' but *pa·hə*,[3] not 'a dish of cornflour' but *ŋəmni* 'a (quantity of) cornflour,' not 'a piece of meat' but *sikʷi* 'a meat.' The language has neither need for nor analogies on which to build the concept of existence as a duality of formless item and form. It deals with formlessness through other symbols than nouns.

PHASES OF CYCLES IN SAE AND HOPI

Such terms as 'summer, winter, September, morning, noon, sunset' are with us nouns, and have little formal linguistic difference from other nouns. They can be subjects or objects, and we say 'at subset' or 'in winter' just as we say 'at a corner' or 'in an orchard.'[4] They are pluralized and numerated like nouns of physical objects, as we have seen. Our thought about the referents of such words hence becomes objectified. Without objectification, it would be a subjective experience of real time, i.e. of the consciousness of 'becoming later and later' – simply a cyclic phase similar to an earlier phase in that ever-later-becoming duration. Only by imagination can such a cyclic phase be set beside another and another in the manner of a spatial (i.e. visually perceived) configuration. But such is the power of linguistic analogy that we do so objectify cyclic phasing. We do it even by saying 'a phase' and 'phases' instead of, e.g., 'phasing.' And the pattern of individual and mass nouns, with the resulting binomial formula of formless item plus form, is so general that it is implicit for all nouns, and hence our very generalized formless items like 'substance, matter,' by which we can fill out the binomial for an enormously wide range of nouns. But even these are not quite generalized enough to take in our phase nouns. So for the phase nouns we have made a formless item, 'time.' We have made it by using 'a time,' i.e. an occasion or a phase, in the pattern of a mass noun, just as from 'a summer' we make 'summer' in the pattern of a mass noun. Thus with our binomial formula we can say and think 'a moment of time, a second of time, a year of time.' Let me again point out that the pattern is simply that of 'a bottle of milk' or 'a piece of cheese.' Thus we are assisted to imagine that 'a summer' actually contains or consists of such-and-such a quantity of 'time.'

In Hopi, however, all phase terms, like 'summer, morning,' etc., are not nouns but a kind of adverb, to use the nearest SAE analogy. They are a formal part of speech by themselves, distinct from nouns, verbs, and even other Hopi 'adverbs.' Such a word is not a case form or a locative pattern, like 'des Abends' or 'in the morning.' It contains no morpheme like one of 'in the house' or 'at the tree.'[5] It means 'when it is morning' or 'while morning-phase is occurring.' These 'temporals' are not used as subjects or objects, or at all like nouns. One does not say 'it's a hot summer' or 'summer is hot'; summer is not hot, summer is only *when* conditions are hot, *when* heat occurs. One does not say '*this* summer,' but 'summer now' or 'summer recently.' There is no objectification, as a region, an extent, a quantity, of the subjective duration-feeling. Nothing is suggested about time except the perpetual 'getting later' of it. And so there is no basis here for a formless item answering to our 'time.'

TEMPORAL FORMS OF VERBS IN SAE AND HOPI

The three-tense system of SAE verbs colors all our thinking about time. This system is amalgamated with that larger scheme of objectification of the subjective experience of duration already noted in other patterns – in the binomial formula applicable to nouns in general, in temporal nouns, in plurality and numeration. This objectification enables us in imagination to 'stand time units in a row.' Imagination of time as like a row harmonizes with a system of *three* tenses; whereas a system of *two*, an earlier and a later, would seem to correspond better to the feeling of duration as it is experienced. For if we inspect consciousness we find no past, present, future, but a unity embracing complexity. *Everything* is in consciousness, and everything in consciousness *is*, and is together. There is in it a sensuous and a nonsensuous. We may call the sensuous – what we are seeing, hearing, touching – the 'present' while in the nonsensuous the vast image-world of memory is being labeled 'the past' and another realm of belief, intuition, and uncertainty 'the future'; yet sensation, memory, foresight, all are in consciousness together – one is not 'yet to be' nor another 'once but no more.' Where real time comes in is that all this in consciousness is 'getting later,' changing certain relations in an irreversible manner. In this 'latering' or 'durating' there seems to me to be a paramount contrast between the newest, latest instant at the focus of attention and the rest – the earlier. Languages by the score get along well with two tenselike forms answering to this paramount relation of 'later' to 'earlier.' We can of course *construct and contemplate in thought* a system of past, present, future, in the objectified configuration of points on a line. This is what our general objectification tendency leads us to do and our tense system confirms.

In English the present tense seems the one least in harmony with the paramount temporal relation. It is as if pressed into various and not wholly congruous duties. One duty is to stand as objectified middle term between objectified past and objectified future, in narration, discussion, argument, logic, philosophy. Another is to denote inclusion in the sensuous field: 'I *see* him.' Another is for nomic, i.e. customarily or generally valid, statements: 'We *see* with our eyes.' These varied uses introduce confusions of thought, of which for the most part we are unaware.

Hopi, as we might expect, is different here too. Verbs have no 'tenses' like ours, but have validity-forms ('assertions'), aspects, and clause-linkage forms (modes), that yield even greater precision of speech. The validity-forms denote that the speaker (not the subject) reports the situation (answering to our past and present) or that he expects it (answering to our future)[6] or that he makes a nomic statement (answering to our nomic present). The aspects denote different degrees of duration and different kinds of tendency 'during duration.' As yet we have noted nothing to indicate whether an event is sooner or later than another when both are *reported*. But need for this does not arise until we have two verbs: i.e. two clauses. In that case the 'modes' denote relations between the clauses, including relations of later to earlier and of simultaneity. Then there are many detached words that express similar relations, supplementing the modes and aspects. The duties of our three-tense system and its tripartite linear objectified 'time' are distributed among various verb categories, all different from our tenses; and there is no more basis for an objectified time in Hopi verbs than in other Hopi patterns; although this does not in the least hinder the verb forms and other patterns from being closely adjusted to the pertinent realities of actual situations.

DURATION, INTENSITY, AND TENDENCY IN SAE AND HOPI

To fit discourse to manifold actual situations, all languages need to express durations, intensities, and tendencies. It is characteristic of SAE and perhaps of many other language types to express them metaphorically. The metaphors are those of spatial extension, i.e. of size, number (plurality), position, shape, and motion. We express duration by 'long, short, great, much, quick, slow,' etc.; intensity by 'large, great, much, heavy, light, high, low, sharp, faint,' etc.; tendency by 'more, increase, grow, turn, get, approach, go, come, rise, fall, stop, smooth, even, rapid, slow'; and so on through an almost inexhaustible list of metaphors that we hardly recognize as such, since they are virtually the only linguistic media available. The nonmetaphorical terms in this field, like 'early, late, soon, lasting, intense, very, tending,' are a mere handful, quite inadequate to the needs.

It is clear how this condition 'fits in.' It is part of our whole scheme of *objectifying* – imaginatively spatializing qualities and potentials that are quite nonspatial (so far as any spatially perceptive senses can tell us). Noun-meaning (with us) proceeds from physical bodies to referents of far other sort. Since physical bodies and their outlines in *perceived space* are denoted by size and shape terms and reckoned by cardinal numbers and plurals, these patterns of denotation and reckoning extend to the symbols of nonspatial meanings, and so suggest an *imaginary space*. Physical shapes 'move, stop, rise, sink, approach,' etc., in perceived space; why not these other referents in their imaginary space? This has gone so far that we can hardly refer to the simplest nonspatial situation without constant resort to physical metaphors. I 'grasp' the 'thread' of another's arguments, but if its 'level' is 'over my head' my attention may 'wander' and 'lose touch' with the 'drift' of it, so that when he 'comes' to his 'point' we differ 'widely,' our 'views' being indeed so 'far apart' that the 'things' he says 'appear' 'much' too arbitrary, or even 'a lot' of nonsense!

The absence of such metaphor from Hopi speech is striking. Use of space terms when there is no space involved is *not there* – as if on it had been laid the taboo teetotal! The reason is clear when we know that Hopi has abundant conjugational and lexical means of expressing duration, intensity, and tendency directly as such, and that major grammatical patterns do not, as with us, provide analogies for an imaginary space. The many verb 'aspects' express duration and tendency of manifestations, while some of the 'voices' express intensity, tendency, and duration of causes or forces producing manifestations. Then a special part of speech, the 'tensors,' a huge class of words, denotes only intensity, tendency, duration, and sequence. The function of the tensors is to express intensities, 'strengths,' and how they continue or vary, their rate of change; so that the broad concept of intensity, when considered as necessarily always varying and/or continuing, includes also tendency and duration. Tensors convey distinctions of degree, rate, constancy, repetition, increase and decrease of intensity, immediate sequence, interruption or sequence after an interval, etc., also *qualities* of strengths, such as we should express metaphorically as smooth, even, hard, rough. A striking feature is their lack of resemblance to the terms of real space and movement that to us 'mean the same.' There is not even more than a trace of apparent derivation from space terms.[7] So, while Hopi in its nouns seems highly concrete, here in the tensors it becomes abstract almost beyond our power to follow.

HABITUAL THOUGHT IN SAE AND HOPI

The comparison now to be made between the habitual thought worlds of SAE and Hopi speakers if of course incomplete. It is possible only to touch upon certain dominant contrasts that appear to stem from the linguistic differences already noted. By 'habitual thought' and 'thought world' I mean more than simply language, i.e. than the linguistic patterns themselves. I include all the analogical and suggestive value of the patterns (e.g., our 'imaginary space' and its distant implications), and all the give-and-take between language and the culture as a whole, wherein is a vast amount that is not linguistic but yet shows the shaping influence of language. In brief, this 'thought world' is the microcosm that each man carries about within himself, by which he measures and understands what he can of the macrocosm.

The SAE microcosm has analyzed reality largely in terms of what it calls 'things' (bodies and quasibodies) plus modes of extensional but formless existence that it calls 'substances' or 'matter.' It tends to see existence through a binomial formula that expresses any existent as a spatial form plus a spatial formless continuum related to the form, as contents is related to the outlines of its container. Nonspatial existents are imaginatively spatialized and charged with similar implications of form and continuum.

The Hopi microcosm seems to have analyzed reality largely in terms of EVENTS (or better 'eventing'), referred to in two ways, objective and subjective. Objectively, and only if perceptible physical experience, events are expressed mainly as outlines, colors, movements, and other perceptive reports. Subjectively, for both the physical and nonphysical, events are considered the expression of invisible intensity factors, on which depend their stability and persistence, or their fugitiveness and proclivities. It implies that existents do not 'become later and later' all in the same way; but some do so by growing like plants, some by diffusing and vanishing, some by a procession of metamorphoses, some by enduring in one shape till affected by violent forces. In the nature of each existent able to manifest as a definite whole is the power of its own mode of duration: its growth, decline, stability, cyclicity, or creativeness. Everything is thus already 'prepared' for the way it now manifests by earlier phases, and what it will be later, partly has been, and partly is in act of being so 'prepared.' An emphasis and importance rests on this preparing or being prepared aspect of the world that may to the Hopi correspond to that 'quality of reality' that 'matter' or 'stuff' has for us.

HABITUAL BEHAVIOR FEATURES OF HOPI CULTURE

Our behavior, and that of Hopi, can be seen to be coordinated in many ways to the linguistically conditioned microcosm. As in my fire casebook, people act about situations in ways which are like the ways they talk about them. A characteristic of Hopi behavior is the emphasis on preparation. This includes announcing and getting ready for events well beforehand, elaborate precautions to insure persistence of desired conditions, and stress on good will as the preparer of right results. Consider the analogies of the day-counting pattern alone. Time is mainly reckoned 'by day' (*taLk, -tala*) or 'by night' (*tok*), which words are not nouns but tensors, the first formed on a root 'light, day,' the second on a root 'sleep.' The count is by *ordinals*. This is not the pattern of counting a number of different men or things, even though they appear successively, for, even then, they *could* gather into an assemblage. It is the pattern of counting successive reappearances of the *same* man or thing, incapable of forming an assemblage. The analogy is not to behave about day-cyclicity as to several men ('several days'), which is what *we* tend to do, but to behave as to the successive visits of the *same man*. One does not alter several men by working upon just one, but one can prepare and so alter the later visits of the same man by working to affect the visit he is making now. This is the way the Hopi deal with the future – by working within a present situation which is expected to carry impresses, both obvious and occult, forward into the future event of interest. One might say that Hopi society understands our proverb 'Well begun is half done,' but not our 'Tomorrow is another day.' This may explain much in Hopi character.

This Hopi preparing behavior may be roughly divided into announcing, outer preparing, inner preparing, covert participation, and persistence. Announcing, or preparative publicity, is an important function in the hands of a special official, the Crier Chief. Outer preparing is preparation involving much visible activity, not all necessary directly useful within our understanding. It includes ordinary practicing, rehearsing, getting ready, introductory formalities, preparing of special food, etc. (all of these to a degree that may seem overelaborate to us), intensive sustained muscular activity like running, racing, dancing, which is thought to increase the intensity of development of events (such as growth of crops), mimetic and other magic, preparations based on esoteric theory involving perhaps occult instruments like prayer sticks, prayer feathers, and prayer meal, and finally the great cyclic ceremonies and dances, which have the significance of preparing rain and crops. From one of the verbs meaning 'prepare' is derived the noun for 'harvest' or 'crop': *na'twani* 'the prepared' or the 'in preparation.'[8]

Inner preparing is use of prayer and meditation, and at lesser intensity good wishes and good will, to further desired results. Hopi attitudes stress the power of desire and thought. With their 'microcosm' it is utterly natural that they should. Desire and thought are the earliest, and therefore the most important, most critical and crucial, stage of preparing. Moreover, to the Hopi, one's desires and thoughts influence not only his own actions, but all nature as well. This too is wholly natural. Consciousness itself is aware of work, of the feel of effort and energy, in desire and thinking. Experience more basic than language tells us that, if energy is expended, effects are produced. *we* tend to believe that our bodies can stop up this energy, prevent it from affecting other things until we will our *bodies* to over action. But this may be so only because we have our own linguistic basis for a theory that formless items like 'matter' are things in themselves, malleable only by similar things, by more matter, and hence insulated from the powers of life and thought. It is no more unnatural to think that thought contacts everything and pervades the universe than to think, as we all do, that light kindled outdoors does this. And it is not unnatural to suppose that thought, like any other force, leaves everywhere traces of effect. Now, when *we* think of a certain actual rosebush, we do not suppose that our thought goes to that actual bush, and engages with it, like a searchlight turned upon it. What then do we suppose our consciousness is dealing with when we are thinking of that rosebush? Probably we think it is dealing with a 'mental image' which is not the rosebush but a mental surrogate of it. But why should it be *natural* to think that our thought deals with a surrogate and not with the real rosebush? Quite possibly because we are dimly aware that we carry about with us a whole imaginary space, full of mental surrogates. To us, mental surrogates are old familar fare. Along with the images of imaginary space, which we perhaps secretly know to be only imaginary, we tuck the thought-of actually existing rosebush, which may be quite another story, perhaps just because we have that very convenient 'place' for it. The Hopi thought world has no imaginary space. The corollary to this is that it may not locate thought dealing with real space anywhere but in real space, nor insulate real space from the effects of thought. A Hopi would naturally suppose that his thought (or he himself) traffics with the actual rosebush – or more likely, corn plant – that he is thinking about. The thought then should leave some trace of itself with the plant in the field. If it is a good thought, one about health and growth, it is good for the plant; if a bad thought, the reverse.

The Hopi emphasize the intensity-factor of thought. Thought to be most effective should be vivid in consciousness, definite, steady, sustained, charged with strongly felt good intentions. They render the idea in English as 'concentrating, holding it in your heart, putting your mind on it, earnestly hoping.' Thought power is the force behind ceremonies, prayer sticks, ritual smoking, etc. The prayer pipe is regarded as an aid to 'concentrating' (so said my informant). Its name, *na'twanpi*, means 'instrument of preparing.'

Covert participation is mental collaboration from people who do not take part in the actual affair, be it a job of work, hunt, race, or ceremony, but direct their thought and good will toward the affair's success. Announcements often seek to enlist the support of such mental helpers as well as of overt participants, and contain exhortations to the people to aid with their active good will. A similarity to our concepts of a sympathetic audience or the cheering section at a football game should not obscure the fact that it is primarily the power of directed thought, and not merely sympathy or encouragement, that is expected of covert participants. In fact these latter get in their deadliest work before, not during, the game! A corollary to the power of thought is the power of wrong thought for evil; hence one purpose of covert participation is to obtain the mass force of many good wishers to offset the harmful thought of ill wishers. Such attitudes greatly favor cooperation and community spirit. Not that the Hopi community is not full of rivalries and colliding interests. Against the tendency to social disintegration in such a small, isolated group, the theory of 'preparing' by the power of thought, logically leading to the great power of the combined, intensified, and harmonized thought of the whole community, must help vastly toward the rather remarkable degree of cooperation that, in spite of much private bickering, the Hopi village displays in all the important cultural activities.

Hopi 'preparing' activities again show a result of their linguistic thought background in an emphasis on persistence and constant insistent repetition. A sense of the cumulative value of innumerable small momenta is dulled by an objectified, spatialized view of time like ours, enhanced by a way of thinking close to the subjective awareness of duration, of the ceaseless 'latering' of events. To us, for whom time is a motion on a space, unvarying repetition seems to scatter its force along a row of units of that space, and be wasted. To the Hopi, for whom time is not a motion but a 'getting later' of everything that has ever been done, unvarying repetition is not wasted but accumulated. It is storing up an invisible change that holds over into later events.[9] As we have seen, it is as if the return of the day were felt as the return of the same person, a little older but with all the impresses of yesterday, not as 'another day,' i.e. like an entirely different person. This principle joined with that of thought-power and with traits of general Pueblo culture is expressed in the theory of the Hopi ceremonial dance for furthering rain and crops, as well as in its short, piston-like tread, repeated thousands of times, hour after hour.

SOME IMPRESSES OF LINGUISTIC HABIT IN WESTERN CIVILIZATION

It is harder to do justice in few words to the linguistically conditioned features of our own culture than in the case of the Hopi, because of both vast scope and difficulty of objectivity – because of our deeply ingrained familiarity with the attitudes to be analyzed. I wish merely to sketch certain characteristics adjusted to our linguistic binomialism of form plus formless item or 'substance,' to our metaphoricalness, our imaginary space, and our objectified time. These, as we have seen, are linguistic.

From the form-plus-substance dichotomy the philosophical views most traditionally characteristic of the 'Western world' have derived huge support. Here belong materialism, psychophysical parallelism, physics – at least in its traditional Newtonian form – and dualistic views of the universe in general. Indeed here belongs almost everything that is 'hard, practical common sense.' Monistic, holistic, and relativistic views of reality appeal to philosophers and some scientists, but they are badly handicapped in appealing to the 'common sense' of the Western average man – not because nature herself refutes them (if she did, philosophers could have discovered this much), but because they must be talked about in what amounts to a new language. 'Common sense,' as its name shows, and 'practicality' as its name does not show, are largely matters of talking so that one is readily understood. It is sometimes stated that Newtonian space, time, and matter are sensed by everyone intuitively, whereupon relativity is cited as showing how mathematical analysis can prove intuition wrong. This, besides being unfair to intuition, is an attempt to answer offhand question (1) put at the outset of this paper, to answer which this research was undertaken. Presentation of the findings now nears its end, and I think the answer is clear. The offhand answer, laying the blame upon intuition for our slowness in discovering mysteries of the Cosmos, such as relativity, is the wrong one. The right answer is: Newtonian space, time, and matter are no intuitions. They are receipts from culture and language. That is where Newton got them.

Our objectified view of time is, however, favorable to historicity and to everything connected with the keeping of records, while the Hopi view is unfavorable thereto. The latter is too subtle, complex, and ever-developing, supplying no ready-made answer to the question of when 'one' event ends and 'another' begins. When it is implicit that everything that ever happened still is, but is in a necessarily different form from what memory or record reports, there is less incentive to study the past. As for the present, the incentive would be not to record it but to treat it as 'preparing.' But *our* objectified time puts before imagination something like a ribbon or scroll marked off into equal blank spaces, suggesting that each be filled with an entry. Writing has no doubt helped toward our linguistic treatment of time, even as the linguistic treatment has guided the uses of writing. Through this give-and-take between language and the whole culture we get, for instance:

1. Records, diaries, bookkeeping, accounting, mathematics stimulated by accounting.

2. Interest in exact sequence, dating, calendars, chronology, clocks, time wages, time graphs, time as used in physics.
3. Annals, histories, the historical attitude, interest in the past, archaeology, attitudes of introjection toward past periods, e.g. classicism, romanticism.

Just as we conceive our objectified time as extending in the future in the same way that it extends in the past, so we set down our estimates of the future in the same shape as our records of the past, producing programs, schedules, budgets. The formal equality of the spacelike units by which we measure and conceive time leads us to consider the 'formless item' or 'substance' of time to be homogeneous and in ratio to the number of units. Hence our prorata allocation of value to time, lending itself to the building up of a commercial structure based on time-prorata values: time wages (time work constantly supersedes piece work), rent, credit, interest, depreciation charges, and insurance premiums. No doubt this vast system, once built, would continue to run under any sort of linguistic treatment of time; but that it should have been built at all, reaching the magnitude and particular form it has in the Western world, is a fact decidedly in consonance with the patterns of the SAE languages. Whether such a civilization as ours would be possible with widely different linguistic handling of time is a large question – in our civilization, our linguistic patterns and the fitting of our behavior to the temporal order are what they are, and they are in accord. We are of course stimulated to use calendars, clocks, and watches, and to try to measure time ever more precisely; this aids science, and science in turn, following these well-worn cultural grooves, gives back to culture an ever-growing store of applications, habits, and values, with which culture again directs science. But what lies outside this spiral? Science is beginning to find that there is something in the Cosmos that is not in accord with the concepts we have formed in mounting the spiral. It is trying to frame a *new language* by which to adjust itself to a wider universe.

It is clear how the emphasis on 'saving time' which goes with all the above and is very obvious objectification of time, leads to a high valuation of 'speed,' which shows itself a great deal in our behavior.

Still another behavioral effect is that the character of monotony and regularity possessed by our image of time as an evenly scaled limitless tape measure persuades us to behave as if that monotony were more true of events than it really is. That is, it helps to routinize us. We tend to select and favor whatever bears out this view, to 'play up to' the routine aspects of existence. One phase of this is behavior evincing a false sense of security or an assumption that all will always go smoothly, and a lack in foreseeing and protecting ourselves against hazards. Our technique of harnessing energy does well in routine performance, and it is along routine lines that we chiefly strive to improve it – we are, for example, relatively uninterested in stopping the energy from causing accidents, fires, and explosions, which it is doing constantly and on a wide scale. Such indifference to the unexpectedness of life would be disastrous to a society as small, isolated, and precariously poised as the Hopi society is, or rather once was.

Thus our linguistically determined thought world not only collaborates with our cultural idols and ideals, but engages even our unconscious personal reactions in its patterns and gives them certain typical characters. One such character, as we have seen is *carelessness*, as in reckless driving or throwing cigarette stubs into waste paper. Another of a different sort is *gesturing* when we talk. Very many of the gestures made by English-speaking people at least, and probably by all SAE speakers, serve to illustrate, by a movement in space, not a real spatial reference but one of the nonspatial references that our language handles by metaphors of imaginary space. That is, we are more apt to make a grasping gesture when we speak of grasping an elusive idea than when we speak of grasping a doorknob. The gesture seeks to make a metaphorical and hence somewhat unclear reference more clear. But, if a language refers to nonspatials without implying a spatial analogy, the reference is not made any clearer by gesture. The Hopi gesture very little, perhaps not at all in the sense we understand as gesture.

It would seem as if kinesthesia, or the sensing of muscular movement, though arising before language, should be made more highly conscious by linguistic use of imaginary space and metaphorical images of motion. Kinesthesia is marked in two facets of European culture: art and sport. European sculpture, an art in which Europe excels, is strongly kinesthetic, conveying great sense of the body's motions; European painting likewise. The dance in our culture expresses delight in motion rather than symbolism or ceremonial, and our music is greatly influenced by our dance forms. Our sports are strongly imbued with this element of the 'poetry of motion.' Hopi races and games seem to emphasize rather the virtues of endurance and sustained intensity. Hopi dancing is highly symbolic and is performed with great intensity and earnestness, but has not much movement or swing.

Synesthesia, or suggestion by certain sense receptions of characters belonging to another sense, as of light and color by sound and vice versa, should be made more conscious by a linguistic metaphorical system that refers to nonspatial experiences by terms for spatial ones, though undoubtedly it arises from a deeper source. Probably in the first instance metaphor arises from synesthesia and not the reverse; yet metaphor need not become firmly rooted in linguistic pattern, as Hopi shows. Nonspatial experience has one well-organized sense, *hearing* – for smell and taste are but little organized. Nonspatial consciousness is a realm chiefly of thought, feeling, and *sound*. Spatial consciousness is a realm of light, color, sight, and touch, and presents shapes and dimensions. Our metaphorical system, by naming nonspatial experiences after spatial ones, imputes to sound, smells, tastes, emotions, and thoughts qualities like the colors, luminosities, shapes, angles, textures, and motions of spatial experience. And to some extent the reverse transference occurs; for, after much talking about tones as high, low, sharp, dull, heavy, brilliant, slow, the talker finds it easy to think of some factors in spatial experience as like factors of tone. Thus we speak of 'tones' of color, a gray 'monotone,' a'loud' necktie, a 'taste' in dress: all spatial metaphor in reverse. Now European art is distinctive in the way it seeks deliberately to play with synesthesia. Music tries to suggest scenes, color, movement, geometric design; painting and sculpture are often consciously guided by the analogies of music's rhythm; colors are conjoined with feeling for the analogy to concords and discords. The European theater and opera seek a synthesis of many arts. It may be that in this way our metaphorical language that is in some sense a confusion of thought is producing, through art, a result of far-reaching value – a deeper esthetic sense leading toward a more direct apprehension of underlying unity behind the phenomena so variously reported by our sense channels.

HISTORICAL IMPLICATIONS

How does such a network of language, culture, and behavior come about historically? Which was first: the language patterns or the cultural norms? In main they have grown up together, constantly influencing each other. But in this partnership the nature of the language is the factor that limits free plasticity and rigidifies channels of development in the more autocratic way. This is so because a language is a system, not just an assemblage of norms. Large systematic outlines can change to something really new only very slowly, while many other cultural innovations are made with comparative quickness. Language thus represents the mass mind; it is affected by inventions and innovations, but affected little and slowly, whereas to inventors and innovators it legislates with the decree immediate.

The growth of the SAE language-culture complex dates from ancient times. Much of its metaphorical reference to the nonspatial by the spatial was already fixed in the ancient tongues, and more especially in Latin. It is indeed a marked trait of Latin. If we compare, say Hebrew, we find that, while Hebrew has some allusion to not-space as space, Latin has more. Latin terms for nonspatials, like *educo, religio, principia, comprehendo*, are usually metaphorized physical references: lead out, tying back, etc. This is not true of all languages – it is quite untrue of Hopi. The fact that in Latin the direction of development happened to be from spatial to nonspatial (partly because of secondary stimulation to abstract thinking when the intellectually crude Romans encountered Greek culture) and that later tongues were strongly stimulated to mimic Latin, seems a likely reason for a belief, which still lingers on among linguists, that this is the natural direction of semantic change in all languages, and for the persistent notion in Western learned circles (in strong contrast to Eastern ones) that objective experience is prior to subjective. Philosophies make out a weighty case for the reverse, and certainly the direction of development is sometimes the reverse. Thus the Hopi word for 'heart' can be shown to be a late formation within Hopi from a root meaning think or remember. Or consider what has happened to the word 'radio' in such a sentence as 'he bought a new radio,' as compared to its prior meaning 'science of wireless telephony.'

In the Middle Ages the patterns already formed in Latin began to interweave with the increased mechanical invention, industry, trade, and scholastic and scientific thought. The need for measurement in industry and trade, the stores and bulks of 'stuffs' in various containers, the type-bodies in which various goods were handled, standardizing of measure and weight units, invention of clocks and measurement of 'time,' keeping of records, accounts, chronicles, histories, growth of mathematics and the partnership of mathematics and science, all cooperated to bring our thought and language world into its present form.

In Hopi history, could we read it, we should find a different type of language and a different set of cultural and environmental influences working together. A peaceful agricultural society isolated by geographic features and nomad enemies in a land of scanty rainfall, arid agriculture that could be made successful only by the utmost perseverance (hence the value of persistence and repetition), necessity for collaboration (hence emphasis on the psychology of teamwork and on mental factors in general), corn and rain as primary criteria of value, need of extensive *preparations* and precautions to assure crops in the poor soil and precarious climate, keen realization of dependence upon nature favoring prayer and a religious attitude toward the forces of nature, especially prayer and religion directed toward the ever-needed blessing, rain – these things interacted with Hopi linguistic patterns to mold them, to be molded again by them, and so little by little to shape the Hopi world-outlook.

To sum up the matter, our first question asked in the beginning is answered thus: Concepts of 'time' and 'matter' are not given in substantially the same form by experience to all men but depend upon the nature of the language or languages through the use of which they have been developed. They do not depend so much upon *any one system* (e.g., tense, or nouns) within the grammar as upon the ways of analyzing and reporting experience which have become fixed in the language as integrated 'fashions of speaking' and which cut across the typical grammatical classifications, so that such a 'fashion' may include lexical, morphological, syntactic, and otherwise systematically diverse means coordinated in a certain frame of consistency. Our own 'time' differs markedly from Hopi 'duration.' It is conceived as like a space of strictly limited dimensions, or sometimes as like a motion upon such a space, and employed as an intellectual tool accordingly. Hopi 'duration' seems to be inconceivable in terms of space or motion, being the mode in which life differs from form, and consciousness *in toto* from the spatial elements of consciousness. Certain ideas born of our own time-concept, such as that of absolute simultaneity, would be either very difficult to express or impossible and devoid of meaning under the Hopi conception, and would be replaced by operational concepts. Our 'matter' is the physical subtype of 'substance' or 'stuff,' which is conceived as the formless extensional item that must be joined with form before there can be real existence. In Hopi there seems to be nothing corresponding to it; there are no formless extensional items; existence may or may not have form, but what it also has, with or without form, is intensity and duration, these being nonextensional and at bottom the same.

But what about our concept of 'space,' which was also included in our first question? There is no such striking difference between Hopi and SAE about space as about time, and probably the apprehension of space is given in substantially the same form by experience irrespective of language. The experiments of the Gestalt psychologists with visual perception appear to establish this as a fact. But the *concept of space* will vary somewhat with language, because, as an intellectual tool,[10] it is so closely linked with the concomitant employment of other intellectual tools, of the order of 'time' and 'matter,' which are linguistically conditioned. We see things with our eyes in the same space forms as the Hopi, but our idea of space has also the property of acting as a surrogate of nonspatial relationships like time, intensity, tendency, and as a void to be filled with imagined formless items, one of which may even be called 'space.' Space as sensed by the Hopi would not be connected mentally with such surrogates, but would be comparatively 'pure,' unmixed with extraneous notions.

As for our second question: There are connections but not correlations or diagnostic correspondence between cultural norms and linguistic patterns. Although it would be impossible to infer the existence of Crier Chiefs from the lack of tenses in Hopi, or vice versa, there is a relation between a language and the rest of the culture of the society which uses it. There are cases where the 'fashions of speaking' are closely integrated with the whole general culture, whether or not this be universally true, and there are connections within this integration, between the kind of linguistic analyses employed and various behavioral reactions and also the shapes taken by various cultural developments. Thus the importance of Crier Chiefs does have a connection, not with tenselessness itself, but with a system of thought in which categories different from our tenses are natural. These connections are to be found not so much by focusing attention on the typical rubrics of linguistic, ethnographic, or sociological description as by examining the culture and the language (always and only when the two have been together historically for a considerable time) as a whole in which concatenations that run across these departmental lines may be expected to exist, and, if they do exist, eventually to be discoverable by study.

NOTES

1 As we say, 'ten at the *same time*,' showing that in our language and thought we restate the fact of group perception in terms of a concept 'time,' the large linguistic component of which will appear in the course of this chapter.

2 It is no exception to this rule of lacking a plural that a mass noun may sometimes coincide in lexeme with an individual noun that of course has a plural; e.g., 'stone' (no pl.) with 'a stone' (pl. 'stones'). The plural form denoting varieties, e.g., 'wines' is of course a different sort of thing from the true plural; it is a curious outgrowth from the SAE mass nouns, leading to still another sort of imaginary aggregates, which will have to be omitted from this chapter.

3 Hopi has two words for water quantities; *kə·yi* and *pa·hə*. The difference is something like that between 'stone' and 'rock' in English, *pa·hə* implying greater size and 'wildness'; flowing water, whether or not outdoors or in nature, is *pa·hə*; so is 'moisture.' But, unlike 'stone' and 'rock,' the difference is essential, not pertaining to a connotative margin, and the two can hardly ever be interchanged.

4 To be sure, there are a few minor differences from other nouns, in English for instance in the use of the articles.

5 'Year' and certain combinations of 'year' with name of season, rarely season names alone, can occur with a locative morpheme 'at,' but this is exceptional. It appears like historical detritus of an earlier different patterning, or the effect of English analogy, or both.

6 The expective and reportive assertions contrast according to the 'paramount relation.' The expective expresses anticipation existing *earlier* than objective fact, and coinciding with objective fact *later* than the status quo of the speaker, this status quo, including all the subsummation of the past therein, being expressed by the reportive. Our notion 'future' seems to represent at once the earlier (anticipation) and the later (afterwards, what will be), as Hopi shows. This paradox may hint of how elusive the mystery of real time is, and how artificially it is expressed by a linear relation of past–present–future.

7 One such trace is that the tensor 'long in duration,' while quite different from the adjective 'long' of space, seems to contain the same root as the adjective 'large' of space. Another is that 'somewhere' of space used with certain tensors means 'at some indefinite time.' Possibly however this is not the case and it is only the tensor that gives the time element, so that 'somewhere' still refers to space and that under these conditions indefinite space means simply general applicability, regardless of either time or space. Another trace is that in the temporal (cycle word) 'afternoon' the element meaning 'after' is derived from the verb 'to separate.' There are other such traces, but they are few and exceptional, and obviously not like our own spatial metaphorizing.

8 The Hopi verbs of preparing naturally do not correspond neatly to our 'prepare'; so that *na'twani* could also be rendered 'the practiced upon, the tried for,' and otherwise.

9 This notion of storing up power, which seems implied by much Hopi behavior, has an analog in physics: acceleration. It might be said that the linguistic background of Hopi thought equips it to recognize naturally that force manifests not as motion or velocity, but as cumulation or acceleration. Our

linguistic background tends to hinder in us this same recognition, for having legitimately conceived force to be that which produces change, we then think of change by our linguistic metaphorical analog, motion, instead of by a pure motionless changingness concept, i.e. accumulation or acceleration. Hence it comes to our naïve feeling as a shock to find from physical experiments that it is not possible to define force by motion, that motion and speed, as also 'being at rest,' are wholly relative, and that force can be measured only by acceleration.

10   Here belong 'Newtonian' and 'Euclidean' space, etc.

35 The Biculture in Bilingual

Michael Agar

It is now a cliché to observe that – whether due to political and economic migration, participation in the global economy, intrastate nationalism, or simply media and travel – normal everyday life is now carried out in multicultural worlds. The shifting and shifty relationships between co-occurrent languages and cultures – at the level of adult L2 use as well as the level of community – contain the key that will unlock an interesting and useful ethnographic future.

These are grand claims that legitimate an interest born of personal experience. Though I'd tried on different L2s before – Kannada, Spanish, and a taste of Demotic Greek – 1989's adventures as a linguist in Vienna led me deeper into an L2 world than I'd ever been before. The story begins in 1962, at the age of 17, when I went to a small town in Austria as an American Field Service exchange student.

I had never studied German. My 15-year-old Austrian 'brother' and I hammered out a pidgin made of Latin, which we had both studied; English, which he'd begun to learn; and Austrian German, which I was picking up. By the end of my $4\frac{1}{2}$ months, I was fluent in the limited role of obnoxious teenager. When I returned to the United States, my high school, and then my university, didn't know what to do with me. I'd chat comfortably – most of the graduate students couldn't do that – but only in the adolescent male vocabulary that I'd been exposed to, with a grammar and lexicon that were disasters.

The story goes on and on through several visits with my exchange family over the years, but for now I'll skip to the Fall semester of 1986, when I lived in Vienna and studied at the Linguistics Institute at the University, the first time since 1962 that I'd spent substantial time in Austria.

It was terrible. I couldn't have an interesting conversation, discuss things with colleagues, pass the time of day at the corner store, understand TV or movies or the paper, never mind the professional literature. And this, to add insult to injury, in a language that 'felt' comfortable. *Sprachgefühl*, they call it.

By the end of that semester I knew I was on the way to something but didn't know exactly what it was. Exchange family, neighbors, colleagues,

Source: 'The Biculture in Bilingual', *Language and Society*, **20**, 2 (1991) pp. 169–81.

acquaintances, friends, and a lover had helped me toward an appreciation of everything from high-level premises about the world and how it worked down to how to ask for a drink in Austrian and the various semantic spins all those prefixes gave to verbs.

In 1989, I returned to Vienna and lived there the entire calendar year. For the Spring semester I was an official *Gastprofessor*, taught three classes, and worked with students in Austrian German. The rest of the year, I continued working with colleagues and students; wrote papers; gave lectures – sometimes in English; dealt with the kinds of people I'd known before, only in more interesting ways; talked elaborately (if clumsily) without being exhausted after a couple of hours; watched TV; went to the movies; read the papers; made a few jokes that worked; and began to feel the web of associations that echoed in certain things I said and heard.

At the end of the year, I met someone I hardly knew in a coffee house, and we sat and conducted an elaborate conversation across several topics that I'd never 'rehearsed,' though a couple of times I couldn't get things out. I was invited to give a lecture at the Austrian linguistics meetings and wrote an original paper from scratch in German that went over well, though the best discussion question at the end was beyond my capability to spontaneously handle. I cracked a joke about Vienna's mayor that kept a taxi driver laughing for a block, though he'd had trouble understanding my description of the location of my apartment. I thought of myself as being in the bilingual basement.

I left with regret. I dreamed that I tried to step away from Vienna but fastened to my back was the narrow end of a net that grew ever larger with distance, a net whose ends eventually disappeared into the city. Another net, of course, holds me to the United States. Now that I'm back, many of the pieces of the two nets overlap nicely, some are close but of a different weave, and some are made of entirely different material. This chapter is a step in the direction of trying to figure out what those differences are and why they obtain. ...

In an article in the magazine *American Film* some years ago, Salman Rushdie wrote of a new 'immigrant sensibility,' a view of the world where multiple cultural systems combine as a matter of course, however awkwardly or smoothly, in the same situation. He was writing of the growing number of films that combine story, setting, actors, and crew from multiple cultural traditions. But the biculturalism that the literature points toward, the sensibility that Rushdie wrote about, hints at a mentality, one that may increase as we enter the next century, one that transcends what we ordinarily think of as 'culture.'

Whatever that is. Years ago two of the founding anthropological fathers gathered a collection of definitions into a book (Kroeber & Kluckhohn 1966), and that was before Derrida. *Culture* is – always was – a highly problematic term, to put it mildly. Terms from pragmatics, like 'background knowledge,' or from sociology, like 'members' resources,' just dress the problems in different clothes. Yet some sort of notion is essential, not only because the bilingual literature points at it, but because culture or background knowledge or member's resources are what make the difference between the speechless master of L2 syntax and the L2 speaker who is communicatively competent in a nonnative world.

Let's return to the situated use of L2 and rebuild culture from the ground up. By 'use of L2' I mean something rather specific. Among the many features used to distinguish different kinds of bilingualism, two are relevant here. The first differentiates between *child* L2 acquisition before the critical period that ends at ±11 years and *adult* acquisition. The second feature differentiates L2 acquisition in an L1/L2 *bilingual community* and L2 acquisition in a world where the learner's L1 is not ordinarily part of everyday life. Here, I'm dealing with adult acquisition of L2 in a non-L1 world.

Next, a view of language is necessary that unites language and culture rather than treats them as separate entities. Friedrich (1989) suggested 'linguaculture,' which is appealing on several grounds, but the term creates problematic associations with 'agriculture' and so on among English speakers. Recent notions of 'discourse' may do the job, because some, at least, use the term to mean social practices involving language, language together with the resources that go into its production and interpretation (Brown & Yule 1983; Fairclough 1989).

Some principles that underlie this notion of discourse have become fairly well established (see overviews of the field such as Brown & Yule 1983; Bulow-Moller 1989; de Beaugrande & Dressler 1981; Stubbs 1983).

1. The sentence has lost its privileged status as the primary focus. Discourse is the data; the sentence or utterance is only a special case.
2. When you lift up a piece of discourse – be it lexical item, utterance, or extended text – interpretative strands of association and use stick to it like putty.
3. The putty is reshaped by the analyst into interpretive frames, and with 'frames' I mean to call up the elaborate literature in artificial intelligence that deals with knowledge structures, just as the cited overviews of discourse do (see also Agar & Hobbs 1985; van Dijk 1979).
4. The frames, therefore, are built from sources other than the language at hand – from the analyst's best current knowledge about contexts of culture, situation, and speech; and from such strange sources that make the difference between good and mediocre analysis as intuition and insight.
5. From this point of view, then, the key problem for the study of language is the methodology and theoretical basis for the construction and validation of interpretive frames.

With the term 'frame,' I mean to move the discussion of 'nets' and 'putty' into a world of self-conscious systematic analysis. 'Frame' and its kin – like 'script' and 'schema' – have already proved themselves useful in a variety of fields (see Casson 1983, for examples of their use in anthropology). Frames are structures of interrelated expectations into which a particular expression fits. Frames provide a context in terms of which an expression makes sense, knowledge in terms of which the expression can be discussed, and links in terms of which the poetic echoes (Friedrich 1986) can be made explicit. Frames vary in scope, link to other frames, and in general offer a useful systematic fiction in terms of which the analyst can make explicit a way to understand, a way to interpret, a problematic piece of language.

Now I would like to use discourse as a departure point and develop an approach to L2 acquisition as the study of interpretive frames. The story begins with an epistemology, one that I developed for ethnographic research a few years ago in *Speaking of Ethnography* (Agar 1985). The heart of that epistemology, based on Gadamer's hermeneutic philosphy, holds that when two languages are brought into contact, some connections are fairly simple to forge. Others, in contrast, are striking by their difficulty.

The problem is Whorfian, with a simple twist. Unlike Whorf's the argument about language differences is not a global one, that two languages, *in general*, constitute an insurmountable or difficult barrier, depending on which version of the Sapir–Whorf hypothesis you hold to. Instead, the argument is that points of contact vary – some, perhaps most, are easy jumps; some are traversed only with difficulty; and a few are almost impossible to connect. Rather than a Whorfian wall, a Whorfian Alps would be a better image, a mountain range with plenty of valleys and trails and a few vertical cliffs.

When two languages are brought into contact, the most interesting problems for an L2 learner with the goal of communicative competence, the problems that tend to attract the learner's attention, are the vertical cliffs. The cliffs are difficult because – on one side of the language barrier or another, or perhaps on both sides – the problematic bit of language is puttied thickly into far-reaching networks of association and many situations of use. When one grabs such a piece of language, the putty is so thick and so spread out that it's almost impossible to lift the piece of language out.

I need a name for this language location, this Whorfian cliff, this particular place in one language that makes it so difficult to connect with another. I will call it 'rich,' with the connotations of tasty, thick, and wealthy all intended. The rich points in one language are relative to the other language that is brought into contact with it. The juxtaposition of American English and Austrian German may highlight rich points in both that a juxtaposition of English and Hopi wouldn't, and conversely.

But, in principle, as a prediction in the tradition of comparative linguistics, let's say that a language has rich points that emerge across comparisons with several other languages. We then suspect that those rich points are so intricately and uniquely tied into a language-specific putty that they are not just rich points relative to Lx, Ly, and so on, but that they are rich points in the language, period.

A second prediction, based on my experiences working in 1989 in Austria, is that rich points are also areas that native speakers recognize instantly and then disagree over when they discuss them. Because the putty is thick and broad, different native speakers can take different interpretive trails through it. The comparative test that I mentioned earlier signals rich points from outside; immediate native speaker recognition followed by disagreement signals rich points from the inside.

Rich points, then, are surface forms that tap deeply into the world that accompanies language, where that world cn be represented by systems of interpretive frames. To the extent that those frames enable communication with native L2 speakers who share a particular social identity, we can speak of a culture of that identity, from the L1 speaker's point of view, and characterize it in terms of just those frames that enable an L1 speaker to become communicatively competent.

This is a peculiar notion of culture. First of all, following the ethnographic epistemology outlined earlier, it is a model of new interpretive resources the L1 speaker requires to understand and produce the L2 rich point in a communicatively competent way. Second, the coupling of frames with social identity allows for a variety of 'partial' cultures – traditional cultural labels (the Apache), ethnicity (Chicano), class (the elites), occupation (mechanics), gender (women's language), lifestyles (yuppies), regions (Southerners), states (Austrians), and so on. This suggests variable cultures within any human aggregate, and within any human speaker within that aggregate. The complicated image that this notion of culture evokes is, I think, the right basis for an understanding of the 'immigrant sensibility' that Rushdie described.

During my recent year in Austria, students in my 'Pragmatics and Culture' class did an ethnographic investigation of one rich point in Austrian German labeled *Schmäh*. *Schmäh* is difficult to translate, and native speakers disagreed over what it meant. It acts like a rich point. We investigated it using three methods:

1. A systematic interview in the tradition of ethnographic semantics around the concept of *Schmäh*. Such interviews take an abstract, prestructured frame, place the concept in the center of it, and then pose systematic questions that represent frame relationships and place the answers to those questions in the appropriate frame slots.

2. A collection of anecdotes of *Schmäh* use encountered in everyday life. The notes that result are like the fieldnotes traditionally collected in participant observation. These data yield information about the context of practical action within which the concept occurs, or which the concept labels.
3. An informal ethnographic interview about *Schmäh*. Such interviews allow the native speaker to discuss the concept in whatever way he/she chooses. Methods of discourse analysis can be applied to such data to make explicit the underlying folk theory that contains the concept.

To sum up the results, *Schmäh* is a view of the world, a 'life-feeling' (*Lebensgefühl*), that rests on the basic ironic premise that things aren't what they seem, what they are is much worse, and all you can do is laugh it off. Such an attitude is hardly unique to Vienna. What is unique to Vienna, perhaps, is that the world view, with all its complicated strands, is puttied into a single piece of language, and that the rich piece of language is, in turn, used as a badge of self-identification.

The *Schmäh* world view finds expression in at least two different speech events that are also labeled *Schmäh*: one, a humorous exchange that grows out of the moment that is based on a negative portrayal of the other's motives or situation; two, a deception designed to attain some instrumental end. Both specific examples fit the general philosophy – things are not what they seem, what they are is bad, but the fact that the difference exists is not to be taken seriously.

The description of *Schmäh* in the article is tentative, and the interpretive frames were presented in informal prose, but the outlines of some very thick putty did take shape. And, in retrospect, the reason this piece of language appeared so rich – in other words, appeared so problematic when brought into connection with American English – becomes clear. Over the course of the semester, the students and I played a game repeatedly, trying to link a specific example of *Schmäh* with an American English equivalent or with other German-language varieties such as the *Berliner Schnauze* or the *Kölner Schmoos*.

Such links are, of course, possible, on an utterance-by-utterance basis. Assume I equated one *Schmäh* example with my old high school verbal game, 'cut lows,' glossed another as a 'con', and then linked the world view with New Yorkers. Would I have understood the concept? No, I would have destroyed it.

I would have destroyed it because I would have taken a rich piece of language, cut the putty at different levels in different ways, and reputtied the different pieces I'd cut into another language in a way that was not only piecemeal, but that didn't quite match or didn't match very well at all.

Schmäh isn't really like the cut-low game; *Schmäh* as 'con' isn't the right fit either; and though New Yorkers may be *Schmäh*-like in their world view at times, they don't encode it in a lexical item and celebrate it as a badge of identity. The glosses might work to get by a single example, but in general they'd add up to confusion and distortion.

And that would only be the beginning of the damage. The point is that when we lift *Schmäh* out of Austrian German, the putty that comes with it drags along the raw material for a complicated but coherent set of interpretive frames, with potentially wider links to history and political economy that are only hinted at in the article. The ease with which it is used in Vienna to characterize situations and persons and verbal and written expressions is a testament to its centrality and power, as are the disagreements when people discuss what it means. *Schmäh* is a laughing surface laid over an ugly world, a way of seeing and at least two specific ways of talking within it.

The analysis of *Schmäh* tapped deeply into the world of Viennese discourse. At its highest level, *Schmäh* as 'life-feeling' feeds back down into many other details, ways of speaking and hearing, or writing and reading, of viewing film and reading the news, of understanding politics and history. *Schmäh* began to pull me into a different way of being, one that made it easier to be in Vienna and use Austrian German and more difficult to return and use American English.

Schmäh is a rich point whose analysis reveals not only the interpretive wherewithal to properly use the lexical item or to properly engage in speech events that instantiate it. It also reveals a core view of things that ramify into most of the details of everyday life. *Schmäh* is the surface signal in L2 of what I began to learn as the Viennese culture of native speakers. Such learning put me into what I earlier referred to as the bilingual basement. Next time around, I hope to move up a couple of floors and get a better view.

The review of word association and projective tests, the experimental studies of the compound/coordinate and two-lexicon question showed that bilinguals – to some extent, in some areas – keep the conceptual systems of their two languages distinct. The discussions of anomie, the self-reports of bilinguals, and the review of translation theory showed, at a more global level, that the differences extend into identity, attitudes, behavior, and feelings of altered connections to the original L1 world. From these results, a theoretical prediction can be derived.

> For L2 learners who want to be *communicatively competent* in L2, rich points are areas that *must* be organized separately and *will* move the bilingual into a metacultural *Zwischenwelt*.

The effort to bring bilingualism/biculturalism together and focus the issue of culture involved a notion of discourse as language plus interpretation and an ethnographic view of breakdown resolution. A second theoretical prediction follows:

> The acquisition of L2 rich points is the acquisition of *culture*, in this sense: the higher the level the interpretive frames required to repair the gap between L1 and L2, and the more those frames can be shown to enable communicatively competent discourse among L2 speakers of social identity X, the more we can characterize those frames as the *culture* of X from the L1 speaker's point of view.

Culture continuous rather than discrete, partial rather than complete, relative to the situation of contact rather than independent – it looks strange given traditional definitions. But it sets out a way of seeing bilingualism that covers the experiments and anecdotes in the literature, accounts for my own recent L2 experience, and responds to popular ideas like Rushdie's immigrant sensibility as well as to fascinating speculations about postmodern consciousness and metacultural states. At this point, as the saying goes, a little more research wouldn't hurt.

REFERENCES

Agar, M. (1985) *Speaking of Ethnography* (Newbury Park, CA: Sage).

Agar, M. and Hobbs, J. (1985) 'How to Grow Schemas out of Interviews', in Dougherty, J. (ed.) *Directions in Cognitive Anthropology* (Urbana, IL: University of Illinois Press) pp. 413–32.

Brown, G. and Yule, G. (1983) *Discourse Analysis* (Cambridge: Cambridge University Press).

Bulow-Moller, A. M. (1989) *The Textlinguistic Omnibus: A Survey of Methods for Analysis* (Copenhagen: Handelshojkolen Forlag).

Casson, R. W. (1983) 'Schemata in Cognitive Anthropology', *Annual Reviews in Anthropology*, **12**, pp. 429–62.

de Beaugrande, R. and Dressler, W. U. (1981) *Einfuehrung in die Textlinguistik* (Tübingen: Niemeyer) [Available as *Introduction to Textlinguistics* (London: Longman)]

Fairclough, N. (1989) *Language and Power* (London: Longman).

Friedrich, P. (1986) *The Language Parallax* (Austin, TX: University of Texas Press).

Friedrich, P. (1989) 'Language, Ideology, and Political Economy', *American Anthropologist*, **91**, pp. 295–312.

Stubbs, M. (1983) *Discourse Analysis* (Chicago: University of Chicago Press).

van Dijk, T. A. (1979) *Macrostructures* (Hillsdale, NJ: Erlbaum).

36 Rules for Ritual Insults

William Labov

TERMS FOR THE SPEECH EVENT

A great variety of terms describe this activity:[1] *the dozens, sounding*, and *signifying* are three of the most common. The activity itself is remarkably similar throughout the various black communities, both in the form and content of the insults themselves and in the rules of verbal interaction which operate. In this section we will refer to the institution by the most common term in Harlem – sounding.

Sounding, or playing the dozens, has been described briefly in a number of other sources, particularly Dollard 1939 and Abrahams 1962. Kochman (1970) has dealt with sounding in Chicago in his general treatment of speech events in the black community. The oldest term for the game of exchanging ritualized insults is the dozens. Various possibilities for the origin of this term are given in Abrahams (1962: fn. 1), but none are very persuasive. One speaks of *the dozens, playing the dozens*, or *putting someone in the dozens*. The term *sounding* is by far the most common in New York and is reported as the favored term in Philadelphia by Abrahams. *Woofing* is common in Philadelphia and elsewhere, *joining* in Washington, *signifying* in Chicago, *screaming* in Harrisburg, and on the West Coast, such general terms as *cutting, capping*, or *chopping*. The great number of terms available suggests that there will be inevitably some specialization and shift of meaning in a particular area. Kochman suggests that *sounding* is used in Chicago for the initial exchanges, *signifying* for personal insults, and *the dozens* for insults on relatives. In New York, *the dozens* seems to be even more specialized, referring to rhymed couplets of the form.

I don't play the dozens, the dozens ain't my game
But the way I fucked your mama is a god damn shame.

Source: 'Rules for Ritual Insults', in Sudnow, D. (ed.) (1972) *Studies in Social Interaction* (Oxford and New York: Blackwell and The Free Press), reprinted in Labov, W. (1972) *Language in the Inner City: Studies in the Black English Vernacular* (Philadelphia, PA and Oxford: Pennsylvania University Press and Basil Blackwell) pp. 297–353.

But *playing the dozens* also refers to any ritualized insult directed against a relative. *Sounding* is also used to include such insults and includes personal insults of a simpler form. Somebody can 'sound on' somebody else by referring to a ritualized attribute of that person.

It seems to be the case everywhere that the superordinate terms which describe a verbal activity are quite variable and take on a wide range of meanings, while the verbal behavior itself does not change very much from place to place. People talk much more than they talk about talk, and as a result there is more agreement in the activity than in the ways of describing it. A member of the BEV subculture may have idiosyncratic notions about the general terms for sounding and the dozens without realizing it. He can be an expert on sounds and be quite untrustworthy on 'sounding.'

THE SHAPE OF SOUNDS

As noted above, some of the most elaborate and traditional sounds are dozens in the form of rhymed couplets. A typical opening dozen is cited above. Another favorite opening is:

I hate to talk about your mother, she's a good old soul
She got a ten-ton pussy and a rubber asshole.

Both of these initiating dozens have 'disclaiming' or retiring first lines, with second lines which contradict them. They are in this sense typical of the usage of young adults, who often back away from the dozens, saying 'I don't play that game,' or quoting the proverb, 'I laugh, joke and smoke, but I don't play' (Abrahams 1962: 210). There is a general impression that sounding is gradually moving down in the age range – it is now primarily an adolescent and preadolescent activity and not practiced as much by young men 20 to 30 years old; but we have no exact information to support this notion. The rhymed dozens were used by adolescents in New York City 20 years ago. In any case, most young adolescents do not know many of the older rhymed dozens and are very much impressed by them. To show the general style, we can cite a few others which have impressed the Jets and Cobras (and were not included in the 20 examples given by Abrahams):

I fucked your mother on top of the piano
When she came out she was singin' the Star Spangled Banner.

Fucked your mother in the ear,
And when I came out she said, 'Buy me a beer.'

The couplet which had the greatest effect was probably

Iron is iron, and steel don't rust,
But your momma got a pussy like a Greyhound Bus.

The winner in a contest of this sort is the man with the largest store of couplets on hand, the best memory, and perhaps the best delivery. But there is no question of improvisation, or creativity when playing, or judgement in fitting one dozens into another. These couplets can follow each other in any succession: one is as appropriate as the other. The originators certainly show great skill, and C. Robins remembers long hours spent by his group in the 1940's trying to invent new rhymes, but no one is expected to manufacture them in the heat of the contest. The Jets know a few rhymed dozens, such as 'Fucked his mother on a red-hot heater/I missed her cunt 'n' burned my peter,' but most of the traditional rhymes are no longer well known. One must be quite careful in using the rhymed dozens with younger boys: if they cannot top them, they feel beaten from the start, and the verbal flow is choked off. To initiate sounding in a single interview, or a group session, we used instead such primitive sequences as 'What would you say if someone said to you, 'Your momma drink pee?' The answer is well known to most peer-group members: 'Your father eat shit.' This standard reply allows the exchange to begin along conventional lines, with room for elaboration and invention.

For our present purposes, the basic formulas can be described in terms of the types of syntactic structures, especially with an eye to the mode of sentence embedding. I will draw most of the examples from two extended sounding sessions in which sounds were *used* rather than simply *quoted*. One was on a return trip from an outing with the Jets: 13 members were crowded in a microbus; 180 sounds were deciphered from the recording made in a 35-minute ride. The other was a group of session with five Thunderbirds in which Boot, Money, David, and Roger sounded against each other at great length. For those 60 sounds the record is complete and exact identification is possible.

There are of course many other sessions where sounds are cited or used; included in the examples given below are some from a trip with the Cobras where 35 sounds were deciphered from one short section of a recording. Where the quotations are actual sequences, speakers are indicated by names or initials.

a. *Your mother is (like)* _____. Perhaps the simplest of all sounds is the comparison or identification of the mother with something old, ugly, or bizarre: a simple equative prediction. The Jets use great numbers of such simple sounds:

Your mother look like Flipper ... Like *Hoppity* Hooper ... Your mother's a Milk Dud ... A Holloway Black Cow ... a rubber dick ... They say your mother was a Gravy Train ... Your mother's a bookworm ... a ass, period. Your mother James Bond, K.C. ... Your mother Pussy Galore.

The Cobras use a number of sounds of this type:

Your mama's a weight-lifter ... a butcher ... a peanut man ... a iceman ... a Boston Indian. Your mother look like Crooked-Mile Hank! ... like that piece called King Kong! ... Quahab's mother look like who did it and don't want to do it no more!

Note that the mass media and commercial culture provide a rich body of images. Such sounds were particularly appropriate on the Jet outing because every odd or old person that passed on the way would be a stimulus for another sound.

Your mother look like that taxi driver ... Your mother a applejack-eater ... a flea-bag ... the Abominable Snowman ... Your mother is a Phil D. Basket (calypso accent) ... Your mother's a diesel ... a taxicab driver....

b. *Your mother got ____.* Equally simple, from a syntactic point of view, is the series of sounds with the form *Your mother got so and so.* The Thunderbirds use long sequences of this type.

Boot:	Your mother got a putty chest.
Boot:	Your mother got hair growin' out her dunkie hole.
Roger:	Your mother got a 45 in her left titty.
Money:	Your mother got a 45-degree titty.
Boot:	Your mother got titties behind her neck.

The Jets use simple sounds of this sort as well. (The first statement here is not a sound: it simply provides the base on which the sound is built, in this case the verb *got*.)

J1:	You got the nerve to talk.
J2:	Your mother got funky drawers.
J3:	Your mother got braces between her legs....

The Cobra sounds on clothes gradually drift away from the basic sounding pattern to a more complex structure that plays on the names of New York City Department stores:

Your momma got shit on...
Bel's mother bought her clothes from Ohrbach's. All front and no back.
You got your suit from Woolworth! All wool but it ain't worth shit!
You get your shoes from Buster Brown – brown on the top and all busted
   on the bottom!...

c. *Your mother so* _____ *she* _____. More complex comparisons are done
with a quantifier, an adjective, and an embedded sentence of the type *b* or
other predication.

> *David*:   Your mother so old she got spider webs under her arms.
> *Boot*:   Your mother so old she can stretch her head and lick out her ass.

Such sounds can be made freely against a member of the group.

> *Roger*:   Hey Davy, you so fat you could slide down the razor blade
>   without gettin' cut.
>   ...an' he so thin that he can dodge rain drops....

Other Jet similes show a wide range of attributes sounded on:

Bell grandmother so-so-so ugly, her rag is showin'.
Bell mother was so small, she bust her lip on the curve (curb).
Your mother so white she hafta use Mighty White.
Your mother so skinny, she ice-skate on a razor blade.
...so skinny she can reach under the doorknob...
...so low she c'play Chinese handball on the curve.
...so low, got to look down to look up.
...so black, she sweat chocolate.
...so black that she hafta steal to get her clothes.
...so black that she has to suck my dick to get home.

The syntax of these similes can become very complex and involve a second
subordination: 'your mother is so _____ that when she _____ she can _____.'
It is not easy to get all of this into one proposition in the heat of the
moment.

> Your mother's so small, you play hide-and-go-seek, y'all c'slip under
> a penny....

d. *Your mother eat* _____. We now return to a different type of sound
which does not involve similes or metaphors, but portrays direct action with
simple verbs. The power of these sounds seems to reside in the incongruity
or absurdity of the elements juxtaposed – which may be only another way
of saying that we do not really understand them.

Boot: I heard your mother eat rice crispies without any milk.
Roger: Eat 'em raw!
Boot: Money eat shit without puttin' any cornflakes on.

The Jets use such constructions freely as well.

His mother eat Dog Yummies.
They say your mother eat Gainesburgers.
Your mother eat coke-a-roaches.
Your mother eat rat heads.
Your mother eat Bosco.
Your mother a applejack-eater.

One obvious recipe for constructing sounds of this type is to mention something disgusting to eat. Yet most of the items mentioned here are not in that class, and as we will see below, less than half of the examples we have could actually be considered obscene. Dog Yummies are not disgusting (they are edible but not palatable) but it is plainly 'low' to eat dog food. Elegance in sounds of this type can also involve syntactic complexity. *Your mother a applejack eater* seems to be a more effective sound then *Your mother eat applejack*. (Applejack, a new breakfast cereal at that time, may be favored because it suggests applejack whiskey). If so, it is a further piece of evidence that syntactic complexity is a positive feature of sounds.

e.   *Your mother raised you on _____*.   This is a specific pattern with fairly simple syntax, particularly effective in striking at both the opponent and his mother. In one Thunderbirds' session, we triggered a series of these sounds:

WL: Your mother raised you on ugly milk.
Boot: Your mother raised you on raw corn.
David: Your mother raised you on big lips.
Boot: Your mother gave you milk out of a cave.
Boot: Your mother gave you milk out of her ass.
           ... when you just born, she say 'Take a shot.'

f.   *I went to your house* ...   A numerous and important series are sounds directed against the household and the state of poverty that exists there. Some of these are complex rhymes, quite parallel to the rhymed dozens:

Boot: I went to your house to ask for a piece of cheese.
           The rat jumped up and say 'Heggies, please.'

(*Heggies* is the claiming word parallel to *dibbs*, *halfsies*, *allies*, *checks*, etc. which was standard in New York City some twenty years ago. Today *heggies* is a minor variant, though it is still recognized, having given way to *thumbs up*.)

Most sounds of this type are in prose and are disguised as anecdotes. Cockroaches are a favorite theme:

Boot: Hey! I went up Money house and I walked in Money house, I say, I wanted to sit down, and then, you know a roach jumped up and said, 'Sorry, this seat is taken.'

Roger: I went to David house, I saw the roaches walkin' round in *combat* boots.

Several sounds from a session with the Aces may be quoted here in which the members noted where they had learned various sounds.

Tony: A boy named Richard learned me this one: When I came across your house, a rat gave me a jay-walkin' ticket.

Renard: When I came to your house, seven roaches jumped me and one search me.

Ted: And I made this one up: I was come in your house; I got hit on the back of my head with a Yoohoo bottle.

Ted's original sound seems weak; it leans upon the humor of the Yoohoo bottle but it departs from the rats-and-roaches theme without connecting up with any of the major topics of sounding. ...

Remarks about somebody's house are apt to become quite personal as we will see below. The Jets did not produce many of these sounds, but the following occurred in quick succession:

J1: I went in Junior house 'n' sat in a chair that caved in.

J2: You's a damn liar, 'n' you was eatin' in my house, right?

J3: I went to Bell's house 'n' a Chinese roach said, 'Come and git it.'

J1: I brought my uncle – I brought my uncle up Junior house – I didn't trust them guys.

The tendency to take 'house' sounds personally shows up in the second line of this series. As we will see below, the charge that 'You was eatin' in my house' returns the accusation of hunger against the originator, and this can have a solid basis in real life.

g. *Other anecdotal forms.* There are many other anecdotal sounds which do not fall into a single mold. Some are quite long and include the kind of extra detail which can give the illusion, at the outset, that an actual story is being told. From the Jets' session we find:

I ran over Park Avenue – you know, I was ridin' on my bike – and – uh – I seen somebody fightin'; I said lemme get on this now. I ran up there and Bell and his mother, fallin' all over: I was there first x x x gettin' it – gettin' that Welfare food x x

The incoherent sections are filled with slurping noises which are an important part of such food sounds – indicating that those involved were so desperately hungry and so uncivilized that they behaved like animals.

One can also deliver an anecdote with the same theme as the rhymed dozens quoted above:

Boot: I'm not gonna say who it was, boy. But I fucked somebody's mother on this bridge one night. Whooh! That shit was so good, she jumped overboard in the river.

There are any number of miscellaneous sounds that can be disguised as pseudoanecdotes.

Roger: One day, Money's mother's ass was stuck up and she called Roto-Rooter.

On the other hand, there are anecdotes which take the form of rhymes:

Boot: I went down south to buy a piece of butter
I saw yo' mother layin' in the gutter.
I took a piece of glass and stuck it up her ass
I never saw a motherfucker run so fas'.

Such narratives typically use the simplest type of syntax, with minimal subjects and preterit verb heads. The anecdotal type of sound appears to be most effective when it is delivered with hesitations and false starts, rather than with the smooth delivery of the other type of sounds. The technique is therefore closely associated with certain types of narrative styles in which the point is delayed to the final clause, where the evaluation is fused with result and coda, as in a joke. It is generally true that all sounds have this structure: the evaluative point must be at the very end.

h. *Portraits.* Just as narrative calls for simple syntax, sounds which present elaborate portraits demand syntactic complexity. The most common are those which place someone's mother on the street as a whore.

J1: Willie mother stink; she be over here on 128 St. between Seventh 'n' Eighth, waving her white handkerchief: [falsetto] 'C'mon, baby, only a nickel.'

J2: Hey Willie mother be up there, standin' the corner, be pullin' up her-her dress, be runnin' her ass over 'n' see those skinny, little legs.

i. *Absurd and bizarre forms.* The formal typology of sounds presented so far actually covers the great majority of sounds used. But there are a number of striking examples which are not part of any obvious pattern, sounds which locate some profoundly absurd or memorable point by a mechanism not easy to analyze. There is the darkly poetic sound used by Eddie of the Cobras:

Your mother play dice with the midnight mice.

Rhyme also plays an essential part in this uncommon sound:

Ricky got shot with his own fart.

We might also cite the following exchange; which develops its own deep complication:

J1:   Your mother take a swim in the gutter.
J2:   Your mother live in a garbage can.
J1:   Least I don't live on 1122 Boogie Woogie Avenue, two garbage cans to the right.

The attraction of trade names like *Right Guard* or *Applejacks* may be their bizarre and whimsical character. In charging somebody's mother with unfeminine behavior we can also observe comical effects:

J1:   Willie mother make a living' playin' basketball.
J2:   I saw Tommy mother wearing' high-heel sneakers to church.

j. *Response forms: puns and metaphors.* Sounds are usually answered by other sounds, and the ways in which they follow each other will be discussed below. But there is one formal feature of a sound which is essentially made for responses: 'At least my mother ain't . . .' Although these forms cannot be used to initiate sounding, several can succeed each other, as in these sequences from the Aces session:

A1:   At least I don't wear bubblegum drawers.
A2:   At least his drawers ain't bubblegum, it's not sticky like yours.
A1:   At least my mother don't work in the sewer.
A2:   At least my mother don't live in the water-crack, like yours. . . .

ATTRIBUTES AND PERSONS SOUNDED ON

A review of the content of the sounds given above under *a–j* will show that a wide but fairly well-defined range of attributes is sounded on. A mother (grandmother, etc.) may be cited for her age, weight (fat or skinny), ugliness, blackness, smell, the food she eats, the clothes she wears, her poverty, and of course her sexual activity. As far as persons are concerned, sounding is always thought of as talking about someone's mother. But other relatives are also mentioned – as part of the speech for variety in switching, or for their particular attributes. In order of importance, one can list the opponent's relatives as: mother, father, uncle, grandmother, aunt. As far as number of sounds is concerned, the opponent himself might be included as second most important to his mother, but proverbially sounds are thought of as primarily against relatives.

One of the long epic poems of the BEV community called 'Signifying Monkey' gives us some insight into the ordering of relatives. Signifying Monkey stirs up trouble ('signifies') by telling the lion that the elephant had sounded on him:

> 'Mr. Lion, Mr. Lion, there's a big burly motherfucker comin' your way,
> Talks shit about you from day to day.'

The monkey successively reports that the elephant had talked about the lion's sister, brother, father and mother, wife, and grandmother.

> The monkey said, 'Wait a minute, Mr. Lion', 'That ain't all,
> he said your grandmother, said she was a lady playin' in the old backyard.
> Said ever'time he seen her, made his dick get on the hard.'

Even more relatives are brought in, which brings the monkey to the inevitable conclusion:

> He said, 'Yeah he talked about your aunt, your uncle, and your cousins,
> Right then and there I knew the bad motherfucker was playin' the dozens.'

What is said about someone's mother's age, weight, or clothes can be a general or traditional insult, or it can be local and particular. The presence of commercial trade names in the sounds is very striking; Bosco, Applejacks, Wonder Bread, Dog Yummies, Gainesburgers, Gravy Train, as well as the names of the popular figures in the mass media: James Bond, Pussy Galore, Flipper. The street culture is highly local, and local humor is a very large part of the sounds. As noted before, one of the best ways to start a loud discussion is to associate someone with a local character who is an 'ultrarich' source of humor. Trade names have this local character – and part of the effect is the superimposing of this overspecific label on the general, impersonal figure of 'your mother' as in 'Your mother look like Flipper.' Local humor is omnipresent and overpowering in every peer group – it is difficult to explain in any case, but its importance cannot be ignored.

The odd or whimsical use of particular names can be illustrated by a sequence that occurred when John Lewis left the microbus at an early stop. As a parting shot, he leaned back in the window and shouted genially 'Faggots! Motherfuckers!' This set up a chain of responses including a simple 'Your mother!' from Rel, 'You razorblade bastard!' from someone else, and finally an anonymous 'Winnie the Pooh!'

Obscenity does not play as large a part as one would expect from the character of the original dozens. Many sounds *are* obscene in the full sense of the word. The speaker uses as many 'bad' words and images as possible – that is, subject to taboo and moral reprimand in adult middle-class society. The originator will search for images that would be considered as disgusting as possible: 'Your mother eat fried dick-heads.' With long familiarity the vividness of this image disappears, and one might say that it is *not* disgusting or obscene to the sounders. But the meaning of the sound and the activity would be entirely lost without reference to these middle-class norms. Many sounds are 'good' because they are 'bad' – because the speakers know that they would arouse disgust and revulsion among those committed to the 'good' standards of middle-class society. Like the toasts, sounds derive their meaning from the opposition between two major sets of values: *their* way of being 'good' and *our* way of being 'bad'.

The rhymed dozens are all uniformly sexual in character, they aim at the sexual degradation of the object sounded on. But the body of sounds cited above depart widely from this model: less than half of them could be considered obscene, in any sense. At one point in the Jet session, there is a sequence of three sounds concerning fried dick-heads; this is immediately followed by

J1:   Your mother eat rat heads.
J2:   Your mother eat Bosco.
J3:   Your mother look that taxi driver.
J4:   Your mother stinks.
J5:   Hey Willie got a talkin' hat.
J4:   Your mother a applejack-eater.
J5:   Willie got on a talkin' hat.
J4:   So, Bell, your mother stink like a bear.
J5:   Willie mother . . . she walk like a penguin.

This sequence of nine remarks contains no sexual references; the strongest word is *stink*. Many sounds depend upon the whimsical juxtaposition of a variety of images, upon original and unpredictable humor which is for the moment quite beyond our analysis. But it can be noted that the content has departed very far from the original model of uniform sexual insult.

Only someone very unfamiliar with the BEV subculture could think that the current generation is 'nicer' and less concerned with sex than previous generations. The cry of 'Winnie the Pooh!' does not mean that the Jets are absorbing refined, middle-class wit and culture. Its significance can only be understood by a deeper study of the nature of this ritual activity.

EVALUATION OF SOUNDS

One of the most important differences between sounding and other speech events is that most sounds are evaluated overtly and immediately by the audience. In well-structured situations, like the Thunderbird sounding session, this is true of every sound. In wilder sessions with a great many participants, like the Jet session in the microbus, a certain number of sounds will follow each other rapidly without each one being evaluated.

The primary mark of positive evaluation is laughter. We can rate the effectiveness of a sound in a group session by the number of members of the audience who laugh. In the Thunderbird session, there are five members; if one sounded against the other successfully, the other three would laugh; a less successful sound would show only one or two laughs. (The value of having a separate recording track for each speaker is very great.)

A really successful sound will be evaluated by overt comments: in the Jet session the most common forms are: 'Oh!', 'Oh shit!' 'God damn!', or 'Oh lord!' By far the most common is 'Oh shit!' The intonation is important; when approval is to be signalled the vowel of each word is quite long, with a high sustained initial pitch, and a slow-falling pitch contour. The same words can be used to express negative reaction, or disgust, but then the pitch is low and sustained. The implication of the positive exclamations is 'That is too much' or 'That leaves me helpless.'

Another, even more forceful mode of approving sounds is to repeat the striking part of the sound oneself.

John L: Who father wear raggedy drawers?
Willie: Yeh the ones with so many holes in them when-a-you walk they whistle?
Others: Oh...shi-it! When you walk they whistle! Oh shit!

Negative reactions to sounds are common and equally overt. The most frequent is 'Tha's phony!' or 'Phony shit!', but sounds are also disapproved as *corny, weak*, or *lame*. Stanley elaborates his negative comments quite freely:

Junior: Aww, Nigger Bell, you smell like B.O. Plenty.
Bell: Aww, nigger, you look like – you look like Jimmy Durante's grandfather.

Stan:	Aw, tha's phony [bullshit]...Eh, you woke me up with that phony one, man...
Bell:	Junior look like Howdy Doody.
Stan:	That's phony too, Bell. Daag, boy!...Tonight ain't your night, Bell.

At another point, Stanley denounces a sound with a more complicated technique: 'Don't tell 'im those phony jokes, they're so phony, you *got* to laugh.'

The difference between these negative terms is not clear. For our present purposes, we may consider them equivalent, although they are probably used in slightly different ways by different speakers. The Cobras do not use the same negative terms as the Jets. They will say 'You fake!' 'Take that shit outa here!' or most often, 'That ain't where it's at.'

These evaluative remarks are ways of responding to the overall effect of a sound. There is also considerable explicit discussion of sounds themselves. In the case of a traditional sound, like a rhymed dozen, one can object to an imperfect rendition. For example, Stevie answers one of our versions with 'Tha's wrong! You said it wrong! Mistake!' Members are also very clear on who the best sounders are. Among the Thunderbirds, it is generally recognized that 'Boot one of the best sounders...he's one of the best sounders of all.' This very reputation will interfere with the chances of getting other members to initiate sounding – they know in advance that they will be outdone. In general, sounding is an activity very much in the forefront of social consciousness: members talk a great deal about it, try to make up new sounds themselves, and talk about each other's success. Sounding practices are open to intuitive inspection. It is possible to ask a good sounder, 'What would you say if somebody said to you...' and he will be glad to construct an answer. Members will also make metacomments on the course of a sounding session: 'Now he's sounding on you, Money!' or announce their intentions, as Roger does: 'Aw, tha's all right. Now I'm gonna sound on you pitiful.'

Furthermore, members take very sharp notice of the end result of a sounding contest, as noted below. In a sounding session, everything is public – nothing significant happens without drawing comment. The rules and patterning of this particular speech event are therefore open for our inspection. ...

THE RULES FOR RITUAL SOUNDING

In the presentation of sounding so far, we have seen that this speech event has a well-articulated structure. These rules can be broken: it is possible to hurl personal insults and it is possible to join in a mass attack on one person.

But there is always a cost in stepping out of the expected pattern; in the kind of uncontrolled and angry response which occurs or in the confusion as to who is doing what to who.

As we examine these examples of sounding, the fundamental opposition between ritual insults and personal insults emerges. The appropriate responses are quite different: a personal insult is answered by a denial, excuse, or mitigation, whereas a sound or ritual insult is answered by longer sequences, since a sound and its response are essentially the same kind of thing, and a response calls for a further response. ...

The following general formulation of the interactional structure of sounding is based upon the suggestions of Erving Goffman, in response to an earlier presentation of this analysis. Goffman's framework isolates four basic properties of *ritual* sounding, as opposed to other types of insult behavior:

1. A sound opens a *field*, which is meant to be sustained. A sound is presented with the expectation that another sound will be offered in response, and that this second sound may be built formally upon it. The player who presents an initial sound is thus offering others the opportunity to display their ingenuity at his expense.
2. Besides the initial two players, a third-person role is necessary.
3. Any third person can become a player, especially if there is a failure by one of the two players then engaged.
4. Considerable symbolic distance is maintained and serves to insulate the event from other kinds of verbal interaction.

These properties, illustrated in the previous sections, are the means by which the process of insult becomes socialized and adapted for play. They may eventually be formalized in higher level rules of verbal interaction. In the following discussion, we will see in greater detail how the first principle operates in ritual sounding. ...

When a sound becomes too ordinary – too possible – we can then observe a sudden switch in the pattern of response to that appropriate for a personal insult. This can happen by accident, when a sound is particularly weak. For example, in the Jet session:

A: I went in Junior house 'n' sat in a chair that caved in.
B: You's a damn liar; 'n' you was eatin' in my house, right?

This is the only instance in the Jet sounding session where a statement is denied, and it is plainly due to the fact that the proposition P is not appropriate for ritual insult. Its untruth is not at all a matter of general knowledge – it is quite possible that a chair in somebody's house would cave in, and that the chair in Junior's house *did* cave in. ... First Junior denies the charge; second, he hits back with another proposition that is again a personal, not a ritual insult: 'You come over to my house to eat (since there was no food in your own), and so what right have you to complain?' Of course, the second part implicitly contradicts the first – if no chair caved in, how does Junior know what occasion is being talked about? . . .

Sounds are directed as targets very close to the opponent (or at himself) but by social convention it is accepted that they do not denote attributes which persons actually possess: in Goffman's formulation, symbolic distance maintained serves to insulate this exchange from further consequences. The rules given above for sounding, and the development of sounds in bizarre and whimsical direction, all have the effect of preserving this ritual status. As we have seen, the ritual convention can break down with younger speakers or in strange situations – and the dangers of such a collapse of ritual safeguards are very great. Rituals are sanctuaries; in ritual we are freed from personal responsibility for the acts we are engaged in. Thus when someone makes a request for action in other subcultures, and he is challenged on the fourth precondition, 'What right have you to tell me that?' his reply may follow the same strategy:

> It's not my idea – I just have to get the work done.
> I'm just doing my job.
> I didn't pick on you – somebody has to do it.

Any of these moves to depersonalize the situation may succeed in removing the dangers of a face-to-face confrontation and defiance of authority. Ritual insults are used in the same way to manage challenges within the peer group, and an understanding of ritual behavior must therefore be an important element in constructing a general theory of discourse.

NOTE

I am particularly indebted to Benji Wald for suggestions incorporated in the present version of the analysis of sounding.

REFERENCES

Abrahams, R. (1962) 'Playing the Dozens', *Journal of American Folklore*, **75**, pp. 209–18.
Dollard, J. (1939) 'The Dozens: the Dialect of Insult', *American Image*, **1**, pp. 3–24.
Kochman, T. (1970) 'Towards an Ethnography of Black Speech Behavior', in *Afro-American Anthology*, Whitten, Jr, N. E. and Szwed, J. F. (eds) (New York: Free Press).

37 The Sociology of Compliment Work in Polish and English

Robert K. Herbert

INTRODUCTION

The study of speech formulae, precoded sentential chunks, conversational and interactional routines, and the like has received substantial attention within the linguistic pragmatics literature over the past ten years. The common thread unifying these phenomena is the notion that some – perhaps a great deal – of everyday speech activity cannot be characterized by the spontaneous creativity attributed to speakers by early generative grammarians. It is now apparent that some important pieces of speech activity consist of stored units which are activated or retrieved in appropriate circumstances (cf., for example, Ferguson 1976, and the papers in Coulmas 1980). These precoded pieces and routines vary in terms of their fixedness in speech from a set of rigid formulae to a set of conversational prescriptions which may be filled in a variety of acceptable fashions. Conversational units of this nature seem especially prominent in situations of social negotiation, that is, when speakers are involved in the common tasks of attending to own and others' face. That such interactional face-work should rely rather heavily on formulae and routines is perhaps not surprising, since such formulae and routines are easily recognized as such, and therefore the social moves committed by the speaker stand less chance of being missed or misinterpreted by the hearer. ...

DEFINITION

There seems to be widespread popular agreement on what it is that constitutes a compliment, and the examples which native speakers cite of

Source: 'The Sociology of Compliment Work: An Ethnocontrastive Study of Polish and English Compliments', *Multilingua*, **10**, 4 (1991) (Berlin: Mouton de Gruyter) pp. 381–402.

compliments are compatible with their folk definitions. Most definitions of complements specify two conditions: (1) an expression of admiration on the part of the speaker, (2) concerning a possession, accomplishment, or personal quality of the addressee. The definition proposed by Holmes (1988) mirrors the above folk definitions:

> A compliment is a speech act which explicitly or implicitly attributes credit to someone other than the speaker, usually the person addressed, for some good (possession, characteristic, skill, etc.) which is positively valued by the speaker.

Several points are worthy of mention here. First, the distinction between explicit and implicit compliments is an important one, corresponding in part to the distinction between direct and indirect speech acts. The former are recognized as compliments outside of context, being realized by a small set of conventional formulae (cf. below), for example,

(1)   Terrific presentation this morning!

(2)   I like your hair short like that.

Implicit compliments are those in which the value judgement is presupposed and/or implicated by Gricean maxims, for example,

(3)   I wish I could manage my work like you do.

(4)   Your husband is a very lucky man.

Note that the literature on compliments, and this chapter is no exception, deals almost exclusively with explicit compliments.

A second point relevant to Holmes' definition concerns the relationship between the addressee and the topic of the speech act. Holmes' definition allows for examples such as:

(5)   [Context; 2 elderly women discussing a new TV newsreader]
       A: Oh, but you must admit that she's got a lovely voice.
       B: She certainly has.

to count as compliments (correctly, in Holmes' view), but she then explicitly excludes such examples from further consideration. It is perhaps better to distinguish between compliments and other statements of admiration/praise (of which compliments form a subclass) by restricting compliments to situations in which the topic of admiration bears directly on the addressee or on a quality or person(s) more or less closely related to the addressee (cf. Kerbrat-Orecchioni 1987: 5; Lewandowska-Tomaszczyk 1989: 74). Thus, (6) counts as and is recognized as a compliment whereas (7) is not:

(6)   Your children seem very well-behaved.

(7)   Your neighbors seem like such nice people.

The issue of stating precisely what is meant by 'more or less closely related to the addressee' is a thorny one, which is not pursued in the present context. This issue is taken up and discarded by Marandin (1987: 76), who replaces it with a functional notion, describing compliments as statements where the speaker pleases or intends to please the addressee.

Finally, there are broad similarities between the act of complimenting and the act of congratulating, noted by Norrick (1980), Marandin (1987), and others. This similarity will be taken up separately in greater detail later in this chapter. It will suffice to mention here that while compliments focus on possessions and personal qualities, congratulations often refer to accomplishments and to good fortune (Norrick 1980: 297).

COMPLIMENT FORMULAE

In a series of articles, Nessa Wolfson and Joan Manes (for example, Wolfson and Manes 1980; Manes and Wolfson 1980; Wolfson 1983) noted that one of the most striking features of compliments in American English is their almost total lack of originality (Manes and Wolfson 1980: 15). Examining a corpus of approximately 700 compliments, they found that about 80% of the compliments depended on an adjective to carry the positive semantic load of the utterance and that two-thirds of all adjectival compliments made use of only five adjectives:

nice, good, beautiful, pretty, great

Most of the nonadjectival compliments depended on semantically positive verbs, for example, *like, love, enjoy, admire, be impressed by*, and the first two of these verbs accounted for 86% of the compliments in this category. Relatively few compliments made use of an adverb (usually *well*) or a noun (for example, *genius*) to express positive valuation. Wolfson and Manes noted that the semanic load of the compliments in their corpus is borne by the several lexical items mentioned above, and they argued that this is strong evidence of the non-creativity of compliments in speech.

More striking evidence of formulaicity in English compliments is found at the syntactic level. More than half (53%) of the data studied by Wolfson and Manes exhibited a single syntactic pattern:[1]

(8)   NP   is   (really) ADJ
            looks
      That shirt looks great on you.

The two other major syntactic patterns were:

(9)   I (really) like   NP   (16.1%)
                   love
      I really like what you've done to your hair.

(10) PRO is (really) (a) ADJ   NP   (14.9%)
      That's a good question.

Only six other patterns occur with any regularity in the remaining 15% of the Wolfson and Manes corpus:

(11) You V (a) (really) ADJ   NP   (3.3%)
      You did a great job.

(12) You V NP (really) ADV   (2.7%)
      You sang that song really well.

(13) You have (a) (really) ADJ   NP   (2.4%)
      You have a beautiful living room.

(14) What (a) ADJ   NP!   (1.6%)
      What a pretty skirt!

(15) ADJ   NP!   (1.6%)
      Good shot!

(16) Isn't NP   ADJ!   (1.0%)
      Isn't that ring pretty!

American English compliments are not mere statements of admiration offered to the addressee: they are highly structured formulae which can be adapted with minimal effort to a wide variety of situations in which a favorable comment is required or desired (Manes and Wolfson 1980: 123). ...

Polish, like English, makes use of a small set of syntactic and semantic formulae for the purpose of encoding compliments. The noncreativity of the compliment act is a striking fact: these are speech formulae. It is tempting to speculate that such noncreativity is directly tied to a need for easily recognizable formulae in status- and solidarity-negotiating gambits in speech. That is, in making a social move of this kind, the use of a formula decreases the likelihood that the move might be misinterpreted or unnoticed by an addressee. The formulae used in Polish and in English differ – as one expects – in interesting ways, and these differences are set within a larger cultural framework below.

ANALYZING COMPLIMENT DIFFERENCES

There are both striking similarities and important differences between the Polish and English compliment data. Syntactic differences in the two languages account for the less rigid adhesion to formulaic structure in Polish, that is, the relatively free word order in Polish contrasts with the fixedness of English word order. More interestingly, one notes the virtual absence of compliments expressed with a first person singular focus (for example, *podoba mi sie* ≈ 'I like', *(ja)lubie* ≈ 'I love/like') in Polish as compared with the high frequency of such first person focus in English (for example, *I like/love NP*). By contrast, the most common Polish formula is *Masz* ('you have') *(INT) ADJ NP*, which accounts for 35% of the sample, compared with a 2.4% frequency for the corresponding English structure *You have (a) (really) ADJ NP*. Herbert (1987) categorized English compliments according to the 'personal focus' of the compliment act, for example,

(17) 1st. I like your hair that way.
            I think you've done a good job so far.
      2nd. Your hair looks good short.
            You've done an excellent job with the sources you had.
      3rd. That's a nice sweater.
            Nice job.

and found that the relative distribution of personal focus was:

(18) 1st   2nd   3rd   (impersonal)
      32.8%   29%   38%

By contrast, the relevant frequencies for the Polish data are:

(19) 1st   2nd   3rd
      5.75%   75.5%   18.5%

The infrequency of first person compliments in Polish is quite marked, and it cannot be attributed to the lack of a syntactic formula of the relevant type. Although *podobać się* 'to like' does not often figure in the encoding of compliments, it is frequently used in compliment responses, for example,

(20) A: *Ładną masz sukienkę*
         'You have a nice dress.'
      B: *Podoba ci się?*
         'Do you like it?'

This response type strikes the English speaker as coy and 'fishing' for further praise. The vast bulk of Polish compliments have second person focus, which, on the one hand, may seem natural since the definition of a compliment is an assertion of admiration for some possession, achievement, skill, etc., bearing directly on the addressee or on objects/persons closely related to the addressee. What is interesting is that almost half of the second person structures focus directly on possession via the formula *Masz ADJ NP/ADJ masz NP* 'You have (a) ADJ NP'. As Manes (1983) noted, compliments are indirect indicators of values held by the society using them, and the very high incidence of possession compliments, especially on new possessions, is outstanding here. In the same way that American speakers report an obligation to compliment close acquaintances on changed physical appearance (for example, changed hair style/length, absence/presence of facial hair, loss of weight [although not weight gain]), Polish speakers report an obligation of the same sort when close acquaintances display newly acquired possessions, especially items of apparel or decoration, for example,

(21) *Widzę nowe kolczyki. Bardzo ładne.*
      'I see new earrings. Very nice.'

(22) *To nowa koszula? Ładna*
      'Is that a new shirt? Nice.'

(23) *O, masz nowe spodnie.*[2]
      'Oh, you've got new pants.'

Manes (1983: 99) noted that appearance is very commonly the focus of American compliments, especially aspects that are the result of deliberate effort and new items. Compliments on skill or performance are the second most frequent type, with a rapid decline in topic frequency. Holmes (1988) provides a quantitative analysis of topic in New Zealand compliments:

(24) appearance   50.7%
      ability/performance   30.6%
      possessions   11.2%
      personality/friendship   4.8% (for example, *You're such a gentle person.*)
      other   2.7%

Using these same categories for topical analysis of the Polish corpus, the relevant frequencies are:

appearance	32.25%	(n = 141)
ability/performance	11.75%	(n = 47)
possessions	49.25%	(n = 197)
personality/friendship	1.25%	(n = 5)
other	2.5%	(n = 10) (for example, *Masz bardzo pracowitą żonę* ('You've got a hard-working wife.')

The most striking point of contrast between the English and Polish data sets concerns the category Possessions, which is the most common topical subtype in Polish compliments, accounting for about 50% of the sample whereas the category occurs in only 11% of Holmes' sample. There is a sharply reduced frequency of compliments on ability/performance in the Polish data. It is important to recall here that the data were collected ethnographically among university student populations in the respective countries. One point of interest arising from the present finding is that it directly contradicts the widely held folk-belief mentioned earlier that compliments are relatively infrequent on account of a lesser importance attached to material possessions in Poland than in Western countries. Without any firm evidence to support the conclusion, it is nonetheless tempting to speculate on the relationship between the high frequency of possession compliments in Polish and life within the consumer-troubled society of Poland [under communism, pre-1989 – Ed.]. The fact is, as readily acknowledged by official and unofficial sources, consumer goods are in very short supply, or they are imported and available only for Western currency or at very high, occasionally staggering, prices. There is a variety of sources through which people acquire the consumer goods which they need and desire. The acquisition of goods, ranging from sheepskin coats to washing machines to the trivial purchases of everyday life, is often regarded as an accomplishment – by oneself and by fellow members of the society (cf. Wedel [1986] for a detailed description of everyday life in pre-democratic Poland). Perhaps for this reason, such acquisitions are often prominently displayed and are prominent topics in conversation. Several speakers of Polish observed *independently* to the author that conversation at social gatherings seems to consist of little more than an exchange of news concerning things one has acquired or 'arranged'. In view of the above, it is perhaps not surprising that possession compliments have such a high incidence in the sample. In both Polish and English, one is struck by the centrality of appearance/possession compliments, reflecting the importance of these features in both societies.

COMPLIMENTS AND CONGRATULATIONS

It was noted earlier that the category of compliments shares a number of features with congratulations. According to Norrick (1980: 297), compliments are made on personal qualities and possessions whereas congratulations refer to accomplishments or to good fortune. The two are further distinguished in that compliments tend to reflect the personal judgment of the speaker whereas congratulations are less personal. This distinction is akin to that proposed by Marandin (1987: 74–6), who attributes the central distinction between the two speech acts to the attitude of the speaker *vis-à-vis* the addressee. Compliments are designed to please the addressee whereas congratulations are not. It would seem, further, that the two are sometimes distinguished on the basis of the attitude of the speaker toward the topic of the speech act. The sincerity condition for compliments specifies admiration as the speaker's experiencing emotion (Norrick 1980: 296), but recognition of an achievement or accomplishment is sufficient for the act of congratulation. Complimenting someone on a new car, for example, expresses admiration for the car and for the addressee's judgment in purchasing it; congratulating someone who has won a new car in a lottery expresses recognition of good fortune and does not commit the speaker to admiration of the car.

Although it is not possible to prove the relationship, there is good reason to believe that the two acts of complimenting and congratulating are more alike in Polish than in English, and, specifically, that the high frequency of possession compliments in Polish reflects the function of these acts as congratulatory on the acquisition of a new possession. Given the difficulties of the consumer supply situation, acquisition is an' accomplishment. Members of the society often remark on this fact. The aspect of the addressee's good taste/judgment in some particular acquisition is not entirely comparable in English-speaking and Polish-speaking societies. When an English speaker in the United States, New Zealand, or South Africa is complimented on a new sweater, new shoes, or a new car, the complimenter expresses admiration for the object complimented and for the addressee's judgment in choosing to acquire this object, the addressee having selected this particular object from the scores of similar objects available in consumer-oriented societies. This situation did not usually obtain in Poland during the period of fieldwork. Some Polish speakers have reported an obligation to comment favorably on an acquaintance's new possession, just as American speakers report such an obligation for changes in an acquaintance's appearance, especially hair. If some comment on a prominent new possession is not forthcoming, speakers seem to assume a negative valuation and may explicitly demand comment, for example, *Nie podoba ci się mój X?* 'Don't you like my X?' When later questioned about the sincerity of their praise, speakers occasionally attribute the act of complimenting to social obligation, noting the obvious newness of the object, its probable cost, difficulty of acquisition, etc. These aspects, as well as any aesthetic appreciation, enter into the act of complimenting. That is, it is often the *fact of acquisition* that is the topic of the speech act, and this situation has much in common with the act of congratulating. Further support for such an analysis comes from the observation that speakers very often introduce the topic of their new possession into conversation by complaining about its high cost, the length of time spent waiting in line to purchase it, or by noting their 'good connections' which directed them to the object. Compliments follow such commentary.

Finally, the link between compliments and congratulations is strengthened by the existence of a token in which the topic of the compliment is, for example, a new refrigerator, a hot-water heater, or an unremarkable kitchen cabinet. Speakers compliment on such objects because they recognize the achievement of acquisition, not because they find the refrigerator aesthetically pleasing.

It is, of course, not possible to prove the validity of an analysis such as that proposed above. One might look at patterns of responses to compliments as a source of relevant information on how addressees perceive compliments. When asked about the appropriate way in which to respond to a compliment in Polish, speakers most often report that the compliment should be downgraded or rejected. Those Polish speakers who are familiar with English often contrast the two languages, reporting that English speakers say *Thank you* and accept compliments offered, whereas Polish speakers will most commonly disagree with the compliment. This folk belief also appears in the scholarly literature; for example, Lewandowska-Tomaszczyk (1989: 75) claims that the convention of avoiding self-praise 'seems to be the highest among Poles, less strong in British English, and the weakest with the American English speakers'.[3] There are certainly instances of this kind in the data:

(25) A: *Ale ładne masz butki.*
          'What nice shoes you have.'
      B: *Ale mewygodne.*
          'But comfortable.'

(26) A: *Dzisiaj bardzo dobrze wyglądasz!*
          'You look very well today!'
      B: *Oo, w tej chwili to nie bardzo.*
          'Oh, not so well at the moment.' ...

(27) A: *Tadeusz, naprawdę masz rewelacyjne spodnie!*
          'Tadeusz, you really have terrific pants!'
      B: *Luz-blues, Ameryka lata trzydzieste!*
          'Slick, America of the thirties!'

(28) A: *Masz ekstra zapalniczkę.*
          'You've got a super lighter.'
      B: *Fajna, prawda?*
          'Neat, isn't it?'

(29) A: *Masz bardzo ładną sukienkę.*
          'You have a very pretty dress.'
      B: *Wiem, jest śliczna*
      B: 'I know, it's lovely.' . . .

The high incidence of such acceptances contrasts sharply with the rate of acceptance among American university students (Herbert 1989) and New Zealand speakers (Holmes 1988). This incidence is also the more remarkable in the light of Polish speakers' claims of not accepting complimentary force. It may be that the compliment formula is used to express recognition of achievement/effort in acquisition, a use to which the formula was not traditionally put, and that this usage elicits bold acceptance as a response.

CONCLUSION

Building upon previous work on English compliments, this chapter has provided a sketch of Polish compliments from a contrastive perspective. Polish compliments, like English compliments, are highly formulaic, with almost 85% of the corpus described as variants on four basic syntactic patterns. Further, semantic expression is highly predictable, especially in adjectival and adverbial compliments, which account for 83% of the sample. Wolfson and Manes (1980) have previously raised the question of why (English) compliments should be formulaic. Unlike greetings, leave-takings, blessings, etc., compliments occur rather freely in conversation. Holmes (1988) found that 21.5% of her New Zealand sample occurred as greetings, 5.6% as closings, and 72.9% as 'other'. It is generally assumed that the formulaicity of compliments derives from their need to be recognized anywhere in discourse as tokens of good will, offers of solidarity, or – as expressed by Kerbrat-Orecchioni (1987: 15) – 'une espèce de cadeau verbal'. Compliments are acts of social negotiation. Addressees must recognize them as such, and addressees are then faced with the problem of acknowledging/ accepting or rejecting/deflecting the offered praise, that is, of responding to the compliment. Compliment responses in English have been analyzed in detail by Pomerantz (1978), Herbert (1986, 1989), and Holmes (1988); cf. Kerbrat-Orecchioni (1987) on French compliment responses.

The prominence of possession compliments in Polish was noted, and this prominence was tied to the anthropology of everyday life in the former People's Republic of Poland. Specifically, compliments on possessions, particularly new possessions, recognize an achievement/accomplishment on the part of the addressee, who has managed by persistence, personal connections, or simple good fortune to acquire some desirable consumer item. In this regard, this subset of Polish compliments blurs the distinction between compliments and congratulations. They are superficially compliments, almost always encoded in the semantic and syntactic formulae described above, but they also operate as expressions of congratulations, a fact acknowledged in many response types and also described by informants. This type of approach to the analysis of speech acts obviously derives from the discipline known as 'the ethnography of speaking', in which language and speech are taken to pattern independently and to interact with other patterns of sociocultural organization, for example, cultural value systems, religion, political organization, an approach championed in the works of Dell Hymes (for example, 1962).

Speech acts are obviously multifunctional. On the other hand, compliments express admiration on the part of the speaker and they also serve as offers of social negotiation (cf. Wolfson 1988). On the other hand, these expressions may be put to particular uses. For example, compliments may be used for personal profit, to which we attach the lable 'flattery', or they may serve as responses to compliments when addressees respond to a compliment by offering a return token, for example,

(30)   A: I like your hair short, Sharon.
       B: Thanks, Deb. I like yours too.

thereby re-establishing the balance between interlocutors. The multifunctional character of compliments is further reflected in their rather free occurrence in discourse.

Compliment events (compliment + response) provide interesting information on sociocultural values and organization. As has previously been noted, the topics of compliments reveal the values which are positively regarded within some particular society. Clothes and general appearance are of great importance in Polish- and English-speaking societies. There are numerous compliments on youthful appearance, but none on aged appearance; many compliments on weight loss, but virtually none on weight gain. In addition to these reflections of cultural values, patterns of compliment events reveal social organization. Who compliments whom, in which circumstances, with what purpose, on which topics, eliciting what response, etc.? Finally, the frequency of the act of complimenting may itself provide some insight into the sociology of compliment work. For example, many non-Americans have commented (often unfavorably) on the high frequency of compliments in American English. These comments come from speakers of other varieties of English, for example, New Zealand speakers (Holmes and Brown 1987), South African speakers (Herbert 1989) and second language speakers of English from a wide variety of linguistic and cultural backgrounds. Judging by their own norms, these groups often report a suspicion that Americans are 'insincere' in their complimenting; cf. Herbert and Straight (1989). When questioned, after having complimented acquaintances on new possessions, Poles often reveal noncomplimentary attitudes toward the objects they had explicitly complimented on moments earlier. The most commonly cited reasons for such acts of complimenting include: (1) an assessment that the item was very expensive, and (2) a report that the item is difficult to acquire. Neither of these values is explicitly encoded in the expression of compliments although both are acceptable topics in conversation; speakers may report with pride on the sum of money paid for an object or on the byzantine circuit of connections and acquaintances that enabled them to 'arrange' (*załatwic*) its acquisition. It may be that the compliment formula serves to offer the addressee an opportunity to introduce these facts in conversation. A view of the subset of compliments on possession as a type in which the compliment–congratulation distinction is blurred is compatible with the above reports. The compliment is not necessarily a statement of aesthetic appreciation, although it bears that form. A traditional form is put to new use in response to changes in the organizational patterns of everyday life. ...

NOTES

The writing of this chapter was supported by a Title F grant to the author to the State University of New York at Binghamton and by research facilities provided by the University of the Witwatersrand. That support is gratefully acknowledged here.

The fieldwork upon which the analysis of Polish compliments rests was conducted over approximately 30 months in Poznań, Warsaw, and Lublin during 1983–1985, 1987, and 1988. Fieldwork was concluded in December 1988, and the writing of the chapter was done during the first half of 1989. There have been significant political, social, and economic changes in Poland since that time. The ethnolinguistic analysis presented later rests upon the ethnography of everyday life at the time of fieldwork. Any difference between the 1983–1988 data and those which might be collected now is a matter for empirical investigation.

The author is grateful to Barbara Nykiel, Nessa Wolfson, and two anonymous reviewers for their comments and criticisms. All errors of interpretation are the author's sole responsibility.

1 The following conventions are used in Wolfson and Manes' statements of syntactic patterns: a. *really* stands for any intensifier, b. all verbs are cited in the present tense, c. *look* stands for any linking verb other than *be*, d. *like* and *love* stand for any verb of liking, e. ADJ stands for any semantically positive adjective, f. ADV stands for any semantically positive adverb, g. NP stands for a noun phrase which does not include a semantically positive adjective, and h. PRO stands for *you, this, that, these, those*.

2 *Nowy* 'new' does not figure in the list of most commonly used adjectives since *nowy* is generally used to introduce the compliment; examples such as (23), where *nowy* carries the complimentary force, are rare.

3 Pomerantz (1978) was the first to note that the difficulty of responding to a compliment derives from the conflict in two conversational postulates: (1) agree with speaker, (2) avoid self-praise.

REFERENCES

Coulmas, F. (ed.) (1980) *Conversational Routine* (The Hague: Mouton).

Ferguson, C. (1976) 'The Structure and Use of Politeness Formulas', *Language in Society*, **5**, pp. 137–51.

Herbert, R. K. (1986) 'Say "Thank You" – or Something', *American Speech*, **61**, pp. 76–88.

Herbert, R. K. (1987) 'Sex-based Differences in Compliment Behavior', Paper Presented at the Annual Meeting of the American Anthropological Association, Washington, DC.

Herbert, R. K. (1989) 'The Ethnography of English Compliments and Compliment Responses: A Contrastive Sketch', in Oleksy, W. (ed.) *Contrastive Pragmatics* (Amsterdam: Benjamins) pp. 3–35.

Herbert, R. K. and Straight, H. S. (1989) 'Compliment–Rejection vs. Compliment–Avoidance: Listener-based vs. Speaker-based Pragmatic Strategies', *Language and Communication*, **9**, pp. 35–47.

Holmes, J. (1988) 'Compliments and Compliment Responses in New Zealand English', *Anthropological Linguistics*, **28**, pp. 485–508.

Holmes, J. and Brown, D. (1987) 'Teachers and Students Learning About Compliments', *TESOL Quarterly*, pp. 523–46.

Hymes, D. (1962) 'The Ethnography of Speaking', in Gladwin, T. and Sturtevant, W. C. (eds) *Anthropology and Human Behavior* (Washington, DC: Anthropology Society of Washington) pp. 13–53.

Kerbrat-Orecchioni, C. (1987) 'La Description des Échanges en Analyse Conversationnelle: L'Exemple du Compliment', *DRLA V-Revue de Linguistique*, **36–7**, pp. 1–53.

Lewandowska-Tomaszczyk, B. (1989) 'Praising and Complimenting', in Oleksy, W. (ed.) *Contrastive Pragmatics* (Amsterdam: Benjamins) pp. 73–100.

Manes, J. (1983) 'Compliments: A Mirror of Cultural Values', in Wolfson, N. and Judd, E. (eds) *Sociolinguistics and Language Acquisition* (Rowley, MA: Newbury House) pp. 96–102.

Manes, J. and Wolfson, N. (1980) 'The Compliment Formula', in Coulmas, F. (ed.) *Conversational Routine* (The Hague: Mouton) pp. 115–32.

Marandin, J-M. (1987) 'Des Mots et Des Actions: "Compliment", "Complimenter" et L'Action de Complimenter', *Lexique*, **5**, pp. 65–99.

Norrick, N. R. (1980) 'The Speech Act of Complimenting', in Hovdhaugen, E. (ed.) *The Nordic Languages and Modern Linguistics* (Oslo: Universitetsforlaget) pp. 296–304.

Pomerantz, A. (1978) 'Compliment Responses: Notes on the Co-operation of Multiple Responses', in Schenkein, J. (ed.) *Students in the Organization of Conversational Interaction* (New York: Academic Press) pp. 79–112.

Wedel, J. (1986) *Private Poland: An Anthropologist's Look at Everyday Life* (New York: Facts on File).

Wolfson, N. (1983) 'An Empirically Based Analysis of Complimenting in American English', in Wolfson, N. and Judd, E. (eds.) *Sociolinguistics and Language Acquisition* (Rowley, MA: Newbury House) pp. 82–95.

Wolfson, N. (1988) 'The Bulge: A Theory of Speech Behavior and Social Distance', in Fine, J. (ed.) *Second Language Discourse: A Textbook of Current Research* (Norwood, NJ.: Ablex) pp. 21–38.

Wolfson, N. and Manes, J. (1980) 'The Compliment as a Social Strategy', *Papers in Linguistics*, **13**, pp. 391–410.

Index